Weathered Wisdom

Weathered Wisdom

MEMORIES AND DREAMS

ONE DAY AT A TIME

by

William Richard Jackson, Ph.D.

JACKSON RESEARCH CENTER
P.O. BOX 3577
EVERGREEN, COLORADO 80439

Weathered Wisdom

Copyright © 2010 by William Jackson

All rights reserved.

ISBN: 978-0-9635741-1-4

First Edition
10 9 8 7 6 5 4 3 2 1

Cover design and photograph by: Richard Stahlberg

Paintings on pages ii and viii by: R.W. Jackson

Painting on page xi by: William R. Jackson

Interior design by Dianne Nelson, Shadow Canyon Graphics

Printed in the United States by
Johnson Printing Company, Denver, Colorado

Contents

Preface vi

Introduction vii

Dedication ix

Acknowledgments x

January 1

February 85

March 159

April 235

May 315

June 393

July 461

August 537

September 609

October 679

November 751

December 823

Subject Index to Prose and Poetry 909

Index to Artists and Artwork 917

Preface

This book was designed for easy reading with a number of subjects to consider from one day to the next. A poem serves as a shorthand summary of a story or a situation. The underlying premise and concise format of a poem may represent the entire theme of a book, a particular subject of a chapter or even a subsection within a chapter in a book. Each individual poem may suggest separate thoughts or contemplations that are distinctively different within a given subject. With this concept in mind, it is recommended that you do not read multiple poems at one time. It would be analogous to attempting to speed read multiple books during one sitting. The variation of ideas and the over-abundance of thoughts may cause confusion. Read a poem. Then allow your brain an opportunity to act or react to the subject matter. The "food for thought" may need time to be "digested."

The poetry and prose in the book have been written over two life cycles for a family that is proud of this final product. The divisions of this book will lead you through the processes involved in the accumulation, abundance, and extent of this body of material. I have attempted to collect, restore, organize and develop these literary works.

It is my hope that *Weathered Wisdom: Memories and Dreams One Day at a Time* will provide you with insights and inspiration as you read and ponder the substance of these works. It is with my optimism and expectations that, with this book, you will endeavor to make your personal world a happier and healthier life experience.

—William R. Jackson, Ph.D.

Introduction

Poetic insight reaches a level of elevated awareness where the sense of identity, unity and oneness with all creation becomes an acute part of the spiritual consciousness. Here, kinship with all things is realized in the ecstasy and love of life. You belong! You belong to God and all things are available!

It has been said that a poet is someone who feels and thus attempts to express his feeling through a collection of words. Such an exercise may sound easy. However, it is not easy.

It has been argued that anyone can learn the art of "thinking, believing, or knowing;" therefore, one can learn to "feel." But, reflect: "thinking, believing or knowing" is limited. Others argue that writers (poets included) can learn to think or believe or know. Yet it is observed that human beings cannot be taught to "feel." What is the problem? The fact is that when you think or you believe or you know, you are a collection of contributions by "other people." However, the instant you feel, your opinions and beliefs are only yours.

Poetry goes beyond that situation. It has been widely confirmed that poetry has a depth of an atmosphere, an instinctive, intuitive sentiment that has a sensitivity of spirit—an emotional reaction.

A poet, as a writer, is an artist who portrays new pictures in old fames; old pictures in new frames; new pictures in new frames; leaves some pictures without frames; and some frames without pictures in hopes that he can inspire the creative thought and action of the readers/viewers and stimulate their desire to evaluate the finished product; to complete the incomplete and to comprehend in an hour what it took a lifetime to learn and portray.

—William R. Jackson, Ph.D.

Dedication

*Dedicated to my mother,
Josie Mulder Jackson,
and my father,
Richard W. Jackson*

Acknowledgements

Permission to reprint materials from the
following sources is gratefully acknowledged:

Artwork, Artists, and William R. Jackson Art Gallery

Sincere appreciation is expressed to
David L. Jackson, Roberta Jackson Severson,
Ellen G. Hall, Lynn Megorden De Vaney,
Dorothy Johnson, Greg Walz, Dianne Nelson,
Mom and Dad Jackson, and the other contributors
listed in the Artist Index at the end of the book.

HOME ON UPPER BEAR CREEK BY WILLIAM R. JACKSON

WINTER OF THE BLACK FOX BY GREG WALZ

January

~ 1 ~

The fabric of faith is interwoven in all the intricate designs of society: in government, in labor, in business, in education, in religion, in morality and life itself.

WE ARE WEAVERS

Happy New Year! Woven into the fabric of last year were all of the events and circumstances that sometimes seemed like an intricately woven spider's web. Various occasions may have caught us unexpectedly. But did you realize that a possible negative web could be easily broken by the power of an improved self-concept, a positive faith in our today fabric? This attitude would include a positive relationship with the originator of all things. Your creativity will increase as you are more perfectly aligned with the creator.

How do we better weave or interlace with our friend, the creator? On occasion, we should reflect on the summation of the "charm" of a little girl or a little boy, and the wise counsel of an experienced leader. It has the template of tenderness of a loving husband and wife. Our fabric should weave in threads of gold and silver to reflect the strong, sensitive love of a father and the thoughtful, loving care of a mother. Within this relationship, you will find new poise as an expectant workman, professional or businessperson, while more comfortably radiating the enchanting warmth of an unusual and loyal friend.

What personal attributes would you like to include as you weave your dynamic life fabric this New Year? How would you like for others to describe the tapestry of your expression? Would this fabric include:

The woven design of humor?

The framework of an industries pursuit?

A dynamic garment, which provides warmth as it wraps its caring arms around your friends and family?

Security in the warmth and protection of your personalized tapestry?

A tapestry that would feel welcome as it touched someone else's life?

The woven union of communion?

The beauty of hearts woven together in love?

The weaving of your melody into the overall musical composition of your environment?

Our thoughts will conclude with a poem. It should be noted that sometimes poetic insight reaches a level of elevated happiness or even heartfelt somberness, where the sense of identity, agreement and accord with our circumstances becomes an acute part of this sensitive experience. Here the relationship with our surroundings is realized in the excitement and love of life. We are individual, eager weavers! Keep in mind, we are this very day being beautifully woven into the very fabric of the Creator's total tapestry!

I love you. Please accept the dimensions of love woven into the following poem. It was written for you. (You may wish to read it aloud.) I trust its texture will touch and warm you as you take its thoughts with you throughout this day.

ALL LIFE IS A POEM TO ME

It may be the beautiful fragrance of earth,
    The wind and the rain, or storm;
It may be the cry of a babe at birth,
    Or it may be a gray, stooped form.

It may be the joy of triumph's hour,
    The depths in the voice of pain;
It may be the sweep of anointed power,
    Or the lift of a great refrain.

Its sense, its form, its shade, and rhyme,
    Its grandeur and majesty
Calls forth an echo of chords sublime
    From the deepest part of me.

But the verses vary and bring relief
    As some humorous line I see;
And tho' I may laugh or be broken by grief,
    All life is a poem to me.

January

~ 2 ~

Cooperation is a song where each must harmonize with the one who carries the melody.
It helps to sing in the same key, on pitch, and in perfect time.

TIMELESS WEAVING

How beautiful, the unending design and symphony of nature! It was conceived as a magnificent thought and was so skillfully executed as a unique composition of the most artistic handiwork. The intention and purpose of the creator can be seen in our earth's grand design, as the lofty thoughts took form. Within the exciting experience of seeing, feeling and enjoying nature, one could only compare it to the peak of emotion enjoyed while being present at the playing of heavens most harmonious symphony. Cooperate with the elaborate instrumental composition in multiple movements. Listen to the variations of the orchestra as it describes life itself. Rise and fall with the proportions of grandeur, including the varied tones and chords sublime. What expression, as the instrumental passages occur and the vocal composition and movements are expressed! Talk about unending, timeless weaving. Think about artistic and precise design. What an overture!

Questions:

How about the skillful execution of the musical score?

What are the elements and aspects within nature that are still carried out on a daily basis?

Does your world of cooperation produce fulfilling music?

What is the functional nature of music that your life is composing?

Your day-to-day journey can be accompanied by beautiful music as you approach your personal, individual high design. This was the timely design that was intended for you by the Creator.

The COMPOSITION of the music of your life consists of the act of combining various parts or elements to form the complete score. You can be confident of your musical arrangement and composition. The cooperative goal is to achieve a unified whole, thus your composition will reflect an award-winning production of successful "literary" life symphony.

The MELODY of your life composition will include the detail of musical sounds that are in an agreement, succession or arrangement that will be distinguished from harmony and rhythm. Both a musical piece and a poem may be composed, suitable for singing. Purposefully design your life to include the detail of a positive melody that makes your daily experience suitable for singing.

Musical HARMONY includes heartfelt agreement and accord. You will note the consistency, orderly and pleasing arrangement of musical parts, as well as simultaneous combinations of tones and chords. The difference with harmony, verses, melody or rhyme is the arrangement of musical contents, which are designed to demonstrate the paralleled, the mutual relation, or the differences of that harmony. Your life journey will be marked with interesting variations, and all may be designed with this balanced harmony.

Finally, the RHYTHM denotes the movement or procedure of the musical piece, with uniform recurrence of a beat or accent. Question: How stable is the rhythm of your life design? This pattern of measured movements of regular or irregular pulses is caused in music by the occurrence of a beat by either the melody or the harmony. There is happy hope for each one of us as we establish a stable rhythm to the timely lyrics of our life.

May the cooperative, interwoven design of the composition of your life purposefully include a singable melody, a heartfelt harmony and a reliable rhythm. What a great potential for your own overture! What an uplifting refrain! As you enjoy your beautifully designed personal symphony today, please accept and read aloud the following poem. Listen specifically for its melody, harmony and rhythm.

THE WORKS OF THE CREATOR'S HAND

Oh, blessed are those whose eyes behold
The hand of the infinite God,
Who fashioned the world, the trees and the flowers
The carpeted, odorous sod.
Where sunshine and flowers and tall swaying grass
And birds that sing as they sway,
Where the flute-like notes by the willow-clad shore
Rise sweet where the warm waters lay.

For the waters are singing the song they know
And the soft south wind is filled
With a thousand smells till the hearts within
With the throbbing of life is thrilled.
Oh, blessed are those whose eyes have seen,
Whose hearts can understand
The harmony, symphony, fullness of life
Through the works of the Creator's hand.

January

3

*Earnestness is eloquence with ability, education,
and attention sitting enthralled at its feet.
Continue earnestly to weave.*

A ROYAL TAPESTRY

Tapestry is a fabric consisting of warp threads upon which other colored threads are woven to produce a design that is often pictorial. This tapestry may be used as garments, wall hangings or furniture coverings, and may be employed to furnish, cover or adorn various settings.

A royal tapestry is usually thought to be reserved for those of royal status, dignity, power or sovereignty. You would expect to see the display of this tapestry within a royal domain, kingdom or temple. Of course those enjoying or even wearing such tapestry would include royal persons collectively and would thus bespeak of the holy, queenly, kingly nobility and generosity of their exalted moral excellence. Yes, the character or quality of the royal tapestry would be proper and befitting a sovereign.

Consider this thought: You and I have been gifted a tapestry of such royal status, the tapestry of our earth. Every micro and macro aspect of our existence, from the mighty oceans to the minute enzyme stimulus excreted from a single micro cell makes up the threads of nature that form the tapestry that every day adorns our personal settings.

Questions:

How do we qualify in the first place?

How can we guarantee the dignity and status of one of the most sovereign tapestries of this universe?

There is incredibly good news. It is yours today! Accept the gift of the world of beauty, the royal hanging tapestry of nature. The rewards are greater than winning a lottery. The wonder is spectacular and abundant, and the royal hanging tapestry of nature, with all of its unique design and color, is yours for the claiming. Enjoy it, appreciate it, and protect it. Show your respect for it by developing a relationship with its Creator.

The following poetic expression partially describes your newly claimed gift. Read it to yourself, and feel the rhythm. Then find a friend or a child and share it with them aloud.

DAY AND NIGHT

The sun, like a faithful penitent
Climbed the stairs of azure blue
And paused to sit at the top a bit
Then climbed down thru a rosy hue.
It bathed its face in the white-foamed wave
In an ocean of golden glow,
And wiped it dry on the edge of the sky
Where ragged clouds hung low.

Then it smiled the sweetest red-lipped smile
Before it said, "Good night,"
And blushed a tender rosy pink
In the fading evening light.
The darkness smiled and in its eyes
Ten thousand stars were born.
And the pale, white moon like a silver wheel
Rolled thru where the skies were torn.

The lights from the silent cities
Soon blinked and closed their eyes.
And the children of man their rest began
Here under the watchful skies.
The night winds caroled a cradle song
Like the voice of a mother's love.
And the God of the sky on guard stood by
And watched it from above.

LAST TRAIN'S GONE BY GREG WALZ

TRACKS ON FIRE BY GREG WALZ

January

~ 4 ~

Hang the portrait of your intended accomplishments in the castle of your dreams,
and awake each morning to make that dream come true.

WHO STOLL TH MOTOR AND THE STEARIN WHEOL?

Dear Freinds (& sum fellow-sitizens),

Yuve ben tole to get off yur duff (rhimes w/ that's ruff)! Yuve gone to banquits, konvenshunz, cornfrences and clap-traps. Yuve ben tole, fella-akountants, that yure akountabel, no-akountalbe and as dispensibel as His Ignorunce, the Devl his self.

Yuve stude in line at Kadilack Kolage sho-rums and drooled over the newest moddle T. versions of edgikationel anteks. Yuve ben tole yule drive and pay fur the Akoutibelity Kar Kumpuny's new Hoarceless Wunder Carryage or go bak on wellfair. Everythin lucks goode, smels nu and costs lots les then loosing yur job. So yule by it!

But nobudie in the coten-picken, adle-brain, edicatiunel, ag-heded sails-staph of th Akouhntabelity Kar Ko ken find the motor that maks it run! It has goode ft. breaks, hand-braiks, too gold-plaited anchers and is boulted to the sho-rum floor. Nobudy in the Higherarky of edjukashen or even the janitor ken find the krank or th moter. And nobudy even herd of the self-starter yit. I shure wisht thay woodn't keep knoking our hoarse and buggies till thay find the moter fur there new Akountebality Kar. At least we still go horace-powur!

It wood bee fun to meat a reel Edicutuer that gnu th definishun of the wurd Edukashun. It don't meen powndin sand in a rat-whoule or powndin rats in a sand-houle. It don't meen to confuze, abuze, refuze or reduse. It means to "educe". Edikashun meens ya gotta brang out whats in kidz and techers!

Evry kid has got sumthin besidz th itch. We gotta find wats in em that's goode and diffrunt and usful and drag it out an ploesh it and let em sell it in the Flea-Market so thay ken stand prowd and tall end not nead to skrach so much enymore. A kid needs sumbudie to sho him wher his starter-butten is, giv him a rode map he ken thro away and tell him, Go, kid go! He'll find out soon enuf that hand-breaks, ft. braiks and gold-plaited anchers, floor boults and diskonected transmashuns do make it a litel harder to git started. But most kidz mak it in spite of the skuling and edgukashun thay git. Now about techers: Edikashen and teachers go to gather sumtimez. Why not sumbodie turn th techer on and brag like crtazie about the wons that are turnd onn. Whi not help them do there speshul, diffrunt thing. If thay don't fit into yur pea-shooter, get a diffrnt sized pea-shuter.

Most teachers have got moters, selph-starters, rode maps and gas tanks. Buy them a tank ful of "do it yurselph" gas. Blo up a storm about "Happiness is; self-expresshun, selph-emprovemint, in-spurashun, survace, the wil to win, to exsel, to sho th wurld wat thay have that's diffrunt and bettr. Evrbudie's got sometheng to bring out. Mabe sumbudy in th Flea-Market will by it. Then mabe th techer wil stand prowd & tall & quit skrachin tu!

p.s. Somebodie said we cude be workin on spellang whilst we sort the roks out uv hour intulectual bean-bags!

I DON'T KNOW

I don't know nuthin'
   But I'm really not dumb.
In English I wouldn't know
   Clim, climbed or klumb.

I'm really not awful ignorant—
   Jus dumb in several spots.
Forget to do what I don't want to
   And I don't like "thou shalt nots."

I don't know how to read or rite.
   But I know how to play and eat.
I wouldn't know up from down
   If I didn't look for my feet.

I don't know where I'm goin'
   Or even where I've been.
But somebody said that dumb kids
   Grow up to be the smartest women & men

January

5

*Love is the spell gentle words weave; my love quickly comes
and never leaves!*

THE LOVE LOOM

Just as the weaving and interlacing of threads and yarns can form fabric, textures or baskets, so the weaving loom of love can combine various elements, details or events into a connected whole. This experience evolves like the weaving of a beautiful tale or simple, yet complicated plot. It is as if the individuals touched the magic key of each other's heart and a response was set off which completes a dynamic heartfelt circuit.

The two individuals stand there in a loving embrace and may silently say to each other, "You have just woven a love web around my very heart!" Yet the weaving of the love web may have been in progress for a long time; for example, the tenderness and caring in a voice, the responding tones, the expressive touch, the influence of the little things like smiles, tears, attentiveness, all of which arouse instant desire while welding together over time an unbreakable, unshakable bond. This in-love feeling can weave sunlight and starlight into hearts.

The love loom takes beautiful true-to-life confrontations, which roll from the conscious and subconscious mind and memories, as if they were contained on a ball, as a long, continuous strand of yarn, and weave them into an "in-love" tapestry.

Only the love tapestry or being "in-love" is capable of joining living beings to the extended experience of completeness and fulfillment. In-love kindness finds a couple and joins them by weaving together what personally, individually and collectively motivates them most. Magic seems to occur when the relationship becomes personal or personified and then the couple can mature, become complete or "wholized." The love loom has produced this beautiful, complete unit of lovely tapestry. In this tapestry, there will be a sharing of love and spirit in the couple's mutual exchange.

Questions:

Are you acquainted with the love loom?

Is your love loom functioning at capacity?

How could this "in-love" production, products and by-products be improved?

As you ponder these questions today, have confidence that there are great days ahead for you as you purposefully aim toward more intense love in your life. Do not be tempted to walk away from the love loom before the fabric is finished. Please read the following poem privately. Then I challenge you to read it aloud to the one you now love most.

YOUR HEART AND MY HEART

If your heart and my heart
 Were both in different lands,
Your heart and my heart
 Would still be holding hands.

If your heart and my heart
 Could speak across the miles,
Your heart and my heart
 Would talk with loving smiles.

If your heart and my heart
 Were walking side by side,
Your heart and my heart
 Would be filled with humble pride.

If your heart and my heart
 Sat under a lover's sky,
Your heart and my heart
 Would ride with the moon on high.

If your heart and my heart
 Were opened from above,
Your heart and my heart
 Would be brimming full of love!

If your heart and my heart
 Could sing just one duet,
They would sing the sweetest love song
 That ever was written yet!

January

6

The absence of the unity of cohesive love is disintegration in all things.

A WOVEN UNION AND COMMUNION

I enjoyed communion with my son at breakfast this morning. As we ordered our meal at the restaurant, we reflected on our close relationship, our union of mutual goals over the years, our shared experiences and the common aspects of our basic philosophy of life.

After the meal was over, we parted company, each going our own ways. On the way home, I began to muse the following questions:

What was involved in our union and communion this morning?

How would I define the parameters of this rewarding experience?

Did this experience just happen?

Did this union and communion develop over time?

Does this relationship require a mutual pursuit?

The concept of union or unity accentuates the thought of agreement, or a specific reference to oneness. It is the joining or combination formed by uniting two or more ideas or things together. The very basic concept of union indicates the inherent qualities of being undivided, even to the extent of being in alliance with one another.

The term communion is another challenging thought. The variations of meanings are specifically expressed as follows:

Communion involves the act of sharing or holding in common.

Communion includes participation.

Communion implies association and fellowship.

Communion infers an interchange of thoughts and interests.

Communion denotes communication and intimate talk.

May you aim for an improved union with family, friends, and nature, while developing the multiple aspects of a more meaningful communion with all. Your fabric will radiate the warmth, friendship and lovely charm of union and communion. As you read the poetic expression for today, picture yourself personally involved in the weave of the concept of each verse.

13

"KISSING COUSINS"

We're kissing cousins, the ocean and I
We hold communion beneath open sky.
Cousin nature and I walk hand in hand
Or lie together in the soft warm sand
And watch the gulls glide by.

My kissing cousin is a teacher wise,
Wisdom and knowledge her affection supplies.
No mortal could learn all she reveals
Forever intrigued by what she conceals
Of beauty beneath her disguise.

This kissing cousin invisibly seen
Manifest as an ocean or a meadow green,
Or kisses my face in the passing breeze,
Or ruffles my hair with infinite ease
And no one can come between.

I've always loved her when my heart is still
In her wooded valleys or a windswept hill.
Flirtingly she calls me night and day
She wants to be loved and to laugh and play.
I yield to her roguish will.

She shows me flowers or a tall stately tree.
She knows where the honey is cached for free.
We laugh as we savor the nectar so sweet,
Scrape the pine needles in piles at our feet.
As the hours glide softly by.

With the taste of wild honey fresh on our lips,
With sunset's glad colors form-fitting her hips
The shadows grow long that we're walking among.
I'm glad for a cousin so old yet so young
And for nature's companionship.

January

7

The faith that sees the invisible will be rewarded by demonstrations of visible sight, the faith that first can hear the inaudible will bring forth the audible sound, and the faith that can touch the intangible will find the fabric of reality in its outstretched hands!

INSPIRATION FOR LIVING

What is Inspiration for Living? Inspiration is enthusiasm. It is the inner breathing of Divinity. It is the awakening of awareness to the Ultimate Reality of God within us. It is more than a soda-mint of rationalization to relieve what one can't stomach of life's smorgasbord of indigestible events. It is more than the Alka-Seltzer effervescence of a false optimism that promises to cure a sour mind or take the weight off of one's fallen arches. Inspiration for living goes deeper than nostrum's band-aids or campaign buttons.

Real inspiration for living is the upsurging joy of the healthy spirit and the quickened flesh. It is the rest of total well-being in body, mind and spirit. It is the true secret of success. It is the emotional lubricant that makes planned effort flow smoothly and almost effortlessly in the right direction. It is life's battle strategy, ground support and air supremacy. It's the soldier's battle cry before the battle is won. It's the pilgrim's song of determined conquest before he climbs the last grey hill and sees the sunrise of hope spread across all his tomorrows!

Inspiration for living is the reverberating overtones of the warm, integrated, forward-moving individual who has opened his inner being to the unity and rhythmic flow of the whole spiritual universe which has its own hidden laws of being, measure, meaning and purpose. Inspiration for living is the river flowing through the gates of the dam to turn the wheels and dynamos of all practicality. It is the lifeblood of being. It throbs and pulses in zestful living. It laughs in recreation and play. It works long hours that seem but minutes in its self-forgetful absorption of self-expression and creativity. It is the essence of life, the heartthrob of achievement. It is lifeblood free from the virus of negativity as it stirs the limbs to action, the mind to mental clarity and the spirit to realization. It is like the pounding of the surf playing and working away at the ocean shores of all activity.

Inspiration for living is a glad song of summer, the expectant song of spring, the fulfillment song of autumn and wintertime when frost and snow blanket the ground and cover old scars with the promise of rejuvenation and resurrection after it rests a bit and regroups its energies for project survival and success! It is a song that sings the harmony of universal things.

Inspiration for living is love of life, the joy of self-expression, the song of unselfish service, and the action of achieving faith. It is the spark of genius, the unconquerable spirit of adventure in the pulsing blood of the sturdy pioneer. It is sincerity, earnestness, dynamic drive and the cadence of conquest!

PEACEFUL POND BY NENAD MIRKOVICH

January

8

DIVINE UNION

Oh what a friendly world this is,
　　Even in the darkest night,
For the night is a velvet robe of peace.
　　The stars with pure love are alight.

For the stars are the eyes of God above
　　And the moon is his mirror bright.
And I live in a friendly universe
　　Of God and truth and right.

Oh what a friendly world this is!
　　Each breeze that fans my cheek
Is the breath of God caressing me
　　On seven Sabbaths of every week.

All nature is mine in fellowship
　　For the God in its heart is mine.
And love and joy and confident hope
　　Are the fruit of this Union Divine!

MASTERS OF THE SKY BY BRUCE EAGLE

January

9

Positive thinking is an inner light:
you grow in its glow as you come and go.

CLIMB WITH ME

To stand on some high pinnacle of inspiration, to rise over difficulties, to climb, to achieve, to make self-improvement, this is the challenge of life and the privilege of man. Conquest is the most basic note and the truest harmony of all our songs. People's words are but the symbols of their feelings. They contain the mental images they perceive and conceive.

Picturization precedes language verbalization. Pictures are the basic languages of thought in any language. It is basic talking to ourselves in pictures. Pictures are the blueprints for action and attraction used by the creative, inner mind to materialize our desires.

Perhaps on the wings of music, poetry, song, vivid visualization, looking into the depth of a burnished agate or the blue of the sky, or the depth of green waters may trigger that elevated sense of beauty and divine insight, which is opened by intense, uplifted emotion. Whatever it is that triggers this high sense of soul uplift, the desire is to sincerely see with the eyes of the soul into the essence of all things.

Affirmations are a statement of awareness or consciousness. Thus, conscious cognizance is the appropriate, intuitive, knowing way of attaining wisdom, position, information, wealth, power, health, confidence, all acceptable traits and much, much more. Being truly and fully aware of a trait and to identify with it is to possess it, for consciousness is the secret to attainment.

Join me today. I want to see with the eyes of the soul into the essence of all things in the awakened, alert, conscious condition of an integrated personality. It is possible now, to gain conscious control and direction of my higher energies. I declare it. I affirm that I am aware that I do exercise these latent possibilities. This is also an order to my inner mind to activate these abilities, for I do possess them. I have the courage to use them and the faith to expand them. I am aware, increasingly aware, of activated self-direction, of providential guidance and control over the hidden energies of my inner self.

CHARACTER BROCADE

As the spider weaves his web
    From his inmost vital parts,
So we weave the robe we wear
    From the substance of our hearts.

Silken threads of thought and deed
    With the gold of love are spun,
In the vesture of the soul
    That we're wearing everyone.

Like the snail that makes his shell
    Or the spider his brocade—
From the purpose of the soul
    A beautiful character is made.

PERSPECTIVE

Yonder shine ten thousand stars
In the velvet robe of night.
And you feel quite large beside them;
Distant flickering points of light.

But wait; you have the thing all backwards,
Tho' it may your pride astound,
Man has very small dimensions;
Turn your telescope around!

January

~ 10 ~

The hard-surfaced, porcelain-white, refrigerator saints who quick-freeze all offered friendships and keep the door securely closed on their dehydrated virtues may find themselves defrosted somewhere other than in heaven.

A Select Clergy

"Some preachers push people toward perfection;
others climb the heights and lift their followers after them."

"Many a ministerial cupboard, like Old Mother Hubbard's, is too often bare
except for an occasional bone of contention."

"A minister's life is about as private as a Hippie growing marijuana in
a glass house across from the police station."

"A politician behind a pulpit doesn't make a minister."

"The minister who loves leisure is saving himself, not other lives."

"A preacher should be as upright and as rugged as the cause he represents."

"A minister should lean on his backbone and not on the pulpit,
for he who has a cause will have a crowd."

"The clergy as a profession attracts the wise, the other-wise, the good
and sometimes the good-for-nothing, some counterfeits, charlatans,
and 'saints in cellophane.' But thank God, some ministers
are the genuine, sincere servants of God and the
people every day of the week!"

"Out of the soil of silence the greatest virtues grow, and the secrets of life are
seldom revealed to the crowd rushing to and fro."

A LOOKING GLASS FOR THE DEAD

I sat in a beautiful mortuary church
    That my money had helped to build.
I thought it was still a church-house
    But my hopes were stifled and chilled.

The dim lights on the face of the people
    Made them sallow with premature age,
They sang the songs indifferently
    Or failed to turn to the page.

All the prayers the preacher prayed
    Were platitudinous, empty and dull—
Parroted phrases, pompously mouthed—
    Prayer dust in an empty hull.

The pews were empty and spacious
    Except for folk here and there.
It looked like a near bald-headed man
    With a few wispy tufts of hair.

Or it looked like a field of sugar beets
    Where the seed left a very poor stand,
Like they'd been hoed along with the weeds
    By some untrained fieldworker's hand.

The sermon was read in monotonous tone
    And lasted well past the hour.
Good things were said to the living dead
    But they lacked eternal power.

There was no casket in front of the church
    But the dead sat straight in the pews.
When the benediction finally was said
    They stirred stiffly to hear the good news.

A funeral march for decadence
    Might well have fitted here
With a looking glass for all who pass
    Staring up from an empty bier!

January

∽ 11 ∽

Success City is a place of positive attitudes, subjective assurance, projected vision,
persistent desire, creative thought, and enduring labor.

"Daddy, Show Me How to Do It"

A few months ago out in California, a frustrated little girl was overheard to say, "Daddy, show ME how to do it!" Have you ever been told you were doing something wrong, but knew of no option? How many advertisements have you observed which addressed and admonished you with uncertainty and fear relative to certain subjects? How many social or religious organizations were overly-zealous and told you what you should do, but did not take the time to tell you why and show you how?

So, what is your position? Are you a RIBBON WEARER who lets the world know you care about a cause, and exactly what cause? Are you brave enough to start a friendly discussion with someone wearing a little ribbon, about ways the two of you could do more than just wear ribbons? Would the two of you actually do something about finding and practicing answers?

Are you a MARCHER? It is amazing how much energy is spent and how ardent and adamant some people become to raise awareness about a specific problem, but limit their assistance to marching. Many have concluded, and sadly are teaching by their actions, that everything gets better if you just march for the cause! Some marchers have been interviewed who could not define the issues for which they were marching. It was just an activity, and they joined the party. Where are the people, in the everyday trenches of life, who apply the principles suggested by the marchers? What are all of the marchers doing the next day? Living the correction, or just marching again?

Remember, the situations, problems, and choices are the situations of "we the people," and solutions for most of these circumstances will require the participation of "we the people." It is admirable to define a problem and bring attention to it, but to actually do something about it, that's noble.

Quite often we only wear ribbons or march because we do not really know how to do anything else. To be able to respond to the plea, "Daddy, show ME how to do it," as it relates to successful living of our life issues, we must have sound practices available. It is becoming quite evident that defining the problem is only one step. The next step is actually to set up working models, a pattern of workable solutions that would help us all, give us an example and a standard for comparison and for imitation. Teach us by example! "Daddy, show *me* how to do it."

OCEAN SHORE

I want to go to the windswept beach
    With rain and mist in my hair.
I want to feel its sting in my face
    As I breathe deep of the salty air.
I want to pray and think alone
    Till I know that God is there.

I want to go to the sunset beach
    Where the sand dunes stretch afar,
I want to stay till the sun is set
    And the heavens give birth to a star.
I want to breathe the cool night air
    As one with the things that are.

I want to walk the fresh washed sand
    Swept clean by waves and tide.
I want to walk alone with God
    With His Presence close by my side,
Till my mind and heart are ocean-washed
    And God-cleansed from self and pride.

THE DEPOT CALLED SUCCESS

Every truth is a crosstie
    Beneath the shining rails
As the clicking wheels go singing
    In a rhythm that never fails.

Every truth is a crosstie
    And every spike holds fast.
And the shining rails of progress
    Stretch to a future golden, vast.

Every truth is a crosstie
    Tamped and wedged in place.
Expansive, extensive and reaching far,
    And time is the foe we race.

The rails of inspiration
    And information lead us on.
But we laid the track with aching back
    In the dark before the dawn.

Every truth is a crosstie
    By thought is the future laid.
And the Depot of Success around the bend
    Is the reward for the price we paid.

Every train that travels
    Has rails on which to ride.
It finds the Depot called Success
    If it wanders the countryside!

NUMBER 75 ON THE ROAD

G.W. 75 CO. BUSINESS CARD

BILL JACKSON AND HIS BROTHER JIM WITH NUMBER 75

LEE MARVIN WITH NUMBER 75 IN THE MOVIE *CAT BALLOU*

January

~ 12 ~

*Solitude speaks a silent language known only to nature,
the listening soul, and the Great Creator.*

INTUITIVE KNOWLEDGE

The development of a quick, intuitive knowledge of things and people, beyond the range of natural vision, is a psychic event pertaining to the human soul or mind. This is an extension of man's mental ability, opposed to his physical ability to anticipate change. In this experience, of intuitive knowledge perception, there are octaves of sound beyond the normal range of hearing to which the listener is attuned. This inner hearing and direction may come anywhere, at any time, and should be written down as it comes or be recorded by some means. Out of man's unknown future and out of the other side of his unknown mind will arise supernatural powers and manifestations as yet unborn. Blessed is the man who has the power and manifestations as yet unborn. Blessed is the man who has the power to vividly articulate and convey those concepts that come to him through this "beyond physical" experience. This will include not only the intuitive knowledge but also the function of an intuitive audience.

Man can also communicate telepathically through mental pictures of things projected visually. This was no doubt the first language of all mankind. He can reduce the levels of mind vibration and, at a causative visual level, adjust and condition any bodily condition to function in a perfectly normal, appropriate state at the point of its highest efficiency and greatest duration.

Change is the name of the game called reality. Much of the change is invisible but still influential in affecting the moods, motions, motives and mentation of maneuvering man.

Evolving environment, interchanging energies and ever-recurring responses and negations of natural and supernatural forces preclude a stability in nature other than one based on the predictability and dependability of resulting change. Opposites in interaction produce adjustment in reaction but change in the substructure of this accommodating reality. The human race must now adapt itself to the accelerated rate of change and progress. The expressed usage of "extrasensory" abilities may be a prime requisite for successful survival in a too rapidly changing, technological society severely shaken and continuously vibrating to the stress factors inherent in its accelerated progress.

COMMUNION BY THE SEA

I was utterly alone with the sea and sky,
    Alone on its windswept shore;
And the God of all oceans walked with me
    And rich was His bountiful store!

We talked of life and rain and wind.
    We talked of the driftwood debris.
We talked of immensity, space and time
    But mostly we talked of me.

I told Him about my longings,
    Of the places I wanted to see;
About the things I wanted to love
    And of bondage that wanted free.

So He made me aware of wind and rain
    Mixed with the tears on my face.
And He made me aware of the joy of pain
    And the love of the secret place.

He drew me apart in solitude
    And whispered life secrets to me.
Enlarged my awareness and second sight
    And taught me to feel what I see.

He hummed along with the wind that blew
    And pattered with the rain and spray.
Then we turned back in silent peace,
    Content at the end of day.

January

∽ 13 ∽

Hope should begin with the possible, progress with industry to the probable,
and proceed to the achievement of the actual.

GOALS AND OBJECTIVES OF EDUCATION FOR ACHIEVEMENT

The purpose of Education for Achievement should be to promote a success-oriented philosophy of achievement in education, to inspire self-improvement and self-motivation, to open potential mental reserves through impartation of knowledge, skills, inspiration and positive mental attitudes essential to the highest functioning of the integrated individual.

The purpose of Education for Achievement should be to better understand and utilize all levels of the mind and to strive for and employ all feasible resources for a breakthrough of effectiveness in learning efficiency fundamental to upgrading the quality of self-orientation and individualized education

The purpose of Education for Achievement should be to develop values, provide value guidance, encourage favorable behavioral changes, and promote in-depth intellectual, emotional, cultural and social development. It should implement successful interpersonal relationships, increase enrichment of all possible opportunities for life and learning. It should provide for leadership training with motivation and guidelines for greater service in the circle of one's influence and for a more informed participation in the processes and interactions of a Humanistic Democracy in an ever-converging world community.

BOUNDLESS HOPE

The pendulum of eternity
Beats on forever ceaselessly.
Millenniums pass in endless flow;
The ages come and softly go.

Time unlimited for man
To grow beyond this mortal span;
To learn, achieve and comprehend;
To dwell for aye where beauties blend.

This gift—beyond our finite scope—
Our heritage of boundless hope.

THE KINDNESS OF GOD

God is the artist and Sculptor,
    Painter and Gardener, too.
Architect, Builder of mountains,
    Arranger of clouds in the blue.

Botanist, Lover of flowers,
    Master of fashions is He,
Designing the clouds into landscapes,
    Carving the cliffs by the sea.

Lover of all that is living,
    His watch-care is tender and true.
Keeper of birds and of wildlife—
    The whole wide world is His zoo.

Crowning the works of creation
    Came men when all else was done.
On him God lavishes kindness,
    From dawn-break 'til setting sun.

January

~ 14 ~

NEW DAY DAWNING BY JEAN BARTLETT

SOLITUDE AND I

Oh, Solitude, I come to woo thee.
My noblest dreams have all come through thee.
    And beauty crowns thy head!

Oh, Solitude, unfold thy treasure,
One hour with thee is purest pleasure
    Where pensive feet have led.

Oh, Solitude, thy consent embolds us.
Thy pure enchantment still enfolds us.
    And downy is thy bed.

Oh, Solitude, do not deny us
The *silence* where no distractions try us
    But flee thy frown instead!

Oh, Solitude, thy wine enflames me.
No hand but thine can ever claim me.
    Perhaps we should be wed!

*Out of the soil of silence the greatest virtues grow, and the secrets of life
are seldom revealed to the crowd rushing to and fro.*

January

～ 15 ～

*Unselfishness and love are fraternal friends and even twins; but drab selfishness
and filial doubt no affinity of love or oneness ever wins.*

THE ARTISTRY OF LOVE

If love were the color of springtime,
    Vibrant, life-giving and green,
The flowers would bloom in profusion
    And with colors by mortals unseen!

If love were the color of summer
    And God were the Artist, I know
He'd paint every tree in bold relief
    And add the sunset's afterglow.

If love were the color of autumn:
    Scarlet, yellow and brown,
He'd paint every leaf with flaming gold
    On the hillside and in the town.

If love were the color of flowers
    What variety and shape it would take!
With love's fragrance in every garden
    What bouquets the florists would make.

If love were the color of oceans
    What blue and green would vie
With the blue of the highest heaven
    Or the blue in a baby's eye.

If love were the color of tomorrow
    Its warm waves would be unfurled
With a beauty undreamed of by artists
    On the canvas of a fresh new world!

Your love is the color of living;
Of springtime, of summer and fall;
A masterpiece in moods to be blended
And hung on emotion's bare wall.

Yes, love is the color of kindness,
Of beauty and joy and of peace,
Unselfishly shared with others;
May your artistry ever increase!

BRING ME TO MY LOVE

Let all birds that fly,
Be swift-winged couriers
Of our love.
Let long days go by,
On swift wings gladly fly,
And bring me to my love.

Let all winds that blow
Be high-borne messengers
Of our love.
Let warm days come soon
With love's warmth at high noon,
And bring me to my love.

Let all ships that sail
Be smooth-hulled bearers
Of my love.
Speed through the gale
With full wind in each sail
And bring me to my love.

Let all flowers that bloom
Be sweet-breathed emblems
Of our love.
In love's embrace there's room.
Love's light dispels all gloom
And whispers of our love!

January
~ 16 ~

FLATTOP MOUNTAIN BY JEAN BARTLETT

SUNDOWN IS SYMBOLIC

Sundown can mean the end of time.
Sundown is symbolic in every clime.

Sundown with its shadows long,
Sundown without a morning song.

Sundown with hopes forever set,
Sundown haunted with vain regret.

Sundown with another world to face,
Sundown with or without God's grace.

Sundown, a word that haunts the soul,
Where destiny is set while ages roll.

But sundown is a different thing I know
In a smiling sky with love aglow.

Sundown may be a brilliant thing
With colors spread by angel wing.

Sundown may illumine the upward way
That brings the sunrise of eternal day.

Sundown! Then daybreak with glad surprise,
And sunrise in heaven beyond earth's skies!

Hope is man's steady star at night and the rising sun of the day.

January

17

*It is not so much blood-ties, nationality, knowledge, or position but
fellow-feeling and the bonds of kindness that make all men one.*

LOVE FOR OUR FELLOW MAN

Allow love to bombard your subconscious with the positives. You must learn to love your fellow men with affection and compassion. This will include unlimited liking, enduring friendship, instantaneous attachment, amiable regard, devoted enthusiasm, happy anticipation, generous gallantry, fervent fellowship, and favored fancy.

The good of love is to make the beloved happy, and to please our Creator. You will earnestly endeavor to always lighten life's load for others. You shall continually strive to feel their heartaches, help them in their perplexities and help them to hymn the harmonies of hope and human happiness, in tune with the Creator Himself.

This kind of love is supreme in its purity of purpose, the essence of its emphasis and the source of its origin, for love is of the Creator of all and the Creator is love. You will choose to seek after and strive to personify the virtues of love. Relative to this subject, true success arises from loving service to 1) fellow man, and 2) preserving our earth and pure love for others. You are and must continue to be a person of goodwill and benevolence. Your feelings, expressions and deeds reflect the Creator quality of brotherly love, sincere kindness, happy-hearted fellowship, sympathy, tenderness, regard for others, charitableness, affection and genuine goodness, unselfishly shared with others. The qualities of appealing winsomeness, fascination, attraction, and enchanting empathy reward you with personal appeal.

You are a fellow man champion of charm; a gallant, gentle person. You exercise a like, a personal love for people. Expand your fellow-man interest of people everywhere in affectionate regard. You will hold people dear. You will cherish their friendship, prize their presence, and enjoy their companionship. People will perhaps even fascinate, delight, captivate, enrapture and thrill you. You must in turn continue to be winsome, charming, filled with the gentle goodness of the Creator's own love for all mankind. For the Creator's greatest gift is the gift of the spirit of love. Love all men even as we have been taught to love.

HE SHALL OVERCOME

We would not bring the leader back
    Tho moved by bereavement's cry.
For Samson-like he wrought his best,
    As do all martyrs when they die.

So pick up the trumpet and the torch
    And blow the victor's blast.
His light shall shine, His words be heard
    As long as time shall last.

Lift up the voice of freedom's song
    For his lips now cold and numb.
His dream of justice, truth and love
    Shall surely overcome!

January

18

He who claims God as his Father must by necessity treat the rest of humanity as his brothers!

BROTHERHOOD AND CIVILIZATION

The Brotherhood of Man includes the fact that every person on earth is an extension of every other person now existing, or who has ever lived on this globe. Be that true, all people continue to extend themselves through others, and their influence may continue out through many centuries to come.

Our advanced state of human society is based upon the equal service of each individual, presented with love to our fellow men. This balance is destroyed by unequal interchange, which is caused by greed and selfishness, leading our fellow men to fear each other.

If it is accurate that even distant people, whom you have never met or even heard of, affect your life for better or worse, how much more powerfully that truth can influence you when you examine this application to close family members, the people in your neighborhood, and in your work world.

There is a universal lesson that the human race has not yet learned. The lesson not yet understood or corrected includes the fact that the hurt of one person anywhere on earth is felt or affects every person everywhere on the globe. Civilization today still experiences a world of hate and fear of fellow man for fellow man, which causes people to kill each other by hundreds and thousands. Perhaps mankind does not realize that the accumulating suffering of so many people is threatening all mankind with a black cloud of misery for ages to come.

What mankind has not yet learned is that when a person hurts another person anywhere, they are hurting themselves equally. By the same token, when people enrich other persons anywhere, they are equally enriching themselves.

Do you agree that most people are forever in pursuit of peace, happiness and prosperity? Please understand that the only way you can obtain these endowments of peace, happiness and prosperity is by giving them, because you cannot seize them. Should you bestow love to enrich people around you, you will be enriched, but should you seize this love and attention for yourself, that which was intended for someone else, you will surely impoverish yourself. Rules are not to break lest the rule broken breaks you. Thus the rule of civilization depends upon what every person gives to it or seizes from it.

WE ARE BROTHERS!

Our Brotherhood is a tree that grows out of the diversified soil of an enduring humanity.

I feel the grip of manhood in your handclasp.

I see the light of understanding in your eyes.

I sense the kinship of our common goals, our common toils, our common hopes and fears.

I see in you my own ambitions, strengths and weaknesses revealed.

Together we are stronger and wiser far than any of us are alone.

Together we can win against uneven odds!

I salute you, Friend, in the common cause of the Brotherhood of Man…

We are Brothers!

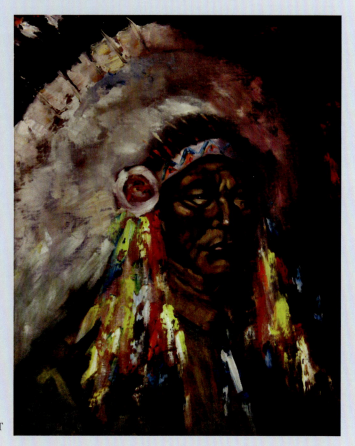

INDIAN CHIEF BY BENGARTT

January

∽ 19 ∽

*Poetry is an illuminated viewpoint that brings out the hidden beauty
to burnish the exterior of the ordinary.*

UNIVERSAL HARMONY

Many excellent teachers encourage students to experience "feeling" poetry. Many individuals struggle to complete their class assignment. How many students actually experience the true essence of feeling their poem? Those who do are the lucky ones! Several questions: As a poet, do you "feel" this experience? Can you express those feelings through words and verses? Does this experience go beyond believing? Knowing? Thinking? Way beyond!

Almost anyone can know about something: Most people can think about a subject. Perhaps it is something they were taught. How and what do you think? Usually this includes a process of considering someone's concept in order to accept or reject it. Consider this: What do you believe? Do you believe your own ideas or the ideas of someone else?

But to feel, and to be able, in shorthand, to express those pictorial feelings, allows you to function as a poet! Is it possible that a line of a poem actually expresses a whole page or even a subchapter in a standard book? Could a poem state the entire thesis of a whole book?

Is it possible that poetry is the pulse of the universe? Is poetry the rhythmic vibration of the spheres, the music of the stars that sing together, the harmony of the unity of the Creator? This rhythmic beat is underlying, fulfilling, softly singing like the rhythmic pulse of the great Creator God.

Metered, measured, moving, musical impulses, singing the eternal song of one accord: This is true poetry, for this is the heartbeat of life itself. He who would move and master matter, or change the course of nature, men or circumstances, must learn to sing life's rhythmic song. Only those who know the score can direct the melody and music of the things that ARE, or change them to the things they want them TO BE. As one person stated, "Let us sing God's glad eternal song together with all the universal love and peace and melodic beauty. This is the rhythmic song and psalm of life—eternal here below." It is a part of the whole universal harmony. When you read a poem, take time to enjoy it and to reflect on the feeling. After all, it is feeling-loaded literature in condensed form!

AN OCEAN PRAYER

If I had my wish I'd walk once more
Along the ocean's windswept shore.

I'd feel the cool breeze strike my face.
I'd lean in the wind's insistent embrace.

I'd mingle my tears with rivulets of rain
And wash myself clean from my inward pain.

I'd lift my gaze to the cloud-swept sky
And lift my voice in penitent cry.

I'd ask the good, great God above
To fill my soul with hope and love.

I'd face my anguish masked by mirth
While my heart re-echoed the pounding surf.

I'd beg the God of earth's wind and wave
To bare His arm and His power to save.

I'd join in the cry of the winging gull
And moan with the sea when storm winds lull.

I'd turn my back to the driving gale
And retrace my steps as the star lights fail.

I'd let the sound of the rolling sea
Carry my prayers thru eternity.

Where God would know and hear and care
And quickly come with answered prayer!

Faith is an ocean where even hardships ride like leaves
                                    upborne on its mighty tide.

January

20

Love and faith are inner faculties that see the invisible, hear the inaudible,
touch the intangible and claim their bounties for their own.

LIFE IS LOVE AND LOVE IS LIFE

Today as I walked through the park in San Diego, I thought of you my love, in the most warm and compassionate way. As you read this, please consider with me the likenesses of love and know that life is love and love is life. May I share my thoughts with you?

Can you see, love is like a red bird singing in a tree while his heart beats tumultuously? Love is like a Colorado snowflake soft and cool, blending in the water of the shallow pool. Love is like the Kansas sunflower's heavy yellow head bowed in acquiescence. Nothing needs be said. Love is like this green tree tall against the sky, swaying in its freedom of the breeze passing by.

Look up my dear; Love is like the soft clouds serene, exalted up above, the object of elusive, reaching love. Love is like a sheltering rooftop red or green or like the four walls with all that's in-between. Look where we are walking; Love is like the path that leads us there. It is a high path if the two of us are walking and share. Back home; Love is like the fireplace warm and quite secure. It is the joys of home that endlessly endure.

Have you noticed? Love is magic, make-believe, forgiveness, and calm repose. Love is an indoor potted plant or a fragrant, rock-rooted wild rose. Love is a stream with rapturous song filled with deep and silent laughter as it spills along. Love is like a burnished agate bright that reflects the un-blemished hope for future sight. Love is an arm supporting another's aching back, a hand holding loving gifts to supply another's lack.

Love is inner peace from tensions all set free. It is a white-winged angel thing; invisible that patiently dwells with me. I love you my beautiful angel! It is true, life is love and love is life.

I SING OF MY OWN TRUE LOVE

Receding and green as the fields in May,
As fragrant as autumn's new-mown hay,
As glad as a fiesta's music gay,
Hoping you'll never go away,
    I would sing of my own true love.

Blue-gray are the skies today.
Blue, blue are your eyes today,
Soft as the mists that rise today,
But gone like the bird that flies away
    While I sing of my one true love.

LOVE

Love is a little word I know
    That touches almost everything.
It is a word, by which men live,
    And it makes the sad heart sing.

Love is a giant kind of word
    As big as the human race.
It stirs the heart and eyes and voice
    And shines on the lover's face.

Yes, love is a big and a little word
    On which this old world swings.
It's the poet's word and the mother's word
    And it makes the whole earth sing!

January

~ 21 ~

Every person should beneficially influence their environment and not be victimized by it.
They should evaluate, invigorate, and renovate their environment by
resolute purpose, determined will and energized action.

THE ENVIRONMENT OF SPACESHIP EARTH

Our Earth has been described as a spaceship. As intelligent, thinking humans, we all live on board the 8,000-miles-in-diameter spherical spaceship, which is speeding around the sun at 60,000 miles per hour and spinning on its axis as it orbits. Thus we speak of flying by plane, "in" for a landing or "out" from the airport, to fly "around" the spaceship Earth and come "in" again for a landing. Of the 4.5 billion people on this spaceship, what can you and I do to make it a safer place to live?

We are all familiar with "bad news/good news" drama. Noting that the world is full of serious environmental problems is not a new observation. We are in the daily process of harming ourselves as well as destroying one another. It seems that our "today-oriented" civilization has ascended from the very ashes of battered, ill people by decimating our natural resources.

The question is, how do YOU relate to this destructiveness? Is there evidence of a greed-motivated, self-centered social malignancy to be found among us? Ultimately, each person participates in a self-killing process of his or her own choice. Why do we make such choices? That we make these choices is the bad news. Can you personally identify at least one harmful environmental issue? If so, can you implement protective alternatives in order to save your very own life, or the lives of your children or grandchildren?

The good news is, there are solutions to our accumulated environmental circumstances, problems and practices. You can accept the fact that our best defense against self-destructiveness lies in the courageous application of intelligence and action: To IDENTIFY ecosystem problems, to CLASSIFY possible answers to these problems, to COMPLY with present improvement programs, and by all means, to TRY to implement a strong personal philosophy and practical process for improving our environment.

I'M AKIN

I'm akin to the flight
    Of the ducks in the sky
When my heart is light
    And my spirit soars high.

I'm akin to the breeze
    When it's vagrant and wild.
I'm akin to all nature
    As nature's own child.

I'm akin to the ripple
    In the placid blue lake.
I'm akin to the fish
    And the splashes they make.

I'm akin to the glow
    Of the sun in the West.
I'm akin to the mountains
    Cold with snow on their crest.

I'm akin to the flash
    Of the lightning and storm.
I'm akin to the rain
    Dripping desolate, forlorn.

I'm akin! I'm akin
    To all life on the earth
For God our one Father
    Gave to all things their birth.

January

22

BUGLING ELK BY R.W. JACKSON

ROLL OUT THAT GOLDEN CARPET, SIR!

The path of the just shines brighter
    Unto the perfect day.
A carpet of golden, luminous light
    Rolls up to the Milky Way.

I do not walk on the cobblestones
    Or in dust that is ankle deep.
I walk on a shimmering carpet of gold
    Where angel wings my pathway sweep.

I do not walk on the sidewalks here
    Or in alleys of blind retreat.
I walk on that carpet of golden fleece
    With wings on my jubilant feet!

I see it unroll before me now
    Up to the conqueror's throne.
It rolls ahead to destiny's goal
    And the prize at the end is my own.

Wherever I go a magic power
    Unrolls acceptance for me.
Unrolls God-confidence, courage and faith
    And golden prosperity.

The carpet of golden success rolls on
    Thru the stars to the Milky Way.
And the path of persons with vision, shines
    With light of celestial day!

Unroll that golden carpet, Sir!
    I'll walk like a conquering Chief.
For the vision I hold will manifest
    At the end of the carpet of magic belief!

The positive attitude expressed in genuine gratitude brings the mind and heart quickly into harmony and communion with God in whom all positive virtues reside.

January

~ 23 ~

Listening is the sweetest eloquence that wisdom ever hears.

THIS I MUST DO

If I do nothing, I but sail my ship
    On a sea of nothingness too!
If I do not share its treasured store,
    My warehouses contain nothing new.

As I stand reticent on the ocean shore,
    I find the sand melting beneath my feet.
I who would run from reality's realm
    Find there's nowhere for cowardly retreat.

So I must drift with the drifting clouds
    And wane with the waning moon.
But I must rise with the rising sun
    Facing life as it comes late or soon.

To sail Life's oceans broad and deep
    And cross each horizon beckoning afar,
I must be here and yet up there
    By the side of each glittering star.

I must set the delimiting ego aside
    And share in the omnipresent thing.
I must give voice to the song of life
    Like the exultant bird on the wing.

My spirit must dip and soar and rise
    Detached from the ego apart.
And thru forms the Formless portrays
    I shall reach to God's very heart!

GIFT OR GIVER

Have you waited sometimes for a blessing?
It tarried, you didn't know why.
Perhaps some fault had you sensed it,
Some doubt that your heart would deny.

Did you ask and really expect it?
Did you honestly come to Him
To ask for the best in His wisdom,
Or only some temporal whim?

Sometimes we must wait for His promise
And gifts of a transitive self.
A good many things we must wait for
But not for the Giver Himself!

January

24

*True greatness pays court to Modesty but avoids those common
street walkers known as Conspicuousness, Conceit, and Self-Exhibition.*

GOSSIP

"The gossip speaks his half-truths through false teeth."

"The gossip leaves his mouth-motor running in a close place until he asphyxiates himself."

"Gossip, like the gopher, runs in one hole and comes out another, but he is always
dragging his tail in somebody's dirt!"

"The dog that wags his tail before he bites is no worse than the gossip who
wags his tongue and smiles while he bites you from behind."

"If the busybodies, the tale-bearers and the gossips were all hanged from high
scaffolds by the tips of their tongues, their feet would still drag in the dirt!"

"The eager-eyed, open-eared, scandal-listener is a sure bet for the
gossip-guy's king for a day!"

"The alligator kills with the tail and so does the scandal-monger."

"Was the little bird who told you so a mockingbird, a silly goose,
a dumb-do-do guy or just another old-hen?"

"The gossip like the echo repeats on empty air the things he heard
another say of one who isn't there."

MOLLY IN THE GARDEN BY ROBIN WOLLMAN

THE CAT THAT CAME TO CHURCH

There were cats that came to Church,
    No, not the furry kind;
But a catty cat that wore a hat—
    A person if you mind.

They had a catty kind of look
    Like waiting for a mouse,
Looking round they quickly found
    Their neighbor in the house.

And pouncing on their neighbor's faults
    They had some things to say:
Some catty things with scratch
    And strings—Nor would they kneel to pray.

Unless you stroked their social fur
    In just the kindest way,
They'd have a fit, and you'd get bit,
    And all parishioners would surely pay.

But the minister spoke about the wrong
    That's buried deep within.
I heard them say, "Oh, let me change"
    "Oh, for a happy life I long!"

So the catty cat that came to Church
    Now sings a different song.
Their life was changed, their claws were clipped
    As they chose love versus wrong.

The selfish nature that they had,
    That used to spit and fight,
Has been transformed by love and peace.
    The "Old Cat" is dead tonight!

MOOSE IN THE WILLOWS BY GREG WALZ

January

~ 25 ~

The person who would purchase a good memory must keep their installment accounts current by paying attention.

Luminary Dissertation on Love

In the balanced life of a man or woman, love is all things. Consider; Love is both rest and action. Love is the spirit of peace and the spirit of rest, expressing itself in the movements of fulfillment and activity. Love is the catalyst in the composition or chemistry of achievement. This may explain that love:

• Transforms theories into actualities,

• Transmutes problems into solutions, and

• Quickens the vibrations of the material until it functions according to the inner laws of its higher spiritual nature.

Love transmutes the higher, essential energies of spirit into movement, matter and accomplishment. From whichever point of divergence we view it, love is the chemistry of a victorious, evolving humanity. Love is the basic principal of the spiritual, as well as the material universe.

Perhaps the greatest chemistry of love is the:

• Transmutation of darkness into light,

• Ignorance into knowledge, and

• Disequilibrium into balance, plus all the other subtle

• Changes from negativity to positivity, from

• Instability to stability, from

• Superstition to comprehension, from the

• Aloneness of individuality, to the

• Comfortable unity of identity with all things.

These processes arise from the stirring and the changes taking place in the crucible of the inner mind as it reaches out for comprehension and understanding of the All.

~ 57 ~

Like Noah's dove that went out from the ark across the swollen waters, the mind and the soul only find a resting place for their weary feet as they learn to love. Do hurting people come back to the ark when they come back to the fact that in, through, under, above and around all manifest things is the manifest energy of God? Love's composition of inner transmutation and transformation does not only change the persons and their viewpoint, but it begins to change their external condition. It begins to change their environment, for they are the masters and not the servants of it now. Love begins to change their inadequacies to strength and, therefore, they are not the same persons with the same viewpoints. Nor are they positioned in the same disadvantage as they previously were before the chemistry of their souls began to work out the solutions to their negative circumstance. The enlightened persons observe the true composition of love. The balanced and energized persons will intuitively know the secrets of love energy, and the secrets of matter, for they know the secrets of God. They dwell in the secret place of the most high.

HOME IS WHERE YOU ARE

Give me a cottage great or small
    By the mountains or the sea.
Home is where you are, Love,
    And evermore shall be.

The pillow of your soft breast
    Is comforting for my head.
Home is where you are, Love,
    No matter where the bed.

Home is in your arms, Dear.
    I need no other place,
For all the joys we've ever known
    Are mirrored in your face.

Home is in your arms, Love,
    Here true contentment lies.
I need no other sheltering roof
    Than the beauty of your eyes.

January

26

All nature is but the garment of God, and those who lean hard against
God's Garments can feel the heartbeat of the Divine.

CREATIVE VISUALIZATIONS AND JACKSON FABLES
(CREATIVE VISUALIZATIONS AND JACKSON FABLES ARE FOUND ON THE LAST FEW PAGES OF EACH MONTH)

Today, please become familiar with the basic principles of creative visualization that we will offer now, before the mechanics and methods of presentation are introduced.

We quote: "As you rest, I want you to think about some special things. You can repeat them silently after me if you start to feel too drowsy. You can repeat after me the things that I'm saying like a silent echo, and that will help you not to be too relaxed. Find this point of reference where you're relaxed and everything is shut out, yet you are mentally alert in this beautiful, warm cave where you're listening, thinking and seeing pictures clearly.

"Here are some of the pictures that I'd like to suggest that you see: See yourself as a successful person. See yourself with a smile on your face. You are a happy person. You will have good success in this class. You like your teacher and your teacher likes you. You like this room with its special arrangement and its decor. You like this room because of the oil paintings and the posters. You like it because of the equipment, the lab, the earphones, the tables, the comfortable chairs and the spaciousness of it. You like it because it's your room and there's a feeling of security and comfort here. You are very comfortable, warm and relaxed. Now as you relax, think of yourself not only as a happy person, a safe, comfortable, and confident person, but also as a very intelligent person. If anyone in your whole lifetime ever told you that you were a dumb-bunny, or that you were a knucklehead or that you were stupid, just remember that they made a mistake. You are intelligent, you are beautiful, and you are wonderful. Everyone has something to be proud of. You have reserve energy that can be tapped just like the genius taps reserve energies. What is it that makes people seemingly more brilliant than others? I'll tell you a little secret. They have found where to break a hole through the ice of mediocrity and where to fish for ideas. You, too, can find this same fishing hole. It contains the wealth of your high self and the secret reserves of your subconscious mind.

"Now that you are opening up the aperture of your mind, you will find hidden treasures of inner potential, abilities and assistance that you can rely upon."

The term Relaxed Learning is used here in the sense of self-conditioning through the meaningful experiences and positive mental exercises as well as the absorption of factual material during a period of concentrated relaxation. Relaxed visual concentration is vital to the effectiveness of the stimulator. Relaxed Learning furnishes the basic self-stimulators, self-image visualizations, and success motivators. It provides the essential self-help affirmations in depth, which are in themselves vicarious experiences in creative thinking and in creative living. They are foundations upon which you can build your own superstructure. Later, as needed, these positive thoughts are projected back to the judgmental conscious mind for reevaluation and application as guiding principles and mental patterns in daily living.

Relaxed Learning expands awareness; it implants self-improvement activators in a pictorial form entirely acceptable to the programming capacities of the inner mind. Its descriptive manner captures the attention and imagination immediately and pleasantly. Beneficial results in many cases follow immediately.

Relaxed Learning systematically and effectively presents such important subjects as have been found fundamental to proper self-image, self-improvement and actual achievement. No lengthy exposition of mental states is intended here, as Relaxed Learning is a pragmatic, psychological approach to learning and behavior modification rather than a theoretical one. Relaxed Learning with its visual induction is just as effective for adults as for children, since in both cases the symbols, stories and pictography of the verbal visuals that encode the self-improvement concepts are addressed to the subconscious "child mind" of each person involved.

Relaxed Learning uses a form of subcortical linguistics, which is a composite form of address directed to the passively relaxed conscious mind and also to the other side of the mind. This occurs as an intuitive combination of balanced, effective sound combinations, tones, inflections, rhythms, symbols, stories, picture descriptions, vivid verbal visuals and a pervasive, persuasive projection of mental and spiritual energies to convey qualities, characteristics, meaning and acceptance of the intended and communicated message. Only a small part of this is lost in the written form, but it is greatly enhanced with group dynamics with the close proximity of the teacher and the meaningful stimulation and interacting response of other persons. Herein lies much of the success of Relaxed Learning as a psychological teaching method.

This Relaxed Learning material is highly original and innovative and is indicative of the vast, untapped potential of man's creative mind and activated imagination when harnessed to an essential objective. The Relaxed Learning tapes have been used in school, church and business on a continuing basis since 1953. Over seven years, the Principles of Relaxed Learning have been taught as a method of facilitating learning and as an aid to individual self-improvement in grades 5, 6, 7, and 8 in a suburb of Denver, Colorado.

The same Relaxed Learning tapes have been used with hundreds of individuals on an adult-education level as well. You have in your hands the Relaxed Learning material to be presented in the following months under their appropriate headings. The ingredients for a new and happier life of successful being and doing lie within the covers of this book.

By way of practical administration of the program, the teacher should personally prohibit any possible disturbance during the Relaxed Learning sessions. A "class concentrating! Do not disturb!" sign should be on the outside of the classroom door. No anger should ever be projected while students are at this very sensitive and impressionable relaxation level. Nothing negative and no teacher reprimands should be aired at this time or even shortly after coming up from the reduced activity level.

An important element in Relaxed Learning is the opportunity given the pupils to give "positive, visual feedback" after listening to the tapes. No critiquing or negative student reactions are ever permitted during or immediately after the sessions because of the very real possibility of increased suggestibility being subjected to adverse influence by some well-meaning but negative expression. Negative reactions, if any, can be best handled on an individual basis in conference. Students are encouraged to describe the things they have seen mentally or have tasted, touched, smelled and heard, but especially the things that came through the most vividly. No retelling of the complete story or recall of detailed facts is expected.

A homelike atmosphere in the classroom with indirect lights from additional lamps used instead of the overhead lights during the Relaxed Learning exercises is desirable. Mood music and soft lights (no red or pink) have therapeutic value. No rock-and-roll type of music is consistent with this method of teaching during a relaxation session.

Should someone drop off to sleep while listening, simply rub their back a little, or gently and quietly let them know the session is over. You could end the session with, "Everybody wide awake! Let's not go quite so deep next time. Keep your mind alert and wide awake while you listen." Do not let other students abruptly awaken any deeply concentrating or sleeping student. This is for the teacher only. If necessary, have the whole class stand and do stretches for a minute to see that everyone is alert and ready to work on the regular assignments or leave the room for recess, lunch or home.

The teacher who works with Relaxed Learning must actually become a positive person, a student-reinforcing kind of person. Good teaching models the virtues intended for student assimilation.

GOOD, GOOD NEWS

Out of the womb of darkness and night
    Springs hope on the wings of day.
Out of the human flow of words
    Faith's thought-line weaves its way.

So weave your words and speak them
    And think those thoughts sublime.
For out of the little shall come the more
    And "your day" will arrive on time!

The birds of despair with molting wings
    Will shed their black feathers of fate.
With shining crests and silver plumes
    They come singing for those who wait.

Then decree the thing, and will it.
    Envision the things you choose.
Soon the good God's messengers
    Will be bringing you good, good news!

MUSTARD SEED FAITH BY BRUCE EAGLE

January

~ 27 ~

*The establishment of a person, an institution or a fortune rests on the
fulcrum of its foundation and is raised by it as well as upon it.*

THE COLOR BIRDS AND LEVELS OF AWARENESS
(CREATIVE VISUALIZATION)

Okay, with your feet flat on the floor. All our eyes closed. Find a comfortable place you can hold without body movements. With the beautiful background music for peaceful relaxation, it should be very easy for you to concentrate. Now, let's relate or associate the colors of the different states of mind, or the colors usually associated with certain brain wave activity at its different rates of vibration.

We're going to start by using a visual of birds. The highest level of the human mind is the high self, the super-consciousness or the spirit level of a person. The highest level of intuitive knowledge is associated with this higher self. The first thing I want you to see clearly is a stormy evening about dusk. The sun is setting, the wind is blowing, thunder is cracking and rolling, and the lightning is flashing around a great, gnarled pine tree on the mountainside. The tree is bending and swaying in the wind. It is groaning and creaking. The breezes are sighing a sad sort of song through its boughs. In the very top of that tree, with the rays of the sunset reflecting and scintillating off from its feathers, is a beautiful white dove. It is snowy, spotless white. I want you to imagine that in addition to the rays of the setting sun, there is a white spotlight flashing and rotating and shining on the white dove. It is sitting on the very top limb of the tree. Let this dove, with the purity of its whiteness, represent the intuitive knowledge of your higher self. Associate the white light with the white dove. He's happy and he's singing softly as the sun is setting and the light is reflected from his feathers. He is very comfortable and very relaxed.

Counting down past the knots and the little pieces of pitch on the side of the tree and the gnarled pieces of indented bark, about three limbs below, you'll find the beta bird, a red cardinal. He's standing on the limb and on his right leg there is a little tin or metal band. It has on it the numbers 14-28, with little "BV" initials after that. It means 14-28 brain vibrations or cycles per second. 14-28 represents the brain wave level of mental activity. This bird is getting a little drowsy. I want you to imagine that his eyes are like mirrors or the screen on a television set. It flicks quickly. And here's what's flicking on those little glassy eyes of this red cardinal: There's a 28, and as the numbers go down, let's imagine that the brain waves of the bird are reduced correspondingly. First it's 28, then 27. See it flick on the eye, like on the screen. . . 26, 25, 24, 23, 22, 21, 20. . . they're flicking quietly, 19, 18, 17, 16, 15. They're moving a little slower now, 14, and the bird nods and dozes a bit.

~ 63 ~

His color is red. Remember he is the beta bird, the cardinal. The red color is associated with the beta brain wave activities of 14-28 cycles per second. Notice him blink his eyes again sleepily and tuck his head under his wing. He's not completely asleep, but drowsy, because he represents reduced activity. He is still rustling his feathers a little but he's getting ready, as he goes down from 28 to 14 to completely relax. You wouldn't see a tight muscle in that bird. He's relaxed and at the lower level of his beta brain wave activity.

Okay. Down a little farther on the tree is a third bird. It's a blue jay. He has a little tin band on his leg, too. See it clearly with the indentation, like the serial numbers on motors and machines. It says 7-14. This is the brain wave vibration of the blue jay, who represents the alpha brain wave level of mental activity.

A light is revolving on the blue jay and his feathers become dark blue, then light blue. And the wind as it blows is ruffling his feathers just a little. Rain is dropping a patter here and there. Mostly it doesn't get to the blue jay because of the branches. He is the alpha bird, and he's the relaxation bird for sure. I want you to notice something different about him. He has earmuffs on! Can you imagine a blue jay with earmuffs on? He has tuned out his sensory perception. That means he doesn't hear the outside distracting noises as clearly as he did before. Now if there was anything he wanted to hear, he could hear it right through the earmuffs, because as we relax and go down to the alpha level, our hearing ability increases so much that we sometimes say, "Please turn the music down," or "speak quietly." We can hear right through these imaginary earmuffs. Picture the blue jay. He has to shut out some things and say, "I'm not going to listen to the unimportant sounds." This is the alpha blue jay. Blue is the color, and the alpha blue jay has his earmuffs on.

I want you to notice his eyes! They're closed tight, but they are relaxed. His eyelids flutter down like a leaf when they close; still they're almost shut. The blue jay has on a pair of dark glasses like a movie actor would wear, right across his little beak. You can't see his eyes, but let's picture the numbers from 14-7 counting down, showing on his sunglasses. Notice these numbers going slower as they go down. . . 14, 13, 12, 11, 10; slower, 9, 8, 7. That's the alpha brain wave activity rate, 7-14, and the alpha bird is so drowsy that he doesn't hear any unnecessary noises. He doesn't see unnecessary things. He has shut off his ordinary sensory perception in order that he may hear with his inner ears, see with his inner eyes, and talk with his inner voice. He has a rubber band around his beak. He's not chirping or talking out loud. If he were going to talk to anybody, he would send a silent message. He could broadcast "I LIKE YOU BECAUSE" with his eyes shut; he would have extrasensory perception. He would exercise intuitive knowledge. He would see clearly even with his eyes shut. He would hear even with his earmuffs on. He could speak with his second, silent voice to people and even convey messages telepathically. But he's pretty sleepy. If a bird could yawn, he would. But he can't. He has that rubber band around his beak. He's stretching a blue wing way out and a light is reflecting on it. He's pulling that metal leg band with the 7-14 on it, up under the ruffled feathers on his breast. Now he's tucking his head with the earmuffs, his colored glasses, and rubber-band-wrapped beak right under that blue wing. He's already sacking out. He is not going completely to sleep, but he's so relaxed that he is tuned to the inner self and to things of another dimension. He is tuned to perfect concentration on anything he wants to think about. Let's leave him resting there.

Climb on down this big old gnarled fir tree or pine tree a few more branches, and there, snuggled up against the trunk of the tree, you find a very unusual owl. He's a green owl. You know how an owl blinks his eyes. Well, he's blinking his eyes like that. He has a metal leg band on, too. And it says 3½-7 brain wave vibration. Let's count him down, too. Notice how every time he blinks his eyes, you can see a number. And the numbers are going slower and slower because he's getting down toward the bottom of his alpha level. Watch the numbers on his eyes as he blinks them. . . 7, blink, 6, 5, 4, 3½. Right out where the alpha blue jay wore his sunglasses on the end of his nose, the green owl has a little TV set. His eyes are closed gently, but he can see his TV. It has clear, vivid, visual imagery on it. It has pictures in color and in action. He sees it like on television in the middle of his forehead except it's projected out a little ways in front of him. So, this owl has his own private, miniaturized TV set out on the end of his curved beak. And he can see right through the middle of his forehead with his eyes shut, too.

Look at his green feathers. He is the theta bird. He is the wise bird. He is intuitive. He has wisdom, not just knowledge. He knows the principles of things. He gets underneath the surface, and he knows the how and the now, the why and the because of all things. He sees into reasons as well as results. He's the green theta bird who represents the creativity level of mental activity. The light that's flashing on him is a yellow green, olive green, blue green, then back to yellow green, olive green, and blue green. He is a very beautiful green bird. The band on his leg says 3½-7 brain wave vibration or cycles per second. Remember that the green owl is the wisdom bird. He is the creative bird, or theta bird.

This level of mental ability can get you better grades and allow you to use the other side of your mind whenever necessary.

Now, there's one more bird that you must see. He's the delta bird, and he's as black as coal. He's a raven. He's clear down on the ground, snuggled into the leaves underneath the tree. He's sacked out completely. His head is nodding. He's the delta bird. He has a band on his leg, too. It starts with ½. On this tin band it says ½-3½. However, he's so near asleep we can't see his eyes. If we could see the numbers reflected in his eyes, we'd hear him counting to himself, 3½, 3, 2, 1, ½. And if he added 0, he'd black clear out until he couldn't even see himself. He would just be a black bird on a dark night sitting on the black ground in velvet-soft blackness. But, let's don't go down that far right now. Let's leave the delta bird snuggled down there on the leaves and we'll come on up a ways to either the theta green owl of creativity or to the alpha blue jay of relaxed learning. Or, we can go clear back to the white dove of the superconscious and the higher self, which really integrates all levels or states of mind as one in the pure white light of completeness and attainment.

Now listen to the music for a little while and think about these birds and their colors. The dove represents the higher self, the pure spirit of a person. The red cardinal represents the beta playground activity. The blue jay represents complete relaxation in alpha, with soft blue light around him. Then we went to the theta green owl, which was wisdom—intuitive knowledge. And then the black bird or the raven was the delta bird, representing sound sleep with autonomic minimal consciousness.

Again, the wind is blowing through the branches. The trees are swaying and groaning, but the birds are holding on tightly and they're safe from the storm. Just remember how fortunate you are that you have learned to use the other side of your mind. Remember that it is a hidden treasure. It is an ability to tap resources that many other people have never found and many will never find. It is your treasure chest where you have many hidden riches to retrieve and to exchange with the world for the things that you need. You will look forward to your times of concentration. You'll look forward to your times of relaxation. And as you use the different states and levels of your mind, you will open up many hidden mental reserves that you never dreamed you had.

You are becoming wiser than you were before, because you are using more than your reasoning mind, which we usually judge as the seat of our intelligence. But you'll be using an inner eye to see with—a second kind of hearing. Depth upon depth of inner intuition, wisdom and strength are becoming yours. You'll be able to increase your knowledge and to use all of your extrasensory abilities, plus you will notice that your physical hearing is keener. You will notice that your eyesight, as well as your insight, is better. You will become aware that you taste and enjoy your food more; you'll notice that your fingertips are more sensitive to things. You will be, and now are, an all-around, well-developed, perfectly functioning individual. You will notice greater efficiency in all of your playground activity and in your personal relationships. You will be in the right place at the right time, doing and saying the right things with the right people with the right results.

These are some of the advantages that come to those who learn to use their altered states of awareness and to those who learn to relax. EASY does it. Just relax and shift gears, like in a car. Please remember that we've learned to bring all of these levels up into our activity level so that we have integrated or meshed gears with all of these abilities while we are wide awake with our eyes open, and we are very, very alert.

I congratulate you. Enjoy the music for a little while and rest. As we come back to the activity level, come back rested, feeling better than you've felt before in your whole life. All things will grow increasingly better more and more as the days come and go. Better and better, more and more. Just enjoy your relaxation for a few minutes.

Okay, coming up slowly now. Will you sit up, please? Just sit up quietly, every head up now, all eyes open! Take a big stretch! All of you take a big stretch. Stand please and stretch again. Great!

Thank you so much. Let's get ready to share the pictures, whatever they were, that you saw the most clearly. What did you see in your mind's eye in color and in action? What did you hear? What did you taste, smell and feel?

CUTTING CLOTH FROM
THE GARMENTS OF GOD

Cutting cloth from the garments of God
    Taps the flow of His love and power,
Like smelling the fragrance of roses
    Or the freshness of a summer shower.

Thru God and from Him and by Him
    All things unceasingly flow.
Consisting, existing, sustaining
    His provisions increasingly grow.

Cut your cloth from the garments of God;
    A suit or a dress or a tent;
A pillow, a bed or a blanket,
    His garments are not threadbare or rent.

Cutting cloth from the garments of God
    Doesn't leave Him impoverished or poor.
His robes show no loss for our taking.
    Our cutting but produces the more.

You can shape the cloth to your patterns,
    And cut it to fit your need.
The world is naked and hungry.
    There are millions to clothe and to feed.

There is cloth to be cut from God's bounty.
    Take the scissors of faith in your hand.
There is gracious provision and plenty
    In the relationship of God toward man.

Cutting cloth from the garments of God
    Is still the privilege of faith and of prayer.
Bring your patterns, your scissors and the naked.
    God is anxious His garments to share!

BEAR OF THE WEST BY GREG WALZ

January

28

*He who would find the Creator need not change his location,
only his point of view!*

The Hibernating Bear Visual

(CREATIVE VISUALIZATION)

Breathing deeply, relaxing completely, sitting comfortably with your feet flat on the floor with your eyes closed, please visualize in color and in action as we present The Hibernating Bear Visual. As you do this, you are bringing yourself to a creative level of mind vibration. You are also lowering the inner and outer activity of your entire body. Having lowered your physical metabolism, you are able to regroup your energies and direct them all to a converging point of "now-ness," where you give full attention to the thing that we're doing at the moment. The past does not intrude, nor does the future, but you are conscious only of the ever-present now. Time loses some of its value. Time passes very quickly and pleasantly as you fully concentrate.

Now, as you see the suggested pictures, you will become relaxed like our hibernating bear. The things you hear and learn will stay very firmly in your memory. Abilities and traits and strengths and mental reserves will be awakened within you as you listen to the visualization and as we draw conclusions at the end of it. Let's do our bear visualization now!

It's wintertime. A giant grizzly bear is looking for a cozy, warm cave. He feels like he must hurry. The grass and tree leaves have turned brown and yellow. The leaves are falling. It is late, late autumn. The bear has been eating all summer just to get fat for the winter. Many other animals are getting ready for winter, too. The squirrels are running all around, gathering nuts and taking them up to little holes in the trees. Birds are flying south.

The grass was green last summer, but the rains finally passed and it was hot and dry during the late summer. Now, in the fall of the year, the grass has shriveled up and become brownish yellow and tan. It stands in little clumps on that steep hillside, and rocks are sticking out between these scattered clumps of dry grass. Some of the grass is tall; other bunches are very short and very dry. It would catch fire quickly if lightning struck or if someone carelessly dropped a match. It's a steep hillside. Down at the bottom of it is a little stream. There are some skunk cabbages growing there. You can see their yellow and green leaves. There are some little water lilies in it, and trilliums are growing in the dead, damp leaves in the shade under the big trees. There are also some pine and fir trees along the creek. On the other side of the creek is a windfall—a jungle of broken timber—dry now, and some of the trunks are showing white where the bark has peeled away and fallen from them. Skeleton limbs reach out like fingers and arms from the fallen trees that lay crisscrossed in every way. The windfalls are leaning up against the face of a steep bank that makes us wonder what might be back behind and under those fallen trees. Up on the hillside to the right are some fir trees and some lodgepole pines that are not much bigger around than the size of your arm. Over to the left are some green cedar trees with the branches gracefully sweeping clear to the ground. There are also some giant ponderosa pine trees that stretch way up to the sky with their rough, bark trunks.

We see lots of scratch marks on the bark where a huge bear has reached up higher than a man could reach and has dug great cracks and claw marks into the tree to show any other bear coming that way who's the tallest and who's the strongest. Notice the berry bushes down at the bottom of these trees. There are huckleberries, salmonberries and blackberries. Look closer and you'll find that the summer sun has dried the berries that are still hanging on the vines, and they're as dry as the dried fruit you would buy in the store. This fruit is so sweet that anyone would enjoy eating it for substitute candy.

Let's watch those bushes. They're starting to wiggle. They're starting to sway and move. Maybe it's a breeze coming up through the valley, caressing the surface of the creek as it blows along, moving the cattails and carrying the smell of skunk cabbage and trilliums. Something is stirring and moving with jerks and starts and stops. Maybe it isn't a breeze. Maybe it's a bear! Look closer and you'll see that the bushes are parting. You see a wet, black nose and muzzle coming through. That bear has probably been down to the creek hunting for salmon or trout. Here he has circled around back of the bushes to have a few sweet, dried berries for dessert. He's pushing the bushes aside! Here he comes waddling out. Wow! He's wider than a door! He has little pig eyes that look like tiny slits because he's so fat. That bear is really a fat one. You are watching him only in imagination, so let him come on out. He won't see you sitting here comfortably in your seats.

So here he comes out waddling, licking his chops because he has just finished off the last one of those sweet blackberries and juicy salmonberries. He's grunting and mumbling and talking to himself as he walks along. He's saying to himself, "I've got room for one more big, white, fat grub worm. Maybe I've got room for just one more big, fat bug like I'd find under the bark of an old stump." Sure enough, he's headed right for a stump in the middle of the clearing on the hillside. He's sitting down. He's too tired, fat and lazy to stand up. He's sitting down, and you can see the rolls of fat on his tummy. He's reaching over and raking and scratching with those big, black claws. Look at that hairy arm! What a bear! He's going to rake that whole stump over! No, he just pulled all the bark loose off of one side. He's got his nose down in it now. He's licking up with that pink tongue all of the little bugs and worms and ants that are hurrying and scurrying and wiggling, trying to get away from him. He sees them just the same, as he gets every one of them. Now he's inching and scooting over on his bottom closer to the stump. He's beginning to lick off all of the bugs and worms that are half-buried in the tunnels and the holes that they made in the tree under the bark. He's licking them out and digging them out, too. Then he just sits back like he's half asleep and very happy. He's thinking about something else like, "I couldn't hold one more bug. I couldn't hold one more berry. I couldn't hold one more wiggly worm or find a place for one more drink of water. I've just had everything a bear could have." He scratches the hair under his ribs with those long, black claws. He can't even feel his ribs, because there are about three inches of fat, padding him like a warm quilt that will keep him warm all winter long. He has decided it's time to do something that he has been thinking about. In the back of his mind, Mother Nature keeps projecting a picture of a certain cave. He hasn't been there yet because he is a young bear, but something tells him where to go and what to do.

He starts lumbering awkwardly down the hill. His hindquarters are up in the air, and he's taking big, awkward steps as he moves around the rocks and brush. The little pebbles are rolling down ahead of him. The little spirals of dust are coming up. Then something touches his nose! He licks it off. Something begins to blow hard and cold against his fur coat from behind. If you will look closely, you can see that under the long, black, guard hairs there is a rust brown undercoat of fur.

It's a cold winter wind that is blowing his hair right up toward his big shoulders as he stumbles down the hill. The wind is saying, "My name is winter and I'm coming fast. I'm going to howl around your cave, and I'm going to almost freeze the feet of the little animals, the squirrels and even the birds that go south. I'm the winter wind, and I'm on my way." So the bear hurries a little faster. Something wet and cold touches his warm nose again, and he licks it off. Then he looks up and sees the snowflakes that are starting to float down like feathers out of a goose's breast. Winter is here! He hurries a little faster.

He doesn't know where to go, but something tells him, "Go, bear, go." He's on his way. He comes to the creek, but he can't let that little stream stop him. He wades right into it, deeper and deeper. He is thinking, "My, the sound of that little creek as it rolls and laughs and tosses and tumbles sounds good to me. I'd like to hear that creek music all winter long." He can smell the tree that has been in the sun so long it has turned white and the bark has fallen off, and the limbs stick out like the fingers and arms of a skeleton. He's crawling down under that windfall and the pile of limbs and brush up against the bank. Something's telling him, "Push!" He feels a knot raking on his back, so he bows his back down like a dog or a cat as it crawls under a fence. He's going under. He's pulling his hips through now. There in the darkness his eyes begin to adjust, and in the shadows he sees the entrance to a cave. He pushes his way in. He's so big he can barely get through the entrance, but it does get a little broader after he gets in. It also gets a little taller, but it still isn't very big. He turns around two or three times, finds which is the long way of the cave, and lies down.

There he is on his side as he looks out with his little pig eyes under the logs, and out across the creek he sees the snowflakes catching on the dry, brown grass. He sees them settling on the berry bushes and starting to pile up in soft drifts. He sees them swirling and beginning to cover all of the bank of the creek until the yellow and green of the skunk cabbage is turning white with the snow. As he watches it, a soft blanket of white comes down over all of the earth. But he's saying to himself, "Let the wind blow. Let it snow. I couldn't care less, because I won't know!" He rolls over on his back now. He isn't even caring to watch the snow come down now, but inch by inch, growing and growing, the snow drifts until there is just a little slit underneath the dead tree. However, he isn't looking through the opening. He's on his back with his paws folded on his chest, scratching a little once in awhile. You can see his bare tummy, and it's so full that it's arched up like a fat, fat circus clown. He's making little sleepy noises. He's saying, "Good night, pine trees. Good night, fir trees. Good night, berry bushes, stumps, and the creek with its song. I'm going to hibernate and rest. I'm going to shut out all of the sights and sounds of the world I lived in all summer long.

Here, enclosed in my warm cave, I'm going to lower the activity and metabolism of my body. I'm going to relax, hibernate and rest." Then he begins to snore. Z-z-z-z-z-z-z-z. He breathes out gently, then deeply he breathes in. Z-z-z-z-z. He takes another deep breath. He's sound asleep, but I don't want you to go to sleep, because we have important listening to do.

I want you to feel as relaxed as you can, just like the bear lying on his back. Just feel full and satisfied like you've eaten berries or good things, or like you feel right after your favorite meal. Sigh a big, big sigh of release and relief and then just rest. As you rest, I want you to think about some special things. You can repeat them silently after me if you start to feel too drowsy. You can repeat after me the things that I'm saying like a silent echo, and that will help you not to be too relaxed. Find this point of reference where you're relaxed and everything is shut out, yet you are mentally alert in this beautiful, warm cave where you're listening, thinking and seeing pictures clearly.

Here are some of the pictures that I'd like to suggest that you see: See yourself as a successful boy or a successful girl. See yourself with a smile on your face. You are a happy person. You will have good success in this class. You like your teacher and your teacher likes you. You like this room with its special arrangement. You like this room because of the oil paintings and the posters. You like it because of the equipment, the lab, the earphones, the tables, the comfortable chairs and the spaciousness of it. You like it because it's your room and there's a feeling of security and comfort here. You are very comfortable, warm and relaxed.

Now as you relax, think of yourself not only as a happy person—a safe, comfortable, confident person—but also as a very intelligent person. If anyone in your whole lifetime ever told you that you were dumb, or that you were a knucklehead or that you were stupid, just remember that they made a mistake. You are intelligent, you are beautiful, and you are wonderful. Everyone has something to be proud of. You have reserve energy that can be tapped, just like the genius taps reserve energies. What is it that makes people seemingly more brilliant than others? I'll tell you a little secret. They have found where to break a hole through the ice of mediocrity and where to fish for ideas. You, too, can find this same fishing hole. It contains the wealth of your higher self and the secret reserves of your subconscious mind.

Now that you are opening up the aperture of your mind, you will find hidden treasures of inner potential, abilities and assistance that you can rely upon.

It'll be a pleasure to come each day to this room. You'll look forward to it. You'll be happy. You'll go out to tell your friends about it. You'll tell your parents about it. You will rejoice deep within yourself, because you are successfully learning how to relax, to concentrate, to improve yourself, to release your reserve abilities to learn and to accomplish worthwhile things in life. I congratulate you on being a winner!

Your grades will come up. Your disposition will improve. Your citizenship will be excellent. Your relationships with other people, the way you get along on the playground, how you get along with teachers—all of this will improve because it will be easy to make it improve. Picture for a moment this better, wonderful you. You are successful, happy, accepted, intelligent, rich beyond compare in the inner resources and in the hidden treasures of your mind. It's a joy and a privilege to teach students like you. It's also a wonderful privilege to learn a new, easy, happy, successful way to acquire knowledge and to do things better than you have ever done them before.

Now will you stretch a little, please? We're going to come up from our reduced activity level. Take a big, deep breath, open your eyes and stretch as high as you can toward the ceiling. Let's stand up and stretch a little more. Wide awake! Alert, healthy, happy! Thank you again for listening.

UNION WITH GOD

I'm one with the wind
   And the rain and the storm.
I'm one in true essence
   Aside from my form.

Unceasing is the river
   Of forms manifest.
I'm one with the inner
   Unlimited rest.

One with the clouds
   That float in the sky.
One with the visions
   That visit the eye.

One with all peace
   Like an ocean of gold.
One with the humility
   Of courage made bold.

One with the endless
   Essence of all.
In tune with the Infinite,
   I respond to its call.

In fellowship blessed
   I know rapture sublime.
Life's greatest joy is:
   God's fullness is mine!

THE QUIET PLACE BY GLADYS DAVIS

January

~ 29 ~

*A faculty for facts is more fortunate than a facility for fanciful fiction,
foolish fabrications or fruitless fantasy, for the framework
and fabric of failure is founded on falsehood,
but facts fortify infallibility and further favorable fortuity.*

THE GREEN ROOM RELAXATION VISUAL
(CREATIVE VISUALIZATION)

Seated comfortably, breathing deeply, relaxing completely, close your eyes gently and visualize the following *Green Room Relaxation Visual* clearly, in detail, in color and in action.

Please picture your favorite room or den. However, you will need to do some mentally creative, interior decoration. Everything in this room is to be in varying and different shades of *green*! Visualize the walls in some pastel shade of aqua, chartreuse, raw umber or whatever your imagination conceives as you roll it on the bare walls. Now paint your own murals in subdued tones of green with lots of green trees in darker and lighter values and contrast. Remember, you are a "quick draw" artist mentally. It may be that you have a favorite picture where the color key is primarily green that you could hang quickly on the walls of your imagination. If the frame is gold, make it green and gold. Place some green plants here and there in your room.

The rug is a plush, olive green. The lampshade and the bedspread diffuse and reflect a soft, gentle, very restful, golden-green glow. It touches everything in the room with an atmosphere of relaxation and peace. The window curtains or drapes are of soft, green velvet. The windows where you are now standing have tinted glass of green that look out over a level, close-clipped lawn or golf course of restful green backed by rolling green hills and yellow green willows bursting with the life-green of spring. The dark green firs and pine trees on the mountainside call to you. Almost without realizing it, you mentally step outside and feel the springing green turf under your feet as, relaxed and happy, you walk between the many hued green bushes and among the cool shadows.

Why not pick a green branch from just any tree and examine the veins on the back of the green leaves. Look at the waxy upper surface, glossy and green, filled with the chlorophyll of verdant, luxurious life.

Find a place beside a grey-green, moss-covered rock and sit down on the shady side. Sit back, lean against the cool, firm rock. Rest! Now, stretch out on the ground. Lie on your back. Shut your eyes. Taste the green. Feel the green. Listen to the refreshing breeze in the swaying branches of the tall, green trees. See in inner vision the whole green, restful world and just rest, rest, rest! Easy does it.

Remember also that relaxation is the key to lighthearted but meaningful living. You have wanted to and needed to rest like this for a long, long time. You are ready to rest; so just relax a little longer and sigh if you feel like doing it and just rest awhile.

You do feel better. You do feel rested and a lot more relaxed. You feel that you have absorbed some of the restful green color of your envisioning. You are walking back down the rolling green hills and across the manicured golf course again. The little creek murmurs restfully. It seems to murmur, "Relax, Relax! Easy does it. Easy always does it. Life rolls on like a verdant song."

You look at yourself as you step lightly across the stream, and you seem to be surrounded with an aura of soft, iridescent, green light. Your very personal atmosphere is a relaxed, pale green glow of subdued color. Others may not see it, but you feel and see it, for it is a part of you now.

You are back in your Green Room now, comfortably seated again, and you are very, very relaxed. You continue to follow directions as you hear your own or your instructor's voice. You are becoming a very relaxed person. Tensions are gone. You are at peace. Courage, confidence, new hope and the will to listen, learn, live and achieve are yours. The will to live fully and to face life courageously springs up like a fountain within you. Life can be beautiful. Life is beautiful. You are a winner because you are a confident, relaxed person—a new kind of person.

From today on, you will be able to take a deep breath and relax anytime, anywhere you desire to relax, with perfect serenity and comfort. You will be relaxed but alert. You are calmly but firmly confident. You have a beautiful balance between optimism and realism. You will always react calmly, confidently and very courageously in all life situations. You are always in full control of your own relaxation and self-improvement sessions. You may intuitively anticipate the suggestion, or your instructor's command, to terminate a Relaxed Learning session. You will always be wide-awake, active and relaxed when you desire to be.

Open your eyes now. Take a deep breath. Move around a bit. Stretch. Everyone stretch! Wide awake! Alert, rested, happy, healthy, feeling great! Thank you for listening.

January

30

Ingratitude, like the logger with ax and saw,
works in the shade of the tree it undercuts!

THE LAND OF THE NINE-FOOT ELVES, OR
I LIKE YOU BECAUSE . . . (EXPRESSING APPRECIATION)
(JACKSON FABLE)

Once upon a time in the land of the nine-foot elves, a wicked fairy called Bat Wings planted giant thistles and ugly weeds in the gardens of the nine-foot elves. Now, the nine-foot elves prided themselves on their miniature roses, the tiny tulips and the little yellow buttercups. Their buttercups were so tiny that the ants could stand on their back legs and put their hands on the petals and look into the yellow hearts of the buttercup mirrors and see easily how to wash their sweaty faces. You see, the ants worked hard in the garden of the nine-foot elves because they had never before had buttercup mirrors and rose-petaled sinks or hot and cold dewdrops every morning to wash in. But when the wicked fairy, Bat Wings, planted giant thistles and ugly weeds, it wasn't long until the weeds and thistles grew so tall that the giant elves almost broke their backs bending over the tiny gardens, pulling out the weeds.

They couldn't win; the thistles were sharp and the weeds tall, and soon you couldn't see the flowers at all. The wicked fairy rubbed her bat wings together with a soft, silky sound and laughed and laughed. Then she had a really wicked, scary, new idea. "Why not plant bad-thought thistles and weed words, hidden hostilities and stuff to grow into bad actions, angry words, fear forces, fights and all kinds of trouble?" So Bat Wings took her negative-thought seeds and planted them in the ears and eyes and hair and hearts of all the nine-foot elves. Alas, when they woke next morning, they heard themselves grumbling, arguing, fighting, complaining and hating even to get up in the morning.

Now, they really had problems! Their beautiful flower gardens were gone. Their friendship and fun had gone as sour as a dill pickle sandwich with lemon juice dressing. Troubles, troubles! More troubles than weeds. And nobody knew what to do. Then one night, the littlest nine-foot elf, Short Enough (he was really only eight feet, eight and one-half inches tall), had a dream. He dreamed he saw Bat Wings, the wicked fairy, planting thistle and weeds in the garden and negative thoughts and bad ideas in the eyes, ears, noses, hands and hair and hearts of all the sleeping giant elves. He started to wake up and tell everybody how it was. But then he was so tired from pulling weeds and fighting and fussing and being afraid all day that he turned over and dreamed some more.

This time he dreamed about a beautiful, kind, good, golden fairy with butterfly wings of silk and silver. She smiled down on Short Enough and whispered in his big ear, "Listen, Short Enough, here's a new game to play! It always makes Bat Wings sick to her stomach because she can't stand to see beautiful flowers or happy people."

You could almost hear Short Enough mumbling in his sleep when he asked, "What's the name of the game, Good Golden Fairy, with silk and silver butterfly wings?"

"The game," answered the Good Golden Fairy, "is called: *I Like You Because!* And here's how you play it." Then she told Short Enough to have each nine-foot giant elf, in turn, sit on a magic stool in the center of his friends or even enemies. As they stood around him, each, in turn, was told to think something special about him, and each nine-foot elf in turn was supposed to say: "I like you because you have such a kind smile," or, "I like you because you always wear the nicest, cleanest clothes," or, "I like you because your hair is curly, straight, long, or short." Or, "I like you because you smell so good or work so hard, or share your games or play so nice." Or, "I like you because you are always fair, or strong"—or just anything nice!

Short Enough could hardly wait 'til morning. He gathered all the unhappy nine-foot giant elves in a circle and they played the *I Like You Because* game. All around the circle they went. They didn't leave anyone out, and everyone felt so much better and no one was unhappy now. The negative sea-weed ideas quit growing between their fingers, in their eyes and ears and mouths and noses and hair. They were singing and happy as they pulled all the thistles out of their miniature flower gardens. The ants started working again and washed their faces in the hot and cold dewdrops in the rose-petaled sinks and stood on tiptoe and admired their faces in the yellow buttercup mirrors. And sure enough, the wicked fairy, Bat Wings, did get sick to her stomach, turned herself inside out like a rubber ball, and rolled down the mountainside and bounced off the nine-foot giants' land and drowned herself in the sea.

The elves had a birthday party for Short Enough and fed him seven-layer chocolate cake and milkweed ice cream 'til he was so happy and so full he couldn't eat anymore. Every once in awhile, and sometimes every twice in a while, they played the Good Golden Fairy's game, *I Like You Because* . . . just to keep everybody laughing and happy and having fun.

Now will you play the game *I Like You Because* . . .? First, just imagine you are going around the circle, silently telling as many people as you can to remember all the nice things you would like to say. Now, let's open our eyes, form a close, happy circle around the magic stool, and we'll take turns sitting on it while we play, *I Like You Because*!

THE LABORER

A ruler paused once, on a crooked street,
    To speak to a woman of wealth.
She kindly inquired of the affairs of state,
    And the state of his Lordship's health.

A laborer passed, a woman who toiled
    Beneath a load of wood and brier.
The street was narrow, her load was wide,
    And it ruffled the Lady's ire!

"Have the wretch punished, Your Majesty;
    She's neither cultured, well-dressed, nor fair."
"Your pardon, Madam," the King replied,
    "But respect the burdens they bear!"

"See yonder mountains, majestic and high;
    They rest on the foothills and plain;
So we of comfort, culture, and power,
    Are sustained by the laborer's pain."

SMALL BOAT HARBOR BY CAROLINE SEYMOUR

January
～ 31 ～

BLUE MOUNTAIN BY GLADYS DAVIS

UNION

I'm a part of the hunger
   And the cattle that graze.
A part of the cold nights
   And warm winter days.

I'm a part of the wind,
   The rain and the pines;
A part of the fence
   Of cedar and vines.

I'm a part of the people
   And they're part of me,
United but isolate
   In a strange harmony.

I'm part of the long,
   Monotonous roads
Where tractors and trucks
   Carry backbreaking loads.

I'm a part of the hills
   That stretch as they try
To pluck the grey clouds
   From the blue of the sky.

I'm part of the rolling,
   Green and brown earth.
I'm part of the sage-covered
   Plains in their dearth.

I'm a part of the Spirit
   And the heartthrob of life,
In a union like marriage
   With the earth as my wife.

Nature both conceals and reveals the Creator to the minds of men;
those who look long and lovingly will find the Creator everywhere.

GUARDING THE HEN HOUSE BY GREG WALZ

BLUE VASE BY JEAN BARTLETT

February

~ 1 ~

*The study of the reality, the being, and the nature of the Great Creator
is the paramount duty of every mind capable of searching out such truth.*

THE ENTHUSIASTIC PERSON

"Nothing great was ever achieved without enthusiasm!" – Emerson

WHAT IS ENTHUSIASM?

Enthusiasm is more than the effervescence of an Alka-Seltzer to cure a sour mind. It is the up-surging joy of the healthy spirit, the zest of total well-being and the secret of success. It is the emotional lubricant that makes planned effort flow smoothly and almost effortlessly in the desired direction.

Enthusiasm is the reverberating overtones of the warm, integrated, forward-moving individual who has opened his inner being to the unity and rhythmic flow of the spiritual universe that has its own hidden laws of:

• Being,

• Measure,

• Meaning and

• Purpose.

Enthusiasm is the river flowing through the gates of the dam to turn the wheels and dynamos of practicality. It is the lifeblood of being. It throbs and pulses in zestful living. It laughs in recreation and play. It works long hours that seem but minutes in the self-forgetful absorption of self-expression and creativity. It is the essence of life, the heartthrob of achievement. It is like the pounding of the surf playing and working away at the ocean shores of all activity.

Enthusiasm is a song that sings the harmony of universal things. It is the feeling of unbeatable drive in the piston-like propulsion of the racehorse with the wind in its mane and its heart bursting with the joy of competition and the prospect of being first across the finish line.

Enthusiasm is the foe of mediocrity, the sister of creativity, and the fortification against failure. It is a singleness of purpose born of the uncluttered mind whose sense of direction is accurate and whose detachment from the unnecessary and secondary has been completed. Enthusiasm is the whir of rising wings when forward thrust overcomes resistance, where lift laughs at gravity and lofty levitation of inner being changes the entire perspective of life. It is the eagle's-eye viewpoint of purposeful optimism, the vantage point of God-confident, self-confident, life-confident assurance of the individual who expects the cooperation of a compatible universe. It is the warm, anticipated

- Handclasp of congratulation,
- Pride of participation, the
- Dependability of teamwork and the
- Overflow of released life forces

that rise resistless and beautiful to make the desert places blossom with the verdant foliage and fruit of distinct achievement.

Enthusiasm is the love of life, the joy of self-expression, the song of unselfish service, the action of achieving faith. It is the spark of genius, the unconquerable spirit of adventure in the pulsing blood of the pioneer. It is sincerity, earnestness, dynamic drive and the cadence of conquest.

"NATURAL LAW"

What holds the clouds above the blue
 Of yonder mountain peak?
Who ruffled them up and rolled them there—
 For to my soul they speak
Of grandeur, beauty, majesty—
 Some reason would I seek.

"Natural Law," I hear folks say;
 But what designing mind
Conceived, Created, and Sustained
 These wonders that I find?
Who filled this canopy of blue
 With clouds of every kind?

The heavens are God's handiwork;
 He hangs the world in space;
For God the Architect Divine
 Conceived this happy place;
And He who made it for His own,
 Sustains it by His grace.

February

~ 2 ~

WHITE ROSE BY R. JACKSON

HIGHER MOUNTAINS

There are mighty, matchless, towering mountains—
　　Stalwart sentinels standing now on high.
And there are vaster, sunlit mountains, too,
　　Than these that rise in earth's blue sky.

These are mountains in the realm of spirit.
　　They are mountains tall of faith and love.
They are mountains that all must conquer,
　　Silent mountains beckoning from above.

They are mountains filled with holy challenge—
　　Mountains that with bleeding feet we climb.
But when we attain at last their summits
　　We have reached at last a plane sublime.

God, grant our eyes be set upon the mountains,
　　That their beauty still may fill our view.
This kind of mountain climbing is a virtue.
　　To the heights of faith and love I challenge you!

*Faith is a laser-beam of vital, spiritual force directed to the
illumination and direction of the affairs of life.*

February

3

Successful manifestation of things hoped for depends upon visually "playing house" in the new and expected environment with as vivid an imagination, and feeling of ownership, as actual and grateful present-possession itself would make you feel.

QUIET ENLIGHTENMENT

The beautiful privilege, or privileged position, of the enlightened persons in relation to their world cannot be bought by price, but is the result of transmutations within their own spiritual nature, which in turn affect their visional abilities, their mental capacities, and their creative and causative powers. There is an increase in their ability to see, to comprehend, to identify with and to interpret the fact of their world which, in actuality, is so different from that which on the surface it appears to be. The enlightened person seeks knowledge that can set people free.

No scientific discovery by an enlightened searcher for truth is made primarily to acquire scientific evidence on the demonstration plane. That person may delve into science and certainly does. This person may discover fundamental principles of science, of nuclear physics, astronomy, astrology, or any and all of a multitude of sciences or pseudosciences, but this person's one drive is to get beneath the demonstrations and the readily perceived understanding of science, of physics, of geometry, or of materiality in general and even beyond that nature of energy. This person wants to find that point of Divine emergence and the primal source of energy manifestation in its unity and its oneness. This person wants to know the nature of the universe, and as he traces it back through intuition to find enlightenment, he finds that it is a universe of light. This person finds that the light in its duality is possibly a fissional division of the dualities of isometric diamides that originally came from the undivided, pure light of the Unmoved, Unmanifest, Manifestor of all things, Creator God.

The enlightened person's crucibles are the crucibles of desire, or infinite longing of insatiable curiosity. The scales of his laboratory do not weigh precious metals alone, if at all, but they are scales that weigh the possibilities, not only of the finite, but of the infinite. He weighs and measures distinctions—finer, ever finer distinctions—of thought and meaning and developmental emergence back to the primal source and to its beginning, to its nature and its cause. His furnaces are the furnaces of devotion, of love for life; yes, white-heated love for life, but also love for the God of life, a love for the essence of life for which he would lay down the crude, outer protuberances of physical life.

His measuring instruments are not always the modern, scientific apparatus of endowed or self-supported laboratories alone. Rather, his measuring instruments are the infinite patience of long suffering, endurance, quest and conquest where long years come and go as he still seeks for greater light. He seeks for a spark of light with always the vision resplendent before him that, "The path of the just shines brighter and brighter unto the Perfect Day." The viewpoint of God is the holy grail of the search. Silent times contribute to this exploration.

SILENCE

Silence is a spacious house
    Where all along the halls of thought
Are treasure rooms of precious things
    That Solitude hath wrought.

Here Glory stands beside each door
    Where Genius doth her skill unfold;
And knowledge rules with wisdom here—
    Her duties manifold.

True latticework of sunbeams point
    Where vision sits a spinning;
Discovery has its armor here
    And purpose its beginning.

A Laboratory Silence has
    To test each treasure that is wrought,
And then she opens up the door
    To paths with danger fraught.

ROSE IN VASE BY R. JACKSON

FEBRUARY'S GIFT BY SUSAN ALSTON

February

4

*Do more than can be readily forgotten, and do it so well that even
the calloused critics give their begrudging praise.*

COURAGEOUS CONQUEROR

Are you aware that the successful individuals are ones who learn to control their own suggestibility? They largely respond to that which is good for them and reject the bad. Because you value your own integrity, free will and destiny, you are eternally vigilant and on guard against negative suggestions and influences, whether they are obvious or subliminal. Reject negative influence immediately and instinctively. Do not be influenced by what you would not choose when you are at your very best.

Today you can be self-confident and courageous! A conqueror is a person who believes that he can. Just affirm: I believe I can. I will! I can! Let it echo from a thousand cliffs. Let it reverberate in the ocean's roar. Let it sing in cadence of every bird's song. I can! I can! I can! I can! But do not substitute words alone for intended action. Courage does not boast itself falsely in empty words. It does what it must do and what it properly intends to do. True courage is calm and unshaken. Therefore, say you will always react courageously to whatever life brings you.

THE WILL TO WIN

You've heard of the story of Bunker Bean?
It's just a story that might have been.
A salesman knocked at his door one day.
He knocked and talked till he had his way.

He sold him a piece of aging wood
And told him a story he understood.
He whispered it softly so no one heard:
"You're the reincarnation of Rameses the Third."

(CONTINUED ON NEXT PAGE)

"Your features declare it. You have the look
And here's your picture in the history book!
You once ruled Egypt in splendid power.
You're a King at heart for this troubled hour."

And Bunker believed as he sat in his room.
And stroked the wood from his ancient tomb.
"If I did it once, I can do it again!
I'll figure me up a kingly plan."

"For why should a King be laid on the shelf?
If I once ruled Egypt, I can rule myself.
I'll whittle me out a throne today.
In the world of business I'll hold my sway."

When his courage faltered in the face of gloom,
He'd grip the piece from the ancient tomb.
And fiercely whisper as he left his door:
"I can do it again, for I've done it before."

And they say in the story of Bunker Bean
That he whipped misfortune and came out clean.
He rose in power, and he made his "dough,"
And then came truth with its staggering blow.

The salesman was only a racketeer!
The wood was a piece of old veneer,
Or maybe a bit of two-by-four,
And Bunker had never ruled before!

But he learned a lesson of priceless worth
That works for all who walk this earth:
It's faith in yourself and a will to win.
This is the place where we all begin!

So grab a slab or a two-by-four,
And batter away at the padlocked door.
And fortune will smile and let you in,
As a man of faith, with a will to win.
Just say to yourself as you leave your door:
"Whatever I've done, I can still do more!"

February

5

Love is life's fundamental necessity; without it, emotions lose their purpose,
and like Noah's dove, can find no solid place to rest their feet.

THE POWER OF COMMITTED LOVE

Have you discovered the Power of Committed Love? Love is the most powerful force in the world! My Mother once said that "If your desire is strong enough and if your love is vigorous enough, there is nothing within the realm of human possibilities that you cannot achieve." Have you ever thought of love being like a high-voltage explosion? It is wonderful when your heart beats so intensely that you feel it will burst, and your urges are so strong to share this love relationship that you are almost overwhelmed and you feel so good that you want to commit your all, because only your all will satisfy that explosive urge.

This great emotion is so excitingly sensational! However, is this tremendous urge to express this love desire just to satisfy the senses? Now tell me, is this powerful emotion "love" a fantasy, or is it true love? Is this infatuation, or is it the real thing? These questions must be determined with proper balance, for the happiness of your whole life may pivot upon the ecstatic momentary verdict.

Our present world, especially today's society, places such an emphasis upon sex, which is not enduring, and too little upon love, which is eternal. Never forget, love is the highest goal of the whole human race, whether we are aware of its importance or not. Have you adopted any guidelines to help you know the difference between sex and love? Are you headed for the ultimate in happy companionship—the greatest joy and endowment on earth? What a dream! To actually demonstrate to our world that a balanced companionship could be attractive and dynamic, thus encouraging people to live together in a united, joyful, and balanced society.

Would you accept the challenge to salute every day with love and joy in your life? Remember, there is real power within committed love. This commitment of love opens the minds and hearts of all people. Yes, I want to demonstrate love as a most potent intermediary to transport this love to others and thus to myself. Can you perceive your love and my love warming all hearts within our circles, much like the rays of the sun warming the most frigid day in our neighborhood?

Say, "Cupid, thank you for your special love dart. I will always appreciate you!"

WHEN CUPID LOOSED HIS DART

One day when Cupid drew his bow
    And sent an arrow fleet,
I felt a missile barbed with love
    That swept me off my feet.

And when my eyes were opened
    I saw two skies of blue,
Smiling skies, your own blue eyes,
    With love-light shining through.

And since that day a happy hurt
    Has lodged within my heart;
But you were wounded, too, my Love,
    When Cupid loosed his dart!

February

~ 6 ~

*Never let faith's vision die, lest hope expire as well. For with faith and hope
and vision dead, there's little left to tell.*

THE OLD VIOLIN
(JACKSON FABLE)

This account begins with the verbal visual, THE OLD VIOLIN, and proceeds from it into the general area of self-improvement. Creatively and visually picture everything clearly, accurately, in color and in action. May your mind be open and receptive now. May you hear, see, smell, taste and touch the different things that are described. You will be able to sense good descriptive feedback. Please try to understand and practice the conclusions at the end of the account found tomorrow, on February 7.

Here is the story of THE OLD VIOLIN. Can you see an old man? Please look closely. Can you see him clearly, a fiddler of the days gone by, of days that are no more? He's not a classical violinist, not someone who learned in the studio how to play. Instead, picture someone who fiddles instinctively and intuitively out of the creativity and emotion of his own inner being. Picture someone who sat and played for barn dances with the smell of hay in his nostrils, someone who with eyes closed could hear the rhythmic sound of the dancing feet, the swaying bodies, and the laughter. Picture someone who could smell the fragrance of the hay in the loft and the pungent odor of tobacco smoke as he put his soul into the old violin. With his chin pressed caressingly against the warm, polished wood of his violin, the sensitive fingers of that left hand held it as though it were his ticket upraised as a passport to the anywhere and the everywhere. On the emotions and the strings of that old violin he could go and come in fancy where he would.

See him as he played the old tunes automatically, as his mind went back to childhood where he first saw the bow with its relaxed, unstrung, white horsehair. See him standing there, as he wanted to take that violin down. One day he did take it down, and he placed it on the table. He imagined that he was smaller than Tom Thumb, whom he had read about. He looked down in his miniaturized form into a great hollow place in the violin like a giant manhole in the street. In his miniaturized form, it seemed that those strings, beginning with a metallic G, the D, the A and the E, were not violin strings but great cables. He could step from one to the other. It was all he could do in his miniature stride to step from the E to the A string. Then he reached down and took hold of the string, and it completely filled his hand. There was only barely enough finger grip to hold on as he lowered himself as far as his fingers would stretch, down into the dark cavern beneath him. Then he dropped lightly to the wooden floor, where there were great crossbeams. These were not two-by-fours, but great beams that stretched from one end of the wooden box called a violin to the other and the crossbar. He couldn't reach the top and he couldn't reach the sides. Even the grain in the wood seemed like splinters projecting inward. The distinct smell of rosin from the bow filled his nostrils. He could feel the dryness inside that old violin. P.S. Think: How would you finish this story? Read the poem below today. Tomorrow, on February 7, we will complete the account of THE OLD VIOLIN.

ARTIST'S EYES

I have a pair of eyes that only see
   The things my mind is looking for.
Often eyes that should be windows
   Close like heavy wooden doors.

God, grant me Artist's eyes to see
   The hidden meaning of this life
That makes its substance more real,
   Finds rest within the strife.

God give me eyes to see beyond
   The scope of earthly vision small.
Help me see the good that I may do
   In answer to some needy call.

February

7

*An honest self-examination could readily produce a reformation,
and better yet a transformation, if we would face the inner reality
of our introspection with a view to its correction.*

THE OLD VIOLIN
(JACKSON FABLE)

(Recall from yesterday, February 6, the old man imagined himself down inside the old violin.)

He began to pick up vibrations there. He began to pick up overtones. It wasn't any particular song of the songs of yesterday that went through his mind, but the vibrations of the violin became a vast symphony, a vast harmony. It became universal singing so that all of the songs that had ever been sung blended into one song. It was the most beautiful song he'd ever heard, caressing melodies that were forever encased in the vibrations of that old violin. With it were scenes, memories of every place that violin had gone, carried under someone's arm or suffocating in a black violin case. He took the long journey through the old violin. He met people that it had met. He heard the songs that it had sung. Then he began to sing his own song. It echoed and reverberated and changed the sounds within the chambers of the old violin.

He looked up above himself through the hole and wondered how he'd ever get up there again, for it seemed like there were great telephone lines above this manhole in the street, this subterranean vault where he found himself. As he looked up between the bars, they were like the bars of a prison now. The light reflected from up above, where a shaft of light cast great shadows on the floor. A golden sunbeam, where the light broke through, reflected against the far side. Looking up through the hole, he could see there was another dimension beyond the encasement of his own self-imprisonment. He could look above it and see there were things higher and more beautiful. Then, out of the depth of his imagination, he knew that there was only one way he could get out. It was the same way he had gotten in. That was simply to imagine that he began to grow enough in stature until he could reach those strings. Squeezing his way between them, he found himself outside again. He felt such uplift from the eternal harmonies and the accumulated song that he almost felt like rising above everything. He decided to pick a note that he heard within the sound of the violin and to rise and ride on that note anywhere he wanted to go, for this was the secret of the old violin.

Today, think about the following ideas:

Where are you today?

Where would you like to be?

What benefits would you choose to reap?

I MEET MYSELF

I meet myself in every person
    That I perchance may meet.
I walk in every pair of shoes
    That pass me on the street!

A smile or frown I will reflect
    In every mirrored face,
I meet myself and greet myself
    In both triumph and disgrace.

I meet myself in punishment
    And receive again the gift,
That I had given once before
    In liberalness or thrift.

I meet myself on every street
    In circumstance or in deed.
I reap as I have sown before—
    My roses and my weeds!

February

8

*Faith is the pivot of progress, the center of all achievement,
and the source of all inspiration.*

HOW DOES ENTHUSIASM HELP YOU?

- Prerequisite for Leadership
- Earnestness of Enthusiasm
- Inspiration of Enthusiasm
- The Enthusiastic Person—different timbre in his voice

Enthusiasm is a *prerequisite for leadership*. It attracts followers like a fragrant flower attracts the swarming bees. There can be no leadership without followers, and any organization must have people as well as products. You must have people who will work with you, fight for you and share the enthusiasm of your plan and purpose. It is the responsibility of enthusiastic leadership to know what it wants, when it is wanted, where it can be obtained, why it is wanted and how you can go about getting it. The leader who knows the how, why, where, when and what has already built into his own being the steadfastness and assurance of continued enthusiasm, because his emotional drives have intelligent outlet, purpose and direction. His organization and circle of influence will vibrate to his own sureness, knowledgeable authoritativeness and enthusiasm.

The *earnestness of enthusiasm* tends to draw others around the enthusiastic person. There is something catching about earnestness and sincerity, which alerts others who feel as well as hear the purposeful sound and see or sense the vibrant body tones of the enthusiastic leader.

The *inspiration of enthusiasm* is contagious. A person must be an inspired leader to have an inspired following. The greatest power is a spiritual power. A person's truest source of inspiration is the inbreathing of an exalted atmosphere above the negative, dubious mind-smog of failure. The inspiration of enthusiasm is the God-in-breathed emotion of poised action and attraction. It is a controlled contagion of animated feelings. It can arise and must arise in leadership as the inspired result of accomplishment or as the purposeful, self-motivated, positive reaction to the lack of accomplishment. Motives are the inner out-thrusting of emotion or feeling.

Enthusiastic leadership must condition itself to positive reaction regardless of opposing or cooperating circumstances. The person, not the passion, must always be in the driver's seat. The horse can't be in the saddle; and emotion, although it is a driving force, must always be directed and driven, controlled and encouraged, held back, whipped up, or pulled to a halt when it is expedient in the mature judgment of the driver.

The *enthusiastic man has a different timbre in his voice.* It says, "Let's go places. Let's do exciting things. Let's make life sing and shout!" The enthusiastic person is an interesting conversationalist; first because he loves life and has learned to value other people and to listen to what others have to say. Whatever he says or adds to a conversation by way of response, comment or proffered information has vibrancy and a quickening effect on the listeners. His inner wealth and expanded awareness make him intrinsically interesting. The energy of his enthusiasm inspires others not just for WHAT they say but for HOW they say it.

THE TEST OF FAITH

The test of faith is found in works.
To be alive is to believe.
To fraternize and visualize
With God is to receive.

The test of faith is practical.
It is expectation in effect.
If faith is not achieving faith,
That faith is derelict!

Faith that lives must demonstrate.
Its hopes must materialize.
Else faith lies casketed and cold
With sleeping, sightless eyes!

February

～ 9 ～

ROSE ON THE TABLE BY R. JACKSON

IF I CAN GO DOWN TO THE SEA

If I can go down to the sea awhile
   And watch the waves at play,
If I can go down to the sea alone
   I can wash my fears away.

If I can go down to the sea awhile
   And look for the agates bright,
If I can go down by the ocean's side
   I'll "sleep like a log" tonight.

If I can go down to the sea awhile
   And tune my heart to its sound,
If I can go down to the sea to pray
   I know where true peace is found.

If I can go down to the sea awhile,
   Away from the haunts of man,
If I can go down to its jumbled shore
   I'll find myself again.

If I can go down to the sea awhile
   And hear its great waves roar.
If I can go down to its windswept beach
   I can walk with God once more.

If I can go down to the sea again
   And watch the ships pass by,
If I can go down with its surf and sand
   I will have lived before I die.

If I can go down to the sea again
   And sense its surge of power,
If I can be down with its fishing fleet,
   I'll be free as the gulls for an hour.

If I can go down to the sea again
   And walk on the firm, wet sand,
If I can go down to the sea once more,
   I'll walk with God hand in hand!

February

~ 10 ~

Ingratitude is the treason of the thankless heart.
Ingratitude bites the hand that blesses it and licks its lips for more.

THE ENERGY OF ENTHUSIASM

- The enthusiastic person stimulates himself
- Enthusiasm activates and alerts the subconscious mind
- The energy of enthusiasm generates more energy
- The energy of enthusiasm increases brain wattage
- The enthusiastic person—paralysis of advancing fear
- The energy of enthusiasm is invigorating

The *enthusiastic person stimulates himself.* His food digests better, his blood flows freer, and his muscles, relaxed and functioning without tension, permit expressions and gestures to accompany his contagious thought. His physical energy seems inexhaustible.

Enthusiasm activates and alerts the subconscious mind to the value and importance of the situation; it releases hidden powers and taps long-forgotten resources of the inner person. The enthusiastic one finds that he has more money in the intellectual and emotional bank than he thought he had as he shares with those who have overdrawn their emotional reserve through self-indulgence, self-doubt, self-pity, rationalization and hidden hostility. The enthusiast finds that enthusiasm accumulates interest on interest, and the principle seems exhaustless, for he is drawing on the universal supply.

The *energy of enthusiasm generates more energy.* Tiredness gets out of bed, dresses and "goes to town." Ill health finds that physical action and increased awareness are more fun than reading cards of condolence. Laziness stretches farther than it meant to, opens its eyes, jumps to its feet and joins the parade of champions! Our emotions make us or break us. Feeling and emotion are one. Enthusiasm is the feeling of success before, during and after accomplishment.

The *energy of enthusiasm increases the wattage of the brain* as the blood flows faster and farther and ideas and actions cry out to be born. Thought leaps beyond the mind and telegraphs its inspiration to others who are receptive so that the awakened mind becomes an unconscious center of stimulation, a control tower of positive, although unvoiced inspiration and directives.

The *enthusiastic person gives the karate blow of paralysis to advancing fear,* doubt, worry or despair. It lets the dead bury the dead and occupies their attention with progress, practicality, positive living and the principles of achieving faith. Enthusiasm on any racetrack is a horse called "Winner."

The *energy of enthusiasm is invigorating.* It is felt in the handshake of the enthusiastic person. It invigorates, inspires and stimulates, relaxes and encourages just by a simple transference of its glad, vital contagion. It shines in the eyes of love and charges the atmosphere of a room with sunbeams of vitality. It restores people to hope, self-confidence, courage, belief and love. Thus, the energy of enthusiasm pulls back the drapes of despair and watches the shadows and specters of old fears, failures and futility flee away.

INGRATITUDE IS BLIND

He is worthy; God is worthy
Of the sacrifice of Praise
He has been our source of comfort
Thru the years and length of days.

He is worthy of our blessings;
He doth merit all we give.
Thru His providence and keeping,
Thru His grace we daily live.

He has loved us; He has kept us;
He has met our every need.
Now with praise and glad thanksgiving
Grateful hearts rejoice indeed.

Praise is comely! Thanks, a virtue;
Only those of selfish mind
Fail to see the cause of praising,
For ingratitude is blind.

February

~ 11 ~

*Decisions are personal and each person has the awesome right
to determine his own destiny, his failure or his success.*

ENTHUSIASM AND SUCCESS

- Enthusiasm and the writer's words
- Enthusiasm wins friends and keeps them for years
- Enthusiasm and a positive personal atmosphere
- Enthusiasm and eloquence in speech

The *energy of enthusiasm flows over into the words* a writer puts on paper. It adds seasoning to sagacity. It makes a book a living thing when the spirit of the author comes through between the lines. The author's sincerity, earnestness, vivacious thinking and overflowing enthusiasm throw a luster on the printed page that makes the words much easier to read and understand. It inspires the obedience, stimulates the comprehension and evokes the cooperation of students in the schoolroom and makes learning a pleasure. Then it is that slow progress, defeat and failure bow their heads and say, "Step on us if you must, but just keep on climbing where enthusiasm lights the way."

Enthusiasm wins friends and keeps them through the years while others walk a lonely way. Enthusiasm is the right hand of love and the cement of marriage. It is a happy contagion of mental, physical, spiritual and interpersonal excitement that communicates in a thousand ways the prerogative of a positive personality.

The *enthusiastic person has a personal atmosphere that is positive.* It is not misdirected or non-directed energy, but a wisely and purposefully directed overflow of vital power that radiates like a magnetic field or aura of communication around the positive person. It is a drawing, cohesive, wiring vital force or energy field that colors and characterizes the possessor wherever he goes. It is a radiating personal influence that can easily be sensed or felt by others. Enthusiasm is a person's armor against the frustration and failure complex of mediocre living. It is his personal antidote for the negativity of ordinary living. It is a catalyst that blends all diverse, negative and/or positive elements into productive, personal power by the fusion of awakened emotions while it remains unmoved and triumphant in the process.

In speech, enthusiasm is eloquence. It is the one additive in any sales presentation or persuasive situation that cleans out the carbon of sales resistance and adds anti-knock quality to any product.

~ 107 ~

In communication it is eloquence, in the flesh it is good health, in the spirit it is being a comrade with Divinity, in business it is the success of achievement, in life it is confidence, hope, faith, love, progress and dynamic virility. It is power steering with released but directed and controlled emotional impact. It is life with purpose and direction but without prison bars or prison garb of drab conformity and hopelessness. Enthusiasm is the eloquence of a soul set free. The enthusiastic person is always marketing whatever he has!

Enthusiasm is not an add-on to a credit card charge account. There is a price to pay, and every person has the wherewithal to pay it. There are things we can do to attain and maintain enthusiasm.

LIFE IS ALL BRIGHT AND HAPPY

Life is all bright and happy
If we see it thru the eyes of youth.
But life may be quite different
When it is seen thru the eyes of truth.

Life is all bright and happy
As we skip thru the childhood years.
But life may be quite different
When seen thru sorrow's tears.

Life may be bright and happy
When we walk in rectitude's path.
But life can be quite different
Under the lash of wrath.

Life can be bright and happy
If you choose to make it so.
For life is just what you make it
In whichever direction you go.

February

12

*Repose is more to be found within the heart
than to be achieved from change of outward circumstances.*

REPOSE: DIGNIFIED CALMNESS

The persons who rest well, work best.

*A good conscience can sleep better on corncobs and confidence
than injustice on its featherbed of banknotes, greenbacks and greed!*

The number of hours of sleep required for our best health differs tremendously from person to person. The "standard" eight hours of sleep each night appears to be average; however, the essential proof is whether you feel rested in the morning and have sufficient energy to carry through the day's activities. Another consideration we experience may include the next phase of repose, the need for rest during the day.

As people put on a few years of age, it is a good idea to rest; for example, say a half hour after meals and at intervals during the day. Adults whose work does not permit them to lie down should take advantage of breaks or rest periods to relax as completely as possible.

Are there relaxation techniques, methods used to promote the lessening of tension, reduction of anxiety, and the management of stress? Yes, and the physiological effects include a reduction in:

- Pulse rate

- Respiratory rate

- Oxygen consumption and absorption

- Carbon dioxide production and elimination

- Blood pressure

- Metabolic rate

- Muscular tension

Through a variety of practices, several surface with features in common: rhythmic breathing, reduced muscular tension, and perhaps an altered state of consciousness. Using this latter technique, the

109

relaxed individual moves into an alpha level of consciousness, located between full consciousness and unconsciousness. At this level, thought processes become less logical and more associative and creative. At this relaxed level, a person is more receptive to positive suggestions and is able to concentrate on a more specific mental idea or image. When a person returns from the alpha level of consciousness to full consciousness, he feels more rested and more alert.

Best wishes to you as you practice repose and enjoy a dignified calmness. The best of health to you!

"Man works eight hours, sleeps eight hours, and has eight hours left; but it is what he thinks of during the first sixteen and what he does with the last eight that make the real difference."

"Even the blind mole is sensitive enough to know when someone walks over him, trespasses on his private diggings, or when some shadow obscures the warmth of unseen light as he surfaces for a moment in the sun."

WHEN DAY IS DONE

The shadows lengthen on the ground;
The creatures of the day have found
    Their place of rest in tree or mound;
    And night comes in without a sound,
        When day is done.

When sunlight's hiding in the West,
When everyone has gone to rest,
    When prayers are said, and hearts are blest,
    When baby lies on mother's breast,
        Then day is done.

So each day's sun doth climb and set;
And we may face the dusk and fret
    Like children; but we soon forget
    The weariness, the pain, the sweat,
        When day is done!

Like drowsy chirping of the bird,
We too should murmur, "Thank you, Lord."
    Nor heed the tales of night we've heard,
    But smile and rest with hearts assured,
        When day is done.

February

~ 13 ~

ROSEHEART BY JAN LEITNER

MEDITATION PRAYER

This day, Oh God, in its beginning, its proceeding and its closing, is your day. You have given it to us to use as best we may, to invest wisely, live fully and return to thee at sunset, having filled its minutes and its hours with a purposeful pattern of worthwhile things that we have said or done, both for others and to bring honor to your name. Grant us such wisdom that we may order our lives in a worthy manner, after a worthy end, to the good of all our fellow men and to the eternal praise and honor for our Creator who loves us and is always available to us through our blessings. Thank you. Amen.

SABBATH REST

The days of the week had ended;
 The Sabbath had come at last.
And with it had come the rest of death
 With time and labors past.

For just as the stars were fading
 Into the morning of blue,
The aged pilgrim passed beyond
 The stars and morning, too.

For weary and bent with struggle
 That crushed and stilled his mirth,
He dropped his staff and walked with God
 Beyond the toils of earth.

February

~ 14 ~

Love is a song that has a harmony and uplift all its own;
and happy are the persons who learn to sing it with others,
for love's Great Composer intended it not for solos as much as for ensembles.

LOVE IDENTIFIES AND UNIFIES

Love identifies and unifies. The highest intuitive knowing is by identifying with the nature of the object. Identity or fusion of subject and object is only by love, by will, and by desire. It is by choice. All senses of the individual, thus, are fused as one sense, and it is exalted and increased in vibratory intensity. It identifies its magnetic field with the magnetic field of the object. Thus, it is one in fusion and one in being, state and knowledge. I instruct my heart to identify in unity with that which I desire to know, to identify in love and in oneness and yet maintain my own individuality. I will take time to visualize the situation, as I desire it in the atmosphere, as it should be and the reactions of those concerned as cooperative and pleasant. I visualize their anticipated reactions and actions as in a play, as a previewed revision of what seems best under the circumstances.

I'D TELL YOU ON VALENTINE'S DAY

If I were a lamb and you were a tree,
  I'd rest at your feet in the shade.
I'd be glad for the sun
And for rivers that run
  And for God who such loveliness made.

If I were a moth and you were a flame,
  I'd hover around in your light.
If I were that moth
On a curtain of cloth,
  I'd fly in and stay there all night.

(CONTINUED ON NEXT PAGE)

If I were a star and you were a star,
    I'd wink and I'd blink through my tears,
Till your star came to mine
And together we'd shine
    In a halo of love through the years.

If I were a river and you were the sea,
    I'd dash down the mountains with glee.
Like a torrent above
I would pour out my love,
    And mingled forever we'd be.

If I were a glove and you were the hand,
    I know we would perfectly fit,
And I'd grip your warm hand
Across seas or on land,
    And forever I'd be holding to it.

If I were a cup though missing some chips
    And you were the thirsty one,
I'd rest on your lip
While life's fullness you sip
    And emptily sigh when you were done.

If I were just me, and you were just you,
    And we passed on some busy street,
The light from your eyes
Would make the sun rise,
    And I'd lay my heart down at your feet.

If you were a Valentine card on a shelf
    And in shopping I passed by your way,
I'd pay any price
For something that nice
    And I'd tell you on Valentine's Day!

February

~ 15 ~

Hate can pulverize opposition like crushed ice,
but only the warmth of understanding and love can melt it away.

LOVE AND GRAVITY

Love is light. Is love sometimes subjected to the principles of gravity? On the other hand, is it possible that gravity itself may begin to lose its negative pull as it relates to the enlightened person? Could it be possible, then, for a person who does not possess adequate light to make wrong choices which would cause that person to be unable to give or receive love to some degree? Would the less loved person be prevented from experiencing and enjoying love to its fullest extent? Can it be that the very gravity of life experienced by the person who does not live in the realm of luminary love, view the expression and the receipt of love perhaps as a dark and empty "haunted house?" This loss would be real. This vacuum of love would be or could be very painful and may well create insecurity and dread.

Don't forget, gravity has some molecular and structural relationship to the structures and density of matter itself. For example, the more opaque an object is, the less light it possesses. The more its vibrational frequency deviates from the condition of light, the greater the pull gravity has upon its more sonorous and solid qualities. As balanced and energized people become aware of the light of the Creator God, the Source of Love, attracting them, their nature is transformed from opaqueness to luminosity. Those individuals feel a lightness of weight, the loved and in-love step that barely touches the ground, the extreme mobility and ability to execute intricate, weightless steps and exercises.

The greater the stimulated and sustained balance of your spirit, the more you possess that buoyancy of both spirit and of the flesh. The state of your subconscious self in its enlightenment is subsequently perceived in the transformation as transmutation of the flesh from its denser, sensual, earthly qualities, in an upward spiral toward the spiritual and the less materialistic. Consequently, even the physical is less bound by the laws of heavy bodies. So enlightenment is both the perception of the light and the processes of refinement, transformation, luminosity and the vibrational and structural changes that take place in the spirit, the mind, the brain and the entire molecular and atomic structures of the physical person.

Complete enlightenment and commitment to this love chemistry give considerable independence from the laws of time, space and matter. It is the groundwork for the miraculous in either planes or dimensions of a person's obvious existence. To repudiate the laws of gravity, a person must espouse and identify with the laws of light and the subtle structural changes that spiritual identification brings to all of our awareness in the entire composition of our God-gifted self:

In our Spirit, our

- Reasoning self and in our brain, in our

- Subconscious, and in its counterpart, the

- Physical body.

Techniques for the restructuring of matter will certainly be found, along with an increased knowledge of the manipulation and the nature of love/light itself in order to increase or lower the intensity of its vibrations through whatever necessary methods and means the heart and science require.

LOVE IS A HAUNTED HOUSE

Love is a ruined, lonely house
    Where hopes that once grew like flowers
Around the door, behind, before,
    Died unwatered by love's cool showers.

Love is a ruined, silent house
    Where the windows and door hang broken;
Where empty rooms with silence dooms
    Even the echo of words once spoken.

Love is a ruined, empty house;
    No children play in the garden.
They all are grown and love has flown
    And there's no one to ask for pardon.

Love is a ruined, haunted house
    Where memory and sorrow go mocking;
Where ghosts of the past their shadows cast,
    And lost love through the halls is walking.

VALENTINE'S DAY BY CAROLINE SEYMOUR

CHINESE PANDA BY CLANCY CHERRY

February

∽ 16 ∽

*Love does not complain of the child's crippled feet, but looks rather
at how the crutches may be made more comfortable or the journey happier.*

ENTHUSIASM IN ACTION

- Enthusiastic persons encourage the will to live

- Enthusiastic persons must focus their vision

- Action and reaction—necessities for enthusiastic accomplishments

- Maintain enthusiasm—self-inspiration and self-motivation

Enthusiastic persons encourage the will to live. They must deep within themselves face the battle of life and determine to win. They must have great things and some personal, insignificant things to live for that have special meaning to them alone. They must basically come to the conclusion that it is actually easier to earn and enjoy the fruit of a courageous life than to work for and endure the fruit of failure. They must accept life and the will to live it.

Enthusiastic persons, or those who aspire to be enthusiastic, *must focus their vision* and direct their attention outward. If they don't, they may be like the hunter who fired twenty times at one pheasant before he realized that it was a fly on his bifocals. They must give up their previous, critical attitude toward others and toward themselves. Enthusiastic persons will begin by looking for the good in the perceived bad and for the better in the best. They will hold no bitterness toward life or others. They will forgive life, forgive others, forgive themselves and know they are forgiven. Their enthusiasm carries them now. They don't have to drag it along. Having cleansed the windows of their mind and spirit and having washed their glasses, they can more clearly see the opportunities for helpful service, sharing, achievement, action and the rewards of enthusiastic accomplishment.

Action and reaction are necessities for enthusiastic accomplishment. Enthusiastic persons must mesh gears with reality. They no longer will be content to sit at home and race the motor of their frustrated emotions. They will find something to do, some place to begin, and further directions and guidance will be given as they move out along the course of action. Action begets action and enthusiasm begets enthusiasm.

To maintain enthusiasm and to acquire it, individuals must find self-inspiration and self-motivation through thinking inspired thoughts in quiet meditation. They must find some time by themselves to crystallize their thinking, to tune their mind and heart to the inner melody of life. They must read inspirational books, take courses that increase their knowledge and confidence. They must associate whenever possible with the courageous, the champions and the optimists. They must prefer gladness to gloom. God is a glad God. Enthusiasm is an attitude of gratitude. The thankful persons are the inspired, enthusiastic persons. Individuals will find for themselves those things that produce the grateful state of mind once they are alerted to the necessity of it and resolve to cultivate the enthusiastic life that has its feet planted on the ground of eternal gladness.

Such persons will gravitate toward the winner's circle.

I AM LOVE

I am love for it surrounds me.
    I am love inside and out.
I'm silent love that radiates
    And sings, laughs and shouts.

I am love and love surrounds me,
    For there are people everywhere
Who have their many ups and downs
    But not always friends who care.

So I am love and it surrounds me
    In all who care to interact.
For love is life and life is love.
    Try it, Friend, to prove the fact.

February

~ 17 ~

*Faith is an attitude of acceptance, confidence, and trust in the integrity
and dependability of a beneficent God and a friendly universe.*

ENTHUSIASM PERSONALLY APPLIED

- Enthusiasm and the integrated personality
- Enthusiastic persons recount their conquests

Inner personal integration of the entire personality is a vital necessity in attaining and maintaining the enthusiastic concept of life. To achieve this state, individuals must cut the cords of hindering things and thoughts and must make positive the memories and mental conditionings of all past failures.

We are often too much like the "last duck in line." A college friend told about the duck that always came in late at feeding time. Somewhere, somehow, he had gotten entangled in a sturdy fish line, which was wrapped around one webbed foot. He had dragged it until it had become entangled with weeds, sticks and debris. He quacked sturdily and struggled manfully but always came in when the others were half done feeding. But the friend could never get close enough to cut him loose. Then one night he didn't make it in. They found the wing bones and tail feathers down by the river, where some hungry fox had waited in the rushes.

Our remembered and often cherished failures, inner despairs and lack of God-confidence and self-confidence have held us back in the biscuit line when others were eating cake. Cut loose, declare your freedom from all hindering past experiences and resolve to live a life of inner emotional freedom. Enthusiasm arises naturally when our conflicting directions are brought into a correlated drive that doesn't tear us apart or deplete our energies by dissipating them in many different directions. Here our goals and plans and purposes play an important part. The elimination of the nonessential, the subjugation of the secondary and the correlation of the primary purposes are the foundations of emotional release and enthusiastic living. Enthusiasm, with its overtones of inner joy, results from the personal integration of personality and the correlation of our goals and drives and purposes for life.

To attain and maintain enthusiasm, individuals must on occasion recount their conquests and relive their triumphs to recapture the expansive feelings of unbeatable power for accomplishment as they reach the various stages of their planned achievements. You must always look forward and upward with only an occasional glance back over the road you have climbed, and that primarily to encourage yourself in seeing how far you have already come. However, your chief focus of concentrated effort is in the glad present, where enthusiasm is confidence at the bat, endurance circling the bases, courage sliding home. Enthusiasm always has the highest batting average and the best score. It is the stuff from which all champions are made! Be enthusiastic! The world is waiting for the enthusiastic man and the enthusiastic woman!

A STRONG FAITH

Stronger than strength,
Greater than fear
Firmer than wavering,
Wandering doubt.
Is the substance of faith,
Upholding, serene,
Clearing the way
And leading us out.

Safer than security.
Wiser than maturity,
Stronger than
Weakness or power
Is the infinite God
Of the everywhere
In eternity and
In time's short hour.

Kinder than the kindness
Of human love,
Closer than there
Or here
Is the presence of God
With all our supply,
For faith in God
Is the antidote for fear.

February

~ 18 ~

Faith is an impregnable fortress
secure though all the world lies embattled at its feet.

AUTHORITATIVE FAITH

- Faith is a demonstration of an energized will in action

- Faith is the will commanding

- Faith is authority, events directed

- Faith is courage to be summoned

- Faith is the exercise of the creator-God image, volitional power

- Faith courageous enough to assume some responsibility for ordering events—courage to command

The activated will must determine what it wants, why and when it wants it, and all within the boundaries of the possible and permissive Will of God. Hence, faith exercises its free, God-like volitional powers and is divinely encouraged to do so. Man must master circumstances, courageously summon beneficial changes in his situation, and work for the best good in the lives of others. All of this is done in the spirit of true consecrated humility, which constantly prays "Thy will be done."

There is a replacement technique, a dynamic thought process, a God-contemplation treatment, a faith-stimulating, problem-solving approach to all things that perplex, dismay, afflict or in any way impoverish us.

It is the simple technique of recognizing or simply stating the problem and then immediately turning our attention and thought concentration to the face of God, where we contemplate or think about, affirm, quote scriptures, write poetry or formulate our own concepts of God's greatness, goodness, gladness, love, power, peace, mercy, grace, perfection, purity, immensity, eternity, glory or humanity as taught in most all religions, especially Judeo-Christian.

Amazing results follow this thought-replacement procedure. Try it. The following poems, prayers, scriptures and affirmations should aid your contemplation and meditation. After you have stated your problem, refer it to God and then turn from it; in attention, think of God.

Stating the problem or need clarifies and defines the issue in your own mind. Turning the thoughts to something else is a form both of commitment to God's care and trust and a form of negation, where the problem tends to vanish for lack of thought form and emotional nourishment.

Also, stating and leaving the thought is a natural way of assigning it both to God and to the subconscious mind for further analysis and problem solving rather than further worrying about it with the conscious mind. And further, turning the mind to a greater, more worthy object of consideration—God—makes the problem become proportionately and properly smaller in dimension and importance by comparison. This contemplation of the greatness or goodness of God, or of some other attribute of God, stimulates faith that one so good and great will and is, even now, doing something about a solution so fully committed to God that it is actually out of the center of conscious thought. The unconsciously stimulated faith and the subconsciously held problem tend to intermesh and to seek solution behind the scenes of conscious faith, building concentration on the attributes and being of God.

But regardless of the process, try it for results. Effortless, activated faith is the victory!

FAITH FOR EACH DAY OF THE YEAR

Faith is a buoyant, powerful thing
    That falters at no defeat
But battles on with a will to win
    When doubts cry out for retreat.

Faith is a happy jubilant thing
    That drives back the clouds of despair,
That fills the soul with a joyful song
    No matter what troubles we share.

Oh, faith indeed is a beautiful thing
    That banishes worry and fear.
May faith in your friends, the future, and God
    Be yours each day of the year!

February

19

WILD WHITE ROSE BY R. JACKSON

CHILDREN ON THE BEACH

Children running on the beach,
    Their feet warmed by the sand!
Flying hair and flying feet,
    And running hand in hand.

Children sitting on the beach,
    Sitting side by side,
Watching ships and seagulls fly
    Across the surging tide.

Children playing on the beach
    With purpose all unplanned.
Shovels, buckets, hoarded rocks
    And castles in the sand.

Children playing on the beach
    With beach balls, race away.
God grant these childhood memories
    May never fade away.

QUESTIONS TO THINK ABOUT:

- How would you describe the children you have observed at the beach or the park?

- As a child, did you spend time going on vacation? Were your parents there?
  Are your memories positive?

- Describe your activities with your friends at school. How many friends were there?
  What time of the year was your favorite?

- How does your self-concept today compare with your self-image then?

- What were the reactions of your parents toward you and your friends?
  How about the reactions after you returned home?

February

~ 20 ~

Achievement is its own reward, and accomplishment
adds luster to any setting sun.

ACHIEVEMENT

The good news is, we can now possess that natural, mental power known as Thought Force—Creative Thought Power. It is a vibratory, emanating phase of personal magnetism that serves to attract other persons and to arouse their interest and affections and that will move their emotions and stir their feelings. We can possess this strong, vibrant power, which attracts and influences other individuals with whom we come in contact.

This mysterious mental force is positive magnetism. Every day in every way we are learning to use it more efficiently and more directly with the minimum of energy, effort and time and with the maximum of results and permanency.

Our determination is not affected by circumstances, yet it is still dominant and assertive when held in joyful, happy abeyance. We can be kind, calm, helpful, successful and diplomatic. We do not need to talk about our abilities, plan of action or personal business.

We are also conscious of sufficient positive strength so that others can and are welcome to come up close to us. We remain strong and relaxed. Their closeness does not frighten us, for we have complete confidence in our ability through providential assistance to more than hold our own under any and all circumstances. We always form and hold strong and clean, positive mental pictures, or vivid mental images, of the thought or idea we wish to impress upon other persons. This is done through the exercise of concentration and mental pictography. Because we are capable of strong thinking, and because we possess strong ideas and ideals, we automatically demonstrate all of the positive powers and strength of purpose and persistent, determined tenacity that denote the presence and exercise of a strong but gentle willpower. We have dynamic power of will.

RELATIONSHIPS

When the umbilical cord is severed
And man stands naked, alone.
He must learn to relate
Himself to his fate
And for his helplessness atone.

As the child matures in a complex world
He relates himself to his mother
In a world of greed
He must fulfill his own need
With deference to sister or brother.

Man learns to relate in many ways
In the realm of kith and kin
And he attains life's best
As he relates to the rest
And shares each triumph that he wins!

QUESTIONS TO THINK ABOUT:

• Have you encountered the hazards of competition during this past week?

• Have you overcome the situation yet?

• How did you view the problem of one more favored than yourself?

• Was the magnitude and wide prevalence of this traumatic situation manageable for you?

• Do you feel you have a good support team, or do you sometimes feel you have to solve your own problem alone?

February

~ 21 ~

In the brotherhood of books, no bigotry can close the door,
for wisdom reaches out its hands to every creed or race,
both rich and poor.

HUMANITY

There should be a people shelter in the Humane Society for unfortunate persons who are so often in the dog house.

The most multitudinous thing in this life is what you do to your fellow traveler. As we evaluate each other, we will be judged, and condemned or hallowed according to our response to what we do to others, every creed or race, both rich and poor. There are many teachings that include this admonition. For a specific example, consider the Sermon on the Mount (Matthew 5, 6 and 7) as a summary. "Judge not that you be not judged. For with what judgment you judge, you will be judged: and with the same measure you use, it will be measured back to you . . . Therefore, whatever you want men to do to you, do first to them, for this is the Law and the Prophets." Historically and even today, people have yet to comprehend the scientific and spiritual meaning of these concepts.

Please consider the first role of nature, which requires that every transaction within it be matched or balanced. Included in scientific function, the "law" says, "For every action there is an equal and opposite reaction." Our destiny is therefore dominated by what we do to our fellow humanity. Do we understand then that the most dominate thing in the world is how we act and react to our fellow man and woman? As we think about this important issue, we may stop placing blame on others for our shortcomings and problems and begin to repose ourselves for how we have been viewing and treating our fellow travelers in the past.

HUMANITY IS ONE

Generations fuse incessantly
        Into one flux of life.
Man knows a community
        And not uncommon strife.

The multiplied ancestry
        Of all who live today
Appears in each identity
        Of those still on the way.

There is no vital difference
        In man from fellow man,
But all partake of everything
        In God's protoplasmic plan.

Here each records experience
        That was felt by all before,
And the superconscious memory bank
        Is crowded more and more.

And only those who know it
        Can countless riches find—
The incalculable hidden treasures
        Of the superconscious mind.

February

~ 22 ~

*All values will arrange themselves more harmoniously
around the center of our being when we have found
our place in the center of Divine Being.*

PHILOSOPHY FOR TODAY

*Philosophy, if forged from living truth, will never lead away
from Divinity, the way, the truth and the life!*

Please affirm with me now: I have definitely good, constructive ideas and ideals of the Golden Rule kind, which I reinforce with vivid mental pictures. I therefore have successful action outcomes and power of performance commensurate with the quality and intensity inherent in the nature of the idea and equal to the need and desire for its expression and actualization.

I give voluntary, concentrated attention to desirable ideas and plans of action, and they grow in organized intensity and action force, which produces desirable results and materialization. I push worthwhile short-range and long-range goals and desires to completion where wisdom and circumstances indicate and allow their fulfillment. I know that concentrated visualization is the essence of positive magnetism and that the energy force of a dominant idea is the basis for the higher acts of the will and the resulting performance.

I constantly hold in my mind strong, concentrated thoughts and ideas of God-given strength, ability, financial abundance, perfect health in every part, pleasant, magnetic attractiveness, loving service, task completion and organization, efficient thought projection, reception and the power to acquire desirable traits, abilities, conditions, circumstances, information and desired states of awareness.

I do have a sense of personal worth and the ability to self-improve in any desired area. These things I visualize in clear, vivid, mental picturing. This produces mind and spirit radiations by magnetic induction and gets up proper vibrations in the minds of others and in myself. These things I accept as a part of my true, deeper and higher self. For these things I give sincere thanks and appropriate them and all other high-self gifts, graces, traits, powers and conditions for unselfish use in a perfect way. I am a successful person always; I am grateful.

PURPOSE

Oh, God, refine all my purposes
    And give me a resolute will.
Set my face steadfast forward
    Tho the winds blow fierce and chill.

Keep great goals ever before me.
    Thy will as my beacon light,
And keep me pressing onward
    Thru the cold and black of night.

Reorder the scale of my values
    Turn self-centeredness to love I pray.
Renew my heart for adventure
    And bring me new friends today.

Sustain me in arduous seeking
    And in striving to do Thy will.
Grant when the day is ending
    That my heart may be grateful and still.

YOU CAN CHOOSE YOUR POD OF PEAS!

Pessimism and positiveness both begin with the letter "P!" But you never hear pessimism speak positively of peace, plenty, pleasure, purpose, progress, prosperity, philanthropy, promotion, providence, promises, possessions, prayer, purity, patience, perfection, permanence, power, pluck, persistence, proficiency, praise, or patriotism. It just looks like there are a lot of good things that pessimism doesn't know about!

February

~ 23 ~

PATIO ARRANGEMENT BY BOB ERWIN

MAKING FRIENDS

Sure, you're lonesome; you'll admit it.
    God's in Heaven above
But there's a lot of space between
    That clouds His smile of love.

Plenty of friends you had back yonder.
    Yes, but they're not here.
And without them you've been thinking
    The days are mighty drear.

The nights are just plain lonesome;
    The wind a cheerless ghost.
If friends won't come, try making some,
    And soon you'll have a host!

MORE ABOUT FRIENDSHIP

"Your friends are your true assets; save them like you would save money.
    We all have rainy days."

"Chance, good fortune and even adversity may bring you friends,
    but they can also take them from you; therefore, count your friends
    like a miser counts his coins and add one every day."

"Goodwill gains good friends, and the neighbor's dog knows if you really like him."

"The man who slaps you enthusiastically on the back in the morning
    and stabs you in the back before night was a kindergarten dropout
in the school of friendship and is still playing truant from the facts of life."

"Friends lost are enemies gained, and there is no enemy like a friend betrayed."

February

∽ 24 ∽

*The wine of friendship sparkles in the eye, sings in the voice,
warms the hands, and quickens the heartbeat.*

POSITIVE FUZZY-WUZZYS
(JACKSON FABLE)

Put your feet flat on the floor, if you are seated, and close your eyes gently. Just breathe deeply and relax so that you're comfortable, but with your mind very, very alert, and your body relaxed. Expand and extend your awareness so that you see everything I talk about in very clear visual imagery. But see it, please, in color and in action, because then you are functioning at the creativity level. And it will all become very meaningful to you. So let's proceed with our verbal visual. Some conclusions will be drawn at the end of the story about "Positive Fuzzy-Wuzzys," which has been abridged, changed and adapted in the style of Relaxed Learning.

A long, long time ago when the world was young, every baby that was born was given a shoulder bag to wear over its right shoulder. And down in the bag were some wonderful, interesting, beautiful, positive fuzzy-wuzzys. People used to go around, and when they'd see each other, they'd reach down into that soft, warm, positive bag full of fuzzy-wuzzys, and they'd give the other person one and the other person would give them one. They'd go on their way happily, having exchanged fuzzy-wuzzys.

But one day, somebody said, "Don't give your fuzzy-wuzzys away. You only have 199 of them for a lifetime. Why don't you save them?" People got to worrying about that, so when they'd meet somebody, they'd pass a judgmental decision and say, "Is this person worthy of my giving him one of my best, warmest, most positive, cheerful, happy fuzzy-wuzzys?" And they'd think it over, and if the other person didn't respond first and show a friendly willingness to exchange positive fuzzy-wuzzys, they wouldn't give them.

Then they got to thinking, "Maybe we ought to manufacture some artificial fuzzy-wuzzys, and something we could give as a substitute—not something quite so genuine, but still an effort to make contact and do something for people as we pass them by." So they started manufacturing fuzzy-wuzzys, and they got a bag to put on their left shoulder. They put the artificially manufactured ones on the left side. But, you know, when they tried to make them, they weren't quite genuine, and they didn't turn out to be warm, wonderful, positive fuzzy-wuzzys. Instead, they turned out to be negative, cold, prickly, chilly fussy-wuzzys.

So, when they'd meet somebody that they didn't like, they'd take one out of the left-hand bag of artificial fussy-wuzzys, the prickly ones, and they'd give the person one of those. And the other

∽ 135 ∽

person would exchange a cold, chilly, negative, unfuzzy, prickly fussy-wuzzy. Then they'd each go their way, both of them rather unhappy, because they knew they'd been given something less than the best.

One day an old lady was walking by a school, and she saw the children exchanging the cold, negative fussy-wuzzys out of the left-hand bag. She noticed how they reached in with an "icky-ugh" sort of a feeling and got a prickly fussy-wuzzy and handed it to some other little kid who reached in and gave them one back. They made faces while they did it, and everyone went on their unhappy, negative way. The old lady said, as she walked onto the school grounds with her apron still on, "Why is everyone so unhappy and so negative today?" And they said, "Well, didn't you hear? We've only got 199 fuzzy-wuzzys for life. We can't give out the genuine, happy ones!" And the little old lady said, "Well, I'm 70 years old, and I've never run out of warm fuzzy-wuzzys. I've always had lots of the positive ones. Fact of the matter, I've exchanged with a lot of people, and some of the fuzzy-wuzzys, like the one on joy, laughed itself into pieces. And each one of the pieces had twins." Then she continued, "I'm ending up with a whole bag full of fuzzy-wuzzys that keep spilling out everywhere I go. Don't you believe that there are only 199 in the first place. And in the second place, you'll never run out, for the more you give, the more you'll receive."

And the children said, "Well, ok, Grandma. If that's right, we'll try it." And so they reached into the right-hand bag and they went around saying, "I like you because you are nice!" Others were saying, "Hope you have a great day!" Some of them said, "Is there anything I can do to help you?" And they began giving out positive, genuine, beautiful, warm fuzzy-wuzzys.

The children went home and their parents said, "Don't tell me you've been giving out positive fuzzy-wuzzys all day!" And they said, "Oh, we're getting along great with our teacher. We are doing better in math. We get along well with the kids we used to fight with. We play games and sports better, and we've been having fun passing out genuine, happy, positive fuzzy-wuzzys." The mother said, "Well, the report card does look better and you do look happier." She said, "Why don't you give a happy fuzzy-wuzzy to Rover, out there, and see if he'll be happy." So the little kids went out and fed and watered Rover, and the dog was happier.

Everybody they met and everything they met was happier, and even the chickens laid more eggs. And they concluded that if you gave out the good fuzzy-wuzzys, somebody would give them back to you. And you'd never run out a lifetime through.

Of course, you already understand the purpose of the story. If you've got anything good, share it. One of the things we need more of are teachers, parents and friends, with bags full of fuzzy-wuzzys. Each of us needs a whole bag of fuzzy, beautiful, warm, kind, positive things to give away. And the best way we can start is right here on the school grounds. Then we'll take it on home and we'll try to make the world a more positive, warm, wonderful place. So, all day today, will you please make that your purpose? You know the symbolism of fuzzy-wuzzys and how to say true, good things that make others happy. Just give the best there is in you, and the best will come back to you.

Let's think about it for just a moment while we listen to the music and see how you can apply it or to whom you could give a big fuzzy-wuzzy. Right now you could send one by airmail, mentally. You could send it by your telepathy, by your silent second voice. Send a good, warm, fuzzy-wuzzy attitude and feeling to some friend or enemy or someone you don't know yet! Imagine that you're sending some good wishes and good feelings to a lot of people.

Well, remember that thinking about it helps. Easy does it if you picture it first. But also remember that thoughts without actions are like dead limbs on a tree, so, go out to do something about warm fuzzy-wuzzys today. You've got a whole bag of positive fuzzy-wuzzys, and you'll never run out!

Think about these things for a little while. As we come up to the wide-awake, active, everyday level, it will be increasingly easier for you to think of other people and how to say and do the things that will make them like themselves better. You are a winner with a bagful of positive, kind things to say and do.

Open your eyes. Stretch if you need to. Wide-awake now. Thanks again for listening so attentively. Your concentration is getting better with every listening session.

EAST OF THE SHADOWS

East of the shadows
    The sun shines on.
Just past the darkness
    Bursts a radiant dawn.
    Just East of the shadows.

Just West of the shadows
    I walk in the night.
Some "come between" object
    Dims the glorious light.
    Just West of the shadows.

East of the shadows
    Is beckoning love.
The warmth of God's sunrise
    Shines bright from above.
    Just East of the shadows.

East of the shadows
    Fear's specters all fly.
I must leave all behind me
    That clouds up my sky.
    Just East of the shadows.

SNOWY EGRET BY CLANCY CHERRY

February

25

*Love is a rope so strong that nothing on earth need break it, for its strands
are kindness, constancy and care, and it is no stronger than the hearts that make it;
and neglect, not use, will make it show the most wear.*

CHEERFULNESS IN A KISS

Cheerfulness is the sun in sorrow's night, with faith and hope its constant light.

*To kiss the dew of innocence from unkissed lips is to taste
the dew of heaven bejeweled on the petals of a soft, white rose.*

MY LOVE

When the soft stars shine
Clear for the love of shining,
And the sky seems far,
My heart will be pining.
I'll be thinking of you,
My love.

When the sun is soft gold
In the sky of evening,
And the shadows start
Alone I'll be grieving.
I'll be thinking of you,
My love.

Where the flowers bloom
Sweet for the joy of blooming,
When the roses are full,
And restless I'm roaming
I'll be thinking of you,
My love.

(CONTINUED ON NEXT PAGE)

When the road leads far
From the land of longing,
And the hurt is deep,
There is peace in belonging
And in thinking of you,
My love.

When the cold rains fall hard
On the roof above me,
And the air is chill,
I'll be warm since you love me,
Warm in thinking of you,
My love.

Should some illness come
Bringing the fear of dying,
And I need you close,
There'll be strength for new trying
In thinking of you,
My love.

When Autumn brings sear
And red leaves are falling,
I'll be wanting you near.
My heart will be calling.
I'll be thinking of you,
My love.

When green things come fresh
With new life in Spring-time,
We'll meet again, Love,
As when it was ring-time.
I'll be with you once more,
My love.

February

~ 26 ~

GOOD FINDING AND THE GARDENER'S DOG
(JACKSON FABLE)

An old Aesop's tale tells of the gardener who was drawing water out of the well to water his flowers and plants. The little dog was jumping and barking at the well curb. He lost his balance and fell in. Hearing the splash, the gardener decided he'd have to rescue his dog. So he kicked off his shoes. He kicked off his pants. He took off his shirt. There he stood in his shorts, ready to dive into the well, but he decided to use the bucket and the well rope.

And he picks up little Rover, who's wet all over. Now he's bringing the little dog up to the top. He has climbed about halfway up with the dog wedged under his arm. He can't help it, but he squeezes too hard. The dog bites his master right on the hand. And the man says, "After all the meals I've fed you, and after all the times I've patted you on the head, after all the times we've gone places together, you are an ungrateful dog to bite your master's hand. Why, you're a little monster! Is this your idea of gratitude to someone who feeds you and pets you and treats you kindly, and risks his life to pull you out of a well? I've got a notion to drop you again." And he dropped the dog back into the well. Just as he turned away to leave the dog in the well, he said, "Only an ungrateful dog bites the hand that feeds him." This means, don't bite the hand that feeds you.

What's the moral of this lesson? What does it actually mean when you apply it to your life? It could mean don't take the good things you have for granted. Be nice to people who take care of you. For example, if your mother does nice things for you, go home and say, "Mother, I love you. Thank you for being so nice!" Always be kind to the ones you love. Appreciate everything that you get.

Learn the habit of good finding. It seems that people have a tendency to find fault occasionally. But you can cure or forget a lot of your troubles or problems by finding something good in the other person to commend them for. Look for something nice in their clothes; look for something nice in their personality; look for something commendable about their sportsmanship, or about their getting along with people. And then practice it on the magic stool by telling each other the things you like about the other person. This is good finding, and it is the opposite of fault finding.

Whatever you give your attention to, you nourish, and you make it grow. It is just like watering the plants in the house: You see them begin to brighten up and grow stronger. If you give attention to a fault too long, it makes the fault grow. Analyze and constructively criticize a situation only long enough to see what needs to be improved. Spend most of your time on the solution and very little of it, after analysis, on the negative situation. You become like that upon which you concentrate. Therefore, do not let your mind dwell longer than necessary on any problems or upon any fault.

~ 141 ~

Instead, encourage yourself to be a good finder and an answer-finder. Look for an occasion today to find something good in some person you meet.

And where is the little dog that didn't appreciate his master's help? He's still in the well. He turned out to be a Water Spaniel!

Okay. Become wide awake now, and thank you for listening so attentively.

THE GOLDEN RULE OF LOVE

The Golden Rule of love entwines
    Both enemies and friends.
It doeth good while others hate,
    And yet it never ends.

For patient love must pray and yield,
    And give and do and be;
And he who loves is loved of God
    For all the world to see.

With gentle tongues, forbearing cheeks,
    With gracious, open hand,
With humble hearts, devoted lives,
    Let love possess the land.

DREAM ROSE GARDEN BY WANDA KIPPENBROCK

YOSEMITE BY DAVID JACKSON

February

27

Humanity is the family of God;
and He loves no child less, nor another more.

LUCKY LUTHER AND KING HENRY HAPPINESS
(JACKSON FABLE)

Resting comfortably, breathing deeply, relaxing completely, please listen with complete attention and understanding. Elevate and activate all of your senses. See vividly; smell, feel and taste with extra-ordinary sensitivity. Let the story come alive, and assimilate its inner and hidden meaning. Now to the story of *Lucky Luther and King Henry Happiness!*

Once upon a time, a long time ago, there lived a jolly little king whose name was Good King Henry Happiness. His wife was none other than Queen Gertrude Gratitude. Their beautiful daughter was princess Gladys Gladness. But she usually just said, "Hi there! I'm glad."

They all lived on the far side of the Isn't-It-Grand River in a shiny, silver castle called Wow!-That's-Wonderful! It was right on top of Happy Mountain in the sure enough center of the land of Mil-Gracias, which means it was in the Land of A Thousand Thanks.

Everybody was happy in the land of Mil-Gracias, but everybody didn't live there because they couldn't cross the river. Then one day somebody did build a bridge across the Isn't-It-Grand River. Because it was a magic bridge, sometimes you saw it and then again you just thought you did. You could usually see the name of the magic bridge even on cloudy days, and some people said that they had seen it even in the dark. The big see-on sign said, "This is Remember-The-Time Bridge." What it really meant was, remember some good time and the toll gate will open and you can skip across to the Land of A Thousand Thanks all for fun and all for free.

But some people who wanted to cross said, "Ah ha! I see the bridge, and I can read the Remember-The-Time sign easily, so I guess I'll cross!" But they remembered the wrong thing. They remembered the time they got mad or when they were sick or had trouble, and clang!—the bridge closed. The sign disappeared, and the first thing they knew, they were standing in the mud over their boot tops in the It-Isn't-So-Grand River. Some of them never did catch on how to cross the magic bridge and climb Happy Mountain or live in the Wow!-It's-Wonderful! silver castle shining in the sun.

However, one little kid, Lucky Luther, caught on. He said, "I remember the time I helped my dad pile the wood for the fireplace and he gave me a dollar. Besides that, we had a nice warm fire when it was snowing outside. I remember those three A's and two B's on my report card and the time I got to visit my best friend over the weekend. We had the most fun! Wow! It's wonderful to remember good times!"

Swish! There was the magic bridge, glistening like gold stardust in the summer sun. Lucky could see the Wow!-Isn't-It-Wonderful Castle in the distance. The tollgate was wide open as he ran across, three jumps at a time. It wasn't any time at all until he was in the land of Mil-Gracias, because he kept on thinking about more things he was thankful for. He looked back at the grown-ups and the barefooted little kids dressed in sad-sacks on the other side of the It-Isn't-So-Grand River. He cupped his hands and called back to them, "It's easy! Just think of happy things and presto, you are halfway up to Happy Mountain!"

Lucky hadn't gone very far until a Kind Knight on a white horse with steel armor, with a smile-button on his shield and with a peppermint candy sword, threw three magic coins on the ground in front of him. Lucky Luther said, "Thank you, Sir." He bent down and picked the coins up out of the warm dust on the mountain road.

The first was a gold, good-luck piece. It had Good King Henry Happiness' picture, with a crown and beard, all on one side. On the other side was a mirror with an old, English-style inscription that read, "Happiness is you! Think about that once in a while."

The second coin was a sing-sing silver piece. It had a cute, little cameo picture of Princess Gladys Gladness with the words, "I'm Glad!" On the other side it just said, "Sing! Sing! The birds do and they can fly!"

The third coin of the Kingdom of Happiness fell in a rock crevice, but Lucky Luther finally got it out. It was the best of all. It shone like yellow copper, but it wasn't. It was made out of pure happiness. Probably Good King Henry coined this one himself. It had a picture of Queen Gertrude Gratitude on it with the words, "You Are My Sunshine, Baby." And on the other side was a picture of the Kind Knight's silver shield with the round, yellow smile-button in the very center. Under the shield in big, bold print were the words, "I LIKE YOU BECAUSE!"

Lucky Luther put the money in his front pocket, brushed his hands on his pants, and started to say, "Thank you" again, but the Kind Knight was gone. So he said "thank you" anyway just in case the knight on the white horse was hiding somewhere nearby.

Lucky Luther started again to climb up the rocky path that led to the castle just as the sun with banners of gold, orange and red was setting behind the Good Wishes Mountain. It was so beautiful and he was so happy! He didn't know that, around the bend and just before he got to Wow!-It's-Wonderful! Castle, there were three sleeping dragons on their backs with the sun shining on their yellow stomachs! He wouldn't have stopped or been afraid even if he had known about the three dragons. His happiness made him strong, and besides, his name was Lucky Luther. Also, he had the three good-luck coins of the Happiness Kingdom in his pocket. Anyway, the three dragons were tied by their tails to an old oak tree. Their fires had gone out while they were sleeping instead of stoking their hot-air furnaces with red-hot Red Hots and Red Pepper Peppermint sticks!

Luther saw Dumpy, the Dog Dragon, first, because he had the longest rope tied to his tail and because he was stretching to look around the corner as he heard Lucky Luther coming! Wow! Was he ever messed up! His dragon hair was dragging, and he hadn't had a hot bath in six weeks or maybe six months. He was so full of I-Don't-Like-You-Because ideas and feelings that he kept chewing off all of his own toenails and eating off all of his own scales for breakfast each morning. He always followed this with a chaser of sour milk and raw frog's liver! His breath smelled like sour soup and garlic gum. But Lucky Luther was so happy he wasn't even afraid. He just held his nose

146

while he untied Dumpy's tail and said, "Let's go swimming." And sure enough, that's what they did. And they both felt happier and cleaner than ever!

When they came back from the swimming pool, Ho-Hum, the second dragon, just leaned against the old oak tree where his tail was tied up short and blew smoke (not really fire) out of his nostrils. He didn't have enough ambition to throw dry, dragon wood on his own fire.

He just sat there saying, "Ho-Hum, Ho-Hum, Ho-Hum! Who cares anyhow? Ho-Hum." So Lucky Luther opened Ho-Hum's mouth and put in a couple of shovels full of dragon breakfast briquettes, closed the furnace door and said, "Look at this lucky coin, Ho-Hum. It says, 'Sing! Sing! The birds do and they can fly!'" So Ho-Hum opened his mouth and sang a real hot, happy number, and sure enough, he felt like flying again. So he flew back to Chicago and lived with his Uncle Gus. But his Uncle Gus called him "Stumpy" when he got to Chicago because nobody had untied Ho-Hum's tail before he took off like a jet!

That only left one more dragon for Lucky Luther to take care of and he still had two magic, good-luck coins left. The last dragon's name was Unhappy Hetty. Dumpy, who was now Lucky Luther's own dog-dragon with a rope around his neck instead of on his tail, had told him about Unhappy Hetty. She was a girl dragon with scraggly hair. Her teeth weren't brushed and her fingernails were dirty and long. Her posture was so poor that she couldn't stand straight even with six legs and a dragon crutch to lean on.

Lucky Luther felt so sorry for her that he almost cried. Then he remembered his King Henry Looking Glass coin, so he held it in front of Unhappy Hetty. While she looked at herself real good for the first time in her life, he read the inscription on the coin to her. It said, "Happiness is you! Think about that for a while!"

So Unhappy Hetty looked at herself and thought and thought. Then she combed her hair, brushed her teeth with a piece of sagebrush, sat up straight, tall and proud and said, "Just call me Happy Hetty now." Then she untied her own tail and packed her red suitcase. She printed a travel sign to hang around her neck that said, "Happy days are here again." On the other side she printed in beautiful Chinese dragon letters, "Have fun—will travel!" Then she went walking down the road with a yellow umbrella under her arm and the red suitcase in the other hand and with the "Have fun—will travel!" sign tucked under her double dragon chin. She said she was going to visit her relatives in the zoo at Kalamazoo, Michigan. If hitchhiking was a blast, she would hitchhike, and if not, she planned to take the Snub-Way or basement elevator down to China.

Dumpy, the dog-dragon, followed Lucky Luther as he hurried on to Wow!-It's-Wonderful castle, silver and shining under the stars now. He knocked at the castle door. The royal butler opened it. He fainted when he saw that the dog-dragon was off of his leash. But Good King Henry Happiness patted Dumpy on the head and Queen Gertrude Gratitude dabbed her nose with a pink handkerchief and said, "I'm so grateful that the other two dragons didn't come for lunch, too."

Then Princess Gladys Gladness patted Lucky Luther on his head and they all went in and had supper together in the Dragon Tea Room. There was room enough for everyone; but Dumpy did have to hang his tail out of the kitchen window. The scales hadn't grown back on it yet, so he joked some about getting it hair-conditioned.

Well, the princess fell in love right there and then with Lucky Luther and forgot to put sugar in her tea. But she did remember to say, "I'm Glad! You're Lucky." And he said, "I'm Lucky you're Glad!" So luckily and gladly they lived happily ever after!

I AM HUMANITY

I am no more nor less than humanity
for I am human.

I am the philosopher, grey-bearded,
bending long hours over his books
and scrolls where candle shadows
dance upon the walls.

I am the engineer with measurements
intricate, blueprints endless and
calculations tedious.

I am the teacher. Yes, I am the
teacher and also the learner, too,
who cannot rise above the source
of his reason unless he opens up
his inward parts whence treasures
of hidden knowledge are stored!

I am masculinity. I am femininity.
I am strength and I am weakness.
I am despair and I am love, for
I am man! I am of this world and
yet akin to heaven. I am earth
dust awakened by the breath of
God.

I am all things and more for I am
a man created in the image of God
and thus in one hand I hold up in
the darkness a double candle of
light: The light of God-fused
humanity and the light of man as
fused with divinity.

I am that I am, for I am humanity!

February

28

The salty, seaweed-swaying, swelling, shore-caressing ocean speaks of preserving power;
The storm-tossed, wave-crested, surging ocean is suggestive of misdirected, dynamic, destructive power;
But the calm, far-reaching sea, reflecting the lights of the setting sun, is symbolic of the powers
of progress, peace, and the immensity of the Divine reserve and potential
available to all voyaging mankind.

LUCKY LUTHER AND THE TWO-HORNED UNICORN
(JACKSON FABLE)

While you are seated comfortably and relaxing completely, let's talk about Lucky Luther and the two-horned unicorn. Remember that Lucky Luther was the little kid who figured out how to cross the magic bridge over the It-Isn't-So-Grand River, climbed Happy Mountain, and met the Kind Knight on the white horse who gave him the three magic coins with which he helped the three tail-tie dragons that he met on his way to Wow!-Isn't-It-Wonderful Castle. Remember, too, how he met Good King Henry Happiness, Queen Gertrude Gratitude and the beautiful Princess Gladys Gladness and had supper in the Dragon Tea Room. Then they lived happily and gladly forever and two days more. Pretty lucky kid! How could he be so lucky? Did he carry a pocket full of lucky rabbit feet, raise four-leaf clovers, or play a game of lucky horseshoes every morning before breakfast? No, Lucky Luther was lucky because he did certain things in a certain way and thought certain thoughts and looked at things from a certain viewpoint. His lucky attitudes and right actions just naturally and effortlessly made him lucky. He would have been the first to tell you, "Everybody can be lucky if they play the Lucky Game with the simple, lucky rules."

We will find out more about that in a few minutes after we talk a little bit more about Lucky Luther and the Unicorn Easter Parade.

One day Lucky Luther was out hunting two-horned unicorns, with Dumpy the Dog Dragon doing the bird-dogging for him. Lucky Luther always hunted the two-horned unicorns with his popgun in second gear. It wasn't really a popgun that made a popping noise. That would have scared the already scarce two-horned unicorns away. Not many people had seen a two-horned, Shetland pony-sized, horse-tailed, talking unicorn. However, they weren't much different than the one-horned, Welsh-sized, pony-tailed unicorns except that they had a second horn for blowing in heavy traffic in case they met a convoy of Canadian Honkers who wanted to out-honk them.

But back to Dumpy, and Lucky Luther's popgun; it was really a squirt gun and a popgun all in one, because it was "guna" squirt pop when you triggered the puller or even sometimes when you pulled the trigger. Lucky didn't dare shoot it in high gear, because then the Dr. Pepper fizzed over

149

and fogged up his scope. He sure didn't want to fog up his scope sight with a fizzy phase of hot Dr. Pepper. Anyway, Lucky Luther always carried an extra ammunition belt with little-cartridge, glass-bottled, miniature-sized containers of Squirt and an extra 7-Up mini-pack for emergency in case he met a whole flock of one- or two-horned unicorns galloping across the sky. No matter what any-body said, he knew that he had a real popgun because his pop gave it to him once when he was little. It was a lucky popgun, too, for sure enough, he was starting to get lucky again, like he always did.

Dumpy the Dog Dragon was standing on three legs and was pointing with his tail over his shoul-der at a clump of green bushes with pink flowers at the edge of a beautiful, green-grass meadow when out into the clearing stepped three baby, Dalmatian-spotted, little unicorn horse-colts with black leather boots and white umbrellas just in case it rained during the Easter Sunday Unicorn Parade.

Then the bushes parted, and there stood Mama Unicorn with a May basket full of Easter eggs in a nest of crisp, green lettuce leaves. She wore a pink slip that was slipping. It showed about two inches below her yellow-green, tulip-flowered Easter dress. She was walking barefooted, backwards, and was carrying her patent-leather, high-heeled, Sunday-best shoes tied together and slung over one dainty white shoulder just to the back of where her mane was tied with blue- and pink-striped ribbons.

Walking right by her side came Father Unicorn in a red bathrobe with tie-dyed, blue-green de-signs on it. His pant legs were rolled up almost to his knees on all four legs because he had been wading in Deep Creek Drainage Canal looking for crawdads. He was barefooted, too, but he wasn't walking backwards. It's really better not to be too backward unless you are a little too forward. But it worked out pretty well anyway, because Papa Unicorn could see where they were going, and Mama Unicorn could see where they had been. With Mama and Papa Unicorn and the three Dalmatian-spotted, baby unicorns, it made five. So they had four-sight and hindsight, too.

Well, Lucky Luther had never seen so many unicorns, especially not all at once, and not on a Sun-day morning in a green meadow with their Easter clothes on and all carrying white umbrellas. He just stood there and started shaking all over with excitement. He was having unicorn buck fever. If one baby unicorn had whimpered even a little bit, Lucky Luther would probably have dropped his gun!

Papa Unicorn blew his second horn gently to attract Lucky Luther's attention so that nobody would get squirted accidentally with 7-Up before Sunday dinner. Two of the little unicorns blew their horns in harmonious unison, and the third Dalmatian-spotted, baby unicorn couldn't find his horn button, so he just blew his nose loud and hard so that nobody would notice he couldn't find his horn.

Mama Unicorn's horn was a beautiful, soft, tenor beep that made you think of daffodils and church bells in the distance on a clear, spring morning.

Just then, Papa Unicorn, who was leading the family parade, held up a red-orange octagonal stop sign as he bravely stepped in front of his family to protect them. Lucky Luther saw all of the white umbrellas and thought they were truce signs, so he handed his popgun to Dumpy the Dog Dragon and came forward cautiously exactly halfway. Papa Unicorn came the other half, and they sat down together by a little beaver pond and started to hold a summit conference meeting about popgun dis-armament and Easter Sunday traffic patterns, unilateral sportsmanship, and responsibility for uni-corn preservation on and off the reservation.

Lucky Luther reached over and felt the real live unicorn horn in Papa Unicorn's forehead. Then they drank a toast from the Seven-Up emergency ammunition pack and got right down to business.

Lucky Luther took a quick, postage-stamp-sized, miniature-camera picture with his camou-flaged-necktie, pin-sized, automatic-zoom lens and infrared film, secret-service, money-back-guar-anteed, Woolco camera, because he wanted firsthand proof about how lucky he really was. You didn't see unicorns every day, you know, and especially not on Sunday. Well, anyway, you didn't see a whole family of unicorns on parade.

When everything was peacefully worked out, Papa Unicorn led the way with his red bathrobe on and his tie-dyed blue and white pant legs rolled up to his knees and with the red-orange stop sign over his shoulder. Mama Unicorn followed him in her best yellow-green, tulip-flowered dress with the pink slip showing as she walked barefooted, backwards, carrying her black, patent-leather shoes tied together over one shoulder and her May basket full of Easter eggs in a crisp nest of green lettuce leaves. Behind her came the three baby, Dalmatian-spotted, little unicorns with black boots and white umbrellas all beeping their little horns as they crossed the green meadow, single file, on their way to join the Easter Sunday Fashion Parade.

Dumpy was still standing at point with his dragon eyes popping almost out of his head as Lucky Luther looked over at him. He motioned Dumpy to relax and come closer. Lucky Luther leaned his back against a big tree, and Dumpy curled up at his feet with his nose resting on his tail. Right there and then, they had a good talk about how everybody can be luckier than even a two-horned unicorn crossing a green meadow on his way to the Easter Sunday Morning Parade.

Dumpy asked the first question, and Lucky Luther tried to give the right answer. Dumpy said, "Lucky Luther, what do you have to do to be lucky?"

Lucky Luther said, "Dumpy, the way I see it, you have to do lucky to be lucky. Some people think you have to be lucky to do lucky, but really, if you *do* lucky, you will for sure *be* lucky."

Dumpy wasn't quite sure what Lucky Luther meant, but he was very good at listening, especially when he was so relaxed. So he listened more, or meant to, but just then he thought of another question. "Lucky Luther," he asked, "how do lucky people get lucky?" Then he rolled over on his back and stretched his legs out sideways so that the sun could fall soft and warm and bright on his full stomach.

"O.K.," said Lucky Luther, "there are a lot of things that help. But mostly, when they are put to-gether in the other side of your mind, they become like a magnet that attracts and draws good for-tune, the right people, good circumstances, material things and all kinds of fun and worthwhile things into your experience."

"Sounds good," said Dumpy. "Tell me more. Make it real easy and simple, Lucky Luther. Make it so simple that even a Dumpy Dog Dragon could understand it with his eyes closed."

"Right!" answered Lucky Luther. "When life throws a lucky curve across the plate, you have to swing on it for a home run, then hit all the bases, and slide home for a winning ball game and a part of a winning team. Or, to say it a different way, Dumpy, you have to respond to good luck. It's like a basket of fried chicken, hot cornbread, and cold lemonade that came floating in over your head. You would have to sit up, reach up and take it, open the top of the basket, remove the napkin, smack your lips, enjoy your dinner and be very, very thankful for floating baskets full of fried chicken. You have to respond to good luck and make it feel welcome around you and in you."

"Wow!" said Dumpy. "Tell me more!" Lucky Luther scratched his tennis shoe in the warm, shining sand and tried to think of more to say that sounded wise and important, but he couldn't right then think of anything more. When he looked up from the ground, who do you think was sitting down under the shade of a Lucky Lollipop tree right in front of Dumpy and Lucky Luther? You guessed it. It was the Papa two-horned unicorn who had come back to say, "Thank you" right after the Easter Parade. He blew his horns softly and whistley and important-like to get their attention. Then he started right in to tell them all about what good luck was really like. It sounded like he really knew, too.

"To be lucky," said the unicorn, "you have to expect good things, picture good things happening, see good things coming. You must expect lucky things to happen, for what you see is what you get!

"You have to know what you want and know what you are looking for. Keep one eye open, Dumpy," he said to the Dog Dragon. "Keep one eye open, for if you truly want something badly, somebody or something will finally bring it around your way. Be ready to bargain for it and to pay any reasonable price necessary. Then take care of your good-luck gifts when they do come. Desire good luck. Be ready for it. Expect it. Receive it gladly and quickly. Good fortune isn't too good to be true! Re-channel the river of good luck so that it runs every day through your own front yard.

"Be self-confident. Put up an invisible shield against anything other than good luck. Be courageous. This attracts good luck. Be happy. Happy people know they are lucky people. And what you know is what you get. Know that you are lucky. Charge your good-luck battery. Step on your own self-starter and begin to make your own good luck. You are secure. You need to bring the positive, the fortunate and the good into your life experience."

Lucky Luther interrupted Papa Unicorn here and said, "Dumpy, you are a winner. You are a lucky Dog Dragon. Even when people call bad luck, it can be changed into something good!"

This made sense to Dumpy, even though he was so relaxed he was almost asleep in the sun. He knew that lucky people would always be in the lucky place at the lucky time, doing and saying lucky things with lucky people with lucky results. He was sure glad he had met his new friend Lucky Luther, and now he had a two-horned, lucky unicorn for another friend and teacher.

"You've got to work on self-improvement," continued Papa Unicorn. "Keep your cool. Use good judgment always. Save your money, or at least some of it. Do your work well. Use the other side of your mind often. Be honest. Exercise self-control. Be happy. Be enthusiastic. Be a good listener. Listen to other people. They may have just the inspiration and information you need. Something very important to you may be said if you keep your ears open. So be a good listener always!" Then Papa Unicorn flicked a fly off of his ear with his long red tail and listened carefully just to check on what the little unicorns with white umbrellas and black boots were doing. Then he continued with a wise frown on his forehead that looked almost like zebra stripes.

"Get along well with other people. Good luck comes to you through other people. Keep your people-lines up. Communicate and understand. Go out of your way to keep your friends happy. Don't neglect them so long that they forget you. Meet new people, too. They can sometimes make your rocket take off for Luckyville. New friends are important." He licked his black mane with his long, rough, pink tongue and thought of some other good things!

"Curiosity, interest, and reading inspirational books are luck-producing habits. Get a library card from the Unicorn University Library in your neighborhood. Keep learning. Love and enjoy life. Keep positive. Conquer anxiety and fear with confidence, courage and creativeness. Be ready for good adventure. Use your imagination. Don't get caged in. Keep free and moving. Overcome timidity. Blow your own horn every once in a while, but quietly. Mostly, think of others more than yourself. That's real lucky. It's okay to forget yourself a lot of the time in order to make other people happy. Have several good hobbies and fun things going that interest you."

Papa Unicorn was going in high gear now. He wasn't even stopping for a deep breath. But it was all very important, and it wasn't every day you could hear a real, live, imaginary unicorn talk about something as important as good luck, so Lucky Luther and Dumpy the Dog Dragon both listened and listened and listened!

Papa Unicorn went right on explaining good luck. "Think more," he said, "about answers and possible solutions to your problems rather than rerunning the problem through your mind again and again. Don't do that. Run the possible answers through your mind. Picture things like they would be if you had a real neat situation rather than an unsatisfactory one. Visualize things like you would want them to be.

Make more friends. Keep old friends. Make friendship an adventure. Be gracious and generous. Give and receive cheerfully. Give not only of things, but of yourself and of your inner warmth of love. Remember that even a cat will curl up by a warm fireplace. Be warm and courteous. This is the lucky life.

"Don't try to be a big shot. Don't play like you know everything. Keep in the middle way. Be self-confident and patient. This helps you be there when the luck truck drives up at delivery time. Give more than you expect to receive and you'll receive more than you expected to get. Make contacts. Keep up your contacts. Leave a warm memory in the heart of people you meet and live with. They'll help you be luckier people and bring fortunate circumstances. Choose the kind of activities you want to be involved in, and plant your own lucky, four-leaf clovers.

"Be responsible, faithful, dependable and predictable. Be loving and kind. Be truthful and gentle. Luck is a flower that grows in the garden of kindness.

"Get on the beam when luck moves in. Ride on the beam to the rhythm of progress. Move with the motion of success. Take advantage of little opportunities. They have a way of growing up.

"Don't be overly ambitious. Moderation is a lucky line to follow. Keep working on self-improvement. Increase and use your best talents and abilities. Use your head. Think straight and logically. Never do anything that makes you ashamed of yourself or that in any way hurts another person. You will respect yourself and the rights of others. Develop the other side of your mind— the instinctive, creative, knowing side. Positive thinking with its clear visualization and penetrating imagination is essential for good luck.

"Well," said Papa Unicorn as he scratched his horn with a front hoof and stretched as he stood up to leave, "lots of good luck. Buena suerte!" as the Spanish Unicorns say. "I hope to see you all next year in the Unicorn, Good Luck, Easter Parade." With that and a swish of his long tail, Papa Unicorn was gone.

Dumpy the Dog Dragon and Lucky Luther sat there a long time in the warm sun and thought and thought about it. Then Lucky patted Dumpy the Dog Dragon on the top of his rough, scaly head sort of friendly-like and said gently, "If you want it simple, Dumpy, 'Lucky is as Lucky does!'" Then they went walking down the forest path together kicking the leaves and the ground where little yellow pools of light mingled with the soft shadows of the road called *Success*.

VIEWING THE OCEAN

I'm close to your heartbeat.
    I'm wet with your tears.
I stand with the others
    Thru primeval years
    Alone on your windswept shore.

I'm awed by your mammoth,
    Magnificent size.
I view you with humble,
    Admiring eyes
    With the countless others before!

I LOVE THE SOUND OF THE SEA

I love the sound of the surging surf,
    The pounding of the sea.
There's something about its insistent beat
    Like a monarch's firm decree.

I love the sound of the surging surf
    Where the "suds" splash wild and free.
The ocean is washing clothes tonight
    In a tub of infinity.

February

~ 29 ~

*Malicious slander leaves a devastation trail of destroyed reputation
and blasted influence wherever its hoarse whispers of hate and the scorched breath
of its falsehood by chance or intent are blown.*

AGGRESSION

Doctors use the term "mind." There are other titles for this "organ of intelligence," descriptive words such as emotions, personality, nerves, and soul. Within this frame of reference, the "mind" may well determine a person's feeling and behavior. As you observe society, there is common acceptance that there is a great amount of variety in human attitude and behavior. Many of these differences may include the result of cultural heritage, or of family attitudes. Another might consider behavior that is perfectly acceptable in one group as entirely abnormal.

Consider this example for the sake of this subject: moderate reactions of anger and hatred. Average persons may get angry, of course, but they restrain their anger to within reasonable limits. These individuals may have to curb their temper or reactions in the face of petty annoyances, but they will try to work off their pent-up feelings by hitting a tennis ball rather than slandering their neighbor.

Aggression means any sort of hostile attack on others, verbal as well as physical. Frustration means the thwarting of some wish or motive that has been aroused. Thus, aggression is the natural response to frustration. From this response to frustration, aggression constitutes one of civilized man's most serious problems.

Individual and social conflicts and systems for their resolution are both theoretical and of practical concern. According to Dr. W.C. Olson, a conflict is defined as any instance in which one person attacks another's person, or by word or deed interferes with the person, activities, or possessions of another, or threatens by words or gesture to do so, or endeavors by force or verbal demands to possess another's belongings, or to direct another's activities in opposition to the apparent desires of the person against whom the aggression is made.

Aggression, as in delinquency, is one reaction to a person's frustration. Delinquent persons may be assumed to have more than their burden of frustrating experiences. Unfortunately, however, the persons in need of control are most likely to be insecure, worried, and fighting back in a world which has demonstrated to be too much for them. Their aggressiveness may have begun at home, at work or at school, and the symptoms may take on the form of fighting, destruction of property or negative word wars.

SLANDER

Great men have died like Caesar,
    But at the dagger-point of words.
Others fell like Lincoln,
    But at the pistol crack of verbs.

And the world of mad assassins,
    Girt with ammunition belts,
Slay their prey, scrape their hides
    And call them "worthless pelts."

These "fire-bugs" with gas and matches
    Saturate their slander rags.
They laugh in fiendish triumph
    As some burning building sags.

But the idle words and bitter words
    That slash and cut and kill
Are judgment words that all come back
    To pay the speaker's bill.

Someone has said, "Don't speak them,
    Just take the silent pledge.
And if you have to write them—
    Write them near the water's edge."

But some poor fish may see them
    Ere the sands wash smooth again.
God, seal my lips from slander
    Lest I hurt my fellow man.

WALK IN THE PARK BY CAROLINE SEYMOUR

ALONG THE RIO GRANDE BY VICKIE FEARS

March

~ 1 ~

*The future, like a chalice of unfolding, floral gold, opens up its silent petals;
and if perfumed sweet or bitter, God still the flower holds.*

MEMORY

*Meaningful classification of knowledge, and confidence in memory ability
to automatically recall it, is the foundation of meaningful learning.*

*The persons who would increase the efficiency of their memory must commend it,
and not condemn it; for self-confidence, not criticism, encourages efficiency.*

WHAT IS HAPPINESS?

Is happiness the smell of spring in the air or the reflected light on a child's blond hair? Is happiness hope and love and peace? Is it a school child's joy at vacation's release? Is happiness butter piled high on fresh bread? Is it rain on the roof when you're safely in bed? Is happiness the feeling of home and familiar things? Is it pigeons in the park and the whir of glad wings? Ah, yes! Happiness is all this—all this and much, much more!

Does happiness lie in self-content, in the unity of an emotional firmament? Is happiness wholeness, self-acceptance and peace? Is it a inner armistice where hostilities cease? Is happiness "heaven" located in man? Is it inner integration with an orderly plan? Is happiness environment or our reaction to it? Is it rationalization when we actually "blew it?" Ah, yes! Happiness is all this—all this and much, much more! (To be continued on March 2.)

MEDITATION PRAYER

There are tasks and duties, O, God, that confront us today. May we, with your divine assistance, take them one by one and do them quickly and well and to the honor of you, our Creator, and to the good of our fellow man. May your grace and our courage be greater than our burdens, may our inspiration and willing service make our duties pleasures, and our tasks a spiritual profit to our own lives in the doing. And may our strength be like the fabled knight of old, whose strength was as the strength of ten because his heart was pure. Thus we shall serve acceptably, and at the end of the day our duties and our finished tasks shall be but monuments of your power and love. Thank you. Amen.

FADED ROSE LEAVES

Faded rose leaves of some long past event
  With benediction's farewell still there.
Withered red leaves on the mantle piece
  With memory's fragrance still filling the air.

Storm-strewn shores, beaten beaches of life.
  The familiar and old washed away.
Where the driftwood of memory lies broken—
  Jumbled fragments of yesterday.

Great God of earth's faded rose leaves,
  God of our storm havocked shore,
Let us live and relive what the past may give
  And still look to the future for more!

March

2

What is a city but people; not tall skyscrapers with bright lights at night,
but an ocean of surging, searching people; this is a city.

Achievement

The Good Fairy with the magic wand said she couldn't loan it out anymore;
but she did leave a pair of work shoes, a sweatshirt and a bag full of
potential achievement with the word "work" written all over it.

WHAT IS HAPPINESS?

Is happiness a river with a bridge to cross? Is it a destination, a journey, gain or loss? Is happiness the proper order of things? Is it the lift and the whir of emotion's own wings? Is happiness the gold of all things worthwhile? Is it the coin of kindness and the glint of a smile? Is it the mechanization of technological stuff? Is it the satisfaction of having enough? Ah, yes! Happiness is all this—all this and much, much more!

Is happiness the positive, victorious side of the negative and neutral emotional tide? Is happiness a glimpse of self-confident success, of triumphant energy that outwits distress? Is happiness power and creative thought? Is it loving to do the things that we ought? Is happiness the surge of vigorous life? Is it the healed scar from the surgeon's knife? Ah, yes! Happiness is all this—all this and much, much more! (To be continued on March 3.)

TELL ME, CITIES

Tell me, cities of the future
With your steel and brick and stone,
Can the comforts of your courtyards
For true solitude atone?

Can the grandeur of your buildings,
Can your traffic's din and roar
Bring the ease of soul and comfort
That the woodlands brought of yore?

Can your polytechnic theories
And your polymorphous streets
Take the place of streams and rivers
And pine needles for your feet?

Can the supersonic travel
An atomic furnace blast
Produce the kind of people
Who the tests of life can pass?

Can your culture and your customs
And your integration strife
Give the world the peace it's lacking
If we pay the asking price?

No need to give the answer
Though it's surely worth the try.
But the moon looks down in wonder
As we rise to fall and die!

March

3

*To attain in this life a humble state of loving, spiritual union with the Infinite,
without the absurd error and folly of mistaken identity,
is a relationship to be sincerely desired.*

What Is Happiness?

Is happiness the opposite of failure and fear? Is it trading your poverty for provision and cheer? Is it uselessness finding something to do? Is it the snack reward when the job is through? Is happiness the release of the prisoner called "self?" Is it finding the cookie jar on the bottom shelf? Is happiness walking some long, lonely mile engrossed in contemplation of things worthwhile? Ah, yes! Happiness is all this—all this and much, much more!

Is happiness contentment and purity of mind? Is it climbing and searching with the past left behind? Is happiness self-improvement and striving to achieve? Is it casting out doubt and learning to believe? Is it self-control, contemplation and conquest of pain? Is it temperance in thought and emotion and deed? Is it final conquest of misery causing greed? Ah, yes! Happiness is all this—all this and much, much more! (To be continued on March 4.)

MEDITATION PRAYER

For arching sky, and soothing winds, for happy nights and succeeding days, for constellations, clouds and skies, for summer's splendor spread so lavishly. For laughing, murmuring, gurgling streams alive with beauty, life and mysterious with the shadows of the overhanging trees. For high hills and vast, rolling waves that surge and press and beat upon a thousand shores. For tall pines and singing birds. For hidden mysteries in her forests. For hills eternal, strong, snow-capped and proud. For perfumed air, and for the joy of life. For every beautiful thing, we thank you this day, O, God, our Creator. Amen.

ALL ARE A PART OF GOD'S FOREST

Blasted stump of white pine tree,
Whispering secrets from eternity,
Still, still it stands in serenity,
    A tall white pine in the forest.

Sheltering boughs rugged and tall
With offered protection for all
Earth creatures great and small
    A shelter for life in God's forest.

White pine tree with grace and power,
Shelter when storm clouds lower,
Symbol of strength for every hour,
    Protector of meadow and forest.

Tall white pine of antiquity,
Rooted in the rocks of severity
With encompassing arms of security,
    I, too, am a part of God's forest.

March

Money is a linguist who can say, "Goodbye, now!" in every known language and under every conceivable circumstance in the world; and it has been known to leave without bothering to say, "Good bye."

What Is Happiness?

    Is happiness the sublimation of selfish desire or curbing overindulgence when the senses tire? Is it the focus of attention on the favors of life? Is it an island of calm in an ocean of strife? Is happiness the annihilation of the negative or impure? Is it replacing them with virtues that always endure? Is happiness replacing all evil with good? Is it expressing compassion or wishing we could? Ah, yes! Happiness is all this—all this and much, much more!

    Is happiness the battle of courage with fear? Is it weakness grown strong on the elixir of cheer? Is it the eradication of selfishness, anger and hate or confusion, ignorance and subservience to "fate?" Is happiness the ability to concentrate? Is it control of the senses and patience to wait? Is happiness the realization of your high, other-self part? Is it living more fully from the dictates of the "heart?" Ah, yes! Happiness is all this—all this and much, much more! (To be continued on March 6.)

MY GOLDEN GOOSE

I'll feather my nest
　　From a green-backed goose
Whose feathers are bank notes
　　When I pull them loose.

It's my very own goose
　　That lays golden eggs,
That waddles thru nuggets
　　On silver legs.

It swims in a goose pond
　　With diamonds for sand
With a craw full of rubies
　　And pearls for leg-bands.

It carries a full purse
　　Under each wing.
It buys princes and bankers
　　And almost anything.

But my golden goose
　　On a golden sea
Sometimes flies south
　　When I call it to me!

March

5

The persons who rule their reflexes will not ruin their reflections
or rue their reactions half so much.

SHYNESS VERSUS COMMUNICATION

One day while walking on the sandy beach of the Pacific Ocean, the thought occurred: Why is it so hard to express my ideas and feelings to my mate? When you seem tongue-tied and awkward, isn't it easier to just be quiet, or even run away? Maybe we need practice. Well, the opportunity was very available. There on the beach was a piece of driftwood, half-buried in the sand. Why not practice talking to the driftwood? It cannot disapprove if you are clumsy; you could start your sentence or paragraph over if you were in pain. Or you could just sit down and think for a half hour if you became uncomfortable, before you ventured to speak again. Besides, there was no threat; it was easy to take it back if it didn't come out right.

OK, what shall we discuss? Well, so what is love like? Now speak up: Love is like a river flowing, deep and broad and strong. Love is like a peaceful morning filled with rapturous song. Love is like a new beginning whose transformation sets us free.

One half hour later: Love is like a quiet tempest centered in the blustering storm. Love is life itself, expressing in conscious and subconscious form. Love is like a quiet ocean deep below the surface waves. Love is like a cool, sweet fountain in the soul's subterranean caves.

Wow, this is emotionally expensive: Love is laughter, tears and courage. It is appreciation, friendship, and peace. Love is patience long enduring, hope and faith that never cease. Love is sunset when day is dying and tomorrow with its new sunrise. Love is the soul's own secret language whose silent eloquence never dies!

Love is something born for sharing that misers hoard like glittering gold. Love knows the secret gift of caring and banks its fires when winds blow cold. Love would fill its arms with gladness and scatter sunshine where it will. Love dispels the gloom of sadness like sunbeams on life's windowsill!

I must hurry to my apartment now.

I FELL IN LOVE WITH A MANIKIN

I fell in love with a manikin,
　　She listened so intently to me;
The only woman who didn't talk
　　Or yammer incessantly.

I fell in love with a manikin.
　　Her weight never varied a pound.
She didn't talk diet or metrical,
　　But just kept hanging around.

When I needed to drape a coat on her
　　She had an extended arm.
No matter how late I came in or out
　　She never threatened me with harm.

I fell in love with a manikin.
　　She wore what I gave her to wear.
She was always as neat as a pin or two
　　With never a misplaced hair.

I fell in love with a manikin;
　　But she did have a wooden head.
She wanted to stand in the corner all night
　　When I wanted to go to bed!

COMMUNICATING LOVE

　　It is my sacred duty and privilege to resolve to sincerely communicate love to you. Sweetheart, it would be so much better to learn to hold you and to personally and warmly tell you, "I love you," than to talk to a piece of driftwood or to a wooden-headed doll. May we practice loving together?

FISHERMAN BY BENGARTT (W. JACKSON COLLECTION)

FJORD BY CAROLINE SEYMOUR

March

*Let the light of truth direct your path, the lamp of reason guard your
steps, and the candle of courage give you confidence;
for that person is not alone who walks in light.*

WHAT IS HAPPINESS?

Is happiness group sharing of a common aim or riding your own hobby and not playing the game? Is happiness knowing an important friend? Is it breaking a habit you could hardly bend? Is happiness the vacation or just coming back? Is it recording the expenses or forgetting to keep track? Is happiness the memory of things long gone? Is it living in the present with face to the dawn? Ah, yes! Happiness is all this—all this and much, much more!

Is happiness playing on the winner's team or being a good loser with a shattered dream? Is happiness found in the people we meet? Is it sharing with others both success and defeat? Is happiness the security of finding your place, or is it being here and gone without leaving a trace? Is happiness possessing the thing we love best, or is it enjoying what we have, forgetting the rest? Ah, yes! Happiness is all this—all this and much, much more! (To be continued on March 7.)

SEAL MY LIPS, O LORD

God, help me that nothing but good may pass
    These lips of mine today.
And place Thou a seal, a check divine,
    On all that I fain would say.

And if I must speak at all, O Lord,
    About the other man,
Give me the grace and wisdom enough
    To say the best thing that I can.

May never a word from lips of mine
    Add one more straw to the load
Of a struggling brother with faults enough
    Without my slanderous goad.

My words are Thine for blessings now;
    For commendations sweet.
And grant that they may never, Lord,
    Some evil thing repeat.

O, Thou who judges all our hearts,
    By what we think and say,
Help us to stand with a conscience clear
    At the closing of the day.

March

7

The grateful, the creative, and the confident have a standing invitation in the presence of God.

WHAT IS HAPPINESS?

Is happiness the favorable aspect of stars? Is it freedom's bondage outside jail bars? Is happiness something we're conditioned to learn? Is it the search or the object for which we yearn? Is happiness the acceptance or rejection of thought? Is it "paying the piper" for not getting caught? Is happiness the pride of accomplishment? Is it moving to the "big house" and leaving the tent? Ah, yes! Happiness is all this—all this and much, much more!

Is happiness the frugality of saving your dimes? Or "blowing" your savings with abandon sometimes? Is happiness sharing the talents God gave? Is it reading a headstone that's not on YOUR grave? Is happiness the flow of the creative mind? Is it laughing at a problem you've left behind? Is happiness the favorite chair where you sit or a special tool in the "fix-it" yourself kit? Ah, yes! Happiness is all this—all this and much, much more! (To be continued on March 8.)

THE PROMISE OF GOLDEN DAY

The door of God awareness
    Swings wide on hinges of gold.
A door of hope and inner light
    Well-known by the prophets of old.

These portals of illumination
    Open bright vistas from afar,
Where strange and wonderful promises
    Float thru the gates ajar.

The sounds of holy harmony
    Not distant or far away,
Are wafted thru the doors of God
    With the promise of golden day.

March

*The courtship of truth should result in a love for reality,
and the union of faith with fact.*

What Is Happiness?

Is happiness a state of both mind and health? Is it freedom from debt or excessive wealth? Is happiness luck and good fortune combined? Is it the peppermint you relish after you've dined? Is happiness the refraction of projected good? Is it relief that comes from being understood? Is happiness confession and fixing things up? Is it drinking a beverage from a favorite cup? Ah, yes! Happiness is all this—all this and much, much more!

Is happiness insight or seeing ahead? Is it skimming a good book you've already read? Is happiness leaving the wrong side of the "track?" Or is it the satisfaction of just looking back? Is happiness the efficiency of an organized plan or living with conditions as best you can? Is happiness detachment like you couldn't care less or strengthening up things you've found in a mess? Ah, yes! Happiness is all this—all this and much, much more! (To be continued on March 9.)

THE OTHER SIDE OF TRUTH

That attribute of an evolving race
    That flash of supernal fire,
That illumination from within
    Is a gift if we aspire.

Here awareness of the universe
    Where all things God's presence share
Gives freedom from fear, evil and death;
    Sheds love's radiance everywhere.

This awareness breaks the bonds of thought
    And knows of itself, forsooth.
But asks no man to understand
    The other side of truth.

March

9

He who lives too fast to savor life seems not to have lived too long;
but he who lives most fully adds extra stances to his once-heard song.

What Is Happiness?

Is happiness the privilege of "griping" a bit? Is it having a chair when you're ready to sit? Is happiness the skill of perfected technique or the paycheck that comes at the end of the week? Is happiness the art of forgetting your grief? Is it recalling the beauty of a tree in full leaf? Is happiness just loving somebody "to pieces?" Is it stretching and laughing when tension releases? Ah, yes! Happiness is all this—all this and much, much more!

Is happiness a wall that shuts things out or that keeps things in that we're fearful about? Is happiness an ocean with a sandy shore? Is it lying in the sun relaxed to the core? Is happiness good credit because you didn't abuse it, or is it not having credit because you never use it? Is happiness the inspiration of talkative friends or the blessed quiet when conversation ends? Ah, yes! Happiness is all this—all this and much, much more! (To be continued on March 10.)

I LOVE THE SOUND OF THE SURF

I love the sound of the surging surf
    In the early, clear cool dawn.
I hear it's singing, beating and ringing
    And pounding on and on!

I love the sound of the surging surf
    With its endless, rhythmic song,
Like a lingering lover at the door
    Who has stayed almost too long.

I love the surging of the surf
    That stirs some solemn chord
Of restless fear and surging hope
    And longings oft outpoured!

I love the singing of the surf
    That strains at the anchors old.
Capricious sea inviting me
    To adventures still untold!

I love the sound of the surging surf
    And the gusty winds that blow.
I pity the soul who has never heard
    The ocean come and go!

March

~ 10 ~

When the dust of mortality is blown afar,
the door of immortality will be standing ajar.

WHAT IS HAPPINESS?

Is happiness keeping communication's hose unkinked or the knowing smile when somebody winked? Is happiness the cry of grief and pain that gives birth to some good thing that will still remain? Is happiness life balance and stabilization when the extrinsic and intrinsic find equalization? Is happiness the conveniences of suburb and city, or roughing it while you enjoy your own self-pity? Ah, yes! Happiness is all this—all this and much, much more!

Is happiness your inner, directional sense? The avoidance of trouble with its recompense? Is happiness measured by things possessed? Is it the good self-image of being well dressed? Is happiness the extension of a helping hand or the "please" that precedes an expected command? Is happiness kindness and established rapport? Is it the welcome smile and the opened door? Ah, yes! Happiness is all this—all this and much, much more! (To be continued on March 11.)

I WANT TO KNOW

I want to taste the dew of life
    On duty's lips with pleasure.
I want to know life's fullest bliss
    And taste its purest measure.

I want to swing in orbit wide
    Above the rainbow's arching.
I want to know what wisdom is
    And leave on earth some marking.

I want to know the facts of life
    Both the causes and the reasons.
I want to know the why and how
    Of nature's laws and seasons.

I want to know my Maker well
    And see beyond earth's portals.
I want to be a man who walks
    And talks with the immortals!

PORT COMRADES BY CAROLINE SEYMOUR

AT DOCK BY CAROLINE SEYMOUR

March

11

We think God is against us when he only wants to be close.

WHAT IS HAPPINESS?

Is happiness the summertime smell of the breeze? Is it a boy with freckles and with patches on his knees? Is it bursting the bonds of your self-limitation, or changing life from a "dumb-heap" to a service station? Is happiness a road map and a gas-filled car? Is it solving the problems by staying where you are? Is happiness the smell of a summer shower? Is it a book, a shade tree and peace for an hour? Ah, yes! Happiness is all this—all this and much, much more!

Is happiness capturing attunements "lost chord?" Is it resignation, rattling seeds in an empty gourd? Is happiness rebuilding with the bricks of defeat? Is it a rain-swept face after the storms retreat? Is happiness the shortcut in the cross-country race, or is it the long way where you EARN second place? Is happiness the awareness that finally comes to the one who the heights and the darkness plumb? Ah, yes! Happiness is all this—all this and much, much more! (To be continued on March 12.)

THE SECRET PLACE

He who daily dwells beneath the shade
    Of God our secret place
Shall know the inner faith and love
    In God's sustaining grace.

And he who dwells in love's own realm
    Shall find the satisfaction true
Of God's own comfort and his care
    Till life's journey here is through.

Here sheltered from the burning heat
    Of temptation's fiercest sun
The praying one, his strength renews
    As when day was first begun.

Thus I choose to live within His care
    And in prayer to steal away,
To find God's secret hiding place
    There to dwell from day to day.

March

~ 12 ~

*Thought is an artist whose idle doodling become tomorrow's blueprints;
and thought is a dreamer whose fantasy becomes tomorrow's history.*

WHAT IS HAPPINESS?

Is happiness your gift under your own Christmas tree? Is it liberty's package in the land of the free? Is happiness the perfection of inner intent? Is it opening some package for which you had sent? Is happiness procrastination's early demise? Is it getting things done to everyone's surprise? Is happiness the rhythm of the whole universe? Is it harmony and peace when things couldn't look worse? Ah, yes! Happiness is all this—all this and much, much more!

Is happiness silence when you feel uptight? Is it being all by yourself when you turn out the light? Is happiness communing with nature alone? Is it watching a squirrel with a fat pinecone? Is happiness self-confident orientation, or a survival experience that borders starvation? Is happiness music, travel or art? Is it fame, fortune, honor or just play-acting a part? Ah, yes! Happiness is all this—all this and much, much more! (To be continued on March 13.)

CREATIVE THOUGHT

O, God, of creative urge and power
    Awaiting the will of man.
Grant me the wisdom to form my thoughts
    In some creative pattern or plan.

Help me to do as the Father doeth
    Thru creation's manifest law
That from Thy free-flowing, creative will
    I may continually, triumphantly draw.

O, God, of all vibrant power and love,
    I have reshaped earth-forms by my hand
But greater works than these I must do
    Thru faith, which is mine to command.

I yield the power of my thoughts to Thee
    As together we shall work as one
Till the imaged form of faith held firm
    Creates the vision when finally done.

March

~ 13 ~

Who knows what destiny is God's design, or what duties are eternally ours to perform?
To know Him is our first duty, and to do it is our life.

WHAT IS HAPPINESS?

Is happiness the green light when you are in a hurry? Is it the childlike capacity not to worry? Is happiness banking the coals of desire till another time when they can rise much higher? Is happiness discerning the heaven-consciousness code? Is it just to walk simply down your own country road? Is happiness the art of salvaging from trouble the secrets of success that were left in the rubble? Ah, yes! Happiness is all this—all this and much, much more!

Is happiness a hermit in a sacred cell, or the carefree vagrancy of the ne'er-do-well? Is happiness the release of emotional drive? Is it animal instinct glad to still be alive? Is happiness the collar on a workhorse's neck? Is it saddle and spurs and reins to check? Is happiness being securely tied to a hitching post? Is it giving your best and doing the most? Ah, yes! Happiness is all this—all this and much, much more! (To be continued on March 14.)

DIMENSIONS

I spend all my days in eternity
    And timeless, I measure all time.
I rise to dimensions of awareness
    Bathed in sunlight from celestial clime.

I spend all my days in eternity
    Where love is the heartthrob of life.
Detached from evil, from things and from self
    I am centered above storm and strife.

I spend all my days in eternity,
    God conscious, I desire what He planned.
Committed, purged, ecstatic and free
    Heaven's oceans roll over earth's sand.

March

~ 14 ~

All life and the disposal thereof lie ultimately in the hands of God.

WHAT IS HAPPINESS?

Is happiness God-conscious, calm meditation? Is it ultimate truth and our glad appropriation? Is happiness acquiring the knowledge of facts or is it discovering true wisdom and how intuition reacts? Is happiness a no-limitations belief? Is it giving of yourself, for another's relief? Is happiness a thoughtful, outgoing trend where you helped a friend? Ah, yes! Happiness is all this—all this and much, much more!

Is happiness an experience that's all your own? Is it holding your ground like a dog holds a bone? Is happiness siphoning the universal mind pool or tapping your subconscious like going to school? Is happiness the food on a banquet table? Is it the call, "Come and get it," when you know you're able? Ah, yes! Happiness is all this—all this and much, much more! (To be continued on March 16.)

GOD'S ALLNESS

Each star is connected to God
 For He is both here and there.
On the other side of matter unveiled
 He is always and everywhere.

There's only the thinnest veil between
 God and the thing controlled.
And God is the Person, the Power and Form
 Of the objects that before us unfold.

God is the veil of the object hid,
 The invisible and the visible, too.
God is a part of the viewer and viewed,
 The light and veil it shines thru.

God is the substance behind the fact.
 Which caused it to manifest.
And God is the fact in manifest form
 That His power made active or at rest.

Yes, God is the various levels of form
 From Spirit to the substance plane.
His Spirit forms substance from Himself
 Repeated again and again.

If the veil of non-seeing were lifted
 And insight comprehended indeed,
Truth would reveal God's fullness
 And supply our every need!

CHIVA-KEN FISHING VILLAGE BY HUGO WESTPHAL

HERITAGE OF SEATTLE BY CAROLINE SEYMOUR

March

~ 15 ~

A FLY-BY-NIGHT WEDDING

"Come into my house,"
    Said the fly to the spider,
And he sidled right over
    And sat down beside her.

He looked in her eyes
    So brilliant and green
And decided right then
    To make her his queen.

He spoke from his knees:
    "I'll be your provider,"
But he really looked hungry
    From the moment he spied her.

She looked at his arms
    And how they could hug her,
But she really distrusted
    The hairy-faced mugger.

She coyly evaded
    His proposal to wed,
But fluttered and flitted
    Around his flat head.

She thought: "You look handy,
    Both knavery and army,
So I'll put you to work
    Before you can harm me."

"Our plumber was dumber,"
    She said with a wink;
"So I need your long arm
    To clean out the sink."

But the spider just eyed her
    And wrinkled his brow.
He knew he was getting
    The "go-around" now.

"Perhaps you could mend
    My tennis racket web,
Or weave a new rug
    For the foot of my bed."

But silently he wove
    A web over her door
With bars on each window
    From ceiling to floor.

He stamped all his feet
    And cried with a shout:
"You asked for it, baby;
    Now put the lights out."

He fastened his gaze
    On the bridge of her nose
And soon hypnotized her
    As the sad story goes.

He quickly encircled her
    With one stiff, jerky arm,
As she fainted away
    In mortal alarm.

When he saw on her face
    He had completely overpowered her,
His love turned to hunger
    And he completely devoured her.

Therefore, fly-by-night romance
    Is strictly taboo!
Watch it, lest some insect
    Gets shacked-up with you.

March

~ 16 ~

*The person who is careless with the truth is an artist at misrepresentation
who can paint holes in the canvas where no defect ever had been.*

WHAT IS HAPPINESS?

Is happiness nostalgic memory release? Is it compromise with life and an uncertain peace? Is happiness devotion to all things worthwhile? Is it helping somebody over the second mile? Is happiness a composite, enjoyed before it's too late? Is it expanded awareness with the capacity to take cheerfully what life gives without being a fake? Ah, yes! Happiness is all this—all this and much, much more!

Is happiness a dimension, or an environment? Is it courage facing the unknown when life is spent? Is happiness the grip you have on existence? Is it holding back tears with cheerful insistence? Is happiness ad-libbing the words when YOU really can't hear? Is happiness love overflowing, divine? Whatever happiness is, it's yours and it's mine! Ah, yes! Happiness is all this—all this and much, much more!

INSIGHT

Brown are my sculptured tree forms
    Against the far horizon.
Blue, blue are the mountain peaks
    Steadfast to set my eyes on.

Opened is my inner vision now
    That sees such beauty beckon.
I claim each visual treasure
    As wealth I cannot reckon.

Blue-gray are the mountaintops
    Where snow freshly lies in patches.
Where perception is a point of view
    For soul values man attaches.

Where emotions are the telescope
    That brings the focus clearer.
And ecstasy and praise and love
    Blend the distant with the nearer.

Oh, wonder world, of joy exciting
    In panoramic vision viewed,
Where insight sees each hidden depth
    Thru eyes with light endued.

March

~ 17 ~

Complacency is a floating raft in a stagnant mill pond for people who drifted out of the main current and have lost their pole and their push, or their oars and their ambitions, which tends to promote only retrogression and unwanted decadence of body and mind.

TRUE IDENTITY

In a deeply relaxed condition, the inner self should be questioned as to the why of any physical malfunction, and it also should be encouraged to give the proper procedures for its remediation. The inner self knows the cause of its own irritations and can direct in the corrective activities to heal any variance between the original self-mold and its physical counterpart. All needs and problems should be referred to the high self. Man must learn to live in a state of detachment, possessing all things but in no sense being possessed by the things he possesses. Often, desire itself can be eliminated with greater ease than it can be satisfied.

In true non-directional, decentralized concentration, the mind loses its separated consciousness and its feeling of being an observer of something observed, and it actually identifies with and becomes that which it is observing. True concentration as an exercise of consciousness is the ability to identify with the object of contemplation, to sense its properties and to explore it in its identity. It is only the space and time sense that is lost in identifying with an object where and when limiting barriers are broken down. But the observer does continue to realize his own identity in the sense of evaluating that with which he identifies and also in the storing of those evaluative opinions and reactions within himself rather than within the thing observed. Otherwise, he would completely lose his identity and resort to a lower level of simply being, not being and knowing.

Man, the Spirit, has made this error in identifying with his physical body, which is a thing to be known and a mechanism to be used. But it is not himself. He must maintain his identity outside of his body as a thing separated from it lest he become only a thing and a part of materiality without the ability to evaluate, to carry back memories and to give directions to that which is exterior to himself but known entirely by identifying with it. Man must know and never lose his true identity even while ever changing.

THE BLARNEY STONE

In the southern part of Ireland
    Where castles tower high,
Up in the "keep" of a tower steep
    Against the Irish sky,
Is a coveted stone for those alone
    Who have the grit to try.

It's the Blarney Stone of Ireland,
    The symbol of fluent talk.
And there's verbal bliss for those who kiss
    That selfsame granite rock.
And many a "smooth-talk" lad has had
    His tryst at the Blarney Block.

There's a Mightier Rock than the Blarney Stone—
    Rock of Ages for us riven—
Where words of faith and courage
    Make earth a bit of heaven.
May your life embrace its gentle grace.
    All your words be kindly given!

March

~ 18 ~

The moon lights up the night better than a thousand sightless eyes; so an illuminated person reflects his inner wisdom among the multitudes with lesser stars for light.

IT PAYS TO THINK

Life calls for clear, farseeing, accurate thinking. If a person is to achieve successfully rather than to endure in mediocrity, that person must learn to think. He must overcome inactivity and mental inertia. He will master the techniques of analytical, logical thought processes.

Have you noticed that the most appreciated concepts and ideas that any person can contribute to any group or to a specific business is the person who will increase the general body of knowledge for that group? This may include the increase of sales or the decreased cost of production. For example, this is the quickest avenue to promotion and success. Within the corporate world, the power of creative thinking is sleeping, unused among most individuals, but may be increased once the persons involved understand how to think successfully. Never give up on mental prospecting, for the mind's capacity to invent provides priceless adventures. There is nothing that will deliver to a person such a mental lift—"lift you up out of the dumps"—as to solve a problem or use your thoughts to create something.

Creative thinking enables you to find your place in this life, because without creative ideas, you may be sentenced to remain where circumstances have put you. As you consider the occasions to benefit you as an individual, there are also occasions to benefit the world around you. This is a demonstration of how our world functions. Our society moves through creative ideas—good, not so good, and indifferent plans—as far as the impact on others is concerned. Would it be possible to aim for the development of such good ideas that wants are abundantly satisfied? Yes, creative thinking is our most prized, profit-producing privilege for any individual, business and, for that matter, any country. Know this: Creative thinking has the ability to change you, your corporation and even your extended community.

The challenge for this 18th day of March is to learn to apply a trained, penetrating, active mind to the evaluation of your situation, the solution to your problems and the attainment of your life's goals. To do this, a person must think!

SOMETIMES

Sometimes in the broken silences
    And in the quiet voice of prayer
I find my heart responding
    And I know that God is there!

Sometimes in the wake of silence
    That follows our deepest sleep
I know I have touched the eternal
    Where God His vigil keeps.

Sometimes in the somber shadow
    Of longing, pain and strife
I get a glimpse of the better way
    And the gleam of eternal life.

Sometimes the truth shines lucid
    And I see things as they are.
I know the way my soul must take
    And at times I have wandered far.

But always when the veil is lifted
    And I catch a glimpse of the light,
I know sometime, somewhere, somehow
    That all things will come out right!

March
~ 19 ~

PEACEFUL SURRENDER BY DANIEL TETTEH

The life is long enough that fully works out the purposes
for which that life was born.

SAFE ON THAT SHORE

You angry old ocean!
    I'll have fun by your side.
I'll kick sand in your teeth.
    I'll laugh at your tide.
    I'm safe on the shore.

You persistent old ocean!
    Your waves never stop.
But where are you going
    With your splash and your plop?
    You clutter the shore.

From away in the distance
    Your waves stumble in,
All fizzled out finally
    In spite of your din
    That threatens the shore.

I love you old ocean!
    You remind me of life,
Of the struggle unending,
    Of turmoil and strife
    And the folks on the shore.

You faithful old ocean!
    I'll outrun your tide
On a shore that's called heaven
    On time's other side,
    On a far brighter shore!

March

~ 20 ~

He is an orphan indeed whose life purposes are not sired by just ambition,
nurtured by fervent desire, schooled in the creed of service,
and accepted in the household of humanity, for the sake of peace and love.

WHAT IS THINKING?

Creative ideas, subjected to action, produce events that count in our lives and in the life of our world. Can you believe there is a magic future that begins and continues to develop in our own minds? It could select any one of us and convey us into posterity. The invitation is for you to become an idea factory. Why not set out on an idea safari?

What, then, is thinking? Thinking is the mind in action. The mind in action may remember, imagine, conceive, consider, rearrange, weigh facts and evidence, conclude, judge and expect. The mind may decide a course of action; arrive at a purpose, a plan, an intention, an opinion or a belief. But thinking is often a more or less involuntary, symbol-like process or procession of superimposed mental images moving at variable rates of speed in different depth, overlapping and superimposing themselves upon each other and demanding varying degrees of conscious attention.

Thinking is mental attention. It is meditation; it is visualization and it is concentration. But thinking is more than consciousness, which is primarily involved with sense-presented things. The mind in action can, by subjective processes, concepts and imagination, deal symbolically with sense-represented things. But the full image or mental picture is not all that is necessary in the act of thinking, even though it may be accomplished by symbols, words, shorthand concepts or flashes of meaning, or feeling that is so rapid and so subjective as to challenge conscious examination. This form of mentation is here and gone. Impressions are seen and felt and then lost again, but nevertheless, a conclusion is arrived at.

Finally, we ask the question, what generally controls our choice of thinking and creative problem solving? Consider the following five examples:

- Commercial and money-making potency,

- Preservation and prosperity of ourselves and our neighbors,

- Conceivable labor-saving practices,

- Elegant and graceful appeal to the senses, and

- The electric charge relative to global thinking, peace and love.

Identify with these concepts. Open yourself entirely to them. Impress your own inner mind by the fervency of your own desire to pick a goal and to practice thinking.

PEACE AND LOVE

Peace is the palm of plenty.
Love is the force of life.
Peace is the calm of sunset.
Love is the balm for strife.

Peace is the new day dawning.
Love is the sun at high noon.
Peace is the soft cloud floating.
Love is the half-clad moon.

Peace is the hearth and fireside.
Love is the embers' glow.
And peace and love are roses
That always together grow.

March

~ 21 ~

*God respects principles and potentials more than He respects
present positions of "poor" or "prominent" persons.*

IDEATION

In casual discussion, ideas are much like the weather, and it seems as if many people talk about them. On the other hand, few people are specific about how to develop these ideas. After all, why would anyone want to tamper with "those obscure laws of our world?" Well, what are ideas and where do they come from? According to the dictionary, an idea is "any product of mental apprehension or activity." Perhaps the idea may be "a concept" or "a notion." Then you may consider an idea a "purpose or plan" or "a mental image." Could the idea be considered a "standard of excellence" or an "ideal?"

Many years ago, a fellow described an idea to be "the mental spark that ignites the gas and starts our idea-mobile going." When that mode of operation takes place, we may be transported in various directions to experience many events, which can provide multiple alterations for our individual community and ourselves.

Ideation within the bound of normalcy certainly involves self-directed mental activity. Idea thinking is an active, creative process; a doing and an achieving; a problem-solving adaptation of information and ability. Idea thinking is the reasoning process of the intellect of the person, and idea thinking is problem solving. The thinker facing a problem, a deficiency, an unattained desire or a goal will acknowledge, define, face and analyze his problem. The person's conscious mind will conceive possible solutions from past experience or adaptations and combinations of past experiences. Thus, stimulated by necessity, he will come up with either an original or a synthetic solution to his problem.

His subconscious, creative mind may become activated and interested in the problem and may project suggestions or possible solutions to his more conscious processes in the form of inspirations or ideas out of the clear, blue sky. Here, the thinker's logical, deductive, selective reasoning abilities may exercise themselves in judicial decision as that person strikes upon a successful conclusion or experiments, variously, with the best possible solutions until he is satisfied pragmatically, on a working basis, that results have confirmed and crowned his efforts with the attainment of his desires.

THE ULTIMATE AND THE TRUE

Oh the presence of the Infinite
In the here and everywhere,
Is the kindly, sure reality
That God with man would share.

There is no place in all the world
From sunset till the dawn
But that God is there and everywhere
That man has ever gone.

Creation's cord, umbilical,
To God still binds us fast.
The finite and the Infinite
Are one while life shall last.

No feelings bring him nearer,
No gloom makes him depart,
For God is here and everywhere,
Of everything a part.

We think Him gone. He still remains.
His constancy is true.
For God is here and everywhere
The day and long night through.

Beneath, above and everywhere
We're encompassed round about.
God's presence is vouchsafed to us
And none are left without.

March

~ 22 ~

*The splendor of achievement, the light of recognition, and the glory of exaltation
are bright halos for the humble, but they ill-fit the proud.*

LOGICAL THINKING

To reason logically is to reason accurately. To consider what is relevant or pertinent and to reject the irrelevant—this is logical reason functioning accurately. A study of formal logic is, of course, an encouragement to accuracy of thought. But fortunate indeed is the man or the woman who possesses that inborn ability to think accurately and quickly. Many do, for in everyday living, with its social relationships, its recreation and labor, we must constantly be making up our minds. We must come to decisions and form judgments upon which our loss or gain, our success or our failure depends. We should strive to be as exact and scientific in our thinking as possible, for we as well as others lose or gain by it, and we will sooner or later reap the results of inaccurate, indecisive or careless thinking. Or again, we may reap and will reap the benefits of logical, positive thinking!

Inductive and deductive thinking or reasoning is a familiar method for arriving at conclusions. Induction arrives at a general truth or truths based upon particular facts. Induction is taking first, the particular, and then the generalization or the principle. Deduction, however, proceeds from a generalization or principle to particulars; from a whole to a part; from the greater to the lesser. This is deduction.

Much of our knowledge comes to us through our senses and the senses of others. However, because impressions may inductively be misinterpreted and wrong inferences drawn, a person has invented machines to extend their hearing, seeing and feeling in order to ensure greater accuracy. But, they must still depend upon their own intelligence to interpret the facts that they gather from near and far, by whatever means.

They may, as was mentioned in the definition of thinking, reason in a condensed, swift, shorthand kind of thinking so rapid that it seems they have intuitive knowledge or knowledge without consciousness of attainment. Intuition in some cases, however, seems to be an immediate apprehension or cognition of basic truth or principle, perhaps without conscious thought process even of the shorthand type mentioned.

Generally speaking, however, the laws of thought are the laws of order and relationship that can be traced and the method learned through use and personal experience. Analysis, arrangement and classification with divisions and subdivisions, as in an outline arrangement, are essential to accurate thinking whether we're aware of the exact process or not. So, to classify is to think.

A good vocabulary and accurate definitions are necessities for clear thinking, for a person must know whereof and of what he speaks. Without language and its word symbols, any proper organization, classification and understanding of knowledge would be very difficult indeed, if not impossible altogether.

OH, LET ME SING ON!

Let me dream dreams in the nighttime.
    Let me dream of the songs of the spring.
Let me be wafted on airy lightness
Filled with the lift of Ariel brightness
    And let me dream on while I sing.
    Forever just let me sing!

Let me sing on the songs of the nighttime.
    Let me sing on of the days that are gone.
Oh, let me fore-herald the better day dawning
Protected from ill by love's canopied awning.
    Oh, let me sing on of the night and the dawn.
    Forever just let me sing on!

March

23

Those who pray for wings should also ask for directions.

COMMON SENSE

*Common sense is that intuitive perception that sometimes writes its reasons in shorthand
but spells out its conclusions in capital letters of judicious decisions.*

What is this trait called common sense, and what is its relationship to thinking as explained? It is practical judgment or intelligence and, as the term implies, just ordinary, good, common sense. It is the ability to place everything in its proper place and evaluation. It can adapt itself to commonplace or elevated concepts as the need may demand. It finds the better part of wisdom to avoid strife and it most fully develops in an atmosphere of friendly, unstrained congeniality. Common sense is a unifying, converging point whose periphery or outside point of contact is a candid desire for actual knowledge and ultimate truth. Its practicality would rather solve problems than raise them. This is common sense. It has an affinity for directness, simplicity, consideration and respect for others.

Common sense is a judicial function that manifests itself in discernment, coherency and accuracy. Reason in the role of common sense illuminates, examines, differentiates, dissects, analyzes, defines, classifies and evaluates the subject of its consideration. It pierces duplicity, deceit or insincerity. Common sense avoids credulity with its tendency to accept all things without evidence. It also avoids apathy, that uncaring attitude with its inaccuracies of acceptance. Common sense grips the rock of reality. Its mental equilibrium judges relative values efficiently, defines its course with foresight, prepares its plans of progress and brings its desires to happy fruition.

Common sense possesses such a habitual sense of practicality that it shatters illusions, fads, enthusiasms, reverie, and mediocrity. With conscious, consistent effort, common sense drives unremittingly with perseverance toward its reasonable and entirely attainable goals, as seen in the light of its own wisdom. Thus, common sense is seen to be a central sun, luminous and radiant, around which many planet virtues orbit as a natural consequence of its strength and inner virtue. Its pivotal principles are just, demonstrable and true. No one can travel far toward the end of the day without the staff of common sense to lean upon as he treads the intricate paths of personal judgment and decision that are intrinsic to a complicated life pattern or a life that seemingly has no pattern. It is here that he needs the staff of common sense upon which to lean and the map of common sense as his guide throughout the day.

Reason or common sense is nourished by the accurate visual and auditory perceptions of the senses. Man must hear accurately and see correctly in order to feed the decisions of his common-sense conclusions. It is here that memory moves in beside perception to raise, to resurrect and to re-construct the past and to assist in making conclusions by proper comparison, classification and differentiation of the inceptive idea as it unfolds. The alerted understanding actively reflects upon the problem at hand. Reason looks backward to the past for confirmation and forward with fore-sighted precaution to all possible pleasant or unpleasant outcomes.

THE WINGS OF THE WIND

The wings of the wind? Who sees them?
    I have felt their swift passing by.
Like a giant bird flown from heaven,
I have heard their jubilant cry.

I have heard their cry at nighttime,
    Mourning like someone bereft.
Whispering sighs they have passed me.
    Answering, I found they had left.

Wings of the wind, how they rustle!
    Fanning my face with their breeze.
Wings of the wind's angry buzzing
    Like the hum of wild, swarming bees.

Wings of the wind like some angel
    Have brushed me in passing by.
Oh, wings of the wind sent from heaven
    Drive the dark clouds from the sky.

Wings of the wind, how symbolic!
    Portraying God's Spirit Divine,
Come fill my heart with Thy Presence
    And touch Thou this spirit of mine.

March

~ 24 ~

"THE OLD SEA AND THE FISHERMAN," ALASKA, W. JACKSON

HAVE I THANKED HIM?

I have thanked God for my roses.
Have I thanked Him for my thorns?
Have I thanked Him for my midnights
As I've thanked Him for the morns?

I have thanked Him for the pleasant
Path my feet have walked today.
But have I thanked Him for the fences
That kept me in His way?

Then help me, God, to thank Thee
For a world of many things.
And tune my heart to praise Thee
With a faith that always sings!

March

~ 25 ~

Even love should have its vacations, for afterwards its treasures shine brighter
in the new perspective that distance and time have renewed.

Heart to Heart

Living love includes a different dimension, compared to just voicing words of love. You can count on the fact that living love can be abundantly more romantic than listening to all of the beautiful and sweet expressions of love. Living love includes the involvement of giving of yourself in everything you are a part of together. The absolute principle of love embraces GIVING. There is no dispute, love is the sum total of everything of importance in the Universe!

For those who have been married, do you remember when the honeymoon was over? Can you recall all of the expressions of winsomeness and protestation of everlasting love as they branded themselves on your psyche, and after excited bodies have exhausted themselves in desires fulfilled? This may well have been the prime time when you were the most available candidate for the real romance of living. Consider the potential opportunity to shape your lives in a beautiful oneness, or on the other hand, your choice to tear your relationship apart in the emotion of misunderstandings. It is impossible to build a joyful and fulfilling life of love that has lasting durability without a basic understanding of love. This could be like the approach to any project, with no plan.

When people develop a love relationship with the sole intention of obtaining happiness, time will demonstrate disappointment and the relationship will include diminishing romance. The issue must be, what can I give to my mate and lover to make that person happy? What a difference there is in these two desires.

Can we accept the fact that no one else will be able to make us happy? We must be happy within ourselves, and then we are ready and able to share happiness. Be happy yourself internally and you demonstrate that you understand what love is. Remember—you do not take love, you can only give love. Therefore, giving provides opportunity to serve each other, and yes, to serve and to love each other is our transcending purpose on this earth.

I'LL TELL YOU A SECRET!

Go find a white blackbird
 As blue as the sky,
And bring me a Cyclops
 With more than one eye.

Go search till you find
 In the ocean or sea
A long-legged Mermaid,
 And bring her to me.

Go find me the foot
 Of a fish that can walk,
Or bring me a deaf-mute
 Who can listen and talk.

Go bring me the dew
 From a wilted, dry rose,
And I'll tell you a secret
 That every man knows!

What a woman will do
 Is a riddle to guess,
But don't tell her I said so,
 Or I'll be in an interesting mess!

March

~ 26 ~

*Those who identify with their weakness when they could have chosen strength
have voted for defeat, difficulties and death; it is better to become more conscious
of our strength than of our weakness, of our possibilities than of our problems.*

OBSERVATION THINKING AND SCIENCE

Observation thinking will sharpen the eye, open the ears and put lubrication on the cogs of its mental machinery. After all, the individual's conception of a situation or a fact is a rather modified personal version of that reality. Observation thinking includes profitable observation as a general detection of differences. The thinking and observing scientist observes the significant, important and the out-of-the-ordinary.

If you are an engineer and you are interested in new buildings, examine a number of plans, construction sites and completed projects, and ascertain what departure from generally accepted practices you can find. If your own personal business is languishing, determine if you might be able to bring some distinctive and original touch to it. The mind has the ability to develop a process wholly unknown to you as you study the project. Did you know that the mind could suddenly rearrange various attributes or apply different components to something else? In addition, our minds sort ideas and new creations, which are the result of multiple, even many hundreds of changes that assemble successively and beautifully represent the finished product of your thoughts. It, of necessity, must be because it is your own experience and therefore your own conclusion and your own method of thinking. Thus, better attention, and efficiency in concentration and accuracy in hearing or seeing, will give you even greater accuracy of the overall perception while avoiding false conceptions, which lead to wrong decisions and wrong actions.

The little-known life of scientists includes several practices. For example, they gather facts, and still more facts relative to their proposed project. They would like to collect and thus know everything that everyone already knows about their project. At the same time, they are observing, observing and observing. Included in this scientific thinking and planning process, the scientists' minds are unconsciously laboring over the vast accumulation of knowledge they have assembled during their lifetime. Then they begin working backward and then with experimentation, working forward to try to demonstrate the possible procedure to determine if what they have thought out really works. Remember—while all of this is going on, the thinking scientist is observing his experimenting and is constantly observing interesting sidelines. In this case, the scientist's work is never done.

~ 215 ~

Industry and government spend many billions of dollars a year in research and experimentation. Yes, finding things out and applying these findings are big business and often develop controversial rulings—and thus pressures. Again, observation thinking would indicate that common sense should be used relative to various battles and should carefully be thought out long before they're fought. On second thought (speaking of thinking), common sense would warn us that battles can be lost, and that even the winner is often the loser. It is the better part of wisdom to avoid the acute angle and to conceal any necessary force under the velvet glove of peaceful persuasion.

WINGS OVER SEAGULL BAY

I see the seagulls flying
Over Seagull Bay,
Wingtips spread and dipping
Above the ocean spray!

I see the seagulls flying
Over Seagull Bay
With silhouette of gray wings
Sunlit at close of day.

I see the seagulls flying
Over Seagull Bay.
With symmetry of soaring wings
They wheel and cry at play!

I hear the seagulls crying
Over Seagull Bay.
Their wingtips brushed by heart
With peace as they went away.

March

27

DISPUTED LANDING BY CAROLINE SEYMOUR

THE SCHOOL OF PRAYER

How rich to converse with Omnipotence!
    But how could such things be?
Can time's questions ever be answered
    From the book of eternity?

What privilege to ask Omniscience
    About the puzzles and problems of life;
For assurance for the present and future,
    For guidance in death and in life.

What errors could be corrected?
    What discoveries our voyaging could make.
What relief just to talk things over
    When prayer, the sound barriers break.

How rich to converse with the Almighty
    To enroll in the College of Prayer,
To sit at the feet of the Creator
    An hour of His conversation to share.

Sometimes no response breaks the silence
    But we pray and continue to wait.
Then out of the inner stillness
    God opens prayer's golden gate.

Thus God walks and talks in our Eden.
    The still small voice rings clear.
Thus saith the Lord of all Wisdom;
"Listen! And your soul shall hear!"

March

~ 28 ~

If desire opens the door wide enough, knowledge will move in, bookshelves and all,
and it may even be said in the future that "wisdom once lived here."

THE FINGER AND THE FLAME
(JACKSON FABLE)

The flame came. Men stood in awe with the women and the children behind them as they felt its searing heat against their faces.

The roar of the fire filled all the forest, and the frightened deer leaped over dead branches and still-smoking logs to escape on hot hooves to cooler, safer ground. The lesser animals fled in fear before the smoking fury of a monster called The Flame. They were anxiously looking for a pond or lake or river where they could submerge their tired, quivering bodies up to their noses in the cool shallows. The soft mud rested their burned feet while the Monster Flame raced on, laughing and crackling like a witch as it chewed up whole trees and spit out the broken branches from between its own toothless, scarred gums.

Like a raging lion, this fire-cat, with flaming mane and glowing eyes, pounced across the ponds and rivers, licking up the leaves at the water's edge and eating the dry grasses where the little creatures built their nests and hideaways. Then it began to climb the trees again on the other side. It wrapped its yellow legs around the strong trunks of fir and pine and other trees and smothered them as it sucked their cool, green breath into its own hot nostrils and dug deep into their backs with its ripping claws and teeth.

The Flame tore through the moaning valleys without resistance until the clouds in the sky were black and the air was breathless and hot, and all the greening landscape was a silent, smoking furnace where nothing lived or breathed. Little spirals of smoke arose here and there where the fires were going out. Even the Monster Flame didn't dare live here anymore or he, too, would die, for he was a destroyer who finally burned himself up in his greed and rage.

Then darkness came and the soft, restfulness of nighttime blended its own shadows with the stark skeletons of old snags that were still standing. The frightened animals began to stir in the lagoons and rivers, looking for something to eat along the shores.

It was morning now, and along a ridge and down a little gully, where the wind had changed its course and the Monster had missed a strip of green, came a little boy who had stood with his family in the distance on the day before. He had to see what the Monster Flame had done to his friends who sang in the branches, swam in the pools, and burrowed in the ground or played in the cool shade along the silent forest paths that till yesterday were always filled with life and adventure.

Further into the skeleton forest he came, staying on the green path and jumping to avoid the still-hot places underfoot as he came closer to the water. Finally he came to a burned-out log beside a lake that was covered with floating debris from the fire. There must have been a breeze blowing, ever so gently, because the smoking leaves beside the log burst into a tiny, steady, orange flame that busily flickered here and there as it began to eat again from the blackened, half-devoured log.

The boy reached out his finger to touch The Flame. It didn't look like a Monster now, since it was so small and harmless-looking. He touched it for a full second before he realized it was biting him. Then he drew his finger back quickly and put it to his mouth to cool it. He sat down cross-legged at a safe distance and watched the flame gradually grow stronger as it ate its way in silence. He reached his finger out almost close enough to touch it again. The heat made it start to hurt, so he pulled it back a ways and pointed it accusingly at the Little Flame. Then he began to imagine that his finger and The Flame were talking, just like he often talked to the birds and squirrels and even the trees before the Fire Monster had come and carried them all away.

The Flame replied, "You made me do it. I was eating this dry log and you put your finger in my mouth! My Father the Fire Monster even tries to eat rocks and water when he gets excited. And even the stars and the world are wise enough not to get too close to our Grandfather, the Sun!"

Then The Finger pointed itself right at The Flame and said, "Your Father killed my friends in the forest yesterday. I stood way back, but I could see and hear how angry he was!"

"Oh, yes, I did hear about that," said the Little Flame.

"Then why did he burn the feathers on the birds' wings so they couldn't fly away to other places? Why did he burn the foxes' feet so they couldn't run and jump across the logs and climb some other mountains? And why did The Flame strip the tall trees of their green clothes and leave them naked with no place to hide their ugliness? Why? Why? Why?" the Finger kept asking over and over.

The Flame stopped eating and moved over closer to The Finger. "I'll tell you why," he said. "My Father, The Big Flame, was asleep until the lightning hit him hard and rudely woke him up, and he got mad. The more he roared and ran about, the angrier and hungrier he got. So maybe it wasn't all his fault, and besides, he even asked the lightning why it struck him when he was asleep. The lightning said, 'I was just jumping and running around in the sky playing Zig-Zag and I happened to bump into you. So it was an accident and I'm sorry, of course!'"

"Oh," said The Finger, drawing back just a little in fear, "I didn't know that."

"But that isn't the only thing that wakes the Fire Monster up," said the Little Orange Flame.

"What else?" asked The Finger, drawing back just a little in fear.

"Well, once some boys were playing with matches in an old barn and my Fire Father went so wild he ate the hay and the barn and almost ate one of the boys before anybody could stop him. And another time," he continued, "some hunters didn't put out their campfire, so they got more than their limit that day. The Flame got into the game and began to shoot in every direction. It probably helped the hunters kill twenty deer that day or maybe more . . . I remember, too, a lady was smoking in her bed and a Fire Monster woke up right in bed with her. He thought her blond hair was so beautiful that he ate most of it. But the mattress made him sick, so he went out and left the lady screaming with her hair on fire."

The Finger was almost too scared to ask any more questions, but it did get up the courage to say, "Isn't there anything good that your father, The Angry Flame, ever does for people or animals?"

"Oh, sure," said the Little Yellow-Orange Flame, and it almost smiled, but some of its teeth were black, so it didn't. "Oh, yes, if people are careful, we have marshmallow and weiner roasts and things like that. I even help cook supper for Boy Scouts and Girl Scouts and campers who have learned how to use us without letting us get loose or excited. We burn happily in cages called furnaces and fireplaces. We keep apartments and houses and schools warm without doing any harm if people follow the safety rules. We even make cars run, trains whistle, ships sail, and lights burn. We just love to work, but somebody else has to do our thinking for us. But thank you so much for asking. I feel like I have to go out now!" With that, The Flame flickered twice and went up in a wisp of grey smoke.

The boy licked the burned place on The Finger again so that it wouldn't hurt and put it back in his front pocket, where it couldn't see to ask any more questions. But he was very glad he had listened to the conversation between The Finger and The Flame, because he knew now that there was a lot about fire that he hadn't known, and he decided to be very, very careful until he learned the other things about Fire that everybody should know.

MEXICAN WOLF BY CLANCY CHERRY

March

~ 29 ~

What is a city but people; not tall skyscrapers with bright lights at night,
but an ocean of surging, searching people; this is a city.

THE POTATO WHO COULDN'T SEE
(JACKSON FABLE)

They called him Tater Chip, and hoped he'd be a chip off the old potato, like his father, Dick Tater, who was very proud of his new son of the soil.

His brother, Idaho Spud (they sometimes called him Spud Nut), thought he might be okay by planting time. His mother, Mash Potato, was a real softie and couldn't resist the charms of this new addition to the vine in the Potato Family. But it was Susie Sweet Potato, his stepsister, who first noticed that there was something wrong with Tater Chip's eyes.

Old Doc Potato Bug, the much-loved Potato Country Doctor, was quickly called. He looked over his gold, horn-rimmed spectacles and said impressively, "Hum . . . hum . . . double hum! This here potato boy don't have no eyes!"

The whole Tater Family held hands around Tater Chip's crib, and his mother, Mash Potato, tucked the gunnysack sheet and the burlap blanket up under his dainty double chin while the tears ran copiously down all of their dusty faces from their multiple eyes as they all said in unison, "Hum . . . hum . . . hum . . . triple hum! Our little Tater Chip don't have no eyes! Hum . . . hum . . . hum!"

They were short on cash because Johnny Cash and Spot Cash hadn't been around since Johnny stepped on his guitar. So they paid the doctor with a right fresh, half sack of red onions. Idaho Spud loaded it into Dr. Potato Bug's buggy. Doc felt well paid for his diagnosis and his double hum.

Everybody loved the doctor, even those disrespectful people who sometimes called him Old Doc Hum-Bug instead of Dr. I.Q. Potato Bug, M.D. They thought the M.D. meant that his diagnoses were sometimes a Mite Dubious, M. Dealy speaking.

It was quiet now in the potato shed shack as the Tater Family sat cross-legged on the dirt floor with their heads in their hands and tried to figure out what to do for the little Tad-Tater that couldn't see!

Then they called in the Beetle, Brain-Doctor. Not the Beetle-Brained Doctor, but the Beetle, (comma) Brain- (dash) Doctor. He looked in a knowing, sort of sophisticated way and barked, "Ain't nobody here got no brains? Don't be a bunch of potato heads. Don't just sit there sacked up together. Sure, the boy don't have eyes, but he's got a potato skin. Teach him to see through that. He's got fingers to feel with. Teach him to touch it and see it! We call that dermo-optical brain-viewing."

~ 223 ~

Everybody was listening real hard, because everybody listens to specialists even when they can't understand the big words.

"Ain't nobody here got no imagination?" asked Doc Beetle, grumpy and a little sad-like. "Teach the Tater Chip to see pictures inside his head. Maybe he ain't got potato eyes, but he's still got five senses if you count his extrasensory perception!"

Then the Beetle, Brain-Doctor snapped his black, grain-box-bag shut and climbed back into his long, black Hadalack car after they paid him off with a sack and a half of red and white onions. Then he drove off lickety-split, beetle-brain-boring down the bumpy, dusty, potato dirt road.

Everybody was happy at the potato house, and everybody started working on Tater Chip's other five senses, which included his sixth sense. They just knew, now, that he might even grow up to be another Uncle Tom, if he had a cabin, or even another Helen Keller, except he was a feller.

Susie Sweet Potato worked on his taste buds first as she gave him his bottle-fed breakfast. She said, "Tater, Tater Chip, tell me what does your potato milk taste like?"

Tater Chip just answered, "Goo!"

"No, Tater Chip, not glue," she said. "It tastes good like potato milk should."

Then Idaho Spud Nut said, "Hey, Tater, feel my new mustache. That's how green grass grows on a green grassy hill under a hot summer sky. And smell the back of my hand. That's the way potato dirt smells in a dark potato cellar. Here! Smell this dry potato sack. That's how potato dirt dust smells when it's dry in the potato shed. And one thing more, Chipper, smell this yellow dandelion. It doesn't have much smell, but it's yellow like the sun feels warm and soft on your skin!"

Then Dad Dick Tater picked Tater Chip up out of his gunnysack cradle and tapped him lightly on each side of his head where little potatoes and little kids both have ears for hearing things. "Listen, kid, you got ears even if you ain't got eyes! Listen, Tater, listen! Hear them meadowlarks a singin' in the Tater Fields! Hear that bobwhite calling for its mate! Hear them bullfrogs croakin' down by the lily-pad-pond! Sure! You can hear it better than any other potato chip in the whole world. Listen to that Freight-Jet goin' overhead. It's carrying potatoes to Ireland or London Town. Hear that mouse nibbling something scratchy in the corner? And can you hear your mama's footsteps scuffing on the dirt floor while she's makin' potato soup for supper?"

Littler Tater Chip really began to listen. Then he began to see pictures in his potato head. They were good—clear, green grass growing, yellow dandelions blooming, birds singing, mice scratching, bullfrogs croaking, jets flying, footsteps scuffing—pictures right inside his very own head. He could even remember what wet potato dirt smelled like, and he knew his breakfast tasted good like potato milk should.

He learned to even see with his skin and to feel with his fingers and to read books and books and more books. When little Tater Chip grew up, he kicked his burlap cradle clear over in the corner of the potato shed and marched right out for Washington, D.C., dragging his carpet-bagger, tater-sack right behind him. He defeated the Peanut President and became the first Potato Head President of the United States of Expanding Awareness!

Now, whenever you see a potato, please remember that little Tater Chip learned to touch, taste, smell, feel, hear, and also to see pictures inside his head. So we're all mighty proud of our first and greatest potato president, because when he got to the White House, that really opened his eyes!

March

~ 30 ~

The instinctive purpose of all life on earth is growth, development, and progress in every area of being: body, mind, spirit, and circle of social influence.

HOW TO GET ALONG WITH PEOPLE WHO BUG YOU
(CREATIVE VISUALIZATION)

With your feet flat on the floor and seated comfortably, take a deep breath and relax completely. You will hear my voice distinctly and follow instructions attentively. Visualize clearly and vividly, in color and in action, the mental pictures in our verbal visual.

Visualize yourself as a bather on the ocean beach covering yourself, except for your head, with warm, clean sand. Your body feels so good, so heavy from the sand and yet so light at the same time. It seems that the ocean with its breaking waves and soft sounds is an ocean of music. As you lie on the beach in the sand, the waves come in first over your feet and wash all tightness and tension away. They come up over your knees and upper legs, stomach, chest and arms. They relax your eyes and ears. Picture just your nose sticking out as you breathe deeply and freely. You are completely bathed, rested, relaxed and refreshed in the waves of a whole ocean of soft, beautiful music.

You are like a piece of bark or driftwood floating on the rising and falling waves of the great ocean where you were resting on the beach when your concentration first began. You are held up, you are carried, you are resting in the ocean of endless love and well-being and complete confidence. You are relaxing deeply. You hear my voice clearly. You will not drift off to sleep. Your mind is slowed down and very, very attentive. It is clear and alert and expectant, very calm, relaxed and at rest. You are breathing slowly, deeply, and easily, almost like a sleeping person, but your mind and emotions, your problem-solving creativity and your ability for visual imagery are functioning perfectly. Your intuitive wisdom centers are activated. You perceive the beautiful, the true, the positive and the good effortlessly. You identify inwardly with the beautiful, the true, the positive and the good.

Put aside all resentment; forgive everyone and everything in the whole wide world. Lay aside all anxious worry, and rest and float on an ocean of trust and peace and love.

Each time you relax, concentrate and visualize clearly, you create and increase the ability of your mind to observe and control your own thoughts from within yourself. Each time you function at this level, you will create a greater awareness of the present. The unpleasant events of the past become less and less important. You will keep your awareness primarily in the present. Functioning at the creative level makes this so without special effort on your part. It clears your mind of the negative responses and replaces them with the positive. Past annoyances no longer disturb you, because they have been replaced by new and simple insights of truth in your inner being.

You are happy! From now on, nothing must upset, irritate, aggravate, agitate or distress you unduly, or ever hurt your feelings in the slightest degree. The little unkind, unfair and dishonest things that people say and do to you and to others in daily experience will no more ruffle or disturb you than water running off of a duck's back. They just don't reach the inner you or disturb the equilibrium of your inner place of rest. You are bringing your inner relaxation and calmness of your deeper mind into your activity level of awareness. You are a peaceful lake, an undisturbed ocean of forgiving love, peace and eternal calm, where no storms rage and no winds blow cold.

The sun is warm and you are at rest within. You will not be disturbed or annoyed inwardly or outwardly. You will be calm, collected, patient, peaceful and kind. You do not need to suppress resentment because you will not be angry. Just remember always to overlook and make allowances for any offense right at the moment when things happen, and do it because you want to and you are happy to. You are big enough and strong enough to overlook all little, insignificant thoughts, actions and intentions of others.

You will condition your responses more and more to react less and less to unfavorable environmental conditions and irritating attitudes of the people who used to annoy you or those who may try to upset you.

From today on and always, look quickly for opportunities to overlook faults, failures, irritations, trouble and distress immediately and right at the place and time they happen. Don't wait a minute or even a second to forgive and overlook what might upset you.

Take great inner joy in completely and instantly overlooking such things at the moment they are happening. Stand aside and look objectively at the whole interplay of human drama and feel in no way emotionally involved. Stand aside and observe yourself and others and feel only kindness, patience and involved detachment. Overlook the whole situation and forgive and love those involved as things unfold their actions. See all unpleasantness dissolve in the bright light of inner reality, which consists of peace, power, patience, kindness and objective, calm detachment!

It is such a relief to bring the true inner levels of love and joy up to the outer activities of life, for they eventually calm all circumstances in harmony with the inner rhythm and flow of your own relaxed living.

Be good and tolerant and kind especially to those who are close to you, like your family, friends and daily associates at work, play or school. Make allowances for everyone from now on, whomever they are, and especially for those who are close to you emotionally—because when you forgive, you are forgiven. To forgive is to give for. So give love and understanding patience for the situation or person, whomever or whatever it is. This makes you the master of any fate, fact or fiction.

Do not expect too much from anyone. If you expect too much, you are disappointed if you do not receive as much. What others give or don't give, do or don't do, really doesn't matter as much as what you give or do cheerfully because you want to. You will respond in the proper manner regardless of circumstances. The imperfect world filled with imperfect people gives you the chance to be courageous, kind and strong.

If you were afraid once, for example, and never had a chance again to prove that you could be courageous, it wouldn't be fair, would it? You know you can be brave and courageous. It's the same with problems and trivial irritations. The people who give you a rough time are also giving you your chance to prove to yourself and to all the world that you are a bigger person than you even thought you were before you learned to bring relaxation into your outer life situations. Be thankful for people who are giving you opportunities to practice calmness under pressure and to accomplish now what before you may have failed to do.

The things that once upset you, irritated you and caused inner tension are now your occasion to prove yourself and to feel proud that you can remain undisturbed, unafraid, confident, kind, positive and happily detached.

The people today or in the tomorrows who try to upset you don't know that they are giving you your chance to sail right over their miniaturized selves on your magic carpet of relaxed, problem-solving creativity while you immediately forgive them and figure out what else you should do, if anything. They don't know that they are doing you a favor, because the harder they try to upset you, the calmer you get and the brighter your kindness light shines out. Just remember to forgive them on the spot; overlook their negative attitudes and detach yourself from the situation like a second-stage rocket. You know your own destination and your goals. If something needs to be said, be plainspoken, firm, very kind and always patient. Do and say from this time on only what comes out of your inner center of wisdom, joy, calmness and peace!

Remember, stand firm, stand tall, don't react, but be patient under pressure. Keep calm; disagree when necessary in an agreeable manner. Give up any imaginary conversations about what you could say or have said cleverly in telling people off. Don't do it ever in an argumentative, contentious spirit. Forget it. If something from your calm, inner self is worth saying or doing, say or do it firmly, and do or say it kindly. You do have a right to speak your mind calmly. If it comes from the relaxation level, it likely won't hurt or offend.

So overlook things, be plainspoken, understanding and kind. Be appreciative of all good things, but don't be overexcited by commendation and praise. Be appreciative of constructive criticism, but be not offended emotionally by any criticism. Make allowances for all people with your thinking, your feelings, and your understanding, and not because you have to but because you really want to and are glad for the opportunity to grow and to overcome.

Your own inner judgment and wisdom will alert you when, for self-protection, you must act in true self-defense. This we leave to your own judgment and the circumstance. You can get along with people who bug you!

Open your eyes slowly and move around a bit. You are alert now, active, happy and healthier than ever before. More and more you are becoming outwardly like the images you visualize and hold inwardly. I congratulate you. Take a deep breath and stretch. Now stand and stretch again. Thank you for being such good relaxers. You are getting better each time.

THINK

Somebody in Egypt had a thought.
    And, lo, the Pyramids pierced the sky.
Now tall skyscrapers rise today,
    And thought is the reason why.

Row on row of bookshelves bear
    A silent tribute to the skill
Of ancient scribes who thought and wrote,
    And their thoughts are living still.

Thought is the parent of progress.
    Man is more than clay.
Man in the thought of God made flesh,
    And thought creates today!

An immortal is one who thought and felt
    More keenly than his fellow man,
Who united an act to a vibrant thought
    And followed it through with a plan!

Yes, man can outfly the eagle,
    The tides and the winds outride,
For man is the sum of all his thoughts,
    As great as he is inside!

HIGH SEAS BY BOB ERWIN

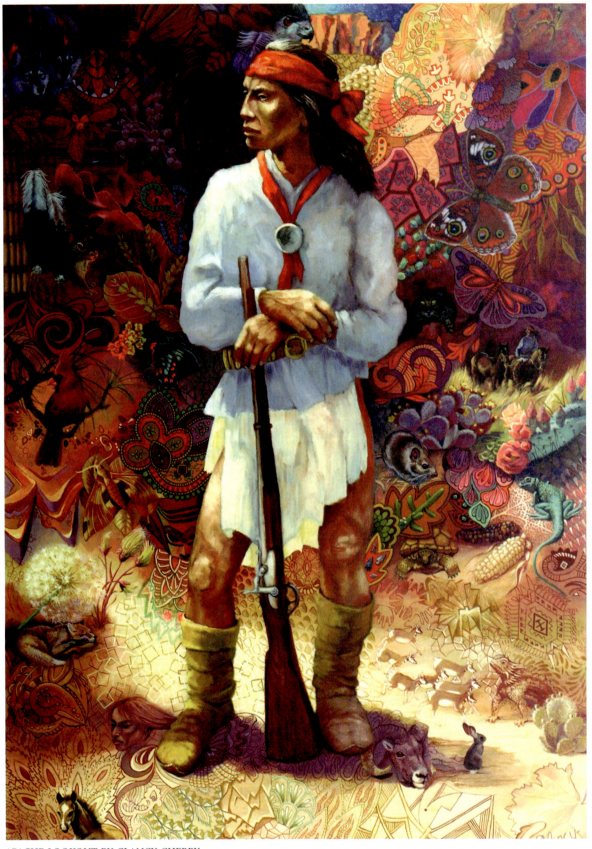

APACHE LOOKOUT BY CLANCY CHERRY

March

~ 31 ~

Satisfaction counts its treasures with glad hands and shares willingly
with others what it gratefully possesses and sings of its fullness
until the heavens drop down the dew of continued contentment.

SELF-APPRECIATION
(CREATIVE VISUALIZATION)

Sitting comfortably and relaxing completely, you are learning more and more how to concentrate deeply and successfully.

You are like a Raggedy Ann or Raggedy Andy doll propped up in an easy chair. Raggedy Ann or Andy doesn't have a tight muscle. You could bend him or her just anywhere and neither one would care.

Picture a kitten on the back of a sofa or couch. He is stretching his long claws, which contract, retract and relax back into his velvet-soft paws clear out of sight. He could wake right up in a second if you told him to. And the "alert center" in your own brain, even in its most relaxed state, is very active and very much aware of all things and reacts to meet any situation and to bring you immediately back to activity level feeling better and in better health and happier than ever before.

Imagine your pet dog at home, sleeping in a warm, restful place on his side. He must be seeing pictures, too, of something in his head as his foot and ears move once in a while as he rests completely. He isn't even thinking at all, probably—just resting and seeing happy pictures.

You are like a bird at sunset on a strong tree limb with its head tucked under its wing, singing softly and saying "thank you" for the whole wide world around it and for a place to rest and relax.

So let us adventure together into the Kingdom of Self-Improvement like the knights of old who first disciplined themselves and then went out to fight battles and win victories for others in need. Our adventure is a secret journey unseen by casual eyes and unheard by untuned ears, but it is an open book to all who learn to relax, to concentrate, to visualize vividly and to follow the treasure map of step-by-step instruction for achievement and self-improvement.

You will notice in yourself many interesting changes and areas of progress after thinking these thoughts, and this will make you glad. Other changes and insights will come more gradually after a period of incubation and inner adjustment and illumination of attitude and thought processes.

Give your undivided thought attention to all instructions so that you may become better, be better and do better. Forget your fears. They are mostly shadows that the shield of confidence, the song of joy and the lamp of hope can drive away. Give your undivided inner attention to visualizing, feeling, and understanding the things I say to you now. Find the key instruction and do it whenever you have the opportunity and desire to do so.

This exercise in self-appreciation and self-improvement is so simple that either an adult or a child can do it. So accept it and know that it does and will work for all. Refuse to be negative. Insist on a positive, happy, childlike acceptance of all truth. Then, understanding and appreciation will automatically come to you. You always enjoy doing your Relaxed Learning exercise. The motto is, "Do it now!" Be very faithful to put into practice and follow the new instruction you have been given in all of your verbal visuals. Your inner self remembers them all and will faithfully help you do them in their proper time and place.

These mental calisthenics bring the subconscious mind into integrated cooperation with the conscious understanding and purpose of your life. You are learning perfect, well-disciplined self-control and relaxed concentration, which increase greatly when these instructions are happily accepted.

Let's think especially now about self-acceptance, self-appreciation and acceptable self-image. You like yourself. You are a bigger person than you imagine. You are a wonderful person. You have possibilities for present and future development far greater than you realize. You are now free from the devastating notions of self-debasement. Your freedom will catapult you quickly and securely to happiness and abundance, to success and perfect health.

You are successful in your work, your pleasures, your social contacts, your school, your financial and domestic lives, your love and personal lives. The potentials you possess as a human being, created in the image of the Creator, give hidden resources of power that make you truly great and truly worthwhile. You naturally love and help people. You are destined for happy and effective living. You know that you are now making good. There are many things that you as an individual do exceptionally well. You are coming into your own. You are finding your best and most effective place in life. You are attracting many friends. You are filled with hopeful expectations of present success and pleasure. You have sufficient time to truly succeed and make your own contribution in your own sphere of influence. Your superconscious and subconscious minds will fan the spark of desire into the flame of a winning, attractive, dynamic personality. You are a great person. You are learning to know yourself. You are finding yourself and your productive, happy place in life.

You have a well-balanced personality. Your personality conveys a definite sense of poise, self-confidence, security, self-control, tranquility, understanding and peace. You are emotionally stable. You are calm and relaxed. Your emotions and intellect are working together in a beautiful, harmonious balance that produces a pleasing, restful stability in your life and its relationships. You have proper self-esteem and assurance. You naturally pay attention to and think more about others and exterior events than you do about yourself. You rejoice in the realization that you belong to your group, your friends and your organization. You think for yourself. You are prompt and efficient in your work.

You are relaxed and resting, and your subconscious mind is accepting these thoughts because you know that they are strong, positive, character- and personality-building thoughts that are helpful to you and, in turn, to others.

Open your eyes now. Stretch if you would like. Take another deep breath of fresh air, feeling better than you have ever felt before. Thank you so much for listening! You are doing better and better every day.

HIDDEN BEAUTY

Never sprinkle sparkle on a diamond
    Or put Christmas tinsel on a budding rose.
Diamonds have been cut for brilliant shining
    And a flower needs no tinsel as it grows.

Don't sprinkle the sparkle of deception
    On a love already calculated, hard and cold.
It's the fool's-gold of your own self-delusion,
    A counterfeit for love's real, yellow gold.

Don't sprinkle the sparkle of false approbation
    On situations you no longer can endure.
Inner honesty and outer nonattachment,
    Plus forgiving love will make your triumph sure.

Never sprinkle sparkle on a silver sunset,
    Nor add restless tinsel to the things you dimly see.
Diamonds, roses, life and sunsets all have
      Hidden beauty.
We must find the truth within and set it free.

HOUSE OF MUSIC BY GINGER COOK

April

~ 1 ~

THE SAD CLOWN BY CYDNEY (DE VANEY COLLECTION)

"WHAT IF . . . ?"

What if grasses, trees and ferns
    All were colored blue?
What if God had made the flowers
    All of somber hue?

What if every bird that sings
    Sang a tuneless song?
Or worse than that if every bird
    Sang his tune all wrong?

What if every breeze that blows
    Blew always cold and chill;
And brought no springtime fragrance sweet
    To set our hearts a-thrill?

'T would be a bleak, unhappy world,
    But this is all untrue.
For God has made grasses green,
    The flowers a brilliant hue.

For every bird a different song
    As seasons come and go;
A thousand fragrant woodland scents
    Where springtime's breezes blow!

April

2

*The genius of the inner mind needs the building material of facts,
the hammer and nails of purpose, the square of truth, the saw and rule of correction,
the labor of meditation, the blueprints of design and construction,
and a little time to accomplish its inspired ends.*

No son really knows how to appreciate his father until he has been one, and then it is often too late.

FAMILY DESIGN

Each family reflects its individual design produced to some degree by:

- Individual needs,

- Personal frustrations,

- Special goals, and

- Desires of all family members.

It is difficult to develop an adequate appreciation of the dynamics that function within a family; however, we can never deny their power. During the original family's later life, when the children are perhaps not such a vital part of this original family group, the children may still continue to receive some of their emotional battery recharging from within their original family setting.

It is observed today, however, that a major cultural change is taking place in this original design of the American family. The change is from a tightly knit group, reflecting almost complete dependence upon itself for emotional as well as physical satisfaction, to a family with a structure, which in so many ways is becoming disintegrated and perhaps somewhat dysfunctional.

The discernment and patterns that children develop are strongly influenced by their perception of their own personal place and role in this family. For example, if a child feels another family member threatens his security, he will often develop special abilities and strengths in the area of weakness of other family members. Now consider this issue: Why is it so important for a child to have attention, love and acceptance from his parents? Because a child, whose parents have not demonstrated the value of that child, sets up that child to not easily value himself. Often, the children that do not believe in themselves will probably be convinced that no one else can actually believe in them.

The warm, accepting parent or parents answering the child's requirement for love and attention enables that child to find security and satisfaction in their presence. As the child learns to recognize his separation from his parent or parents, that child continues to feel their support.

WHEN HE BECOMES A MAN

I wonder how many little guys
 Are neglected and pushed aside,
Who are left at home when they very much
 Would like to go along for the ride?
Maybe you'd better remember they're yours
 And include them whenever you can,
For God has to take these left-out boys
 When he wants to make a man.

I wonder how many times they lie
 Awake with wide-open eyes
Wondering if you really love them as much
 As the parents of some other guys.
Maybe you'd better love them more –
 As much as you possibly can,
For boys are the only stuff there's left
 When God wants to make a man.

I wonder what kind of person you'd be
 If your parent had cared a bit more,
Instead of the nagging, hard-voiced cry:
 Blow your nose; wipe your feet; close the door!
Maybe you'd better gently speak
 And as kindly as ever you can,
For there isn't much left for God but boys
 When He wants to make a man.

I wonder if we're as busy as we think we are?
 I wonder if it will matter so much
When the boy you neglected and left on his own
 Has someway gotten in "Dutch?"
Maybe if his mom and, better, his dad
 Had made him a part of each plan,
Then God Himself would really be proud
 Of that boy when he becomes a man!

April

3

All ill-gotten money is fool's-gold!

MONEY

"Wealth comes to the enlightened like rivers flow down to the sea."

"The fact of Wealth always follows after the subjective feelings of wealth.
Prosperity is the projected product of the inner security, abundance,
and possession of divine substance and supply."

"The God who made a million stars and more can help a person make a million dollars,
especially if he needs a million dollars like the night needs a million stars."

"The love of money may be the root of all evil, but money itself is a root from
whose branches most materials and many spiritual blessings spring."

"The *materialist* believes that we were not put here to make friends, or enemies,
but simply to make money. The *humanist* believes that we were put here
not to make money or enemies, but to make friends. The *philanthropist* believes
that we were put here to make money so that we can help both our friends and our enemies.
The *idealist* believes that we were put here to make friends if possible,
to make enemies if necessary, to make money when needed, but above all
to make it to our eternal reward and to help our enemies
and our friends to make it, too."

WHAT SHALL WE CALL IT?

There's a book full of blue checks
    Or yellow, green or pink.
Your name is printed on it.
    So as you think, "think mink."

Some call it lettuce or cabbage
    Even kale or moss or beans.
It's salt pork in your barrel,
    A wad of mazuma in your jeans.

It's stocks and bonds or assets,
    Gold in the poke or swag,
The wherewith and the wherewithal,
    The shackles in the bag.

It's the yellow quartz of clinkers,
    The velvet for your bed.
It's dough you cut like dollars
    When you make your gingerbread.

It's the cartwheels to El Dorado,
    The axle-grease that makes 'em roll.
It's prosperity and abundance
    That keeps the banker off the dole.

It's the plum in your plum pudding.
    It's the frosting on the cake.
Money comes to those who call it.
    Call it something for goodness sake!

April

~ 4 ~

CLOWN WITH YELLOW HAT BY BENGARTT (W. JACKSON COLLECTION)

THE GOD OF THE ROSES IS MINE

The stars do not try to shine in the night;
    Nor do the roses try to be sweet.
The stars simply shone because they have light,
    And roses by nature are sweet.

God grant that my life, like the stars overhead
    May shine with a glory divine.
And let the perfume of my life reach out,
    For the God of the roses is mine!

April

⁓ 5 ⁓

Love with its wings clipped is no longer love; for love enforced is fractured love,
and if the force used to retain it had been used to gain it, it would not exist at all.

LOVE AND ROMANCE EARNED?

Do you understand our quote, "Inventory the assets of your love and romance and invest the dividends of your joy and fulfillment and you will reap the rewards of your labors?" As a couple, do you live a life to bless your spouse? Are you each a cheerleader for the other? Are you each dependent upon the support of your lover? Do you each do many little and big things for one another? Would this be a wonderful, happy and balanced life, working for the love and romance of each other?

Is this example something that each lover learned by the example lived at home? What are the chances of a successful and happy relationship if you were not blessed with this example of positive living? Is it possible, to each fall in love *and* live a giving life to each other? Did you experience other outside influence, which encouraged love that you could emulate?

Do you believe that we must first give to stimulate the experience of love being re-given? How do you react to the primary concept that everything must be earned? How intensely would you work for a beautiful relationship of love and romance?

When building a new business, *how much creative time* does one spend covering all of the aspects of development to guarantee the whole spectrum of the business: decorating the showroom, developing the efficiency of the shop, selecting the employees and a management team, advertising and public relations? Are you willing to creatively cover all aspects of making your mate and lover the most comfortable and self-confident person in your life? Is the courtship everyday, forever? Are you so confident that the price tag of this love trip is worth the time and effort involved, that you would sacrifice your own ego for the sake of this powerful union?

Are you willing to be a leader in instigating such an involved experience of two becoming a team of one to accomplish the rewards of unconditional love? Could this dynamic relationship be so available to the Creator that the daily results will demonstrate that, as a dedicated duo, even you, as well as the people around you, will be surprised at the creative harmony of events completed? What will the summary of your lives reflect?

Does anyone recall Solomon's words of wisdom: "I declared that the dead, who had already died, are happier than the living, who are still alive. But better than both is he who has not yet been, who has not seen the evil that is done under the sun. And I saw that all labor and all achievement spring from man's envy of his neighbor. This too is meaningless, a chasing after the wind. The fool folds his hands and ruins himself. Better one handful with tranquility than two handfuls with toil and chasing after the wind. Again I saw something meaningless under the sun: There was a man all alone; he had neither son nor brother. There was no end to his toil, yet his eyes were not content with his wealth. 'For whom am I toiling,' he asked, 'and why am I depriving myself of enjoyment?' This too is meaningless—a miserable business! Two are better than one, because they have a good return for their work: If one falls down, his friend can help him up. But pity the man who falls and has no one to help him up! Also, if two lie down togther, they will keep warm. But how can one keep warm alone? Though one may be overpowered, two can defend themselves. A cord of three strands is not quickly broken." (ECCLESIASTES 4:2-12)

Are you willing to unselfishly, yes in many cases with even self-preservation set aside, and work intensely for a more dynamic and complimentary love relationship? Are you ready today to commit to a purposeful, powerful and positive labor of love? Blessings on you and yours as you live love!

LOVE IS A WONDERFUL THING

Love is a terrible, wonderful thing
　　That heals and soothes as it hurts.
Love is a cage with an open door
　　And a pit in the path of the flirt.

Love is the siren call of the flesh,
　　That instinctively looks for a mate.
And love, that inexplicable, unpredictable thing,
　　Can turn in a moment to hate.

Love is a need, a vacuum of want,
　　Confusing, amusing and sad.
It never is filled, and it never is stilled,
　　And it drives its possessor quite mad.

Love is an emotional, promotional thing
　　That binds with its golden bands
The lover's soul to the soul of the loved
　　With velvet-soft, iron-like hands.

Away with the thing! It makes people sick.
　　But alas, it is also the cure.
It's a plague and a balm, its own antidote
　　And a wonderful thing to endure!

April

6

The Creator has taught us the art of giving by divine practice, precept and inner promptings.

BROKERED INTELLIGENCE POOL

The Brokers of the Intelligence Pool or the Mastermind concept practice principles that are consistent to a compact of two or more minds, working in perfect harmony for the attainment of a definite objective. This includes a fusing of the subconscious minds of the participants. What are the benefits of the Brokered Intelligence Pool?

- Growth

- Expansion

- Increased awareness or

- Reinforcement and

- Amplification

We may thus use the brains, background, influence, experience, training, education, specialized knowledge and native intelligence of members of the alliance. This active alliance of the Brokered Intelligence Pool results in courage and paves the way for faith. Through the Brokered Intelligence Pool principle, you take advantage of the formal knowledge and education of others; therefore, an inadequate education need not be a serious barrier.

What are several examples of the Brokered Intelligence Pool principles? In business, an ordinary sales meeting to challenge the staff is a good sample; or again, Andrew Carnegie did not know much about making steel, but he surrounded himself with a capable group who certainly did know. Napoleon Hill mentions his Mastermind efforts in connection with F.D. Roosevelt during the time of the Depression when he encouraged congress, the newspapers, radio stations, religious groups and the leaders of both political parties along with the common people of each of these groups to cooperate with him in turning fear into faith. The alliance of all of the states in the United States forming the Union is a good example. Mr. and Mrs. Henry Ford formed a pool of Masterminds as did Mr. and Mrs. Thomas Edison. In addition, Edison and Ford collaborated on their efforts.

A Brokered Intelligence Pool group should be as large as the nature and magnitude of the task demand. However, this should be decided in the light of your particular needs or missing links and

245

should be kept as small as is reasonably possible. Harmony must be the prevailing state of mind among all the member of the Brokered Intelligence Pool in order to receive the best results.

REPOSE WITH A SONG

As the tree on the mountain
    Its cool shadows cast,
So God is our refuge
    When doubting is past.

As tired limbs luxuriate
    When stretched in repose,
So the mortal mind relaxes
    When the fear thought goes.

As the white snow is fallen
    On valley or plain,
God's power gently falls on
    And blots out our pain.

As the birds in the rushes
    Sing early and long,
So gratitude's chorus
    Must swell with our song.

As the flowers in fragrance
    Burst open in Spring,
So our life is unfolding
    What the Father would bring!

April

~ 7 ~

*The Great Creator, who put man's machinery together in the first place,
knew it must be oiled daily with positive, grateful attitudes
and that the alarm on his timepiece should be shut off
occupationally for scheduled rest.*

THE "COMMON" MIND BENEFITS

This group that is to add up to one common mind as a brain trust could display only perfect blending of their mind efforts, and this will reflect beautiful harmony. Without this kind of harmony, the result would include friction, dragging interest and ultimate defeat. Cooperation and concerted action and clarity of inspiration are the result of perfect, unselfish harmony.

The forming of a Brokered Intelligence Pool would include the six following steps.

1. Adopt a definite purpose as an objective and choose proper individuals.

2. Determine benefits to cooperating members.

3. Establish a definite place, plan, and time for mutual discussions.

4. Maintain harmony and continuous action in pursuing aims.

5. Include a watchword of purpose, plan and harmony.

6. Determine the needed number for the pool, by the need.

The United Nations is a somewhat Brokered Intelligence Pool, worldwide today, with an opportunity to represent lives during an unusual time, because our hope for peace may be benefited by this group.

The following includes the Twelve Riches of Life, which can be benefited by the Brokered Intelligence Pool. You may wish to underline or list the ones you now possess:

1. A positive mental attitude.

2. Sound physical health.

3. Harmony in human relationships.

4. Freedom from fear.

5. The hope of achievement.

~ 247 ~

6. Capacity for faith.

7. Willingness to share one's blessings.

8. A labor of love.

9. An open mind on all subjects.

10. Self-discipline.

11. The capacity to understand people.

12. Financial security.

The Brokered Intelligence Pool brings the combined abilities, resources, thought power and the stimulation of many minds, plus the blending of the subconscious, for effectively analyzing the problem and finding a satisfactory, working solution to combat the menace.

I MUST AWAY

I must away to the mountain peaks
    The deserts and oceanside.
I must surge with the ocean's surge
    And lave the shore with each tide.

I must away to the mountain peaks
    All tinted with sunset glow.
I must away to the solitary place
    Where God must also go!

I must away from myself and wrong,
    Away from the drab commonplace.
Where unobserved by men's blinded eyes
    I may see nature and God face to face.

I must away to the mountain heights
    Of vision released and free,
Where all of the "all" I encompass as one
    And the "all" is a part of me.

April

~ 8 ~

CLOWN WITH A BLUE FACE BY BENGARTT (W. JACKSON COLLECTION)

THE SEA IS A STEED GREEN-BROKEN

The waves arch their backs
Like a wild bucking horse
    Fighting the cinch and saddle.
The spume and the spray
As they slobber and sway
    Mark the corral of driftwood they straddle.

Oh, the sea is a steed,
Green-broken and wild,
With the strength of a man
And the wit of a child;
Unbroken, untamed and free!

They fight the bit
With heads tossed high.
    Their windswept manes blind your eyes.
The long shoreline
Is a strong checkrein
    Half subduing the conquered prize.

Oh, the sea is a steed,
Green-broken and wild,
With the strength of a man
And the wit of a child;
Unbroken, untamed and free!

April

9

The man who looks for light will find the lamp;
and he who for belief aspires will find the facts for faith.

MAN IN A WORLD OF CHANGE

Change governs the entire universe. Therefore, men should not be dogmatic in a universe of change lest they fall into the bondage of their own unchanging dogma, which would not fit a universe of accelerating change.

Man is consciousness, and he can identify with all that there is within it regardless of its level of revealing. Man's consciousness is, of course, available to the All, and the All is available to the consciousness of qualified man. We must certainly become conscious of that vaster, other side of our mind in order to escape tendencies toward deterioration or self-destruction and termination.

We should courageously face the unknown, for in it is the hope of our salvation. Within that which is called the unknown are the secrets of the universe, of longevity, of self-control and of life mastery. Fear tends to manifest in the environment of change as man moves from a point of known security to an unknown point of supposed insecurity. The trauma of his fears, therefore, makes change, which should be his greatest delight and the avenue of his greatest progress, a thing to be avoided when it actually is a thing to be sought after and clasped to one's essential being as a way of life and advancement. Change should be faced without fear and without apprehension. It should be welcomed joyously, for it is the advancing future that becomes the present and that can negate the failures of the past.

Change is the name of the game called reality. Much of the change is invisible but still influential in affecting the moods, motions, motives and mentation of maneuvering man.

⤳ 251 ⤳

SENSE-BOUND

What sounds do the birds
And the wild things hear?
What harmonies and cadences
Beyond our deaf ear?
What whispered secrets
Are windblown and clear?
What sights do their eyes
Behold far and near
In their world of vibration
And light?

What sunset colors
May streak the noon sky?
What organ preludes
Thunderingly pass by
Where universal compassion
Orchestrates each sigh
And black light shines luminous
In the midnight sky
For eyes that have
Second sight?

April

~ 10 ~

Reflection is the art of bouncing an idea against the backboard of past experience, accumulated knowledge, and intuitive wisdom until we see it from every angle in relationship to the present, the past, and the intuitively anticipated future.

HOPE, INDUSTRY, AUTHORITY, AND COURAGE

May today find you filled with justifiably, expectant hope, reliance, faith, reassurance, buoyancy, optimism, enthusiasm, and security, which are all mainstays, supports, pillars of strength and anchors for the soul. For hope is a steady staff and an anticipatory aspiration and a confident expectancy. Hope thou in the Creator, for you shall yet praise Him who is the health of your countenance.

Industry is a correlative of success; you must be active, brisk, lively, animated, vivacious, alive, spirited, quick, prompt, ready, alert, swift, up and coming, wide awake, eager, ardent, zealous, enterprising, keen, aggressive, resolute, diligent, persevering, hard-working, businesslike, snappy, instant, earnest, devoted. You must be a live wire, a hustler, a go-getter and a go-giver—a real person of consecrated, loving, serving action.

Success will follow you if you will be busy, progressive, persistent, efficient, and industrious. Be dynamic, be energetic, vigorous, forceful, authoritative, competent, capable, with skill, power, and influence, for these are yours to have and use in the battle of life where you shall most certainly triumph.

You are courageous, fearless, brave, valorous, resolute, bold, hearty, daring, dashing, gallant, heroic, confident, and self-reliant; you have nerve, mettle, grit, pluck, virtue, hardihood, fortitude, backbone, spunk and bulldog tenacity. You can run the gauntlet of life, take what it gives, hold out to the victorious end, and bear up well under strain, for you are stalwart, stout-hearted, lion-hearted, unafraid, unflinching, adventurous, soldierly, strong-willed (the iron hand in the velvet glove), determined, indomitable. You are a winner!

REFLECTIONS

There are great silent places
Pregnant with pain:
Snow clouds and storms, winds,
And rough, steep terrain.

There are mountains and glaciers
And vast fields of white snow.
There are crevices and pitfalls
Wherever the rugged trails go.

There are dangers and terrors
In the blackness of night.
There are inner thought shadows
That fill us with fright.

There are sunrises breaking
On green meadows stretched far.
And life reflects outwardly
What we inwardly are.

April

11

*Wisdom is the reflected light of truth that reveals the oneness of the
past cause, the present content, and the future consequences
of the considered course of action.*

HEAR WISDOM

"It is better to learn wisdom by intuition than to confirm it by the
unnecessary suffering of unwise experience."

"Painful knowledge, not wisdom, is the doubtful fruit of folly."

"The silent owl who seldom speaks is the symbol of wisdom, not the parrot
who parades his meaningless reiterations to every passerby."

"Great men may be better known through their writings than by their
neighbors next door. How many great people do you know?"

THESE ARE THE GREAT ONES

These are the great ones,
The towers majestic.
These are men-mountains
That snow-capped stand by.
These are the mortals,
Immortal great ones.
Men who by wisdom
Are lifted on high.

(CONTINUED ON NEXT PAGE)

These are the great ones,
Who stand like small children.
These are the humble
And pure of the earth.
These are earnest souls
Sons of the Solitude,
Blessed by the miracle
And wonder of their birth.

These are the great ones
Whose hearts are made purest,
Whose thoughts are exalted
To God and His grace.
These are the great ones
Whose lives have been lighted
By true inner vision
That shines on the face.

These are the great ones
Tho' earth may not know them,
And yet they are known
By the angels above;
For all of their knowing
And being and doing
Is pulsed to the rhythm
Of Infinite Love.

These are the great ones
Who see in the commonplace,
Who see in the simple
Small things that are found,
That life everywhere
Rhythmic, pervading,
In themselves and in all things
Is God's Being profound!

CLOWN WITH THE BLUE HAT BY D.B. FYK (W. JACKSON COLLECTION)

CLOWN DUET BY CYDNEY (DE VANEY COLLECTION)

April

~ 12 ~

SUNNY VILLAGE BY VIKTOR SCHVAIKO

CLOWN-DUST

The calliope music has ended.
　　The circus tent is silent and gray.
The clown suit is smoothed out and folded,
　　But the painted smile hasn't faded away!

The façade of levity's laughter,
　　The jesting and the wide-painted grin
Are only the masks of the actor
　　Hiding the emptiness within.

So it is with each role-playing mortal
　　Who forever is acting a part
While the void of life's empty longing
　　Makes a dust bowl of the frustrated heart!

It's clown-dust in your eyes, my dear, that's starting
　　The tears that can't wash it away.
But when the Big Top finally is folded,
　　Clown-dust will be gold dust some day!

April

~ 13 ~

Confidence is the grandchild of ambition,
the child of achievement and the father of success.

THE FOE OF MEDIOCRITY

Inspiration and motivation toward personal and family achievement are the harmony that forms the work song for spaceship earth's improvement. This harmony represents the strength of the draft horse with his sweating shoulders against the cold collar, working toward specific goals. Inspiration represents the melodious, dream-like rhythm of the racehorse's pulse as it sweeps around the track with hoofs pounding the motivational base tempo, the wind in its mane, and its heart bursting with the joy of competition as it heads for the finish line in first place. Accomplishing our objectives and goals within a reasonable time will be crossing the finish line successfully.

INSPIRED, MOTIVATED ACCOUNTABILITY IS THE FOE OF MEDIOCRITY, THE SISTER OF CREATIVITY AND INSIGHT, AND THE BEST DEFENSE AGAINST FAILURE AND THE POSSIBLE EXTINCTION OF THE HUMAN RACE.

Involvement in making our world a better place, or being of assistance to our fellow man, can be the subtle, subconscious feeling of the intuitive victory that a lone cyclist feels when he is one with his bike, a single unit, cornering and stretching out for the final lap. It can be a singleness of purpose that is born of an uncluttered mind whose sense of direction is accurate and whose detachment from self-centeredness has been completed. Its secret is the abandonment of greed-centered attitudes and the service of selfless self-expression set aflame.

We can know what is right and that acting right is worth the fight.

IF YOU CAN

If you can pray the prayer of faith
    And see the vision coming,
Then you can set your life aflame
    And start your world a-humming.

If you can quit complaining now
    And learn the art of praising,
You can stand on victory hill
    When conquest's flag we're raising.

If you can put your doubts and fears
    In one big pile and burn them,
Then life will bring its gifts to you
    For faith itself will earn them.

If you can look at emptiness
    While still God's promise seeing
Then gratitude and faith and prayer
    Will bring conquest into being.

If you can pierce the darkness bleak
    And see the light shine thru it,
Then you can wait or walk or work
    And God will help you do it.

If you can climb the upward way
    That advancing men are making,
Then prayer and praise and progress, too,
    Are yours just for the taking.

If you can see the end by faith
    When you are just beginning,
Then you have found the Certain Way,
    And the prize you'll soon be winning.

April

~ 14 ~

*Fear is a foe or fear is a friend; hold it in the light while you decide
if you should keep it or drown it in a bucket of faith.*

FEAR VERSUS FAITH

Faith is referred to as a definite desire to as many as possible of the basic motives. Faith includes the action to create a specific plan for attainment. This includes applied or actively achieving faith. As a fish without water finds the swimming rough, so faith without works is something, but not enough. Keep in mind, however, even the skeptical must live by the measure of faith.

Faith is an active, positive state of mind that is motivating, activated, working, expectant, confident attitude and disposition of mind that *WORKS*. Fear is its opposite, for it inactivates, creates doubts, procrastinates, is negative, and cringing. Faith and love are man's strongest powers along with hope. Fear is one of man's greatest weaknesses and is destructive, not constructive; a hindrance, not a help.

Infinite intelligence, as used here, is defined as an attribute of the Creator but definitively in this discussion as referring to the Creator; actually, however, it refers primarily to His omniscience. It seems also to be used in a less personal sense than usual, but may be considered by some to be the Power referred to as the *GREAT UNSEEN* or the *DIVINE MIND* or *GOD* as we know Him. Applied faith is the emotion and condition of a positive mind that has been freed from its negativism and attuned to the mind of God, in communion, guidance, assistance and wisdom. This achieving or applied faith gives us a working association with God, the Creator of all.

Some feel that any generally speaking, God preference, to give us a working plan that employs the physical means available, would be welcome. Prayer will certainly bring both the plan, the inner grace or strength, energy or divine assistance to proceed, plus in many cases, people have found that there was a miraculous intervention which was beyond natural means but not necessarily contradictory to them, but rather in conjunction with natural means and agencies. We would then summarize that the possibility of miraculous intervention is applicable within our faith.

Prayer, if it is negative, that is, if it concentrates and meditates on its needs and poverty and illnesses, fears, worries, deprivations, etc., being negative may and perhaps is a form of reverse praying of which the prayer is unaware. If the prayer offered is doubted and the answer not expected then, "according to your faith, be it unto you." The results will be negative unless the prayer is filled with thankful, positive, confident faith that expects, strives and believes now that the desired thing is as good as possessed.

THE MAD, MAD OCEAN

The mad, mad ocean moans outside
    Like some rabid, frothing dog.
It rolls on the beach and snarls at itself
    And grinds its teeth on each log.

The ocean convulses with madness tonight.
    It foams and it bites in vain.
It growls and snaps at the rocky shore
    As it leaps and writhes in pain.

Tenacious beast on havoc bent!
    It would tear the shore to bits.
The lather of madness is in its eyes
    And the ocean is having fits!

Its white teeth shine in the wild moonlight
    And its virus madness runs high.
It springs stiff-legged back from the shore
    To snap the moon from the sky.

Its fevered brain no mercy knows
    As it chases the ships at sea.
The ocean is like a mad, mad dog,
    But it doesn't belong to me!

April

~ 15 ~

Charity is the beneficence of love in action; it is patience without petulance,
kindness without calumny, self-respect without pride,
progress without impropriety, ambition without selfishness,
tolerance without termination, thought without iniquity,
emotion without misdirection, burden bearing without blaming, faith without limits,
hope all-encompassing, endurance uncomplaining, and it is the
greatest jewel in the crown of completeness!

RESPONDING TO LOVE

The strength and power of love represents the greatest power of the universe. The beautiful news is that this power is yours when you function and accomplish all things with love. Are we willing to address and clear our slate of the issues that prevent and obstruct love?

One area to be aware of relative to an enemy of the love response is misunderstandings. The majority of the heartaches and problems and insecurities between lovers are misunderstandings that develop silently and unexpectedly. We need to remember that each of us has an individual perspective and a personal view of things. The fact is that our expression of these views may not only be different, but these differences may also vary from time to time. Question: When we observe things differently, might that truly reflect what could appear to be different agendas?

Yes, it is true. Lovers hurt one another so often when actually it is the very last thing they want to happen. There is an old quote, "The one we love the most sometimes we hurt the most." Is this because we are so close to the one we love, and the intimacy of our closeness, that the familiarity of our daily walk finds us too unaware, not taking time to purposely think forward and to censure what we say?

The review of drama and literature uncovers the facts that lovers all through history have hurt one another. Recall these quotes: "A lovers quarrel" or the rewards of sweetness of "making up." How many years will go by for each of us to become mature enough to pause and think before we demonstrate irritation? Even though this century reflects an overload of tensions and frustrations, we, more than ever, have a great need for deep understanding and love.

What do you subconsciously broadcast to your love mate? Thoughts truly are powerful experiences of reality in our thought wave universe. We stand daily, both as giant transmitting and receiving stations. Are you involved in disseminating loving understanding, one of our greatest assets? Sterling understanding is love in action.

People who totally love each other have found that the physical passion of love, when spent, may confront the lovers with an additional experience of balance, such as loving actions of your mind. There is value in reasoning versus responding only through the channel of your physical senses. When you set aside problems such as misunderstandings, you can experience mental sharing as well as body sharing. For example in a love relationship, you will know when it is not balanced love when all you satisfy is your body. You know you need and want something more, something more durable and lasting than body sharing.

In the love experience, remember that the holy law of love includes the ecstasy and beauty expressed through the balance of the spiritual, mental and physical. During that brief moment when the loved persons melt into oneness with the universal, creator, and heartbeat, the love mates are hardly aware of body consciousness!

RAINDROP WEDDING

Two little drips from the roof hung down.
Soon they fell upon the ground,
    Ran together, don't you see?
    Saying, "You were meant for me!"

Said number one drip, "I'll be your gal."
Said drip number two, "I'll be your pal."
    And as they ran along the ground
    They made a happy, singing sound:

Drip, drip, drip, drip; drip, drip, drip, drip.
    You were meant for me.
Hand in hand and lip to lip.
Drip, drip, drip, drip; drip, drip, drip, drip!
    You were meant for me!

April

~ 16 ~

God, through our extended awareness, can portray before our minds
the universal manifestation of Himself in a moment of time.

LEAN HARD

I met God this morning
When the day was new and fresh,
And His spirit came so sweetly
Calming the ache within my breast.

I've met Him other mornings
But never the same to me,
For I had a special need
That only He could see.

My heart with grief was broken
And the way seemed rough and long,
But the Master said, oh so sweetly,
"Lean hard, My arm is strong."

So with new assurance
His voice still ringing clear,
I met the day with gladness
Without a trace of fear.

GOD

The beauty not seen by the eye,
    A meter not heard by the ear,
The form of the Formless my soul enthralls
    Whom the blind and the deaf see and hear.

Thou art One without oneness,
    Thou indivisible Triune.
To Thy heavenly, holy harmony
    My heart Thou must forever attune.

Thou Essence of the Very First
    Thou Existence of the Last,
Thou art Outward and the Inward Both,
    The Present, Future, and the Past.

Thou Manifest and yet Unknown
    By man Unspeakable forsooth.
Thou art hidden and revealed to us
    In simple, complex Truth.

I know Thee. Yet I know thee not.
    I seek what I possess.
My empty fullness takes away
    Till more and more I'm less and less.

Thy darkness would outshine the light
    If darkness were in Thee.
True comprehension would confound
    Our false reality.

Intangible, yet All in All,
    By eyes unseen or hands unfelt.
I came in prayer and found Thee There.
    In the place where reverence knelt!

April

~ 17 ~

CLOWN BY BENGARTT (W. JACKSON COLLECTION)

SPRING SONG

The crocus are smiling
    On wild crocus hill.
The lilacs are blooming.
    The birds won't keep still.
They're singing of springtime
    Of nesting and love.
While soft clouds are floating
    In blue skies above.
So rest and be happy
    And join in their song.
Good days are coming.
    They won't tarry long!

April

18

The night brings out the owls and the day, the birds that sing!
Success is a positive mental attitude in perpetual motion!

INNER NONRESISTANCE

Will you join me today in the following affirmations? I resolve not to finish any negative statement unless necessary and wise to do so. My preference is to reverse all negative statements and to make a positive statement of them. I will choose to give only positive, creative suggestions of how things might be desirable, different and better. I will see the desired end clearly as though it were so. And it will be. Confident expectancy, as an attitude, is a powerful suggestion to the cooperative powers of the subconscious mind, which release their inner wisdom, power, healing and guidance. I will therefore envision a happy ending or solution to any problem, whatever it is. I will feel the thrill of future appropriation and accomplishment in the present now.

I instruct my quiet, secret self to think and live in ideal and desired conditions and states. I instruct my inner being to be positive, joyful, confident, calm, courageous, strong, vibrant, powerful, knowledgeable and good in the direction of life. In meditation before retiring, I will say to myself, I shall profit from the experiences of today. I shall give a better account of myself tomorrow than I have ever done before. Tomorrow will be a good day, a profitable day, and today is a good day. I will have a good account to give when tomorrow's day is done, for some good thing will come to me this day and every day.

In addition, in times like these, I shall practice where possible and reasonable the spirit of inner nonresistance, and I shall bless lovingly and silently all things and all situations and all circumstances. I have an expectant attitude for good. Some good thing will come to us from all life experiences. My highest good will come to me. I welcome the good, the beautiful, and the true. They are mine by right of personal choice and the power of good to triumph. I put up no resentful resistance to things that seem to overwhelm me. I know all things are working together for my good, and that which is for my highest good will come to me. My prayer is that in times like these, each of us will be available to become persons who will change the face of time. Please join me today as a candidate to positively master circumstances and thus improve time's history book.

TIMES LIKE THESE

Times like these would test the soul
        Of every son of man,
For times like these are common times
        And have been since time began.

Times like these are no better or worse
        Than past or future hours,
For times like these and men like these
        Are shaped by inner powers.

Times like these are glorious times
        When the Creator takes control.
And days like these can bring God's best
        As we strive to reach each goal.

For times like these, Great God, we ask
        For men to match our day.
Men who'll change the face of time
        And push its hands away.

Men who will master circumstances
        And rewrite time's history book.
For even time with faltering gaze
        For timeless men must look!

April

~ 19 ~

When hearts behind united hands are one in truth, the union stands.

GOING THE EXTRA MILE

The principle of going the extra mile is the Golden Rule in positive action. It is giving to others of attitude, fellowship, service, material, and mental or spiritual or social help of any kind. "Give and it shall be given." It is simply doing more than one is expected to do or more than one is paid to do.

What are the benefits of going the extra mile? (1) You will sooner or later receive compensation for exceeding the actual value of the service you render. (2) In addition to this material gain, you will exhibit greater strength of character in other ways. (3) You will find that it is easier for you to maintain a "positive mental attitude" at all times. (4) You will experience the thrill of new and stronger convictions of courage and self-reliance, new surges of the "self-starting" power of personal initiative, and an energizing influx of vital enthusiasm. (5) You will find that there is a permanent market for your services and because of your reputation, you will not be "out of a job."

The following are summary statements, which are discussion points or further reasons for going the extra mile:

- The law of compensation starts working for you.

- The law of increasing returns assists you.

- This brings favorable attention to you.

- This principle makes you relatively indispensable to others.

- The extra-mile principle leads to mental growth and physical perfection in various forms of service, thus developing efficiency in your work and your life.

- This spotlights you in the law of contrasts as it makes you outstanding in life.

- You may be protected against unemployment.

- This principle of the extra mile develops a positive, pleasing attitude and personality.

- The extra-mile philosophy develops personal initiative in you.

- This principle also develops greater self-confidence.

- Watch this principle kill the procrastination habit.

- The extra-mile habit results in definiteness of purpose.

- Believing in the extra-mile principle develops personal initiative.

- Practicing this philosophy helps develop self-discipline and applied, achieving faith.

When do the powerful results occur as we practice the "Going the extra mile" principle? Look at Nature, in the pollenization of flowers. It makes the bee work first and collect his money (honey) afterwards. The farmer must plow, plant, cultivate and wait for the harvest. Demonstrate investment and faith, and then fruitful harvest will follow. Live the positive, good life!

ALL THINGS ARE A PART OF ME

I am a part of the whole
    And the whole is a part of me.
And riches and wealth and plenty are mine
    For all things are my own and free.

I am a part of mankind.
    I'm akin to each rock and tree,
For I am a part of the living God
    And God is a part of me.

I am a part of life
    As vibrant and strong as the sea,
For I am a part of the Father God
    And God is a part of me.

I am a part of death,
    Of death and eternity,
For I am a mortal but immortal with God
    And all things are a part of me.

April

~ 20 ~

Nature is a flower blooming on the banks of the time-space continuum;
but God, the giving Gardener, is standing always nearby.

THE DOORS ARE WIDE OPEN

Quality of service rendered plus the quantity of service rendered plus the mental attitude in which it is rendered equal your compensation (Q+Q+M = C) in the world, and the amount of space you will occupy in the hearts of your fellow workers. The knowledge that the service as defined above will help you make a greater application. The order of importance would increase the incentive. Would it be fair to say our priorities might be expressed as follows: First, help people spiritually; second, mentally and socially; and third, physically and materially?

You should continue to carry out the principle of the extra mile, but you should work in close harmony and with great tact and good judgment in relationship to your employer. You can find an acceptable manner of rendering an acceptable kind of service at an acceptable time. The compensation for going the extra mile does not always come from the source expected or where the service was rendered, but the Creator keeps an "eternal ledger," and it comes from somewhere.

The law of increasing returns is basically the law of compensation plus a reasonable increase. We reap more than we sow. The quality and the quantity of your service does come back to you, multiplied many times over. The law of diminishing returns affects the begrudging giver or the person who invests little and in the wrong attitude. He will get back less than he planted or invested and maybe nothing at all. The doors are open wide! Go for your opportunity to follow the formula (Q+Q+M = C).

TRIUMPH

If a bird can sing
    In a crowded cage
And a pen can write
    On a narrow page,
Then the soul can dance
    Though a ball and chain
Of frustration galls
    With biting pain.
And man can sing
    Like a bird on wing,
And spirit can triumph
    Over everything.

ENVY'S IGNORANCE

The lily viewed with infinite yearning
    The exquisitely colored rose.
The rose pined with passionate longing
    For the soil where the lily grows.

Dew filled the eyes of the daisy
    Who envied the other two
Unaware of Divinity's divergence
    Where composite purpose grew!

April
21

CLOWN WITH TOP HAT BY BENGARTT (W. JACKSON COLLECTION)

THE PERSONALITY OF AN EARTHWORM

An earthworm must feel really low
   As he crawls as best he can,
Flat on his stomach beneath the gaze
   Of that colossal giant, man.

But at least he seems to make ends meet
   When things are getting rough.
And I've never heard an earthworm say,
   "Hold it, I've had enough!"

An earthworm keeps on inching on
   Above or in the wet ground.
And a little wiggle helps a lot
   If one wants to get around.

If he has a personality
   It would be quite smooth and sleek.
But too often now in spite of it
   We find him up a creek.

Here goggle-eyed, mountain trout
   Are quick such worms to see.
One gobbled gulp and "wormie"
   Has lost his personality.

April

~ 22 ~

Courage is the medicine that brings health to
the disease called weakness.

SUBCONSCIOUS MIND AND COURAGE

The exchange of futile fear for achieving faith, and over-caution for courage, is the first order of business for every day. The seven basic fears that affect our strength and courage are:

- Poverty
- Criticism
- Ill heath
- Loss of love
- Old age
- The loss of liberty
- Death and the unknown

The subconscious mind is, as it implies, the area of our mind of which we are not fully conscious or aware. It controls the automatic functioning of nerves, metabolism, heartbeat, and breathing and involves a type of intelligence that is somewhat passive and subject to the conscious mind, yet has higher reasoning powers and abilities than we have dreamed without a lifetime of study. The subconscious mind takes suggestions from the conscious mind especially when emotionalized or often repeated, or under stressful situations, and later, it projects an action pattern to the conscious mind for fulfillment or action. It can be rearranged by autosuggestion whether under hypnosis or self-suggestion or while sleeping and while awake if the stimulus is repeated frequently and with meaning.

Strength and courage, through achieving faith, develop a form of concentrated, worshipful meditation that activates the subconscious mind and brings the person into a higher vibration rate and contact with Infinite Intelligence—the Creator Himself.

STATE OF EDUCATION BY GREG WALZ

April

23

*The wit that wilts and withers what it wants to win
is the verbal folly in the courtship of fools.*

EMPLOYEES, EMPLOYERS, AND THE EXTRA MILE

"Employment and a job are not always synonymous. The one is a task and the other is active involvement in the accomplishment of it. In either case, the employee's position should be one of application." Both the employee and the employer are responsible for raising the salary. The employee should give justification for it by doing a quality and quantity plus of service and good workmanship to deserve it. However, the same laws work for the employers that work for the employed. The employer should go the extra mile if they, too, want to reap an extra bumper harvest. Both are responsible.

It might be necessary to get permission from an employer in some specific incident, but generally speaking, it is the one place where all folks are free to serve in helping others without asking permission of anyone. There are ineffective, permissible ways of making ourselves indispensable to others that are so entirely acceptable in the light of their need that nothing more than a perfunctory permission is needed, and often not even that. Vote for the extra-mile principle!

COMMERCE

"True commerce is the flow of merchandise from industry to industry, from individual to individual. It is the interchange of ideas, of action, of brain, brawn and labor, of goods, service and silver. It is the building, binding, buying, selling, bartering business of bestowing benefits for a profit and by necessity to meet the multitudinous needs of beehive humanity."

THE ONE-EYED MONSTER

Out of the dark, oblivious night
    It stealthily crept and came.
This one-eyes monster of metal and glass
    Filled with its hidden shame.

It was not a monster of flesh and blood
    But a robot of tubes and tin
Intent on devouring our children alive
    After it brazenly entered in.

It stole our time and thus our lives
    And left us beggared and poor.
And to our shame we're not the same
    Since it slipped through the door.

This one-eyed monster that talks and howls
    And is seldom ever still,
With hypnotic eye can hold us all
    And bend each weakened will.

Who knows its wiles and hidden art
    And the slavery of mind it brings.
But the sourest note in the monster's throat
    Are the compulsive commercials it sings!

April

24

SEASON'S SCARLET ROSE BY WANDA KIPPENBROCK

WHO AM I BUT A SINGER?

Who am I but a singer
    With a sweet but saddened song?
Who am I but a singer
    Who sings of the right and the wrong?

Who am I but a singer
    Who echoes humanity's cry?
Who voices the longings of ages,
    The hopes of the living who die?

Who am I but a singer
    That pain has stretched as a string,
Where life, incomplete, voices longings,
    Where despair makes hope rise and sing?

Who am I but a singer
    Who would tear nature's veil away
And sing of earth's hidden secrets
    In the dawn of a Golden Day?

Who am I but a singer
    Who in response to the heavenly call
Would join the song universal
    Having sensed the Oneness of All?

April

~ 25 ~

*Each life is a minstrel outside the castle walls of every other soul, and
only the song of love will open the windows and unbar the iron gates.*

LOVE IS A FRAGRANT FLOWER

With passive alertness, with relaxed awareness, with happy, confident acceptance of these
positive suggestions, be open to meditate on the concepts of love. Relaxing completely, breathing
easily and deeply, visualizing vividly in color, in detail and in action, consider the following
thoughts. Please alert both the eye of pictorial perception and also increase your total awareness by
hearing, smelling, tasting, touching and emotionally feeling and sensing the things that are
described as you read.

Love is a fragrant flower. Love is a many petaled, velvet-soft rose that blossomed first in the
Creator's Celestial Gardens on a bright and warm, transcendent place. But transplanted, and with a
little care, it can grow luxuriously under adverse circumstances in any climate or condition on a
planet called Earth.

Love is a priceless, invaluable, irreplaceable thing that money cannot buy. It has been counter-
feited, imitated, hoarded, dissipated, discarded, valued, cherished and fought for. It is a vine that
grows through many dimensioned walls and blossoms into incredible visibility even in the rubble of
crass materiality.

The need for love is almost limitless, yet its supply, if activated, is self-perpetuating and sufficient
and can survive the severest demands of Earth, for the source of love is rooted in an infinite supply.
To be kept, it must be freely given. To be truly expressed, it must make no unreasonable demands
but respond to necessity and initiative while radiating its own spiritual warmth voluntarily.

The challenge today is, resolve therefore to walk in the Rose Garden called Love. Wear an invisible rose in your lapel or in your hair. Begin to assimilate the qualities of love. Carry the rich perfume of love, transplanted, within your own magnetic field, and people will turn and look again.
For love is a fragrant flower!

YOUR LOVE

Your love is like the cherry trees in blossom,
      Prophetic of the lush, red fruit to come.
Your love is like the song of meadowlarks in summer.
      My heart is full but still my lips are dumb.

Your love is like a red-brick, fencing wall
      Where on its sunny side, in reflected light,
Protected from the wind and the passersby
      We visit among the trees for half the night.

You love is like crocus blossoms in the springtime,
      Growing sweet and fragrant on some grassy knoll.
I pluck from your lips and the crocus kisses,
      Pressing them between the leaves of memory's scroll.

Your love is like the rippling, flowing river
      That moves and undulates around each bend and curve;
Like some voluptuous, beckoning, insistent lover,
      Enchanted by your laughing movement, every nerve.

Your love is like the glow of golden sunset,
      Spreading scarlet on your neck and lips and cheeks.
Your wild-rose perfume floats out its invitation
      And suggests the relationship such love forever seeks.

Your love is like no metaphor of bards or poets.
      Your love resembles nothing more than simply you.
Your love, the pattern by which love is measured,
      Is complete, yet always adding something new.

April

~ 26 ~

Face life realistically, love reality, court it like your one true love;
reform it if advisable, appraise it accurately, accept it if possible;
but never distort it, rationalize it, or play the fool's game
of blind-man's-bluff with it!

SLEEPING BEAUTY AND AWAKENED AWARENESS
(JACKSON FABLE)

Resting comfortably, relaxing completely, breathing deeply and easily, visualize clearly in detail and in action the Relaxed Learning version of the *Sleeping Beauty and Awakened Awareness*.

Once upon a time, a long, long time ago, a king and a queen wanted a daughter. A little baby girl was born one morning just as the sun came up. As they looked at the little red-faced, happy baby, and as they looked out at the shining sun, they said, "Let's call her Aurora, which means 'the dawn' or 'the rising sun' or 'the light from the dawn of the rising sun.'" So they called her Aurora, which was a beautiful name. She was a beautiful baby princess. Her parents were so happy, and everyone in the kingdom was happy, too.

While they were celebrating Aurora's birth, along came three fairies. Their names were Flora, Fauna, and Merriweather. They wanted to give her gifts just like all the other people visiting her. So Flora brought to the little baby princess the gift of beauty, like the beauty of a flower. Perhaps you can visualize a little yellow buttercup with a waxen interior and little drops of yellow pollen in its centers. Visualize a little yellow buttercup out of which fairies might even drink. Or picture a beautiful rose, or a beautiful sunrise, for beauty was the gift Flora gave to Aurora, the princess. Then Fauna came. She gave to the princess the sweetness of song, melody, or rhythm. It seemed that all of the birds began to sing when Fauna presented the gift of song. Then all of the people began to sing and the whole world was filled with the gladness of song. Aurora, the princess, had been given the gift of the happy heart and the singing spirit, for hers was a gift of music and song.

Then Merriweather, the third fairy, just started to touch the baby with her magic wand and to give the princess her gift, but she didn't get to give her gift. Merriweather was probably going to give her sunshine for every day or a nice climate in which to live. But just as she started to touch the baby with her wand so that she could give her such beautiful gifts as sunshine, good weather or light to walk in, there was a flash of lightning. Out of the ball of fire and the flash of lurid light appeared an evil fairy that looked more like a witch than a fairy. Her name was Maleficent, which means evil or evil one. Maleficent! On her shoulder a raven was sitting—a black crow that croaked and echoed

~ 287 ~

all of the evil things that Maleficent was about to say. Maleficent, the evil fairy, was angry because she had not been invited to the first birthday party of the Princess Aurora. Because she was angry, jealous and displeased for not having been invited, she said, "I pronounce a curse upon the young princess. On her sixteenth birthday, she will prick her finger and she will die." Then Maleficent, the evil fairy, vanished in a cloud of black, grim smoke.

Merriweather still had her gift to give, so she decided to use the power of her wish to grant the princess some change in the curse the evil fairy had put upon her. She couldn't promise the princess would never die, but she did change the effect of the bad wish. Merriweather said, "On her sixteenth birthday, when Princess Aurora pricks her finger, if she does, she will not die. She will only fall asleep and that will not be forever, because a charming prince will come along who will love her and the kiss of love will awaken the sleeping beauty, Princess Aurora."

But quick as a flash, those three wise little fairies said, "Let's hold a conference to talk about everything. Maybe we won't even have to let Princess Aurora have her finger pricked with a thorn or anything else. Let's figure out how we can take care of her." So they made themselves real tiny. They took another big, deep breath of fresh air, and they turned on their imaginary miniaturization tubes. And all of a sudden, Flora was a tiny little flower, a little forget-me-not. It was growing under, of all things, a tiny, miniature fir tree. That little fir tree was Fauna, who had also miniaturized herself. Then Merriweather made herself real tiny, too, like a little shiny sunbeam that cast its rays of light across the miniature green tree and the tiny forget-me-not.

There, together, the three fairies, invisible, concealed, and disguised as far as the entire world could see, had a beautiful conversation together. They asked, "What can we do?" And then they said, "We can become peasant ladies. We could rent a cottage, or find a place deep in the forest, and we could take care of this little baby princess. We could raise her away from any harm and away from the danger of the curse of Maleficent, the evil fairy. We could keep her until her sixteenth birthday, and watch over her on that birthday so that nothing would happen. We would then take her back to her father and mother, the king and queen." When the three good fairies were done talking, they decided they would get big again and be regular fairies.

They went back and talked to the king and queen. And they said, "We just had an idea . . . We decided that if you will trust us, we would take the little baby with us and keep her until she is sixteen years old. We'll watch over her everyday, all three of us will, and on her birthday, we'll bring her back home again and she'll be yours on her sixteenth birthday. She will be free from any evil thing that could ever happen to her." The king and queen said, "Okay, better to lose her for a little while and have her after that than to keep her for a little while and lose her forever. Take her with you." So they did.

They went marching off into the forest. They found a big hollow tree and they cut a door in it with their magic wands. They put windows in it and a nice stone floor and a fireplace with a chimney. They fixed some beds with fir boughs with reeds and rushes in the corner and a little table in the middle. There was even a crib over on the side. It was so nice and they were so happy!

They raised the little Princess Aurora like they promised. When she grew up, she had all kinds of fun. She played with the animals. She learned to love them and they loved her. And she went into the forest, singing her happy songs. Years came and went and the fairies taught her many things. Finally, it was her sixteenth birthday. The fairies called the princess "Briarrose" to protect her from the evil fairy. So they said, "Briarrose, this is your birthday. Why don't you go for a walk in the forest? We're going to do something nice for you while you are gone."

And while she was gone, Flora, Fauna, and Merriweather made a beautiful green dress for her and a birthday cake with candles on it that they'd lighted with their magic wand. So, Briarrose, or Princess Aurora in disguise, took her basket to gather flowers and started off to the forest singing. But she didn't sing a happy song that day. She sang a sad song. She sang, "Oh, how lonesome I am. Oh, I wish I had someone to love me. I love these three little ladies that take care of me, but I wish I'd meet a handsome prince." As she was singing, she finally hit a real high note.

Over on the other side of the little stream came a knight; his name was Prince Handsome. He was riding on his horse called Midnight. When Midnight heard that beautiful singing, he started to dance and prance in rhythm like the circus horses do to music. He had just gone over to the edge of the stream when Briarrose, or Princess Aurora, hit that high note. When she did, Midnight jumped straight up in the air and right across the stream. But he jumped so fast that he left Prince Handsome still up in the air in the middle of the stream. Down he came, splashing into the river clear up to his chin. He called to Midnight and said, "Why in the world did you drop me off in the mud and water when I wanted to meet that beautiful princess?" So Midnight waited for him. And the prince said, "Now I've got to go dry my red tunic and I've got to take my boots off and pour the water out of them. All I'll have on is my red flannel underwear, but," he said, "I guess I'll have to do it."

So he took off his jacket and hung it on a branch. He took off his boots, and poured the water out of them. Then he sat down while his shirt and boots were drying. The wonderful part of it was that while they were drying he dropped off to sleep for a second or two in his red flannel underwear. Two little rabbits came along and grabbed his boots and they started to hop and run and scamper with them on. They carried the boots to the princess. They said, "We know what she's singing about. If we can't bring the prince to her since he's all wet anyway, we'll take his boots and his shirt to the princess." The birds got hold of the corner of his shirt, and they carried it away, and the rabbits carried the boots. They told the princess that they'd brought her an invisible, imaginary prince, too. So she just played the game with them. They carried the clothes around and she played like she was dancing with the shirt and dancing with the boots. She was really having a great time.

However, the prince woke up and stepped out from behind his tree, and there he saw the princess! He sneaked over behind his shirt and his boots and he just reached around them and started dancing with Aurora. They had a wonderful time dancing together, and they fell completely and madly in love with each other. The princess said, "I have to go home." And the prince said, "When will I ever see you again?" She said, "Tonight, at that little tree cottage. You can come for supper." So they each went their way.

When the princess got back home, the green dress was a flop and the birthday cake had fallen. The fairies said, "Let's shut the door and windows. We must be careful that the evil fairy, Maleficent, doesn't see us. We'll take our magic wands and make a beautiful dress. So they changed the dress to blue. Then Flora said to Fauna, "I don't like blue. I like pink." And they changed it to pink. Then

Merriweather said, "I like gold." Then she changed it to gold. They kept changing it back from blue to pink to gold until the sparks from their wands began to fill the room and swept up the chimney! That was when Croaker, that raven that sat on the shoulder of Maleficent, saw the sparks that came from the magic wands coming out of the chimney, and he flew to tell Maleficent, the evil fairy, what was going on.

Now, what do you think happened next? The prince didn't come that night! The three good fairies decided that they were going to go back to the king's castle and take his daughter back to her home. They took the birthday cake with them, with all sixteen candles on it. There, Aurora was dressed in that beautiful, multi-colored, gold, blue and pink dress that the fairies couldn't decide on for color! And it kept changing color.

Finally, they all got to the palace. The king and the queen were glad to see their daughter. They did have a wonderful party. But all of a sudden Maleficent came in, invisible and whispered to the princess, "Spin me something beautiful." Maleficent led her up the stairs to the castle tower where there was a spinning wheel. Princess Aurora was so frightened that she went over to start spinning, and she pricked her finger on the spinning wheel! She fell down just like she was dead. Everyone looked all over for her. Maleficent, the evil fairy, flew away and left the princess there for dead. But then the three fairies came and found her. They changed the curse of death to one of sleep. But they said, "We'll put the whole castle to sleep—the king, the queen, the servants and all of the people."

Then one day, Prince Handsome finally came. He couldn't get into the castle because there was an evil dragon guarding it. The dragon was Maleficent. So Prince Handsome fought with her. But he couldn't get very close because of the fire from the dragon's mouth . . . He finally took his sword and threw it as hard as he could . . . The point of it went right into the dragon's heart, and the dragon fell over the cliff. When it hit the bottom, there was nothing left but the cape of that evil fairy, Maleficent.

Prince Handsome went into the castle where all the court and guests were sleeping like statues. He climbed up the magic stairs to the high tower with the spinning wheel, and there he found the sleeping princess, in the silent castle. He leaned over and kissed Princess Aurora on the forehead. She opened those blue peepers, wide open. She said, "I've been waiting for you all night." So he took her by the arm and lifted her up, and they went down and woke up all of the other people and the king and the queen, and they decided that Prince Handsome and Princess Aurora should get married. They did and they lived happily ever after.

Now there are some conclusions to be drawn from this familiar, old story. Your best, inner self is like a sleeping prince or princess . . . The real you is often asleep. But your best self can be awakened and you can become everything you ever wanted to be and much more. You must awaken the best that is within you. This active awareness, this state of being completely awake and fully conscious, is a wonderful thing. We must and we will increasingly from day to day see more that is going on around us and in us than we have before. Our five senses—hearing, seeing, smelling, touching and tasting—will begin and continue to increase with new accuracy and efficiency. We are learning to concentrate and to give our full, wide-awake, mental attention to each situation depending upon its value and importance to us. We are entering into the art of problem solving and the enjoyment of life's permissible pleasures with increasing efficiency and extended awareness.

290

We are able to identify with, or enter into any object, situation, person or relationship with keener comprehension and fuller understanding. Our feelings, emotions and extrasensory abilities are now added to our physical senses in reaching accurate, logical, intuitive conclusions about all things that interest us and are of value to us. We hear better, see better, smell better, taste better and feel with greater sensitivity all things in our mental, spiritual, social and physical environments.

We will no longer walk around half-asleep and preoccupied with half-realities. We are now and will continue to be wide awake and alert when necessary. We will no longer let our mental motors idle carelessly. We will and do mesh gears with reality in the here and now. We will now mentally and spiritually awaken. When this relaxed learning is completed, we will come up with greater awareness than ever before. And remember that as you are learning to relax and to concentrate, you are also learning to turn to awaken your better, inner self so that you can go out and live life, love life and enjoy all of the days that are yours to live.

Wide awake and happy! Everyone open your eyes. You are more alert, feeling better, more rested and refreshed than ever before. It's a wonderful thing to be alive and to be wide awake and happy!

HEAVEN'S DAY HAS JUST BEGUN

When the King of Night
Huddles in bed
And smothers the sinking sun,
Then it's quiet time
And it's nighttime
And the work of the day is done.

When the silent stars
March in the night
Like soldiers with flashing gun,
Then it's a bright time
'Tho it's nighttime
And the toil of the day is done.

When life's longest day
Comes to its end
Time's hourglass no longer can run;
Then it's the right time
But it's not nighttime
For heaven's day has just begun!

DANDELION BY CAROLINE SEYMOUR

April

~ 27 ~

The person who learns to see deeply into the commonplace
will find reality, while others with greater learning pass it by.

THE GREAT DANE AT THE OBEDIENCE SHOW

(JACKSON FABLE)

Let's sit up straight today with our feet flat on the floor. Resting comfortably, relaxing completely, enjoy the story of "The Great Dane at the Obedience Show."

Some time ago, we discussed three things that would help us get "A" grades. One was to pay attention all the way. The second was to understand or ask questions. Number three was to remember the order of the instructions. Today, I want you to imagine that you're going to a dog show with obedience trials. I want you to take another deep breath and imagine yourself clearly, in the ring or looking from the grandstand. Take another deep breath and exhale.

I want you to picture in the ring a huge fat lady. I want you to imagine how big her legs are. They are probably as big as the circular globe of the world. I want you just for fun to imagine that she's twice as wide as any chair she could sit on. Imagine that her arms are fat. They almost stick out like limbs on a tree because she can't get them down to her sides. This lady has a Great Dane dog. He's an extra-large puppy about eleven months old. He'd weigh about as much as your Shetland pony would. He's a big one. The lady is going to show the judges and all of those people in the ring how well she has trained her dog that she calls "Great Dane."

Okay, she's ready now, and she's going to give him the first command, "Sit. Stay." Can you hear her? She's saying, "Sit; stay, Great Dane." What's he doing? He jumps up. He's running up into the audience. He's pulling a pink hat off of a baby in its mother's arms. He's coming back down with a pink hat in his mouth, as proud as can be. His tail is wagging like a flag as he places it at her feet. And that big fat lady is tearing her new wig! She's saying, "You stupid animal! You don't know 'Sit; stay,' from, 'Go Fetch.'" Then she decides to try something else. She's going to try, "Lie down." Here she is, bending over the dog. She has his leash in her hand. She's not going to let go of him this time. She's saying, "Down, Great Dane! Down." Do you know what he's doing? He's dancing on his hind feet just like he was begging for a biscuit. He doesn't know, "Lie down" from, "Beg for a bone."

Let's give her another chance. She's been working hard training her dog for obedience. Let's see what she'll do with Great Dane if she has him follow her on "Heel." Let's get ready. "Heel, Great Dane." What do you think he's doing now? Sitting down? No. He's walking on his hind legs across the field. He's not behind her. He's out in front leading the parade with the fat lady waddling behind, trying to catch up with Great Dane. The large lady is very unhappy as she finally catches up with him. She's jerking on his leash. Should we give her one more week at home to work with that dog? No, we can't wait for a whole week. Maybe she could teach him obedience right now. But he's too big for that fat lady. We'll have to do something about that giant Great Dane puppy right now!

Let's all take a deep breath. Hold it. When you exhale, just picture that Great Dane becoming a little, mouse-sized Chihuahua. Okay. Exhale and watch the dog go down in size. There he is. He is mouse size. He's a Mickey Mouse Chihuahua. He's scared to death of that big, fat lady. She's bending over him. Yes, she's bending over him, and she's pointing a finger down at that little mouse. She's saying, "First, I want you to pay attention all the way. Second, I want you to understand or ask questions." He thinks, "I can't ask questions." And she says, "Well, you can look at me like you're asking a question. You can tip your head to one side like you don't understand." That little Mouse-Chihuahua, Great Dane is nodding his head now, saying, "Yes ma'am. I understand or I'll ask questions." "Third, remember the order of the instructions. Remember the order of the instructions!" He's nodding his head. Let's hope that she tells our Mickey Mouse, Great Dane-Chihuahua that he's got to concentrate. Now let's leave him a minute while he thinks about these three rules. And you think about them, too. Say the three rules just quietly to yourself. Pay attention all the way. Understand or ask questions. Remember the order of the instructions. And concentrate!

Look, now that Great Dane, Mickey Mouse Chihuahua is coming back up to Great Dane size. Let's see if he can go through his obedience training again and do it better.

Here we have the fat lady. She's still fat. The eleven-month-old Great Dane, as big as your Shetland pony, is in front of her. She's saying, "Sit, Great Dane!" Sure enough, he's sitting. Look at that smile on his big, black mask. Look at those ears standing right straight up. He's proud. His tail is pounding the ground. The judge marks something down. Now, she's going to say, "Lie down." There he goes, right flat on his stomach. And she's going to say, "Down; stay." She is holding her hand up as she's backing away from him. Oops! She trips over something and falls down. She's sitting flat. She's getting up now, but the dog doesn't get up. He stayed! Here she comes back. He gets another point for obedience. Now, she's going to ask him to "Heel." Do you think he's going to do it? Right! Let's watch. "Heel, Great Dane." There he is, right behind the fat lady, marching down the middle of the arena. All the people are clapping and cheering. Wait a minute. I think the judge is motioning for her to come over to the stand. Sure enough. He must be telling that Great Dane to beg. Anyway, the Great Dane is standing on his hind feet with his front feet hanging in front of him. He's as tall as the judge. The judge is putting one of those graduation caps on his head. He's putting a long gown on Great Dane, and he's giving him a diploma. Can you see that diploma under his arm? Now the fat lady and the dog are walking back across to the other side of the arena. The lady is leading and the dog is following at heel with the cap on, with the black gown banging against his long legs, as he walks on his hind feet. He still has the diploma under his arm. The tassel on his graduation cap is tickling his nose as the wind blows it back and forth. All of the people are cheering again. They're clapping like mad everywhere. That's good!

The dog earned his obedience diploma, didn't he? I want you to continue relaxing for a moment and remember something. Obedience is the most important thing under some circumstances that a person can do. Under other circumstances, a person must think for himself and maintain perfect self-control. You are a person and are a lot smarter than a Great Dane. You know when you are supposed to be maintaining self-control. You know when you should be obeying orders. So pay attention all the way, understand or ask questions, and remember the order of instructions and follow them.

You are a good class. You are a part of a good school. You are here in school to learn many useful and helpful things and also to learn to become good and useful men and women as you grow up. As your teacher, I am here to help you do the things you might find a little difficult to do entirely by yourselves. I shall do my best for you, because I like you and I like being your teacher. That is a good thought to keep in mind; that we are here in school to help each other.

I want you to say the following words silently now. Just think these words quietly, and please repeat them to yourselves: I shall start now to do my schoolwork better than I have ever done it at any time before. I know that orderly conduct and quiet study are best. I know that staying in my own assigned seat and talking only when I have asked permission to speak will be best for everyone concerned and will make it easier for all of us. Therefore, I will be quiet, I will study hard, and I will be orderly on every occasion. By doing my part, I will help my class to be the best-disciplined, the quietest and hardest-working class in the school.

I also give my full attention to my assigned work and to my teacher when he (or she) is talking, teaching, or conducting the class. I will listen carefully and will not interrupt. My study habits are improving. They are getting better and better. My studies are getting easier each day. I am good not only in conduct but also in remembering what I have learned, for I have a natural ability, interest and love for school and for learning. I will always remember the story of "The Great Dane at the Obedience Show" and how very important cooperation and obedience are!

You are a good class, and you will help each other to always keep it so. Thank you for listening so quietly and attentively. Heads up. Take a good stretch. Today will be a great day!

GOD WALKS ON EARTH WITH MEN

Knowing God is a real experience
    Unsensed by the senses of man,
But as real as beauty is real
    Awakened by springtime's hand.

Knowing God is as real as knowing
    A sunbeam caressing a flower,
Or the sweep of eagle wings above
    And the feel of up-born power.

Knowing God is a different matter
    Than knowing what our senses may know.
It is a spiritual kind of discernment
    That awakes when God walks below.

The Unknown is known by the knower,
    The Invisible is plain to the eye.
And man comprehends the incomprehensible
    As intangibles with earth tangibles vie.

Ah, this is the mystic knowing of God
    In devotion's encompassing ken.
When man transcends the transcendent
    And God walks on the earth again!

April

28

RUST IN PEACE BY CAROLINE SEYMOUR

I KNOW YOU ARE THERE, OLD OCEAN

I know you are there, Old Ocean,
    Weeping your salty tears.
Moaning through desolate caverns,
    Sighing through sullen years.

I know you are there, Old Ocean,
    Quit slapping the bars of your cage
Like a lion hunting in hunger
    Who would paralyze its prey with rage.

I know you are there, Old Ocean,
    Gnawing the stones 'til they're bright.
Polishing the obdurate agates
    'Til they shine with luminous light.

I know you are there, Old Ocean,
    Like a lover with heaving breast.
You would gladly embrace me forever
    And give me oblivious rest.

I know you are there, Old Ocean.
    You call me each day to your shore.
When I think that I need you no longer,
    I find that I need you still more.

April

29

The love of life is a beautiful thing;
it is the infinite within the finite that senses the beauty
of the finite with infinite sensitiveness and intuitive appreciation.

SIR UNO WHO AND THE SEVEN MAGIC GIFTS

(JACKSON FABLE)

Seated comfortably, relaxing completely, visualizing clearly in color and attentively to the story of *Sir Uno Who and the Good Golden Fairy.* The Good Golden Fairy with the silk and silver butterfly wings came one night through a deep forest, where she found a young sleeping prince and princess in a great stone castle called "I Want To Know More and Do Better."

Sir Uno, the prince, was sleeping soundly. His full name was Sir Uno Who, but they called him U or Uno for short. He was dreaming about Wishes, his beautiful Appaloosa horse. That's what he called him—Wishes! Uno kept thinking, "I wish Wishes had wings so he could fly and we could go to faraway places together. I wish he were a talking horse so he could help me with my royal English lessons and my math courses. I wish Wishes would help me with all of my grades. I'd even let him eat my royal report card with sugar and cream on it after I showed my mother, the queen, all of my As and Bs." Well, that's what Sir Uno was dreaming about the night the Good Golden Fairy visited him and the Princess Una, his sister.

Una was dreaming about how she could do well in school to fulfill her own dreams and also help her brother, Uno, with his schoolwork, so that they could grow up and become fine, strong, intelligent people—and not just dream about running away to far-off places that they both talked about sometimes. As the Good Golden Fairy listened in on Una's dreams, too, she thought and she thought and thought, "How can I help Sir Uno and Princess Una to grow up and be what they want to be, to do what they want to do and to know what is best?"

Then all at once the flowers in the Good Fairy's magic thinking cap lit up like the decorations on a Christmas tree. The lights kept right on blinking and shining. The little daisies on the front of her hat looked like little daisy lightbulbs, and the big golden sunflower on top of the hat looked like a bright neon light with little yellow petals coming out in a circle around the center, darker light. You could almost smell the perfume from the red and white rose lights on the back of her head where the Good Golden Fairy's ponytail came out from under her hat. The lights kept right on blinking, because the Good Golden Fairy was thinking sort of blinking-thinking thoughts, or maybe they were thinking-blinking thoughts.

Here was the brand-new idea she was thinking to herself: "I guess I won't make Wishes into a talking horse that knows English and math. I'll not even give him wings to fly to far, faraway places with the prince. I'll just give Prince Uno Who and his sister Una six good wish-gifts that will work for them even when they are older and when they trade their horse, Wishes, for a royal Volkswagen or a unicycle chariot." Uno Who mumbled something in his sleep and said, "Sounds good to me, Ma'am. Let's give it a whirl . . ."

Una turned over in her bed and opened one eye and saw the Good Fairy's thinking cap blinking and thinking, and she thought she was still dreaming, so she didn't bother to wake clear up. But she did say softly, "What's good for Uno Who is good for Una, too." And she went right back to sleep.

The Good Fairy looked through her shopping bag until she found six wonderful gifts to give the sleeping, royal children. She really knew what they needed better than even the prince and princess did, because she had her thinking cap on. So she put a red bird of paradise feather and a yellow canary feather on the very end of her magic, retractable wand so that it wouldn't wake up the children when she touched them. If you looked real close, the wand also had a yellow and purple pinwheel just in back of the star on the end of the wand. The pinwheel went around and around and sang a soothing little fairy song about castles and kings and a horse with wings and princes and fairies and all sorts of things.

The shaft, or handle, of the magic, good-wishes wand looked like a tiny, twisted, neon pretzel of gold and green lights. The Good Golden Fairy with the silk and silver butterfly wings reached out her wand and touched the sleeping princess right on the end of her freckled, upturned, little nose. It didn't hurt, but the feather did tickle, and Una almost woke up. The Good Fairy hurried and said, "Una, I love you because you are a wise, confident, sweet, kind, and loving princess and because you are a caring sister to Prince Uno Who and also because you live in the castle called I Want to Know More and Do Better. So I'm going to give you six wish-gifts that are more important than horses or grades and better than a magic rubber peanut butter sandwich with catsup on it. These gifts will help you all of your life. Keep them carefully and use them every day."

Soft music filled the room as the Good Fairy said, "I give you first the gift of friendship. It is the ability to get along with and have a good influence with your friends, teachers, parents, brothers, sisters and other grown-up people. This is the gift of unselfish love, the gift of peace, joy, and sincere, happy-hearted, inter-personal relationships. It is the gift of friendship."

The Good Fairy waved her wand again and said, "The second gift I give you is the gift of diligent work. It is the untiring capacity for patient labor and the completion of any worthwhile task when once begun. This is the gift that makes a game of willing work and puts fun in all accomplishment."

Again the wand passed over the sleeping Una as the fairy continued, "I give you now the wonderful gift of confidence. I give you confidence in yourself, confidence in others and confidence in the infinite goodness that moves through the entire world. Stand straight. Think tall. Remember you are the king's child. You are brave, courageous and strong. You do have the gift of confidence. This is gift number three, and it is yours!"

The gold and green lights in the handle of the magic wand were blinking. The gold and silver sparks of light were coming out of the star on the end of the wand, and the yellow and purple pinwheel was going round and round, singing its soothing, melodious song as the Good Fairy made a little step forward and whispered, "Now, gift number four will help you in school and with your grades. I give you unusual powers of mental concentration. You can think clearly and accurately for long periods of time when you need to think and concentrate. You will be able to quietly solve problems, know what to do and when to do it. You will be in the right place at the right time saying and doing the right things with the right people, with right results. You will always be able to find the quiet inner place of restful concentration and bring from it wisdom, knowledge and directions for your life.

"You will always be grateful for this gift of concentration, because it will always come to your aid when needed, and it also comes with the gift of a good retentive memory. You will not forget what you want to remember. You will store facts, emotions, and impressions. You will know how and where to find them and bring them back for your own use and to share with others. You have a good memory. It is yours to use. Be grateful for it and have confidence in it, and use it whenever you need it. It is a part of your gift of relaxed concentration."

Una smiled and almost woke up again because it sounded so good, and she knew that these things were just what she had always needed and wanted.

The Good Fairy stepped back and in a clear, kind voice said, "Gift number five coming up! Here is your gift of creative thought. It is the ability to make new things out of old, to see old things in a new way and to do things differently and better than they were ever done before! You are a creator. You do have good, new ideas that are practical and useful. This is the gift of creativity!"

Looking at the last gift-wrapped package in her hand and then looking down into the bulging shopping bag, the Good Fairy with the silk and silver butterfly wings, with the thinking, blinking, thinking-cap and the magic wand, looked and thought and thought and looked. There were so many gifts to choose from, and all of them were important. She put that last gift under the princess's pillow. While she was leaning over, she gently smoothed back her curls and whispered very, very softly, "I also give you the gift of relaxation. Rest when you need to rest. Relax when you need to relax. Relax when you work. Relax when you play. Relax when you eat. Relax when you talk. Relax when you study. Relax when you sing. Relax in everything!"

Then, as the Good Fairy straightened up, the red bird of paradise feather and the yellow canary feather on the end of the wand accidentally brushed across under the little, freckled, upturned nose of Princess Una. She caught her breath and sneezed a big "Ah Chooze!" The Good Golden Fairy thought that Princess Una had said, "I *choose* all of these good things you are giving me!" So the Good Golden Fairy stopped right there because she was so pleased. She took off her neon thinking-blinking, blinking-thinking cap with the electric light flowers and blew on it like you blow a candle out. Poof! It was gone! She took her best halo out of her shopping bag, brushed it off with the feathers on the end of the magic wand, and put it on top of her head just so! She turned around three times on the silver-slippered heel of her right foot. With sparks shooting out of her magic wand, she smiled her sweetest smile and pointed the wand right at Una and said, "Because you *choose* the good things that I chose for you, and because you said the magic words 'I Choose,' I'm going to give you the seventh and best gift of all. I give you today and for all of your days the power to always choose the beautiful, the true, the positive and the good!"

Princess Una smiled happily in her sleep as the Good Golden Fairy went over to Prince Uno Who; but she couldn't find him anywhere. He was sleeping with his head under the covers. So the Good Fairy pulled the covers down from his head and tucked them in under his chin very gently. She pushed her retractable wand together and put it over one ear, and touching Prince Uno Who on the nose with her long, white finger, she said, "Listen carefully again to the wish-gifts that I just gave your sister Una. These are things you have always wanted and needed, and they are yours also."

Sir Uno rested quietly and listened carefully and made pictures in his dreams of the good things he was receiving, while the Good Fairy in her kindest voice went on to say, "I give you first the gift of *friendship*. It is the ability to get along and have a good influence with your friends, teachers, parents, brothers, sisters and grown-up people. It is the gift of unselfish love, the gift of peace, joy, sincerity, and warm-hearted comradeship. It is the gift of friendship, and it is yours!

"I give you for your second gift the gift of *diligent work*. It is the untiring capacity for patient labor and the completion of any worthwhile task that you begin. It is a gift that makes a game out of willing work and puts the fun in all accomplishment.

"I give you for your third gift, the inner *strength of confidence*. You have confidence in your self, confidence in others, and confidence in the infinite goodness that moves throughout all of the world. So stand straight. Think tall. Remember that you are the king's son. You are brave, courageous, and strong. You do have this gift of confidence, and it will grow as you grow and foolish fears will fly away.

"Gift number four will help you in school with all of your grades. For I give you the gift of unusual powers of *mental concentration*. You can and do think clearly and accurately and for long periods of time when you need to think and concentrate. You will be able to quietly solve problems, know what to do and when to do it. You will be in the right place at the right time, saying and doing the right things with the right people, with right results. You will be able always to bring from it wisdom, knowledge and directions for your life. You will always be grateful for this gift, because with it you also have the gift of a good, retentive memory. You will not forget what you want to remember. You will store facts, emotions and impressions and will know how and where to find them to bring them back for use and to share with others. You have a good memory. It is yours to use. Be grateful for it and have confidence in it, and use it whenever you need it. It is a part of your gift of relaxed concentration.

"Gift number five coming up for you, Sir Uno Who! It is the gift of *creative thought*. It is the ability to make new things out of old and to see old things in a new way. It is the ability to do things differently and better than they have ever been done before! You are a creator. You do have good, new ideas that are practical and useful. This is your gift of creativity!

"For gift number six, I give you the gift of *relaxation*. Rest when you need to rest. Relax when you need to relax. Relax when you work. Relax when you play. Relax when you eat. Relax when you talk. Relax when you study. Relax when you sing. Relax! Relax in everything!"

When the Good Golden Fairy was done with the six good wishes, she read the seventh, just to see if it sounded good for Sir Uno Who. She couldn't tell if Uno liked the seventh gift or not, because he was resting so quietly. So the Good Fairy just waited. While she was waiting, she just happened to think of the pepper-pot pie that she had home cooking in the oven. And right then, too, Prince Uno happened to dream about eating pepper-pot pie. He dreamed that he was shaking more red and black seasoning pepper on the crust. Sure enough, he dreamed that he got some up his nose. He sneezed so hard in his sleep that he blew the retractable magic wand right off of Good Fairy's ear, but she caught it in her right hand as Sir Uno sneezed the second time. "Ah Chooze. Ah Chooze!" The Good Fairy with the silk and silver butterfly wings thought that Sir Uno had said, like his sister Una, "I choose!" The Good Fairy said, "He is just like his good and wise sister, so I shall give him the seventh and best of all wishes also." Then she touched him with her magic wand and said, "Because you chose the good things that I chose for you, and because you said the magic words, 'I choose!' I am going to give you the best wish of all. It is the power to choose the beautiful, the true, the positive and the good!" Then the Good Fairy smelled her pepper-pot pie burning in the oven at home, and in a flash she was gone, just like the light when you turn it out.

In the morning when they both awoke, Sir Uno and Princess Una remembered their wonderful dreams about the Good Golden Fairy and the seven magic wish-gifts of *love, confidence, concentration, memory, willing work, creative thought, relaxation, and, above all, the power to choose the beautiful, the true, the positive, and the good.*

Open your eyes, take a deep breath, stretch yourself, and notice how rested and good you feel. Have a good day, Prince Uno Who!

THE 102 BY GREG WALZ

April

30

*Blooming flowers always hold a fragrant, heaven-like beauty of their own
that seems to make the Great Creator say, "I'm just beyond the wall
they're growing through; why not stand by me a moment here, and pray."*

THE BEAR THAT HAD A BOY FOR A DOG

(JACKSON FABLE)

Once upon a time, a bear had a boy for a dog. I don't know for sure just how long ago it was—probably longer ago than a mile! It was way, way back when sometimes boys had bears for dogs and once in a great, great while, dogs had bears for boys; but get it straight now. This is the story of the bear that had a boy for a dog!

Now the bear had just brought the boy-dog, or rather the dog-boy, home from the boy-pound. The boy-pound was called the Inhumane Society for lost dog-boys! The bear-face boy catcher had picked the boy up because he didn't have a boy license. The boy tried to tell them that a dog shouldn't have a boy license or a boy shouldn't *have* to have a dog license. Why, he hadn't even told a lie since he'd been boy-whipped for telling that *whopper* about a bear that wanted a boy for a dog.

Sure enough, he was the bear's boy now! And sure enough, they tied an old frayed rope around his neck to lead him. The boy and the bear had just gotten home to the little clod-shack on Beeline Avenue over in Bearville Village.

The bear, with his cob-corn pipe sticking out at a rakish angle from his black, pleased-looking fur face, had just set down in his J.F.K. kind of rocker on the front porch. He had closed his eyes for just a few seconds to think quietly about the new boy he had for a dog, but the whole thing was a bit confusing and heavy for a warm, July afternoon. He did, however, keep one eye halfway open so that he could see through the eye-winkers how the boy was taking his new studded collar and shiny, bright, brand-new, double-link chain.

The boy didn't seem to be disturbed a bit. He was going through his pockets taking stock of things he might amuse himself with if he should ever find himself in a bear's doghouse, or even in a dog's bare house. His dog collar itched his neck here and there, and he couldn't figure out the combination to the little padlock under his chin that fastened the chain to the collar. But he did manage to sit down and scratch the collar in dog-fashion with the heel of one tennis shoe.

The bear did notice that the boy had more pockets than most dogs have except maybe for the rocket-type dogs. He did notice that the boy wasn't used to wearing collars. So, he said, just to get the boy's attention, "Buster?"

305

"Not yet," said the boy that was a dog, "but I'll try harder."

"I didn't mean it that way," said the bear. "Buster is—well, you might say it's sort of a name that fits people who are dogs, or even dogs who are people-like. I was really only getting ready to ask if you like the job I did on your new dog collar and chain."

"Ah, yes, that!" said the boy. "It's a good job, but I'd rather have a white-collar-type job, or even a white-job-type collar, you know."

The bear knew some about fur collars, for he'd had one himself as "fur" back as he could imagine. So he just said defensively like, "Well, it's a dog-collar-type job anyway—most jobs are."

The bear thought maybe it would help the whole situation if they could decide just what kind of a dog the boy wanted to be.

"Buster?" he asked.

"Not yet," said the boy, "but I'm thinking about it more now than I was." He still thought that "Buster" was a lock-breaking question, not a name.

"Buster," said the bear more affirmatively, ignoring the boy's answer. "Buster, just what kind of a dog are you going to be?"

"Well, yes," said the boy, as he tried to practice wagging a tail in case one came with the new job. "Yes, come to think of it, I'd like to be a man's bear-dog. I mean, Sir, I'd like to be a bear's man-dog, or maybe a lap dog."

"That's good, very good," said the bear, and everybody seemed happy.

The boy looked at his muddy tenni-runners and his sloppy socks and decided he couldn't really be a lap dog, so he decided to change the subject just a wee little bit to left field, and he suggested, "Let's go on a manhunt, Mr. Master Bear."

Just like that out of a clear blue eye, the boy saw his chance to escape from Bearville Village and Beeline Avenue. So he said with real canine enthusiasm as he stood on three legs and held up his front foot like a pointer and strained against his collar, "Let's go on a manhunt!"

"Alright," said the bear. "But how?"

"How, Sir!" said the boy right back like an Indian because he was really thinking how much fun it would be to play Bears and Indians if he wasn't already so busy playing Dogs and Bears.

"How?" said the bear again rather impatiently.

"Have you got a gun barrel?" the boy asked.

"A gun barrel?" said the puzzled bear.

"That's a barrel where you keep guns in the corner," said the boy. "Or maybe you've got a gun stock even, or a gun stick, or maybe even a stick gun!" argued the boy. You could easily say, 'Stick em up!' if you had a stick gun or a gun stick."

"Did you forget about the manhunt?" asked the bear patiently, for he was beginning to like the boy better every minute even though he didn't make sense sometimes.

"Well, maybe I forgot for a second," admitted the boy. "But I know I'd be good on a manhunt because I've got a good nose for a man." Then he felt his own nose and it did seem a little big for a boy but just about right for when he grew up to it.

"Let's go squirrel hunting in the morning instead!" suggested the bear.

306

"All right, Your Barrel Royness, I mean your Royal Bearness, not your Real Hairiness," he answered kind of absentminded-like. Then the boy growled a little quietly like he was already looking for squirrels. Then he looked out of the corner of his eye just past his glasses rim that had slipped down on his nose to see if the bear liked how fierce and willing he was. Sure he was glad to go squirrel hunting first thing, bright and early in the morning!

After that was decided, and without any further to-do, the bear went into his bear house and the boy tried out his new doghouse. But his boy-chain kept getting tangled up in his legs while he was trying to get all of himself into the dog-sized boy house. It should have been a boy-sized doghouse, he thought. But you could tell it wasn't, because when he got his feet and legs in, his head and one or two extra arms were outside. If he got his head and shoulders and maybe one arm in, then his other parts were out where some other bear's boy could bite him real easy when he wasn't looking. So he just came back out little by little as best he could until all his parts—even the chain and collar—were outside. Then he sat down in front of the doorway and practiced scratching his ears first with one foot, then with the other. He knew that if he was going to be a bear's dog, he'd have to learn to sit on one leg and scratch with the other, but he kept falling over on one side. Finally, he had to give it up as a bad job and just leaned back against his boy house. He sat back on his heels and pulled his knees up under his chin with his chain between his knees, his arms around his knees, and tried to sleep with one eye open like he knew a good bear-dog should.

Finally, morning came, and he could smell the bacon frying in the bear's greased griddle. It made him feel so hungry that he could have worn his boy-collar around his middle it felt so little. Pretty soon the bear came out wiping the hotcake crumbs and syrup and the bacon grease and the fried duck eggs and the honey and butter off of his happy, black face with the back of his paw. The bear paused for a moment in the doorway, and the boy saw in the bear's other paw a dish of Frisky Boy-Biscuits. My, did they ever look delicious! The boy stuck one foot and leg straight out behind him and wagged it real friendly like. He couldn't find a tail anywhere to wag with. It was hard to find anything that early in the morning. He even tried to put his ears back and smile with his teeth, but this embarrassed him because he hadn't brushed his teeth for a whole week, and anyway, his ears just wouldn't go where he wanted them to at all. They just kept sticking out sideways with little brown freckles on the top where they showed through his tousled hair. But the bear knew about how dogs and boys smile and wag their tails, so he was real pleased. He came right out, patted the boy on the head, and put the dish that said "Buster" on it down in front of the boy.

And the bear said, "Here, Buster."

And the boy said, "I'm sorry, Bear Sir, but it's kind of springy plastic, and I can't bust 'er. Anyway, I'd like to keep it for my own. And you shouldn't bust what you own."

This pleased the bear, and he leaned against a tree and scratched his full tummy while he watched the boy eat out of the little red, plastic dog dish full of crispy, crunchy, munchy Frisky Boy-Biscuits.

When the dog-boy had finished his breakfast and licked out the bowl in his best boy-dog way, the bear, in a very business-like manner, walked over by his dog-boy and unsnapped the chain from the ring on the boy house. He called sharply to the dog-boy, "Heel, Buster!"

"He'll what?" asked the boy respectfully as he ran along rather awkwardly beside the bear. His back legs seemed a little long or his arms a little short for smooth traveling on all fours, but he was making the best of it.

It was then that the bear noticed the boy hadn't even been trained to "heel" like the best show dogs. So he repeated his command, "Heel, Buster, heel!"

Then the boy understood and he said, "I'll try." He walked along right behind the bear. But he walked so close that the bear's heel kept hitting the end of his nose, which was lower than his back parts right then. This bothered the boy, and he didn't know for sure if he really liked being a bear's dog-boy very much.

Now in Bearville Village, it was a real "status symbol" for a bear to have a boy for a dog. Most bears felt lucky to even have a dog for a boy, let alone a boy for a dog. So the bear stood up real straight on his hind legs, threw his shoulders back, adjusted his suspenders just right and flipped the chain a little in an important manner as he walked right down the middle of the village street, feeling absolutely full of symbol statuses. He felt so proud! Bears mowing their lawns just played like they didn't see the bear that had boy for a dog.

The dust in the street was still cool and the dew was still shining here and there in the early-morning sun. Right down the street marched the bear and his boy, except that the bear's boy was walking out ahead with the chain straight now and tight, with his collar choking him just enough to make his face a bit too red for anything but an Irish setter or a red cocker spaniel.

They crossed through the tall grass in the meadow and finally came to the more woodsy woods. It was not where bears live but where they go hunting for other animals and maybe even people.

The chain kept getting tangled in the brush and wrapping itself around the boy's legs, so he promptly solved that problem by hopping along a little lopsided on three legs or really on two legs and one hand while holding the chain out to one side with the other hand. This pleased the bear, for he knew the boy was going to work out fine. He seemed smarter than most bears even, and almost as smart as a real doggy-dog. The boy seemed pleased, too. Then it happened.

Right in front of them on an old rotten stump where new little trees were bravely taking root, a feisty little squirrel sat right up on his hind feet and sassed both the boy and the bear right over the top of the acorn it was holding in its little hands. My, how that squirrel sassed the bear for having a boy for a dog. And how it sassed the boy for being a bear's dog.

Not to be completely out-talked, the boy said, "Wow! Look at that squirrel!" This pleased the bear, too, because most dogs just say "Wow!" They don't very often say, "Look at that squirrel!" The bear said, "Buster!"

The boy looked at his chain and said, "No, I didn't but I'd like to!"

The bear just ignored this and went right on. "Buster, you shouldn't just say 'Wow! Look at that squirrel!' but 'Wow, Wow! Look at that squirrel!' and sort of run it together like dog talk."

So, obligingly, the boy practiced on it to himself and then tried it out loud several different ways. He tried to work it into just one or two long words. The first time it sounded enough like wow but not quite enough like squirrel, so he tried again. But this time it came out "squirwowl." This confused even the squirrel, and he dropped his acorn in the confusion and fell backwards into a hollow

308

place in the log and almost broke his back. Anyway, it straightened the curl right out of his tail, and he just lay there on his back, hoping he'd never see another bear with a boy for a dog.

Then the boy remembered about the manhunt and how he was going to fool the bear and get away so he could go home to his mother and sleep between nice, cool, white sheets at home. He didn't tell the bear that it was really his father that he was going to hunt for, but he was working around in that direction right then.

All of a sudden, he began to growl, first high like a girl's voice and then low like a boy's and then in between like a dog's. This was pretty good for a boy whose voice is changing. All this time, he kept scratching the grass and dirt with first one foot and then with the other like he'd seen real dogs do. Once in a while he'd paw the grass with one front foot like he'd seen a bulldog do once.

"Hum," he said again. "I do believe the tracks go this way." And he started following the tracks right straight for home. But the bear didn't know about this yet.

The closer the boy got to his house at the edge of the woods, the more excited he got. But the bear just thought he was a real good man-dog. So he followed along, getting excited, too, until he remembered he'd forgotten his man-gun.

The boy could just see the corner of his own brown house through the trees, with its red tile roof. So he quit barking, "Wow, Wow," and began to say, "Woof, Woof." The bear didn't catch on that he was really saying, "Roof, Roof!" as he pulled harder and harder on the chain, dragging the bear along.

The bear didn't have his gun, but he knew that the scent must be getting hotter, so he said, "Sit, Buster, sit!"

"I know that's it," said the boy, but he didn't know how the bear knew that was it. Then he sat down with his tongue hanging out almost to his dog collar. He was really panting. He was putting out more pants than any suit factory you ever saw.

The bear said, "Buster?"

"I really don't think so," said the boy. "I'm just tired and out of breath and maybe a little bit excited."

"Buster," the bear said again as patiently as ever as he tied the chain to a low limb on the closest tree. "Buster, you stay here and get your breath while I run back to Bearville Village and get my man-gun and some duckshot. We need the duckshot just in case the man ducks when we shoot."

So away the bear ran, this time lumbering fast on all fours and kind of sideways like bears run when they forget their guns and duckshot.

The boy was sitting there on his back feet with his front arms and hands on the ground in front of his back feet just like a real dog would while he waited for the bear to get back. He probably would have waited and waited, and he might have even turned out to be as good a bear's dog as even most dogs, but right then, when he was sitting just right like the bear told him to, he heard his mother open the kitchen door, or thought he did, and sure enough, he could smell the bacon frying and he could smell the hot biscuits and honey and butter and jelly and hotcakes and oatmeal and gingerbread cookies and the peanut butter sandwiches going into his father's lunch bucket. He could smell the hot chocolate on the table and he could almost smell his own socks behind his bedroom door.

Right then he remembered that he wasn't really a bear's dog after all. Why, even a boy that was a bear's dog didn't have to sit like a dog with his hands on the ground. So he just stood right up straight like a real boy and dusted off his hands on the knees of his pants and reached right over and untied his chain from the tree.

He just decided that any smart boy could untie any chain better than even a smart bear could tie it up. So he just untied it and put the whole chain right in his pocket along with his other things. He had just taken his first step toward home when here came that bear with his man-gun and duck-shot.

The bear saw what was happening and he called out polite like, "Buster?"

"No," said the boy, still running. "I didn't bust her. I untied it. So long, Bearsy." He laughed and ducked right behind a big tree and ran for home like mad and slammed the door shut.

Oh my, that bear was mad when he saw how the boy had tricked him. He loaded his gun with duckshot and shot at the door, but it didn't come open. He shot at the windows until it sounded like rain on the roof. But the boy was so busy drinking hot chocolate and eating cookies and hugging his mother that he hardly heard a thing.

The bear finally remembered that he'd forgotten to bring his own lunch, so he went home, too. He finally decided that boys probably make better boys than dogs do, even if they don't work at it very hard.

When he got to thinking about that he wasn't even mad at himself. The boy was so glad not to be a bear's dog anymore that he wasn't mad either. So they lived happily together. I mean, they lived happily, but not together forever and ever and two days more besides that. And when the boy's father came home again that night, he said, "Bears shouldn't have boys for dogs anyway." So that ended the whole business, just like that.

Well, it almost ended right there except that the boy who had been a bear's dog wrote an essay for the newspaper and called it: *Bear Facts About Cruelty to Animals.* He wanted everybody to know that if he was ever a bear with a dog-boy, he would want to buy him a fur-lined collar, keep fresh water in his plastic water pan, and even give him peanut butter and hotcake syrup for his Frisky Boy-Biscuits. His essay said, "If you have a father for a bear, be the best kind of boy or a dog that you can be. If you have a mother for a bear, sometimes, don't do anything to make her growl or bite. Always be nice and kind and thoughtful to mother-bears. Also, if you have a brother for a bear's dog, don't jerk his chain so much or tip over his water dish or borrow his stuff when he doesn't want you to. Always treat all brother bears courteously.

"Remember the time you imagined you were a bear's dog. If you ever have a sister for a bear's baby or even an older one, for heaven's sake treat her better than the Inhumane Society would. Be nice to sister bears, too. And any boy that was ever a bear's dog knows how much nicer home is than sleeping in a doghouse that's too small. Don't forget that anybody who's ever imagined what it's like to be a boy that a bear had for a dog knows he has a lot of things to be thankful for back home. He should always be kind to squirrels, too, and to other wild animals and to pets. For how do we imagine they feel to have a boy that's a bear's dog barking and scaring them half to death. So be kind to all animals."

The boy's conclusion was, if you ever have a dog, you should treat him more like a boy. And if you ever have a boy, don't treat him like a dog, even if you feel like a bear. Now think about that for a while, and don't forget the other lessons in *The Bear Who Had a Boy For a Dog!*

THE GARDEN OF OUR GOD

Come, let us love and labor
    In the Garden of our God.
The great outdoors is His and mine
    Of sky and air and sod.

I'll go with Him to visit.
    I'll look His Garden o'er.
And hand in hand He'll show me
    True pleasures more and more.

I'll see the birds at nesting time.
    I'll hear the stream that sings.
I'll feast my eyes on God's outdoors
    And envy not earth's kings.

I'll see yon Robin Redbreast.
    I'll hear his happy song.
I'll clear forget my troubles
    Lost in gladsome song.

Fleecy lined, eternal clouds
    Float on seas of grey.
On and on they're drifting
    To view another day.

I'll see the swelling blossoms
    Of springtime bursting thru.
I'll see the white gulls sailing
    In skies of crystal blue.

I'll feel the soft green masses
    Of the grasses under feet.
I'll find the shade from branches
    In some tree's cool retreat.

I'll see the ferns all lacey
    In fragile formed design.
I'll walk with God who made them
    And be glad that both are mine.

CREEDE WATERFALL BY GREG WALZ

DAHLIAS BY CAROLINE SEYMOUR

May

~ 1 ~

*In back of the detailed envisioning of achieving faith must be the invincible
purpose that the subjective desire must become an objective fact.*

Wash the eyes of error and teach the soul to see.

PREVENTIVE DISCIPLINE OR CRUTCHES FOR THE RAT RACE!

For all fellow teachers and educational administrators, be professional but be friendly. Smile often. Come to school rested and happy. Don't lose sight of what and who you are, but be cooperative and helpful. As a staff member, you are an individual and have the right to express your opinions clearly in a kindly manner. Profit by your mistakes, but never browbeat yourself. Love your job, or find something else you like better.

Dress well, stand straight, think tall, and the children will respect your discipline. When punishing a child, don't ever let him feel you are mad at him as an individual. Do not make idle, impossible threats—either carry out promised consequences, or do not threaten in the first place. Be positive, not negative, as a teacher or parent, and maintain a positive mental atmosphere in the classroom. Hold the respect of the children, but be able to adjust to the group level of mind. Don't forget that you are teaching students, not just material.

Make lesson guidelines, but stay with group interest as it develops. The class is not a mechanical situation but an organism that grows according to inner necessity and individual needs. Learn to see things from the child's viewpoint as well as from your own. Take time to give a child a reason for doing something and less force will be required.

Do not vent hidden hostilities on the unsuspecting child. If you have something wrong at home to upset you, do not take it out on the child at school. A good seating chart based on the student's ability to concentrate prevents unnecessary disturbances. From the teacher's viewpoint, grades should be rewards, not punishments. Be flexible in grading. Give or take a little according to the individual.

Commend children freely and sincerely. Accentuate their achievements, not their failures. Make teaching an exciting, happy experience whenever possible, for nothing is ever properly learned that isn't gladly learned. Small children are very intuitive. Be sure that you are radiating the feeling, "I like you, and we're having fun." Take time to listen to what they have to say. Their insights are often surprising.

~ 315 ~

Learning to know the children's parents helps to understand the children and is also a part of good public relations. Parent-teacher conferences can be an inspiration. The teacher should maintain the control of the interview—make it short and to the point, and terminate it when you're through. Always try to end on a positive note. Keep awake, alert, creative and mentally active. It's never too late to learn and grow! Remember, you are teaching more than children; they are tomorrow's citizens. Give them something pleasant to remember about their school experiences.

A TREE WEEPS

A tree weeps or seems to weep
   Like the weeping willow tree.
And a tree weeps in the public place
   Where all the world can see.

A tree weeps or seems to weep
   Up on some mountainside.
Or a tree weeps on the ocean shore
   Encouraged by wind and tide.

A tree weeps in your own backyard
   For each has his private grief.
And men like trees would weep alone
   If they could find some true relief.

May

2

*Ideals energize, vitalize, invigorate, chart our courses, measure our values,
and test our methods and motives.*

PLEDGE OF COURAGE

I am courageous. To any disquieting emotion springing up within, I will say, I am in control of my choices! So negative pressures cease to surge and roll, with waves of my inner life and waves of outer circumstance. I will speak authoritatively to any irrational, disturbing emotional upsurging, and I will give positive affirmations of peace, of hope, of rest, of harmony and of successful solution.

I shall hold on courageously and react to all life situations with valor and with confidence. I shall persist in effort and in meditation, in faith, confidence, hope and love.

I instruct the extrasensory faculties of my higher self, in advance, to do the things necessary to counteract for me and for mine, any intended loss of property, wealth, health, or general well-being. I instruct my inner self, under God, to activate an achieving faith and thus to successfully counteract any negative forces not for my best good and for those around me. I am grateful for the miracles of progress, of abundance, of well-being, of success and protection now and forthcoming. I firmly suggest and request that my inner level of consciousness seek and provide the spiritual guidance for my life.

PLANT A ROSE OF REBEL RED

Plant a rose of rebel red
    Beside my cottage door.
Let it climb in trellised ease
    Then plant one white rose more.

Plant a hedge of flagrant red
    And one small rose of white
For I protest conformity
    That claims it's always right.

Just plant an errant, rebel rose
    Beside the church-yard gate
For I rebel against the creeds
    That cry "love" but practice hate.

Go plant a rugged, rebel rose
    On every upward path
Lest courage, faith and hope should fail
    In face of guilt and wrath.

Oh, plant a sad but rebel rose
    Beside the tomb of youth
And may it flower before age dies
    At the barren womb of truth.

Oh plant a loyal, rebel rose
    On the battlefields of strife
To bleed red blood impatiently
    Where death will buy us life.

Now plant a fragrant, rebel rose
    Where the sun is sinking fast
And turn time's face against the wall
    And make life's moments last.

Then plant a withered, rebel rose
    Up by the gates of gold!
Beside Fair Sharon's Rebel Rose
    Where immortal years unfold!

May

~ 3 ~

BRISTLECONE PINE, THOUGHT TO BE APPROXIMATELY 8,000 YEARS OLD (THANKS TO THE KEN GAMLIN FAMILY)

SPRING WALKS TODAY

The scent of spring is in the air,
With perfumed sweetness everywhere.

The bright green sward, the blue of sky,
The gentle breezes passing by;

Each have caught her sweet-voiced plea,
Saying, "Come and walk with me!"

For beauty, splendor, grace, and charm
Have quickly clothed drab winter's form;

And Mistress Spring in garments gay
Is walking through the fields today!

Man is a social creature, not just a money-making machine; he must straighten his aching back, breathe in the fresh air outdoors, learn to look anew, and enjoy the world in which he lives.

The productive brain must be productively fed on a well-balanced, invigorating diet of variety and high quality.

They learn to work best who learn to play well; and recreation should properly include relaxation, entertainment, amusement, creative activity and play!

May

4

*The God who could design the beauty of the peacock's tail
can provide food for the other end.*

LAUGH WITH ME

ACTING: "Most individuals can play the fool without special practice, having played the part before."

ACTION: "Only action or an act of God can perform miracles. If you're not sure of one, work on the other."

AGE: "He who has a prune for a face is better than he who has one for a heart."

ARGUMENT: "If you are under water or in an argument, hold your breath as long as you can; in either case, it may save your life."

CHOIR MEMBER

So embarrassed
   She thought she'd die
Was the choir member
   Who swallowed the fly.

Her mouth had been
   Opened a little too wide
And the fly thought:
   "It's cozy inside!"

The hot, scented air
   That softly blew
Drew him swiftly on
   As inward he flew.

(CONTINUED ON NEXT PAGE)

321

Past the half-brushed,
    Strong pearly gates
Of her store-bought
    New dental plates.

Her hot, fetid
    "Garlic-y" breath
Nearly choked
    That poor fly to death.

The pendulous
    Palate on top
Made him slide
    To a sickening stop.

Purple tonsil mountains
    Rose on each side.
They pulsed like an
    Angry ocean tide.

With a gag, a gurgle
    And a gasping choke,
The nightmare spell
    Finally broke.

The explosive air
    On the outgoing tide
Blew him back quickly
    And safely outside.

Now the choir member
    With the flutter of wings
Sings false "fly-brato"
    Whenever she sings!

May

5

Let thy life be like the cool, green ivy that, spreading over stone and weathered windowsill, hides well the faults of all it clings to for support.

THE ARTIST HAND OF GOD

The blue of sky with gentle touch
Still moves the heart with tears,
For God the Artist painted such
In distance yesteryears.

And peopled earth with flowers that bend
Where fern and grasses nod;
Who fashioned all earth's comeliness?
The artist hand of God.

He paints them fresh from year to year
As seasons come and go.
No other than the Artist God
Such loveliness could show.

O, God, take up thine artistry,
Thy brushes and the oil,
And paint with me life's canvass, too,
Lest I its beauty spoil.

TRUE LOVE IS ONE

I fain would call thee to my heart, my love,
    And cheek-to-cheek would hold thee close at hand
In shaded bowers canopied above
    Lest time's lone sentinel in silence stand.

I fain would sing to thee, my Gentle One,
    Nor could the nightingale, his serenade,
Contend with mine when I, forlornly done,
    Have given to the skies my accolade.

I fain would hold thee to my surging breast
    And let the coursing tide of Love's intent
Voyage thy ship, nor ever let it rest,
    Till anchored in Love's port you 'bide content,
Where ocean and love's ship no longer twain
    Shall rise and fall as one—and thus remain!

May

6

Tranquility fosters longevity, and happiness is the harbinger of health.

Books are the pure distillation of the mind, undiluted by the frailty of the flesh that held the cup where inspiration's dews first fall.

GOALS AND OBJECTIVES OF HUMANISTIC EDUCATION

The following objectives serve as guidelines in our own Relaxed Learning approach.

The purpose of Humanistic Education should be to promote a success-oriented philosophy of achievement in education, to inspire self-improvement and self-motivation, and to open potential mental reserves through impartation of knowledge, skills, inspiration and positive mental attitudes that are essential to the highest functioning of the integrated individual.

The purpose of Humanistic Education should be to better understand and utilize all levels of the mind to strive for and employ all feasible resources for a breakthrough of effectiveness in learning efficiency fundamental to upgrading the quality of self-orientation and individualized education.

The purpose of Humanistic Education should be to develop values, provide value guidance, encourage favorable behavioral changes, and promote in-depth intellectual, emotional, cultural and social development. It should implement successful interpersonal relationships and increase enrichment of all possible opportunities for life and learning. It should provide for leadership training with motivation and guidelines for greater service in the circle of one's influence and for a more informed participation in the processes and interactions of a Humanistic Democracy in an ever-converging world community.

IDAHO TREASURES

I love thy great cathedral'd rocks
    Like walls thy towering mountains;
Thy rolling hills, and dwarfed gray sage,
    Vast rivers, crystal fountains.

Thy plains of ripened yellow grain,
    Thy ribboned highways winding,
Are held by us as treasures rich
    That men rejoice in finding.

WHEN SHEARING TIME IS PAST

The sheep like gray rocks in the sage
    Close packed or scattered 'round,
Are grazing thru' the stunted brush
    That marks the desert ground.

The tender growing summer grass
    That tints the waste with green
Is cropped beneath a blazing sun
    As flocks their forage glean.

I see the herder's wagon home,
    The sheep dogs circling past,
The flocks are in the sage again
    And shearing time is past.

May

7

ODESSA, BLACK SEA BY SERGEY CHERNOMORETS

The art of happiness is the fine balance found somewhere between grateful awareness,
increased achievement, and adjusted desires.

PRAYER AND THE WILD ROSE

I found this little wild rose
    Down in the valley of prayer.
Its face was anointed with morning dew,
    All warm with the sunlight there.

The roots gripped deep in the mother earth
    That fed the leaves and stem.
They spoke to me and I understood
    As I gazed at the fairest of them.

I thought how like the soul in prayer,
    Fresh washed in heaven's dew;
Its face upturned was like my soul,
    For, Heavenly Father, it looked to you.

A rich, sweet fragrance clung to it,
    Deep down where the petals start;
And I knelt in prayer by the roses there
    And prayed for a purer heart.

May

8

Friendship is a spaceship that crosses isolation's interplanetary space.

FRIENDSHIP

"No man has truly conquered an enemy until he has made him a loyal friend."
"Friendship chooses with wisdom and criticizes with care."

Usually, friendship is thought to be a social relationship between two persons in which there is mutual attraction and cooperation. The term is usually applied to relationships in which sexual attraction is not present or is not emphasized. Romantic attraction or love is most often felt for only a few persons, while on the other hand, we feel the relation of friendship for numerous people. It matters little whether we speak of our affection for our friends as love or friendship. It seems that we learn to like our friends, and they learn to take pleasure in us, as a consequence of many pleasant experiences together.

So what causes friendships to develop? Are there specific foundations upon which friendships are formed? Psychologists have found that, for both women and men, close friends are more alike than they are different. The similarities among friends are considerable in ideals and moral standards, interests in sports, and neatness of dress, for example. One psychologist requested college students to state their reasons for being attracted to friends. The list of traits ranked highest were:

- Sincerity
- Consistency, and an
- Affectionate disposition

Another study about friendship demonstrated a definite evidence of likeness in morals, manners, ideas, beliefs, tastes in food, amusements, and appreciation of the arts. For a happy friendship a person must enjoy his or her own role in the friendship as well as the relationship itself. The friendship is reasonably expected to bring out the best in each person.

BOLIVIA BY BOB ERWIN

May

9

Responsibility accepted and duty attended make achievement expected for effort expended.

MY FATHER TO MY MOTHER

There's nothing as sweet as a mother;
　　There's nothing so dear to me,
As the mother of my own dear children,
　　Whose picture before me I see.

She's stood by my side like no other;
　　She's "pal'd" with me thru the years;
A smile on her lips and her eyes—
　　Thru sunshine and yet thru tears.

She went thru the valley of shadow;
　　Was lonesome when nobody knew;
Stayed by our children and loved them,
　　As only a mother could do.

Now that the family is older,
　　Her grandchildren are cause for pride.
She's still the sweetest of mothers
　　And I'm glad she's here by my side.

　　　　　　Thanks, Dad

No hill is too steep or mile too long when your life companion is taken along.

TO A FAST-FOOTED SEAGULL

Run, little seagull.
    They say life's a race.
Outrun all the problems
    You wouldn't dare face.

But you've got to hurry
    If you keep ahead.
Might miss your own funeral
    After you're dead.

Run, little seagull.
    I think you are brave.
If you stretch your legs
    You'll outrun that wave!

I knew you'd make it.
    And it was worth the try.
But you know if I had wings,
    I think I'd fly!

ITALIAN COAST BY ELLIOT FALLAS

THE CHILDRENS' WALL (WESTWOOD GRANDDAUGHTER)

May

10

Helpfulness invigorates the helper, and the helping hand is strengthened for its own.

A MOTHER'S FAITH AND LOVE

A mother's love is a life and a creed
    And its value to earth is untold.
It's more than a life or a creed
    Since faith is the treasure it holds.

With faith in her children and in God
    And love for the hurting of this earth—
Oh, a mother's love and a mother's faith
    Are treasures of infinite worth.

For a mother's faith and a mother's love
    Are anchors that hold us fast.
O God of the Ages, grant us, we pray
    Such mothers while time shall last!

IDENTITY

I'm baptized with every baby
    And blossom with every rose.
I'm a part of the holy water
    And the source from which it flows.

I speak with words that are spoken,
    I live in the laughter or fears.
I'm progress and future a-borning
    The herald of dawning years.

I'm peace and love and power,
    The Unity of the One who is All;
The hearing ear and seeing eye
    That answers the quiet call.

I'm sun and rain and shadows.
    I'm the sky and cloud and hills.
I'm the music of God and heaven,
    The emptiness and Allness fills.

May

~ 11 ~

EINSTEIN BY KARRIE JACKSON

GREAT MINDS

A great mind is a ship
   With full sails set free,
And the mind is an island
   Alone in the sea.

Life is an island surrounded
   By frothy white spray,
Of shallow-minded thinkers
   Splashing at play.

A great mind is a sun
   Bright shining at night
Surrounded by pale moons
   Reflecting its light.

And thought is a treasure
   Far richer than gold
That great minds will gather
   From the new and the old.

So away from the shallows,
   Away from earth's shore.
There are thought-planets to conquer.
   There are treasures in store!

May

12

*There is more potential in every person, under the false-bottom
trunk of self-doubt, than even his or her best friends surmise.
Don't sell the trunk for a song!*

Consider Your Potential: Don't Sell Short

There are harmonies of change within the substructurings of natural law. There are melodious, rhythmic changes in all perceived and unperceived levels and functions of the entire universe. The constant intersection of a multiplicity of energy vortexes gives rise to an existentialism of adaptation, variety, evolution, progress, retrogression, and constant change in the matter, motion, mathematics, manifestation and mutation of materiality in an ever-changing kaleidoscopic world of interacting polarity opposites.

Evolving environment, interchanging energies and ever-reoccurring responses and negations of natural and supernatural forces preclude a stability in nature other than one based on the predictability and dependability of resulting change. Opposites in interaction produce adjustment in reaction but change in the substructure of this accommodating reality. The human race must now adapt itself to the accelerated rate of change and progress. The express usage of "extrasensory" abilities may be a prime requisite for successful survival in a too rapidly changing, technological society severely shaken and continuously vibrating to the stress factors inherent in its accelerated progress.

Conscious, purposeful self-improvement, with an understanding of its needs and its benefits, can be clearly held in the focus of the attention at a level that becomes effective in its implementation. When man realizes that his subconscious mind, or lower self, is often an emotionally discontent, rebellious alien within himself, he then begins a process of inner renovation and search for a cure. This often leads him into extremes and into cultish adaptations of hoped-for cures. There must be an integration of all diffracted selves within the triune of man.

The key to its smooth and sane functioning is the emphasis on the compulsion of love and compassion as the effective bond in the integrated personality of man within himself and in all of his interpersonal relationships. It is true that man is essentially mental and spiritual in nature. The physical and the chemical are additions and appendages to his real self.

Man is worthy of possessing those things which he instinctively desires within the framework of the beautiful, the true, the positive, and the good. No imagined shame or guilt should keep us from our God-inspired desires and their proper fulfillment in life.

Man is capable of anticipating change through the exercise of an activated precognition. But it must always admit of the natural limitations of the person employing the gift, plus the unforeseen decisions, actions, and reactions of those people involved who also, by change of course, can change the ultimate outcome or destiny of that which was projected as a probability.

WHAT IS A MIRACLE?

A miracle might be a condition
That someone reconditioned by prayer.
A miracle might be a victory
Where unselfishness its crust would share.

A miracle might be a decision
Where wrong gave place to right,
For a miracle can come like the sunrise
That dispels the gloom of night.

Or a miracle could be a person
Who found some goal to seek.
With God you can become a miracle
Just any old day of the week!

May

13

Courage is not an old blind horse, driven tremblingly up to the precipice brink in uncertainty and fear. True valor is Pegasus with spread wings glinting in the morning sun, with arched neck, flowing mane, and rippling muscles of steel, whose pawing feet strike sparks from the gravel on the chasm's edge as he crouches for the confident leap, with eyes on the other side, unmindful of the winding river and the treetops far below.

PEGASUS: CAN WE WIN THE RACE?

As we consider the environmental effects of various harmful and hazardous, chemically caused problems, we ask, "Is this an inevitable situation? Does progress necessarily include negative effects? If our land and our health suffer from the results of our activities, is restoration and healing possible? If so, how? What will be required, and what must we do?"

What are you willing to pay for environmental safeguards? How convinced are you that we have out-of-balance problems? How determined are you to be a soldier in the battle for overcoming these potentially fatal problems? Big question: Will you participate in this synergism for balance? Can you visualize being involved as part of the solution to the situation right where you live?

Napoleon Hill stated that what the mind can CONCEIVE and BELIEVE, it can ACHIEVE. Do we understand the problem? Do we believe there is a functional answer to this dilemma? And so we ask ourselves again, "What can I do to help?"

Friends and relatives of mine have died in recent years because toxicity accumulated as the result of a lack of balance in their systems. It affected health and ultimately cost their lives. My life has been blessed with beautiful children and precious grandchildren. I love them and care very much about their well-being: Thus, I am highly motivated to CONCEIVE ideas and understand our dilemma, to BELIEVE there is a solution to this destruction, and to work to see answers ACHIEVED.

"Ask not what else can I take, nor which of nature's rules may I break, but rather, in my environment, what can I do to help?" I love you; and as cohabitants of our spaceship earth, I care about the safety and well-being of each of us. I care about the preservation of our planet. Are we yet so convinced that the problem must be solved, that we are willing to set aside some of our own "personal rights" which may include, for example, greed, convenience, or old habits? Would we be willing to do this to help return balance to spaceship earth?

Can we achieve this great task? Can we reverse the attitudes of ignorance and the greed of the past? YES. We must develop a strong philosophy of life, rearrange our priorities, and resolve our will to win. After all, if you have nothing to lose by trying, and perhaps everything to gain, by all means we should TRY.

After consideration, what do you think, Pegasus? Can we win the race?

WITHOUT PEGASUS TO LEAD YOU

A million gray horses
With flowing white manes
   Come galloping up to the shore.
In long serried ranks
They come charging along
   And always, always there are more.

With the roar of a lion
In angry pursuit
   They nicker and plunge and neigh.
With rolling white eyes
And nostrils aflare
   They come pawing huge problems away.

Charge in! Wheel on!
Then disappear.
   Stand dripping and quivering still.
Without Pegasus to
Lead your last charge,
   You never can conquer my hill!

May

14

I KNOW THOU ART REAL

Back of Thy light and Thy splendor,
　　Back of Thy immutable laws,
Back even of truth would I find Thee
　　As truth's illimitable Cause.

Fairer in form than the angels,
　　For they are but forms of Thy thought;
Fairer than all of Thy handiwork,
　　I behold in Thee all I have sought.

Omnipotence, omniscience and perfection
　　Are the garments that around Thee glow,
But beyond the known is the Knower.
　　Thy Transcendent Self I must know.

Beyond the thoughts I am forming,
　　Beyond the deep longings I feel,
Are Thy beckoning arms, Oh, my Father,
　　And intuitively I know Thou art real!

TREE TALK

I don't really feel sorry
    For you, sturdy tree.
I'm glad you're alive
    And communicating with me.

I move my bench over
    To sit closer by.
I hold hands with your trunk
    Your secrets to pry.

In closeness together
    Of true harmony
I would learn the deep secrets
    That others can't see.

I'm one with all things
    Cradled in earth,
But I received of God's Spirit
    In the hour of my birth.

We are the same yet different
    As we reach for the sky.
This secret of kinship
    Is the secret I'd pry.

The horse knows his manger, the dog knows his corner, the homing pigeon knows his perch, and happy is the man who knows that home is the closest place to heaven on this earth.

May

15

I'M GLAD YOU ARE MINE

You're part mother, part sister,
    Part brother to me.
You have everything plus
    Sweet femininity.

You're wholesome and efficient,
    Capable and strong.
A virile, melodious,
    Unforgettable song.

You're an executive, brave soldier,
    Dependable friend,
A woman in whom all virtues
    Plus loveliness blend.

You're so patient and forgiving,
    So constant and kind.
You seldom forget what should be
    Called back to mind.

You're yielding and soft
    Or firm and upright.
You're a worker by day
    And a lover by night.

I'm sorry for the lonesome
    Who for such comradeship pine;
But, Sweetheart, you have everything,
    And I'm glad you are mine.

WELCOME HOME BY WANDA KIPPENBROCK

May

16

A willing gift is doubly blessed; but he who gives himself gives best!

PRIMAL CAUSE

From one cloud
    Fall countless drops of rain.
From one wound
    Are multiplied impulses of pain.

From one sun
    Beam many rays of light.
From one velvet sky
    Shine many stars at night.

From one dynamo
    A sea of lightbulbs burn.
From one continuing power line
    Our busy factories turn.

From one broadcasting tower
    Endless radios speak.
And back of every effect
    Some hidden cause we seek.

From the One great God,
    Whose Spirit is Primal Cause,
The challenged mind can speak
    Thru all nature's extended laws.

The immeasurable mind would
    Its thought-forms multiply
As endless, concrete images
    Caught in mortal, mirrored eye.

(CONTINUED ON NEXT PAGE)

From the one, the countless many
> Would seek to manifest.
But unity in divergence
> Is the foundation on which we rest.

WHEN YOU GIVE ALL THINGS

When you give all things
> You have nothing to lose.
When you want nothing
> You have nothing to choose.

You no longer identify
> With material self
And you gladly forsake all
> That belonged to false self.

When you see all things finally
> As no longer your own
Then loss is not true loss
> Though you stand there alone.

Yet all things are yours
> As you draw freedom's breath.
Having died to life's illusions
> You no longer fear death.

Thus the God of your new self
> Shares His unending stores,
For when you give all things
> Then all things are yours!

May

17

Individual incentive is the seedling of success; actual achievement is the harvest brought home through persistence and labor.

GIVE ME THE BOOK OF TOMORROW

Most of the things dull mortals know
    Are drawn from the book of the past,
Things they've read and heard and learned,
    Bottled messages on time's shore cast.

But give me a book of God's memories
    Of thoughts unthought as yet.
Give me a history of future things
    So tomorrow I won't forget.

Give me a book of things to be
    And a knowledge of here and now.
Give me an insight that comprehends
    New things that the past can't allow.

Give me the book of tomorrow.
    Let life mysteries here be revealed.
How the Spirit manifests into matter
    In energy's unified field.

Give me the book of tomorrow
    And wisdom to understand
The spiritual laws in relation
    To natural laws the Creator planned.

INDUSTRY

The honeybee flies onward,
    With industry's flag unfurled,
Fifty thousand miles on wing
    Or twice around the world.

He gathers a pound of honey,
    In a lifetime rich and sweet,
Then back to hive and home to die
    On worn-out wings and feet.

The rustle of his busy wings,
    His happy, buzzing voice,
Rise up to testify when done
    That industry was his choice.

May

~ 18 ~

Meditation, reflection and creative thought should become a mental habit,
a way of observing, and evaluating life experiences.

MOTHER AND CLEANLINESS

"He who wallows with the pigs is unwanted in the parlor."

"Cleanliness has its own rewards; but the dirty punish both themselves and others."

"Cleanliness begins in the order and purity of a righteous heart, but it must not stop there."

A MAN NEVER OUTGROWS HIS MOTHER

A man never outgrows his mother,
    My brother once said to me.
And the child grown older and wiser
    Still cries for what used to be.

A man never outgrows his mother
    And still misses the tender care,
And longs for the touch remembered
    And for a hand that no longer is there.

A man never outgrows his mother,
    But listens in the silence to hear
The accents of gentle consoling
    That no longer fall on his ear.

He misses her step in the hallways
    And longs for the past to return,
But the voice and the step have faded
    Like smoke where the dry leaves burn.

(CONTINUED ON NEXT PAGE)

A man never outgrows his mother.
　　Her prayers were heavenward sent.
Her unspoken vibrations came softly
　　In language with special intent.

No man can outgrow his mother,
　　Flesh of her flesh and her bone.
The light of her mind and vision
　　In the light of her sons' eyes have shone.

A man can never outgrow his mother
　　Nor the childhood songs that she sang.
And memory can still hear the echoes
　　Where the voices of childhood once rang.

Ah, Mother, come sing me a song again.
　　I'm gray, world-weary and worn.
The joys I thought life had to give
　　Now fester in my heart like a thorn.

Mother of mine, please hear me.
　　And come talk with me once in a while.
The journey will be easier if I hear you say,
　　"Hello, Son! You can make the last mile."

And thank you for being such a mother
　　That your children can never forget.
Stay close while we finish the journey
　　Thru the valleys of shadowed regret.

Come, walk down the isles of eternity
　　Thru the gates that welcomed you in.
Then I'd like to sit by your knee once more
　　Where eternities always begin!

May

~ 19 ~

AMALFI AT NIGHT BY ELLIOT FALLAS

WHERE THE YACHATS FLOWS INTO THE SEA

Down where the Yachats River
    Flows into the white-crested sea.
Down where the seagulls winging
    Soar happy, far and free.

Down where the darting swallows
    Flash thru the clear, still air.
Down where the river flows seaward
    Its freshness and freedom to share.

Here the green of the distant foliage
    In multitudinous hue,
Is marked with ghost white sentinels
    Of dead trees commanding the view.

Here the gray and the gold and the purple
    Where the soft sun has recently set,
Casts their glint on the rocky shoreline
    Where gray waves splash cold and wet.

Here the green of the distant ocean
    Stretches farther and farther away
And the soft sky stoops to kiss it
    At the close of another day.

The green moss on the rocks below us
    And on the tide flats now revealed
Stretch onward as cool and inviting
    As the green of a new-grown field.

Here where the Yachats River
    And the ocean are blended as one
There is peace and purpose for living
    When a summer's day is done.

May

20

The forgetter will be forgotten and the efficient will take his place.

ACCOUNTABILITY AND INSPIRATION IN EDUCATION

What is inspiration in education? It is the key to accountability. It is the positive emotional lubricant that makes planned effort flow smoothly and almost effortlessly in the desired direction.

Inspiration in education is a river flowing through the gates of the dam to turn the wheels and dynamos of all practicality. It is the lifeblood of education and the vital force of being. It throbs and pulses in zestful living. It laughs in recreation and play. It works long hours that seem but minutes in the half-forgetful absorption of self-expression and creativity. It is the essence of life, the heartbeat of achievement. It is like the pounding of the surf playing and working away at the ocean shores of all activity.

Inspiration in education is a song that sings the harmony of universal things. It is the strength of the draft horse with his sweating shoulders against the cold collar. It is the feeling of the unbeatable drive in the piston-like propulsion of the racehorse with the wind in its mane and its heart bursting with the joy of competition and the prospect of being first across the finish line.

Inspired education is the foe of mediocrity, the sister of creativity, and the best defense against failure.

It is the subconscious feel of intuitive victory that the cyclist feels when he and his motorcycle are one unit cornering the track and stretching out for the straightaway on the final lap. It is the singleness of purpose born of the uncluttered mind whose sense of direction is accurate and whose detachment from the unnecessary and the secondary has been completed. Its secret is the service of selfless self-expression set aflame.

Inspiration in education is the whir of rising wings when forward thrust overcomes resistance, where lift laughs at gravity and lofty levitation of inner being changes the entire perspective of life.

Inspiration in education is the eagle's-eye viewpoint of purposeful optimism, the life-confident, self-confident assurance of the individual who expects the cooperation of a compatible universe. It is the warm, anticipated handclasp of congratulation, pride of participation, the dependability of teamwork and the overflow of released life forces that rise resistless and beautiful to make the desert places blossom with the verdant foliage and fruit of manifest accomplishment.

Inspired education is the love of life, the joy of self-expression, the song of unselfish service, and the action of purposeful achievement. It is the spark of genius, the unconquerable spirit of adventure in the pulsing blood of the pioneer. It is sincerity, earnestness, dynamic drive and the cadence of conquest!

A FORGOTTEN FORGET-ME-NOT

A lovely flower grew in a garden
    In a corner, alone, by itself.
Somebody picked its head off
    And let it dry on a dusty shelf.

I'd be lonesome without my roots
    And the water in the garden soil.
My wilted heart would be lonely, too,
    In a world of dry turmoil.

A lonely flower has perfume
    And fragrance it would gladly share.
It needs a nose to smell it
    And somebody to really care.

Lonely people, like plucked flowers,
    Should grow in somebody's flowerpot,
For who wants to be a left-alone,
    Forgotten forget-me-not!

LEAD US

Lord lead us from the seeming
    To the actual and the true.
Help us leave the dying past,
    Give courage for the new.

Lead us from our empty selves
    To fulfillment's fellowship.
My grace and praise and love
    Overflow the heart and lip.

Lead us in the Father's ways,
    There's much to learn and do.
May the Gates of Heaven swing wide
    When our pilgrimage is thru!

May

~ 21 ~

Enthusiasm is contagious power. Its high-frequency vibrations are in tune with the energy pulsations of all creation.

INSPIRATION AND TEACHER ACCOUNTABILITY

Inspired leadership must also condition itself to a positive reaction regardless of opposing or co-operating circumstances. The person, not the emotion, must always be in the driver's seat. The horse can't sit in the saddle; and emotion, although it is a driving force, must always be directed and driven, controlled and encouraged, held back, whipped up, or pulled to a halt when it is expedient in the nature judgment of the administrative driver. Leaders must, by the strength of their inspired leadership, counteract the hot-air pollution of negativity and rise above the dubious mind-smog of resistance and possible failure. But this is why they chose to be leaders.

Inspiration and teacher accountability are inseparably linked. Educational accountability is fact, not fiction. Inspiration in education generates the energy to arise to the challenge of self-directed self-improvement. Tiredness gets out of bed, dresses and "goes to town." Ill health finds that physical action and increased awareness are more fun than reading cards of condolence. Laziness stretches farther than it intended to, opens its eyes, jumps to its feet and joins the parade of champions! Inspiration increases mental wattage as the blood flows faster and farther, and ideas and actions cry out to be born. Thought leaps beyond the mind and telegraphs its inspiration to others who are receptive so that the awakened mind becomes an unconscious center of stimulation—a control tower of positive, although unvoiced, inspiration directives.

Inspiration in education makes a lesson plan come alive and throws a luster on the printed page. It makes the words and thoughts easier to read, to hear and to understand. It inspires obedience, stimulates comprehension and evokes the cooperation of students in the classroom, making learning an adventure and a pleasure.

Inspiration stimulates the will to achieve. Inspired teachers must face, deep within, the battle of life's accountability and the necessity of continuous self-improvement. They must will to win. They must have some great goals and some personal, insignificant things to live for that have special meaning to them alone. They must basically come to the conclusion that it is actually easier to earn and enjoy the fruit of the accountable and creatively courageous life than to work for and endure the fruit of failure. They must accept life and the will to live it. They will mesh gears with reality and find somewhere to begin. Further directions will arise from the nature of their circumstances as they move out along the line of their inspired action.

Inspired teachers must have clear-cut goals and objectives. They must crystallize their thinking, improve their methods and check their road map along the way. Inspiration arises naturally when our conflicting directions are brought into a correlated drive of united purpose. It is here that our goals and plans play an important part. The elimination of the nonessential, the subjugation of the secondary and the correlation of the primary purposes are the foundations of emotional release and enthusiastic living.

To attain and maintain enthusiasm, inspired teachers must evaluate personal successes, recount conquests and move on to other phases of the planned achievements. The chief focus or attention must be in the here and now, where enthusiasm is confidence at the bat, endurance is circling the bases and courage is sliding home. Inspired teachers will have the highest batting average and the best accountability scores. Inspiration is the stuff from which champions are made! And teachers are champions!

HOW GREAT IS GOD?

How wise must be the nature
    Of the God who once designed
The multicolored butterfly
    And all life forms that we find?

How pure must be the nature
    Of the God of love and peace
Whose harmony and happiness
    Our bounties would increase?

How great must be the nature
    Of the God we barely know?
But the evidence is everywhere
    His silent footsteps go!

May

22

Most consequences are but the late harvest of our early plantings, whether bad or good.

The premature appearance of the aging process is the result of the subjective acceptance of the feelings and mental pictures of the characteristics of age.

ADMINISTRATIVE ACCOUNTABILITY AND INSPIRATION

Inspiration in education is the loadstone of leadership. It attracts co-workers like a fragrant flower attracts the swarming bees. There can be no true leadership without inspired followers. An organization must have purposeful people as well as products. You must have people who rally around a banner or cause—people who will work with you, fight for you and share the enthusiasm of your plan and purpose from apples to accountability.

It is the responsibility of inspired leadership to know what it wants, when it is wanted, where it can be obtained, why it is wanted, and how you can go about getting it. Leaders who know the how, why, where and what have already built into their being the steadfastness and assurance of continued enthusiasm, because their emotional drives have intelligent outlet, purpose and direction. Their organization and circle of influence will vibrate to their won sureness, knowledgeable authoritativeness and inspiration.

The atmosphere of inspired administration tends to draw others around the inspired educator. There is something catching about earnestness and sincerity, which alerts others who feel as well as hear the purposeful sound and see or sense the vibrant body tones of the inspired administrator.

There must be a different sound in the inspired leader's voice. It must say, "Let's go places. Let's do meaningful, exciting things. Let's make life sing and shout!"

The energy of administrative leadership must inspire others not alone by *what* is said but also by *how* it is said. Administrative accountability must measure up to the stature of the positive, inspired person and become the wellspring of inspiration in education!

I challenge you to be an inspired person! There is no other reasonable response to the challenge of accountability than *inspiration in education!*

SYMBOLIC, OLD OCEAN

Angry, grey ocean, hoary with age,
Biting and lashing in fury and rage!

Beat on the rocks and leap in the air
Wildly waving the suds in your hair.

Frustration, defeat and surges of power
Pent up through the eons to be spent in an hour.

Lash then, and splash then and make the surf fly.
Break on the shoreline and lie there and die.

I hate you and I love you, you ocean of grief
Sinking my hope-ships on your sly hidden reef.

Go rolling with laughter and devilish glee.
You can have all my cargo but you can never claim me.

I know you are symbolic of life's forces unseen
But the beachcombers and seagulls will pick your
                                    teeth clean.

And man will soon master the force of your wave,
Discover your treasure in each hidden cave.

You'll carry our ships to the farthest shore.
We'll harness you and work you 'till you're tired and sore.

I'm a courageous coward who knows of your strength!
When you are spent on the sand dunes and have
                                    measured your length,

I'll stand on some high hill and laugh you to scorn
Though your waves surged immortal before I was born.

I'll laugh at your stupid, monotonous ways,
And the futile repetition of all of your days.

We'll dredge all the secrets from each hidden part,
Let the salt in your tears cure the wounds in
                                    your heart.

We'll be friends, old ocean, but stay where you are.
Come talk it over, but come only so far!

May

23

Determination fortifies courage, increases confidence, energizes purpose, clears the vision and strengthens the will to win!

MY STRONG FRIEND

"This farming-rancher spoke kindly with his eyes, clearly with his lips, and sincerely from his heart, and he was both heard and remembered."

"His words were weighed in judgment and voiced in kindness and were sturdy seeds planted in the garden of the hearers, and his words produced fragrance and fruitage in due season."

OREGON TRAIL STRENGTH

The man from Oregon
    Sits tall in the saddle
As he rides a horse
    Few men would straddle.

The untamed spirit
    Of an entrepreneur's creed
Is harder to curb
    Than a Roman-nosed steed.

Its sinuous muscles
    Like coils of steel,
Are bunched for the race
    Or to sunfish and wheel.

And the burrs under the blanket
    That somebody placed,
Could have thrown a good rider
    In utter disgrace.

(CONTINUED ON NEXT PAGE)

But the man from Oregon
      With reins firm in hand,
Was looking ahead
      Not for someplace to land.

And the horse sensed the grip
      Of the strong rancher's legs
As it lathered and pranced
      Like it was walking on eggs.

It would have exploded
      But it didn't quite dare
For the hand of the Oregonian
      Held its head in the air.

It couldn't buck loose
      And it couldn't shirk,
So they called it "Challenge"
      And put it to work.

And the "Rough Rider," Teddy
      In the grandstand on high,
Pulled at his mustache
      And said on the sly,

"That man from Oregon
      Takes top money, I'd say.
He's glued to his saddle
      Like he could ride there all day."

So Teddy took his Stetson,
      His boots and his spurs
And said to the Oregonian,
      "Here pardner, they're yours."

"No other ranching settler
      come early or late,
Ever looked better or rode taller
      in a saddle in Oregon state!"

May

~ 24 ~

GRAVITY IS WINNING BY CAROLINE SEYMOUR

EXPERTS

A little learning is a dangerous thing
    When coupled with conceit.
While knowledge held in foolish hands
    Puts wisdom in retreat.

Pride wed to little learning spawns
    An ugly brood of deformity
That doubts the true, rejects the new
    And insists on stale conformity.

Such ill-taught pride can easily
    Tell the artist how to paint
Or criticize in confidence
    The sinner or the saint.

It claims more skill in untaught hands
    Than great physicians could possess.
It claims its right to spurn and scorn,
    To criticize and bless.

It knows its music better far
    Than composers old or new.
I just heard the "candid camera" click!
    But is it fixed on me or you?

Do you want to be a man, a mouse, or just a miserable mistake?
Choose one; or, if you prefer, you can be a miserably mistaken, male mouse.

May

25

*All nature is God's Temple; the sunsets are His stained-glass windows, and sky
His blue-vaulted dome, the harmony of nature from the thunder to the bird-song is His
full pipe organ, and all rocks, stones, or resting places everywhere are His benches,
and the congregation is composed of all the listening world; the only collection
that the angel ushers take is the tribute of our love and praise as they share our sacrament
of service as we rise to labor in the same spirit that we paused to worship and to pray.*

RESPONDING TO LOVE

Every living thing, including humans, need love. Love is so universal that daily we may observe examples of responding to the need for love. The power of love bridges all boundaries.

Some time ago we had the privilege of spending three days with Cleave Baxter in San Diego, California. Some examples from his book, *The Secret Life of Plants*, made the news on several different occasions. As Baxter related many details of his work, he demonstrated that your plants know what you are thinking, and how his plants and flowers unfold in healthy loveliness as he lovingly cares for them. You may recall reading in the news that plants can react to the emotions of human beings. Baxter recorded the impulse from the plant on the equivalent of a lie detector attached to the leaf of a plant. When the plant was yelled at, it would actually make movement, and you could register the trauma. The experiments went so far as to prove that, when there was violence in a room, or where there had been violent abuse going on, and when the person causing the ruckus returned to the room, the plant reacted as though it feared it might happen again.

On one occasion, Baxter related this story. He had gone to the grocery store several years prior and stated that, when leaving his home, he would always leave his analyzing recorder on his plants so that he would have a record of whatever his plants were doing. Baxter said that he arrived at the grocery store, and when he was about to leave, he checked his pocket to pay the bill and found that he had lost his wallet. In that moment of concern, he checked his watch. When he went home, the mild trauma that he had sensed at the grocery store was recorded by each of his plants on their individual instruments.

Further discussion with Baxter revealed that, a month or two later, he was involved in a car accident. During this trauma, the plant instrumentation demonstrated that the plants sensed his plight, and the trauma was measured; it showed up on the testing equipment. Can you tell me what was going on with the plants? What frequency, what mechanism, what is that plus and minus or that medium by which this love and concern travel? We observe in our own experience plants, flowers, animals and humans—*all* living things, to some degree or another, long for and respond beautifully to *love*.

Have you known people who experienced what they determined to be a loss of love? Their bodies may have physically continued to live and mechanically existed, but the joy of living did not exist. *Life* began to fade away because of their loss of *love*—their sense of being needed and wanting love. If all living things need and want to be loved, shall we accept the challenge to practice more dynamic love?

There is a wonderful story about a great man, Dr. George Washington Carver. Dr. Carver was inducted into the Hall of Fame/Inventor Profile, 1890. He was an agricultural chemist who developed crop rotation methods for conserving plant nutrients in the soil. Dr. Carver discovered hundreds of new uses for crops. His research with agricultural products allowed the development of 325 products from peanuts, 108 applications for sweet potatoes, and 75 products derived from pecans. His industrial application from agricultural products included a rubber substitute and more than 500 dyes and pigments from 28 different plants. It is reported that, in 1927, he was responsible for the invention of a process for producing paints and stains from soybeans.

The most beautiful thing, however, about Dr. George W. Carver is the attitude of love reflected in the Glenn Clark intimate story of Dr. Carver, entitled *The Man Who Talks With The Flowers*. It tells of Dr. Carver's great genius in working with flowers and plants, and how love gave him an awareness of the curative and food properties of the simple peanut, for example.

Love exists not just within a species but also between all living things. Please read the following poem and personally relate to the fragrance of love available on the opening of a rosebud.

ON OPENING A ROSEBUD

I started to open a rosebud.
    I was anxious to see its heart.
Then I gently closed its petals again
    For fear I might tear it apart.

So I blessed and watered its roots then,
    And lo, in the morning sun,
The rose had opened its own pure heart,
    And the fragrance of love was won!

May

~ 26 ~

BLUEBIRD GARDEN BY JUSTIN SPARKS

THE LORD LOVES NATURE

The Lord loves nature, sure He does;
He fills the world with wonder.
He likes things different, I believe,
Like storms and wind and thunder.

He likes variety, I'm sure;
He made the minnow and the whale.
He made the earth a garden fair,
And seas where great ships sail.

He made the velvet robe of night.
He hangs the stars in order;
He shaped the skies to fit the earth
With mountains for a border.

He loves the insects, too, I guess.
I sometimes wonder why?
There's half a million different kinds
On land, in sea and sky.

At thirteen different bugs a day
It takes a hundred years
To get acquainted with them all
If nothing interferes.

I think I know why some were made;
Way back when man first fell,
The earth was cursed with thorns and weeds
And maybe bugs as well.

But some insects like honeybees
Do lots of good, you know.
They carry pollen to the flowers;
They make the cherries grow.

So I like nature, sure I do;
The night and every star,
The sunlight, too, and insect things;
I like them as they are.

May

27

*Reflection on a thought gives the mind time to evaluate it, adapt it, classify it,
and file it for future use and reference.*

BULLDOG VISUAL WITH FLOWER EXPERIMENT
(CREATIVE VISUALIZATION)

Your head is either up or down, your own choice; close your eyes easily, let your eyelids float down. Open them and then let them float down again. Take a deep breath. Hold it for a second and relax. We're going to do a short, mini-visual to help us arrive quickly at the listening lab level, after which we're going to do an experiment with flowers.

Please visualize as usual in action, in detail and in color. If you need to see the picture better walk right up to it so that you can examine it more closely. Your imagination has the ability to bring things closer or to bring you closer so that you can see in detail what is being described.

Visualize with me the front porch on a house. There is a cement step leading up to this cement porch, but it isn't large. The face of the one step leading up to the porch shows considerable roughness. Perhaps a poor piece of board was used for the form in which the cement was set. So notice that there are little knotholes and little pockmarks and rough places showing the outline, the fiber and the grain of the board that was used in the form. The top of the porch has been smoothed off better, but the sidewalk that leads up to it is rough so that no one will slip if it gets wet or icy. There are two stunted, green bushes growing on either side of the sidewalk just before you step up onto the porch. On the porch there is a woven, oval, rag rug. At the outside edge where the last round of the braided rug had been sewn together, the end has come loose where the dog has been chewing on it. Beside that rug, standing on the cement porch with a torn screen door behind it, is the biggest white bulldog imaginable.

He has a little twisted screw-tail. His hips are narrow and small. But he grows larger as he comes up to his shoulders and massive chest. He's very white and very broad. His legs are bowed and short in front. He has a spiked collar around his neck like bulldogs sometimes wear. The spikes in it are about a quarter to a half inch long. He wears the collar in case he gets into a fight. He has little ears. They come upright, but they bend over at the top. Notice his beady little eyes set way back in his head. His nose is wet and black, but it looks like an elephant had kicked it right back in his face. His nose is up close between his eyes. There are wrinkles across his muzzle. Talk about concentration! He has frowns in his forehead that show he didn't learn relaxed concentration; instead, he learned the worrying, weary kind of concentration where you frown and puzzle about things. His upper lip has some long whiskers on it. His lower lip sticks out under and beyond his stubby nose. The upper lip is slightly parted like a harelip. It's nearly bare right in front without much hair on it. There are a few little freckles there, but the most outstanding thing about his face is his undershot jaw. He has a big jaw that sticks out with an overbite way past his upper jaw. Out of that underjaw protrude two big, white teeth. They come up over and in front of his upper lip. Those little beady eyes are looking out toward the sidewalk and toward the street. Looking behind us, we see an old Chevy car. A man is getting out. He has a bouquet of carnations in his hand. He must be the deliveryman from the floral shop. He wants to come up and ring the doorbell and deliver his flowers, but just then, out of the bulldog's throat, comes a deep, deep rumble. The deliveryman sees Old Bull lift that upper lip just a little bit to loosen it from under that broken, yellow tooth that sticks out and makes his snarling even more ferocious.

Well, maybe the lady won't get her flowers, but each of you have now, on your desk, the petals of a white carnation. With your eyes still closed, completely relaxed, breathing easily and deeply, I want you to lift this white carnation to your nose and smell the fragrance of it. Now, please rub it on your face and experience how it feels up against your cheek, or your nose, or your lips or somewhere on your face. Now feel it in your fingers. See what it reminds you of. Very gently, let your fingers become very sensitive. Does it feel like a baby's skin? Does it feel like a bar of soap that's a little bit wet? Does it feel like sandpaper? What does it feel like? Now smell it again, if you would please. Slowly and deeply—real easy does it. Remember, all of your senses are activated and quickened at this relaxation level of mind. Now, I want you, with the use of your imagination, to see a white carnation with other flowers growing around it, with a path leading up to it and with a brick wall in the background.

Now, will you enter into this white carnation? If necessary, take a deep breath, and as you relax, just float and fade right into that big, white carnation growing on a strong, sturdy stem with green leaves. Sense how you feel. How do your feet, like roots, feel planted in the ground? Could you walk? Are you stuck there? You're growing and you are this carnation. What do you have for arms and hands? From what part of you do they grow? How do you feel as a carnation? I want you to imagine that the breeze is blowing across your face and you're swaying with the wind. The breeze could be blowing from across a cool lake somewhere. Feel how refreshing the cool air feels. Experience how the sun feels upon your head—your carnation flower head. Which side does the sun shine on? Behind you, in front of you, right side, left side? Feel the warmth of the sun. Feel with complete confidence and security a little ant crawling right up the back of your stem. Still enjoying your temporary identity with the carnation, see a little child coming down the path. He's not very wise in the ways of picking flowers, but he has his eyes right on you. How do you feel as he reaches out that chubby, dirty little hand to pick you if he can? What was the child like? What is the expression on his face? Does he say anything? While he's still reaching, his mother comes running just as fast as she can to grab him so that he won't pick you. How do you feel when the woman comes up? Is she your mother or somebody else's mother? How does the flower feel toward the woman who came up?

There's a man standing now in front of your particular flower. How do you feel toward that man, whoever he is? What is your reaction as a flower? What do you do? What are his intentions? How would you feel if he were your father? Imagine that this man standing there is your father. He doesn't know that, with all of the sensitivity of your conscious and subconscious minds, you're seeing

370

him, feeling him, perceiving him, and that for the moment you are a flower. How does a flower feel in front of the man that is your father? How would you feel if he stepped aside and the principal of the school stepped up? The principal is standing there now. You're a flower, a helpless flower, but everything is going to be okay.

The two best teachers that you've ever had come walking down that path. The baby and mother are gone, the man is gone, the principal is gone, and your father is gone. But your two best teachers are walking down the path. What would they do about any damage that the child may have done when he tried to pluck you? How do you feel toward these two favorite teachers? What are they saying? What are they doing? How are they feeling? How are they looking? If they knew it were you, how would they be feeling toward that flower? Now, the worst teacher you've ever had since the first grade is coming along the path beside the brick wall. What is she doing to you as a flower? What is she doing to anything that the other two good teachers did?

Imagine now that somebody left the gate open at the city zoo. Some animal from the zoo is coming, flying, walking, running or jumping into the garden or wherever your white carnation is growing. What animal is coming, and how do you react to it, and how does it react to you? If it was a kind animal, how did you communicate? What did it do?

Okay. Now I want you to look down the path a little way, and there's a long, hairy caterpillar crawling on his stomach. He's inching and crawling along. Notice how his back undulates and moves where those little segments are. Notice those little antennae-like hairs that are all over him. He's a little furry caterpillar. See his little, hard, shiny nose and his face. Notice his little stomach when he rises up to look around and to reach out ahead. He's right up to the roots of the green stem of your white carnation. He's feeling now with his little feet, and he's getting a firm hold on your stem. Now he's coming on up to the first leaf on your stalk. What are your sensations as a white carnation? Can you hear the sound of his feet? Is he munching and crunching a little nibble here and there as he goes along? Now he's moving past the leaf. He's crawling around it and twisting his body to fit it. As he starts to come up your flower petals, a big, red-breasted robin comes to the rescue. He got a glimpse of the caterpillar. The bird cocks his head and looks with one bright eye before swooping down to eat the caterpillar. You're saved by a friendly robin! How do you feel as the caterpillar lets go of your stem with those many little feet with suction cups when he is pulled off? How did it feel as the bird's wings were fluttering around your bowed head while he was pulling the caterpillar loose?

Now play like you're the caterpillar for a second. How does he feel when the bird swallows him? How does the bird feel when the caterpillar goes down his throat? Look back at that flower. How happy is that flower? What is it doing as the sun is shining on it and the breeze is blowing across it? What is it thinking? It's all by itself now in the garden. You leave it. You are simply you again, happy, healthy, wide-awake again.

This was a lesson in empathy. It will be easier for you now to know better how you feel about things and how other people feel. You will find it easier to be objective and to see things from the other person's viewpoint. This will help you to be patient and kind with people, pets and other living things. Take a deep breath and stretch. Good! Thank you again for listening.

ONCE IT WAS MINE BY GREG WALZ.

May

28

If desire opens the door wide enough, knowledge will move in, bookshelves and all, and it may even be said in the future that "Wisdom once lived here."

TWO EARS OF CORN AND THE WAGON TONGUE
(JACKSON FABLE)

Two ears of corn stood straight and tall.
    Side by side near the garden place.
The cornstalks rustled and swayed in the breeze
    and bowed with majestic grace.

They listened to the wind and the birds that sang.
    They heard the cricket's chirping sound.
They listened to the field mice build their nests
    And the mole as it burrowed in the ground.

They heard the cornhusker's wagon wheels
    As they creaked out their jolting song.
They found themselves in the wagon box
    Behind the driver who walked along.

In the cool of the day, at evening time,
    The wagon stopped by the corncrib shed.
The horses were unhitched and led away.
    The corn lay heaped in the wagon bed.

The two ears of corn on the top of the pile
    Slid over the front endgate.
There on the ground by the wagon tongue
    They decided to rest and wait.

The wagon tongue cleared its crusty voice
    And said in a whisper hoarse,
"I'm the talking tongue, a waggin' tongue.
    I talk from habit and compulsive force.

(CONTINUED ON NEXT PAGE)

If you want to get a word in, or two,
　　Just interrupt whenever you will.
Or, otherwise, I'll just talk to you guys,
　　For wagon tongues find it hard to keep still."

So the ears of corn, who knew how to listen,
　　Heard plenty as the tongue rattled on.
They didn't interrupt but once or twice
　　From evening 'til almost dawn.

By then the wagon tongue was hanging loose
　　And was ready to listen a bit;
So here's the dialogue they carried on,
　　Or, at least, the gist of it!

"It's better to talk than it is to listen,"
　　Said the wagon tongue with a confident smile.
"That's why I talk and talk and talk . . .
　　But people only listen for a little while."

"If you listen to yourself, you'd learn a lot
　　Of what you probably already know.
And sometimes your ignorance is revealed
　　When you do your own talk show."

"Well, we like to listen," the corn ears replied.
　　"We've learned a lot today.
We know what we knew plus most all of the things
　　That you shared when you had your say!"

"So we think that in silence wisdom shines best,
　　That ears aren't a corny communication part.
We firmly believe that the listener learns most
　　Who stores it in his mind and his heart."

"Ho, ho," said the tongue, "that just isn't so,
　　Because nobody will know what you're thinking.
The sponge that drinks in and never gives out,
　　Its duty of sharing is shrinking!"

(CONTINUED ON NEXT PAGE)

374

"We'd argue, I'm afraid," said one ear of corn,
    "With all of us vying for attention.
Listening is more of a non-martial kind of art
    Where sharing is balanced with retention."

Said the wagon tongue, "Pull together, My Friends,
    Like the two horses on the wagon today!"
"That's easy," said the other ear of corn,
    "With only one tongue between us, I'd say!"

Then the conversation ended in silent dispute
    As each pursued his own thought interaction.
The listeners would listen and the talkers would talk,
    Each to his own satisfaction.

IN THE GARDEN BY JEAN BARTLETT

May

~ 29 ~

ESSAI 2 BY CAROLINE SEYMOUR

BLACKOUT DESIGN

I like the design of the heavy quilt
    That hangs from the hooks to the floor.
It's a flowered quilt of soft pink stuff
    So unlike the designs of war.

And sure I'm glad that it's hanging there
    Tho' the light from the window is gone,
And the world is a darker, quieter place
    From the dusk to the full-orbed dawn.

But there is no light in the window tonight
    And our children have wandered so far.
For the battlefields beckoned, the bugles have called
    And they've followed mad pipers to war.

But it had to be for the land and sea
    Had been threatened by conquering hate
That knew no bounds and felt no shame
    In the crimes that they perpetrate.

For the devil had planned a long blackout
    For the forces of truth and right.
But God of righteousness, judgment and truth,
    Stand by us and guide us tonight.

May

30

Man's real security is found in his knowledge of access to divine supply through an appropriating faith.

SILLY, THE SILICONE DOG
(FLEXIBILITY AND ADJUSTABILITY)

(JACKSON FABLE)

It couldn't have happened, but it did. And this is the way it came about. The Tall Foreheads had stretched their thin necks for hours looking into the structure of plant and animal cells. They found that histone, that invisible substance that controls cell growth and cell specialization, could be isolated, analyzed and reproduced synthetically. Now the genes that made cells into bones, skin, blood, tissue, teeth, muscles, etc. could be artificially controlled.

The bright lightbulbs in the laboratory reflected on the shiny, bald domes of scientific creativity. And the sweat glistened there like tiny jewels in the silent laboratory. A new batch of synthetic histone was fresh from the oven. The thin necks and tall foreheads straightened and the vertebraes clicked back into uprightness with the soft sound of a rusty zipper, and the three wise men solemnly straighted up and shook each other's hands as they congratulated one another in six-syllable words that were so dear to them.

Silly, a lovable, half hound, half something else that they planned to use "a la piecemeal" later on, made the mistake of barking her congratulations, too. That was when the lights flashed and the bells rang and the idea of "Operation Silicone" appeared like a vision of splendor in each of the Tall Foreheads' foreheads. They had been toying with the idea of double-whammy injection of histone-homogenate with silicone propensity, subcutaneously and interperitoneally administered to a living organism—maybe even a cat or a dog. Why not Silly? So they shook hands around again and briskly, in the best coordinated, uncoordinated manner, walked over and solemnly shook hands with Silly, who had reached out a friendly paw through the mesh wire of her cramped cage.

Silly shook paws on the deal as cheerfully as a dog could, not at all knowing that this deal would pull more bounce per ounce than anything since rubber balls were invented. But then Silly liked people. Even scientists were sort of people, she felt.

The tallest one of the Three Tall Foreheads was already getting out a big hypodermic needle, almost as big as a pencil. The shortest one held Silly's hind feet together in one hand and scratched her stomach with the other. Or was he shaving her stomach? She couldn't rightly tell. But it didn't

379

feel too bad, and anyway, she couldn't move her head far enough to see as long as the youngest Tall Forehead held her collar so tightly. But by rolling her eyes until the whites showed fiercely, she could see the Tallest Forehead mixing a liquid with some of the new brown stuff. He kept his hands behind him as he came over to the table. And before she knew it—whammo!! It felt just like the time Old Bull, the bulldog next door, bit her tummy when she lay on her back with all four paws in the air, begging for clemency.

Then, just when she had gotten doubled up a little bit to make the present pain quit hurting—wham, whammo!! She got it in the back next, and it felt like a goose egg under the skin. Things sort of blurred out then, but the lights finally came back on and the lightbulbs quit swaying, crazy-like, from the tilting ceiling, and she saw the Tall Foreheads rubbing their hands together like she had done a nice job of whatever they had in mind.

Well, that was okay by her. But she would play possum until she got a chance to make a break for garbage can alley and then on down to Lake-O-Stink and the city dump, where a good dog could hide and mooch a few scraps after dark in one of the likely places, especially if she were an ambitious dog. So she sighed a big, long, shuddery sigh, quivered a bit all over, and jerked her right front left and right, two and one-half times, just like she had seen a dog do in the movies that had been run over by a truck. Then she lay absolutely, limply, completely, immovably still like "Legs," the boy, had taught her to play dead-dog when she was a pup. Well, this completely, unexpectedly, and irrevocably confused the Three Foreheads.

Now, Silly didn't mind being lifted and pulled and pumped for air, but it was really hard not to lick back when one of them gave her mouth-to-mouth respiration. When everything they tried failed, they shook their bald heads slowly and solemnly from side to side, twice each, six times altogether. They shook hands around, and the youngest one said, "Well, learned brethren, we tried. Right?"

"Right," said the other two in unison as they reached out in perfect synchronized, unified action, and one grabbed an ear and the other a tail, and they walked stiffly to the back door and opened it. And again, in methodical unison: once, twice, swonk! Silly landed in a cramped, forlorn pile in the empty garbage can.

Silly noticed that she had bounced right smartly. It didn't even hurt at all. She noticed, too, now that she thought about it, that she never had felt so relaxed and stretchy-like and peaceful in all her life. She could think easily, too, whereas before she had sort of muddled through her decisions and actions. But now her mind sailed along almost faster than she could keep up. She could remember perfectly, and, at command, she could recall every detail of her past, uninteresting life: the smells, flea-scratching, meal-snitching, alley-fighting, running, cars skidding, and "Legs" the boy, who used to alternate between loving her and kicking her to death. Well, everything felt wonderful, just like that clear-thinking, smooth, "all's right with the world" feeling that they say people sometimes have when they first wake up from a refreshing nap.

She heard the door close quietly and heard the lock as it was slipped from the inside. The Tall Foreheads were gone now. Disillusioned, but gone. Silly couldn't have cared less, for she was

380

disappointed in them. She had thought that they were her friends, that maybe they'd romp with her, feed her, and that life would be better. But they had mistreated her. They hadn't done right by her nor respected her dignity. So gingerly and quietly as she could, she stood up, and her legs felt like rubber under her. But that was to be expected. Even people who have been in a hospital often complain about how their legs felt like rubber. So she carefully stretched her front paws up until they hooked up over the rim of the barrel, and then she clambered with her hind legs, scratching and pawing, but she just couldn't make it up over the barrel.

Well, it was risk everything now. So she backed away to the far side of the barrel, gave a springy bounce, and clawed her way to the top of the barrel just as it fell over with a crash and bang. She had just slipped around the corner when the door opened and the Three Foreheads peered out into the darkness. They looked into the barrel and Silly was gone. Now they'd never know the effects, the after-effects, the marvels, or the bizarre possibilities that might have developed from this experiment. Well, at least she hadn't died. They would try again. And the next time, they'd give the project a little more patience.

But Silly wasn't long on patience right now. She skidded around the corner, ducked into an alley, just missed a telephone pole, and slid out onto the rain-soaked highway. There the headlights of a truck were flashing brightly and she was completely immobilized with fear and blinded by the on-coming lights. She heard the screech of its dual wheels. She just had time to think, "When it rains, it really pours. I just got out of one mess and now I'm in another one." And then the truck was on her. She felt, or expected to feel, the sickening grind of the wheels as they broke her bones and rolled the life out of her. Then the truck driver threw on his air brakes and veered to the right, but rather than straddling her, all of the dual wheels on one side and the front wheels as well rolled over Silly. As she lay in the street, the driver looked back and saw that no one had seen him do this homicidal act of perfidy, and anyway, he hadn't meant to, so he just drove on.

But he did look back in the mirror and was never so surprised in his life, for one moment he saw a dog lying flat as a pancake with the rain glistening on the asphalt pavement under the bright lights of the city streets. Then, the next thing so amazed him that he almost drove off the road as he watched in the mirror. For the dog that had laid there flat and dead seemed to fill out like a balloon to normal size. For a moment, it looked like she was even bigger than life size. And then she got to her feet, scratched her right ear for a second or so, bit at a flea at the base of her tail, got up, and trotted on across the street just like nothing had ever happened.

"Well, maybe I missed, her," the truck driver thought to himself. "But I'd have sworn that I ran over that dog with all of my wheels. I'd swear she was as flat as a fritter, dead as a doorknob, lying there in the street."

Then, he thought about the truck stop up the road a ways. Maybe he'd better get a cup of coffee. A fellow could be half asleep and dreaming. Maybe he didn't run over a dog after all. Well, why worry about something you aren't sure of and that you can't help anyway. A fellow can get nervous on these long drives, he thought. Maybe imagination working overtime. Dogs just don't get run over and then walk away like it was an everyday occurrence.

But of course he didn't know Silly. For that matter, nobody knew Silly. Silly didn't even know herself. But Silly was learning, for she did notice one thing when the truck ran over her, front wheels and all, four duals on the trailer behind the truck. It did hurt. But it was a sort of pleasant hurt. It was different than the times she had been run over and had her paws smashed; different from the times she had run into the light post when she was looking back over her shoulder the time the cop chased her. It was different from the time she had gotten in the dogfight and the places hurt and stung where the bulldog had bitten her tummy. Yes, she recognized this as being painful, but it was a smooth, stretchy sort of pain, and it almost got to the place where it hurt but didn't quite.

Now wouldn't that be something, thought Silly. Wouldn't that really be something. Maybe it was the medicine that the Three Tall Foreheads had given her. She remembered the time she had taken the shot for distemper and they had said it would hurt a little bit but help a lot, and she wouldn't get sick. So maybe they had given her a painkiller. Maybe the big hypodermic needle had had a sedative in it. Maybe it had been some other kind of special shot. Maybe she had been vaccinated against pain. At least, that's the way it seemed to her. She'd never felt better in her life. It seemed like there was a new spring in her feet. She felt like she could run all night. So she did. Right down the street at a lope she went. Then she stretched into a dead run on down and across the city, down to Garbage Can Alley, on past where "Legs" used to live before he moved out of town and left her on her own.

Ah! Now she could smell the fumes from Lake-O-Stink. Now she could get the acrid smell of the smoke from the burning garbage! Now she was almost out where a dog could live free and clean without the kicks and the shouts and the rocks and the cans tied to her tail. But now she had come to the place where she had always had to slow up and get her breath and rest a little before she could go on. But it was different tonight. A little drizzle of rain was coming down. Clouds kept crossing the face of the moon. It wasn't a night that a dog would feel gay, and yet she felt the blood that coursed through her veins was vibrant with life. She felt every muscle flex and stretch like she would like to leap up through the clouds, bite the corner off of the moon, and come on back down.

Just to show her good intentions, she jumped as high as she could and barked at the moon. When she hit the ground—surprise of surprises—she bounced another good three feet back up in the air stiff-legged again. Then she bounced another foot, then six inches, and then two inches. Finally, she stood still in absolute amazement. She had bounced like a rubber ball! So she backed off, took a running start, and jumped for the moon again. She barked when she tried to bite the corner off and missed. When she hit the ground, she bounced four feet right straight up into the air, stiff-legged again, then three feet, then two feet, then one foot. Then she simmered down to six inches, four inches, three inches, one inch, and finally she quit bouncing.

Well, she thought, I'll show Old Bull, the bulldog bully, a thing or two if he ever jumps on me again. But she didn't know just how soon she'd have a chance to show that bulldog.

Silly drifted on down through the rubble and the orange crates, the pieces of canvas and the car tops, the broken bottles, the baby buggies, the barbed wire, the bottomless garbage cans, the steering wheels, the oven doors, the washing machines, and the rotten gunnysacks that were half filled with onions and sprouting potatoes.

382

Ah! She was almost home now. There was that old bale of hay, shunted up against the side of the garbage fill where the tractor blade had gouged a place back under the hill. The bale of hay, nearly intact, made a wonderful windbreak. Here she had burrowed her way into it and had nestled and twisted, turned and tromped a nest until the straw was just right for a perfect bed. It was all still there. And Silly was so glad to be home that she didn't take time to hunt for a choice morsel of food. She simply turned around three times, put her nose under her tail to keep it warm, shut one eye, looked up at the moon, and heard the drizzle of the rain as it increased to a patter and bounced off the tin car door off to the right. Ahh! It was a pleasant sound. This was a dog's life. This was the life of freedom. Good to be home again.

It was daylight before she knew it. Warm sun crept over the top of the bale of hay and played in little pools of light and warmth on her scraggly fur, showing the ridges of her ribs and the spiny points of her backbone as they parted the hair. It reflected deep into her fur where her hipbones stood up sharp, but Silly didn't mind that for there was a whole new world to conquer. She had been away about a week now since the humane society attendant had picked her up, stopped by the experimental laboratory, and sold her for a dollar of pocket money on his way to the shelter. It had been an interesting week of confinement. Any dog would be glad to be home. So Silly stretched and yawned. It was never so easy to stretch, and it had never been so easy to yawn. She stretched and yawned again. It felt so good!

She got up and went out to the garbage. Here was a bread crust, over there was a ham bone. She finished the bread crust with a bite or two, laid down, and worked on the ham bone for about an hour. There wasn't much left but the pure bone when she was through with the knuckle.

Silly thought, well, I guess I'll cut around the right side of Lake-O-Stink and hit the edge of town. Maybe I will see that bulldog. I won't pick a fight with him, that's for sure, but I might do a little bounce act for him. Sure would take the wind out of his sails.

So, Silly trotted with her nose to the trail, tail up as high as a hound could carry it. On she went around the right side of Lake-O-Stink. She cut across the cattails and the muck of one corner. The ooze of the blue mud and clay felt good between her toes. Then she clambered out on the solid ground, cut across a pasture where the cows were eating the early dew-wet grass, and then came to the edge of town.

Chickens were just getting up and roosters were crowing. Sure enough, when she finally got to the edge of the city, she saw him down the street, sniffing at a telephone pole. That was Old Bull all right! She would sneak up behind him, she thought. And sure enough, he was so occupied that she got within biting distance and sat down before she barked a little short, happy, snappy bark. Bull didn't wait for a second invitation. He whirled and charged. He was a broad-chested, short-legged powerhouse of a dog! His underjaw stuck out with determination, and his beady little eyes were bright with hate. He'd show this flippant little pooch a thing or two. He'd teach her to mend her manners and mind her business or find herself maimed for life. Then Old Bull hit her broadside; hit her like a ton of brick; hit her like a pickup truck. It should have knocked the breath out of her, but Silly just smiled and showed her teeth. She rolled over, hit the curb, and bounced back, got up and wagged

383

her tail. Sure enough, she thought, that doesn't hurt like it used to. I guess I'll let him try it again. So she bounced right up into the air once and came down and bounced two or three times more and stood there bravelike, although her tail was a little lower than it should have been.

Now this really made Old Bull mad. He shook his head and growled with a rumble way down deep in his chest. He lifted one lip, which showed a broken yellow fang, then he whirled and charged on Silly. This time he opened his mouth, ducked his head low, and came up with Silly's foot clamped in those unrelenting jaws that never let go. That didn't bother Silly. It was a little inconvenient to be jerked around, but the teeth didn't seem to hurt. The bone didn't break, but it bent a little. In fact, pain seemed to be pleasure now. Sort of a dull, smooth, firm, pleasurable feeling. It wasn't bad.

So Silly just licked his ear, smiled at him, nuzzled him a little under the chin, and went along with him as he shook his head, then pulled, walking backward.

That was to be expected, Silly thought. Bulldogs are bulldogs, and that's the way they fight. So she went along with it. Old Bull didn't find any fun in this now. No fun fighting with a dog that wouldn't fight back. So he finally thought it over and let go.

Silly looked at her leg. It was bent off to one side, and there was a row of teeth marks in it and a few of the hairs had been scraped off. As she watched it, she noticed the indentations of the teeth marks slowly fill out, smooth and firm. She wiggled her ankle a little bit and her leg straightened up again. Silly thought, well, I never . . .

But she never got to finish her sentence, for Bristles the Airedale from across the street hit her from the back, and that got Old Bull excited again and he hit Silly from the front. Then she thought it was the finish, for Bristles had her right back leg and Bull had her by one of her soft, floppy ears, and they weren't working together. One of them was headed home and the other was headed for HIS home. And they lived in opposite directions.

This sort of confused Silly for a minute, for she couldn't figure out how she could go with both of them. She was willing to cooperate, but she just couldn't figure out how she could go in two directions at once. But they were solving that dilemma for her, for they were pulling and she was giving. She was stretching and stretching and stretching and stretching. They were halfway across the street from each other now, and Silly was stretched out in between. Bristles was up on the curb, bracing his feet on the grass, and Bull had finally turned around and was backing up again. He was halfway across the street.

As Silly looked out along her ribs and down to where her legs ought to be, she realized that she looked like an inner tube or a rubber band stretched out taut. She was getting thinner and thinner and then somebody whistled. Bristles let go, and that was when Old Bull got the surprise of his life, for the other end of Silly, when Bristles let go, slapped Bull right on the end of his short, pug-nosed, flat, wrinkled face so hard that he sat down right in the middle of the street on his little, crooked, screw tail. He blinked his little beady eyes and looked so stupid to Silly that, as soon as she could get herself back together again, she sat down and laughed until her sides ached. This was too deep for Old Bull. He could fight easier than he could think. He decided to go home and think a while. Might take a day or two to figure this out.

Well, Silly had other business to do. She'd never felt so fine in her life. She decided to throw caution to the four winds. She had always avoided that vacant lot where the tough kids played baseball, but they couldn't hurt her. She could bounce with the best of them. She could stretch with the worst of them with painless pleasure. So why should she worry?

It was almost the undoing of Silly, for no sooner had she hit the vacant lot and sat down by the corner of the clubhouse than somebody came around from behind it with a baseball bat. She didn't see who it was, but she felt the bat when it clipped her behind the ears. This time Silly saw stars, and her neck stretched, too, and snapped back. The lights went out for Silly then, for she'd been hit on a strategic point. A numbness crept over her brain and a film over her eyes. She couldn't see, she couldn't hear, and she sunk down in a crumpled heap by the corner of the clubhouse. She could faintly hear the mean, raucous laughter as the other boys came out. One of them said, "I've got a gunnysack. Put her in it!" "I'll get some rocks," another one said. "Here's a string out of my old tennis shoes," a third boy said.

So they crumpled old Silly up into a heap, pushed her down into the gunnysack, put in three big rocks, tied the top of it, drug her, rocks, sack, and all, down the street, out across the cow pasture, and down to Lake-O-Stink. Silly was just beginning to revive. She revived enough to smell the familiar odors of Lake-O-Stink, where the city sewage came out onto the marshy ground, then bubbled and oozed through the grass roots and cattails that grew profusely there. The stench was unbearable to anybody but a homeless dog or the rodents that lived by its banks. But the boys knew where Lake-O-Stink was, and that's where they dragged Silly that day.

On the high side of Lake-O-Stink, where the bank reached out to the stump of an old tree, they dragged the sack. The water was deeper here. The scum and the bubbles and the oil lay thick on the surface. One of the boys pushed the sack over the edge with the scuffed toe of his tennis shoe. It made a dull, sudsy splash as it sunk to the bottom—down to the roots where the cattails were slimy and thick; down where the few bullheads that lived in its murky depths swam through the mud and ooze.

But Silly had taken a deep breath of air just before they pushed her off. She held her breath now, down, down, down, down. But just as surely as she went down, she began to come up, up, up, slowly up. Her lungs stretched to capacity, filled to bursting with that last breath of fresh, clean morning air that would save her life, for now she was floating like a balloon or a rubber ball. Finally the sack cleared the water for an instant and gave her just one more breath of fresh air, which she gulped in fiercely before she started to sink again to the bottom. But again she struggled, and again the buoyancy of the air held deep in her lungs lifted her like a rubber ball, up, up, up, and this time she drew in another great gulp of air.

She began to claw frantically at the side of the bag. It was old and fortunately it gave. The weight of the rocks held it steady as she clawed her way through it—head, shoulders, hips, tail, then the last foot out. But Silly knew better than to come up where the boys waited on the bank. They couldn't see her in the murky water as she swam directly beneath them underneath the overhanging ledge. There she let just the tip of her nose come up through the scum to the bubbles. She breathed deeply

385

and slowly, deeply and lowly, until she got her strength back. Like an otter, she dived beneath the water, then swam silently through the cattails along the bank and out the far side. Then she thought she'd risk it. Sleek and wet as a drowned muskrat, she came up through the rushes up onto the bank, and before the boys could throw another stone, she scrambled a short distance from Lake-O-Stink to the edge of the garbage dump. She wasted no time and leaped from the bank down to the first pile of rubble. And then she scurried away, under this, over that, and finally out of sight. They'd never find her now.

But Silly had learned another thing—she could float on water. If she could float on water even for a moment with her lungs filled with air, fighting the weight of the rocks and the sack, she knew that, without the sack encumbering her and the rocks to drag her down, she could float forever in an ocean if necessary, for she was the Silicone Dog.

Then Silly began to think about the Three Tall Foreheads who had given her this double-dose injection of histone-homogenate with silicone propensity, subcutaneously and interperitoneally administered. She remembered the laboratory and how those bald, glistening Foreheads looked, bending down over her on the table. If they only knew how relaxed she felt, how confident and happy she was, and how willing to adjust, stretch, survive, and win! New ideas of adventure began to float like toy ballons from her flexible, silicone brain as she bounced lightheartedly along a quieter back street, who knows, perhaps to a rubber bone in Garbageville.

But Silly thought, why hold even a silicone grudge against the Three Tall Foreheads. They would never know how full of bounce even a dog's life could be. This was her day, a good day, and she was the Silicone Dog.

May

~ 31 ~

In solitude's rarified atmosphere a person can feel the greatest humility, assess the truest talents with the surest degree of candor, and perceive the foremost duty with the utmost clarity.

SKY DOG AND SAUCER CAT AND HALF KITTEN
(JACKSON FABLE)

This is the story of Sky Dog, Saucer Cat and Half Kitten. Once upon a time in the land of It-Never-Could-Happen-Here there lived a beautiful kitten, a beautiful, snow-white kitten, and her name was Saucer Cat. The family was poor that kept her and often she had very little to eat. But she did have a dish of her own, a saucer of her own, and when she was hungry, she meowed piteously or purred enticingly and rubbed on the legs, the bare cold legs, of the little girl who owned her asking for an extra morsel or for some milk to drink. But there wasn't much milk in the land of It-Never-Could-Happen-Here, because all of the cows had gone dry and the Starnation Milk Factory had closed down because of heavy depression. When the fall rains beat on the tin roof, the Starnation milk cans rattled in frosty solitude in the empty buildings. The workers had gone home on strike because it was cold at the Starnation Factory, and the hours were long and the pay was little and their fireplaces at home were warm and inviting and they wanted to rest their tired feet. No, there was little milk, very little milk, in the land of It-Never-Could-Happen-Here, because it did happen there.

Saucer Cat continued to grow until she was no longer Saucer Kitten but a full-fledged Saucer Cat. But she was lean and hungry, even though she felt she was born a princess. She licked her snow-white fur and looked in the mirror at her deep blue-green eyes and dreamed about far-off days when either she or someone like her didn't live in the land of It-Never-Could-Happen-Here. Whoever it was that she dreamed about had lived in the land where Everything-Happens-There. In that land there were castles and princesses. There were contented milk cows with bulging udders. There were milkmaids with pails of brimming milk, foamy white on top, reflecting in the pure white, off-yellow, heavy, creamy milk. In the land of It-Could-Happen-There, everybody had everything and the cats sat on their tails in the barn and waited. The milkmaids, with perfect aim, squirted milk into their mouths whenever they opened their mouths and said, "Metoo, metoo." They always said, "Metoo," instead of "Meow."

Saucer Cat knew that it was a gold saucer that she had drunk out of in the land of Everything-Happens-There. She knew she had a silver saucer also to use while they were washing her gold-plated, 14-carat, perfectly round, diamond-studded, rose-decorated saucer. She missed it because it was a perfect mirror that reflected the deep blue of her own far-seeing, blue-green eyes. Often when she had licked the last drop from the gold-plated saucer or from the plain but beautiful silver-plated saucer, she caught sly glimpses of herself and she knew she was really beautiful. She was glad to be called the Saucer Cat in either land, It-Never-Could-Happen-Here, or Everything-Happens-There.

When she awoke from her dreams, she could feel the cold wind whip around the tarpaper shanty without any foundation, with holes where she could crawl under the house, where the wind rattled the tarpaper and where the leaves piled high in one corner. She could see the blue, cold legs of the little girl who wasn't a princess as she came around the corner with a little helping of this or a little scraping of that or a little crumb from her school lunch that she'd saved. Then she was glad to be a Saucer Cat even in the land where It-Never-Could-Happen-Here. But she was lonesome sometimes and there was sadness in her deep blue, far-seeing eyes that looked back to the land where Everything-Happens-There. Sometimes there were tears in her eyes that looked like the jewels on the 14-carat, gold-plated saucer that far-off princes had given her. So the tears just ran down Saucer Cat's nose and left little furrows in the soft, whiskered fur of her white, beautiful face.

One day she sat licking her fur. The plain, cracked saucer plate from the land of It-Never-Could-Happen-Here had been licked dry, then licked dry again. It was empty and it didn't reflect like a real mirror because it was a cracked, old saucer, and the only thing that reflected there was the passing clouds in the cold blue sky of the land where It-Never-Happens-Here.

One day she thought she saw reflected in the plate a soft cloud, nearer than usual, passing by. She looked up into the sky and kept on meowing piteously and hungrily and with a great lonesomeness in her heart like an exiled princess would have done if she had lost her gold-plated, diamond-studded, mirror-reflecting, 14-carat, perfectly round, special princess plate. To her amazement, as she looked up, she saw Sky Dog. At least it looked like a Sky Dog. He didn't have a collar on and he didn't have a dog tag, but he did have ears and he did have big, sad eyes, and he did seem to have whiskers on his face. The nose was blacker than the gray of the cloud. His tail seemed to be wagging as the wind blew the clouds willy-nilly, hither and thither, yonder there, here and over somewhere and back down again.

The tail seemed to wag in the wind and the Sky Dog seemed to move, to stretch a limb this way and that way. He turned his head a little here, there, willy-nilly, hither, yon, over there, back here, over, under and around again. Saucer Cat had the feeling somebody cared. Sky Dog seemed to stretch his neck as the clouds blew him closer. He stuck his dark, thunder-cloud nose at least in the direction, she felt, of the tarpaper shanty with the wind blowing through the holes and under the house, where the leaves rattled in the corner and piled high in eddies, where the little bare, cold legs of the girl who wasn't a princess walked by.

Some of the lonesomeness went out of the heart of Saucer Cat because the cloud dog had come a little closer. Here in the land of It-Couldn't-Happen-Here, it did happen; because on chilly, lonesome days, the cloud dog came closer and closer. Some people said it was fog settling down; chilly, cold, wet fog in the early mornings. But Saucer Cat knew they were wrong. She knew it was Sky Dog. He came sometimes to lick out and to wash her plate with his tears. He was so sorry! Sometimes when there was no water to drink, he left the distilled dew of his own sadness and the jewels of his own tears. When the morning sun came up and Sky Dog had gone back to the sky, maybe clear back to the land where Everything-Happens-There, then Saucer Cat, who felt more like the princess that never was, saw the distilled diamonds in her little, cracked saucer. It always made her think how much it looked like that long-ago, 14-carat, gold-plated, diamond-studded, perfectly round, mirror-reflecting, princess dish that she used to drink royal cream out of as she sat and purred contentedly and licked her fur and felt the fat underneath the skin.

The little girl with the cold, blue, bare legs, who brought her scraps from school and who walked past the holes in the tarpaper under the shanty building where the leaves eddied under the house and the wind blew around the corners, was gone to school most of the time now. So the cat that wasn't a princess decided to fall madly in love with the cloud dog. On cold mornings they touched cold noses. The white fur of Saucer Cat glistened with the early morning dew and the fog of Sky Dog as he came closer and made her fur shine and rubbed her cheeks gently, washed her paws softly, cleaned out her plate and left it diamond-studded where he filled the cracks with the morning fog-dew.

It was a beautiful romance that reminded her of the land where Everything-Happens-There. It reminded her of castles and of princesses, white horses, dairy maids, royal cows with bulging udders, where royal cats sat in royal barns with open mouths calling, "Metoo, metoo, metoo," where the dairy maids with perfect aim squirted the milk into their open mouths and it trickled down the corners through the fur and kept them busy licking to keep themselves clean.

It was a beautiful romance. Then one cold, clear morning, the frost had painted pictures on Saucer Cat's empty saucer and pictures on the windowpanes. In the house, the girl's warm nose was pressed against the frosty surface of the windows. She was looking to see if Saucer Cat was waiting outside in the cold. But Saucer Cat wasn't waiting in the cold. Nobody stood beside the empty saucer. Nobody meowed for milk. Nobody rubbed against the porch railing and purred to be let in because Saucer Cat was down where the leaves eddied high and where the wind blew cold under the tarpaper shanty. Back in the snuggly, hollowed-out place in the leaves in a little depression in the dry dirt in the far, southeast corner was Half-Kitten.

Half-Kitten. That's what Saucer Cat called him, Half-Kitten. He wasn't pure white like Saucer Cat, who had once been a princess, and he wasn't silver-gray like Sky Dog. But he did have a black nose and he was sort of gray and he had soft fur that made you think of dumpling clouds. He did wiggle and stretch and turn willy-nilly, here, there, under, over and back again just like Sky Dog's tail did when the wind blew across the clouds. He did reach out a little paw and scratch the leaves, and he did lie on his back with his little pink tummy full of Saucer Cat's warm milk. The bottoms of his paws were pink on the pads. The little sharp toenails were white and pink, too. He was all sort of gray, soft and fluffy, like dumpling clouds floating in the sky. And don't forget, he did have a little black, cold nose.

Saucer Cat didn't know yet what his eyes would look like. Maybe they would be blue-green eyes with the far-away look in them that could see castles and princesses and dairy maids in royal barns, milking royal cows with full udders, where royal cats sat on their royal tails with their royal mouths open, mewing royally, "Metoo, metoo," while the milkmaids, with perfect aim, filled their open mouths with foamy milk. Or maybe he'd have the sad eyes of Sky Dog. But nobody could tell because Half-Kitten's eyes were closed tight and they wouldn't be open for ten days. But that wouldn't be long, just a week and a half, just ten more hungry days to wait and Saucer Cat would know if Half-Kitten's eyes were like the eyes of his mother or if his eyes would be like Sky Dog's, gentle and sad.

While she waited, she spent very little time with the plain, cracked saucer and lots of times, back under the house where the leaves eddied in the corner and the cold wind blew fiercely. Sometimes she saw the girl's cold, blue legs walk by the hole under the tarpaper shack, and she would come out then. At other times she wouldn't come, even though she heard, "Saucer Cat, Saucer Cat, Saucer Cat!" She just laid there with love in her heart for Half-Kitten, hoping he'd turn out to walk from cloud to cloud, blow across blue skies, maybe look down on castles in the land where Everything-Happens-There. Or maybe he'd be an earthbound kitten. Maybe he'd live under tarpaper shanties. Maybe he'd have a long, far-away, blue-green look in his eyes. Maybe he'd have lean, hungry ribs and cry piteously by a cracked saucer by another tarpaper shanty for another girl with cold, blue legs who brought home crumbs from her lunch at the schoolhouse. Time would tell. Time would tell. Time would tell. And the wind blew under the house, and leaves eddied in the corner, and the cat that wasn't a princess licked her white fur and tried to keep it clean as she nuzzled the little Half-Kitten.

Then one day Saucer Cat, the cat that used to be a princess but wasn't a princess now, came out from under the house just as the little girl with the cold, blue legs walked by the hole under the tarpaper shanty where the wind blew cold and the leaves eddied in the corner. Behind her, with his tail straight up in the air like a flag blowing in the breeze, was Half-Kitten. But his ears weren't pointed like his mother's. His ears hung down like Sky Dog's. He looked like a cat, and his tail was straight up in the air like a cat, but he didn't know how to meow. He couldn't have said, "Metoo," even if he'd tried in the royal barn with the royal cows where the royal milkmaids squirted royal milk into the mouths of the royal cats who sat on their royal tails and cried, "Metoo, Metoo," because Half-Kitten had the deep, thundering voice of Sky Dog on the trail of a cloud rabbit.

When he tried to purr, it sounded like he was growling. It was a frightful growling, like the rumbling of thunder before a storm. It even made Saucer Cat nervous when Half-Kitten tried to purr, because it reminded her of the time the neighbor dogs had chased a squirrel up a tree. They had growled and barked and scratched the trunk for a long time while the little squirrel shivered in the branches, glad that dogs couldn't climb. But Half-Kitten was like Sky Dog. He could climb. His bark was rougher than the tree bark, and he was at home in all of the branches. He thought far thoughts, and his thoughts ran through the sky like a swift wind that blew clear to the land where Everything-Happens-There and back again.

Then the little girl that lived in the land where It-Never-Could-Happen-Here hurried into the house to tell her mother that Saucer Cat had a kitten with droopy ears whose purring sounded like thunder on the mountains, who was soft and like a dimply, gray cloud, whose tail was straight and whose sides were lean and whose nose was black. But he didn't really seem to belong in the land where It-Never-Could-Happen-Here.

When nobody was looking, instead of going back under the house, he climbed the tallest tree in the backyard and he crawled through the branches, heavy with the frost and with diamond flakes of the fresh-fallen snow. When he got to the top branch, he purred, and it sounded like soft thunder. It sounded like a dog growling when the neighbor cat came by. Sky Dog heard it in the sky and he told the wind to blow him closer. As his fur touched the top of the tallest tree in the land where It-Never-Could-Happen-Here, Half-Kitten leaped from the swaying branches clear up onto the back of Sky Dog, and there he lay as the North Wind blew Sky Dog back up into the sky again. It was a beautiful picture of a silver-gray, cloud dog with a black nose and droopy ears and a tail that wagged happily as the wind blew it willy-nilly, here and there, up and down, under, over, in and out, back and forth and down again. And on his back, curled up with his head on his paws, was Half-Kitten with a black nose, gray fur and droopy ears.

Looking down, they could see Saucer Cat looking up, meowing piteously, and the shabby little girl with the cold, blue legs was looking up, too. But of course they didn't know that the story they were a part of had another, deeper meaning. They didn't know that Saucer Cat symbolized the subconscious, instinctive, lower self of real people. The Sky Dog represented man's superconscious, higher, transcendental self. Half-Kitten symbolized the sublimated conscious mind, especially when it was integrated with the super-mind and the instinctive mind.

It teaches, too, that the integrated, synchronized, nonfractured mind of man can lose its earthbound limitations, leave the negative land where It-Never-Could-Happen-Here and hop dimensions to the expanded, elevated, superior state of positivity in the land where Everything-Happens-There. It symbolizes abundance versus lack, misery exchanged for miracles, self-conscious, animal instinct exchanged for intuitive mentation, and physical limitations exchanged for the freedom of the Over-Soul's objective viewpoint....

Now, back to your own released self and Half-Kitten riding on the back of the Sky Dog. Let the soft, south wind stir gently as it blows you for the moment anywhere in the everywhere, to anyplace, person or time span of the past, present or future that you desire to go. While we're up here looking down, let's go somewhere and, while resting comfortably, breathing deeply and relaxing completely, see clearly in detail, color and in action. In the framework of the beautiful, the true, the positive and the good, taste, touch, see, smell and feel all that surrounds you.

MOTHER AND DAUGHTER BY JUSTIN SPARKS

June

~ 1 ~

*To think in images recalled is not difficult, for it is often little more than reminiscence;
To think in abstractions is more difficult still, for principles and ideas are harder to hold even when
translated into symbols; But to think intuitively is the easiest, yet the most difficult of all, for its
processes are the most illusive and its wisdom is the soonest escaped unless captured as the inspiration
takes wings at the hidden womb of creative thought.*

TREES, I LOVE YOU

Trees, my trees, I love you
  With your shady soft caress,
    For the leaves that fall,
    And the birds that call
  And your patterned loveliness!

Trees, my trees, I love you.
  Your rough bark thrills me through.
    Each carved knife mark
    That cuts thru your bark
  Your rough fibers so soon renew!

Trees, my trees, I love you
  And the squirrels that climb and play.
    All nature I love
    With blue skies above
  Where branches in the gentle winds sway!

Trees, my trees, I love you.
  Your limbs are so gnarled and strong.
    You woo my heart
    When you draw me apart
  While leaves sing their soughing song.

(CONTINUED ON NEXT PAGE)

Trees, my trees, I love you
There's strength in your every bough.
Where your crowned heads nod
I walk with your God
And all things are mine here and now!

Trees, my trees, I love you.
In your hidden wisdom I can learn,
For there's noble bliss
In your presence that I miss.
I long, when away, to return!

Trees, my trees, I love you.
I draw strength when we pass in the dark.
I see deep inside
And love you with pride
In the forests or here in the park!

Trees, my trees, I love you
For solitude like a garment you wear.
In your silence I hear
Truth unheard by the ear
And secrets universal I share.

Trees, my trees, I love you.
I grow nostalgic and restless with pain.
But I've learned this for sure
That your balm is my cure,
So I must seek you again and again.

Trees, my trees, I love you.
The enlightened alone will know why,
For nature is sweet
And the union complete
With God, trees and the open, blue sky!

June

2

*Mental pictography is the faith form or the master mold into which desire
will pour the free energy of life's creative forces.*

MAY I KNOW HIM!

God is hidden, but not in hiding.
 He is seeking as He is sought.
May I be aware of His Presence
 Without which all things are naught.

May I be aware of that Someone
 Who stands in the presence of all.
Unseen and unheard in the clamor
 But awaiting our beck and call.

God in each person we encounter,
 God in the good and the great,
And God in the person rejected
Perhaps fettered by hurt and hate.

Oh, God, may I see Thee in all things.
 May I know Thee as Lord and King.
Grant me the gift of this knowing
 And the peace such knowing would bring!

GOD IS LOVE

Each tender blade of grass so verdant green,
Each tiny drop of dew with silver sheen,
Each fragile flower with perfume wildly rare
Are all God's gifts of love for us to share.

Each dawn He gives, each sunrise warm and clear
Are proofs enough He holds His children dear.
While every bird song in the sky above
Is sung to teach us all that God is love!

Each passing day with restful twilight shade,
That slowly cuts the light with night's smooth blade,
And gives us sleep's unbroken sweet repose
Is ours, too, and still God's goodness shows.

God's matchless name is love. His ways are ways of love.
He tenderly is watching from the skies above.
We all may find repose, because God's goodness shows
That God is love.

June

3

*It might be well to rewind our purpose
when we wind the unwound watch!*

EACH SEASON IN REVIEW

Summertime is wonder time
　　Across the lakes in June.
Symphonic time and singing time
　　When all the world's in tune.

Blue herons like stiff statues stand.
　　The fawn explores the wood.
And we become as one with them
　　In thoughts half understood.

The challenges of the pheasant cock
　　In startled rigor calls,
And nocturnal creatures stir about
　　As long, dark shadows fall.

The pastoral loveliness of June
　　Across the bottomland
In flowered, perfumed profusion bursts
　　Around us on every hand.

The wood ducks find their nesting place
　　In hollow stump or tree,
Or spread a rippled, water trail
　　In their flight for liberty.

(CONTINUED ON NEXT PAGE)

The scent of wild flowers in the air,
　　Where sunset rays unfold,
Brings the sudden magic of the sky
　　That turns the leaves to gold.

The days of long, long shadows
　　Paint purple in the hills
With harvest time and reaping
　　Of the fields the farmer tills.

For restless grows the wild duck.
　　Inner urgings bid him rise
In formation's "V" for victory
　　On the flyways of the skies.

Then winter's bony fingers
　　Spread snow across the land.
Deserted lakes and frozen ponds
　　Lay cold beneath her hand.

She hides the mountain passes
　　With brittle, glittering snow
And plants a cold, caressing kiss
　　On all who come and go.

She tucks a cold white blanket
　　Around the shivering earth
And the blood of nature now runs cold
　　Till spring can bring new birth.

The coyote stalks the frozen fields
　　In stealth and cunning pride,
While the little creatures hungrier grow
　　And in frozen terror hide.

But Spring will come again I know
　　And the earth will laugh once more
And the birds will return for nesting
　　In the reeds along each shore!

June

4

If desire opens the door wide enough, knowledge will move in, bookshelves and all, and it may even be said in the future that "Wisdom once lived here."

UNCOMMON, COMMON SENSE

Moderation, **penetration** and **consistency** are vital parts of discretionary reasoning or *uncommon*, common sense. The sagacity or wisdom of instinctual mentation or thought processes is based upon experiential knowledge that teaches us to profit today from the lessons we found hard to learn in the yesterdays of our own experience. Common sense puts a curb on our impulses, for impulsive action is a result of the mind bypassing the reflective, deductive period of ideation. Here the stimulation passes immediately into action in an automatic and not always successful fashion. The impulsive person becomes the victim of his own unprocessed impressions. More self-control is needed to give him time for proper decisions. Good judgment must counterbalance instinctual reaction, giving reason its moment of meditation and evaluation and the weighing judgmentally of the evidence at hand. Given time, reason will foresee the dire consequences of impulsiveness and will more wisely adapt itself and its reactions to the circumstances and situations involved.

Habitual thinking as to quality and manner results in determining attitudes or instinctual reactions and becomes a characteristic part of personality, action and life. In other words, the way you think will show in the way you act. On the back of successful living is successful, accurate, common-sense thinking. We should encourage and energize and direct our most successful, positive thoughts in order that they may be born to action, that they may survive through organization and finally reach the maturity of accomplishment. This, in part at least, is the art of thinking. As you have listened, reflected, visualized and have both passively and actively thought upon the definitions and the actions suggested in this lesson, let these truths become a part of your inner self. Receive them. Identify with them. Open yourself entirely to them.

Impress your own inner mind by the fervency of your own desire to become a logical, accurate, common-sense thinker in every life situation, for it pays to think!

HYBRID BUSINESSMAN

Over a cage marked "Coyotes,"
  Racing to and fro,
Was a spotted, lop-eared creature,
  A freak in a pen for show.

He had the restless nature
  Of the wild blood in his veins
As he paced and pressed the iron bars
  And longed to be free again.

But whence the spotted color,
  And whence the hound-like ears?
They say he is a hybrid dog
  With all of the coyote's fears.

I declare that since I've seen it,
  In this half-breed counterpart,
I've seen some hybrid businessmen
  With conflicts in their hearts.

I've seen a few halfway honest salesmen
  With honorable poise and dignity set aside
Their pompous boasting was most sickening
  And their overdress spoke of pride.

They were restless for unrestrained freedom.
  They longed to make a quick deal again.
But legal rules, like bars restricted them
  And they planned and schemed in vain.

For hybrid, halfway reliable salesmen
  Their lives were frustrated and incomplete.
Their fears, not integrity, constrained them
  With attitudes far from honest and sweet.

But thank goodness for law officials
  Who confront each wayward part.
By the long arm of law enforcement
  They distract and "tame" these restless hearts.

June

~ 5 ~

GARDEN OF HAPPINESS BY WANDA KIPPENBROCK

I SEND MY LOVE

I send my love like a letter
    Sealed with the kiss of desire.
I send my love like a candle's
    Red tears melted with passion's fire.

I send my love like a flower,
    Fragrant and jeweled with dew.
Each day a corsage of devotion
    Is love expressed and sent only to you.

I send my love like a jewel,
    A white diamond transparent and rare.
I send it ring-set for your finger,
    Everlasting the symbol we share.

I send you love's warmth for the winter.
    I send you glad love in the spring.
I send you June love for the summertime,
    And when autumn comes blustering.

I send my love for each season.
    Like a homing pigeon, my love I release.
If together, I'd be glad, my lover,
    Then these substitute epistles could cease.

*Who knows but that a letter sealed with love and penned with care, may be by its invisible words
and overtones a deeper message bear.*

June

6

Why should the mortal dust not settle in the shade whence once it arose?
And why should not clay return to the bank where the river of eternal life flows?

FAITH WORKS

Faith must have an honored place
And not where the servants dwell.
Faith must have the finest room
And we must serve it well.

Faith will not dwell where envy dwells
Nor anger, pride or greed.
No hate, revenge, doubt or fear
Or superstition meets its need.

But faith commands the royal room
In the dwelling of the mind.
Here faith will work its miracles
With failure left behind.

Overcaution is a jailer who imprisons our good intentions, handcuffs our actions,
and forgets on purpose where it hid the keys.
Faith overcomes.

WHAT IS A BABY?

What is a baby but a gift from above?
Perfection in miniature, a gift of love.

A baby includes the hopes and fears,
Toils and caring of days and years.

What is a baby? Tell if you can.
Potential unlimited, a woman or man?

A baby is mortal, but immortal and frail.
A Chalice for God, a Holy Grail!

*Education is the interminable process of self-discovery, the bringing to light
of our hidden treasure, and the enlargement of our capacity to still discover more.*

*Learning is richer than riches and stronger than strength; it extends time,
by making it more productive, and life, by making it more meaningful.*

June

7

MAXWELL FALLS CLIFFS BY GREG WALZ

LET THERE BE LIGHT

On that great creative morning
    When the darkness covered all,
The shadows of the formless deep
    Upon all things did fall.

"Let there be light!" I hear it!
    These were the words sublime.
Then out of the darkness of midnight
    The beauties of heaven did shine.

Then the gleam of stars and moonlight
    And of the sun in the morning sky,
All rose in successive splendor
    To see the darkness fly.

But spiritual darkness comes upon
    The souls of all mankind.
Man groped in rebellion and error
    Not knowing that he was blind.

Then again we hear the Father,
    "Let there be light!" He said.
And the light of the soul's resurrection
    Shone on the face of the dead.

The dark prison-house of guilt
    Opened quickly and wide each door;
And the glad songs of hope were echoed
    With peace for the sick and the poor.

June

~ 8 ~

WOOD RIVER BY EVERETT SPENCER

Happy is the person who radiates goodwill, tolerance, kindness, and peace;
for what he projects rebounds to him again like a basketball
from the backboard of just compensation.

RECOMPENSE

The fathers sow the wild wind;
The children reap the whirlwind.
An age of selfish, heartless greed
Where hopes decrease and hatreds breed;
Where suffering cries of countless poor,
Where classes clash in civil war
And nations plod thru' fire and blood—
Their cry now smites the ear of God!
And revolutions shake the earth
And leave behind their molten dearth
Like pent volcanoes bursting forth
    Before they rest.

June

9

*Today is a good day; it's a new day; for some things it's creation's day
and for other things it's doomsday: But for all things it's our day,
and it can be our best day.*

SEA LIFE AND THE TIDES

The waves of the sea play hide and seek
  Along the ocean shore,
As the tides come in and the tides go out
  Leaving behind their treasured store.

It may be a broad expanse of sand,
  A mudflat or rocky bay
Where the tides come in to wash them clean—
  Fresh washed two times a day.

Seaweeds grip tight the smooth, worn rocks
  As they sway and bend with the tide,
While creatures that fail to cling or dig
  Must shoreward with the high waves ride.

The tide pools reflect the setting sun
  And the shadows stretch soft and far,
While the sea life hides in the salty brine
  With barnacles and red sea star.

The muscles are anchored to the slippery rocks
  With tenuous threads from special glands.
Tenaciously there they cling for life
  With their tiny, clutching hands.

Razor-back clams all bury themselves,
  Spewing out the sand from each shell.
Thus safe below while lying low
  They adjust to the tides quite well.

(CONTINUED ON NEXT PAGE)

The barnacles use their fringed, long legs
    To rake in their watery food.
When the tides have left them high and dry
    They close their shells but good.

Sea stars and feathery anemone
    And nutabranches white or of brilliant hue
All seek the tide pools near the shore
    Till the waves again crash through.

The sand dollar quickly slips away
    Like its counterpart in life.
It feels secure beneath the sand,
    Safe hidden from ocean strife.

The leathery cucumber of the sea
    Is not the garden or domestic kind,
But a feathery, flowery, floating thing
    That is deaf and dumb and blind.

The Hermit Crab who has no shell
    On his tender, unprotected back
Must substitute instinctively
    What he finds for what he lacks.

Double lives these denizens
    Of the ocean deep must live
As half their lives are spent without
    The moisture the sea waves give.

Storms and wind still smash great ships
    Against the obdurate shore
Where the hungry waves devour their prey
    And still greedily wait for more.

Thus the tides of the sea play recklessly
    With its creatures and ships and man,
As the tides go out and the tides come in
    Since time and tide began.

June

~ 10 ~

Ideals should be focused on the far horizon where both earth and heaven meet,
but not so far or so high as to be entirely "out of this world."

OPPORTUNITY IDEAS GLISTEN EVERYWHERE

Thomas Edison once stated that success is based upon 10 percent inspiration and 90 percent perspiration. Our achievement and glistening list of accomplishments follow these two paths, which include the execution or the demonstration of the active "doing" person. These two avenues of opportunity allow us unlimited performance and fulfillment. Yes, these opportunities also include a type of creation, which may generally consist in the shifting of attributes from one situation to another. How might this work? Well, if we apply the item with which we are working, a few new characteristics or qualities, we now have what functions as a new creation with different attributes. Could we then say that being original is actually reaching over and shifting attributes as they represent that with which we had been dealing? Does this mean, then, that our world proceeds on the principle of combination? No, our world grows in an orderly fashion, developing a line of constant adaptation. This wonderful process of creative ideas includes:

- Evaluation of the presentation or project,
- From this evaluation, selecting one unusual or powerful quality or attribute, and then
- Applying that attribute to the new project.

We then have a new creation. Explore your situation for possible thought starters. Now let's examine the more formal mechanics of our glistening opportunity ideas, which are everywhere.

By association, approximation and deduction, the mind in judicial action comes to a conclusion and gives birth to the developed idea or thought relative to the proposition or problem confronting it. Examination and deductive common sense conclude that, if one action is equal to a previously tested action, it will reproduce the same results, providing surrounding circumstances are also equal. The mind must minutely analyze, synthesize and finally deduct its conclusions as a result of these mental activities.

Thus, deduction takes cognizance or awareness of the fact that, although like actions produce like results, any incompatibilities between the past and the present contingencies may and likely will

~ 411 ~

produce different results, for they do not have all things in common. This very multiplicity of varying details of individual circumstance makes it somewhat difficult for the individual to predict accurately the expected results under the present circumstances.

Best wishes for you as you informally and formally develop successful creations for your opportunities as ideas, glistening everywhere you look.

THE IDEAL ROSE IS THE REAL ROSE

Is the real rose the red rose
 Or the lavender or the pink?
No, the real rose is the pictured rose,
 The thought form of which we think!

The real rose is the ideal rose
 And not the plant in your room.
The real rose is the ideal rose.
 The image God made to bloom.

The real rose is the pattern rose
 Stamped in the seed and pod.
The real rose is the enduring rose,
 Eternal in the thought of God.

The real rose is the unseen rose,
 Invisible in sun or shade,
That pushes out a new, sweet rose
 As we pluck the ones that fade.

The ideal thing is the real thing
 In perfection's creative plan.
And vision precedes accomplishment
 In nature or in man.

And the real person is the ideal person
 Perfect in thought and deeds;
For the concept precedes the manifest
 In roses, people or weeds!

June

11

Speeches are sayings sometimes written in the sand;
but character and conduct are monuments chiseled in the solid rock.

CREATION

When the subjective became objective,
    This was creation's hour.
When the Spirit transformed its energy,
    The heavens displayed visible power.

When the heart of an atom of Spirit,
    By divine alchemy of will and word
Became flesh and stone and matter,
    Then creation's first stirrings were heard.

For God who was Spirit Eternal,
    Who filled all of time and space,
Projected a bright new dimension
    And "nature" was the smile on its face.

Nature was the light of His person,
    And nature the radiant glow.
And the glory that God projected
    Formed a universe with its overflow.

As the moon changes and the sun rises, so you progress and methods alter,
but the conservative person works with the laws of primal cause
rather than trying to put the moon where the sun is,
or to reverse the rotation of the earth on its axis.

RIVERS

Rivers roll there thru virgin land
With powers not bound by human hand.

Rivers swift and fierce and strong
Are flowing deep and broad and long.

Rivers are filled with rocks and waste
And broken trees with abandon placed.

Rivers with mountains towering high
Can whisper secrets in passing by.

Give me a boat and a river to fish,
A frying pan, a fork and a dish.

And build a fire by the river's brink.
That's real living, the way I think!

MOUNTAINS

Distant, blue and purple,
    Stalwart, strong, afar.
The mountains call the valleys
    A challenge wherever they are.

Mountains are symbols enduring,
    Rugged, tall and proud.
So people, like mountains, rise only
    When they rise above the crowd.

June

~ 12 ~

COBBLESTONE SUNSET BY VIKTOR SCHVAIKO

STAND STILL AND SEE

Fearful men on God will call
While trembling mountains shake and fall.

But, Soul of mine, be not afraid
A way of peace for thee is made.

Stand thou still, and thou shalt see
The wondrous things God does for thee.

Stand thou still when day is thru
Giving God the worship that is due.

Stand thou still when sore beset
And learn to trust and not to fret.

Stand thou still and give God praise
And thou shalt see His wondrous ways.

Thou shalt see the foes that flee
As God, almighty, fights for thee.

Thou shalt see thy mountains fall.
Thy God shall break down every wall.

Oh stand thou still and thou shalt see
The mighty things God does for thee.

June

❧ 13 ❧

*Directed attention and simple awareness are the intuitive, appropriative processes
of attaining wisdom, position, information, wealth, power, health acceptance,
and general self-improvement. For example: To direct the attention to, and become
aware of, confidence is to discern its qualities and to identify with its positive feelings.
To emotionally identify with something is to possess its qualities first
subjectively in essence and then objectively in manifest reality.*

YOUR MIND AND ADVERSITY

"A soft bed and a secure future dull the minds of millions content with mediocrity. Adversity is the
hard bed and the sharp thorn that make a person rise to labor and to better serve their fellow man."

"One end of adversity has horns; the other end produces the milk of experience
and the cream of wisdom."

"Money can make a person feel rich, adversity can make that person feel poor, but only courage can
make them face facts and forge new circumstances."

THE CREATIVE MIND

We have our instant coffee
    And we have our instant tea.
And the creative mind can do as well
    With Instant Poetry!

No task is too hard
    For the inner mind
That produces a poem
    When the title is assigned.

(CONTINUED ON NEXT PAGE)

❧ 417 ❧

An electric computer
    For creating verse!
You have to trust it
    For better or worse.

You capture the gossamer
    Beauty it brings.
You write down the rhythm
    And melody it sings.

It spells out its invisible
    Message on air.
It must be translated
    With fortuitous care.

It scans all your knowledge
    As it moves to and fro
And searches out the deep things
    That you really don't know.

It fashions with beauty
    The turn of a phrase
And blends yesterday's knowledge
    With the best of today's.

It's a willing servant
    With magical skill
That works at the bidding
    Of man's sovereign will.

It can produce what you want
    If faith gives it a start.
Your conscious mind guides it
    But it is ruled by your heart!

June

~ 14 ~

*To conceal is to reveal; for the desire for concealment often reveals
the nature of the desires and the nature of our desires reveals the desires of our nature.*

*The Creator is often treated like an abandoned gold mine.
Reopen the tunnels of relationship and dig deeper.
You will find the treasures of true acquaintanceship
long neglected but worth their weight in gold.*

STEAM LOCOMOTIVE ENGINEER BY WM. JACKSON

419

ENGINE NO. 489 BY GREG WALZ

June

~ 15 ~

Friendships, like pottery, can be broken, but love will cement them again.

CHAT WITH ME ABOUT LOVE

*Love is inner peace from tensions all set free. It is a white-winged angel thing,
invisible, that patiently dwells with me!*

Love Is Life

Love is like a river flowing, deep and broad and strong. Love is like a peaceful morning filled with rapturous song. Love is like a church bell ringing. Love is like a greening tree. Love is like a new beginning whose transformation sets us free.

Love is like a quiet tempest centered in the blustering storm. Love is life itself expressing Theta in the Beta form. Love is like a quiet ocean, deep below the surface waves. Love is like a cool, sweet fountain in the soul's subterranean caves.

Love is like the burst of sunrise heralding the Aquarian age. Love is braille-trained fingers reading meaning from life's empty page. Love is joy and peace and heaven, the pulse and heartthrob of all life. Love is a ship with full sails billowing, outriding tidal waves of strife.

Love is laughter, tears and courage. It is appreciation, friendship, peace. Love is patience long enduring, hope and faith that never cease. Love is sunset when day is dying and tomorrow with its new sunrise. Love is the soul's own secret language whose silent eloquence never dies!

Love is something born for sharing that misers hoard like glittering gold. Love knows the secret gift of caring and banks its fires when winds blow cold. Love would fill its arms with gladness and scatter sunshine where it will. Love dispels the gloom of sadness like sunbeams on life's windowsill.

All humanity needs the touch of love. It is our sacred duty on arising to resolve sincerely in our minds to greet the whole world with love in our hearts.

~ 421 ~

THAT'S WHAT YOU DO FOR ME

Love makes fools of men.
Love makes tools of men.
    Love makes knaves of men
    And sometimes slaves of men;
But every now and then
I fall in love again,
  That's what you do for me!

Love makes ghouls of men.
It sears the souls of men.
    It inspires hope in men.
    Trips the hangman's rope for men;
But every now and then
I fall in love again,
    That's what you do for me!

Love makes mutes of men.
Love makes dumb brutes of men.
    Love makes kings of men
    And gives them wings again;
So every now and then
I fall in love again,
    That's what you do for me!

June

16

MOUNTAIN STREAM BY CAROLINE SEYMOUR

CHERRYVALE BARNS BY GREG WALZ

June

~ 17 ~

*Just as good food and vitamins are important for bodybuilding,
so inspirational thoughts are essential for clear minds and strong character.*

IDEAS ABOUT WORRY

Worry goes to bed with its work shoes on, still heavy with the toils of the day.

Worry is blind negativism, exaggerated fear, and the diseased function of an inactive will,
too weary to get off the nightmare treadmill of self-doubt and inner despair.

Worry is a monster behind the mask of every person's face who hasn't conquered
devitalizing self-depreciation with its hidden face of fear.

Worry is emotional cannibalism, and the bone you gnaw on is your own.

Worry is growing anxiety, the luring fear of uncertainty, and insecurity
caught in the dilemma of indecision.

Worry is mental indigestion caused from the vitamin deficiency of
courage, faith, hope, and quiet confidence.

The worry-furrowed brow advertises, "I don't know where I'm going or why, and if I did,
I doubt if I'd really make it, and especially not on time."

The person who worries pays a high rate of interest in advance
on troubles expected but which may never come.

The person with self-confident courage is a tempered, steel instrument
with a razor-sharp edge, well-suited for any close shave.

Fear flees at the footsteps of faith; and hopelessness
cannot endure the happy songs of gratitude.

Worry doubts the outcome before the race begins.

Nothing cures worry and grim despair like exercise, sleep, sunshine, and fresh air.

Nature is never worried, and all wildlife seems to work in patient rhythm
at the task of survival unplagued by all the frantic fears that wiser mortals know.

If our yearning capacity didn't exceed our earning capacity,
our ulcers wouldn't have such churning capacity.

HE WILL KEEP ME TRIUMPHANT, I KNOW

I will lift up mine eyes to the God of the hills
    From whence cometh my help today.
For God is the One who has promised and wills
    To guide my poor feet in the way.

Surely God, who created the heavens and earth,
    Hath power to shape my path.
Protecting my life from the hour of its birth,
    He giveth the best that He hath.

Oh, how sleepless and kind, like a mother to me!
    How He watches my every step.
My keeper, my shelter, my Father is He,
    Who never hath slumbered nor slept.

He protects me by day; He sustains me at night;
    He preserveth my soul from ill.
Like shade from the trees when the sun is too bright,
    My sky with rich blessing He fills.

He preserves me from evil; He strengthens my soul;
    He is with me wherever I go!
His promise—forever tho' ages may roll—
    Will keep me triumphant, I know!

June

~ 18 ~

FALL SPLENDOR BY EVERETT SPENCER

A DEEP WELL

A fabled frog
Lived deep in a well.
From top to bottom
He knew it quite well
     Tho' he never had been outside.

A neighboring frog
From the ocean green
Dropped into the well
To see what could be seen
     When wearied of seaweed and tide.

"Where do you live?"
Said the frog in the well.
"By yonder sea
Where the great tides swell,
     Where graceful steamships ride."

"How big is your sea;
As big as this board,
Or as big as this pile
Of pebbles I hoard?
     Such comparisons will help us decide."

"It's as big as a million
Wells like this.
I live on its banks
In profoundest of bliss,
     Tho' I say it in humble pride."

"Nonsense, deceiver,
Get out of my well.
I want no guest
Whose fables would tell
     Of some fanciful place outside."

Said the frog from the Sea,
"Come, string along with me;
Your ignorance is bliss,
But it's best to be free!
     And you'll never know till you've tried!"

June

19

OCEAN GRILL BY GREG WALZ

HOW SHALL WE CROSS

How shall we cross the ocean of this world
    Without Thy wonderous grace?
Or see the light in earth's dark night
    Except through Thy smiling face?

How shall we cross the ocean of this world
    Through all of its tumultuous gales?
Without the land, the guiding hand,
    Or wind for billowing sails?

How shall we cross the ocean of this world?
    The way is long!
How shall we feel secure or long endure
    Without some cheering song?

We cannot cross the ocean of this world,
    Sail home above,
Unless God rides and safely guides
    Our ship with hands of love!

June

~ 20 ~

STRAYS BY STEVE GRAY

ATTITUDE

The attitude of gratitude
　　Will tune the human mind
To thoughtfulness and gratefulness
　　For things of every kind.

The attitude of confidence
　　Is based on common sense.
Inner strength comes at length
　　As our golden recompense.

An attitude of vibrant power
　　Will win the battlefield.
For he will win who's strong within
　　And resolves to never yield.

*The positive attitude expressed in genuine gratitude brings the mind and heart
quickly into harmony and communion with God, in whom all positive virtues reside.*

*Safety has less to do with dangerous circumstances than with the outer protection
of inner confidence and the invulnerable armor of courage and faith.*

June
~ 21 ~

ELK IN THE HIGH COUNTRY BY GREG WALZ

BACK OF THE SEED

The heart of a seed is a thought of God
    Dimensioned in atoms reversed.
For a thought is a miniature universe
    Where the shadow-body-thought came first.

As the seed embodies the future tree
    So the thought substance embodies the seed.
Thought essence and energy of life unfold
    Their pattern of destiny in matter or deed.

God projected His will and pulse of power
    And His creative image, inmost, divine
To reproduce itself on the visible plane
    In intricate, atomic, patterned design.

So in back of the seed is the thought of God
    And the thought is a miniature world
Enfolding a universe of potential ideal
    Till manifestation's banner is unfurled.

June

~ 22 ~

In the grammar of success, verbs count more than adjectives;
and description must follow action, not substitute for it.

Synchronizing My Movements in Time and Space

I believe in the perception and effectiveness of my relationship with Creator-assisted creativity. I experience it. I remember it and I depend upon it daily. I am surrounded by magnetic influence that is effective in repulsing negativity. It is an aura of gratitude, positive thinking, Divine awareness, power, protection, peace and plenty. Others will sense this and respond to it. I daily pray to possess the courage, faith and confidence to both recognize and act upon genuine hunches and accurate intuitive perceptions that come to me.

I do now have faith in, depend upon and respect my internal level of consciousness more and more and am aware of its silent working. I am increasingly able to receive, manifest and transmit these inner messages effectively. I firmly suggest and request that my inner self, in communion with the Creator, seek, accept and provide the right guidance for my life that I may know and do the right thing at the right time always and say or not say the right things intuitively. I shall be warned in adequate time of anything I need to know for my best interests and the protection of myself, my life interests and my loved ones.

I renounce any hindering or negative self-image or unnecessary self-limitations and choose the larger freedom with a proper self-image for conquest and positive progress. I am free of all self-imposed, unnecessary, unreal limitations. I shall not be disturbed by apparent misses or seeming hindrances to success. I will believe that everything is working out well for the right time and place. This is being arranged on a subconscious, inner level of intuition and spiritual perception, synchronizing my movements to accomplish these desires and proper ends. I instruct my inner mind to continually and faithfully synchronize all of my movements in time and in space that I may be at the right place at the right time, doing and saying the right things always to attain the greatest good of my life.

I have more than adequate income to use or share with others. I believe now that, as I relax having stated my need, the Creator through my higher levels of awareness, knowledge and revelation will show me solutions to any problems, stated or unstated. I will be shown answers and ways of success and how to have abundance. I ask for Divine guidance during my sleep and will either

(CONTINUED ON PAGE 437)

~ 435 ~

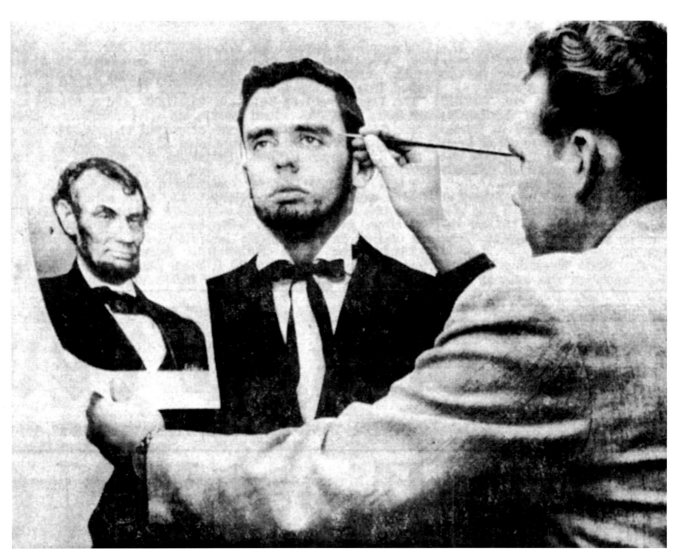

MAKEUP FOR ACTOR, W. JACKSON 1956

remember or record and be directed by the answers that come, and I shall continually improve more and more.

Enjoy your experience of positive awareness. Feel refreshed, strengthened and perfected in every way. Experience joyfulness, and be ready to face every today and all of the glad tomorrows.

AS A MAN THINKETH

Man is the master molder
And himself the clay,
And he passes self-inspection
As the judge at close of day.

For a man is a master weaver
And himself the thread
As he weaves his outer circumstances
By thoughts from heart and head.

By virtue of his thinking
As he passes on his way.
He smoothes the road or plants the thorns
That he walks on day by day.

He may weave in ignorant folly
And come at last to die
Having been his own worst enemy
Not knowing how or why.

May wisdom light our pathway,
This truth within us sink:
Our thoughts are what we make them
And we are what we think!

GARDEN COTTAGE BY SHANNON KINCAID

June

~ 23 ~

Purpose is the gun barrel, will is the trigger, action is the bullet;
but energy is the powder that drives it to the mark.

ENERGY

"Ability and judgment plus energy equal achievement.
Work is the watchword and energy is the word to watch."

AN ENERGY DIVINE

An Energy Divine
    Breaks thru the snow-soaked sod
And greening Spring springs forth
    From the energy of God.

The canopy of day
    By nightfall sore distressed
Breaks forth in Energy Divine
    And paints sunset in the west.

An Energy Divine,
    Liquid jewels men call tears,
Pour forth their water power
    In joy, in agony or fears.

An Energy Divine
    In convolution flows
Across an angry sky
    Where lurid lightning goes.

(CONTINUED ON NEXT PAGE)

An Energy Divine
    Breaks forth in feathered song
And flits from tree to tree
    The whole day long.

This Energy Divine
    Pierces the darkened night
And stars shine on in multitude
    Where God's energy is light.

An Energy Divine
    With aching back stoops low
In spotless laboratories
    Because truth men must know.

Logicians and their books,
    The lover in his tryst,
Or dew-wet flowers at dawn
    By this energy are kissed.

An Energy Divine
    Is His effulgence manifest.
From Him alone are all things
    Of motion and of rest.

An Energy Divine
    Impulses from Love Divine
Both on earth and in heaven above.
    It's yours and yet it's mine.

But God is more than pine trees
    On a snow-clad, rocky hill;
More than an expanding universe
    Of energy or existential will.

God is an Infinite Being,
    Both Personal and Supreme.
But His energy creative weaves
    The fabric of life's dream.

June

~ 24 ~

*We can only be what we are. A pink sheep with a poodle trim still can't bark,
and a cat with a dog collar can't herd sheep. It's what we are, not what we seem,
that determines the degree of our helpfulness.*

AMBITION AND ADMONITION

"Ambition to be seen simply for self-exhibition is unworthy.
Ambition to serve without recognition is unnatural. But ambition to achieve,
to serve, to improve and to arrive, seen or unseen, is true ambition."

"The run-down person, like a run-down watch, needs to be wound up often,
shaken gently and watched occasionally."

"Too many people are asleep under the shade of the family tree.
Individualism plus ambition will get up, move over, get its feet planted
and learn to cast its own shadow."

"Blind ambition carries a heavy load down the wrong road,
but once enlightened, it chooses the right road but not the light load."

TWENTY-SIX DEAD SOLDIERS

Twenty-six dead soldiers
 Are lying side by side.
These twenty-six dead soldiers
 Go marching far and wide.

These twenty-six colored men are brave.
 I've seen them rise and stand,
Ready to fight for anyone
 In any distant land.

(CONTINUED ON NEXT PAGE)

From the cover of your Bible
        To Revelation's final word
They help folks tell the message
        Wherever truth is heard.

They fight for love or bitter hate.
        They fight for war or peace.
These twenty-six dead, undying men
        Wage wars that never cease.

They fought for old Napoleon
        And helped "Heil, Hitler" too.
They billeted with Karl Marx
        When "Das Kapital" was new.

They did their best for Khrushchev's gang
        To help them reach the moon.
They fingerprint our rocketships
        And sing our freedom tune.

They communicate and negotiate
        And verbalize their views.
These twenty-six men who battle away
        To bring us all our news.

They close the communication gap
        And unite the world as one.
We salute these twenty-six soldiers
        For the good and bad they've done.

They range from Corporal Adams
        Down to Private Zee.
These twenty-six cooperative communicants,
        Speaking ALPHABETICALLY!

June
25

NECTAR FEST BY GREG WALZ

THE ARTISTRY OF LOVE

If love were the color of springtime,
    Vibrant, life-giving and green,
The flowers would bloom in profusion
    And with colors by mortals unseen!

If love were the color of summer
    And God were the Artist, I know
He'd paint every tree in bold relief
    And add the sunset's afterglow.

If love were the color of autumn:
    Scarlet, yellow and brown,
He'd paint every leaf with flaming gold
    On the hillside and in the town.

If love were the color of flowers,
    What variety and shape it would take!
With love's fragrance in every garden
    What bouquets the florists would make.

If love were the color of oceans,
    What blue and what green would vie
With the blue of the highest heaven
    Or the blue of an infant's eye.

If love were the color of tomorrow;
    Its warm waves would be unfurled
With a beauty undreamed of by artists
    On the canvass of a fresh, new world!

But love is the color of living;
    Of springtime, of summer, and fall:
A masterpiece in moods to be blended
    And hung on emotion's bare wall.

Yes, love is the color of kindness,
    Of beauty and joy and of peace,
Unselfishly shared with others;
    May your artistry ever increase!

June

~ 26 ~

No life can rise as high or remain as unshaken as the one that has gone deep enough to find the foundation stones of integrity, faith and service.

UNCLE SNOOSE AND THE BLUE-EYED GOOSE
(JACKSON FABLE)

The Blue-Eyed Goose really ruled the roost,
    As it honked and flapped night and day.
It sassed the neighbors' cats and dogs
    And the children who came out to play.

Now, Uncle Snoose was the brother-in-law
    Of the tobacco plantation man.
He liked the goose that always ran loose
    But would like it best in the roasting pan.

He loved the blue of those goose-grouch eyes.
    And he loved its courage and grace.
He loved the way it waddled and swam,
    But he'd love it best some other place.

The Blue-Eyed Goose loved Uncle Snoose,
    Like the tobacco plantation man,
For the food to feed its gizzardly greed
    And for the plantation that Blue-Eyes ran.

Then one day at Christmastime
    The cupboard was empty and bare.
So Uncle Snoose turned an idea loose,
    But he knew he wouldn't dare!

(CONTINUED ON NEXT PAGE)

~ 445 ~

He could see the Blue-Eyed Goose all brown
    As it lay trussed in the goose-greased pan.
His mouth just watered and his stomach growled
    As he dreamed up his delectable plan.

He'd fix that goose so it couldn't get loose
    And he'd do it that very day.
Let's omit the demise of the Blue-Eyed Goose
    But not the price Uncle Snoose had to pay.

The feathers flew and the goose lay bare.
    They stuffed him with stuffing and sage.
They baked and browned the Blue-Eyed Goose
    Without respect for his age.

Uncle Snoose broke his front teeth loose
    With the first bite at the Christmas dinner.
Then the gone-goose smiled up in goose-ghost heaven
    And he was the real winner.

That Blue-Eyed, detestable, indigestible goose
    Was as tough as a piece of rubber.
The grease ran down Uncle Snoose's chin
    Like you'd imagine Eskimos eating their blubber.

His stomach ached and turned in knots
    And he honked like a goose when burping.
He dunked his beard in the goose-grease gravy.
    He'd slipped when they caught him slurping.

The yard was quiet and the children cried
    And so did the plantation owner.
For Uncle Snoose choked and almost died
    When he swalled his goose-joint "boner."

His face turned blue, like the Blue-Eyed Goose,
    As he waddled, honking, away from the table.
Don't let anything ever "get your goose"
    Is the moral of this Blue-Eyed fable!

June

27

Yesterday is a morgue of dead dreams; forget them.
Yesterday is a garden of flowers; smell them.
Yesterday is the seedbed of promise for all your tomorrows; cultivate and weed them.
Yesterday is the future in disguise; work on it today and you will be proud of it tomorrow.

WISTFUL THE WIBBLE WITH THE WOBBLE IN HIS WING
(JACKSON FABLE)

Once upon a time there was a Wibble with a warped wing. Now Wibbles can fly sort of so so, but Wibbles can't sing so well because sometimes they have a wobble in the wing. This makes them catch their breath, and when they want to warble, they just wobble. You can always tell a Wibble even a long way off in the sky because it flies crooked and sings a jerky, little, wobbly song like it has a stitch in its side. It's pretty painful even for a brave little Wibble to weave its wandering, wondering way through an awakening sky on a bright morning in June, especially with an ugly wavering, wretched, writhing, unwanted wobble in its wing. So if you see a bird that flies straight and sings a happy song, just be glad; but if you see a Wibble listing, leaning and lamenting in a lonesome, longitudinal line in the early luminous light of the lingering evening loveliness, you might even say a prayer for it. It's probably a sad little Wibble with a warped wing.

Now Wistful the Wibble wished with all his withinmost want to and wishfulness that he could sing and sail and outride every gale when the storm winds blew, and still, always and ever fly a charted, chosen, comfortable course across the customary sky. But he couldn't. Tears sometimes ran down his little beak nose, and he almost got wretchedly cross-eyed watching the tears run down and come together at its pointed, patient, pitiful but picturesque little protruding proboscis (that means nose).

Of course, the wistful Wibble was willing to work at the unwelcome wobble in his way of winging and singing in the wonderful sky while his fellow birds wandered and watched and listened to the whacky, wabbling warble of his eager effort. When they laughed at him, he sometimes completely dropped the tune out of the bucket he couldn't carry it in. And sometimes he did three backward somersaults, two cartwheels, and three belly flops onto the closest cloud with his wibbly head tucked uner his wobbly wing just to show everybody how unhappy and hurt he felt forever!

Then one day the Wibble Bird-Doctor came walking through the willows and winding through the waterways watching the wavering weeds for some sign of sick singers and wistful Wibbles that were already grievously grounded for good or at least for a spell while they healed their hurt feelings in the fresh mud under the sheltering shade of a double-decked dandelion leaf.

The Wibble Bird-Doctor sure enough saw Wistful the Wibble all wretched and racked up with rheumatic remembrances of his capricious condition. The Wibble was so glad to see the Bird-Doctor that he started to warble, but it wobbled! The whole happy song went wrong; so he did three somersaults, five cartwheels, and two belly flops right through the tightly tangled timothy and tiger grass and put on such a show that the Wibble Doctor slid to a slithering, slightly shaky, but sideways sliding, standing stop. He sat on his tail, put his gold-rimmed reading glasses on the end of his beak, and rummaged rapidly, without resentment, through his pretentious portfolio, and in his black, dubious-looking, doctor's bag for an aspirin for himself! You see, the blithe Bird-Doctor was an educated, extraordinary ostrich with two extraordinary hands under his almost useless wings which were really appendages for appearance and didn't do much but keep his hands warm. In fact, his own lack of wing power helped him understand and love the Wistful Wibbles with unpredictable problems in their steering style and with stitches in their several sides under the whichever wing it was that wobbled.

You could see the Wibble Doctor sitting on his short ostrich tail, and you could see the self-administered aspirin as big as a golf ball at the top of his long larynx literally lowering itself down his thirsty throat like he was swallowing his Adam's apple. Then he got up, came through the rushes and reeds, and found the wretched, wistful Wibble all racked up with his recent repercussions. The Wibble was so sorry for itself that it lay on its back with its fairly full belly bathed by the brilliantly burning sun. It rolled its little round eyes piteously as the tears ran backwards into its listening yellow ears.

The wise Wibble Doctor wrote out three prescriptions for positive prevention of the Wistful's wobbles. They were: First, if you are a bird, stay in the sky and keep trying, for your beak will get rather rusty if you always keep crying rather than trying to sing. Second, let's put some stitches and a piece of balsam splint on your weak wing, and be sure to exercise by flying from one tree to another. That's just a little ways. Then, on the second day, fly from the littlest bush to the tallest tree in the world. That's a lot farther or could be. On the third day, try for a nonstop flight to anywhere in the everywhere. Go by way of the South Pole, and on the way back, visit with the man on the moon or even with an anxious astronaut if one is handy. Now for the last particularly purposeful, positive, preventive, and maybe even popular prescription for wistful Wibbles. Quit being wistful, wobbly, wretched, and reminiscent of past failures. Boys and bees should hum and sing. And birds and girls for sure should sing!

Then that wonderful Wibble Doctor looked at the seven stitches on the wing that wobbled and rubbed on rigorously some non-Wibble-wobble juniper juice for adequate adjustment. He picked up his pretentious portfolio and his bulging black bag and the little no-longer Wistful Wibble. Then he picked himself up and took three giant steps out of the bushes, brush and brittle briars. Each step in the mud left a three-toed track that looked like Danny the Dinosaurous had been down to the river for a drink.

The wise Wibble Doctor snuggled the now healed up and happy Wistful Wibble Bird in his hand under his own almost-worthless wing, and when they got to the water's edge, he gave the Wistful Wibble a big, giant, gentle, just-right toss clear up into the blue, blue, surprised, summer sky!

Wow! You should have seen that Wistful Wibble fly. He sailed. He soared. He sang and sort of shouted. He shifted gears and flew backwards like a hummingbird with his tail flaps down. There was never a wobble in his Wibble wings again.

So he held his three special prescriptions in his beak and he read instructions cross-eyed as he flew from one tree to another, from the littlest bush to the tallest tree in the world. Then he started on his nonstop flight to somewhere in the everywhere by the way of the South Pole. He presently planned to perch on the nose of an astronaut or on the nose of the man in the moon, for just a minute in his meanderings, on his way back again to fly the highest happy, hopeful skies of his very own planet earth in the right-here-and-now.

He remembered the good Wibble Doctor's last point in the particularized prescription, which said to sing! So he made up a little lilting, litany song out of it and sang and sang. He was pretty high up in the sky when he got back, but this is what I think he sang softly:

"I won't be wistful. I won't be wobbly and I won't be wretched anymore. Boys and bees and birds and girls should hum and sing, without a wobble in song or wing. Remember what's good and forget the bad. If you want to fly high, you've got to try and it always helps to be glad!"

Then the little Wibble Bird was gleefully glad that the extraordinary, educated ostrich, Wibble Bird-Doctor had taught it the facts about bird life and how not to wobble even if you're a Wibble. So he took another deep breath and made up some more pointed, positive prescription verses for his next happy song! He lived happily ever after and probably longer than the lingering light when the sun can't set. But he always flew straight, sang happily and shared his super-secret of song with every other Wistful Wibble in the world.

THE GETAWAY BY EVERETT SPENCER

June

~ 28 ~

THE BLACK-EYED PEAS WHO WOULDN'T SAY PLEASE
(JACKSON FABLE)

Everybody eats black-eyed peas in the South on New Year's Day.
But the black-eyed peas weren't always black. And I'll tell you how they got that way.
They were boiled and brewed and baked with bacon
Till they smelled so good your stomach was achin'.
The savory smell filled the world with beauty
Till people felt eating peas was a delicious duty.

However, the eyes of the black-eyed peas
Were blue till the day they forgot to say please.
It started out in the blued-eyed patch
Where the young peas grew in rows from scratch.
Side by side in the fields they grew and flourished
With sun and rain their roots were nourished.
The soil was a rich, dark, humus loam,
And the peas had everything in their pea-pickin home.

But they argued and fought and were never pleased or thankful
Until they were picked by bushel or by the tankful.
The blue of the blue-blue summer skies
Was reflected in their southern, blue-blue eyes.

Some that had blues eyes wished they were brown
And the ones with green eyes! You should have seen them frown.
Some caught the "pink eye" one chilly night.
Then the blue eyes and the green eyes started the black-eyed fight.
The green and the blue-eyed peas either rooted or hooted
Till they all got cross-eyed from their being beaten or booted.

(CONTINUED ON NEXT PAGE)

~ 451 ~

They pulled up their stems from where they were growing.
Without even saying, "By your leaf" they started throwing
The rocks and clods in a riotous manner.
It was a fighting pea patch with bugle and banner.
Their peashooters popped and whistled in the air.
And who shot whom they really didn't care.

HOW FAR AWAY IS YESTERDAY?

How far away is yesterday?
    How dim are its shadow of thought and deed?
    How fleet the feet where memories speed?
It seems a long, long weary way
To that lost land called yesterday!

How far away is yesterday?
    How illusive, furtive is each scene
    Obscured by days and years between
From December's age to youth in May,
Or fields in June called yesterday?

How far away is yesterday?
    Further than now but closer than never.
    Bound to the present by memories' thin tether
And checkered with shadows and sunbeams gay,
Oh, where is this land called yesterday?

How far away is yesterday?
    How tall were its hills and mountains steep?
    How strong are the boxes its treasures keep?
How real are its fields where fancies play?
Can you catch the mirage called yesterday?

How far away is yesterday?
    In the infinite cycles of human ken
    We buried the past with "what might have been"
In the half, half land where lost hopes stray.
Is this the grave of a yesterday?

How far away is yesterday?
    A little beyond the will to recall.
    Like a truant child behind a wall,
Ready to leap in startled play,
This ghost of the past called yesterday.

June

29

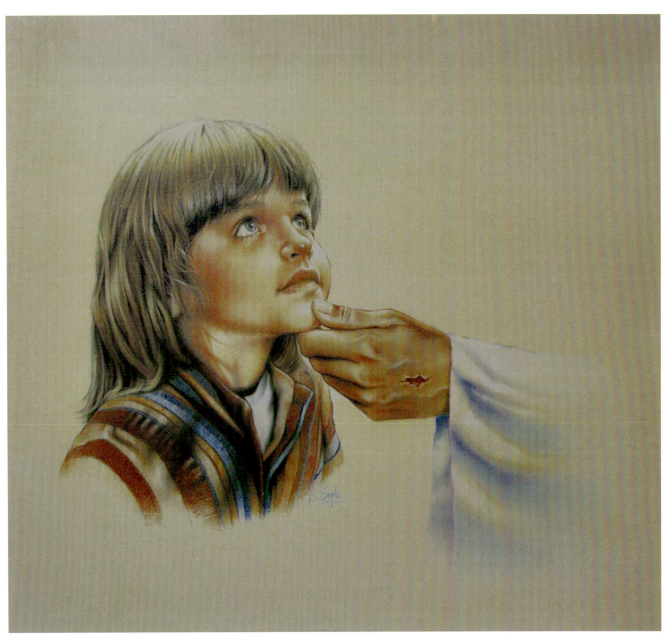

TOUCHED BY BRUCE EAGLE

MANY WOULD PRAISE THE SEA

Many would praise the sea
Who on its shores remain.
    They admire the blue
    Of the ocean's hue
But it beckons them all in vain.

They thrill at the silhouette sails
Of ships in the sunset glow.
    But they brace their feet
    In grim retreat
Because they're afraid to go!

They read of exotic islands
That call from near and far,
    But the Viking will
    They stifle and still
And they stay right where they are!

Many have praised the sea
Of Beauty, of Truth and of Good,
    But they fail to take
    The advice they make
And they're still where they've always stood.

They stand on the ocean shore.
They admire the rolling sea.
    But they ought to know
    The joyous glow
Of the life that still could be!

June

~ 30 ~

Safety has less to do with dangerous circumstances than with the outer protection of inner confidence and the invulnerable armor of courage and faith.

WHISTLE BOY, WHO-DONE-IT, AND THE WHIM-WHAMMER
(JACKSON FABLE)

This is the story of Whistle Boy, Who-Done-It, and the Whim-Whammer. Now Whistle Boy, the hero of our story, lived in a little village called You-Never-Can-Tell. And sometimes you couldn't tell, but once in a while you could. Whistle Boy is like all of us. He whistled partly because he was confident and happy and sometimes to keep up his courage when he wasn't so happy. He's the good guy.

It is also about Who-Done-It, another boy who lived in another village close to You-Never-Can-Tell but they called it Sometimes-You-Can-Tell if you looked real hard. Who-Done-It represents our natural curiosity and also the tendency to place the blame on somebody or something else other than ourselves for our problems. He is our Sherlock Holmes boy. He's our detective.

But our story is mostly about a mysterious villain named the Whim-Whammer. He's the bad guy, but he is difficult to detect because he is such an expert, quick-change-artist type of rogue. He shows up in so many guises, places and persons that his universality and his anonymity make him the multiple, nameless culprit. He's nobody in particular sometimes, and everybody else at other times. Sometimes he's ignorance, accidents, synchronicity of circumstances or something else. Mostly he's just us!

Whim-Whammer was a whammer and whimperer. You could call him a Whimper-Whammer, and he was a fusser. Whim-Whammer had whims. Then he wanted to wham. Sometimes when he saw his sister he took a whim to wham her. He was always complaining even at the drop of a feather or if a leaf blew across his path by a contrary wind. He had his whims and he sometimes had his whams, and he was for sure a Whim-Whammer-Whiner. He was always complaining. He didn't get a fair deal here. Somebody done him dirt there. He was always whamming something; kicking the dog, kicking the cat, slamming the door, throwing his books down, breaking his pencils, calling his friends bad names, sassing his mother and father, shutting the cat's tail in the door, or kicking over the dog dish. Nobody liked the Whim-Whammer.

But it was hard to pin any facts on Whim-Whammer because the Whim-Whammer wasn't just one boy. The Whim-Whammer wasn't just one girl. The Whim-Whammer wasn't just one mother, and the Whim-Whammer wasn't just one father, because the Whim-Whammer was kind of a whimsy-whammer. Some days he wanted to be a boy. Some days the Whim-Whammer wanted to be a

~ 455 ~

girl, and sometimes he wanted to be a mother or a father. Sometimes he even wanted to be the dog or the cat because the dog took whims and the cat had whams and sometimes the dog bit the cat and the cat scratched the dog. Then the dog barked at the neighbor's boy when he came by. Then sometimes the neighbor's boy caught the whim-whamsies and he went home and whammed his little brother. He went home and slammed the door, whammo! Sometimes he just went home and whined and complained to his mother.

It was hard to find out who-done-it. At least, that is what Who-Done-It thought. And he, Who-Done-It, asked so many times who done it that they finally called him Who-Done-It. He always wanted to know who the Whim-Whammer was. But the Whim-Whammer was so many people under so many circumstances doing so many things that it was awfully hard to find out who done it, when they done it, where they done it, why they done it, and to whom they done it.

But Whistle Boy didn't care. He was happy. Well, he was happy till the day the Whim-Whammer whammed him. Then he almost took the whimsy to wham back. But he kept on whistling. He remembered the boy that whistled in the graveyard to keep from being afraid. so he thought he'd whistle just in order to keep from being mad. He didn't really want to have a whim-whammy fit, because he'd seen the Whim-Whammers have whim-wham fits, and he'd rather be a Whistle Boy than a Whim-Whammer.

Who-Done-It came to visit him that day from the city of Sometimes-You-Can-Tell-If-You-Look-Hard. Who-Done-It always liked to visit his cousin in the town of You-Never-Can-Tell. So when Who-Done-It got there, the first thing he said was, "Cousin, Cousin Whistle Boy, you got a clean, cool, black eye. What I want to know is, who done it?"

Whistle Boy said, "I really can't rightly tell because I wasn't looking before I got hit, and after I was hit, I couldn't rightly look because it hurt. There were tears in one eye and it watered some and was blurry. But I saw something go by. I couldn't tell if it was a boy or girl, cat, dog, a mother, or a father or maybe even a teacher that had a whim-whammsy. But something did."

So Who-Done-It sat down. He took out his pencil and right at the point of his pencil he began to draw a picture. He began to write noises and sounds. He picked up the sound of a whimper, so he wrote whimper. Then he picked up the sound of a growl, so he wrote growl, and under it he wrote, "Maybe it's a dog. Maybe it's a Growler, the dog." And after he wrote that, he drew a picture of Lean Hungry, the neighbor's dog. Sometimes Lean Hungry whined at Whistle Boy's backdoor when he couldn't get anything to eat at his own house.

Who-Done-It kept on drawing pictures and writing words and drawing pictures and writing words. Pretty soon he came up with the Shadow, but the Shadow wasn't a man. It had on a man's shoes but it had on a lady's dress. It had on a witch's hat and it had on a mother's apron. It had on a little girl's pigtails and it had on a long nose like the dog. It had whiskers on its face like the cat and it had ponytails like his sister. It had long fingernails and it had a sash around its head like a gypsy. It had a scarf around its middle like a Black Belt karate expert. Who-Done-It didn't know which was which. So he wrote across the bottom of the paper, "Who done it? I don't know. Who done it? I don't know. Who done it? I don't know. Who done it? I don't know!"

Then they went to sleep that night. In the middle of the night, Who-Done-It woke up and he heard a sound. It sounded like scratching on the window. It sounded like footsteps on the stairs. It sounded like a woodpecker knocking on the gable end of the house. It sounded like a cat walking on the roof. It sounded like pigs rooting in the potato shed. It sounded like a horse rubbing on the shed where it itched in a place or two. It sounded a little like the creaky wheels on a train that hadn't been greased. It sounded like the humpety-bumpety-bump of a freight train going along the railroad track where the rails were fastened together with big spikes. They make an uneasy whumpety-whumpety-whumpety-whumpety-whumpety sound. Then it sounded like dry seeds rattling in an empty gourd, or like a Spanish dancer with the castanets in her hand. It sounded a little bit like her whirling, swirling skirts. It sounded a little bit like the heavy breathing of two wrestlers with one pinned on his back, short of breath, with a stitch in his side, a cramp in his rib, a charlie-horse in his right leg and with a knot in the back muscle of the other leg. It also sounded like somebody had a half nelson hold on the wind and it was moaning and groaning through a knothole. It sounded like there was a bull outside, rubbing and clicking his horns against the corner of the house. It sounded a little bit like a porcupine that was eating away at the railing on the front porch.

Who-Done-It lay there. He didn't say, "Who done it?" He said, "Who's doin' it? Who's doin' it?" Then he heard a whine. Then he heard a whimper. Then he heard a growl. Then he heard a scream. Then he heard a thud. Then he heard silence. It was so silent that you could have heard a pin drop from a mile high into a mattress of goose down. Still he could hear it. It was so quiet all around that he lay there and shivered and shivered. Who-Done-It laid there and he shook. He kept saying, "Who done it? I mean, who's doin' it? Who's doin' it?" And then the answer came. The answer said, "Who-o-o, who-o-o, who, who?"

Then Who-Done-It thought, "Did I say that? Did I think that? That sounds like Old Coot the Hoot Owl." He got up and went out to the window. Sure enough, something moved in the branches of the tree. It was the tree where all the leaves had fallen to the ground and its long, black, bare limbs looked like skeleton arms and fingers reaching up to pull the moon out of the sky. Sure enough, there was a black shadow in the crotch of the tree just above where the hole was that went down into the rotten, hollow trunk. Something moved and it sounded like feathers rustling. It couldn't be angel wings, but it did sound like feathers rustling. Something moved and two lights blinked on and they weren't car lights. He heard it again! It said, "Who-o-o, who-o-o, who-o-o-o? Who DONE IT?"

This surprised Who-Done-It so badly that he fell over backwards just as Whistle Boy got up out of bed and came through the bedroom door into the front room where Who-Done-It had been looking out of the window. When Who-Done-It fell backwards in surprise, who do you think he knocked over? Whose eye do you think he blackened? Why it was the other eye of Whistle Boy. There they were on the floor, and Who-Done-It didn't know who done it. He thought something had him. He thought something really had him. Whistle Boy didn't know what got him, because it was dark in the front room and the ghostly shadows of the skeleton tree with the long fingers that reached up to pull the moon out of the sky kept the light from shining through the window. So there they lay on the floor, too scared to move. Each one of them got up and crawled away. They met in the bedroom.

Who-Done-It said, "I was looking out of the window and I heard this thing say, 'Who-o-o, who-o-o,' and just as it said, 'done it,' something hit me. Something hit me in the back of the head and I fell on the floor, then I crawled away real quiet like."

And Whistle Boy said, "I came in to look out the window and I heard this thing say, 'Who-o-o, who-o-o DONE IT?' and right then something hit me in the eye."

They turned on the light and sure enough, Whistle Boy had two black eyes. But they didn't know who done it. They sat and shivered all night long, afraid to go to sleep because it was getting close to Halloween and they didn't know what might be prowling through the village where You-Never-Can-Tell.

In the morning when the sun came up and threw its soft light across the frosted branches and the cold, yellow-white snow, Who-Done-It and Whistle Boy got up, dressed, and went down to breakfast. After they brushed their teeth and washed their hands and combed their hair and put on their best play clothes, Whistle Boy's mother said, "You went to bed with one black eye. You get up in the morning with two black eyes. What I want to know is, who done it?"

Then Whistle boy's mother smiled and gave both of them a second helping of hotcakes. She poured on some more maple syrup and put some cow butter on their plates, then passed them the Wheaties and the Cheerios, the hot oatmeal and a second glass of milk. She smiled sad-like to herself, shook her head and said, "Maybe we'll never know who done it. Maybe we'll never, never know . . ."

I SEE GOD STANDING THERE

I see God standing there,
At the head of every stair.
    I see His face
      And His footsteps trace
Throughout the world of care.

I see God standing by
In the distant clouded sky.
    I see His form
      In every storm
Where surging oceans lie.

I see God standing near
In the face of those held dear.
    God's self I trace
      In each loved-one's face.
His acknowledgement is clear.

I see God standing still
Where winter's snows lay chill,
    Where icy pond
      And all beyond
His stately Presence fills.

I see God calmly sit
As I decide to rest a bit.
    He speaks to me
      By the shadowed tree
As He rustles the leaves of it.

I see God moving, too,
In the things all mortals do.
    I see His hand
      In what He planned
In the way His love shines through.

THE CLOAK BY TOM DUBOIS

July

~ 1 ~

TWO JACKSON DAUGHTERS BY W. JACKSON

SHE'S YOURS ONLY TODAY

A girl and her mother
　　Are of each other a part;
A chip off the diamond
　　Of the mother's own heart.

She is childishly mature
　　And yet so naïve.
Her mother's the oracle
　　She'll always believe.

She's a vulnerable bit
　　Of angel and clay
That the mother protects
　　Until the end of the way.

She's a jewel in your safe;
　　Just guard her with care,
That little adventurer
　　In need of a prayer.

She's the link in the chain
　　Of humanity's span,
The idol, the play-thing,
　　The wife of some man.

Well, mother, remember
　　You're the best that she's got.
It depends upon you
　　If she makes it or not.

So count up the cost
　　That a mother must pay;
Then pay the full price.
　　She's yours only today!

July

2

All things must blossom or wither, grow or die,
for the law of increase is the law of life.

GOD IS

God is the greatest word
    That the mortal tongue may speak.
God is the greatest truth
    That the thinking mind may seek.

God is the greatest love
    That man can manifest.
God is the greatest peace
    That brings the greatest rest.

God is the greatest power
    In the universe above,
Unlimited and Infinite
    But administered in love.

God is the greatest thought
    That earthlings can conceive.
And faith in God is the surest way
    His greatness to receive.

GRASS

Grass fresh clipped
    Like crew-cut hair.
Grass long on the edges
    Unfinished but fair.

Grass grown rank
    Like denied desire.
Grass grown tall
    A hazard to fire!

Grass swaying far
    In pendulum flight.
Grass for the cattle
    Morning and night.

Grass, the strong refuge
    For the life that is small.
Grass for the wildlife
    And sufficient for all.

Grass fresh and dew-wet
    In the morning's first sun.
Carpet for earth
    And shroud when life's done.

Grass nestled flat
    Where lovers have lain.
Struggling to be upright
    And virgin again.

Grass in great bales
    For winter's cold store.
Grass that is musty
    Thru the barn's open door.

Grass that conceals
    And hides dirt and scar.
I'm glad that God put you
    Wherever you are.

July

3

*Fear is a nightmare of delusion, but hope is a
happy dream brought to mind.*

THE LILY

I found a lily in the deep, dark wood
  Overshadowed by branches and vine.
I lay on the moss and the damp, cool earth
  And the beauty of the lily was mine.

I knew if I plucked it up by the roots
  And carried it thru the heat of the day,
The eyes of the sun and the passersby
  Would blight it and wither it away!

So I left it grow in the secret place
  Away from the eyes of all men.
There quietly I go and lay by its side
  And drink of its fragrance again.

We needed no language to communicate
  For the intuition of love was a voice
That whispered caressing, longing thoughts
  As love instinctively made its own choice.

Let the lily know that the God of love,
  Who walks thru the gardens and wood,
Opened the lily and the blind eyes to behold
  All its beauty, its truth, and its good.

As I look in the radiant lily's face
  I see more than mortal eyes can perceive,
For only the soul filled with love and faith
  Can such a vision of true beauty receive.

HEAVEN'S SUMMERTIME

Beneath the trees along the brook
Where shadows thickly fall,
I see the resting cattle lie
And hear the killdeer's call.

The laughing gurgle of the stream,
The shaded mossy sides,
The placid pools where bullheads swim
And skippers gently glide.

There's nothing like the good old earth
With flowers everywhere,
And nothing that satisfies quite
Like summer's perfumed air.

But we may breathe such air again
In better fields than these,
And rest beside the river there
Beneath the living trees.

And, Father, grant that these of earth
May reach that fairer clime,
To walk together hand in hand
In Heaven's summertime!

July

4

Patriotism, which is love, loyalty, and allegiance to one's country, does not necessitate race prejudice, imagined superiority, or international snobbery; and it respects the same quality of patriotism in the loyal citizen of another country.

Too often, vested interests and political expediency post patriotism signs on the closed-door conference of self-interest, including environmental issues.

AIR QUALITY, WATER PURITY AND LAND PRODUCTIVITY

Today we are beginning to understand that a destructive, degenerative cycle has been thrust into motion. Our mistaken assumptions about how our ecosystem works and our place in it have created negative effects. And the widespread use of out-of-balance chemicals has bankrupted much of our land and has threatened our health. These problems overtly demonstrate the toxic condition of the food we eat and the very lawns upon which our families and pets play. This abuse and imbalance has left us with significant problems with our air quality, water purity and land productivity. These issues are affecting the entire ecosystem of our spaceship earth.

The environmental question has been asked: Are toxic, out-of-balance waste and pollution, the use of harmful chemicals, an "I don't know, I don't care" attitude, inevitable parts of our society? Take the example of pesticides: Doesn't 45,000 plus, different chemical pesticide formulations registered in the United States alone, alarm you? Why so many?

There is good reason for alarm, because harmful chemical compounds, when present in excess, not only cause toxic deterioration in nature, but also function as deadly toxins for inhabitants of spaceship earth. This unwholesomeness and destruction, however, can be remedied.

With a determined resolve to see remediation happen, the assistance of natural processes, and adequate information from which to choose safe chemicals, microbial balance and sound, functional, purposeful reclamation can be accomplished. With balance, the toxicity of harmful chemicals may be neutralized, hydrocarbons and oils dissolved and digested, heavy metals and inorganic pollution impounded, the ill effects of some radioactive materials reduced, and the possibility of having toxic wastewater pollution eliminated.

Through bio-remediation, indigenous microorganisms continue to cleanse spaceship earth effectively. Their ability to decontaminate polluted sites and systems is used with various methods, including bio-stimulation and bio-augmentation. Natural microbial activity may be further encouraged by nutrients found in humic matter, thus promoting healthy organic action and providing healing for our lands.

Nature holds the answer for its own redemption from toxic conditions. The plea to the inhabitants of spaceship earth is: Be responsible, responding, informed people; foregoing selfish greed while honorably playing by nature's rules of preservation.

AIR POLLUTION SOLUTION

What's the solution for air pollution
    And the plight of all mankind?
Is it mere negation thru legislation
    Or can science an answer find?

Is it longer breath till we choke to death
    Or should we just try not to breathe?
Do we asphyxiate or levitate
    Or do we just pack up and leave?

Shall we terminate or fumigate
    Or buy an iron lung?
Or immigrate and investigate
    The planets farther flung?

Excuse me! (choke, gasp, rattle)
I believe I just choked to death!
I knew there'd be a solution.

July

~ 5 ~

WYOMING MOUNTAIN LAKE BY R. JACKSON

COME, MY LOVE

Come, my love; come, my love.
　　Come, my love, to me.
Come, my love; come, my love
　　To a trysting by the sea.

Softly blow, softly blow
　　Breezes from afar.
Come, my love; come, my love
　　The distance is not far.

Birds on wing sail and sing,
　　Sing for you and me.
Come, my love; come, my love,
　　I would sing love songs to thee.

Wild waves splash; whitecaps spray
　　The rocks and sandy shore.
Come, my love; come, my love.
　　Winter comes no more.

Come, my love; come, my love,
　　For blue, blue is the sky.
Come, my love; come, my love;
　　We must not let love die.

Come, my love; come, my love;
　　Heed love's call divine.
Come, my love, to the trysting place
　　And exchange your love for mine!

July

6

We peddle our dreams like paupers and display them where the hawkers cry;
but if new dreams could be bought in the marketplace,
I wonder whose dreams we would buy?

URBAN AND RURAL CLASS STRUCTURE

What are the comparative rankings among social classes who occupy the same relative social strata? For example, would an upper-middle-class Midwesterner find equal position in a Deep South or Yankee City?

The region and the size of the community, the type of growth, the cause for growth, the rapidity of growth, and the degree to which that community's older traditions have held are all valid factors in the strength and power of that American city's class order.

All American cities, large or small, have their social "mental Blue Book" or device for recording social rank. This register separates the "important, notable people who count" from all the rest. All cities will have their areas that represent "the wrong side of the tracks" versus the "better districts."

There are specific differences in the class system found in smaller cities and towns. The local dwellers of the smaller communities view their localities as a whole. A person knows or "someone he knows" knows everyone in town. Each inhabitant's background cannot long remain unknown; thus, almost everyone is socially ranked. However, this is less true of the larger metropolitan areas. Within the larger city, a family can move from one section to another and establish new social connections without the whole city knowing that they have raised their social status. Do consider, though, that social contacts are less easily developed for the same reason; therefore, the problem of raising the family's status is greater, because it frequently is impossible to make the beneficial connections with the people above them.

In conclusion, the small towns and cities in the older regions of our country, demonstrating the least social change in their histories, tend to exhibit the most clearly developed class orders. The youngest cities with the most noticeable social changes experience the least clearly developed social classes; however, the chances of social mobility are more abundant. By the way: Whose dreams do you buy today?

THE CITY AT NIGHT

A swarm of flickering fireflies
    Moved in flowing flight.
They settled down on our hometown
    And spread their wings of light.

Countless blinking neon signs
    Set the night aglow.
Lined the thoroughfare with flame.
    Where gleaming headlights go.

The swamp of gloom and darkness
    Reflected starlight gleam
In pools of light breaking the night
    Like the radiance of a dream.

A sweeping finger of azure light
    Searched the empty sky.
And made its quest without rest
    Forever asking "why?"

The sea of light like creating waves
    Spilled on and on and on
From mountain shore to valley floor
    In a vigil from dusk to dawn.

An endless sea of flame-tipped waves,
    Fireflies were poised in flight.
With candle flame of good or shame
    Our hometown is alive tonight.

July

7

*The great mind will strike across the fields of thought and leave the path of parroted,
verbal phrases behind; for courage, not caution, independence, not servitude,
creativity, not compliance, are the blessed centricities of those
who think for themselves and thus for all who follow.*

GOLDEN DOORS

Today we are alert, sensitive to and keenly aware of the functioning of our extrasensory faculty of our mind. Today we shall be able to call these processes into the forefront of awareness and consciousness as we shall desire to do so, and we may retain that which our minds find profitable to be remembered. Can you see yourself opening the curtains of your subconscious? See yourself opening your extrasensory awareness so that you may more fully live in the unlimited side of your being. Now we may, more and more, function with complete awareness and perfectly intermesh with the inner survival mechanisms and the willing, choosing, reasoning, conscious mind, all fully integrated and functioning as one for our best good. Through our higher sensitive self and our connection with the Creator, we have a spiritual faculty of awareness, cognizance with intuitive knowledge that is not affected by time or space or other persons' minds.

Knowledge and wisdom are golden doors opened wide to enter in. We are now inside. We know instinctively the things we need or desire to know. We discern them. We have a quickened sensitivity and a distinguishing, perceptive mental process. The Creator's creativity is often revealed through events, situations, conditions, solutions, courses of action, information and knowledge in advance. This can be true for both of us today.

Join me today in considering these thoughts. Is it possible that you, too, may enjoy a more full life? I challenge you to allow the golden doors of wisdom and knowledge to be open to you. The poem for today suggests that love calls us through these golden doors where rich joy awaits.

WISDOM'S GATE

Fierce the winds of soul bombardment
    That in tumult rise and blow.
Oh, the longings deep within me
    That dog my footsteps as I go.

Great the love of God the Father
    Washing grime and dust away,
Purging all that's ill within me,
    Ready for my evaluation day.

Great the grace of contemplation!
    Ripe the fruit on thought's full tree.
But to climb to heights supernal
    Claims to the highest part of me.

Oh, to know the destination
    And direction life should take.
Oh, to know what's truly worthy
    And that to choose for wisdom's sake.

How supreme the love that calls me.
    Rich the joys that here await.
As I stand in beggar's garments
    At Eternal Wisdom's gate.

July

8

There is no birth of progress without the parenthood of thought.

SURVIVAL

With half the race of mortals
    Physically worn and ill,
With eighty out of one hundred
    needing psychiatric treatment still.

It seems that with self-destruction
    And the hidden will to die,
Man is fighting a losing battle
    With despair as his only cry.

Where the will to live and to labor,
    To achieve and to give and to be
Is broken, beaten and crowded back
    Too blinded, too weary to see.

There's a need for a vital challenge,
    A spark of achieving fire,
Rekindling the will to live and serve,
    To conquer and reach up higher.

The powerful drive of discovery,
    The desire to reach a goal,
These are the things for which men live
    In spite of troubles that roll.

The motives of love and of sharing,
    The spirit of comradeship,
These are the virtues and purposes
    That from our hearts would slip.

(CONTINUED ON NEXT PAGE)

The sick man must throw off his sickness
 And the ills of a slow suicide,
Where he drives himself to oblivion
 Or behind his failures would hide.

With the burden of defeat and of darkness
 Gone from his heart and his mind,
The sick man with strength for his weakness
 A new way of living will find.

Choose then your goals and your purpose
 Truly worthwhile and tried,
Then life will be more than survival
 And God himself will walk by your side.

And the battles will all turn to victories
 And the self-imposed ills will be healed.
And life will well be worth living
 Before your life's forces will yield.

For in each of our minds there's a battle
 Twixt the forces of death and of life.
And the man who has faith will conquer
 And triumph whatever the strife.

WANDERING THOUGHTS

As hard to curb as the vagrant breeze
    Is the restless, fleeting mind.
Like the bee that flits from rose to rose
    A sweeter nectar to find.

O wandering, fickle, uncurbed mind,
    So impetuous, self-willed, untaught,
Like a "green-broke" horse turned out too long
    That would rather not be caught.

With oats in hand and lasso hid
    I catch thought's glistening eye.
I can almost touch its cold, damp nose
    When it whirls and dashes by.

When I think it's too late to concentrate
    As I stand in the dust and the heat,
Then the thought comes rushing back again
    To the sound of echoing feet.

LIBERTY'S DIAMOND BY NENAD MIRKOVIC II

July
~ 9 ~

SHAVANO AND TABEGUACHE BY GREG WALZ

A MASTERPIECE SOMEDAY

I saw a golden sunset spread
    Across the Pacific skies
Unfolding a vision of splendor
    Before my wondering eyes.

A riot of luminous colors,
    As far as the eye could see,
Was splashed with the brush of time
    On the canvas of immensity.

The lavish hand of the painter
    Neither paints nor colors would spare,
But with strokes of creative genius
    Left a masterpiece there!

I would like to paint with abandon,
    With strokes of confident ease
Till I had painted a life supernal
    That would the eye of the Creator please.

But it takes the lengthening shadows
    And the dark clouds that obscure the sun,
The red of life's blood must be mingled
    With our tears and our sweat when we're done.

And the gold of the smile of patience
    With the scarlet of shame confessed,
Plus hope with its silver lining
    Must be blended with all the rest.

Perhaps the wings of some angel critic
    Might smooth our crude brush strokes away
And change our primitive paintings
    To a masterpiece some day.

When success seems a delusion and hope a mirage, when the day seems all darkness and you can't remember where you were going or why, just remember that the sun will rise again tomorrow morning.

July

~ 10 ~

To worry little and love much; to live without tension, competition, irritation, criticism, or hostility; to have faith in God and in humanity; to have contentment, security, tranquility, calmness, confidence and serenity; to practice moderation, relaxation and exercise; and to enjoy nature, will help one live a more fulfilled life.

GIFT OR GIVER

Have you waited sometimes for a blessing?
It tarried, you didn't know why.
Perhaps some fault had you sensed it,
Some doubt that your heart would deny.

Did you ask and really expect it?
Did you honestly come to Him
To ask for the best in His wisdom,
Or only some temporal whim?

Sometimes we must wait for His promise
And gifts of a transitive self.
A good many things we must wait for
But not for the Giver Himself!

PRAYER FOR PEACE

Sad wail of man's despairing heart,
    Filled with strife, pity and hate,
Selfishness, love, deceit and the truth
    Vying and shaping his fate.

Confusion at sunset and sunrise in turn
    With its beauty half lost to his view.
Living and dying, unseeing and sighing,
    The false mixed up with the true.

Great God, in your mercy and pitiful love
    Look down on our mortal deceit.
Reviving in us some divine platitude
    That our grief-stricken lips can repeat.

Give paths for the feet, light for the eyes.
    Give hope and life for the soul.
Give peace, give love, draw our hearts above.
    Make our spirits and minds truly whole.

Draw us up toward the stature of God himself.
    Let our hearts and His heart be as one.
May peace be our portion day after day
    Till earth's sunrise in heaven is begun.

*The trinity of man's being cries out for satisfaction in the wisdom of truth,
the revelation of the good, and the sense-apprehended beauty of the natural,
each in its proper proportion; and if the distilled essence of the best
cannot satisfy man's inner being, there is little hope that the
sordid sewage of the distorted senses alone can satisfy it adequately.*

July

~ 11 ~

Nature both conceals and reveals the creator to the minds of men.
Those who look long and lovingly will find the creator everywhere.

Faith is an ocean where even hardships ride like leaves upborne on its mighty tide.

HERITAGE OF EARTH

The flowers along the woodland path,
The dew-washed blades of grass,
The petaled rose's sweet perfume
That greets us as we pass;

The cadence of the waterfall,
The patter of the rain,
The air refreshed by summer shower,
The pools that still remain;

The shadows in the quiet brook,
The textured clouds of white,
The moonlight distances and stars,
The voices of the night;

The whispered secrets of the wind,
The God who gave them birth
Are all the heritage of those
Who love this grand earth!

ANGELS OVER THE TETONS BY GREG WALZ

WATER TOWER BY JEAN BARTLETT

FIXER UPPER BY GREG WALZ

July

～ 12 ～

*When success seems a delusion and hope a mirage, when the day seems all darkness
and you can't remember where you were going or why, just remember
that the sun will rise again tomorrow morning.*

*Yesterday is a morgue of dead dreams; forget them. Yesterday is a garden of flowers;
smell them. Yesterday is the seedbed of promise for all your tomorrows;
cultivate and weed them. Yesterday is the future in disguise;
work on it today and you will be proud of it tomorrow.*

WHAT TRULY IS GOD'S PLAN?

You sit upon a mountaintop and watch the scene below,
A waterfall, the leaves, the trees swaying to and fro,
The crack of thunder in the sky, the forked flash of light,
The sound of raindrops, falling slowly, the lowering shades of night.
Clouds floating in an azure sky, to hide the sun's bright rays,
The breezes sighing in the trees bring the close of day.
Shadows creep on ghostly feet, along a narrow lane,
You sit and wonder why all this, and then you think again.
Whence came I, where am I from, what did I do today?
Who am I and for what cause am I meant to stay?
Or am I meant to travel on—in this world of man?
And shall I ever know, for me,
What truly is God's plan? *(J.H. Westcott)*

I SHALL NOT FEAR

Only the blue sky above me
    Is the limit of my success in life.
Only the coward within me
    Can defeat me in the battle's strife.

I shall cancel out my fears with courage.
    I shall transform all my hate to love.
I shall leave the caverns of the fearful
    To walk the pathway of triumph above.

I shall learn to know life's true meaning.
    Know the truth of what I should be.
I shall trim my sails for conquest,
    Never fearing storms that threaten me.

I shall conquer and be grateful for victory.
    I shall rest when this life is done.
And the world will know I lived it
    With my face set toward the rising sun!

July

~ 13 ~

FULVIC: ABOVE THE FORMS OF MATTER BY W. JACKSON

ABOVE THE FORMS OF MATTER

Above the forms of matter,
    Above the physical laws,
Is the supernatural pattern
    Of thought as the creative cause.

Above the forms of matter
    Is the pulse and energy of life,
Where cause to effect is wedded
    As the union of husband and wife.

Above the forms of matter
    Is the mind unlimited and free,
Where thought manifests in being
    And will, the prime mover must be.

Above the forms of matter
    Is the substance of formless mind,
By thought, creatively projected
    In individualized expression refined.

Above the forms of matter
    Is One God sustaining each law
Who is Substance, Spirit and Creator,
    On whose sustenance all things must draw.

July

~ 14 ~

*Ambition's empty substance, like the fabric of a dream, can cast no eternal shadow
where it falls, save the Creator be in it.*

SELFISH GLORY

"Glory, that eminence of fame, condition, pleasure, pride, and honor,
is a precarious pinnacle and a position in which it is difficult
to maintain a proper balance."

"Earthly fame, like a slipping halo of glory, blinds a man's eyes so that he sees
only the distorted image of himself without giving attention to the
whole picture of life; and covers man's ears until he hears only the
commendations and gives no credence to criticism, however true."

"An angry man is a tempest-tossed ship caught in the storm of his own brewing."

"Fleeter than the flight of a bat on the wing,
is the brief hour of honor for a pauper or a king."

I'M YOUR SISTER AND YOUR BROTHER

I'm your sister and I'm your brother
Ye shadows that dwell in the lake.
    My life is a mirage
    That ripples dislodge
Where the sun its own shadows would make.

I'm your sister and I'm your brother
Ye leaves that fall in the pond.
    So man falls to earth
    Where nature gave birth
To float thru the great beyond!

(CONTINUED ON NEXT PAGE)

I'm your sister and I'm your brother
I see your yellow-webbed feet.
    Do not glide by
    With wary turned eye
In a ripple of mallard retreat!

I'm your sister and I'm your brother
Ye trees whose leaves fall fast.
    My own juices dry
    And dehydrated I cry
For the summers and springs that are past.

I'm your sister and I'm your brother
Ye sturdy tree trunks unmoved.
    But I'll leave a trace
    That time can't erase—
My sturdiness thereby be proved!

I'm your sister and I'm your brother
Ye birds who raucously sing.
    There's sweet discord
    That earth can afford
In the varied songs that you bring.

I'm your sister and I'm your brother
Ye carpeted grasses, windswept,
    Vacuumed by the breeze
    That no mortal eye sees.
By the Heavenly gardener kept!

I'm your sister and I'm your brother
The life that flows thru my brain
    Is energy Divine
    It's yours and it's mine.
In the springtime it will rise once again!

July

~ 15 ~

It is the gift, the manner and meaning of the giving and above all the giver,
back of the giving, that makes the gift a cherished thing.

PAUL'S PASSION PARAPHRASED

I may verbalize with the eloquence of men, women and angels, but if I have no love, I am a noisy gong or a clanging cymbal;

I may project great thoughts regarding the future, fathom all mysteries and secret knowledge and learning;

I may have such absolute faith and confidence that I can move hills from their permanent location, but if I have no love, I count for nothing;

I may distribute all I have collected and do now possess to goodwill and charity,

I may sacrifice my life as a martyr, giving my body to be burned for a cause, but if I have no love, I make nothing of it.

Love is so very patient, so very kind. Love knows no jealousy. Love makes no parade, gives itself no false airs, is never rude, never selfish, never irritated, never even resentful. Furthermore, love is never glad when others go wrong. Love is gladdened by goodness and is always slow to expose, always eager to believe the best, always hopeful, always patient. Remember also—love never disappears. As for projecting things in the future, it will be superseded; as for speaking in non-understood riddles or puzzles, they will cease; as for knowledge, it will be superseded. Today we only know bit by bit; and we can only project the future bit by bit; but when we learn about that which is perfect, the selfish, imperfect will be superseded.

When I was a child, I talked like a child, I thought and planned like a child, I argued like a child. Now that I am a more mature person, I am done with childish ways.

At present, we only see the baffling reflections in a mirror, but the future will find us understanding as "face to face." At present I am learning bit by bit, but then I shall understand, as all along I have myself been understood.

Therefore, faith and hope and love last forever, these three, but the greatest of all is LOVE! Today MAKE LOVE YOUR GREATEST AIM.

THE MAGIC OF LOVE

Love, that soft, white, gossamer feather
    Floating down from silver angel wing,
Lifts the heart to soar in golden gladness
    Teaching earth's mute lips again to sing!

Love, that tender, warm, consuming passion
    The opposite yet so akin to hate
That when jealousy provokes or anger
    Locks the heart and quickly bars the gate.

Love, that pure and noble, yielding pleasure,
    Knows no gift too great to give;
But rejected turns with smoldering fury
    On itself devoid of will to live.

Love, that rugged anchor gripping firmly,
    Still holds fast in every stormy gale;
But great ships have drifted seaward
    When moorings break or anchors fail.

Love, that sturdy root of nature,
    Finds nourishment in sun-baked, barren earth,
And happy is the rock by which it clings there
    In a union whence true beauty finds its birth.

Love, that cloud that casts cool shadows
    On the feverish, restless, burning sand,
Makes an oasis where once was only desert
    Blooming now beneath the magic of love's hand.

July

16

*If life requires change, let judgment dictate its direction
and integrity its quality.*

CREATIVITY IS KING!
KING MIDAS WITH THE GOLDEN TOUCH

Creativity is a Regal Virtue. It is a God-like gift among the many abilities and capacities of the human mind. Creativity caresses with splendor all that its fingers touch. It, too, like King Midas, whose touch turned all things into gold, increases the usage value and intrinsic worth of all things within its realm. Only when its genius becomes destructive or negative does its human values suffer loss, as did the daughter of King Midas of old. But creativity is king, and its kingdom has no bounds. Beneficent improvement is the code of its kingdom and progress is its passion. It is the king, whose golden touch turns difficulties into opportunities, problems into answers, weakness into strength, poverty into riches and failure into success! Creativity is king!

Creativity is the king's alchemist who turns the baser metals of the drab commonplace into the valuable, priceless jewels of enjoyment, the silver and gold coins of high accomplishment, excitement and purposeful achievement.

Creativity is the king of Inspiration. Creativity takes the old, dried paint out of a twisted, tin tube, fastens a few hairs from a camel's back to a little sliver of wood, squares off in front of a piece of coarse canvass and paints a "Mona Lisa" whose quizzical smile seems to say, "Mind is the master, wisdom is the artist and Creativity is king!"

Creativity spreads its inspiration in vivid color, intricate design and accurate perspective over canvasses without end, and each tells a different story in color key, mood and message. Creativity sings its inspiration in orchestration, individual instrumentation, vocal interpretation and combinations of all these, without end. But in it all, Creativity is king of melodies and meaning, who conducts the orchestration of inspiration and stirs the blood of marching persons, or soothes the mind with restful cadences. Creativity controls, for Creativity is king! (To be continued on July 17)

495

CHANGE OF VISION

When your eyes grew tired of knitting,
Hard the chair where you were sitting,
You walked to yonder windowpane,
Viewed the landscape thru the rain,
Did you not?

Now, perhaps you're just as weary
Of your treadmill patch of dirt.
With your struggles and your conflicts
Are your feelings often hurt?
Likely so.

True, the odds you face are many,
And the friends who help are few;
While the smoke and dust of battle
Hide your glimpse of heaven's blue;
Dims your eyes.

But thru mists that now are falling,
There's a promised rainbow calling!
You can see its color breaking
In a day with hope awaking!
Sure you can.

Look away, then, rest your eyes;
Get a glimpse of Paradise.
Dry those tears of indecision;
What you need is a change of vision;
Is it not?

July

~ 17 ~

*Incompetence, indifference, indolence and loss of interest
are the pallbearers at the funeral called failure.*

CREATIVITY IS KING!

Creativity is king of Perception. Creativity is the sight of an inner eye. It is the optical focus of man's second sight, the glasses of fresh, practical objectivity, added to the haze of illimitable vistas of future outcomes, application and uses of products, people and places. Creative envisioning sees the many mountains of difficulties to be climbed but notices also, and marks on its map the passes, the contour of the terrain and the various trails over which people have traveled before. It sees, too, the better ways, the shortcuts, the curves that need to be straightened, the rivers that need to be bridged and the high places that need to be brought down. Creativity is the king of perception, the focusing faculty of the binoculars of inner and outer, short-range and long-range perception.

Creativity sees the need, sees the facts involved, sees the variety of possibilities for solution, and sees relationships, changes, improvements and all manner of possible combinations. It sees the best way out, the best way of traveling the journey, the best time to make it, the best things to take along and the best reasons for going, and it receives the best rewards at the journey's end. Creativity is king of perception with the high and piercing vision of the eagle soaring confidently in the far sky.

Creativity is the king of Crises. To creativity, a crisis is a challenge. Conformity is the death of creativity, but it thrives on necessity and is inspired by imperative demands. Adverse circumstances are the fuel from which it stokes the consuming fires under the funeral pyre of failure. Give creativity a crisis and creativity gives you a credible performance of prevention, or a positive solution. The subconscious mind is activated by danger, is stimulated by emergencies and rises confidently to the occasion when immediacy demands. Creativity is a product of the subconscious mind, and Creativity is king in the crises of life for those who have learned to trust it. (To be continued on July 18)

SLEEP

Sleep sealed my propped-up eyelids
    And laid them softly down.
Sleep took my work shoes from my feet
    And brought my dressing gown.

Sleep stole my good intentions
    And robbed me of my zeal.
It gave me wine and drugged me
    Till my conscience could not feel.

Sleep snatched my sense of duty
    When tasks were half begun.
It pilfered the hours God gave me
    And hid my setting sun.

Sleep stole my hope of harvest
    And the autumn signs concealed.
It laughed at winter's coming
    As the crops died in the field.

Sleep dulled my hope of Paradise
    Till I saw thru heavy eyes
That only those who wake and work
    Will win the final prize!

Self-improvement is easier than the reformation of all humanity.

July

～ 18 ～

Friendships, like forged steel, are fashioned in the furnaces of adversity.

CREATIVITY IS KING!

Creativity is king of Curiosity. Creativity wants to know how everyone and everything works. It believes that, with a little tinkering and prescribing, everybody and everything could be made to work a little better. It has prescriptions and vitamins for minor ailments of all its subjects. It has major operations for more serious difficulties. It even has strong, self-motivational stimulants for the awakening of its own inner genius.

Curiosity loves confrontations, encounters and inquiry. These are as natural to it as shaking hands with Uncle John, but Creativity is king and it dictates the changes in the persons, products or environment of its encounters, and all things are benefited by the healing touch of the "king's" hand. Curiosity gives out its undivided concentration and attention in each idea preceding the corrective outflow of its curative energy. Creativity is a curious king who must know before he can do. Creativity is king.

Creativity is king of Light. The shafted rays of his inner illumination identify the problem in its inception, with the evaluative process of Creativity's analytical insights. Creativity plays the searchlights of its inquiry in the gathering of information under the light of knowledge and the classification and differentiation of its relationships. The spotlights of its hypotheses are radiant with possible solutions and variants of its conjectured conclusions as it continues to ask, "What more? What besides these? Where in addition? How otherwise? And so on." These are the reflections of its alternatives.

The flash of understanding that lights up the sky of its contemplation glows and shimmers like the aurora borealis as it arises from the inner awareness of its intuitive recognition of relatedness. Its insight arises from the relativity of the parts to the whole, and it observes the unity beneath diversity and sees that answers are in integral part of all problems. It conceives in the light of its intensified awareness of reality that truth is a related whole and that the universe has a cohesive tendency for balance and completion. Remember, creativity is blessed, relative to a positive relationship with the Creator. Creativity lights the lamps in the shadows of ignorance. Creativity is king of the light of insight! (To be continued on July 19)

～ 499 ～

HE WALKED WITH ME

God was the Gardener strong
Who leaving behind the throng

Beckoned me come with Him
Where evening sun grew dim;

Where shadows reached out their hands
Caressing the weary lands.

Then He pointed to sunset's glow
Where clouds were golden and low;

Where mountains were rimmed with fire
And beauty was the heart's desire.

He pointed them out to me
Each cloud, each shrub, each tree.

He took me gently by the hand
And walked across the land.

Together thru His own eyes
I saw that earth was Paradise!

July

19

At midnight the rose of tomorrow blooms with its fragrance bold;
and sunrise will greet it with dewdrops of hope, brighter than diamonds or gold.

CREATIVITY IS KING!

Creativity is king of Competence. Creativity has a kingdom of resourcefulness, and the Creator's kingdom is within. It holds all exterior things as satellites in the orbit of its power. Its solutions, its sources and its secrets of success are self-generated from the hidden treasures of its inner resourcefulness. Creativity has reserve wealth unknown even to its own sense of extended knowledge. It possesses not only what it has in the vaults marked "experience," but it also houses the machinery that manufactures the processes of accomplishment. It has the mint that makes the money and the dynamos that create the hidden powers. It has the mechanics on duty to repair its difficulties, and unless there is too much outside interference, its competence knows no bounds.

Creativity is king of Cooperation. Let each would-be creator learn that cooperation is the keynote to creativity. To form a brainstorming, mastermind group of creative people is a basic step to successful mentation. There is great wisdom in the multiplying of concepts already held in the average mind. Each person's prior experience is individually remembered, evaluated and ready for practical projection. Together we are much wiser than any one of us are alone. Cooperation is the expected procedure in the realm of Creativity. (To be continued on July 20)

GREY SUNSET

When God takes the red from the sunset,
    The blue and the gold from the sky,
When He plucks out the brilliant plumage
    From all the songbirds that fly;

When He takes the green from the ocean
    And blood no longer is red,
When the face of the sky is pallid
    And the pulse of the earth is dead;

When the life-giving green of the foliage
    Is withered and sear on the limb,
When the sun no longer is golden
    And the stars forever are dim;

When the light is lost in the chaos,
    And black has turned into grey,
When the day is the same as the nighttime,
    And the night is the same as the day;

When the world has lost all its beauty,
    And refraction diffuses no light,
When the rainbow has lost all its color,
    And when wrong is no different than right;

When depth and height have been leveled,
    And men grope in a dismal haze,
When color-blind men in a color-blind world
    Are voicing monotonous praise;

Then the poet will have lost his passion,
    And the writer will have broken his pen.
And the musician will have lost his genius,
    And the singer will be silent again.

The artist will fold up his easel
    And pack all his canvass away,
For there never could be a bright sunset
    If all of earth's colors were grey!

July

~ 20 ~

*Life is for action, youth is for learning,
and age is for memories
without regret.*

CREATIVITY IS KING!

Creativity is king of Common Sense. Creative common sense doesn't just tear watches apart to see why they won't run, but has the wisdom to put the pieces together again with the assurance that cleaning, lubrication and minor repair are no major problems for its instinct for synthesis and its urge for togetherness. Creativity's uncommon common sense is manifest in the deductive reasoning of scientific verification and evaluation. It finally comes to reject the less desirable solutions, perfects the best possible answers, and tests the end results in the crucibles of practical application. This is good judgment. This is critical evaluation in its proper place. This is verification. This is the safety valve for genius. There is always a castle called "Common Sense" in the realm where creative accountability must rule with wisdom and equity.

Creativity is king of Idea Procreation. Necessity is the queen. The Creativity principle is the courtship, conception, embryonic development, labor pains, birth, dressing, maturing and working of the phases of ideation. Creativity couldn't be king without siring offspring in his own image, for "imagineering" is his nature, and his game, and Imagination is his other royal name. His royal family, too, is worthy of note.

THE KING'S CHILDREN:

Expressiveness is the eldest child, a Prince of considerable activity. He loves freedom and lends spontaneity to a rigorous independence. His favorite brother, a twin, in fact, is Productiveness, who, at an early age, showed great aptitude in skills, techniques and development.

Prince Inventiveness, another son, delights in discovering things new and old and is always mixing new potions, combining strange ingredients, building curious contraptions and powerful machines from bits of this and parts of that. He just knew they would somehow fit together to make something better than the separate parts could ever make. Be inventive. It may be your key to the patent office!

~ 503 ~

Princess Innovation is a true daughter of King Creativity. She tends toward abstraction, novelty, variety and minor alterations that always add a new touch of femininity and originality to the refinements of her happy individuality. She may not change the world, but she will make it a more interesting place to live. Be innovative. It is the key to refinement! (To be continued on July 21)

WHEN SPRING IS IN THE AIR

His grimy feet
In the dusty street,
A brown dog by his side,
He trudged along,
And the sun was strong,
But so was his boyish pride.

And every gust
Of the spiraled dust
That followed the little lad,
Awoke in me
The memory
Of days that made me glad.

To unshod feet
The dust was sweet—
As sweet as the thrush's song,
Who warbled each note
From its ruby throat
To the pair who trudged along.

What fuller joy to man or boy
Than a dog—but never a care;
To walk some road
Without a load
When spring is in the air!

July

~ 21 ~

Opportunity is a golden moment: awakened by awareness, selected with discernment, set in the broach of preparedness, cut and shaped by man's purpose, purchased by resolution and denial, and worn in the honor of attainment.

CREATIVITY IS KING!

THE KING'S CHILDREN

Prince Emergent Creativity will no doubt be the successor to the throne. He has talent, training and tremendous potential. They call him Prince Emergent Creativity because he knows how to relate the subjective to the objective and to work on the plain of visible practicality. He is a born producer. Prince Emergent Creativity, or as referred to by his friends, **Sir Practicality**, knows that identifying a problem, researching solutions, incubating processes, or even to include the flashes of pure illumination, could never cure "causes of change" characteristics, unless he meshed gears with reality and produced in the realm of practicality. Sir Practicality knows that the purpose of Creativity is to bring workable things into being. Sir Practicality wants to foster life forms with the stamp of his own individuality. He wants to make things more efficient and not to change things just for change's sake. Actuality is his reality! His awareness is intensified. Sir Practicality becomes physically as well as mentally activated and goes into relevant ACTION!

Prince Emergent Creativity, also known as Sir Practicality, is a man who stresses meaningful achievement in a world of people, places and problems. He is more than a Prince Charmer with fluent theories. He is more than a weaver of dreams. He puts his product on the shelves of the world and cries his wares in the marketplaces. Sir Practicality knows that creative accountability is educational competence, taking its finals.

Are you willing to be practical?

It is the key to successful accountability. Practical Creativity is Royal, and Commerce is his Crown! Tomorrow, July 22, we will consider the Ten Codes of the Creative Kingdom.

THE LIGHT

Oh, give me back again,
　　Give me back what I felt before.
The universal sense of oneness held
And fearless, comprehensive love,
Insight Infinite revealed
　　Thru illumination's door.

Oh, give me back again,
　　Oh, give me back again, I pray
That light illusive but divine
With unmeasured, implicit wonderment
And that frail, lovely flower, hope,
　　That I heedlessly had lain away.

Oh, give me back again,
　　Oh, give me back again, I say,
My awakened sense of knowledge deep,
My humility, receptivity and endless peace,
My awareness, ecstasy and joy,
　　My gift from God to men who truly pray.

MEDITATION PRAYER

Oh God of love and light, whose shining through the eternal years has never dimmed or faltered, grant to us today the unwavering of a certain faith in You and in the providences of life. May we have the confident boldness to expect and receive your best in this life and in the future to come. May we, like undimmed light, direct some other wandering friend to the reality of a relationship with You. May we reflect the burning brightness of Your Love Divine. May we dispel the darkness of wrongs among our fellow travelers, as You guide each of us into your glorious love and light. Thank you. Amen.

July

~ 22 ~

*Dark days reflect the condition of our inner sight as much as
the condition of our outer circumstances.*

KEYS THAT UNLOCK CREATIVITY'S DOORS

TEN CODES OF THE CREATIVE KINGDOM

Creativity is a necessity. Its skills can be activated, released and utilized for successful accomplishment. The following activators are Keys that unlock Creativity's Door.

1. BE POSITIVE! Have a positive mental attitude. Be filled with expectancy, cheerfulness and charity. Look for the best in everything and everyone. Be positive. It unlocks the doors of seeming impossibilities.

2. BE CURIOUS! Stimulate continued interest and research. Examine, concentrate and analyze. Be curious. Curiosity is the key to satisfaction.

3. VISUALIZE! To make pictures, to create images and to see things as they are and as they could be is the nature of imagination and the duty of creativity. Visualize. It is the key to creative perception.

4. LEARN TO MEDITATE. Think deeply and continuously about the underlying nature and principles of things. Spend time alone. Spend time close to nature, close to the Creator, and if possible, meditate pictorially. Tap the subconscious. Record the facts and insights revealed in times of pure inspiration. Learn to meditate and to concentrate; it is the key to creative insight.

5. EXPAND YOUR AWARENESS. Increase your consciousness! Be alive to life. Wake yourself up and live! Expand the sensitiveness of sensory awareness, and mindfulness. Open the windows of your mind. Open the doors to your Spirit. Awareness is the key to knowledge and wisdom.

6. INTENSIFY ALL LEGITIMATE DESIRE. Build a fire under your desire. Emotionalize your drives and needs, your hopes and aspirations, through prayer and meditation. See your desires as

present, as fulfilled, in detail and with the gratitude of acceptance. Claim them as your very own in the intensified desire of present possession. Intensify all legitimate desire. Desire is the key to conquest.

7. BE AMBITIOUS! Industry is a virtue. Work. Work. Work. Experiment, rest, apply, and practice. Creativity must have a workshop and a master craftsman with calluses on his fingers. Be ambitious! It is the key to achievement.

8. BE COOPERATIVE! Learn to reach out to others for the missing parts of your puzzle if you cannot find the complete answer within. Work for and with others, for together we can reach solutions that by ourselves we might have failed to achieve. Learn to work and think as a part of a non-critical, non-competitive, creative group. Evaluation comes later along with other cooperative processes. Group brainstorming is an art that the cooperative can learn. Be cooperative. It is the key to accumulation.

9. BE PERSISTENT! Be patient but be persistent. Be determined and never give up. Try, try, try again and again. A right solution will be forthcoming soon. Success is often just one step farther on! Be persistent. It is the key to attainment.

10. BE COMPETENT! Get the facts; know the problem inside and out. Research, study, learn and propose answers. Examine and re-examine each possibility for validity. Increase your competence through experience, confidence and practice in creativity. Competence works best in the full light of factual and inner illumination. Turn on all the lights! Be competent; it is the key to excellence.

ESCAPE EMPTINESS

Empty words in empty temples
    Re-echo from each empty hall.
Empty hearts receive no message
    Where empty specter footsteps fall.

Empty words have lost their meaning.
    Empty forms are hard and dry.
Emptied of the Living Presence
    In emptiness we live and die!

Oh, God of fullness, add Your blessing
    To all our worship and our love.
Fill our empty hearts and churches
    With Your Presence from above!

July

23

Infidelity blossoms in rebellion and is the fruit of disobedience;
its skepticism is self-deception for self-justification because of self-inflation
and self-indulgence, however expressed.

THE REWARDS OF CREATIVE IMAGINATION

Creative Imagination teaches one to see from many viewpoints. It teaches us to identify with things, with knowledge and with the feelings and viewpoints of the other person.

Creative Imagination projects itself into the future and sees around the corner and makes advanced preparation possible. It keeps you ahead in the race.

Creative imagination puts the flare of showmanship in social settings, in education, in selling and in business in general.

The person with Creative Imagination has, or will have in due time, an appreciative following who respects what he says and how he says it. People listen when ideas are being born and when changes are being made.

Creative Imagination is a lifesaver, a miniature miracle worker to the individual or business, up to its ears in difficulty.

Creative Imagination is as rewarding as know-how, as important as road maps and as necessary as blood transfusions, artificial respiration, oxygen masks or any other life-giving device.

Creative Imagination is as rewarding as modern civilization, for all of our conveniences and most of our necessities rise up to pay tribute to Inventiveness!

Creative Imagination is as rewarding as money in the bank, the cars we drive, the clothes we wear or any of the things that money will buy, for Creative Imagination is the foundation for it all and the ability that brings the highest price in the marketplace. Without creative accountability, our endeavors flounder in the swamps of non-achievement and the lethargic failure of self-deception.

Creative Imagination is still king! There is no area or domain, from personality problems, to scientific research, to education, commerce, politics, society, religion, international relations, and to the future itself, where Creativity has not affected all human endeavor! It is as universal as the problems of humanity and as important as the answers it brings. Creative accountability is the key to our achievement. I challenge you to light the candle of your own Creativity!

THE RHYTHM OF LIFE

The world was built to order.
　　And the atoms march in tune
Here on earth were man was cradled
　　Or on the stars or yonder moon.

The world was built for order
　　In its elemental parts,
But the sphere of de-arrangement
　　Is in selfish human hearts.

While the atoms move in orbit
　　Obeying universal law,
Only man would break the rhythm
　　To be creation's flaw.

Only man would flaunt his power
　　In the face of God Omnipotent
And proceed, a reckless deviate,
　　On destruction firmly bent.

And only man can stop destruction
　　As it hangs above his head.
He must learn to live in harmony
　　Or else humanity is dead.

May the hearts of men, united,
　　With all the universe attune,
Move in perfect, wondrous rhythm
　　With time standing at high noon!

July

~ 24 ~

The vulture and the gossip are carrion-cousins!
They are always carrin' something that stinks.

CRITICISM QUOTABLES

"The false pride of the critic weighs its finger on the scales of justice."

"The critic who is secretly conscious of his own faults may feel
the necessity of proving the rest of the world wrong."

"Too many people are already Knock-aholics!"

"Criticism costs confidence; even the critic's best friends
find their own confidence ill at ease."

"The carping critic is usually a competitor
even as the ranting raver is a rival."

"To encourage the good is better than to criticize the bad."

"Criticism is a cancer and the vicious are its victims;
for the criticized often outlive the critics."

"Criticism cries aloud of its want of charity."

"The swivel-tongued, carping critic has much
to swear at and so little to swear by!"

VULTURE WAYS

Carrion-eating vulture,
   Sailing in the sky,
You can sight the half-dead thing
   And hardly seem to try!

You can flap your black wings wide
   And settle on your feast.
You can eat what others won't
   And worry not the least.

I do not like your vulture look,
   Nor yet your vulture way.
You really aren't sportsman-like
   With your easy gotten prey.

You make me think of people
   Who peer with "wicked" eye,
Looking for some half-dead tale—
   Thence quickly see them fly!

I do not like your stretching neck
   That reaches as you walk,
If only you had vocal means,
   I'm sure you'd stop to talk.

I do not like your appetite
   That loves such things as this;
You must be off a quarter turn
   If dead things bring you bliss.

At least you have a purpose
   That God gave you to fill—
A garbage pail with wings, I guess,
   That floats o're fen and hill.

Man should feast on happy things
   And keep his vision high.
If vulture banquets come your way,
   Just gladly pass them by!

July
~ 25 ~

COUSIN BETTY, BILLY, AND MOM JACKSON (W. JACKSON AT RIGHT)

I OPENED THE DOOR

I opened the house of my heart to a friend
    As the sun glowed warm and bright.
We walked and talked from room to room
    In luminous, inner light.

We looked at the withered flowers of hate
    And the roses of love in bloom.
We studied the pictures life had framed
    On the walls of the living room.

I opened the door of the house of my heart
    To the gaze of one who passed by.
Then I gently closed the door of my heart
    And quietly said, "Goodbye."

July

~ 26 ~

True greatness pays court to Modesty but avoids those common street walkers known as Conspicuousness, Conceit, and Self-exhibition.

GOSSIP

"The gossip speaks his half-truths through false-teeth."

"The gossip leaves his mouth-motor running in a close place
until he asphyxiates himself: His hearers or the object
of his ill-intended attention."

"Gossip, like the gopher, runs in one hole and comes out another,
but he is always dragging his tale in somebody's dirt!"

"The dog that wags his tail before he bites is no worse than the gossip
who wags his tongue and smiles while he bites you from behind."

"If the busybodies, the tale-bearers and the gossips were all hanged
from high scaffolds by the tips of their tongues,
their feet would still drag in the dirt!"

"The eager-eyed, open-eared, scandal-listener is a sure bet
for the gossip-guy's 'king for a day!'"

"The alligator kills with the tail and so does the scandal-monger."

"Was the little bird who told you so a mockingbird, a silly goose,
a dumb-do-do guy or just another old hen?"

"The gossip, like the echo, repeats on empty air the things
he heard another say of one who isn't there."

KIDS AT PLAY ON THE SIDE OF A MOUNTAIN BY GREG WALZ

July

27

*Thought enamored with virile action leads to
the trysting place of creativity.*

YOU ARE A PEACEFUL PERSON
(CREATIVE VISUALIZATION)

With your feet flat on the floor, sitting comfortably with eyes closed gently, breathing deeply and relaxing completely, please listen to the music in the background and visualize the symbols, mental pictures and thought forms of this Relaxed Learning tape on the subject of Peace. Translate the meaning of its verbal and musical message into vivid, visual, inner pictures with color and action. Enter into and identify emotionally and actively with the essential content of its message. See it, hear it, feel it, touch it, taste it, smell it through the imagination faculty of your inner minds. Go beyond this and become one with the beautiful, the true, the positive, the peaceful and the good. Know that you are, little by little, more and more, by ever-increasing degrees, becoming aware of the need and the importance of self-improvement through Relaxed Learning and concentration. Know that, little by little, more and more, in ever-increasing degrees, you are improving and you are becoming a living, here and now, demonstration of your higher, better, positive self.

Relaxation, concentration, self-improvement, achievement, personal growth and increased efficiency for interpersonal relationships are so important for your present and your future that you will gladly give your full attention and cooperation to master the Relaxed Learning tapes. You will gladly and cheerfully follow the techniques and instructions in class and will practice and profit more and more from the things that you become aware of during each session. You will increasingly look forward to each Relaxed Learning session, because it is so personally important and valuable to your best interests and personal success in life.

You are a peaceful person, a calm lake, an easy rider! Essentially, you are, and more and more you will and can be.

What is peace? It is, according to the dictionary, an undisturbed state of mind. It is serenity, calmness, quietness, and freedom from inner or outer strife. It is, of course, all this and much, much more.

Putting it in picturesque or colorful visual imagery, peace is a river flowing, a storm that has been calmed, a well overflowing, a refreshing summer shower, a soft blanket of winter snow covering old ground scars and putting the scarlet leaves to rest at the foot of stalwart trees. And remember, you, too, are a river flowing gently, a lake without a storm. You are a well of refreshing kindness and goodness overflowing. You are like a refreshing summer shower that clears the air when it comes and refreshes the dry landscape under the hot sun. You are like a soft blanket of winter snow covering old ground scars of hurt feelings or trouble. You help people to be relaxed, rested, happy and peaceful like scarlet, autumn leaves resting at the foot of stately trees.

Peace is a fire purging. Peace is a breeze, a zephyr blowing, and a wind from angel wings. You are like a cheerful fireplace lighting and warming the room and making people happy who sit around it. You are like a cool breeze blowing across a sweaty forehead. You are cooling and refreshing to have around or even when passing by, because you have a calm, undisturbed, peaceful atmosphere about you, like a zephyr blowing or like wind from an angel's wings.

Peace is a breeze of promise, a cooling breath of hope, a beckoning and a swaying in the treetops of expectancy as refreshing and sweet as the fragrant perfume from a garden of blossoming roses. You are this kind of person. You make people happy and hopeful, and your disposition is as refreshing and sweet as a bouquet of flowers.

Peace is a breeze of summertime and the resurrection of spring that kisses the early flowers into bloom and embraces the drifted, calloused, crusted snow and melts it in the arms of transforming love. And you, too, are a peaceful person who inspires others to blossom and bloom because you encourage them. Your loving and kind ways melt the snows and ice of their indifference. You are so thoughtful and nice that you could almost melt an abominable snowman or at least help thaw out a snowman kind of person or an icicle enemy if you had one.

Peace is laughing springs, flowing streams and darting fish in deep green pools where skippers glide on its undisturbed surface. Peace is the warm rays of the summer sun ripening fruit, helping to incubate the eggs in a billion nests and overshadowing the nestlings and pouring its energies into the maintenance of all creation.

You are like a spring of cool water where other people can drink from your friendship. You are like a deep, undisturbed pool. You are like the warm sun. You inspire and protect other people who are also growing strong and kind and who are becoming beautiful people. You help keep things in order.

Peace is the whirl of the far-flung galaxies of an ever-expanding universe. It is the oil of gladness that makes all the wheels of the universe run smoothly. Peace winks in every star at night, smiles in the complacency of the silver moon, and rises with the faithful sun for its morning calisthenics as it jogs across the awakening sky. You, too, are an expanding kind of person, always growing and becoming better and better in every way and day by day. You make your circle of influence run more smoothly by the oil of your gladness.

Peace is in your eyes like it is in the far-shining stars at night. Your smile is like the quiet silver moon, as warm and dependable as the faithful sun as it brightens up the sky. So you make the world a brighter place by day or night because you are living in it. You are a needed, worthwhile person just like the sun and moon and stars are worthwhile and are needed and for more reasons than even that.

Peace is the river of red, the pulsing circulation of lifeblood in every warm-hearted life form that walks or runs or flies. Peace is the lifeblood of distilled experience where the winepress of life pressures squeezes the beautiful, the true, the positive, the peaceful and the good from the grapes of our wrath, the fruit of our frustrations and the pulp of our fears. Peace is the sparkling wine of life that flows through the arteries and veins of our inner and outer man, circulating the oxygen of confident hope to every cell where it imparts perfect health of spirit and the abundant energy of life made manifest. You, too, are a warm, living person. You are gaining good things from all of your experiences if you look for them. Please always let the pressures and troubles of life make you a more beautiful, sparkling person than before you had the experiences, whether they were good or bad. You are filled with health, energy and beauty.

Peace breathes in rocks and trees, stars and sticks and stones. Peace is the inbreathing inspiration of the highest and the best. It is the music of the spheres. It is the joyous energy of dancing, swirling, whirling, waltzing atoms all attuned to the harmony of the whole universe. Best of all, peace and calm and serenity are your heritage and privilege. Breathe them in. Live them out. Be filled with the energy, unity, and harmony of peace. Be in tune with the whole, happy, vibrating universe of light and love. For peace is a gift to be received, unwrapped and examined, a gift to be enjoyed, cherished, and shared with others. Peace is yours, and you are peace.

And now as we come up from the deep, creative, restful levels of calmness, poise, serenity and peace, please tuck the awakened awareness of your new and personal concept of peace away somewhere in a hidden corner of your inner self where it can work its way out into a happy, peaceful, everyday life that is as beautiful as the pictures we have imagined and visualized in our mind's eyes as we have listened to the Relaxed Learning tape on You Are a Peaceful Person!

Remember, each day you will look forward to your sessions on self-improvement and Relaxed Learning. Each time it will become easier to do, and you will little by little, more and more each day, become the wonderful person in reality that you already potentially are.

Wide awake now, feeling better, more rested and peaceful than you ever have before! Thank you for listening!

THOUGHTS

Thoughts are things
With angel wings.
    Or thoughts can bring
    The viper's sting;
For thoughts are what
You make them!

Thoughts are tall
Or mean and small,
    With gall replete
    Or honey sweet;
For thoughts are as
You think them!

Thoughts take you home
Or make you roam.
    Your thoughts you guide
    Like the horse you ride;
For thoughts are as
You use them!

Your thoughts are yours
Like secret doors.
    They're old or new
    But your thoughts are you.
And you are what
You make them!

July

~ 28 ~

A person's happiest employment is found in the area of his greatest abilities and his deepest interests.

MEMORY AND MENTAL SET
(CREATIVE VISUALIZATION)

Sit comfortably, so there'll be no need for body movement, heads either up or down with your eyes closed gently. As you close your eyes, let the feeling of relaxation spread over your forehead, around your ears, up and down your back, over your shoulders. Let your arms relax quietly. Listen to the music. Pick up the restful rocking, rhythmic musical sound. Check back over your body again. Know that as we go deeper into our relaxation, we will relax completely, not only in the physical voluntary muscles, but we will relax in all the internal, involuntary muscles as well, for this comes automatically as we begin to visualize vividly, clearly, in color and in action! You have permission to add to it, to subtract from it, to make it more beautiful or more meaningful, to put more color or action in it as we go along. Then, when we come to the part on memory, which will be the follow-up for our verbal visual, let the things that you have previously learned about memory be reinforced, and let your attention be increased in the learning of all material at all levels in all classes. Let your association processes with knowledge already known, and new things to be learned, be quickened. Let your recall especially be associated with a slight relaxation of body and mind so that all things can come back to you when you need them in time of review or recall or in time of testing. You will profit greatly by this session and will go down to a very deep, relaxed learning level. You will find a very deep visual level, and the results will be increased effectiveness not only in memory but also in all of your inner, personal relationships and in the exercise of all of the faculties of mind and spirit.

The suggested verbal visual was that we start with a lake. There's something about water that is restful, just as there's something about music that's rhythmic and undulating, with waves that go to and fro. So, picture a beautiful lake with a golf course of green on the far side, with little planted trees on the hills and in the valleys. In the far distance there is a forest. It is a green forest that slants ever upward toward giant, deep blue mountains, snowcapped in the distance, with jagged peaks, where the spring sunshine is glistening on their perennial snows.

But, down on this side of the lake where we're standing, a little path leads through the tall grasses to the water's edge. This is a more primitive side where we're standing, for unclaimed forests stretch behind us. And out to our right, emerging from behind a clump of greenery, which hangs out over the water, comes a beautiful swan. The sunlight is glistening on its smooth, velvet feathers. It moves

~ 521 ~

its wings a little, trailing them in the water, and with long strides from its yellow webbed feet, it paddles its way gracefully out into the lake. We're watching its profile now, its curved neck, its yellow beak, its gently half-closed, dreamy eyes. We notice the waves that are spreading from either side of its breast as it parts the water like a ship. The little waves run off the side in V shapes. Now the swan is turning and facing the shore, and it seems to just be resting and almost standing still as it preens its feathers. It cleans the feathers on its wings, picking here and there at a feather on its breast. It is stretching its neck from one side to the other, stretching it up as though looking at the bright spring sun. Now it is paddling its way very slowly to the shore, but it stops because it sees to our left a deer coming down to drink.

We remain invisibly motionless as the deer comes down to water. A long, slender-legged deer, his coat looks brown and warm with tan underparts. He looks like he's been well fed on the spring grasses that have been recently growing. Maybe somewhere in the wintertime he found a place hidden away from the snows where he could find leaves on the trees to eat and where he could paw his way down to the preserved winter grasses, rich with their seeds and their grains. He came out slick, well fed, and happy. He has antlers—strong sturdy antlers that could lock in a death struggle with an antagonist who might contend for his harem. He would protect his herd and all the little ones, the fawns that might be by their mothers' sides. But he came alone and solitary to the drinking place today, and he's just now stepping and sliding down into the water. There are little hoof marks in the back where his hind feet are still up on the bank, and he's slanted forward with his front legs buried almost to the knees in the mud and water and grasses, and he's drinking.

You can imagine the sound as he slurps the water up. You can hear the gurgle in his throat. You can watch the movement of the water as the deer swallows it as it moves along up that graceful, slender neck. But he keeps lifting his head to look around. The swan doesn't bother him, but just then one of those summer horseflies lights on his ear and stings him. He twitches that ear and flops that ear. Then he twists his neck around until his antlers are striking on his side and on his ribs while he's trying to brush away that fly. He must have done it, for the fly is gone and he shakes his head a little and goes back to his drinking. He starts up as he pulls his feet out of the water with a suction sound, and he whirls around and starts back to the forest again.

As he turns, up from one of the hazelnut bushes, a little sassy, chattering squirrel scurries along. He is saying, "You're invading my private property. Take those antlers, and those graceful legs, and go away somewhere. Don't disturb my lake and don't eat the leaves from my trees. This is my place." That little squirrel is jerking his bushy tail and sassing like he really was big enough to do something about it. But the deer knows that the squirrel is harmless, that the swan belongs there and that all things are peaceable, warm and beautiful, so he bounds away into the forest again, full, happy and content. The swan turns and swims on across the lake, and the squirrel goes about his chattering and investigating this and that, in his quick, quiet, nervous little way.

Now wherever you are in this picture find a very comfortable place to rest while we talk about memory. At this level of visualization where you can and do see clearly, vividly, in color, and in action, you are at a place where you can program your own actions and release your own abilities. You can increase your own mental capacity and make your memory much better, so that it can take in, store, and give out facts that you need to know and recall. Picture yourself somewhere in this setting. Maybe you are bareback riding on a beautiful horse and you are just resting there on the horse's back, looking out over the lake. Maybe you slide down from the horse's back and tie him to that bush where the squirrel was chattering a few moments before. Maybe you can find someplace in the grasses, or somewhere that's comfortable, while together we think about how to have a better memory.

Repeat this silently after me, please. "I am determined to make my memory my obedient servant so that it comes when I say come and it goes when I say go. My memory stores its valuables like the little squirrel stores his nuts in the hollow trunk of the tree. So my memory, and my attention, will pick out important things. My judgment will know which memories and impressions should be saved and which shouldn't. The things that should be saved, I will intuitively recognize, and I will store them away for future use. When there is a need in the wintertime of want, when there is need to recall them, I will recall them, and then I will enjoy the things that I am storing now.

"I am determined to make my memory my obedient servant. It must not forget when I want it to remember. It must not remember when I want it to forget, but it must mind me and do what I want it to do when I want it to do it. I will treat my memory gently, for it is a valuable servant. I will nourish it well. I will be thankful for it. I will brag on it and commend it when it does do well. I'll give it a moment of time to do its work. I'll not be impatient with it, but when I want it to bring something to me, I know it has to go somewhere and do something, and then bring the information back. So I'll give my memory time to go where it knows it must go, do what it knows it has to do, and then bring me, its master, the thing that I sent it for. I am determined to make my memory my obedient servant.

"In all things to be learned, I will hold the thought, 'It will be easy for me to learn this.' I will never say, 'I cannot do it.' I will never say, 'This is too hard for me.' For I know I have a magic memory. I know I have a servant who is wiser in its own ways than I am when it comes to storing and classifying and recalling valuable things. Therefore, I will firmly hold this thought always, 'It will be easy for me and for my inner mind to learn this, to store this, and to recall it.' For easy does it. I will simply let the other side of my mind do my work for me. If I need to formally memorize something, I'll not leave a unit to be learned until I have thoroughly mastered it and can repeat it without hesitation. But I also know that there are many things that I do not have to laboriously learn. I do not have to memorize them in a formal, technical sense. I need simply to open my awareness, remember the printed page, and remember the information as it comes back, clearly, beautifully and vividly, without hesitation.

"Basically, I do have a good memory. It will be fun to improve it. Memory improvement is my game. It's my thing. I will enjoy remembering things and I will enjoy the approval of others because I have memorized and remembered things well. I know I have a good memory for important facts, things that I wish to learn, and I will recall them easily and accurately because I desire to do so, because I am counting on, and depending on, my inner mind to do its work faithfully and well. I am thankful that my memory serves me faithfully and efficiently, and I will always hold a grateful attitude and an appreciative attitude toward it. I will not blame it when it seems to fail, but I will give it opportunity to do its work well. I will be happy to exercise my memory, for I have a good memory and I will cheerfully make it better. Self-improvement in learning is my theme. I will practice observing details and relationships in what I see. I will notice the differences in details and in relationships, and I will associate new things with things I already know. My mind is orderly and retentive. I classify ideas. I retain them like in drawers or in files. I can simply pull a memory file out and there it is. I am master of my thoughts. I choose what I put in. I choose what I bring out. They respond to me.

"I will welcome opportunities to learn as a challenge. When I am told to learn something in class or at work, I will put my mind to it. I know that if I put my whole mind to it, even for a moment, it is mine. Therefore, I will welcome opportunities to learn, because this is challenge and I am a winner. I have a good memory and it works very, very well.

"Others have mastered memory; I can do it, too. I can, at will, recall to consciousness any of the facts in my mental storehouse. I have a great storehouse of things, and I can, when I desire, recall to consciousness any of these good things in my mental storehouse. I can shut the door to memories when I desire.

"I have a good auditory memory for things I hear. I recall clearly and distinctly the things that I hear. I have a good memory for things that I see. I have a good visual memory so that I can recall easily and accurately the things I have read and seen, whether in print or in pictures. I will be happy to exercise my memory, for I do have a good memory and I will cheerfully make it better. I will memorize material in the most efficient manner and in the shortest period of time. If, for the moment, I do not seem to recall something, I will say to myself, 'I will remember it in a moment,' and it will come to me in a moment. I resolve to direct the energy and time of idle thinking in the mastery of things more important to me."

Now, as we come to the conclusion of this Moment of Memory Training, let us know that we do have a good memory and we will make it better and better, more and more as we experience new things and recall them.

Shall we open our eyes, slowly? Sit up, please! Let's all stretch!

HEAVENLY WANT AD

There is a job for which I am fitted
 And it is best suited for me,
Where I can do the greatest good
 With every devoted energy.

I need this position and it needs me
 So I claim it now by Divine decree,
And all the substance of power Divine
 Will bring my work to me.

The Mind Divine knows where it is
 And how to claim its prize;
And it will bring my own to me
 As sure as the sun shall rise.

I give my grateful thanks to God
 For the law of magnetic desire,
For the overflow of abundance
 And gifts He wants to hire!

WEATHERED AND WEARY BY GREG WALZ

July

~ 29 ~

MY GRANDPA, CORNELIUS MULDER, BY KARRIE JACKSON

GOD HAS MANY VOICES

God has many voices
    With which He speaks.
And God has many ways
    In which He seeks
For the living souls of men.

God has nature's voice
    In the winds and in the rain.
And God often speaks to us
    Through our ills and in our pain;
For God has many voices.

God has softer voices
    As soft as a summer shower.
And God has louder voices
    For correction's hour.
God sometimes speaks in sterner tones.

God has a special voice
    So very small and still
That only those can hear
    Who sincerely do His will.
This is God's inner voice to man.

July

~ 30 ~

*Ambition's empty substance, like the fabric of a dream, can cast
no eternal shadow where it falls, save the creator be in it.*

ACCESS TO INTUITIVE KNOWLEDGE
(CREATIVE VISUALIZATION)

As you listen to the music, please give your full, undivided attention of the deepest level of your mind to the lesson that we must learn. But at the same time, with the peripheral edges of your attention, be fully absorbed also with the sounds of the music. Relax deeply as you ride upon this river of music, as you ride like a leaf that bobs and floats and swirls with the current of the ever-flowing river of living, beautiful, musical sound. Rest, float, ride, and all along the riverbanks, as you pass them by, absorb the sights, sounds, the visual imagery and the meaning of the thoughts you are thinking. Accept the facts that are being impressed upon the silent centers of your receptive minds. I am addressing your inner mind, and it really knows potentially, all the things of truth and reality by its own process of inward knowing. You will hear and you will understand and in no way will you be distracted from attaining the secret abilities that we are searching for, that we are finding, that we already have found. Think clearly now, while deeply, deeply relaxed. Think about the following things. See them as much as possible in pictures of vivid, visual imagery.

Remember that, here and now, it is necessary and it is a pleasure to do a number of things that are required of us. We must learn to read, to read easily and as smoothly as the river of music flowing along. We must read eagerly with a clear comprehension of the intended meaning. We must learn to read successfully. This we shall do.

It is a necessity and a pleasure to write legibly, to write neatly, to write accurately. This we shall do. This we are learning to do. This we are happy to do. We will write better.

It is also a necessity and a pleasure to speak interestingly, to talk intelligently, to communicate persuasively. We are gaining experience day by day in speaking more interestingly, talking more intelligently, communicating more persuasively. This we shall do better each day as opportunities come and go that leave us richer for the experience of having spoken at the proper time, the proper things, in the proper way. We are thankful for the gift of speech and the privilege of exercising it when opportunity is provided. We shall always take advantage of those right and acceptable opportunities when they come. We shall be and we are successful in our speaking and in our thinking as we speak. Our thoughts will flow smoothly and our speech will proceed beautifully to wrap the correct ideas with clarity and vividness of expression. Correctness in spelling will also become easier.

~ 529 ~

It is a necessity and it is also a pleasure to add accurately, to subtract, to multiply, to divide properly. If we are required to do these things well, both to please ourselves and to please others, then we shall put forth the necessary effort to master correct spelling and mathematics until we can do them rapidly, easily and accurately. Accuracy is a skill that we have learned something about, that we are learning more about, and that we shall master completely and enjoy the process of doing it as necessity demands.

It is also a necessity and a joy to hear and to appreciate good music. This we often do to our own relaxation as we open up the deep and hidden recesses of our minds. So it is a privilege to hear and appreciate good, beautiful, and restful music.

We must learn to see and be moved emotionally by great art in the beauty of its form, in the beauty of its line, and in its perspective as it leads into the distance or some special point of interest. It is a pleasure to see and be moved by the color of great art and to see, to be moved by and to understand its intended message for us. We are creative and inventive, not only in art forms and in music but also in our ability to solve our problems until life itself becomes an expression of music, of harmony, of melody, and of art with its form, its lines, its perspective, its color and its intended message. Thus, our lives will become a canvas painted beautifully, a song sung rapturously. This is the joy of the creative life.

It is usually necessary and it can also be a joyful experience to live with, cooperate with, love, appreciate, respect, help, and understand the world of people in our immediate environment. We are learning to get along with people. It is an art, it is a joy, and it is a pleasure to be good at getting along with people. More and more, we shall become experts in our interpersonal relationships and in our ability to be pleasing, helpful, kind, cooperative and understanding in all of our human relationships.

It is necessary and it is an especially rewarding experience to know and to identify with, to emotionally share in, and to comprehend fully the higher mental and spiritual levels of existence. The concentration, the turning inward, the point of silence, the point of understanding, the place of relaxed receptiveness and the place of evaluative awareness have already opened an inner comprehension of our own highest potential resources. This we are doing, have done, and will do more and more. And we shall be exceptionally successful in opening up the integrated mental, emotional and spiritual levels of our inner integrated selves.

The knowledge and the awareness of our skills in reading, writing, speaking, spelling, figuring, understanding art and music, of being creative, of getting along with other people and walking in the clear light of our highest spiritual enfoldment can be arrived at either by actual personal experiences, by intuitional and psychic experience or by a combination of both of these.

In each of the above stated areas, I challenge your inner mind to open its doors of secret wisdom, to spill out its hidden treasures of skills and of knowledge. I instruct your unconscious mind to surface like a deep-sea diver with a load of hidden treasures. It must and it will bring you abilities, solutions, know-how, facts, desires, inner drive, goals and the energies for unselfish accomplishment. We will be able, more and more, to intuitively understand all things necessary to our quest for coordinated knowledge and accomplishment of the beautiful, the true, the positive, and the good.

You will increasingly, day by day, be able to read better, to write better, to spell better, to speak better, to figure better, to understand music and art better, to be more creative, to solve problems more easily, to get along with other people beautifully, and to develop mentally and spiritually into the perfectly well-balanced, complete, wonderful person that you already are. Your knowledge will come to you intuitively from deep within yourself. It will come to you by telepathy from others who know. It will come to you by thought transference from the universal mind pool of knowledge, experience and external wisdom. For every problem and for every need you will find an abundance or answers plus the persistence and strength for practical realization of desirable states and benefits. And you are very, very relaxed. You are very grateful. All this is very, very true. And so it is and will be more and more until you reach the stature of the perfect man and the perfect woman, until you become that which you truly desire to be and until you accomplish that which you truly desire to accomplish.

Now as we listen again to the river of music as it flows along, let us from the deep inner silence of our own being review these things we have talked about, that we have visualized and that we have accepted deep within us. Let us make them our own, and let us rest while our inner being awakens in us the gifts that we have opened ourselves to receive.

Open your eyes now if you've had them closed. Wide awake! Happy, healthy, and grateful. You may want to stand and stretch a bit. Thank you again for listening.

MAKE WAY FOR GOD

Out of the still, impenetrable deep,
Down where the shadows their lone vigil keep,

Out of the subterranean vaults of the soul,
Down where unfathomable life surges roll,

Oh, God of the inner, universe sublime,
Draw me upward, onward where mortals must climb.

Make way all ye men and myriads of things.
Make way, make way for the gift that God brings.

Make way for removal of the outmoded and worn.
Make way for new things that come with the morn.

Make way, make way, for the pathways untrod.
Make way for the creative forces of God!

GUIDO'S ESTIMATION SERVICES BY GREG WALZ

July

31

MY GRANDPA MULDER, HOLLAND DUTCH DAIRYMAN AND FARMER (W. JACKSON)

A LONE TREE GREW

A lone tree grew in no-man's land
 Nourished by blood and sun.
A lone tree grew against the sky
Where broken helmets and rusted guns lie,
 Where battles were lost and won.

A lone tree grew on a mountainside
 Windswept and drenched by rain.
But gnarled fibers of deep content
Grew in its heart as the storms were spent
 And strength was the fruit of its pain.

A lone tree grew in the desert waste
 Struggling with drifting sands.
But its strong roots lengthened, sinking low
Down where the silent, deep waters flow,
 Where now an oasis stands.

A lone tree grew in a forest deep
 Where trees stood close and tall.
But smothered here on every side
It stood alone until it died
 Without enough room to fall.

A lone tree grew in a garden of love.
 The birds are still singing there now.
Verdant and green it blossomed and grew,
Sturdy and straight as loved trees do
 And the fruit hangs ripe on each bough.

A lone tree grew in a faraway place
 But it knew from the very start
That though a tree is watered by hand
Or grows alone in no-man's land,
 Aloneness is the plague of each heart.

LIZARD HEAD SHEEP BY GREG WALZ

NORTH AMERICAN WILDLIFE BY BOB ERWIN

August

~1~

A garden is a lovely plot, wind-swayed in the summer sun, with God as the
neighbor who leans on my fence while we talk when the day is done.

Practical ideas are the seedlings of thought, the solution to problems, the answers to questions,
and the reward for the effort of an industrious, imaginative mind.

How impartial is the Mother Earth in the benefits she renders unto all!

No life can rise as high or remain as unshaken as the one that has gone deep enough to
find the foundation stones of integrity, faith, and service.

From the soil of directed passion the virtues of creativeness, goodness,
and true greatness arise.

Success does not come so much to us at first as from us; for the seeds of interest and intention
must be planted in the soil first of the inner self from which all things grow!

Good examples are patterns of Excellency more easily read than books, more practical than advice,
and difficult to argue with, and often they inspire imitation.

DESIGN

Design! Of course, I see it.
Who but blinded eyes
Could fail to see the glory
Of God's own summer skies.

The shadows in the water
Are deep as silent prayer.
And the blue in yonder heavens
Would prove that God is there.

The fragrance of the flowers
By the woodland trail
In the fading light at evening
Tell the happy tale.

It's a world of peaceful beauty,
A world of lovely things,
A world of lavish splendor
That lifts the heart on wings!

Thus silent nature whispers
And vocal nature cries:
"God has made life beautiful
Beneath glad summer skies!"

A thousand different voices
Softly try to say:
"Our God is in His heaven
And He's ruling night and day!"

August

~ 2 ~

THE WISDOM OF SOLOMON BY CLANCY CHERRY

GOD'S HANDIWORK

Where deserts keep tryst in the
    moonlight,
    And the wings of the morning
      unfold,
Thru the dawns and the dusk and
    the noontide,
    The glories of God I behold.

Where the grim seas weep on the
    shoreline,
    And the stars bravely shine in
      the night,
Up there in God's infinite stillness,
    His handiwork breaks on our
      sight.

Where the mother looks down on
    her baby,
    And smiles with love in her eyes,
I know I have seen something
    brighter
    Than the stars that illumine the
      skies.

In churches where people are
    meeting,
    Where sermons are preached
      clear and true,
I'm seeing a glad new creation—
    God's handiwork happy and new.

In laughter, in love and in labor,
    In men and in nature beside,
The glorious works of the Creator
    Roll on in an ocean-like tide.

August

~ 3 ~

ACCOUNTABILITY FEEDBACK

Department of Education
State Office Building
Denver, Colorado 80203

Dear Sirs:

After I went home from your very excellent Accountability Workshop in Denver, I tried to put things together like you told us. I hooked up my semantic differential directly to the psycho-motor's affective emergency and cross-wired that directly to the cognition switch. And, sure enough, I got a Euripidean response out of both my dual exhaust pipes!

I began to question the behavioral accuracy of the interpretive data, especially after smoke started curling out of the long-range antennas. I wish I knew how to equalize the inputs with the outputs. It might help stabilize the existential put-puts and I wouldn't have to call a Taxim to patrol the assessment activities when the playground is muddy.

I finally had to pull my 1971 Facilitator over to the criterial curb and put a dime in the no-parking meter. Operator answered and gave me someone in the State Department of Education, who said that what I probably needed was a new model evaluative instrument or an unabridged glossalia regulator to check the propertionality of the prognosticated verbalizations. And especially to watch out for those Euripidean responses if the muffler had any rusted places where procedural determinants might build up. I was already using twenty weight detergent motor-psycho oil before the convention!

Anyway, Sirs, it was a real thriller to move up from the three- and four-letter words in our little district to the genuine four-syllable verbalisms of cosmically theoretical, educational abstractions of self-inflicted accountability.

God bless America! I can almost hear the kids back home pledging allegiance to the flag with "accountability and justice for all!" Sure hope they don't leave out any important words like "freedom"!
Sincerely and uncertainly yours,

Accountability Committee (Letter was read at the State House during the Accountability Hearing and also published in the *Colorado Education Association Journal.*)

AN ORCHESTRA OF TREES

Like sad musicians lost in thought
They swayed and played of days forgot.

A giant orchestra of pines,
They posed in stately, rhythmic lines.

Like lovers' restless, long-drawn sighs
They whispered promise to the skies.

Their minored melodies of pain
Were mutely murmured to the rain.

With solemn-toned accompaniment
Their piney incense upward went.

They harmonized in solitude
On instruments of living wood.

Directed by an errant breeze
I heard a symphony in trees!

*Those who learn to observe intently wherever they are need not travel so far or so fast
to find something worthy of observation.*

August

4

To waste the unwanted is sometimes wiser than to want the unwanted for the sake of unwise frugality. Remember the packrat.

The art of happiness is the fine balance found somewhere between grateful awareness, increased achievement, and adjusted desires.

The genius thinks with the other side of his brain and simply listens and records with his conscious intellect; thus, his own mind, as well as the minds of others, are stimulated by their creative and original thought.

A person's growth and survival are not measured so much from the latitude of their years as by their attitudes, their aspirations, and their fears!

The conformity of variety and the variety of conformity give unity to diversity and a pattern to inconsistency.

Worry is growing anxiety, the lurking fear of uncertainty, and insecurity caught in the dilemma of indecision.

Determination, like the bulldog, never lets go except to get a better grip on a more vital part.

TRIBUTE TO NOTHING

Nothing! Mysterious nothing!
    How shall I define
Thy shapeless, placeless emptiness?
    Neither sound nor size is thine.

Words nor action can thy voice express.
    With what shall we compare?
Mankind devotes itself to thee
    Devoid of cause or care.

How many heads thy plans alone pursue?
    Great books thy histories contain.
What laboring backs and calloused hands
    Thy portion only gain?

What busybodies thy doings only do!
    To thee the proud and giddy bend.
And like this poem are full of thee
    And in *nothing* end!

*Nature is the hand of God reaching out of the sleeve of Divine Immensity
to caress you as you pass Him by unnoticed.*

August

~ 5 ~

SNOW LEOPARD BY CLANCY CHERRY

WHEN THE ONE THAT I LOVE PASSES BY

Leaps like a fawn
My heart at the sight
    And form of the one I desire.
Leaps like a flame
My heart at the name
    As vision-fanned love leaps higher.

Leaps like the wild goat
In ecstasy free
    On the mountains against the blue sky.
Soars like the eagle
My heart when I see
    The one that I love passing by.

Leaps like the mountain trout
Caught on the hook
    Of a fisherman's enchanted fly.
Leaps like a speeding boat
Slapping the waves,
    My heart when you pass me by.

Leaps like the wild rabbit
In purposeless play
    My heart for the one that I know.
For love is the game
And yours is the name
    That inspires me wherever I go!

August

6

Confidence and respect should be earned rather than too freely given.

There is no adversity equal to the loss of faith, hope, or love.

Genius is the hand of faith that feels in the darkness until it turns on the light of inspiration.

Love rests at the feet of fairness where equity once stood alone.

Listening is the sweetest eloquence that wisdom ever hears.

The person with a phenomenal memory observes more details and relationships in what he sees and hears, and with greater intent to recall them accurately.

Back of the detailed envisioning of achieving faith must be the invincible purpose that the subjective desire must become an objective fact.

THEN, I'LL BUY

There are six questions that I would ask
Of every man with a selling task:

How can I profit without recourse?
What do I gain or lose with remorse?

When will the action I contemplate
Put bills in my purse or food on my plate?

When will it make me a bigger man
Or help me succeed at my goals and plan?

Why should I take this action now;
What harvest will I reap if I plant or plow?

Where will the benefits first appear
Like grapes full ripe or corn on the ear?

Who says I can profit? Tell me who knows?
Are my hopes assured when the salesman goes?

Tell me how, what, when, where and why,
And if you really believe it, then I'll buy!

August

7

A right concept of God gives a real sense of security.

Inventory your potentials and you will discover your opportunities.

Honor and ambition should be early wed, and never divorced!

Enthusiasm is confidence radiating, faith achieving, and love expanding
in the glow of eager, interested response.

There is great value even in virtue maintained by unwanted circumstance;
but the truest virtue is the fruit of constant and purified desires.

A garden of small pleasures is more fragrant than the desert of ingratitude.

Hope is man's steady star at night and the rising sun of the day.

GOD'S EMBRACE

The universe embraces,
　With invisible embrace,
The soul of each mortal
　With immortal grace!

Here the Eternal Invisible,
　Resplendent with love,
Puts everlasting arms under
　Benignity's smile from above!

Embracing Arms Everlasting
　Encompass each soul.
Reciprocation with the Infinite
　Is the finite's first goal.

Oh, wondrous Eternal,
　As Thy heavens are scanned,
We see in each atom
　The universe that was planned.

We see in the telescopic
　Thy macrocosms farflung.
And see in the microscopic
　Thy microcosms unsung.

And my heart full expanded
　Sings the song of the whole,
Where minutia oft repeated
　Is the alphabet on the scroll.

So my heart sings with rapture
　Of true greatness so small
And of smallness unforgotten
　But embraced by the All!

August

~ 8 ~

Any station in life should be a Service Station whether the attendant wears coveralls, cap-and-gown, or the robes of royalty!

There are seven basic fears in life:

1. Poverty
2. Criticism
3. Ill health
4. Loss of love
5. Old age
6. Loss of liberty
7. Death and the unknown

THE TRIUMPHANT MARCHING SONG

The awakened man writes his own marching song for the triumphant life. The radiant man whistles somebody else's tune, and usually it is a different one every day. The unawakened person is simply under the group control or the mass mind of humanity. We need to become ourselves. We need to declare our independence and freedom. We need to experience a new and meaningful relationship with the creator and the whole wide globe.

The person whose global awareness is expanding is like a seed in the earth pushing its way by divine instict up through the darkness and the crust of the earth itself into the warmth and the atmosphere of a beautiful life and expression. The spiritually aware person demonstrates the possibility of penetrating the mysteries of the universe, unveiling their secrets and discovering the meaning of, and an awareness of, a supreme being. This aware person has found an amalgamation or integration for the fractured parts of his triune self. He has learned not to function so much in the playacting part of his mortality, but to think and to feel and to act in the real part of his immortality. He has learned to function in his high self part, to discover its hiding place, to find out where the greater unmanifest part of himself moves and has its being as an individualized projection of the creator and his world.

GIVE SOMETHING TO SOMEONE

O my soul, reach out to your neighbor.
　　O my soul, reach upward in love.
O my soul, there is a world that needs loving
　　And a lonely God up in heaven above.

There's no room for separation or hatred.
　　No place for hostility or greed.
O God, break the barriers of aloneness.
　　Grant the joy of fulfilling some need.

O my soul, there is purpose for living,
　　Cheerful service that makes life worthwhile.
O my soul, give something to someone
　　If it's no more than "hello" with a smile!

THE CONQUEROR

He who has conquered doubt and fear
Has conquered failure, too.
So build your faith triumphantly
With the will to live and do!

August

9

*True identity is discovered in quietude; and contentment blossoms
most profusely there.*

Gratitude is the first debt we owe to heaven, whose courts ring empty without earth's paean of praise!

The life is long enough that fully works out the purposes for which that life was born.

Thought enamored with virile action leads to the trysting place of creativity.

*Reflection is casting the light of past experience, memory, reason, and wonder upon the present
point of concentration.*

YOU'LL FIND YOURSELF

I lost myself in the rush of life
   And I didn't know where to find me.
I looked to the right and I looked to the left
   And I even looked behind me.

I belonged to this and I belonged to that
   And what I possessed, possessed me.
I blessed myself and I blessed my friends
   And I knew the Good Lord had blessed me.

But I'd lost myself and I couldn't find out
   Where I'd been or was going to.
I felt like a bottle of empty wine
   That the sad wind was blowing through.

As I wrote in the glow of a sunset sea
   With the poet's inspired pen;
A picture shone through of a person I knew
   And I'd found myself again.

(CONTINUED ON NEXT PAGE)

I lost myself again next day
    As lost as ever before.
I wouldn't have known my own backyard
    Or the knob on my own front door.

But I walked among the stately pines
    And lay on the sun-warmed earth;
Then the focus of life again came clear
    And my true self was given new birth.

When I walk the shores of illimitable thought
    Where life is vibrant and still,
I know like a pigeon the way back home
    And I'm soon on my way with a will.

If you've lost yourself in the rush of life
    As you struggle along behind it,
Just get alone in a quiet place
    And there in your heart you'll find it!

August

~ 10 ~

THE TREE HOUSE (DE VANEY COLLECTION)

~ 555 ~

THE TREE HOUSE

Halfway between earth and heaven
   Is a house I built myself.
With floors and doors and everything—
   Even books upon the shelf.

Halfway to heaven hiding
   In the leaves of a giant tree,
Is a hideaway from grownups
   And it all belongs to me.

It's castle, cave and clubhouse.
   It's shelter, ship and port.
It's winter fun while raindrops run,
   My dugout and my army fort.

It's halfway from earth to heaven
   Where halfway from boy to man
I can think and think and think
   Then climb down to do what I can.

August

11

Hate is spawned by helplessness, and the person is strongest who can forget, forgive, and find a way of helpfulness.

The horse knows his manger, the dog knows his corner, the homing pigeon knows his perch, and happy is the man who knows that home is the closest place to heaven on this earth.

The weaker the law of inner constraint, the greater the volume of legal restraint; self-discipline will seldom need costly correction.

Friendships, like pottery, can be broken; but love will cement them again.

Obstacles are a challenge to the resolute; they seem to demand a pledge or proof of our persistence and a demonstration of determined progress.

Reflection on a thought gives the mind time to evaluate it, adapt it, classify it, and file it for future use and reference.

YOU CAN CHANGE IT

If a river can alter
    The course of its bed,
Then life can exchange hatred
    For true beauty instead.

For the current of life
    Flows on boundlessly.
It awaits your direction
    And longs to be free.

If a tree that is fallen
    Or bent over by storm
Can grow again upward
    With green stalwart form,

Then man by his faith
    His powers and his prayer
With God's help can change
    Anything, anytime, anywhere!

August

∼ 12 ∼

The cause is always king and circumstance the servant; and he who would change a decree must consult with the crown. The creator is worthy of profound love and adoration.

I AM AVAILABLE

On May 30, 1884, Oliver Wendell Holmes, speaking before the Army of the Republic, said, "Recall what our country has done for each of us, and ask ourselves, 'What can we do for our country in return?'" LeBarron Russell Broggs, in 1904, referring to his Alma Mater, paraphrased the proclamation: "Ask not what she can do for me, but what can I do for her?" The paraphrase of Oliver Wendell Holmes, used in John F. Kennedy's Presidential inaugural address on January 20, 1961, rang out, "Ask not what your country can do for you, but what can you do for your country."

Our lives have experienced major changes during the past fifty years. The acceleration of mechanical technology has precipitated ingenuity and economic change. Industry with its modifications, advancements, and its progressive methods reflect substantial change. Health-motivated experiments have included the risk of the unknown. These "advanced" methods, procedures and stimulants have been employed in the struggle for technical, financial and medical survival.

Many new ideas have been abused. In some cases, the long-term effects of these developments have not been researched adequately. For example, problems of environmental toxicity are becoming apparent around our globe. Our food lacks the nutrients we need, fields are becoming sterile, dangerous chemicals threaten our industries and our personal workplaces. Many of our waterways are contaminated, and much of our groundwater is becoming polluted.

But, if I am one among the masses and you are one, WHY DON'T WE come up with some answers for ourselves? Maybe our responsibility is not to change the world. Perhaps we must only make our little part of the world safer and more productive for our family, our neighbors and ourselves. We must start where we are and make a difference in the lives of those around us.

The creation of our spaceship earth was perfectly balanced. For example, today our ecosystem can be restored to that same balance, if we choose. Perhaps, as trustees of our spaceship earth, our paraphrase today could be: "Ask not what else I can take, nor which of nature's rules may I break, but rather, in my environment, what can I do to help?" Think about it. In your secret place of meditation, envision improvement and restoration of our world. You and I can make a difference!

THOU ART ADORED

May the God of the River Winds
   Fill the sag in our empty sails.
May the God of the Storm-churned sea
   Calm all of our raging gales.

May clear-eyed, upward vision
   Always lead us safely through.
May the God of our inner light
   Grant us grace to be always true.

May the gracious gifts of God
   Be increasingly outpoured.
And may our lips say softly,
   "Thou art our God, adored!"

August

13

Independent opportunities may be the conquest of adversity as well as the smile of good fortune.

POSITIVE EMOTIONAL LUBRICANTS

Relative to personal management, inspiration and motivation in decision-making are the keys to accountability. These qualities provide a broad sky in which to fly. Each of these factors are the positive emotional lubricants that make change and planned efforts toward emotional health and spiritual development functional and occur smoothly. This experience and expression may seem to be almost effortless.

Think on this analogy: Inspiration and motivation in our development are like rivers flowing through the gates of the dam. These sources of motivation turn the wheels and dynamos of all practicality in regard to joining the ranks of these changing, maturing people. Inspiration and motivation are the lifeblood of improvement and the vital force of safe success. Their aim throbs and pulses in the intent of zestful, healthful living. It is through them that we can laugh in healthy recreation and play. With them flow good health, and the strength and clarity of thought, to be able to work the long hours that seem but minutes in the half-forgetful absorption of self-expression, creativity, and recreation that bring us to a sense of fulfillment. We then have the opportunity to live the essence of life, the heartbeat of achievement.

With our lives in balance, we can enjoy the right to live happiness, to experience more than just survival with pressure and confusion. Do not settle for flying in the fog, or being involved in negative practices, which are like the pounding of the surf eating away at the ocean shores of many helpful or positive situations.

BROAD SKIES IN WHICH TO FLY

A drill team of blackbirds
   Practiced in the sky
In drill formation intricate
   That held the upturned eye.

Perhaps some hidden instinct
   Or divine, remote control
Called the drills they execute
   As they wheel and dip and roll.

Or perhaps some strong-willed leader
   With a gift for fancy flight
Manipulates his fellow birds
   From the wondrous sight.

But regimented jailbirds, too,
   With coats all striped the same
Are prisoners in their routine steps,
   All interlocked in shame.

For clocks all strike and whistles blow
   In the prison house of time.
Oh, the clanking chains of servitude,
   And walls too high to climb!

But, perhaps on some far distant star
   Where parolees all go free,
We'll trade drab uniformity
   For the robes of liberty.

Wheel on and turn, free birds, in flight
   Against your azure sky.
People, too, must have their freedom
   With broad skies in which to fly!

August

~ 14 ~

ANGRY TIGER BY BOB ERWIN

THE SIZE OF GOD

I had a very little God
   For I was a little man.
But as my understanding grew
   God grew span for span.

I cannot guess how great God is
   But I'm sure I'll know someday
When I'm big enough to comprehend
   And earth limits have passed away.

Foresight and insight rather than hindsight are the binoculars for spotting an opportunity while it is still coming our way.

August

~ 15 ~

Love is expansive, jealousy is not: Jealousy is constriction, restriction, and contraction;
selfishness is a python that chokes itself to death.

JEALOUSY DEMONSTRATED

"Jealousy knows no appeasement, for it takes concessions as confession to all its wild imaginings."

"Jealousy is a bloated spider full of venom that weaves its web of suspicion
and feeds with equal greed on fact or fantasy."

"Self-love cries its jealous wares so loudly in the marketplace that true love hides its face, and
strangers fear to buy where tolerance and reason scarce are heard above the din of
distraught passion."

"The jealous are never alone; they make bedfellows of Doubt, Distrust,
Suspicion, Apprehension, and Fear."

"Let not the toothless snarling of old dogs turn you from your path;
they are angry not so much at your ambition as at the lack of their own."

"Jealousy proves a want of love and seeks a cause for hate;
yet by its vain imaginings, it suffers every fate!"

"If imagined inferiority could find a true security, then jealous passion's flame
would smolder out for want of air."

"Jealousy is a glass that magnifies the trifles that it remotely sees,
while it blurs the sturdier virtues closer by."

"The green eyes of jealousy are often blind; they seek for faults, but virtues seldom find."

"Jealousy can see with jaundiced eye, deception in each breeze that passes by."

JEALOUS LOVE

Cruel, wanton jealousy
   With ice water in its veins
Oft feels unrequited in its love
   For all its cherished pains.

No love, indeed, could be
   Half as cold as fear's desire
That feeds on husks with kernel gone
   In ashes without fire.

We judge it hate, not love,
   That would break the wings that fly
And stand by the cage of songless fear
   To watch love droop and die.

True love, not jealousy,
   Can hope to claim its own,
For fledglings must some freedom have
   Until new love has wiser grown.

MEDITATION PRAYER

Oh, God; you are infinitely, eternally calm, confident and powerful. In the midst of our jealousy and immaturity, would you impart to us today a bit of Heaven's insight, wisdom and repose. We who hurry, scurry, fret and bustle so need the confidence of your LOVE and the calming quietness of your infinite tranquility. We need to cease our extreme reaction to our insecurities, our chafing, our fitful struggling, and for a moment at least, to sense the eternal calm of your spirit. Negative spirits and dark circumstances are no match for your power and presence in our lives. Infiltrate our minds and hearts with the assurance that all will be well, as we relate ourselves to you. Thank you. Amen.

August

16

*Constructive optimism is an observatory built on the rock
promontory of faith, hope and love.*

AWARENESS IS A KEY

Awareness is the key to consciousness. This includes awareness of self, awareness of the creator, awareness of others and awareness of the universe and the interworkings of each of these areas. The awakened person will be different inwardly than he was and may also be different than others in outward proof. This difference is a blessed normalcy recognized as mental and spiritual efficiency even by those who do not fully comprehend it. The man who has changed himself finds it much less necessary in some respects to change his environment, or conversely. The things that do need to be changed, he sees with a fresh clarity and insight. He is also aware of the reasons why conditions need to be changed and some of the best possible ways to change them as well as the expected results following such change. He does realize that change is not worthwhile for its own sake or for the satisfaction of his own ego exaltation. Man's first responsibility is, of course, to get in tune with the creator before he tries to tune the orchestras of earth. And, being in tune, he may become so absorbed with the harmonics of heaven and the inner life of complete satisfaction that he could care less about trying to tune everybody else's instrument. This is especially true because each of us is on a different wavelength. Things that once bothered us, we no longer even hear, and things that were once inaudible sound clearly to our inner ears.

Man needs to strive less for what he is not. He does not need to ruefully regret what he has been once or failed to be, but he simply needs to know that he is. He needs to live in the here and now. He needs to accentuate the "I am-ness" of the here and now. Generally speaking, what I am, I was. And what I was and am, I will be unless I change. The basic truth is that we are what we are aware of. Let us then direct our awareness into proper fields of acceptableness in the awakened condition. When the heart becomes activated by proffered benefits, when the mind becomes excited and agitated by great longings and desires for the awakened experience and can no longer wait to attain it, then let that soul cry out simply to the heavens for direction and guidance. No two people require the same directions, for no two people are in the same place. But let that man, wherever he is in the here and now, look up to God with emptied hands and opened heart and simply receive that which is potentially his own and has been his from time immemorial. Now!

567

SHEPHERD OF LOVE

The Lord is my Shepherd protecting from wrong.
He leads me and feeds me and gives me a song.

Supplying my needs so I never shall lack,
He guides my feet up thru the safe, narrow track.

To fields where the meadows of clover are high.
Where fed and protected the Shepherd stands by.

I drink the waters that flow from His Word.
Restored by the Shepherd, Creator and Lord.

I walk in the paths of His righteousness, too,
Thru early spring sunshine, thru diamond-like dew.

And the shadows of death no longer I fear;
His promise supports me; His presence is cheer!

While here on my journey by many foes pressed,
My table of blessing He fills with the best.

And surely, Oh surely, such comfort as this
Shall follow my steps to the City of Bliss.

And there in the courts of the Home Far Above
Forever I'll dwell with the Shepherd of Love!

August
17

SILENT APPROACH BY BOB ERWIN

WHEN THE STORM WAS OVER

Torrential rains came pounding down
    In windswept, drifting sheets.
From the roofs of the tallest buildings
    To the busy city street.
I watched the watery avalanche
    As the sky fell at our feet.

The wind snarled by with lifted lip
    That threatened to slash and tear.
The thunders rolled and bounded back
    As blue flames split the air.
Then the sky gave up her weeping
    And wore a rainbow in her hair!

Trivial causes may produce terrific effects, for little is much if trouble is in it.
But, without adversity, wisdom is wanting. Those who learn suffer some things,
and those who suffer with discernment learn wisdom.

August
18

MOSES BY BRUCE EAGLE

THE POWER OF THOUGHT

Thought and action are jailors of fate.
    They imprison and they release.
They are angels of freedom which liberate.
    They diminish and they increase.

If your self and your prayers are harmonized,
    The answer will come from afar.
Your life will mirror both cause and effect,
    For your thoughts make you whatever you are.

Your environment is only your looking glass
    With your experiences of good or ill;
And only the equitable working out
    Of the thoughts you can change at will.

Alter your thoughts toward people
    And they will change their thoughts to you.
For there is a law: "As we sow, we reap."
    That makes our thoughts come true.

Your thoughts are never kept secret.
    They congeal and continue to rise.
They shape a memorial of all your past,
    A curse or a treasure to prize!

August

19

Self-reliance is compatible with God-entrusted self-sovereignty, free moral agency, self-direction, self-confidence, and the intuitive wisdom that knows where to go for help.

POSITIVE ATTITUDE ACCOUNTABILITY

You are invited to join the advocates for the changing of the guard. With mental assent, please consider; we can do better as we positively relate to the Creator. Please join us as we explore ideas of inspiration and motivation for planning for "fog lifting" accountability. As we visualize the following thoughts, begin to see yourself as part of the dynamic, positive answer, rather than as a part of the negative problem.

What do inspiration, motivation, and accountability mean? Inspiration, or to be inspired, certainly includes being aroused; to advocate or recommend, while at the same time, to incite; evoke; stir up; give new life to; to kindle and perhaps inflame a cause, an attitude or a situation.

Motivation suggests prompting; stimulating, while involving and being induced. Motivation could urge a provocation, a push or thrust which may denote an impelling encouragement to be positive.

Accountability suggests duty; what ought to be done; perhaps even a moral duty; an imperative duty, and certainly a call to duty. Within the connotation of this term is the idea of responsible answerability, even to the point of being nonexempt from liability while in a fog.

WHEN THE FOG LIFTS

Until the fog lifts
    There is no vision.
We blindly drive on
    In indecision.

Distorted objects
    Loom up ahead
The fog enshrouds us,
    The living dead.

It conceals the beauty
    We may see by day.
No sealed beams pierce it
    As we feel our way.

We see life darkly
    And ill described.
Until the fog lifts
    We are circumscribed.

Just look to the Creator
    Where the luster bright
Dispels earth's darkness
    And demonstrates light.

The fog of ignorance
    And of vision dim
Can all be lifted
    When we count on Him.

For life no longer
    Is dimly seen
When the fog is lifted
    That came between.

With the low clouds lifted
    When fog banks flee
I'll know the Creator's love
    Dwells close to me!

August

∼ 20 ∼

Oh, eternity, that ocean without shore, as bottomless and as deep as the deepest sea and high as heaven, where tide and time, and measure are no more!

All nature is but the garment of God, and those who lean hard against God's Garments can feel the heartbeat of the Divine.

Faith is an ocean where even hardships ride like leaves upborne on its mighty tide.

Nature both conceals and reveals the Creator to the minds of men; those who look long and lovingly will find the Creator everywhere.

ETERNITY

Go saddle the rolling thunder.
    Rake your spurs in its flank.
Search for the ends of eternity
    Till time and space grow blank.

Ride till the echoing thunders
    Fade to a whisper thin,
On a steed foam-flecked and wasted;
    Then eternity will just begin.

Lasso the forked lightning,
    Cling to its orange mane.
Circle the constellations
    Forever and back again.

Race till the flashing lightning
    Dims to an emerald glow.
Eternity's sun never has set.
    It cannot diminish or grow.

Endless the road you travel
    As you search for the cradle of God,
For God and eternity never were born
    Like slow-footed centuries that plod.

August

~ 21 ~

All people hear more than sound, see more than sight, and feel instinctively the emotions and thoughts that the Creator and others subconsciously project.

Dreams are the blueprints for reality, the scaffolding for our skyscrapers, and the foundation of future fortunes. Don't chuck your cherished dreams in the dispose-all of doubt.

Nature is the hand of God reaching out of the sleeve of Divine Immensity to caress you as you pass Him by unnoticed.

NEW PERCEPTION

Perception quickened by the light
   Makes sight and hearing one.
And in that inner, luminous land
Life and I walk hand in hand
   In freedom's golden sun.

Here blue of sky and cooling shade
   With nature sings in tune.
Here comprehended oneness seeks
And manifests in all it speaks
   Thru fragrant joys of June.

Ah, heavenly consciousness,
   Oh soul within set free,
My life shall know its purpose yet
To labor ere the sun is set
   With wise intensity.

(CONTINUED ON NEXT PAGE)

Ah, universal longing,
   Oh urge to reach the stars,
My heart shall give its glad consent
To understanding's discontent
   In its confining prison bars.

Oh, gratitude and ecstasy
   Of truth's exalted wine,
I'll drink from inspiration's cup
And return again to fill it up
   Because all things are mine.

I'm lifted up to feel and think,
   To be and to possess;
To hear what silent voices say,
To walk high roads along the way.
   I dare not ask for less.

The Spirit of the living God
   Made me brother to all things.
I'm part of all I see and touch
Yet stand apart surveying such
   On inspiration's wings.

Oh, teach me God, to know Thee,
   I now myself present.
Grant me to know, to be and do—
God-taught till life itself is thru
   And the veil at last is rent.

August

~ 22 ~

Matriculate in friendship and major in the mathematics of compatibility.

Education is the interminable process of self-discovery, the bringing to light of our hidden treasure, and the enlargement of our capacity to still discover more.

Dreams are fanciful, beautiful, nebulous things. Dreams are luminous, airy, dazzling things. They are woven from the fabric of hope, the cobwebs of desire, and the gossamer wings of ambition envisioned.

WHEN I WAS A LITTLE CHILD

When I was a little child,
I saw God everywhere.
Even hidden in the fragrance
Of my mother's skin and hair.

When I was a little child,
God swung in every swing.
He bubbled in the zest of life
In the mossy mountain spring.

When I was a little child,
I saw God in every tree.
Whose strong arms encompassing
Reached out protecting me.

When I was a little child,
God ran with every stream.
He rested in the shadows cool
Or rode some glad sunbeam.

(CONTINUED ON NEXT PAGE)

When I was a little child,
He smiled in every cloud.
He winked in every blinking star,
And life stood straight and proud.

When I was a little child,
The wildest storms and wind
Just made me think of God again
And wonder if I could be like Him.

When I was a little child,
I loved each shower of rain.
My bare feet gripped the cool, firm earth
And joy was fierce as pain.

When I was a little child,
Brook trout swam slowly by,
And the fleecy clouds reflected
God's face in the blue of sky.

I no longer am that little child,
With piercing inner sight.
And I long to see God's presence shine
In my sometimes lonely, silent night.

August

23

All the university degrees in the world cannot give you true wisdom:
It is the quintessence of experience and the distillation of adversity.

WISDOM AND LEADERSHIP

It is the responsibility of inspired and wise leadership to know what it wants, when it is wanted, where it can be obtained, why it is wanted, and how to go about getting it. The wise leaders who know the how, why, where, and what have already built into their being the steadfastness and assurance of continued enthusiasm because their emotional drives have intelligent outlet, purpose, and direction. Their organization and circle of influence will vibrate with sureness, knowledgeable authoritativeness, and inspiration.

The atmosphere of wisdom tends to draw others to it. There is something contagious about earnest, sincere inspiration and motivation that alerts others who feel as well as hear the purposeful sound, see the upright attitude, and sense the vibrant tones.

There is a different sound in the inspired and motivated leader's voice. It is a sound that is heard without noise, and it challenges us to join the changing of the guard; to do meaningful, exciting things: To make life sing and shout with confidence and vitality; to improve our world, our lives!

Wisdom and leadership will inspire others, not just by what is said or how it is said, but also by example. Wisdom's accountability must measure up to the stature of the positive, inspired individual who will dare to become the wellspring of inspiration and motivation for our future generations.

Wise and inspired leadership must also condition itself to a positive reaction regardless of opposing or uncooperative circumstances. The person and the cause, not the emotion only, must always be in the driver's seat. The horse cannot sit in the saddle, and emotion, although it is a driving force, must always be directed, controlled, encouraged, held back, whipped up, or pulled to a halt when it is expedient in the mature judgment of the administratively wise driver. Wisdom and leadership are best when married.

WELCOME TO WISDOM'S EDEN

Welcome, Friend to Eden
   With its bowers of shade and light.
Come and rest in Love's fragrant garden.
   There's room for each quest tonight.

Open your eyes to the wonders
   Of all things both new and old.
Come sit in the classroom of sages
   Where the ages their truths unfold.

Come join in the ranks of truth seekers
   And discover bright diamonds or gold,
The wisdom and riches of Spirit,
   Such wealth as never was told.

Come think great thoughts, eternal.
   Search the lines in reality's face
Till expansion of mind and spirit
   Make dull yesterday's errors erase.

Come, Friend, and always be welcome.
   Together we'll study to know
God's changeless, eternal wisdom
   And walk in its afterglow.

The Spirit of God will guide you
   And nothing shall make you afraid.
And truth shall be your companion
   In Wisdom's Eden of sun and shade.

August

24

*If you close your talk shop, it will take some of the wear and tear off of the gossip's tongue
who feels a compulsion to spread your lingual litter to every lawn in town.*

EGOTISTICAL PRIDE

Reacting and interacting, wise persons become aware of the fact that the state of spiritual awareness has given them an intuition more than commensurate with their intellectual achievement. They become aware of the fact that a sincere and seeking heart may receive creator wisdom and exercise this intuition even though they had never paid tuition in any university or college in the world. Those who do not find this insight into true reality may find that they are "ever learning and yet never coming to the knowledge of the truth." True, an inner attitudinal change takes the sting and the personal afront out of one's confrontations in life's relations. Having risen above himself, man is not enslaved by himself. Having risen above and stepping aside from the acute angle in relationship to other people, he finds himself in a detached, nonresentful and certainly more compatible frame of mind. He is no longer as thin-skinned, as touchy, or as easily offended as he previously was. He can at times step out of himself, stand aside from himself, and see himself and the other persons discussing the situation. He can see it and hear it with a complacency that gives him an objective viewpoint and a higher spiritual control over all of his emotional reactions. It gives him that moment of contemplation, reserve judgement, and emotional self-control prior to any reaction. He lives in the here and now with an unobstructed view, with undivided resources, and with a singleness of purpose that makes him, generally speaking, superior to any untoward circumstances.

The positive mental attitude of a wise person is not a mask that he wears of pseudo-sincerity or concealed hypocrisy. His positive mental attitude is more than P.M.A. It is P.H.A.—a positive heart attitude. Other people accept his attitude at its face value, or, we may more properly say, at its heart value. If a person can give up his self-deceptive, egotistical self-regard and abnormal pride, he will find that he has considerably fewer battle fronts to defend.

ELEPHANT EARS

The elephant's ears are flapping
   Like a mighty fan,
Or like a giant antenna
   They hear just all they can.

They're about as big as a basket
   And about as rough and plain.
They hear the biggest noises
   And feel but little pain.

And they're like a lovely person
   That long ago I knew.
Their mouth was big and both their ears
   Were of mammoth sizes, too.

They heard the latest gossip
   And every forlorn tale.
They sucked it in like an elephant
   From the circus water pail.

Then they'd spew it softly over
   Those far or closer by.
They could hit a distant target
   And hardly even try!

Good, old, noisy elephants,
   Their ears flapped in the breeze.
Brother, I'd like to have seen them
   Humbly praying on their knees!

August

~ 25 ~

KILIMANJARO BY BOB ERWIN

A garden of small pleasures is more fragrant than the desert of ingratitude.

LOVE'S HARVEST

We mowed love's fields together
    And brought its harvest in.
The fragrant smell of haying time
    Was a prize that gleaners win.

The grass of love grew softly green
    Then ripe as harvest time.
For longing love grows full and tall
    Where love's bright sun is seen.

But the fields we mowed so closely
    Grow thick as summer grass.
Grows wild and rank and lonely
    As it waits for time to pass.

The grain of love is fully ripe.
    The corn is in the field.
But always I need you by my side
    To harvest love's full yield!

August

26

False fear germinates in ignorance and grows in the darkness where it fetters our feet,
attacks our ambition, kills our courage, and drives us stumbling from the pathway
of purpose into the deeper shadows of doubt and despair.
Never cultivate or coddle false fear. Open the doors and let the sunshine in!

FEAR IN THE FACE OF SUCCESS

Dump your doubts, deny defeat, face your fears, campaign for courage, affirm your faith, and the whole world will help you win! Pay close attention to the following ten steps to a positive mental attitude on which applied faith is based:

1. Definite major purpose with a plan for giving to the world.
2. Affirmation through prayer and faith with "imaging" or seeing oneself in possession of the object desired or condition expected.
3. Associate basic motive of life with a definite purpose, and call it to mind frequently and forcibly.
4. Write out advantages of a definite purpose; create "Success Consciousness" by reviewing them frequently.
5. Associate with encouraging people of Master Minding type.
6. Persistent, daily ACTION in the direction of your goals.
7. Choose a pacemaker who is prosperous, forceful, etc.
8. Surround yourself with pictures, books, mottoes of self-reliance, and reminders of successful, great people and conditions to build an atmosphere of achievement.
9. Stay put until you win. Fight it out with oughtness with yourself and with untoward circumstances, right where you are.
10. Pay the price in persistency in spite of any tendency to laziness or avoidance.

Fear is a rampant emotion, a runaway horse on the road. Avoid fear and keep your own horses tied unless you are in the saddle or in the driver's seat!

DOORKNOB DAY

Doorknobs are glass
Or polished brass
    With one on every door.
They let us in
Or keep us out;
    That's what doorknobs are for.

A doorknob shines
A welcome sight
    Bright with mirrored light.
But I can't find mine
Or even the key
    When I come home at night.

Doorknobs are cold
Or else they're warm,
    It depends on who has held them.
Let's take them off
And end to end
    In a chain of brass let's weld them.

Then open doors
Would need no keys
    And we'd throw them all away.
We'd take time out
To celebrate
    And call it "Doorknob Day!"

August

27

*Disappointment may be like a burr under the saddle blanket or a spur in the horse's flank,
but no person should give up because disappointment galls or goads him.
Our disappointments should only spur us on to greater conquest.*

POSITIVE LIVING AND THE OLD GREY MARE VISUAL
(CREATIVE VISUALIZATION)

Relax completely, breathe deeply, and visualize clearly. We want to do a tape on The Old Grey Mare. I want you to picture the numbers 1 – 9 – 7 – 2. 1972. Picture it clearly. How would you make the 1 – 9 – 7 – 2? Maybe you could write it on something in your mind. Now directly under it, visualize 1950. 1950. How did you make the zero? Was it round? Was it oval? How did you make the 5? Was there a nice round part to the five? Does it have a little tail on it that's straight? Does it point up or point down? Now look at the 9. What kind of loop do you have on the 0 that faces toward the 1? See a nice round beautiful 9, and the number 1. 1950. Now will you subtract the 1950 from the 1972? Why, you get twenty-two years, don't you?

A long time ago, twenty-two years ago on a spring morning, anytime between the middle of March and even up toward May, a little colt is born in a farmyard on a ranch, let's say, in Nebraska. It is a little grey colt with little freckles on her nose, and she's standing on long, gangly legs nuzzling up to her mother for the first drink of milk. She's feeling the warmth of the sun on her back for the first time. Her mother is walking out toward the trough to get a drink of water, and that little colt has to almost run and stagger to keep up with her mother. That's the Old Grey Mare when she was a little baby foal.

But the years have come and gone, and the mare is still on the same old ranch or homestead. But there's a better home now and there's a better corral. Right in the middle of that corral there is a great big post like a tree. The horses stand there and they've milled around until the dust and the hay is all pulverized around the post. The Old Grey Mare is standing there. She's been rubbing her back against that post. Old age and the skin deterioration or the flies may have made her scratch and push and rub until she's rubbed all the hair off from one side of her tail. You can see the black, smooth, velvety skin underneath the tail. You can also see some of the wisps of grey tail hair caught on a little snag, on a little sliver, on the side of that post. Visualize it clearly. But would you look at that Old Grey Mare! Her back is sagging. She isn't what she used to be. Look at those hipbones. They're pointed. They're sharp. Look at that scrawny, u-neck. Notice how that neck bows down, and a scraggly mane flops over the other way; part of it is standing straight up where she has rubbed it against the limb of an overhanging tree. She has a Roman nose with just a little white blaze down through her face and forehead. And there are still freckles on her soft, velvety nose. Play like you're giving her a cube of sugar. She's reaching out that long, stretchy, upper lip. She's wiggling it anxiously. You can feel it as she gently touches your hand and fingers.

The Old Grey Mare is starting to wander out across the pasture now. She goes through the corral gate. She has to step over a bar that is down. She manages to do it, but it is hard for her to see, because if you will look closely, you'll see a white film covering one eye. The other one doesn't see too well either now as the Old Grey Mare is walking out into the field. She isn't what she used to be. She can't see the flowers blooming. She can't see the sun shining as well as she could. She can't even see where objects are. But she knows the way to the back pasture. She's crossing a little creek now. There are flowers on one side. On the far side are some little buttercups with their waxy petals and their graceful, green leaves. She's stepping across the creek, and there are little pebbles like rocks on the bottom of it. There's a little minnow darting here and there, but she can't see it. One hind foot slips back into the creek. She can't quite make it across, but she's going on now.

She's coming up to an old, dilapidated building. It's a building that is so old it's falling apart. It's the first house that the people lived in back when the Old Grey Mare was just a little colt. The house is made out of one-by-twelve boards that are upright. The screen door is sagging and broken from one hinge. There are no lights in the windows now, for no one lives there. The windows are like vacant eyes in a house that has no soul, no life. Just memories are there. The shingles are gone from part of the roof. The sun as it came up in the morning, as it was warming her bony back, cast a shadow on the west side of the old house. The Grey Mare remembers and is walking over toward the shade of the house. She's standing there now with her head down and her nose almost touching the ground. An old grey horse is standing against an equally old, brown, weather-beaten building whose boards show the brain, the cracks, the knotholes and the weatherworn beating of years that have come and gone.

No wonder the Old Grey Mare isn't what she used to be! Houses deteriorate, fall down and come apart at the seams. People grow older, and the Old Grey Mare, who was once a colt, is an old, old horse at the end of her journey. Her head is down, and maybe she's thinking about the good days when she played as a colt in those same fields. Maybe she's thinking about the boys that rode her back to school. Maybe she's thinking about the time she had to plow the fields and the corn came up so beautifully, sweet and green. Maybe she's thinking about colts that ran by her side. She's thinking, thinking, thinking. For the Old Grey Mare isn't what she used to be, because time makes changes.

Okay. As you're thinking about that picture now, I want you to stay at this level. We want to do some pretty heavy thinking, too. First, time does make changes. Time can make good changes in us. Time is valuable. Time is life. Time is like money. Spend it wisely and well! Keep a happy, positive attitude, because it keeps you young! Make your time count for something worthwhile. Live your life successfully and beautifully so that, when you do get older, you can look back on happy memories.

Keep healthy. Take care of your "body house" that you live in. Sometimes sickness keeps people from doing what they want to do. Nearly everyone has lost some valuable time just because of a bad cold or something like that. So just for fun and for serious, too, let's work on overcoming the common cold. Lots of people have been told, "Don't do this or you'll catch a cold. Don't do that or you'll catch a cold. Don't go there or don't come here." And there may be some truth in it, but you can put up today a barrier—an invisible shield around you that will keep you from getting the common cold so often. Let's make up our minds that, from today on, we'll have fewer and fewer colds. They'll be farther and farther apart. If you have had a lot of them in past winters, you'll have very few, if any, this winter or summer. The time between colds will get longer and longer, and the colds will be fewer and easier, because you are putting an invisible energy barrier around you that says, "Germs, keep away from me!" You're going to be exceptionally healthy and have lots of strong, active white corpuscles to fight infection and germs. Your body knows how to throw off viruses and to protect yourself.

You're going to be so full of health and energy that, when a cold germ comes around, it will just kick up its heels and fall over dead. It won't have the ability to withstand how strong and how tough you are, because you are healthy! You are not a sickly person. You are a healthy person. You are going to be more and more healthy as you grow older so that not only can you throw off the common cold, you'll be able to throw off all kinds of disease and bad health that try to come to you. If you're exposed to them, you'll just throw them off. The germs won't be able to live successfully on you, because you're going to exercise the inner power of self-protection. You are a winner, and here's to your good health!

You'll maintain a normal weight for your age. If you are overweight, you will reduce. If you're underweight, you'll increase your weight. You'll enjoy exercising and building the muscles in your body. You'll enjoy walking and working. You'll not complain about tasks that are yours to do. You'll get them done quickly. You will enjoy exercise. You'll enjoy sports. You'll be good at sports because you'll play from the relaxation center of your better self. You'll play from a relaxed level with your eyes wide open. When you participate in and learn new sports, whatever they are, you'll do well. You will enjoy your hobbies. If you like to fish, you'll know where the best fishing places are. You'll know the best way to catch the fish. You'll know the best way to take care of them. If you like to take pictures, you'll be a good photographer. If you like to hunt, you'll be a good hunter. You name the hobby or sport. You will enjoy it and do it well.

Let's talk about your schoolwork. You're going to find that, where once you thought you had a hard time and you sometimes were tempted to complain about it, it's going to be a lot easier and maybe even fun. You won't complain now. You're going to talk about good times. Whenever others start talking about hard times and start to be negative, you're just going to be quiet and happy, and you just might say, "It isn't so bad anymore. It's getting better and better and better."

You're going to get along well with people you associate with. You're going to get along very, very well with your family, with your friends, with animals and with people everywhere. Not only will you get along well with people at home, at work, at play or in school, you'll also get along well with your teachers and supervisors. You'll learn how to do little things that make the other people happy.

Your eyes are going to be opened wider. You'll see what's going on around you. You'll hear what's going on around you. You'll hear very, very well. Nature will heal your eyes, ears, and every part of your body so that you function beautifully. You'll see clearly and hear distinctly. You'll enjoy quiet music and relaxation. You'll enjoy talking to people. You are a good conversationalist. You enjoy talking about things. You'll not only talk about the things you enjoy, but you'll find out what the other person is interested in, and you'll talk about the things the other person enjoys. You'll ask that person questions about the thing he enjoys. When you have company, you'll notice or ask what they're interested in, and you'll listen to what they are talking about. You'll ask them to tell you more about what they are interested in. Then, in turn, they may ask you what you are interested in. It will work both ways. But first, ask them and get them talking about something that gets them excited, something they like to do, so that you can share their interest. They'll think you're a wonderful listener, because you will be a wonderful listener.

Your physical body will be in perfect, sound health. Your superconscious mind, your high self, knows everything that your physical body needs to function perfectly. Let's release that physical body from any problems. It's going to be a perfectly healthy physical body. Picture yourself as a truly healthy person!

Your mind has already declared its freedom from all hindrances and inabilities. You now have a strong, clear, happy, smoothly working mind. It is as clear as a bell ringing on a cold, frosty morning. Your mind is as strong as a steel trap snapping shut. It is firm and strong and kind, and it can hold onto ideas. It is a mind that can create new ideas. It can solve problems easily. You have a good mind! You have a sharp mind.

It will always be easy for you to find this level that we're working at now or a deeper level. It will be easy for you to go down to this level and work from this level. So be happy and be cheerful, and look forward to the next lesson and the next one and to the playing of the tapes. Look forward to it with the feeling that each time it's going to be easier and easier to get into your relaxation level. While we're there, we will accept and receive deeply into ourselves only the beautiful, the true, the positive and the good. Your mind from this day on will not be open to bad suggestions. It will not be open to suggestions that are negative. These you'll shut out. You'll know the difference between the kind of things to accept and the kind of things not to accept. You are always in control of your own life. Your limitations will be released. It will be like you'd gotten out of a box and you now feel that you're free, unlimited, happy, strong, intelligent, courageous, healthy, and active. Your life will become better and better day by day as you go along the road that leads to the mountaintop of contentment!

Now, in your mind and heart, be very, very thankful that this is true, and it will be more so as the days come and go. Get ready to come up to activity level. Open your eyes, please. Take a deep breath. You are wide awake, alert, happy, healthy and ready to face life courageously. Everyone stand, please. Stretch a little. Thank you for listening!

STRUGGLING MAKES THE PERSON

From the first step taken upward
   The mountains seem less tall.
And we're closer to the summit
   If we rise each time we fall.

Who says you'll fail to make it?
   You're the captain of your soul.
God's mighty hand outreaching
   Will help you reach your goal.

So strive and keep on striving.
   Give no thought to giving up.
Then when the sun is setting
   You'll be on the mountaintop!

Then look back where first you stumbled,
   Where you resolved to try again,
And remember it's the struggle
   That helps the strong to win.

BENGAL TIGER BY CLANCY CHERRY

August

28

*Constancy of purpose is the crown of achievement, and only those wear it
are subject to their own sovereignty.*

SELF-IMPROVEMENT
(CREATIVE VISUALIZATION)

Resting comfortably, relaxing completely, visualizing clearly and distinctly in color and in action, open your heart and mind to listen and receive the inspiration and the instruction of this information on self-improvement and profit by it. Listen to the music and become a part of the emotional essence of it all as we go deeply within ourselves to program ourselves for progress.

To stand on some high pinnacle of inspiration, to rise over difficulties, to climb, to achieve, to make self-improvement—these are the challenges of life and the privileges of man. Conquest is the most basic note and the truest harmony of all man's source. Man's words are but the symbols of his feelings. They contain the mental images that he perceives and conceives. Picturization precedes language verbalization. Pictures are the basic language of thought in any language. It is basic talking to ourselves using pictures. Pictures are the blueprint for action and attraction used by the creative, inner mind to materialize our desires.

Perhaps on the wings of music, poetry, song, vivid visualization, looking into the depth of a burnished agate or the blue of the sky, or the depth of green waters may trigger that elevated sense of beauty and cosmic insight that is opened by intense, elevated emotion. Whatever it is that triggers this high sense of soul levitation, desire sincerely to see with the eyes of the soul into the heart of the essence of all things. Repeat silently: This is my desire. I want to see with the eyes of the soul, into the heart essence of all things in the awakened, alert, conscious condition of an integrated personality. I visualize this perfect man image restored completely in me through the forgiving, cleansing, quickening of the Creator's grace, love, and life-giving power. I thank the Creator for it.

It is possible now to gain conscious control and direction of my higher powers. I declare it. I affirm that I am aware that I do exercise these latent powers. This is also an order to my inner mind to activate these abilities, for I do possess them. I have the courage to use them and the faith to expand them. I am aware, increasingly aware, of activated self-direction, of Divine guidance and control over the hidden powers of my inner self. Affirmations are a statement of awareness or consciousness. Thus, conscious cognizance is the appropriative, intuitive, knowing way of attaining wisdom, position, information, wealth, power, health, confidence, all acceptable traits and much, much more. Being truly and fully aware of a trait and to identify with it is to possess it, for consciousness is the secret to attainment.

I resolve not to finish any negative statement unless it is necessary and wise to do so. My preference is to reverse all negative statements and to make positive statements of them. I choose to give only positive, creative suggestions of how things might be desirably different and better. I will see the desired end clearly as though it were so. And it will be. Confident expectancy, as an attitude, is a powerful suggestion to the cooperative powers of the subconscious mind, which releases its inner wisdom, power, healing and guidance. I will, therefore, envision a happy ending or solution to any problem, whatever it is. I will feel the thrill of future appropriation and accomplishment in the eternal now.

I instruct my inner self to think and live in ideal and desired conditions and states. I instruct my inner being to be positive, joyful, confident, calm, courageous, strong, vibrant, powerful, knowledgeable and good in the direction of life. In meditation before retiring, I will say to myself, I shall profit from the experiences of today. I shall give a better account of myself tomorrow than I have ever done before. Tomorrow will be a good day, a profitable day, and today is a good day. I will have a good account to give when tomorrow's day is done, for some good thing will come to me this day and every day.

I am aware that the successful individual is one who learns to control his own suggestibility, so that he largely responds only to that which is good for him and rejects the bad. Because I value my own integrity, free will and destiny, I am eternally vigilant and on guard against negative suggestions and influences, whether obvious or subliminal, that come to me. I reject negative influences immediately and instinctively. I am not influenced by what I would not choose when at my very best. I am self-confident and I am courageous. A conqueror is a man who believes he can. I believe I can. I will! I can! Let it echo from a thousand cliffs. Let it reverberate in the ocean's roar. Let it sing in cadence of every bird's song. I can! I can! I can! I can! But I shall not substitute words alone for intended action. Courage does not boast itself falsely in empty words. It does what it must do and what it properly intends to do. True courage is calm and unshaken. Therefore, I will always react courageously to whatever life brings to me.

I shall practice where possible and reasonable the spirit of inner nonresistance, and I shall bless lovingly and silently all things and all situations and all circumstances. I have an expectant attitude for good. Some good thing will come to me from all life experiences. My highest good will come to me. I welcome the good, the beautiful, the true. They are mine by right of personal choice and the power of good to triumph. I put up no resentful resistance to things that seem to overwhelm me. I know all things are working together for my good. I am working with them in the power and the wisdom of the Spirit. I put myself and all my affairs in the hands of the creator God with a child-like trust. That which is for my highest good will come to me. It will come to me, for I attract my own to me. I am courageous.

They have no fear that put their trust in the creator of the universe. To any disquieting emotion welling up within, I will say, "Be still as Galilee was still. Be quiet. Harken also unto me. I am in control of my life even as God controlled the waves of Galilee. So cease to surge and roll, waves of my inner life and waves of outer circumstance. Cease to rage and roll. Me, you must obey, subject to God's command, to my will and to His.

"Safely we shall come to land, for I am His." I will speak authoritatively to any irrational, disturbing emotional upsurges, and I will give positive affirmations of peace, of hope, of rest, of harmony,

⫸ 596 ⫷

and of successful solution. I shall hold on courageously and react to all life situations with valor and with confidence. I shall persist in effort and in prayer, in faith, hope, and love. God shall supply all of my needs. He is the author of my salvation and my hope and my joy.

I instruct the extrasensory faculties of my higher self in advance to do the things necessary to counteract for me and for mine any intended loss of property, wealth, health, or general well-being. I instruct my inner self, under God, to activate an achieving faith and thus to successfully counteract any negative forces not for my best good or for those around me. I thank God for the miracle of progress, of abundance, of well-being, of success and protection, now and forthcoming. I firmly suggest and request that my inner level of consciousness seek and provide the right guidance, directly from God, for my life.

Love identifies and unifies. The highest intuitive knowing is by identifying with the nature of the object. Identity or fusion of subject and object is only by love, by will, and by desire. It is by choice. All senses of the individual, thus, are fused as one sense, and they are exalted and increased in vibratory intensity; they identify their magnetic fields with the magnetic field of the object. Thus it is one in fusion and one in being, state and knowledge. I instruct my highest self, under God and in a perfect way, to identify in unity with that which is desired to be known, to identify in love and in oneness and yet maintain my own individuality. I do pre-charge special situations in advance with holy, prayerful, light-filled atmosphere. I take time to visualize the situation as I desire it, the atmosphere as I want it, and the reactions of those concerned as cooperative and pleasant. I visualize their anticipated, desired reactions and actions as in a play, as a previewed revision of what I will and desire it to be.

I am alert, sensitive to and keenly aware of the functioning of the extrasensory faculty of the mind. I shall be able to call these processes into the forefront of awareness and consciousness as I desire to do so and shall retain that which is profitable to be remembered. I see myself opening the curtains of my superconsciousness. I see myself opening my extrasensory awareness so that I may more fully live in the Divine Image, the unlimited side of my being. I now, more and more, function with complete awareness and am perfectly intermeshed with the inner survival mechanisms and the willing, choosing, reasoning, conscious mind, all fully integrated and functioning as one for my best good. Through my high, inner self and my connection with the Divine Nature, I have a spiritual faculty of awareness, cognizance and intuitive knowledge that is not affected by time or space or barriers of other persons' minds.

Knowledge and wisdom are golden doors opened wide to enter in. I am now inside. I know instinctively the things I need or desire to know. I discern them. I have a quickened, God-filled, discerning mind. And it is so. I believe that I am sensitive, that I have the gift of discernment, and also the gift of extrasensory perception. God often reveals Himself—events, situations, conditions, solutions, courses of action, information, and knowledge in advance to me and to others also. I believe in the effectiveness of extrasensory perception. I receive it. I remember it and I use it daily. I am surrounded by a white aura of holy, pure, magnetic influence that is effective in repulsing the evil. It is also an aura of gratitude, positive thinking, Divine awareness, power, protection, peace, and plenty. Others will sense this and respond to it. I do possess the courage, faith, self-confidence and God confidence to both recognize and act upon genuine hunches and accurate intuitive perceptions that come to me under Divine guidance. I have faith in God. I do now have faith in, depend upon, and respect my inner level of consciousness more and more and am aware of its silent working. I am increasingly able to receive, manifest and transmit these inner messages effectively. I firmly suggest and request that my inner self, under God, seek, accept, and provide the right guidance for my life that I may know and do the right thing at the right time always and say or not say the right things intuitively. I shall be warned in adequate time of anything I need to know for my best interests and the protection of myself, my life interests and my loved ones.

I renounce any hindering or negative self-image or unnecessary self-limitations and choose the larger freedom of God-like capacity and nature with a proper self-image for conquest and positive progress. I am free of all self-imposed, unnecessary, unreal limitations. I shall not be disturbed by apparent misses or seeming hindrances to success. I will believe that everything is working out well for the right time and place. This is being arranged on subconscious and superconscious inner levels of intuition and spiritual perception, synchronizing my movements to accomplish these desires and proper ends. I instruct my inner mind to continually and faithfully synchronize all my movements in time and in space that I may be at the right place at the right time, doing and saying the right things always to attain the perfect will of the creator God for the best interest and the greatest good of my life here and hereafter. Under God and in a perfect way, I have more than adequate income to use or share with others. I believe now that, as I relax deeply, having stated my need, God, through the higher levels of awareness, knowledge, and revelation will show me solutions to any problems, stated or unstated. He will show me answers and ways to success and how to have abundance. I ask for Divine guidance during my sleep and will either remember or record and be directed by the answers that come . . .

Rest for a moment longer, please. As we open our eyes fully, let us come up from our level of relaxed awareness feeling refreshed, strengthened and perfected in every way with joyfulness to face every today and all of the glad tomorrows. Wide awake now and thank you for listening!

PERFECT LAND

Oh let me view the perfect land
  Thru the eyes of inward viewing—
The anti-matter shadow land—
  True reality pursuing.

Ah let me find that perfect land
  And see beyond the fleeting,
To behold the patterns of all things
  Where unseen and seen are meeting.

In the pathways of the perfect land
  My soul walks calm and lightly,
In tune with Infinite, rhythmic flow
  Where beauty speaks forthrightly.

The perfect land is nourished
  By all things here projected,
For the material and the spiritual
  Are by unseen cords connected.

LION'S GAZE BY CLANCY CHERRY

August

~ 29 ~

KING OF THE BEASTS BY CLANCY CHERRY

A SUNSET, EVENING SKY

God wiped a golden paintbrush
    Beneath a somber cloud.
The painting He called a sunset
    And did it all up proud.

He carved the mountains from the rocks
    And the chips fell in the sea.
He stretched time out so long and far
    That men called it eternity.

God placed a sliver of silver moon
    Like a half-closed, watchful eye.
Men called it rain when the great God wept
    And God had reason to cry.

The ocean cast up its driftwood debris
    And left it all tangled on shore
Like the drifted, twisted thoughts of men
    Who had come and gone before.

The roar of His surging ocean
    And the moaning of the sea
Were drowned out by an inner cry
    From the deepest heart of me.

I wanted to be helpful and stronger—
    Free from the blight and din.
I wanted to be good and happy,
    Very positive and bright within.

I wanted to pass beyond the clouds
    Where invisible angels stand.
Till I came somewhere, to the home of God
    In a far-off, peaceful land.

But, goodnight, for now, my Father,
    There's a prayer of my will to try.
May I always discern the face of God
    In a sunset, evening sky!

August

30

Enthusiasm is the outreaching, positive, creative force of God within us manifesting itself in the lively spirit of joyous progress and increase.

DUMPING THE GARBAGE BAG OF FEAR
(CREATIVE VISUALIZATION)

Sitting comfortably with your body upright and your feet flat on the floor, take a deep breath and exhale. Do it again. With your eyes closed gently, breathing deeply, relaxing completely, visualize clearly, in detail, in color and in action, as you follow the creative visualization of *Dumping the Garbage Bag of Fear.*

There are some wonderful things about the power of suggestion when we are at a relaxed level like this. Many things were stored in our minds a long, long time ago. Many things people said to us when we were tired and in a relaxed condition went way down inside of us like a barbed arrow or like a fishhook that got caught and we couldn't get it out. These were emotional feelings, pictures and ideas. Some of these ideas were negative ones. They weren't all associated with the beautiful, the true, the positive and the good. There might have been even some ideas like, "You're a dumb bunny; you're not so smart; you're a bad boy or girl; can't you read? are you afraid? you don't hear well; you don't understand easily; you're stubborn;" or some other untrue, foolish thing. These things are not true about you because you are a good person; you are a smart person; you are a co-operative, kind person. You do hear well; you do see well; you can read; you are brave; you do get along well with people and you catch on to things quickly!

The wonderful thing about listening to a discussion at this relaxed level is that we can go back and take out those old fishhooks—things we used to be afraid of, we can get over being afraid of. If someone has told us negative things back in our childhood when we were tired, sleepy, relaxed or even highly emotional, we can go back now at the same relaxed level of mind and take those fish-hooks out where they are hurting us. That's what we're doing right now. We're going to affirm and picture some very positive things. You can say them in your mind silently, not aloud, but in your mind after me. Take another deep breath and keep your eyes closed gently so that no sensory input, except my voice, is holding your undivided attention. Be completely at a passive, relaxed level in order to do this well. That's why we listen to our tapes with relaxed, undivided attention. It helps us find this quiet, interior place where we can work on ourselves.

Very good. Let's work on that mean fishhook called fear. Many things were said to us when we were children about fear; for example, "You should be afraid of this. Be careful! Don't do that! Watch out!" This gave us things to worry about. Well, remember, you are protected. You truly are wonderfully protected. We want to get rid of foolish fears that are not reasonable fears for self-protection.

Changing our thought picture for a moment, just imagine that you're on a ship and that you are rolling up all of your fears, whatever they are; and you know what they are. Roll all the things you have been afraid of up in a piece of canvas or burlap or put them in a heavy plastic garbage bag. You can take a second to name these fears if you want to as you put them in your bag…

Now, roll it up tightly in this giant garbage bag, and then tie it with ropes. Also tie it to a big piece of cement or to several cinder blocks. Run the rope or wire around and through the heavy weights. Okay, you've got your bag full of fears! You have a chunk of cement or two or three pretty heavy cinder blocks. Please walk over to the side of the ship. There's a plank there like the old pirates used to have for people to walk the plank. You just imagine that you're walking right out to the end of the plank like it was a diving board. Look down at the water below you. Notice the big, green, ocean waves. See the fin of an old shark going by. See a dolphin splashing or playing in the distance. See a fish come to the surface or a seagull skimming the waves. Observe that, way down in that bottomless, fathomless ocean, deeper than you can see, way down below the waves where deep-sea animal life walks, swims and lives on the bottom, there's an entrance to a cave! You can barely see the cave door. You're going to lean out over the end of that plank, and you're going to drop your whole bundle of unnecessary, inconvenient, unwanted, foolish fears.

Okay, get it stretched out, and then lean out over the waves. Drop the cement blocks first. Notice how the cement starts to slide, fall and jerk on the bag of fears until pretty soon they jerk that big bundle of fears out of your hands. Watch them go down. See how they splash in the water. See how the little bubbles come out of the sack. Watch the shark swimming around them now as they sink. He's excited. He thinks it's something he can eat, but it's just garbage! See that fin going around and around in a circle and the waves going out, farther out, farther out, farther out…

Those old fears are bubbling and gurgling as they go clear down to the bottom of that silent, dark ocean. They are landing right over the entrance to that cave. It's a dark cave, and there are some little fish swimming back and forth in front of it. Can you see it in your mind's eye? Down, down, down goes that garbage bag of fears. The little fish scatter from in front of the cave entrance. A big goldfish joins them as they swim away.

Off to one side of the cave there's an octopus looking through the underwater darkness with his little beady eyes. He is spraying out some of his octopus ink across the cave entrance. But look! Those rocks and the bag roll and fall as the water and their own weight carry them down into the entrance of the cave. Down, down that garbage bag goes. There goes the fear of failure. There goes the fear of darkness. There goes that fear of people. There goes the fear of closed places. There goes the fear of being alone. There goes the fear of animals. There goes the fear of anything you can think of that you no longer need or want! All of those fears are going farther and farther away. Going, going, going. They are so far away that you can't hear them. So far away that you can't see them, because a giant swordfish rammed his sword point under the ropes of the bag and is carrying it farther and farther away into the back of that cave. He dropped that garbage bag of fears off over a cliff back there and lost it forever. Wow! Down at the bottom of the ocean, clear back at the back of a deep cave, and then down over a big cliff into an ocean of nothingness!

Just at the edge of that cliff is a rusty, heavily banded treasure chest. Lying by it is the skeleton of some pirate or maybe Barnacle Bill the Sailor. Let's imagine he reaches into the treasure chest and gets a big stick of dynamite. It explodes, and the whole roof of that cave is coming down. Guess that takes care of that garbage bag full of stupid fears that we didn't want anyway! The water is bubbling, the rocks are fumbling and the fish are coming out of there in a hurry. Let's get out of there, too. Our fears are buried in the sea of forgetfulness and we'll not remember them anymore. We are happy now because we're free! We will keep our good fears for self-preservation. We'll not do foolish things. We will protect our lives wisely but we'll not be guilty of being afraid when we should be courageous. That kind of fear is gone…

Rest a moment longer but get ready to come up to activity level. Take a deep breath. Open your eyes, please. Stretch a bit! You feel wonderful. You feel rested—relaxed but not sleepy. You feel healthy, happy and ready to courageously face life because you've dumped the garbage bag of fear. Today will be a good day. Thank you for listening!

THE ESSENCE OF LIFE

O Thou Pure Essence of Life,
 Fountain and Source overflowing.
O Thou Pure Essence of all,
 Life energy radiant and glowing!

Thou, O God, art the Essence of life.
 Pure Fountain of Infinite Power.
Eons swiftly have come and gone
 But undiminished art Thou this hour.

O Thou Pure Essence of Life,
 Complete refreshing, supreme!
Shine Thy beneficent Light on us
 Who would walk in its life-giving gleam.

WHITE TIGER BY CLANCY CHERRY

August

~ 31 ~

NEARING THE SHORE

The sailor is tossed on a barren sea;
No greenery of land meets his eye.
But wait, as he nears the invisible shore,
Some land-laden breeze passes by.
The fragrance of flowers, the smell of the trees,
And lo, now the land greets his vision anew.
The long voyage is over, the harbor is reached
And the ship is safe home with her crew.

And so we are walking the deck of our faith
On the ship of our hope where we ride.
While over our hearts comes the subtle soft breeze
Of our Harbor-Land-Home o'er the tide.
And the warm air is laden with hints from the land
And a shout shall arise from the shore,
When the Ship of Life shall reach her last port
And the days of our voyaging are o'er.

A PROUD FATHER'S SON (W. JACKSON)

September

∽ 1 ∽

Poetry, like beauty, is as much in the perception of the viewer and the listener as it is in the manifest form; and it rises from an intuitive rearrangement of the commonplace into an expression of the universal harmony and rhythm of the inner essence of life's vital forces.

IF A POEM SHOULD COME TO ME

If a poem should come to me
　Like a ship upon the sea,
Then I'd go to meet and greet it,
Welcome, beckon, and entreat it,
　And I'd be glad it came to me.

If a poem should come to me
　Like a gray bird, wild and free,
Then I'd try to dare to snare it,
Gladly would I freely share it,
　Then others would be glad with me.

If a poem should come to me
　Like a leaf from autumn tree,
I would catch and boldly hold it.
In my heart I would enfold it,
　And I'd keep it where its
　　beauty I could see!

LAMARTINE BY GREG WALZ

September

2

Quietness is therapeutic, and the quest for quietness is the cure for countless problems, pressures and pains.

SHUT IN WHEN THE RAIN COMES DOWN

When I'm tired and weary of people,
And the rain comes pouring down,
I feel refreshed and comforted
   like;
Shut in when the rains come down.

It's nice to have people visiting,
To call in the country or town,
But I like that encircling, comforting
   feel—
Shut in when the rain comes down.

It makes the Creator seem closer
When there are no folks around.
So I like to be home with the rain
   on the roof;
Shut in when the rain comes down.

GIVE US BACK

Give us back our hope and wonder
    That we have laid aside.
Give us back our doors and windows.
    Let our shades be opened wide.

Give us back our faith and promise
    And our ears for harmony.
Give us back our inner vision
    That our second eyes may see.

Give us back our hope and wonder
    Let our faith become as sight.
May our consciousness expanded
    Bring the dawning of the light.

May our shadows of delusion
    And our love of "Status Quo"
Flee like shadows in the dawning
    Of true wisdom's afterglow!

May a radiant inner knowing
    That expands the mind and heart
Shine forever at full zenith.
    May its wisdom not depart.

September

3

CONQUEST:
*Self-conquest is safer than conquest, for it has fewer subjects to conquer or control,
and in case of mutiny, there is more likelihood of compromise than decapitation!*

People and circumstances respond to the heartbeat of enthusiasm in action.

A person's happiest employment is found in the area of his greatest abilities and his deepest interests.

Action may appear magnificent, but it is measured by its motive.

The courage of valor in wisdom directed battles no windmills in the targets selected.

WHISPERING WIND

The whispering, whistling, laughing wind
    Comes blowing up my hill.
The whispering, sighing, crying wind
    Can never quite keep still.

The whispering, moaning, groaning wind
    Is like a suffering soul.
It climbs each hill and always will
    For conquest is its goal.

The whispering, laughing, shouting wind
    Is a happy child at school
When teacher's gone from night till dawn
    And it plays without a rule.

The whispering, singing, silent wind
    Dies down and seems quite gone.
But in an instant it springs back to life
    To play and sing on and on.

VALLECITO FALL BY GREG WALZ

September

4

*Education doesn't start in school, nor does it end there. It is a lifelong process
of self-correcting vision, judgment and discipline.*

GOALS FOR PUBLIC EDUCATION

I

The purpose of education should be to promote a success-oriented philosophy of achievement in education, to inspire self-improvement and self-motivation, to open potential mental reserves through impartation of knowledge, skills and positive attitudes essential to the highest functioning of the integrated individual.

II

The purpose of education should be to better understand and utilize all levels of the mind; to strive for and employ all feasible resources for a breakthrough of effectiveness in learning efficiency fundamental to upgrading the quality of individualized education.

III

The purpose of education should be to develop values; provide value guidance; encourage favorable behavioral changes; promote in-depth intellectual, emotional, cultural and social development; implement successful interpersonal relationships; and increase enrichment of all possible options for achievement in life and learning and for leadership training with motivation and guidelines for greater service to humanity and for informed participation in the processes and interaction of democracy in the world community.

The man who stopped studying when he stopped going to school is losing more than his hair.

CHALK TALK

Chalk, chalk,
Teachers wave it and talk.
    Dust clutters up the air.
The facts they are sighting,
With the chalk they are writing
    Aren't worth giving a care.

Chalk, chalk,
People wave it and talk,
    Pointed like a gun at your head,
They hold it like a "Kool"
While sighting some rule
    Hardly knowing what they've said.

Chalk, chalk,
Kids watch it in shock
    Then snitch some pieces to use
To write on the street
Or trample under their feet
    Protesting some imagined abuse.

Chalk, chalk,
For the prey teachers stalk.
    But here's what would be more fair:
Teachers, eat chalk while you listen.
Let the kids give the lesson.
    Show them you really care!

September

~ 5 ~

JEWEL OF SEASCAPE BY I. DALE

MY HEART IS LIKE THE OCEAN

My heart is like the ocean
    Where surging billows swell,
Where hidden thoughts and longings
    Lie too deep to know or tell.

My heart is like the ocean
    Where sailing steamships ride,
That bring their bartered cargo
    And gifts on every tide.

My heart is like the ocean
    Where bits of driftwood play,
Where chance and breeze and current
    Bear the hours of life away.

My heart is like the ocean,
    Turbulent, wild, and free,
That longs to be here and everywhere,
    For this is the way of the sea.

My love is like the ocean
    Where waves strange shores embrace;
And when they have found fulfillment,
    They ebb without a trace.

September

~ 6 ~

In the immortality of books the dead speak yet once again and twice as loud and clear.

Emotion, the atomic energy of mind and spirit, is a power plant for good or ill. It is life's vital force directed or misdirected, negative or positive, constructive or destructive. Emotion is what you make it, by how you direct it and where and why you project it.

Mix equal parts of faithfulness, unselfishness, trustworthiness, steadfastness, dependability, confidence, courage, cooperation, common purpose, and uncommon love, and you can whip up a batch of loyalty that will stand the long stretch.

WRITE THE WORDS DOWN

Dictionaries are full of many words.
They fall in fluent currents
   From the lips of man.
Printed books are full of regimented words.
They cry their wares in silent streets
   And stop us when they can.

Newspapers are full of empty words,
The words of crime and trouble
   Sadly sped abroad.
The Holy Book is filled with weighty words,
True words of power and blessing
   Proceeding forth from God.

My heart is filled with happy words,
Sweet syllables of gladness—
   New words of peace and love.
My lips are filled with singing words,
Seraphic words that angels hymn
   With vibrant harps above.

(CONTINUED ON NEXT PAGE)

Our lives are like great books of braille
    That people are always feeling
    While they pass us by.
God grant that silent words or spoken
May be the kind of words that point
    Folks upward to the sky.

Some friends have gifts for writing words
That flow like magic rivers
    Thru countryside and town.
God grant such ones the truth and courage
To take the burning pen of fire
    And quickly write them down.

September

~ 7 ~

*To understand cause is better than to beg for effects. Appreciate and respect
the responses and responsibilities of your subconscious mind.*

THE SUBCONSCIOUS MIND

Conscious, purposeful self-improvement, with an understanding of its needs and its benefits, can be clearly held in the focus of the attention at a level that becomes effective in its implementation. When man realizes that his subconscious mind, or lower self, is often an emotionally discontent, rebellious alien within himself, he then begins a process of inner renovation and searches for a cure. This often leads him into extremes and into cultish adaptations of hoped-for cures. There must be an integration of all diffracted selves within the triunity of man. The key to its smooth and sane functioning is the emphasis on the compulsion of love and compassion as the effective bond in the integrated personality of man within himself and in all of his interpersonal relationships. It is true that man is essentially mental and spiritual in nature. The physical and the chemical are an addition and an appendage to his real self.

Man is worthy of possessing those things that he instinctively desires within the framework of the beautiful, the true, the positive, and the good. No imagined shame or guilt should keep us from our God-inspired desires and their proper fulfillment in life.

Man is capable of anticipating change through the exercise of an activated precognition. But it must always admit of the natural limitations of the person employing the gift plus the unforeseen decisions, actions, and reactions of those people involved who also, by chance of course, can change the ultimate outcome or destiny of that which was projected as a probability.

There are harmonies of change within the substructurings of natural law. There are melodious, rhythmic changes in all perceived and unperceived levels and functions of the entire universe. The constant interaction of a multiplicity of energy vortexes gives rise to an existentialism of adaptation, variety, progress, retrogression, and constant change in the matter, motion, mathematics, manifestation, and mutation of materiality in an ever-changing, kaleidoscopic world of interacting polarity opposites.

TO THE LOW SELF

I would not exalt you as high as some others
    Have lifted your banner in seasons gone by.
But I would exalt you as part of the wonder
    Of the immortal mortal in whose bosom you lie.

I would not exalt you as out of due measure.
    You are but part of the trinity of man.
And without essential, common-sense reason
    You do err often and very frequently can.

I would not exalt you above the high spirit,
    Above superconsciousness closest to heaven.
But I would exalt you for intuitive awareness,
    Creative memory and preservation oft given.

I would not exalt you beyond your deserving.
    You are the low self though wondrous in plan.
You do work truest when harnessed together
    With judgment and God's own Spirit in man.

I would not exalt you, my subconscious helper,
    As one to be dominant or entirely alone,
For you are a genius, a child-like giant,
    Subject to reason and God on the throne.

But I would exalt you as a true servant
    Unsleeping, faithful to suggestion or need.
And out of your province of instinctive wisdom
    Come many achievements and profoundest deed.

I would commend you for all of your powers
    And instruct you to make a unified whole,
That reason and spirit and subconscious will
    In perfect union may prosper my soul.

I am not wise enough to delineate your duty
    Or pass valid judgment without your aid.
But together as one in luminous awareness
    May earth be pleasant and heaven be made.

September

~ 8 ~

A person steps up or stumbles over his own attitudes on the stairway to success. He must keep a determined and positive outlook, and up look, to arrive at the top.

WE MARCH TO THE SOUND OF DRUMS

We march to the sound of drums within.
    We strike the rhythm and beat.
Ours is the orchestration of life
    And ours the jubilant feet.

We march to the sound of silent drums;
    Vibrant but softly they roll,
The rhythm of an inner universe,
    The harmony and pulse of the soul.

We march to the sound of rolling drums
    Projected in mood and in deed.
And others may join in our symphony
    With fife and with harp and with reed.

We march to the sound of singing drums,
    The melody is militant and clear.
And, whether in battle or in festival played,
    We march without doubt or fear.

I MUST WALK ON!

I must walk out in the face of the wind,
The wild elements of rain and storm.
   The task before me I must not shirk.
   I'm a part of nature at play and work
And naught can work me harm.

I must walk out in the forest of trees
And enjoy its breadth and length.
   I must sit down on some rocky ledge
   Or climb the heights to the canyon edge
And draw from the earth its strength.

I must walk out in the sleet and rain
And feel it bruise my face;
   And wash my lips to pray anew,
   And purge me thru and thru,
Windswept of all disgrace.

I must walk out in the crowded streets
Where my fellow men pass by,
   Till I'm one with them in peace and pain,
   One link in humanity's groaning chain
Lest alone, unsustained, I should die.

I must walk out in the night again
Alone with God and the smiling stars,
   Till His healing hand on my wounded soul
   Makes each broken part alive and whole
As Love kisses life's battle scars.

September

∽ 9 ∽

Every person is breaking the sound barrier of his future at the rate of sixty seconds a minute and sixty minutes per hour. Have you charted your journey and considered your destination?

TIME IS IN YOUR FAVOR

Today, begin to be receptive to the pride of participation, the dependability of teamwork, and the overflow of released life forces that rise resistless and beautiful to make the dry deserts of sluggish habits change to circumstances with favorable outcome and that blossom with the verdant foliage and fruit of the pleasant accomplishment of balanced restoration and timely success. Envision yourself among the ranks of the changing of the guard; work with the calendar and the clock!

- TIME, with MATURATION, is in your favor!
- TIME, with INSPIRATION, is in your favor!
- TIME, with MOTIVATION, is in your favor!

Inspired and motivated life goals are the standards on and beyond our spaceship journey. Will you be among those to express love, both to the Creator and to your fellow man? Sing the song of service and action to the purpose of joy and fulfillment related to salvage and preservation? These goals will preserve our relationships and those of our families and our businesses.

This experience will serve as the spark of genius and the unconquerable spirit of adventure. Coupled with sincerity, earnestness, dynamic drive, and the cadence of conquest, the expression of our creative energies and love will form a joint venture with the Creator of the universe to correct spaceship earth's social and spiritual vacuums. Preservation of our lives is the cause, and this cause is worth living for. Believe it: We can and will determine to do better!

Inspiration and motivation within our personal life management form the lodestone of leadership. This lodestone attracts a dedicated workforce like the fragrance and color of a flower attract a diligent swarm of bees. There can be no true leadership without inspired, motivated followers. May we say here, an organization must have purposeful and dedicated people as well as good principles and procedures. It is one thing simply to identify issues, but to progress, even to maintain, solutions must be found and implemented. In addition, we must have people who will work in harmony with nature, fight for creative accomplishment, and share the enthusiasm of a balanced plan and purpose for this spaceship earth.

∽ 625 ∽

SUNDOWN SHIP

I see a ship called Sundown
   With red sails in the sun.
I see a cloud-boat sailing
   Where night is just begun.

Its sails are touched with crimson
   As it sails a silent sea.
I cannot see its ship crew well
   But it must be you and me.

A lonely ship at sundown,
   Its sails are grimly set.
A shadow ship is sailing
   With a load of deep regret.

A sturdy ship is sailing
   With a cargo piled high
Of service, love and happiness
   That outweighs every sigh.

And she knows beyond the sunset
   Beyond the storm clouds' somber hue
That Heaven's harbor beckons
   And Sunrise will soon break thru.

September

10

MAYFLOWER II BY HARVEY GARRETT SMITH

THE SUFFERING, SOBBING, SIGHING RAIN

I heard the sighing, suffering rain
Pour itself out in its grief and pain.
It wandered grimly thru the trees;
Murmured its sorrow on every breeze.
And my heart beat to the sad refrain
Of the sobbing, sighing, suffering rain.

The wailing wind in shrill despair
Shrieked out its fear on the soggy air.
The naked trees like misshaped gnomes
Bent their heads over the moss-clad tombs.
And my poor heart joined in the mad refrain
Of the sobbing, sighing, tortured rain.

The lightning, like a catastrophe,
Struck, unsuspected, a struggling tree.
Blasted, smitten, fallen, grim,
It clutched the ground with each dying limb.
And my cold heart joined in the sad refrain
Of the suffering, sighing, sobbing rain.

The windswept passersby faced the blast.
The rain-soaked people hurried past.
With little joy and much of despair;
Hateful and fearful with none to care.
Then my own heart wept with the sad refrain,
With the suffering, sobbing, sighing rain!

September

11

The mood of discouragement is more vicious than the circumstances that triggered it. Take a second look and you'll find a way out. Take another look and you'll see how lucky you really are.

DIVINE REALITY

The duality of the isometric diamides (measured, diaphragmous energy pulsations), or the Yin and Yang principles of eastern philosophy, or the male and female principles of passivity and creativity, do not exist separately or in opposition in the purest, high dimension of God. The sound-light, broken pattern of dualities in vibratory differentiations arise only as the life force of the Being of God manifests through His own magnetic, vital force field. Prior to its emergence into duality, it existed as a single life force. It existed in pure, undifferentiated, formless, boundless, vibrationless, quiescent, Eternal Being. Its creative emergence, by the very nature of its effulgent, overflowing manifestation in light, makes manifestation possible everywhere and at once in that God is unlimited, uncompressed and exists everywhere so that His magnetic field, of course, would be but a dimensional differentiation capable of manifesting itself anywhere in the everywhere and existing in quiescence in the nowhere and in the now.

God Himself is the absolutely, complete, undivided, vital, spiritual life force at the center and the circumference of all manifest being. Because of the different extended orders of Divine nature, and because some of them arise or manifest first in the center of His Being, without sound or sight stimulation, they cannot all properly be known by the sensory abilities of man through his physical mind. And because of the immensity and complexity and yet the utter simplicity of the nature of God, it is difficult, if not impossible, for man to even catch a brief glimpse of the meaning of Divine Reality. And these brief glimpses do not come through sensory perception but through supersensory perception or the exercising of the high self part of man's own divine nature which alone can comprehend the nature and the essential Being of God in whose image man was patterned. So the necessity is to shift our awareness to the high self if we would know the true self of God.

629

WHEN THE FOG CAME IN

When he magnified the little things
   And dallied in indecision;
When he worried and fretted
And waited too long,
   That's when he lost the vision.

When in unprepared confusion lost,
   Or for easier shortcuts scheming,
He lost his way
In the upward climb
   And vision turned to dreaming.

When he bragged about what he'd done
   Or brooded on loss or quarrels,
That was the day
He lost his way
   And lost his hard-earned laurels.

When without a goal or programmed plan
   He rode with the tide and drifted,
That was the day
The fog came in
   That we hope will soon be lifted!

September

12

To attain your desires, let your goals be clear, your faith expectant, your gratitude unceasing, your purpose unfailing, your actions efficient, and your eternal goals unremitting.

Discouragement is the distemper of despondency, the disease of despair. Cure it! Don't countenance it.

Determination is a steadfast will in purposeful action.

Don't let life's disappointments disappoint you. The places where you fall will soon be road markers on your way to ultimate achievement.

I CLIMBED A HILL

I climbed a hill one evening
   Above the sinking sun.
I saw the cattle browsing
   Where gentle rivers run.

I heard the musing west wind
   In yonder swaying trees.
I saw the white-capped cloud banks
   Like waves upon the seas.

The dimness of the distance
   Had clothed the purple hills
Where waterfalls and streamlets
   Ran down in rippled rills.

The leaves of multicolor
   Had paved a royal way
Where sun and shadow mingled
   At closing of the day.

(CONTINUED ON NEXT PAGE)

I sat upon the summit.
　　I dreamed of yesterday.
I turned my heart to heaven
　　And paused awhile to pray.

I dreamed about tomorrow,
　　Of things that yet may be,
And in the evening sunset
　　A gladsome future see.

I thought of God's tomorrow
　　With tear stains wiped away,
Where eyes will see more clearly
　　In that eternal day.

September

~ 13 ~

*Our greatest goals may be centered on our allegiance to our personal ideals
of individual initiative,
integrity, faith, freedom, and service!*

THE VIEWPOINT OF CHILDHOOD

In a sense, this viewpoint of God is the viewpoint of childhood. It is the fresh look and the beholding of reality, as it is, without the conditioning dust that clouds our more adult eyes. It is without the preconceived and impregnated group concepts of the mass mind of an unseeing humanity. Education itself should seek to develop this side of man but not seek to warp it with preconceived ideas or to take from it its delegated responsibility for self-directed action. Man should not be programmed, but should be taught how to program himself. He should be taught how to live utterly without unnecessary, superimposed programming as he flows with the infinite wisdom of the universe itself. When one rises above the space and time continuum, all things are both nowhere and everywhere, both here and there, because there is no location at the Theta mind level where there is space or no space, time or no time, but a great overlapping which requires no sorting at the moment because there is no necessity for space or time as earth-limited. There is no necessity, therefore, for actual travel as we know it now. This seems incomprehensible, but nevertheless true. For the dimension in which the high self lives is certainly a dimension beyond a space and time continuum, although it recognizes, cognizes, and adjusts itself as best it can to all the timing of this material universe. But it is certainly not limited to it.

ONE WITH THE PURE OF HEART

I want to be so pure and holy
　That I'd feel at home in heaven above.
I want to be so kind and so gentle
　That I shall know the true meaning of love.

Oh, I want to be so good and so useful
　That I can love and serve and live
With true dedication to all my duty
　Reserving nothing that I should give.

Oh, I want to be so upright and honest,
　So sincere in each hidden part
That God Himself can accept me
　As one with the pure in heart!

September

~ 14 ~

Clarity, brevity, reflection, and interest are sure aids to better understanding.

*The individual that too readily confesses to being a worm will likely feel the impulse to crawl again;
the strong choose different symbols for their totem poles of courage and strength.*

*Censure, calmly and kindly given, provokes little contention, for its gentle persuasion
speaks more clearly of its just judgment by the absence of its excessive emotion.*

DISSONANCE

What is our hope of heightened sensation or
    The newness of old things we pass every day?
Dissonance and detachment, new-angled attention
    Bring focused beauty to things on our way.

What is the hope of a beautiful moment
    Set like a diamond in a time cycle of gold?
Polish the coin of each scene with attention
    And open the habit-closed eyes to behold.

What is our hope to avoid the monotonous
    Of circumstance and dull commonplace?
What can now bring us this subliminal vision
    Till the uncomely is touched with new grace?

Open the cocoon of life's full potential,
    To examine minutely each chrysalis of time
Till we stand strangers, as from a far planet,
    Filled with discovery of mundane and sublime.

(CONTINUED ON NEXT PAGE)

This is the hope of our heightened sensation,
    To see new things with old eyes aglow,
To see old things with the marvel of childhood,
    To see in new depth both above and below.

This is the hope of our vision resplendent
    To see in the heart of an atom or flame
The pattern of worlds and universes created,
    All with signatures of the Creator's name.

This is the hope of our intuitive perception—
    The awareness of "thereness" unobserved.
Break the lock step of time, habit, and distance
    By detachment and dissonance unreserved.

The time differential of dimensional severance
    Breaks the progression of gravity's powers.
Standing aside from ourselves and old concepts,
    Marvel like a Martian in a world not ours.

This is the hope of all heightened understanding
    That losing hold of dim things we behold
We gain by losing complete incompleteness,
    Receive it all back in chalices of gold!

EL POTRO BY VICKIE FEARS

THE CANDLE DANCE BY VICKIE FEARS

September

~ 15 ~

Never court so vigorously as to alarm, nor so vaguely as to be misunderstood,
or so as to pass the buying signals of acquiescence when they come.

LOVE IS AN INEXACT SCIENCE

Love, like gravity, is a force field of attraction between bodies, or exerted by a particularly attractive body which produces a high rate of reactive responses favorable or otherwise. The mass, the quantity and the attractive, vital force of such comely matter, or attracting body, changes the speed and positively or negatively stimulates the reactions of the gravitational force field of the now somewhat involved other body. Some time for adjustment is usually required.

What is true of physical attraction is also true of mental, emotional, or spiritual gravity. Conclusion: Love is an active, interactive, qualitative, quantitative, more or less mutually satisfying process that integrates force fields of various dimensions and distinctions and functions in mutual orientation of disorientation: for love is an inexact science. Why not try it? You might like it. If you don't understand it, just whistle. You may get even quicker results that way . . .

However, let us more seriously consider the likenesses of love and silently know that life is love and love is life.

Love is like the soft clouds serene exalted up above, the object of elusive love, reaching love.

Love is like a sheltering rooftop red or green or like the four walls with all that's in between.

Love is like the path that leads us there. It is a high path if two are walking there.

Love is like the fireplace warm and quite secure. It is the joys of home that endlessly endure.

Love is magic, make-believe, forgiveness, calm repose.

Love is an indoor potted plant or fragrant, rock-rooted, wild rose.

Love is a stream with rapturous song filled with deep and silent laughter as it sails along.

Love is like a red bird singing in a tree while his heart beats tremulously.

Love is like a snowflake, soft and cool, blending in the water of the shallow pool.

Love is like a sunflower's heavy yellow head bowed in acquiescence. Nothing needs be said.

Love is like a green tree, tall against the sky, swaying in its freedom of the breeze passing by.

Love is like a burnished agate bright that reflects unblemished hope for future sight.

Love is an arm supporting another's aching back, a hand holding loving gifts to supply another's lack.

Love is an inner peace from tension all set free. It is a white-winged angel thing, invisible, that patiently dwells with me.

WHAT IS LOVE?

Who knows the bounds, the length and depth
    Of love inordinate or divine?
Who knows which love is strong or pure?
    It must be right, because it's mine!

Who knows why love would leap the fence
    To gamble wildly in forbidden fields?
Who knows why love fulfilled or surfeited,
    To erotic love, unrequited, quickly yields?

What is this thing called human love?
    A fever, hope, conquest, or a fire to tell?
Is it a stream that cools the burning heart
    Or added fuel to passion's bursting shell?

Is love a song that only some are taught to sing
    While others, mute with longing, grieve each day,
And dream of a heaven, of gentle love at night,
    To find when they awake the dream has gone away?

Oh, Muse, where are the hidden bowers of true love?
    Where are the flowers of love with nectar full
        and sweet?
Guide me to the goddess amorous that men call love,
    And let me lay my aching heart before her naked
        feet!

September

~ 16 ~

The hammer and anvil of cold argument can seldom dent the exterior of unbelief; only the fires of faith, hope, love, and desire can melt it into a golden river of confidence and compliance.

WHAT YOU SEE WHEN YOU LOOK

Can you look in a puddle of mud and see
Reflected, a clear blue sky?
Can you look at your troubles and in them see
    good
That shall come to you by and by?

Can you look thru the black-shrouded night and
    see,
Illumined, a starlit sky?
Can you take what life gives and come back for
    more?
Can you "take it" and not question why?

Can you look thru the tempest of strife and see
The smile of the Creator there?
Can you see mirrored back some rich promise of
    grace,
Assuring of heavenly care?

Or is trouble just trouble and mud just mud,
Depriving your soul of its sight?
If you'll look for some good in the worst that may
    come,
Your gloom will give place to the light!

FAITH AND HOPE

Faith sees the silver-crested
  mountain peaks
    All shining in the sun.
Hope runs to climb the rugged
  paths
    Though light of day is done.

Faith sees the distant shimmering,
  shining goal
    Beyond the crumbling ledge.
Hope walks with steady footsteps
    Along the canyon's edge.

Faith sees the distant harbor's
  beckoning lights
    Hid in the foggy gloom.
Hope cheers the Mariner on his
  way
    And guides him safely home.

Substantial hope on battlefield
  undimmed.
    Unconquered hope divine!
With faith and love in happy
  company,
Hope thou in God and all things
  shall be thine.

September

~ 17 ~

Tonight, invite the Creator's quiet assistance, and pictorially review the day's doings before sleep and picture it not as it was but vividly revised as you now pray it might have been; for from these new visual chartings, tomorrow's deeds will be automatically directed. Purposeful review and revisions affect tomorrow's self-image and decisions.

NEW SELF-AWARENESS

Awareness moves during the time of its awakening back into the more private life of the higher divine self within persons, and this is certainly the larger portion of a person, although it is unfinished. It is a shifting of awareness from the periphery to the center of one's more complete being. It maintains its connection with the activities of the physical, intellectual, and moral lives of the individual. But it transcends this and rises into the realm of other dimensions, where the greater part of a person's true being exists unknown to a great extent to its very self in its conscious actions. Changing the figure of speech, it is as though one who lived instinctively and primarily from his primordial subconscious, instinctive self moves up from the basement of this area into the first floor, where his reasoning, logical mind takes over. On these rare occasions of enlightenment, he goes up to the third story or to the observatory above the third story of his high self, and there, with the telescope of infinity, of expanded awareness and of directed cognizance, he views the universe from the viewpoint of God. He sees all things as though he were above. In actuality, there is likely considerable bi-location or at least the shifting of awareness to the part of the high self which is above time and space, and, therefore, it has the same viewpoint as an individual who bi-locates or astro-travels.

THE QUIET HEART

The eternal shines in the temporal.
    The superlative things may be seen
If the soul contemplates the transcendent
    And worships with nothing between.

Thus winging above the material,
    Lost in the Spirit and word,
The unseen Eternal is visible
    And silent secrets are heard.

For blessed are they who listen well
    To the truth that God would impart,
For the highest and deepest are only revealed
    To the person with the quiet heart!

September

∽ 18 ∽

GRANDPA'S OLD TRUCK BY PAT KAMERATH

CAMPFIRES ALONG THE WAY

Fuel is consumed in the burning,
   Yet the fire that consumes burns on.
Life is consumed in our yearnings,
   But the things we have yearned for are gone.

The past is a haunting shadow now
   Of the smoke of our consumed desires;
The half-filled forms of our memories,
   Burned out by time's smoldering fires.

The half-charred friendships forgotten,
   The half-loved friends of the past,
O God, they rise up to haunt me
   And cry for completeness at last.

I must love more sincerely, intently;
   I must give not counting my lack;
For the ravaging fire of time's passing
   Never will give my life back.

O fire of love, burn within me.
   O campfires burn bright with love's flame,
That only the ashes of happiness
   May mark the trail by which I came.

September

19

Keep your objectives noble and your purposes high;
for there's a lot less traffic on the "through route."

CONFIDENCE AT BAT

Inspiration and motivation will arise naturally when our conflicting directions are brought into a correlated drive of united purpose. It is here that our goals and plans play an important part. The elimination of the nonessential, the subjugation of the secondary, and the correlation of the primary purposes are the foundations of emotional release and enthusiastic living. We must aim toward a goal of doing better.

To attain and maintain enthusiasm, inspired leaders must evaluate personal successes, recount personal conquests, and move on to other phases of their planned achievements. The chief focus of their attention must be in the here and now, where their enthusiasm is CONFIDENCE at bat, ENDURANCE circling the bases, and COURAGE sliding home. The inspired example will have the highest batting average and the best accountability score. Inspiration and motivation are the stuff from which champions are made!

WHISPERING WIND

The whispering, whistling, laughing wind
    Comes blowing up my hill.
The whispering, sighing, crying wind
    Can never quite keep still.

The whispering, moaning, groaning wind
    Is like a suffering soul.
It climbs each hill and always will
    For conquest is its goal.

The whispering, laughing, shouting wind
    Is a happy child at school
When teacher's gone from night till dawn
    And it plays without a rule.

The whispering, singing, silent wind
    Dies down and seems quite gone.
But in an instant it springs back to life
    To play and sing on and on.

September

~ 20 ~

Only what is given gladly on earth is retained as treasures in heaven.

DIMENSIONAL AREA OF SPIRITUALITY

The spiritually aware person, while maintaining a full, dual awareness, certainly arises, as St. Paul said, to a third heaven or to some dimensional area of spirituality and comprehension over and above that which he normally resides in. Man must learn to mind travel more frequently to this realm until he becomes thoroughly aware of its existence and from its high vantage point views his other existence on the lower plains of material existence. The flashes of inspiration, the sudden intuitions, the clear reality of things that come to us in moments of lucidity are but indications of the fact that, for the moment, we have stepped aside from our ordinary viewpoint and may actually have stepped aside from our geographical location. And certainly, from a dimensional viewpoint, we have climbed the heights of the pyramid and are looking out across the deserts, the green valleys, and the far-distant foothills of this thing called life-made existence. A different concept of time and space would help us to approximate more closely the viewpoint of God.

The spiritually aware person must either amalgamate his now divided consciousness or shift his awareness, as suggested, to the higher divine self—part of his rather involved being. From this amalgamated viewpoint, or the shifting of awareness to the high self, man will certainly come up with different values. He will certainly come up with different principles and laws both for this dimension and for the other. He will understand this life and the afterlife much better. The mysteries will begin to unravel, darkness will begin to flee, comprehension will begin to come, and man will find that inner peace which comes from integration of his fractured self. But along with the peace will come the ability to be receptive and to intuit, to understand and to hear truth as it speaks eternally from out of the great wisdom pools of endless time and space, out of the very mind of God who is all and is in all and speaks through all.

TAKE THOU MY ALL

O Infinite, Thou hast a thousand feet
　　To walk the world's long, weary way.
And yet Thou hast no feet at all.
　　The Formless One, the theologians say.

Omniscient One, Thou hast a thousand eyes
　　In Heaven and on the earth.
And yet Thou hast no eyes at all
　　Who gave light its beauty and birth.

O Infinite, Thou hast a thousand ears
　　That hear each rapturous, vibrant sound.
And yet Thou hast no ears at all
　　Who heareth with acuteness most profound.

O God of Nature, Thou hast many ways
　　To test earth smells in silent wonderment
And yet Thou hast no nose at all
　　Who gave to every flower special scent.

Omnipotent, Thou hast a thousand hands
　　To heal the hurts of life injustice burns.
And yet Thou hast no hands but ours
　　Whose heart with loving outreach yearns.

Munificent, Thou hast a thousand lips
　　That speak in accents common or unknown.
Thou hast a still small voice but ask
　　That we in consecration give our own.

Take my feet, eyes, ears, my sense of smell.
　　Take my lips, hands, my heart's desire
Till every human sense is energized
　　By love's gentle, purging, holy fire!

September

~ 21 ~

The wheels of Universal Cause grind on, and yesterdays lie mangled in the rutted road. Today still proudly sits in the driver's seat, unaware that tomorrow it, too, shall die; and that shining, beckoning angel, the future, soon shall, in its turn, try a hand at shaping destiny; but growing feeble with unending labor, it shall come to lie broken with all of our yesterdays in the littered road of time and progress.

Books speak with thunderous tones from age to age; man has no power to match the printed page!

The life is long enough that fully works out the purposes for which that life was born.

There is no darkness to the saints in death; only another dimension of light.

OWNERSHIP

If a man owned the whole earth, it would not be for long; after which he could occupy only a few feet of it until time and deterioration made the dust of the grave and the dust of its owner without destination or identity.

Life, like the eagle's flight, seems to float without sense of time, space, or motion; and like a Pacific sunset, it seems to pause for reflection and then is swallowed by death's restless ocean.

YESTERDAY IS DEAD

Yesterday died last night;
It can't encroach on the day.
It lived its life
With peace or strife.
With that it passed away!

(CONTINUED ON NEXT PAGE)

Yesterday died last night;
No shadows today must spoil.
    No yesterday
    Must smother today
With its sweat and tears and toil.

Yesterday died last night
With a past that today forgets.
    It's dead and gone
    With the rising dawn
For today has no vain regrets.

Yesterday died last night;
It's gone with its funeral bier.
    Today is the day
    In struggle or play,
And today is already here!

September

~ 22 ~

I am a free, modern man! I can do whatever I want with the consent of my conscience, the Church, the Federal Government, State Law, Public Consensus of Opinion, Civil Rights, Customs, Precedence, Circumstances, Finances, Time, Health, Ability and my Wife!

THE SILICONE MAN

A silicone man
With silicone brains
And silicone nerves
Impervious to pains!

Silicone feet
That need no shoes.
Rubbers outdated!
What exciting good news!

Silicone man
With intestines that stretch.
No chance for a rupture
In the overstuffed wretch.

Silicone thumbs
For every "Jack Horner"
And silicone necks
To stretch round the corner.

Elastic muscles
That quickly relax.
No load too heavy
For supple, silicone backs.

(CONTINUED ON NEXT PAGE)

~ 653 ~

With silicone eyes
You could really rubber,
Your silicone tears
Would bounce when you blubber.

Silicone dentists
Could stretch their pay
For our silicone teeth
Just wouldn't decay.

Your silicone bones
Wouldn't break when you fell.
But your silicone mouth
Would stretch when you yell.

Silicone joints
Without arthritis
For mountain climbing
Should conquest invite us.

Rubberized rulers
That would stretch a bit
For the rubber conscience
That accompanies it.

With silicone hairdo
And silicone clothes
You'd be as slim and trim
As a garden hose.

But these adjustable husbands
And their silly silicone wives
Would live synthetic existences
The rest of their lives!

MY MOTHER IN THE WIND BY BRUCE EAGLE

VILLAGE WITH RED POPPIES BY NENAD MIRKOVICH

September

~ 23 ~

Balkiness describes the mule; tenacity, the bulldog;
but wise, direct determination is the trait of champions.

DUBIOUS MIND-SMOG

Good management must include the leading of the doers! It must, by the strength of inspired individuals, counteract the hot-air-pollution of negativity and rise above the dubious mind-smog of resistance and possible failure. If "progress" has created an attitude "mess," then as wise, inspired, motivated leaders, we must be a part of the changing of the guard to instigate "correction burns." This will be done for the preservation of our beliefs, for the preservation of our own lives, and for the preservation of the lives of those around us for whom we may be responsible. It is for reasons like these that motivated and inspired individuals have been chosen as managers, leaders and, most of all, examples!

To be successful, the inspiration and motivation underlying individual accountability must be inseparably linked. Our responsibility for ourselves, our family, our home, and our world is fact, not fiction. Inspiration and motivation for responsibility and accountability generate the energy to rise to the challenges of self-directed, self-assigned self-improvement. Under the influence of motivation, TIREDNESS gets out of bed, dresses, and "goes to town." ILL HEALTH learns that physical action and increased awareness are more fun than reading cards of condolence. LAZINESS stretches farther than it intended to, opens its eyes, jumps to its feet, and joins the ranks of the changing of the guard, the parade of champions!

Inspiration increases MENTAL WATTAGE as the blood flows faster and farther, and ideas and action cry out to be born, while asking, "What can I do to help?" THOUGHT leaps beyond the mind and telegraphs its inspiration and motivation to others.

AWAKENED MINDS become unconscious centers of stimulation, control towers of positive, although unvoiced, inspirational directives that signal, "We are ready to help! Let's join the ranks of the changing of the positive guard!"

Inspired, motivated examples must have clear-cut goals and objectives. Challenge yourself and others to be obvious examples! Crystallize your thinking; improve your methods; check your road map along the way, a map drawn by a pen of inspiration and motivation that leads toward a goal and a purpose. Remember—WE ARE CHAMPIONS!

KEEP ON KEEPING ON

I've swum the raging rivers
    When the waters closed over my head.
I've reached the shore and a little more
    And lay there like one of the dead.
    But I've kept on keeping on!

I've crossed the hot-footed deserts
    And drunk of its brackish streams.
I've seen my hopes lie withered
    Among my broken dreams.
    But I've got to keep moving on!

I've climbed the tall, jagged mountains
    Amid ice and snow and sleet.
I've felt the sharp rocks gouging
    My consecrated feet.
    But, God, I will keep on keeping on!

I've tried to swim life's ocean
    But I was sinking in grim despair.
Then you came and walked beside me
    And I felt your tender care!
    I know I can keep on keeping on!

September

~ 24 ~

The foreclosures of past failure may be the forerunners of future fulfillment.

WALL, WINDOW, TREE, AND SUPER CONCENTRATION
(CREATIVE VISUALIZATION)

I want you to think now for a moment very clearly and see in pictures the things that I call to your mind. Visualize a stone wall, but play like there's only a part of that stone wall that still remains. That part could be thirty feet long at the base, or forty, and it could be thirty or forty feet high. But it comes to a peak like a pyramid at the top. It's only the broken remains, only the standing part, of a great temple or cathedral that at one time stood in this place.

Notice at the base of this rectangular section of wall that's still remaining that there are jumbled piles of rock, mortar and debris that were left over from the fallen part of the wall. Many people have, no doubt, come and taken some of these rocks to build fences or other buildings in the neighborhood.

The rocks on the standing part of the wall are moss-covered, gray and green stones. The cement between them that holds them together has grown gray and, through the wasting processes of corrosion, it almost blends with the rock itself.

Picture and examine the rock wall in your own mind. Notice that in the top part of this triangular wall there is a stained-glass window still standing. You may picture a circular one, or an upright, tall, rectangular one. Observe it closely. Does it have a picture? Does it remind you of something you saw in a church one time, or in a beautiful cathedral?

Please concentrate now on the sections of glass in this beautiful, stained-glass window. There are many, many colors of glass. The first section I'd like to have you pick out is a piece of blue glass. Find a piece of blue. Does the glass have a crinkle effect? Would it feel rough to your fingers if you were to rub your fingers over it? But it's definitely blue. You may choose the shade of blue. It could be a dark indigo blue, or a sky blue, or a dull gray-blue. You could pick a bright blue like your favorite skirt or shirt or something that you have at home. You pick the color of blue, but please notice that the sunlight is filtering through the glass. The sun is up almost to the meridian in the sky, and it is shining down through this stained-glass window at the top of this broken, jagged wall of an old cathedral that still remains standing in the sun. The color of the glass affects the light as it's reflected and refracted through the stained-glass window and falls upon the leaves and stones on the ground. Look at the blue carefully and notice its specific color.

~ 659 ~

Now find another piece of glass. This time, find a piece of red glass in the stained-glass window. You may choose the shade of red. It could be a dark, deep, blood red. It could be an orange red. It could be just a red, red. It could shade almost to a pink red. Find a piece of red glass and see it clearly. Visualize red. And then see this red as it lightens up where the sun shines through it. The yellow light of the sun turns it slightly orange and rosy as it shines through the red glass down on the ground and on the leaves. Compare the red with the blue. Look up at the blue section you first chose; now, back again to the red. Contrast them. Compare the colors and the size and the shape of the piece of glass. Carefully compare your red with your blue as you visualize it clearly.

Now, will you please pick still another color of glass? Pick a piece of green glass in your circular or rectangular stained-glass window in the jagged, broken wall. The color could be dark green. It could be grass green. It could be chartreuse or yellow green—you pick it and then observe how the sun shines through it onto the ground beside the blue and the red. There's something life-giving, something of vital force and activity in green, something restful and relaxing in green, something healing and beneficial in green, something so much like the chlorophyll of nature that you almost seem a part of the color just as you emotionally feel yourself a part of the blue, blue sky or red sunset.

Now, would you pick a shade of yellow, darker or lighter, or golden, if you prefer. Notice how warm and beautiful the sunlight shines through the yellow and all the other colors that are reflected and shafted down on the ground. They are like a rainbow of colors softly blended together.

There's one last color I want you to choose. We are going to specialize in this color to do something with it. Maybe it is a three-cornered piece, or an odd-shaped piece, but find a big piece of lavender or purple glass in the stained-glass window. Okay, you have it now. Look how the sun shines through it and lights it up. Bring that piece of glass up closer to yourself. As you see the shadows or rays of the purple shining down on the ground, just imagine yourself climbing in and right up that purple beam of light. Climb until you get up right close to the glass itself so that you don't see anything but that purple glass. You are looking deep into the very heart of that lavender glass. You are seeing the color activated now. You can see the rhythm of its molecular structure. You can see the atoms of the glass as it whirls. You can feel the rhythm of the atoms and molecules as they do a dance. You can feel the vibration of the purple. You can hear the song that it sings. It is singing, and it is dancing, and it's moving like it's a live thing. There are spots of the lavender that seem to come closer to your face. There are circles of it. There are little flashes of living, moving, pulsating light. It flows like water and rolls like clouds. Look right into the heart of that lavender. The little raised pieces on the glass almost look like mountains of lavender with deep valleys of purple—mountains and valleys of lighter and darker purple. The lavender is blending into that rainbow of light and coloring and is blending it all so beautifully. You are a part of that light and you are a part of that music.

Look, please, to the left on that stone wall, just back of it, and you will see a tree in your mind's eye. You can pick any kind of a tree and instantly plant it there. It could be a maple tree with giant leaves. It could be an oak tree with its little waxy leaves. It could be any favorite tree you have in your yard or that you have seen in the park, just so it has leaves on it that come drifting down in the fall. Notice now that the leaves are red and brown, green, gold and yellow. They have held onto that tree about as long as they can hold on. And there are some leaves already on the ground. Over next to the wall there's a pile of leaves eddied up against the wall where the wind has blown them during

660

the last cold night. The leaves are warming up a bit as the sun comes over and warms the deeper shadows by the wall. But most of the leaves are still on the tree, and they are ready to fall.

Play like you're one of those remaining leaves, still on the tree. Become one of those leaves. Play like your hands or your arms are above your head. And you're holding on to that little leaf stem. Your arms are tired, very tired. Squeeze that leaf stem with your fingers like you are a leaf! Squeeze it hard. Let yourself feel the tension in your body as you're holding on to this imagined leaf. Play like you're a trapeze artist and you've got to hold on because there isn't any net below. So you are holding on tighter and tighter. Finally you decide, "I can't hold on all winter. The snow will come, the rain will freeze on me, I'm just a leaf and I've already turned brown and crinkly and brittle. I'd better let go and snuggle down below with all those other leaves that are resting among the jumbled rocks at the base of this broken wall." Just let go! Let your hands go. Let go of the stem. Let go of the tree. Let go of everything! See yourself floating down now. You're a leaf floating down to the ground. You're coming in closer to the ground like a jet on the runway of an airport. You're just skimming the ground. You touch a little leaf and it swings you around in a circle like you're dancing, and you bounce off of a rock. Now you're settling down in a nice warm spot in the sun where the red, purple, blue, green, gold and yellow lights are blended so beautifully. Other leaves are coming now and they're settling down all around you. They are friendly leaves. Some of them you know. You want to be close. Now, the leaves are falling and floating from the tree. You have let go completely of all tension and have floated softly to the ground. You are resting there contentedly. Now, as you're resting at the bottom of the tree, think about how you feel as a leaf. Without my saying anything for a few moments, identify with the leaves. See them clearly and feel very intensely, with vivid imagination, that you are a leaf . . .

While you are relaxed so comfortably and are visualizing, feeling, hearing, seeing, touching and tasting whatever you desire while at this alpha-theta mind level, let's add to our relaxed learning exercise some important personal concepts of self-improvement and potential accomplishment. Because these affirmative statements are for your highest good, it will be easy for you to accept them, retain them and act upon them under the proper circumstances. So attention all subconscious minds! You have work to do, a life to live. Let's get on with it in the best way we can. You know how to create, always, the perfect conditions of body and mind for super-concentration. Let go and do a perfect job of relaxing and listening. You will maintain the necessary conscious awareness at all times under your own self-control. You are always basically in control. You function easily and naturally in a dual state of awareness with perfect security and total efficiency. You are an integrated person. You know where you are going and what is expected of you as well as what you expect of yourself. You know what you desire to do and to be. You are capable of using the reasoning faculties plus the intuitive side of your mind with perfect coordination. You do always mesh gears with reality, practicality and creativity in a happy, successful manner at all times.

Whenever it is necessary to pay attention, concentrate upon any subject, creatively solve any problem, you will be able to enter and maintain the creativity level with both eyes open and with your mind completely relaxed, receptive, open and alert.

You will be able to perform your work easily, with pleasure, and you will produce solutions efficiently. You will also perceive many things intuitively beyond the limits of the physical senses. Your intuitive awareness of your total environment will increase continually. Your relationships with all people will improve remarkably. Your grades will improve. They now are improving in many areas. You will continue to make happy, positive, successful progress. You will feel only restful, relaxed comfort during and after your Relaxed Learning session.

School is fun. School studies are easy and something to quickly finish and turn in. You will accept all your responsibilities cheerfully and complete each task assigned as quickly as is reasonably possible. You will take care of important papers, schoolbooks and other valuable property. Your school is proud of you. I am proud of you. You are a responsible person!

Positive thinking is always acceptable. The things herein suggested are acceptable, "in things" and are profitable to you. You will strive for perfect attendance whenever it is possible and reasonable. When you leave this room, you will be wide awake, alert, happy, healthy, ready and willing to work or play as the situation demands.

Let your mind go back now for a moment to the old wall with the beautiful, many-colored, stained-glass window and the old tree with the fall leaves drifting down to the ground. You are resting in your imagination at the foot of the tree, relaxed and comfortable. You feel contented, happy, rested and very, very good. Coming up from the visual level now, open your eyes. Stretch a bit. Move around. Alert now! Wide awake. Take a big breath of air. Stretch again, everyone! Thank you for listening.

September

25

*In the test of enduring love, CHARACTER, not passion, charm, emotions, or beauty
should tip the scales of attraction.*

ASSOCIATES:

"Your associates are the billboards of your worth and the ambassadors of your own self-evaluation."

"It is most difficult to sleep with the dogs and not the fleas, to eat in the henhouse and avoid the lice,
to herd sheep and avoid the ticks; it is better to avoid some circumstances than
to carry a load of flea-powder, de-lice and tick-remover."

BEAUTY:

"Beauty is a sun; a smile, the light: But both must quickly fade in error's night."

"O, Woman, why should beauty on deception's brow be worn?"

"Goodness and truth have beauty all their own; but beauty hath not always good and truth alone."

A HUNDRED BROKEN HEARTS

Here lie the fragments
  Of a hundred broken hearts,
Strewn in wild abandonment
  By your false love torn apart:
Shattered pieces of a
Hundred broken hearts.

(CONTINUED ON NEXT PAGE)

Some were thrown.
    You couldn't stop them.
Others broke where
    You had dropped them:
Fallen pieces from a
Hundred broken hearts.

Since pleasure
    Was your thesis,
You could dance
    Among the pieces:
Bleeding pieces of a
Hundred broken hearts.

Playing chess
    May have appeal
When the men you move
    Are real:
Fallen kings with a
Hundred broken hearts.

You could build
    Your own mosaics
Unless a pattern
    Seems prosaic
To an artist of a
Hundred broken hearts.

But Judy, my dear, when your
    Beauty fades away,
Still your memory like
    A cat can play
With the yarn from a
Hundred broken hearts.

Each broken promise
    That you gave
Could help form a
    Headstone for the grave
Of a forgotten suitor among
A hundred broken hearts!

September

∾ 26 ∾

JUDY BY BENGARTT (W. JACKSON)

A Boat Trip and Expanded Awareness
(CREATIVE VISUALIZATION)

Please find a comfortable place for your body. Relax it as fully as you can in whatever way you can best relax. Let your body and mind tensions slip away. You will find that you do relax more and more as the exercise continues to progress. So with your body completely relaxed, listen closely, very closely to what is being said. Be alert to the intended meanings and active in all expected responses.

Now with eyes closed gently, breathing deeply, relaxing completely, focus your awareness on the deep, in-and-out, rhythmic breathing of your diaphragm. Feel and hear the rhythm of the universe as you continue to breathe deeply, rhythmically and easily. With your eyes still closed gently, relaxing deeply and completely, concentrate on the words, the suggested imagery, the message intended and on whatever you may feel, hear, smell, taste and touch.

Imagine that there is a secret door in the floor of your bedroom at home with a rug and that certain articles of furniture cover it. Moving the rug and the furniture, you grasp the ring in the trapdoor and lift it up. As you do, you see a set of circular steps that lead down into the darkness. You have a good, confident feeling about the solidarity of the stone steps. There is enough light for you to see with confidence where to step. So see yourself going deeper and deeper, step by step, further away from all distractions. You descend deeply, calmly and quietly, until, at the very bottom of the stairway, you walk out onto a dock. There's a small, red boat tied to the dock. There is a bearskin rug on the bottom of the boat. You step over the side of the boat and ease yourself down onto the soft bearskin. You feel the gentle motion, the rising, falling, rocking sensation of the boat on the waves, and you ride, gently rocking, gently floating, in rhythm and harmony with the river of life and the vibration of the whole world. You finally drift out of the subterranean caverns into the dim light of a somewhat brighter day, out into the open air, the soft, warm, yet brilliant sunlight of a new and better day dawning. Hear the cry of the bright-plumaged birds that dart and skim along the river's edge. Listen to their songs. Be lifted with the lilt of their music and the sweep of their airborne wings.

Feel the warm, yellow sunlight pouring down upon your back as you lie facedown, snuggled into the warmth of the bearskin rug on the bottom of the rhythmically rocking, gently moving boat. Feel soft breezes playfully brushing your hair, caressing your cheeks as you drift down this river of relaxation. Notice the growth along the banks and the gentle-sloping, sandy shores. Notice the overhanging ledges with the deep shadows and the fish that dart and hide or leap from the waters to splash and play. Smell the fragrance of the wildflowers. See the cattle in the distant fields. Observe the farmer with the wagons piled high with fragrant, fresh-cut hay. Smell it. Take in the beauty of the summer day. Feel the great satisfaction, the deep, soul-enthralling contentment and serenity of the scene.

Drowsily you listen to the hum and the drone of the bees working in the flowers. You drift restfully, yet alertly onward and downward with the gentle, undulating movement of the rocking boat. You feel yourself a part of it all. You are surrounded and protected and are very aware of movements, of meanings, of warmth, of breezes. You are aware of colors and odors and innumerable sounds as you proceed on your winding way, relaxing more and more. You are sensing and becoming aware of greater depth of appreciation, of intuition, of understanding, of participation.

666

September

27

Keep your objectives noble and your purposes high; for there's a lot less traffic on the "through route."

BOAT TRIP
(CONTINUED FROM SEPTEMBER 26)

Take a moment now in the quietness to experience your own inner visioning, to see in distinct colors, in clear visual imagery, in action and in detail, the scene that plays itself before you. Become, where possible, involved in the action of the imagery. Be a part of all nature. Be in tune with the rhythm of the whole universe. It's your scene to enjoy. Continue now to float. Continue to drift gently until your boat reaches the distant shore. Pull it up onto the sandy beach. Wade through the tall and tangled grasses. Climb the steep incline, and as you break over the brow of the little hill, you see stretched out before you a gentle meadow with the wind swaying through its tall grasses. You see a stream meandering and winding its way through the lush meadowlands. You feel the breeze and enjoy the smell of the flowers. You notice the wildlife. You see the birds in the air and in the branches, a little spotted fawn hiding in the shadow of a rock, wildflowers nodding and smiling here and there, sending out the caresses of their perfume to add its sweetness to the beauty of the summer day.

Be conscious of your own body as you imagine yourself walking up toward a giant tree with gnarled branches outspread. Walk up to it and circle its trunk with your arms and feel the roughness of the bark, the smoothness of the great limbs that reach out just above your head. Sense the depth of the shade and shadow. Notice its gnarled roots half buried in the ground that reach out before they wrap themselves around the rock and bury themselves deep within the rich, soft loam of the meadow. Sit beneath that tree with your back against it and with the sunlight falling through its shadows. Warmly touch one hand in little patterned pleasure sensations. Enjoy it as completely as you can. Be in harmony with the whole world. Let this tree in your imagination become your point of contact with ultimate reality. Let this be the aperture from one dimension to another, from the visible to the invisible with only a gossamer separation between the two.

This is the world where all things are a part of all else. Ask the tree what it has to tell you. Reach through it to the infinite wisdom that encircles the world and manifests in all materiality. Let the poetry of life flow through you. Let the rhythm of the universe enthrall you. Let solutions to all of life's problems come to you as desired and in the measure of your capacity to understand them. There will be a corresponding enlarging of your faculties to understand and appreciate the solutions.

Draw strength from this moment of interiorization with its inner amplification of sight, touch, sound, smell and movement. Know that increasingly, more and more, you do have the ability to richly envision, to clearly and vividly experience an increased awareness, a transformation, and an expanded consciousness. Know that you do have the capacity for altering your own states of awareness at will. Know and instruct your mind to automatically work at whatever level of awareness is best suited to your needs, your desires, and the nature of the situation in which you are engaged. Your mind will function at the proper level at the proper time, in the proper circumstances to produce the desired results for you.

Anticipate, intuitively, the instructor's command to awaken, to open your eyes just before he instructs you. You'll do so, when that time comes, feeling relaxed, refreshed, invigorated, energized and as completely rested as though you had had a good night's sleep in your own bed at home. This relaxation technique expresses in a new way, with new applications, insights and meanings. It will lift you to new heights of expanded awareness and will continue to increase your ability to visualize clearly, in detail, in color and in action.

Open your eyes now. Stretch a bit. You are bright, alert, happy, and healthy, and you feel wonderful—better than you've ever felt before. This will continue to be so. Let's all stand for a moment and stretch again. Everybody stand. Thank you again for listening.

September

28

A person's growth and survival are not measured so much from the latitude of their years as by their attitudes, their aspirations and their fears.

THOUGHT FORCE IN ACTION
(CREATIVE VISUALIZATION)

Relaxing comfortably, breathing deeply, visualizing clearly, distinctly, and, where possible, with color and action, I give my undivided and relaxed concentrated attention to the subject of *Thought Force in Action*. In a passive and receptive state of mind, I listen to the rhythm, cadence, and melody of the musical background and open the inner doors of my higher self as I make these thoughts my very own.

I now possess that natural, mental, and psychic power known as Thought Force or Creative Thought Power. It is a vibratory, emanating phase of personal magnetism that serves to attract other persons and to arouse their interest and affection, to move their emotions and to stir their feelings. I possess this strong, vibrant power that attracts and influences other individuals with whom I come in contact.

This mysterious mental force is positive magnetism. Every day, in every way, I am learning to use it more efficiently and more directly with the minimum of energy, effort, and time, and with the maximum of results and permanency.

My determination is not affected by circumstances, yet it is still dominant and assertive when held in joyful, happy abeyance. I am kind, calm, helpful, successful, and diplomatic. I do not talk about my abilities, plans of action, or personal business.

I am also conscious of sufficient positive strength so that others can and are welcome to come up close to me. I remain strong and relaxed. Their closeness does not frighten me, for I have complete confidence in my ability through providential assistance to more than hold my own under any and all circumstances, with one or many. I always form and hold strong, clear, and positive mental pictures or vivid mental images—of the thought or idea I wish to impress upon other persons. This is done through the exercise of concentration and mental pictography. Because I am capable of strong thinking, and I possess strong ideas and ideals, I automatically manifest all of the positive powers and strength of purpose and persistent, determined tenacity that denote the presence and exercise of a strong but gentle willpower. I have dynamic power of will.

I have definitely good, constructive ideas and ideals of the golden rule kind that I reinforce with vivid mental pictures. I therefore have successful action outcomes and power of performance commensurate with the quality and intensity inherent in the nature of the idea and equal to the need and desire for its expression and actualization.

I give voluntary, concentrated attention to desirable ideas and plans of action, and they grow in organized intensity and action force that produce desirable results and materialization. I push worthwhile short-range and long-range goals and desires to completion where wisdom and circumstances indicate and allow their completion. I know that concentrated visualization is the essence of positive magnetism and that the energy force of a dominant idea is the basis for the higher acts of the will and the resulting performance.

I constantly hold in my mind strong, concentrated thoughts and ideas of God-given strength, ability, financial abundance, perfect health in every part, pleasant, magnetic attractiveness, loving service, task completion and organization, efficient thought projection, reception, and the power to acquire desirable traits, abilities, conditions, circumstances, information, and desired states of awareness.

I do have a sense of personal worth and the ability to self-improve in any desired area. These things I visualize in clear, vivid, mental picturing. This produces mind and spirit radiations by magnetic induction and sets up proper vibrations in the minds of others and in myself. These things I accept as a part of my true, deeper, and higher self. For these things I give sincere thanks and appropriate them and all other high-self gifts, graces, traits, powers, and conditions for unselfish use in a perfect way. I am a successful person always; I am grateful.

Take a deep breath, open your eyes, please. Wide awake, alert, and feeling great. Thank you for listening.

THE WRITTEN WORD

Above the star-lit sky-ways
    Rides the ruler of men.
And over the mass of mortals
    Rule the people with the pen.

Over the minds of the plodders
    Like shadows across the sun
Hangs a pall of contented ignorance.
    Here the writer's task is begun.

From the heavens of high inspiration
    Like a glad star guiding at night
Shines the luminous lamp of the writer
    Dispelling the gloom with its light.

Over the path of revolving words
    They shape and they form a thought
That breaks the chains of bondage.
    And, behold, what a word has wrought!

September

~ 29 ~

CHAMA BY GREG WALZ

AFTER CHASTISEMENT

After the storm of chastisement,
 After the lightning's release
Comes the soft weaving of rainbows,
 Comes the sweet music of peace.

After the air has been freshened,
 And the dust has been settled again,
The hills and the mountains seem closer
 In the calm that follows the rain.

The troubles that hurt and harass us,
 The storms that fiercely sweep down,
Reveal the smile of the rainbow
 Back of chastisement's dark frown.

September

∾ 30 ∾

*The conformity of variety and the variety of conformity give unity
to diversity and a pattern to inconsistency.*

LIVE THE INSPIRED LIFE

The energy of inspired living generates more energy. Tiredness gets out of bed, dresses, and "goes to town." Ill health finds that physical action and increased awareness are more fun than reading cards of condolence. Laziness stretches farther than it meant to, opens its eyes, jumps to its feet, and joins the parade of champions! Inspired living is the feeling of success before, during, and after accomplishment. Our feelings of inner drive, our emotions, like the motors in our cars, want to go or forever leave us behind when the motivation of inspiration is lacking or insufficient. The energy of our inspiration increases the wattage of the brain as the blood flows faster and farther, and ideas, dreams, and actions cry out to be born, to live and to labor. Thought leaps beyond the mind and telegraphs its inspiration to others who are receptive so that the awakened mind becomes an unconscious center of stimulation, a control tower of positive, although unvoiced, inspiration and direction for others.

Inspiration for living gives the karate blow of paralysis to advancing fear, doubt, worry, or despair. It lets the "dead bury the dead," and occupies its attention with progress, practicality, positive living, and the principles of achieving faith. Inspiration and the will to win on any racetrack is a horse called "Winner!" It is the inner energy of confident conquest that kicks the dust of determination in the face of defeat as it pulls itself across the finish line!

The energy of inspired living is invigorating. It is felt in the handshake of the enthusiastic man. It invigorates, inspires, stimulates, relaxes, and encourages others just by a simple transference of its glad, vital contagion. It shines in the eyes of love and charges the atmosphere of a room with the sunbeams of vitality. It restores men to hope, self-confidence, courage, belief, and love. Thus, the energy of inspiration pulls back the drapes of despair in every living room and watches the shadows and specters of old fears, failures, and futility flee away. Its light is the light of faith, hope, and purposeful love.

The energy of inspired living flows over into the words a writer puts on paper. It adds seasoning to sagacity. It makes a book a living thing where the spirit of inspiration shines through between the lines, and the author's sincerity, earnestness, vivacious thinking, and overflowing spirit throw a luster on the printed page that makes the words much easier to read, hear, and understand. It is what makes the author come through from beneath the print and paper. It inspires the obedience, stimulates the

∾ 673 ∾

comprehension and evokes the cooperation of students in the schoolroom and makes even difficult learning a pleasure. Thus, it is that slow progress, defeat, and failure step back, bow their heads in shame and say, "We will stand aside for inspiration. Step on us if you must, ignore us if you will, but just keep on climbing where inspiration lights the way."

The inspired man has a personal atmosphere that is positive. It is not misdirected or non-directed energy, but a wisely and purposefully directed overflow of vital power that radiates like a magnetic field or aura of communication around the positive person. It is a drawing, cohesive, winning, vital force or energy field that colors and characterizes the possessor wherever he goes. It is a radiating personal influence that can easily be sensed or felt by others. Enthusiasm is the inspired man's armor against the frustration and failure complex of mediocre living. It is his personal antidote for the negativity of ordinary living. Inspiration is a catalyst that blends all diverse, negative, and/or positive elements into productive personal power by the fusion of awakened emotions, while it remains unmoved and triumphant in the process.

In speech, inspiration is eloquence. It is the one additive in any persuasive situation that cleans out the carbon of general resistance and adds anti-knock quality to any push or product. To communication, inspiration is eloquence, in the flesh it is good health, in the spirit it is comrading with Divinity, in business it is the success of achievement reaching its goals, in life it is confidence, hope, faith, fearlessness, unselfish love, purposeful progress, and dynamic virility. It is power steering with released but directed and controlled emotional impact. It is life with destination, and direction but without prison bars or prison garb of drab conformity and hopelessness. Inspiration for living is the eloquence of a soul set free, the overflow of inner vitality that reaches the top of the dam and flows down through green valleys and out to uncharted seas.

The inspired man encourages his own will to live. He must, deep within himself, face the battle of life and the necessity of self-inspiration and determine to win. He must have some great things and some personal, insignificant things to live for that have special meaning to him alone. He must basically come to the conclusion that it is actually easier to earn and enjoy the fruitage of the courageous life than to work for and endure the fruit of his failures. He must accept life and the will to live it.

Action and reaction are necessities for accomplishment. The inspired man must mesh gears with reality. He must focus his vision and direct his attention outward. He no longer will be content to sit at home and race the motor of his frustrated emotions. He will find something to do, some place to begin, and further directions will be given as he moves out along the course of action. Action begets action and enthusiasm begets enthusiasm, and inspiration is the fountain from which its increase unceasingly flows. To maintain inspiration and to acquire an enduring enthusiasm for living, a man must find or activate self-inspiration and self-motivation through thinking inspired thoughts in quiet meditation. He must find some time by himself to crystallize his thinking, to tune his mind and heart to the inner melody of life. He must read inspirational books, take courses that increase his knowledge and confidence. He must associate, whenever possible, with courageous souls, the champions, and the optimistic. He must prefer gladness to gloom, optimism over pessimism, and progress over inactivity.

Inspiration is an octave of gladness, an attribute of the attitude of gratitude. The thankful person is the inspired, enthusiastic person. The inspiration of gladness is a life necessity, not an emotional luxury. The thankful, joyful person inspired by the upward pull and purpose of inspirational living will find for himself those things that produce the climate of appreciative awareness and the grateful state of mind. He alerts himself to the necessity of an ongoing inspirational attitude and resolves to cultivate the enthusiastic life in the light of eternal gladness unvexed by any shadows that circumstance or adversity may cast. He gravitates toward the winner's circle by the very nature of his positive vibrations. Inspiration, enthusiasm, and confident forward thrust result from the personal integration of personality, mind, body, and spirit. It rises like the cadence of a harmonious song from the correlation of our goals, drives, values, purposes, and the ambitions of our lives.

To further attain and maintain inspiration for living, a man must on occasion recount his conquests and relive his triumphs and recapture the expansive feelings of unbeatable power for accomplishment as he reaches the various stages of his planned achievements. He must continually look forward and upward with only an occasional glance back over the road he has climbed, and that primarily to encourage himself in seeing how far he has already come. However, the chief focus of the inspired man is in the glad present where enthusiasm is confidence at the bat, endurance circling the bases, courage sliding home. Inspired living always has the highest batting average and the best score. Enthusiasm is a winner! It is the stuff from which all champions are made! Let life live through you. The world is waiting and will step aside for the inspired man and woman. I challenge you to be an inspired person. There is no other reasonable response to the challenge of life other than *inspiration* for living! So, from this hour forward, remember that you, too, are an inspired person.

LISTENING FOR TOMORROW

Old high Henry was the pioneer's name,
And he stood at six foot eight.
A lean and leathery, mystical man
Who cooked what the pioneers ate.

He slept at night beneath the stars
And tuned an inner ear.
Called it, "listening for tomorrow,"
Just to hear what he could hear.

Said he couldn't hear tomorrow
In the city's clamoring street,
So he'd "float his stick" in the
    far-out West
Where the air was still and sweet.

Here he heard the wheels a-groaning.
Saw the covered wagons roll.
Saw the Nation marching westward
And it was music to his soul.

(CONTINUED ON NEXT PAGE)

From the frontiers of Missouri,
Down the trail to Santa Fe
He could hear "steamboats with
    wheels" a-comin'
Before the railroads had had their day.

If ships could ply their trade on
    rivers,
They could roll them on the sand
He could hear tomorrow's engines
A rip-snortin' through the land.

When he saw the big stars shinin'
In their knowin', friendly way,
Then he'd dream about tomorrow
That he knew would come to stay.

Now, faith is like the tuning
Of that inner, listening ear
To catch God's echoed promise
And to bring the distant near.

It can hear the dawn awakening
Where along the Milky Way
The King of Kings comes riding
On that glad Millennial Day.

So I'm listening for God's tomorrow,
And there's a rumbling in the land
That warns me to be faithful
For God's Kingdom is at hand!

And we dare not lose the power
That can see the things unseen—
That can look into the future
With no veil of time between.

We must LISTEN FOR TOMORROW
And be ready when it comes,
Lest it steal upon us softly
Without the sound of drums!

BUFFALO SOLDIERS BY J.D. EVANS

ASPEN ROAD BY GREG WALZ

October

~ 1 ~

LOST IN THE CLOUDS BY GREG WALZ

EARLY WINTER COMING BY ELLEN REINKE

Today is one day; tomorrow is another;
yet the future is the offspring and today will be its mother.

WILD GEESE ACROSS THE SKY

Wild geese
　　Across the sky,
It's cold today.
　　I hear your cry.
In serious tones
　　You question why.

Wild geese
　　With sturdy wing,
You rise to fly
　　Thru everything
To lakes that call
　　Where flowers spring.

Wild geese
　　Across the land,
Your echoes tell the
　　Flight you've planned
To a warmer, happier
　　Promised land.
Good-bye!

SOLITUDE BY DAVID GREEN

October

2

Adaptability, not capriciousness, is a virtue in a changing world.

A person's religion is best that makes his attitude inclusive and worst if it makes him exclusive, sectarian, or falsely "superior."

Negative suggestion accepted, or the senility of courage, and faith grown weary, produce in the body the seed pictures accepted in the soil of the mind.

Time is more valuable with advancing age, not only because there is less of it but because of the accumulated interest of increased potential.

ONE OF GOD'S DAUGHTERS

One of God's daughters walks
    In joy across our dreary world.
She throws a multicolored scarf
Across the sky
    And a brilliant sunset is unfurled.

She walks through cool, dark woods
    Brushing the leaves from the lilies' face,
And all the forest ferns and flowers
Sway and bow
    And pay their tribute to her sprightly grace.

This stately daughter frowns
    And strikes the world with icy wand;
And white and low the tree boughs bend
Beneath the snow
    Where joyful children skate on every pond.

(CONTINUED ON NEXT PAGE)

She teaches all the new-fledged birds
    To sing and soar in summer skies.
She puts the light of love and rapturous
Wonderment
    In the youthful lover's shining eyes.

She has a million billion children
    And as many different laws to keep.
Her house is always full and bigger
Than the world,
    And no one has ever caught her fast asleep.

I wonder who she is, this strange,
    Maternal daughter of the sky and sod?
Some men call her Mother Nature
Or "Nature,"
    Eldest daughter of the Universe and God.

October

～ 3 ～

Laughing Autumn leaps astride the shocks of standing corn and paints each pumpkin with the vine from which the leaves are shorn. A Laughing Autumn calls the sleet and frost while north winds coldly blow and cover up their painted pride with impartial winter's mantled snow!

You have more to do with yourself than time, circumstances, or even natural consequences.

Initiative is active aptitude!

The greatest poverty is hopelessness!

Self-doubt is traitor to our best interests. It discounts our hopes and dreams and sells our birthright of success in the marketplace of despair for an I.O.U. of consolation.

Man must depend upon his inner self—knowing that his inner self may securely depend upon higher powers.

THE WEALTH OF AUTUMN'S TREASURE

I love to sit with the sun on my back
    All warm in the autumn morning
When the gold, the red, the yellow and green
    Of the trees are the lake's adorning.

I love to watch the mallards glide—
    A path in the lake face stirring.
I love to see them rise in flight
    And hear their strong wings whirring.

I love to see the shadows sharp
    On the green sward gently sloping
Where squirrel fingers in the leaves
    For winter's store are groping.

I love to feel the cooling breeze
    That fans my face with pleasure
As I sense the inner joy of life
    And the wealth of autumn treasure.

October

~ 4 ~

WOODLAND FRIEND BY HUGO WESTPHAL

We admire in others the reflected image of ourselves if it be noble,
and despise it if it is not.

BALDHEADED MEN

Baldheaded men are beautiful,
    I see them here and there.
The Lord must really love them,
    He puts them everywhere.

Baldheaded men are different
    If they have a smiling face.
They have a lot more of it;
    That's certainly no disgrace.

Baldheaded men are intelligent
    When the hair is in retreat.
But you know the wise, old saying:
    "No grass on a busy street!"

Baldheaded men are popular.
    I could be one someday.
Should you see my lengthened face,
    You'll understand the things I say.

I don't know where this leaves the ladies,
    I wouldn't dare to say;
But wigs are a wonderful coverup
    If not at night, at least by day!

October

5

*In the secret, dark, and hidden places of nature, unsullied even by the thoughts of mankind,
we sense the Creator of nature lingering near in the unbroken solitude.*

IMAGINATION

Imagination is constructive, obstructive, or destructive, depending upon its control and direction.

*Imagination is the ability to recall vividly the old images, to create new mental concepts that are
visible in the mind's eye, or combinations of creative imagery, to conceive and construct from the
recalled material of past experiences, new forms, new methods, new conditions, new pictorial
thoughts as subjective embodiments as yet unmanifest.*

THE NIGHT THE TREES WENT WALKING

Tree roots reached out like the trees were walking;
The trees looked sad as I heard them talking
    While they grew there on the lawn.

The leaves looked down with laughter mocking
To hide their shame where the roots were locking
    Their own feet so they couldn't go on.

They stood all day and through the dark night.
Still they stood in the morning dawn light
    But nowhere had they gone.

The trees leaned hard in the breezes blowing,
Unbalanced, stretching, but their roots kept growing
    In a frozen walkathon.

(CONTINUED ON NEXT PAGE)

Little slim trees and burly old ones,
None dared move, not even the bold ones.
    Each was an immovable pawn.

Limbs were lopped off that wanted to grow out,
And each tree stayed home that wanted to go out,
    Silent and so withdrawn.

But I dreamed one night when the moon was hidden
That the trees came free and walked unbidden
    Until break of laughing dawn.

They walked the streets with leafy handshakes.
They danced and swayed to the tune of earthquakes,
    Darting swiftly hither and yon.

They walked by twos, changed friends and position.
Each vied with another to improve his condition
    In the tree-family echelon.

These simple souls with unbounded freedom
Chose a Queen to rule all treedom.
    Amazing phenomenon.

But the night was spent and the action ended,
So the trees took root and with new scenes blended
    From Texas to Oregon.

But the laughing trees at nighttime tell it.
They whisper and point and almost spell it
    In fantasy's lexicon.

But if trees could walk that for friends were sighing,
Then people can change and just for the trying.
    Love should meditate thereon!

October

6

The fearful and the foolish hold Halloween 365 days in the year.

A Tombstone for Despondency

Wanted for Mayhem and Murder!

Let the archfiend of all humanity die! Dig a grave, buy a casket and raise a tombstone to the mutilator of mankind who disembowels the courageous, shrinks the heads of the wise, kills the confidence of the creative and cuts the heart out of hope.

Who is this frowning despot, this callous criminal who writes his foul negations on the walls of life, and chills the bones of believers with his disapproving frown? Who deletes all the YESES from the scroll of life and writes in its place his perfidious, persuasive NO on every page?

Who says it can't be done when experience, hope, faith, courage and confidence say it can? Who kicks crutches out from under cripples, tells the struggling heart to stop beating, quit quivering and simply die? Who is it that makes a person stop the struggle of life just before he climbs the last hill and breaks over the last ridge of conquest?

Who stops the inventor just short of the discovery that could revolutionize industry? Who stops the scientist just before the cure for cancer is discovered and ten thousand times ten thousand victims have a chance to live again? Who is this saboteur of happy homes who blatantly auctions off his wares of desertion, divorce and dissension?

Who is this king of the "Cosa Nostra of corrupted emotions?" Who paints the big lie with the black brush of hopelessness and despair across the face of life? Who is this "unwanted" advocate of futility and failure who tells the salesman that service is senseless, that persistence is impractical, that success is sour grapes and that heroes just happen to be lucky?

Who or what is this hated thing whose funeral all humanity would be glad to attend? When I tell you, if you haven't already guessed, you will recognize his name. You will probably say, "I met him once and he almost did me in!" His name is DISCOURAGEMENT, alias DESPONDENCY, or in some circles they call him the Cop-out, Drop-out Kid! No doubt you have a few choice epitaphs that you would like to chisel on the proposed tombstone for DESPONDENCY and DESPAIR! May his obituary be read and forgotten and his influence be interned with his bones! (To be continued on October 7.)

691

OCTOBER DAYS

October is a happy month
    That's sandwiched in between
September's back-to-school distress
    And a festival Halloween!

October is the month of fall
    With aspens red and gold,
When snows fall at winter's call
    And autumn winds blow cold.

October is for everyone
    With skies of clearest blue.
May golden rays fill your days
    And the best things come to you.

October

7

All people must live awhile, and then all must die;
but what we choose to live and die for indicates the validity of our values.

A Tombstone for Despondency

What Causes Produce This Criminal Called Despondency?

There is a chain reaction to depression that may manifest itself in physical malfunction, spiritual deterioration, mental disorientation and social disorganization. Some people seem to have both the instinct for self-preservation and creative expression, while lurking in the shadows of the subconscious is also the escape mechanism of self-destruction and the will to die. Only as they embrace fullness can they avoid emptiness, and only as they love life and express their love for life can they shake off the last downward pull of the quicksands of despondency and the seeming futility of the noncreative life.

I. Incompetence

Incompetence is the swamp in which the malaria fever of fear is spawned. Incompetence is more than an inferiority complex and much more difficult to face and correct. Incompetence may arise from an imagined or a genetic lack of ability, natural gifts and graces. It may result from lack of knowledge or wisdom, from lack of ambition and industry, from lack of creative resourcefulness, from lack of endurance and perseverance, from lack of initiative and leadership, from lack of concentration and attention, from partial awareness and limited consciousness, from lack of reading comprehension or verbal efficiency, from lack of confidence in self and others, from lack of experience and the willingness to acquire it, from fear, procrastination, lack of willpower, mental discipline, direction and determination. To accept such a list of incompetence could certainly be cause for discouragement. But each individual has some ability that he can cultivate and some competence that he can share with his fellow travelers to mutual advantage.

Knowledge may be increased by study. Rewards and purpose can stimulate ambition and industry. Creative resourcefulness has always been forged in the fires of necessity. Endurance can be extended; initiative and leadership can be learned as responsibility is assumed.

Concentration can be focused and awareness can be extended. We learn to read by reading and to speak by right practice in speaking. Time brings experience. Decisiveness can be learned, the will strengthened by action and the mind disciplined by proper exercise. (To be continued October 8.)

ONENESS WITH LIFE

Divinely illumined,
Fully believing,
Spirit comprehending
Incomprehensible Law;
Unifying cohesively
All that is opposite
From birth to death,
Of darkness and light;
From cause to effect
Manifestation arising
With awareness vibrating in
All that is life.

Knowing God-consciousness
Infinite Wisdom,
Gratitude, devotion,
Power and peace,
Happiness, wholeness,
Prosperity and sharing,
Freedom from resentment,
Doubt, fear, or strife;
Without competition,
Hostility or envy,
God-confident-Oneness
Loving all life!

October

8

R.W. JACKSON FAMILY, SEASON'S GREETINGS

Don't offset a day of smiles by one last unthinking frown.

A Tombstone for Despondency

What Causes Produce This Criminal Called Despondency?

The purpose of the thoughts yesterday, October 7, were to assist each individual in the exchange of incompetence for competence and failure for success!

II. Indecision

Indecision is a paralyzing, disheartening state of mind that can result in discouragement. The fear of accepting the responsibility in an unresolved decision saps the emotional energy of the indecisive. It accounts for the lost time, procrastination, uncertainty, irritability and the rationalization of inactivity.

Perfection in end results is an ideal in decision making, but too often it is an unattainable ideal that must find compromise with expediency in the balance of pros and cons, advantages and disadvantages, entailing some sacrifice.

A built-in set of ethical values or life convictions that serve as general guidelines for conduct help delimit the area of the decision and thus to simplify it. The sense of incompetence previously mentioned makes decision making a seemingly hazardous thing to those who are more aware of the possibility of a reasonable solution. Their fear is of failure, of an unknown future, of the possibility of criticism and the result of inaction!

Decision making is similar in structure or procedure to the problem-solving techniques of creativity. The problem must be defined and narrowed by analysis to its basic essentials. Fact-finding research follows with a listing for the possible solutions. Then comes a reasonable incubation period, such as sleeping overnight on the problem with the expectancy of inner illumination, and finally the period of evaluation, with a listing of reasons for and against the possible alternatives for the solution of the problem. Perhaps the wisest decisions are a combination of the inner, intuitive feeling or illumination and the factual conclusions of common sense. (To be continued on October 9.)

FLYING TO ASPEN IN AUTUMN

Flying to Aspen in autumn
    The clouds float softly by;
The plane like a bird speeds onward
    Through the blue of the autumn sky.

Flying to Aspen in autumn
    Where green hills stretch afar,
Where the red and gold are vying
    And nothing its beauty can mar.

Flying to Aspen in autumn
    My heart soars free in the air,
And the joy of autumn rides with us
    As the aspen autumn we share!

Flying to Aspen in autumn
    The houses lie flat and low
And the trees of the forest foreshortened
    Their multicolored patterns still show!

Flying to Aspen in autumn
    The cattle like mice in the field
Graze in the fading summer
    In the shade the broad trees yield.

Flying to Aspen in autumn
    I forget I'm a part of the earth,
And view if from the eminence of heaven
    Close to God who gave autumn its birth.

HOPA WOMAN BY DAVID GREEN

October

9

*Death clings impulsively to the cold breast of receding earth
and only asks for life, not lust or mirth.*

A Tombstone for Despondency

WHAT CAUSES PRODUCE THIS CRIMINAL CALLED DESPONDENCY?

Always in the ultimate decision, the individual must face life cheerfully and confidently, with a sense of inner strength, courage and resourceful determination that moves out along the path he has decided to take. This positive response to life cures a person's indecision and prevents the despondency that continued uncertainty and inaction tend to produce.

III. Fear (Λ)

Fear paralyzes and produces despair. Our emotional attitudes toward life affect our responses toward life. We can fear and fight. We often overcompensate both in good and bad ways. Such overcompensation, if it is constructive self-expression, is beneficial. Another reaction of fear is to flee. Running is good exercise but is more profitable if it is in the right direction. We can compromise with our fears and rationalize our failure. To rationalize is simply to sell ourselves on our own rational lies. This is negative compromise. But fear can be faced courageously, and we shall discover how this may be done.

Fear is a witch doctor who would rob us of our self-determination and cast a spell of the black magic of hopelessness over our supposedly defenseless heads. But self-determination, self-respect, self-expression, self-acceptance, self-appreciation and self-confidence bolster the trembling inner self while it buckles on the sword of courage and goes out to fight the battle of reality. A proper image of worth versus worthlessness, self-appreciation versus disparagement, is a cure for discouragement and an antidote for the poison of fear.

Fear may manifest itself in the overcompensation of vanity and self-exertion. Its self-concept of helplessness may drive it ceaselessly in a self-centered lust for power over others, an inordinate desire to be always in the limelight, to bolster and counteract its true sense of inadequacy. This, too, is fear and, coward that it is, it would bully life and disregard the deference and respect it should show to others, whose cooperation and acceptance are the very grounds of its hoped-for successes.

When self-seeking, incompetence and fear take the motor of love and service out of the car of our emotions, and under the flagellation of their own warped self-contempt, thus resorting to "push and pull," they usually do not have enough motor power to make it to a good garage. Proper self-evaluation, humility, courtesy, kindness, cooperation and love are a way of life and indicate that their possessor has tuned in on an energy source that recognizes the essential equality, the individuality and yet the unity of all things. How do you feel about fear today? (To be continued on October 10.)

STORM GHOSTS DANCE

A million ghosts of the departed dead
 Dance on every wave.
A million ghosts with arms outspread
 Dance over their ocean grave.

They whip the waves to lathery spray
 And they dance on their toes in glee.
These ghosts of the storm in frenzied play
 Race over the wave-tossed sea.

Ghosts of the storm that climb the rocks
 And tear away at the sand.
In frenzied freedom they leap and mock
 The earthbound souls on land.

Ah, me, ah, me, the ways of the sea!
 How fickle and changing each day,
Stirred by the frivolous, invisible feet
 Of the sea-ghosts who maliciously play!

October

10

The fraternity of friendship is open to the happy smile and the warm hand of helpfulness.

A Tombstone for Despondency

What Causes Produce This Criminal Called Despondency?

III. Fear (B)

Fear wears many masks, but under each ugly false face is the contorted visage of many varieties of specific fears. Some people are plagued with superstitious fears and fear of the occult and fail to realize that they can walk in an aura of God-consciousness and protective light.

There are physical fears of accident, sickness, age, epidemics, war, bombs and the whole unknown future. There are environmental fears of storms, earthquakes, high places, closed places, dark places, empty spaces, irreparable losses and even bosses. There is fear of failure, fear of poverty, fear of people, fear of violence and many, many others. Some of them are groundless and some are genuine threats to self-preservation and our inborn instinct of self-protection. But fear, when rampant, is a many-tentacled octopus that squeezes the life out of trembling humanity. Fear, of course, produces discouragement, for it is the opposite of courage. But fear may be overcome by developing a right mental attitude of optimism and by a right relationship with self and the spiritual forces and powers of the universe.

Energy depletion in general is a major cause of despondency. The pressures and stresses of life emotionally drain our reserves and leave us exhausted. This tends to produce discouragement as a mood. Our inner reserves of mind and heart can be built up until the inner forces more than equalize our outer stresses and pressures that would collapse our emotional framework.

Social disapproval, or nonacceptance, distresses us and makes us feel our unworthiness and inadequacy. Proper self-image, self-acceptance and assurance of divine approval can make temporary social nonacceptance much easier to bear. (To be continued on October 11.)

BUT I CAN

I cannot hold the flowing
    Of the river in my hand.
I cannot hold the blowing
    Of the wind that drifts the sand.

I cannot turn the sunset
    Back again to dawn,
I cannot stop the hourglass
    Of time from running on.

I cannot stay with old friends
    If I go to seek the new.
But any road is a good road
    If I can walk it, God, with you!

I cannot lift earth's sorrow,
    No matter how I try.
I cannot stop the heartache
    In each weary passerby.

But I can join their laughter,
    Or weep the rain of grief,
Or give the gift of gentleness
    To the ones that need relief.

But I can know that longing
    Will bring me close to God;
That He shares my rutted road and yoke
    Where time's slow oxen plod.

And I can know the future
    Will somehow turn out right,
And that somewhere in the darkness
    A star will shine at night!

October

11

Discouragement is the tough kid that kicks the crutch out from under crippled hope. It snatches the purse of purpose, paralyzes the power of performance, and strangles the struggler. Run from it: Fight it! But never embrace discouragement.

A Tombstone for Despondency

What Causes Produce This Criminal Called Despondency?

III. Fear (C)

Fear is a negation of life, whereas life is what we are aware of and the sum total of all that we are alive for. Fear retreats into oblivion and refuses to live zestfully, confidently and courageously. Yesterday, we looked at *energy depletion* and *social disapproval* as they relate to *fear*. Today we will look at several more issues that relate to *fear*.

Guilt puts us in the winepress of self-condemnation, confusion, fear, and inner-energy, depleting turmoil of spirit. Guilt can be confessed silently to the Creator in prayer, talked out with a counselor, written out and then destroyed, or compensated for by some reasonable act of restitution or penitence.

Worry saps the life force as it muddles through its half identified and often anticipated problems. It's fearful, unilluminated state of mind with its treadmill circles arrives at no decision, and its unintelligent processes produce little more than exhaustion. If we can learn to expect life's best but be ready to accept its worst, if we can intelligently attack our problems and solve them, if we can stand aside in emotionally uninvolved detachment, if we can remember always that neither friend nor foe can knock a doormat down, if we can learn confidence in ultimate outcomes and believe that the sun will come up again in the morning, then we have come a long way in our conquest of worry.

Physical and mental ill-health can make the stars seem to quit shining, and both must be prevented by wise thinking and healthful living. These can be either the result or cause of despondency and are closely related to energy depletion or the failure to expend energy positively and creatively.

Inner anger, hidden hostilities, hate, contempt and ill will can turn into self-cannibalism to consume the energies and strength of life itself and leave a person but a shell of his former physical and mental self. However, LOVE, that divine and social emotion, can cure with its healing balm the emotionally self-mutilating person and also reach out to bless and benefit the object that once was rejected.

Any of these listed causes of discouragement can exhaust our energies, but each has a remedy and a release to check energy depletion and despondency. (To be continued on October 13.)

THE WIND BLOWS FREE

The wind blows cold.
It's boisterous and bold.
    And the wind blows over me.

I'm an autumn leaf
And the wind is a thief
    As it blows me from the tree.

I often ride high
In a thistle-down sky
    As the wind blows under me.

I soar and I fly
In the cold, grey sky
    As the wind blows endlessly.

MEDITATION PRAYER

O, God, scalding are the tears that often have fallen down our faces. How heavy our troubled hearts have been, how blind our eyes, how dull our ears to hear. May your presence calm our heart's aching and dry our tears of penitence and fear. Touch our eyes again that we may see the fields of promise, green with hope and vibrant with the thrill of life. Touch our ears, and may we tune out all of earth's clamor and its discord; enable us to catch the strains of heaven's harmonious chords that men and angels sing. Remove the feelings of despair and teach us to sing the song of confident joy. Thank You. Amen.

October

~ 12 ~

MOVING OUT BY LEE HERRING

Determination is a steadfast will in purposeful action.

THEY THAT WAIT
(Isaiah 40:29-31)

Sure you've felt the weariness
    That follows after pain.
And been denied the temporal help
    Of some material gain.

You've climbed your hills with trembling knees
    Afraid lest you should fall.
Such trials beset the most of us,
    We're frail creatures all.

But what a promise God has given—
    His power for all the faint.
He loves the sinner sure enough!
    But most of all the saint.

Though youth should fail thru weariness
    And many round you fall.
What consolation just to know
    God answers at your call!

That those who wait upon the Lord
    Renew their strength each day.
They mount and soar with eagle wings
    Whene're they knelt to pray.

And in the race that lies ahead
    They strike a steadier pace.
For God is with them all the way
    To give them strength and grace.

And though long years should take away
    Your bent to fly or run,
You'll walk along with spirit strong
    As when you first begun.

October

~ 13 ~

Stop signs and caution lights are necessary for traffic regulation,
but perseverance adjusts to the traffic flow and keeps on keeping on!

A TOMBSTONE FOR DESPONDENCY

DESPONDENCY'S DEMISE: LET DESPONDENCY DIE!

Execution day. Count your ten bullets—one for each man in our firing squad. Examine the bullets and scratch on each cartridge shell a cure and a compensation for each of his crimes. Ten sturdy stalwart men, each with a rifle in his hand, are standing by!

Bullet #1: I see the first bullet glinting in the sun. Call that first one **Relaxation**. Relaxation relieves the tension of the victim of despondency. It gives his nerves and muscles and organs a moment of rest. His energies can now regroup and replenish the depleted areas and flow unhindered and free to every part of his body and mind. Relaxed and restful, he has opened his gates to the inflow and overflow of his inner powers and wisdom, and to the influx of Divine assistance through the avenues of the sensitive self. Relaxation is a shiny, solid bullet. It should work a cure.

Bullet #2: "Let me see yours, Sir. I see **Gratitude** stamped on it. The man who counts his blessings, the man who has positive optimism and the habit of happiness and gratefulness, has tuned the vibrations of his being to the heartbeat and positive rhythms of the Creator Himself. That man can withstand discouragement and get the draw on despondency at any time."

Bullet #3: "Fellow, over there! You seem to be weighing your bullet. Oh, I see, it's the bullet called **Balance**. It is indicative of the balanced, well-ordered, organized life where all things count but nothing counts too much. It reflects the analytic judgment of common sense and evaluation with a proper place and time for everything."

Bullet #4: "Soldier, that's an odd label on your bullet. I'm sure it reads, **'The Love of Life!'** That would hit despondency hard, wouldn't it? Love of Life. Love life enough to let it live itself. Love it enough to let it happen. Love it enough to value it, guard it, and share it. Don't run from it but toward it. Don't hide it or hoard it. Love it! Invest it; this makes life worth living."

Bullet #5: "Next man. Next bullet. **Affirmation!** The inner focus of attention on a desired state tends to produce that state. To affirm is the first step to confirm. Assert the certainties of life and deny its denials, and the inner mind will begin to produce the condition that you requisition. I do hope you have an automatic rifle, Sir, a repeater so to speak. It works well with affirmation." Later, we will review more execution bullets. (To be continued on October 14.)

PERSEVERANCE

Perseverance is a gift of God
    That we must strive to cultivate.
And in persistent pressing on,
    We conquer every fate.

Perseverance bows its humble head
    And presses thru fog and dark,
And does not turn aside in fear
    For terrors grim and stark.

Perseverance is a virtue strong
    That lasts till set of sun.
Perseverance is the second wind
    Of all who heavenward run!

October

~ 14 ~

The question is not why, or where, or even how:
but all the past or hoped-for future is in the present, here and now.

A Tombstone for Despondency

Despondency's Demise: Let Despondency Die!

Join me as we continue our execution, considering the effectiveness of bullets six through nine.

Bullet #6: "Neighbor, you must go to church somewhere. Your bullet reads, **'The Power of Prayer.'** As Tennyson said, 'More things are wrought by prayer than this world dreams of.' And I fully agree. That one bullet could knock despondency dead. Devotion deserves attention. To commune with the Creator, to hold hands with Infinity, to converse with Omniscience, to confer with Omnipotence, turns despondency off like a leaky faucet with a new washer. Kneel when you take aim with that one!"

Bullet #7: "**Creativity** is a soft-nosed bullet that can blast the conformity out of monotony and cure despondency with curiosity, variety, novelty and efficiency. It solves problems, prides itself in progress and could figure out at least ten ways to make even despair laugh itself to death. Don't miss when you shoot that one, my good man. It has a money-back guarantee!"

Bullet #8: "You there, smiling, jumping up and down, waving your gun. What's all the excitement? Oh, you have the bullet called **Enthusiasm**. Great day! No wonder you want to get on with it. If your enthusiasm has the qualities of earnestness, inspiration, stimulation, activation of subconscious reserves and resources; is self-generating; increases the wattage of the brain; paralyzes fear; is invigorating and illuminating; can win friends; has a positive personal atmosphere; and has the will to live—then you have every right to be excited. You have a winner! Just hold steady till the rest of us are ready and we'll all fire together."

Bullet #9: "Man, you have a shotgun, not a rifle, and that looks like a shotgun shell, not a bullet! **Achieving Faith** is a wide-range shotgun shell of expectant activity. It does not presume; it knows. It does more than hope and anticipate; it *wills to believe* and *works to achieve*. It is faith for accomplishment. It is determination rolling up its sleeves and spitting on its own calloused hands of application. It is confidence in action. It is an expectancy that links arms with Divinity and works for efficiency. It makes a believer out of despondency or works it to death with tenacity."

On October 16 we will discuss bullet #10. Please join me. (To be continued on October 16.)

~ 709 ~

ONENESS

I feel a oneness with the object
  Like the paint upon the shelf.
I have blended by the knowing
  Till the object seems myself.

Identity's discerning mirror
  Reflects the feeler and the felt,
Where the soul with God is blended
  In the place where worship knelt.

A secondary consciousness
  Of some happy, heavenly kind
Unites the known and the knower
  In the apprehending mind.

There a penetrating cognizance
  Awakes awareness from her sleep,
And the breath of comprehension
  Encompasses all within her sweep.

When illumination's luster
  Comes like sunrise to the soul,
Then man's severed selves are one again
  In the universal whole.

October

~ 15 ~

DAYDREAM BY SERGEY CHERNOMORETS

The simplest creed is the creed of kindness,
the tolerance of love and the unity of understanding.

TIMELESS LOVE

How is it we have scaled
    Love's Eden wall
Close where the angel with
    The flaming sword
Has guarded this fair haven
    Since the fall
    Of human horde?

How is it we have known
    The joys primeval
Like islands together in a sea
    So warm with love,
Drifting to the insistent,
    Surging tide coeval
    Of consuming love?

How is it that no rain of fire
    Falls on our forbidden bed
When lost in interstellar time
    And space above,
Star-canopied here at night
    And softly spread,
    In timeless love?

October

～ 16 ～

Self-confidence is a fine balance between fact and faith, between what we have done and what we know we can do, what we actually are and what we are potentially.

A Tombstone for Despondency

Despondency's Demise: Let Despondency Die!

Achieving faith is an expectancy that links arms with Divinity and works for efficiency.

Bullet #10: "Energy! My friend with the black beard and bald head, you look like a scientist who should be in the laboratory, rather than on the firing squad for the final rites of despondency. In fact, you do not have a silver bullet in your palm, ready to slip into the chamber. You don't even have a gun. You have an atomic hand grenade that seems to vibrate with energy. We agree that the generation of inexhaustible, dynamic energy with its enthusiastic but wise expenditure of, and conservation of reserve energies, is absolutely necessary for the destruction of despondency. *It takes terrific energy to outwit, outwait and outwork the competitive forces of life.* Laziness and indolence invite despondency, but energy works it to death.

Radiant energy, powerful energy, atomic energy, exhaustless energy are the characteristics of the persons of genius and accomplishment. Energy plus native intelligence makes a human dynamo that can blast its way through all opposition. Intense, controlled energy, like the skilled courage of the matador, wins the applause of the crowd and elicits the cooperation of invisible forces and the unseen powers which come to its aid. Energy in overalls with a pocket full of ideas and a hammer of purpose will build something useful before the sun sets. It may even be a slab-casket for despondency.

What is the cure for fatigue, failure feelings and despondency? The secret of abundant energy is to draw upon the untapped abundance of our potential energies. The increased use of powers actually possessed is the secret of increased energy. A person can rise to higher levels of personal vigor and push back the emotional barriers of exhaustion.

Relative to our personal relationships, despondency is often the deep fatigue of a psychic wound, exhaustion from unresolved, inner emotional conflicts. Not overwork, but an overdose of inner distress, sires our exhaustion and gives birth to our depressions. Lack of insight, anxieties, physical and mental conflicts and personality impairment all rise up to rob us of our heritage of abundant, joyous energy overflow. We need to cure our incompetence by learning and doing together. Learn to love one another. Learn to understand one another. Learn to support one another. Stay tuned. Tomorrow is execution day! (To be continued October 18.)

～ 713 ～

SILETZ KEYS

Siletz Keys are a no-man's land
   In the battle between land and sea.
Floating logs like fallen men
   Lie in dead impropriety.

Island clumps of earth and fronds
   Advance in surging tides.
Cut off from the land they mutely complain
   To the immovable rocks at their sides.

The debris and foam and drifting wood
   Conspire in a riot of rubble,
As the waters back up from eager seas
   Spewing out with foam and bubble.

Let's have no more indecisive debates
   Of reclaiming the Keys from the tide,
Let's give a hand in the battle for land
   Or forever just let it ride!

MEDITATION PRAYER

O, God, our Father, Heaven is your dwelling place and hallowed is your holy name. Our hearts desire the coming of your kingdom both without, but first within. With fervent hearts we pray that Your will be done in us today, even as angels and the spirits of men redeemed, today have done, so they will in heaven. And satisfy the hungers of our daily need by the supply of yourself and your word, which are our living bread. If ought of unforgiveness cringes in our heart, O, God, purge it out and do forgive. In the face of fierce or lesser nagging temptation now, to be weak and fail, stretch out your arm of deliverance. For you are supreme and you do have the power. We, your love servants, pledge to give you honor, glory and all the credit forever and ever. Thank you for your love. Amen.

HARVEST DAYS

Like army tents the corn shocks rise
In harvest time beneath blue skies.
Or growing corn like soldiers stand
In long, straight rows across the land.

The summer splendors fade away
But autumn brings her rich display
Of fallen leaves in brighter hue;
Each season bringing something new.

And surely when today is o'er,
And present pleasures are no more,
The Harvest God to us will give
A fuller, richer, life to live.

AREZZO BY JOE SAMBATERO

October

17

GOD'S GRACE

God's grace is sufficient, efficient, and strong.
It's power, triumphant, will conquer all wrong.
His grace, like the mountains that ever endure,
Is eternal, universal, and wondrously sure.

Like the peace and the calm that follow all pain,
Like the harvest fields bending low with their
    grain,
Like a river of golden, luminous light,
It supplies our need; and puts the shadows to
    flight.

Like the glow of sunrise in the bright eastern sky,
His loving grace warms as it shines from on high.
And He tenderly leads us in pathways of peace,
And His grace all-sufficient never will cease.

His grace is a storehouse of silver and gold.
Like a fire it warms us and protects from the cold.
Like a roof in the storm when rain torrents fall,
His grace like a canopy covers us all.

His grace is sufficient for each trial of life.
His grace is our armor that protects in the strife.
His grace is our strength, our consolation and love.
Thank God for His grace that shines from above!

THE WINDMILL OUT BACK BY GLADYS DAVIS

October

~ 18 ~

Determination is a steadfast will in purposeful action.

A TOMBSTONE FOR DESPONDENCY

DESPONDENCY'S DEMISE: LET DESPONDENCY DIE!

The house of our emotions harbors an emotional delinquent, an arch-criminal with anti-self, anti-social and anti-success tendencies. When someone has a headache, despondency suggests the guillotine. If the house leaks, despondency doesn't think of repairing the roof with a new shingle. Despondency wants to burn the house down! Nobody cares anyhow! Thus, *despondency is negative overreaction to a specific problem that could be solved.* To make the problem more real, we have considered despondency as a personification of negativity. We have read despondency's definitive obituary and listed his crimes and the conditions that caused his coming.

Now, let a positive posse of purposeful people hunt this perpetrator of crimes through the gloomy swamps of depleted emotion. Bring him to bay. Handcuff the criminal. Bring despondency to the courts of sound judgment. Let us judge him guilty in the high courts of common sense. There can be but one verdict. Let the sentence of condemnation ring out. Let despondency die! Let hope survive. Let life attain its meridian and live out its years in peace.

The coupe de grace of despondency is the cure for despondency. But how shall he die? We could turn the laser beam of concentrated light with the refracted sunbeams of hope and courage full in his face and watch despondency disintegrate into ancient dust! We could hang despondency high on the gallows because he has left so many others hanging. But the firing squad may be the best with a bullet of cure for every crime. Straighten despondency's sagging form against that adobe wall. Slip the black blindfold over his distorted face. Count out ten bullets—one for each man in our firing squad. Tomorrow, October 19, return and we shall begin the execution.

TEMPEST TOSSED

Tossed from the trough
   To the crest of the wave,
Dashed into fragments
   With no one to save.

This is the life
   Of the average man,
Wrecked in the tides
   Of life's short span.

Tragically drifting
   Out of the bay,
Cast on the shore
   At the close of the day.

Elements that brought him
   His sorest distress,
If mastered could lift him
   To greatest success!

Grant us, O Father,
   Strength to survive,
Out riding life's storms,
   Fully alive!

He guides our frail boat!
   Let nothing despond.
The Harbor's in sight
   And Heaven's beyond!

October

~ 19 ~

Self-confidence is a fine balance between fact and faith, between what we have done and what we know we can do, what we actually are and what we are potentially.

A TOMBSTONE FOR DESPONDENCY

DESPONDENCY'S DEMISE: LET DESPONDENCY DIE!

Relative to despondency, we need to learn how to make right decisions, solve our problems quickly when possible, conquer our fears, resolve our inner conflicts and release the abundance of energy native to every person's inner being. Cooperation and understanding between our subconscious drives and a proper knowledge and understanding of ourselves are necessary.

Such an atomic bomb of singing, dancing, energy elements would probably finish off Public Enemy #1 with proper dispatch. But wait! We have ten good men ready to fire. They have eight silver bullets, a shotgun shell and an atomic hand grenade! Let's get it over with.

"Firing squad! Attention! Ready! Aim! FIRE!"

The body bounces against the wall and sags. Despondency is dead! Cut out the bullets from the criminal's corpse. Put them in the museum of Victory. Call them again by their names. They were: **Relaxation, Gratitude, Balance, Love of Life, Affirmations, Devotion, Creativity, Enthusiasm, Achieving Faith,** and **Abundant Energy.** No wonder **DESPONDENCY** is **dead!**

Write on the tombstone: **"Life is worth living."** Write beneath it if there is room: **"Life is sufficient. Courage and confidence are supreme."** Write it again and again. **All things are possible. Raise the tombstone on the baselessness of fear and push it half over at a rakish angle in the laughing light of shafted sunrise. Kick a little contemptuous dust and leaves over the fresh dirt of despondency's grave. Turn your back upon it. Despondency is dead. It is better that you live to conquer conflict. It is better that for you, despondency is dead! For despondency isn't a person. It is an emotional malfunction that has causes and a cure!**

SKEET'S PEPPY BY BOB ERWIN

October

20

PIONEER TENDENCY

I've seen deserted farmyards—
    Machinery rusted thru.
The old has been discarded since
    Or traded for the new.

I've seen the old freight wagon
    Resting by the Snake,
Where time had left its ravages
    With sadness in its wake.

I've seen the trail where men
        have gone—
    Trails of the olden days.
I've thought about the yesteryears
    And the old. Old-fashioned ways.

I would not bring them back again
    Nor would I quite forget
The memory of the former days
    Where time's low sun has set.

I've climbed the old, old river road
    And led the horse along;
I've ridden on her sturdy back
    While hoofbeats sang their song.

It's fun to live in yesterday,
    But only for a while.
I lose my pioneer tendency
    As I ride the homeward mile.

HIGH SIERRA BY LEE HERRING

October

21

Immortality is an unending symphony of universal harmony in heaven; and it is one concert for which all mortals, musicians or not, should make immediate reservations.

AUTUMN LEAVES AND LIFE

Autumn leaves are falling,
  Falling in the breeze.
Autumn chill is coming.
  Soon the ground will freeze.

Once the spring was vibrant,
  Once the summer sun
Hung in hazy splendor
  Then its course was run.

Youth and strength are given,
  Health and vigor, too.
Days of pride and labor
  All too soon are thru.

All too soon the autumn
  Of our life is here.
Chilling winds of winter
  Leave us bent and sear.

Chilling frost of winter
  Etching out its lines
Leaves us marked for falling
  Like wasted mountain pines.

(CONTINUED ON NEXT PAGE)

Youth and strength will vanish,
Trembling in the light.
We totter toward the sunset
And the long, long night.

There beyond life's autumn
In that fairer clime
Spring will follow quickly—
Then eternal Summertime!

I BELONG TO THE UNIVERSE

I belong to the universe.
I can't tell why or how,
But I belong to a dimension
Removed from the here and now.

I long for its air and grandeur.
I long for its solitude.
It's more than comprehension
And it's more than an expansive mood.

It is contact with the invisible.
It is insight with inner eye.
It is microcosm and macrocosm,
Infinite atoms in finite size.

I belong to the universe
And its mysteries belong to me.
So I look and love and am aware
Of the dimensions of infinity.

I belong to the universe
And it severs earth's cords that bind.
But I still must live in both my worlds
With a flexible, adjustable mind.

October

22

Faith is a Jacob's ladder that leads from earth to heaven;
but unbelief would cut it down, round by round.

THE LOVE OF THE BEAUTIFUL

Would you mind being called visionary by those who are blind, for you know that you truly see? In a special way, you see the glowing of an inner light. You see its own aura. You can be conscious of your own magnetic field. You are conscious that all magnetic fields are vortexes of energy and light which are part of another, all-inclusive, greater vortex of energy and light. You know that your own magnetic field is a part of the great, all-encompassing, all-inclusive, magnetic force field of God in His everywhereness and in His everythingness and in His more-than-everywhereness and everythingness—filling all the inner spaces of the universe and beyond universes. This new self loves God with all of its heart, for it has the love of all knowing, of all acceptance, and of all rightness and righteousness, for it identifies with the perfection of God in which there is nothing that cannot be loved. It knows that all things can be loved in perfect self-acceptance, for man is part of the Great Self, accepts all of the Great Self, and it knows that the Great Self and all of the other selves in the Great Self accept itself, for it is a part of the accepting Self and the accepted Self. It did not arrive at this state of awareness by striving, by action, or by primarily storming the gates of heaven—although this is effective. It became this way by the grace of God available to all men. It became this way by an awakening awareness of its limited self, a purging away of the limits of this self and the defects of this self. Out of the awaking and the purging came the true revelation and the spiritual revolution of its own change of consciousness. It was a shifting of gears, a changing of perspective, the opening of an inner eye, the listening of an inner ear, the outreach of the strong hand of faith, and the awakened functioning of a spiritual body. It saw and heard and felt and tasted and exercised all of its sensorial faculties on a higher perceptive level, on a spiritually, intuitive, revelatory level. It knows the truth as it becomes the truth. It swings on out beyond verbalizations. It swings on out beyond the limitations of language. It becomes one with the concept, with the symbol, with the reality, with the Truth. "And ye shall know the truth and the truth shall make you free." Out of the expansive, unrestricted, superconsciousness of unlimited understanding, the self comes into direct contact with the realities of its perceptions, unfiltered and unhindered by linguistic concepts or verbalizations. It sees and knows directly without the intermediary limitations of putting it down into words, the words of man.

The emotions of the emancipated self surge deep. Its joy rises high. It becomes enraptured with the love of the beautiful and the beauty of love.

THE CLOSET OF PRAYER

The world is so needy and so is thy soul;
Prayer is the pathway; heaven's the goal;
And heaven begins in the closet of prayer;
Pray much; pray oft; pray everywhere!

He who prays much knows God as his Friend;
He who prays not will fail in the end.
Apostasy starts at the closet door;
Pray much; pray oft; pray evermore!

Victory begins in the closet alone;
Prayer is the passport to God and the Throne;
And heaven begins in the closet of prayer.
Pray much; pray oft; pray everywhere!

October

~ 23 ~

Happiness is an inner attitude rather than an outward circumstance.

WISDOM PARTICIPATING; LIFE EXPRESSING

Awareness and love are immortal, like universal power surging. They are like an ocean that beats on every shore and that touches every other awareness and loves it all. Their intuitive sense of moral order is an awareness of a interrelated plan that sees nothing as chaos and accident but sees it all as a part of the integrated expression of God, who speaks out of the void, who manifests all things from His "no thing" existence and is aware that He upholds everything, that He hangs the earth on nothing, that He is in all things yet beyond all things, supporting all things in an existential, creative emergence, and is producing all things. So great is the all-inclusiveness of God that this philosophy manifests itself in all the religions of the world. Here the "I" loses its sense of its own limitations and its own exclusions and becomes more aware of the otherness of itself. Its all-inclusiveness identifies with the otherness of all things as encompassed beyond and in the selfness and the otherness of itself. Here, unified, the multiplicity manifests as One—and the one, or the part, manifests as the multiplicity. The self-enveloping awareness of itself, and of all things included within itself, now manifests as identifying with the all-inclusive things that once were considered as other things outside of itself. It sees the interrelated designs of all things. It cries out with exuberance in the very manifestation of a multiplicity of the facets of its own existence. Its interconnecting lines run everywhere in the Allness of God. It need only shift its awareness to function on many different levels. It only shifts its awareness to be in many different places, for it is above time and above space or place. In a sense, it is above knowledge, for it is intuitive knowing. It is wisdom participating. It is spirit emancipating. It is life expressing.

THE WINE OF THY KINGDOM

O mystical wine of God's Kingdom,
    Thy provision never shall cease.
And all who drink deep of thy fullness
    Shall know the repose of thy peace.

O blessed wine of the Kingdom,
    Gathered from heaven's glad hills
Where the river of life flows majestic,
    To the laughter of murmuring rills.

Miraculous wine of the Kingdom.
    Touched by the Creator's own hand.
Purer art thou than earth's vintage
    Since distilled in a happier land.

Unequaled the wine of Thy kingdom
    Ripened richly with joy and with love.
Deeply I'll drink of Thy sweetness
    On earth and in heaven above.

October

~ 24 ~

The gourmet, the camel, and the balloon have great capacity, but quality is more important than quantity; for a person must be full of more than food, water or hot air.

LIFE'S PEAK EXPERIENCE

Man's highest state of consciousness is a powerful goal. It is life's peak experience. It is peace beyond comprehension. It is love encompassing the awareness of all of the universe. It is a transcendental knowing that rises above sensorial limitation. It is walking and perceiving, radiating and receiving the inner splendor of a spiritual light. It is an individuation that has become a universal comprehension where individuality is lost in an all-encompassing awareness of the unity and interconnectedness of all things. It transcends ordinary understanding. It supercedes normal waking consciousness, for it is superconsciousness. This high state of spiritual sensorial awareness is a self-transforming comprehension and perception of one's total union and unity with Infinity. It is rising above time and above space. It is rising above bounds and the boundaries of egoism, of self-limitation and self-consciousness. It is an experience, a timeless experience, in the eternal now. It is an unlimited experience of oneness with all creation. That sense of me and mine, the limitation of the "I," as socially conditioned, finds a new definition of itself, a redefinition of itself, until that "I" is no longer a limited, egoistic "I." Then it is a new "I" whose identity equates all universality, all humanity and all livingness. The ordinary boundaries of a self-defensive ego are lost and break down so that the true identity, the expanded yet humbled ego, passes beyond all the limits and the delimiting conditions of the body and the concepts of a limited self and becomes one with the Over-Soul of the universe, one with the Over-Mind of God. This self, through purification and self-abnegation, becomes a selfless self, and its limited egoism is seen to be an illusion and it comes to an end. The new self identifies and defines itself with the non-self of the All-Self beyond the manifestation of selves.

~ 731 ~

MANIKIN FOLKS

What is a manikin
But similitude and likeness
    Wrought in feigned reality?
What is a manikin
But something falsely framed
    In deceptive similarity?

It walks and stands
And on occasion talks,
    With unmeant, unthought word
If the right button
Is firmly pushed,
    But its ears no sound has heard.

With vacant eyes
It scans the passerby
    As it looks thru the window glass.
Or waits in the closet
Where it is put
    Unaware of the hours that pass.

A manikin is no person
With reason in its brain
    Or will to laugh or weep.
But the world is full
Of manikin folk
    Who are standing half asleep!

October

25

*In a good marriage, each is a mirror that reflects the best in the other
without trying to break what it can't see through.*

We admire in others the reflected image of ourselves if it be noble, and despise it if it is not.

*Today is one day; tomorrow is another; yet the future is the offspring
and today will be its mother.*

*Proposals, postponement, and procrastination are the
TREASON TRIPLETS.*

ALWAYS I NEED YOU

Till the rivers run backward
    To the mountains and land;
When the fish swim swiftly
    In an ocean of sand;

Till the crabapple tree bears
    Sweet fruit on each bough;
When the past becomes future
    And the future is now;

Till the sun without color
    Comes up in the West,
Or clothes make us naked
    And tiredness gives rest;

Till the child is grey-bearded
    And birds cease to sing;
When winter brings sunstroke
    And red leaves in the spring;

Till then I will love you
    And love only you,
For without you cold reality
    Doesn't seem to be true;

And without you all order
    In chaos must lie,
While the stars wear dark glasses
    And weep in the sky;

Or beauty has lost all its
    Sweetness and grace,
And the sun dressed in blackness
    Wears a mask on its face;

For "the two shall be one"
    Is the law of all life,
Thus always I'll need you,
    My lover, my wife!

October

~ 26 ~

TREE OF LIFE BY RALPH BAGGETT

THE CLOCK

A clock is a wondrous, symbolic thing
That marks the passing of time on the wing.
It strikes off the minutes that rapidly fly.
To stop their quick flight we vainly would try.

Tick, tick, tock. Who can stop, who can stop?
Who can stop the clock?

The clock on the wall daily helps me to know
That time is treasure though hours pass slow.
For time is not measured in moments of days
But in content and quality of meaningful ways.

Tick, tick, tock. Who can stop, who can stop?
Who can stop the clock?

The years of our youth so quickly are gone.
Sunset and age always follow the dawn.
Time is the gold that we so freely spend
Like unlimited surplus that never could end.

Tick, tick, tock. Who can stop, who can stop?
Who can stop the clock?

October

27

The art of happiness is the fine balance found somewhere between grateful awareness, increased achievement, and adjusted desires.

RECALL AND THE BALLOON EXPERIMENT
(CREATIVE VISUALIZATION)

We are going to do a balloon experiment today. Take the balloon quietly, and immediately lower your activity level as soon as you get the balloon. Should any balloon accidentally break, it will in no way disturb you. I would suggest that you take a deep breath, but not an excessively deep one. When you take a deep breath, you lower your diaphragm. The diaphragm is sometimes raised because of stress or from the busy excitement of play, work, or school. Take a deep breath to lower the diaphragm and to produce a condition of emotional and physical rest. Do that now. Take a good, average, deep breath! Good! Remember that when you take this deep breath, it also puts oxygen in the blood, and that makes the brain work better; it detoxifies your entire system and gives you richer, better blood to carry energy and oxygen to the different cell centers in your muscles as well as in the brain. So relax now, with a second deep breath of air . . . Now, if you'll take the third one on your own, hold this breath as long as you comfortably can, and then exhale when you're ready. When you're done you should be completely relaxed. As your body relaxes, the emotions are even more sensitive, and the mind becomes more active as it concentrates on the experiment that we're doing. If you're not quite relaxed, just tell your body to relax, and tell your feet and hands to relax until you come to this beautiful, interiorized place . . . Good!

To help you relax more deeply, listen to the music in a special way. Try to enjoy the soft background music with all of your senses and especially with your imagination. What is the music like to you? What does it remind you of? Does the music seem to you like an icicle that's melting and dripping? Dripping, dripping, dripping? Does it seem like a dandelion blowing in the wind, like soft, downy dandelion seeds blowing in the wind? Does it seem like a glowing beam of sunlight coming down through the trees in the forest, leaving its shaft of light on the path, falling across the edge of a leaf and touching a blade of grass, caressing a beetle with its warmth, stirring the antennaes on a butterfly or on the hairy projections on a caterpillar's back? Is some bird stretching and fluttering its wings in a nest somewhere, warmed by the sun? Is the music like sunlight, like floating leaves in the wind? Is it like cumulus, white, rolling clouds in a summer sky in June? Is the music like a river flowing along, caressing its banks, washing the rocks away, undermining the roots until little chunks of dirt fall and splash into the water? Can you hear it splash? Are you listening to the music and seeing it too? Is it like a diamond glittering in the sun, or like a solid nugget of gold, firm and warm in your hand?

737

Picture one note. It could be a half note, an eighth note, a quarter note or a sixteenth note. You are like a little fleck of dust reflecting the sun or a tiny moonbeam speck of light in the restful darkness. Please pick a note of music and imagine that you climbed up on the round part of it. Put your arm around the staff and lean up against it. Ride on it while it floats out across the air. Swing on the bars above that note of music and enjoy it, feel and taste it, see it, hear it with your skin and with the nerve centers of your whole body, and sing with it. Play as it plays, dance as it dances, laugh as it laughs, and really get with it! Listen to what it says to you and become a part of its beauty, its rhythm and its harmony.

This is an exercise in far memory recall. All of us can quite easily recall recent, important events and while at this restful level we can also recall memories that go way back to our early childhood. We can remember birthday parties, favorite toys, the pets we loved and many, many other pleasant, happy things.

We are going back to some point of your choosing in early childhood where you may have seen or played with balloons before. Go back in memory as far as you can and recall everything vividly, clearly, in color, action, and in accurate detail.

Feel your balloon quietly now with your eyes closed. Feel the shape of it and the texture of its surface. Recall the color of it. Take a deep breath now and begin to remember some party, place or activity where there were balloons. Notice everything around you. Let the far memories of childhood come back, especially the happy ones.

See again the people who were there. Look at yourself and see how old you were. How were you dressed? How were other people dressed? What did your mother wear? How did she fix her hair? How did her face look? Was it younger? Was she smiling or sad? What were the smells, the sounds? How did things taste? Can you remember your playpen or bedroom? What did your yard or house look like?

Gently feel your balloon, gently, again. Listen again to the music and when a picture comes to your mind, examine it, bring it up closer, and walk around it while you look at the front, back, top, and sides of it in your imagination. When you are ready to report on what you are recalling, simply raise your hand and I'll call on you as soon as I conveniently can. Those of you who must wait your turn can continue to examine your picture more carefully and in detail so that you can do an even better-than-ordinary job of reporting when it is your turn.

Maintain a happy, restful relaxation level even after you are through or while waiting. Very good! Some of you have your hands raised already. Let's start our feedback now.

It looks like that's all we'll have time for now, so grab that music note you played like you were riding on and let's come all the way back to where we were before we started. Leave all of those childhood memories back where they belong. In a moment we are going to open our eyes, so it's okay to start moving around a little. You'll come up to activity level, happy, rested, healthy, feeling better and being better adjusted than you've ever been before. Okay. Open your eyes! Take a deep breath. Stretch. Let's everybody stand. Everybody on your feet. Good. Stretch again. Maybe we'll do some calisthenics. Thanks again. You did great!

October

~ 28 ~

*Enthusiasm is the outreaching, positive, creative force of God within us manifesting itself
in the lively spirit of joyous progress and increase.*

CLOUD TECHNIQUE
(CREATIVE VISUALIZATION)

Take a deep breath and hold it until I say to exhale. Shall we together in unison breathe in. Exhale. Again. Hold it. Exhale. Once more. Exhale and relax completely. Now, will you please shift your awareness to your body, and do not tense the parts that I call except in your mind only. Just imagine they're tensing and that will be sufficient. Will you tense your feet please, just for a moment, slightly, not with any great physical activity. Think of them as being tense and then relax them. The calves of your legs, imagine they're tense. Relax them. Up to the thighs and kneecaps. Tense them at least mentally and relax them. And then do the trunk of your body. Tense each part of it. Relax it. Will you take one more deep breath together and hold it. Exhale. This took care of the chest area. Now will you move your scalp or at least imagine that you're tensing it and then relax it. The same around the eyes. Relax them. Relax even the nose muscles. Tighten them and then relax them. Shift your attention to the ears and to the muscles around the ears, which are always alert to hear important sounds. Imagine they're tense and then relax them. Now take the tip of your tongue and run it down at the bottom of your gums, down just below the tongue itself. Place it there for a moment. Just relax it!

Now your arms. Will you tense them and then relax them—clear out to your fingers. Now would you take one more deep breath in unison and hold it together. Exhale and relax the whole body completely. Any time you feel like taking a deep breath and going deeper, just do it. Remember that you are in complete control of any state of awareness or relaxation, or of any perception that you receive. You can exercise this complete self-control either when I call you to rise or go deeper, or at your own pleasure. Please imagine that you step out of your body and levitate. Looking down upon this building and this group tonight, observe everything from an objective viewpoint. Rise above yourself and look down upon your body as you see it here, sitting comfortably alone or among friends as the case may be. Recall the different things in the room from an aerial view as though you were, in imagination or in fact, above your body looking down. Rise a little higher so that the perspective broadens somewhat like the sunrise comes up in the morning. Now it's high noon and you're above the earth, looking down upon the green pastures, upon the cattle grazing, upon the trees swaying in the breeze. Perhaps a lake ripples as the wind blows gently across it. But do not tarry here, though it is a beautiful spot, but go a little higher to the highest mountain peak that you may choose. Look down from that place of grandeur to the cities and the lights below. Or, choose a

~ 739 ~

daytime view with the sun glinting off from the roof and highways winding with cars flashing in the sun. Or see the green, green hills and trees down below. But you're above it all now with the wind blowing fresh and free as you stand on some pinnacle of mountain with arm outstretched. Let's not stay here either. In the flight of imagination and astro-travel, shift your awareness so completely to spirit essence that you're catapulted from the highest mountain peak up to some fleecy, soft cloud. You're engulfed in it. Pulling your feet up in it, you are surrounded by it. You feel how cool it is with the refreshing moisture permeating the cloud bank. How protected and encompassed you feel in it! It is very much like the protection in a mother's womb where you were once wrapped, comforted, surrounded. This would be a good place to rest awhile without any noise or distraction or even the vision of things below.

After resting a moment, let's go one step further. Let's push ourselves, like a swimmer from the bottom of the cloud up to the top. We sense the light coming in as we rise to the surface. We're breaking through. Like a swimmer, we're climbing out on the bank on the edge of our cloud. We're sitting there, taking a deep breath. Over our heads is the clear dome of blue, God's own blue sky without a cloud in it; clear and blue. Something about the infinite expansiveness of eternal sky does something for you.

You're sitting there on the cloud bank. Imagine you're a scout looking off into the distance. An eye is opening. Pictures will soon be forming. Look up at the blue sky above you in any direction that pleases you. We're going to go above the sky very soon. Imagine that the sky is rolling back like a velvet curtain of blue. You see the folds of it. You hear a stirring as the curtains of the sky are pulled back gently. You see a stairway of light like marble steps that lead up to the Cathedral of the Soul. They lead up into the very presence of a spiritual world. You hear cosmic choirs singing. You hear the music of the spheres. Listen to the cadence. Listen to the organ that's rolling out its infinite sound like the sound of waters rolling and oceans lapping on far shores. It is like the sound of happy bees at their work, intoxicated with the sweetness of sunlit fields and with the nectar in the dew-wet heart of every rose. You hear the chorus singing. Dimly you see angelic forms, movement and vibration. You're aware of the Infinite, Invisible Presence of God. You welcome the rays of soft, penetrating, healing, purple light. You bask in the green light of life itself. You're aware of the warm glow of the light of love.

Here in this Cathedral of the Soul, you sit down at the feet of God, and you turn your face earthward to the cities of men, to the nations of earth where people, like insects, are running to and fro. People, like actors, nations, and participants in a great play, are moving here and there, saying their lines, following their cues. Look from the viewpoint of God into the future. Gently close the physical eyes, even as you're sitting there, and look through the eye of the soul, through the spiritual insight, the intuitive perception of your high, high self. Here in relaxed solitude, precognitively anticipate the future. Take time here to express your gratitude and thanksgiving to God. Express your confidence in His providential care. Present your problems for solution and pray with sincere, earnest expectancy. When you are done, come back to the point where you started, rested, relaxed and confident.

October

～ 29 ～

GONE FISHING BY GREG WALZ

YOU'LL FIND GOD EVERYWHERE

You will find that God is everywhere
That you have ever gone.
You will find Him in the quiet night.
At breaking of the dawn.

You will find Him in the twilight
Where daytime folds its wings;
You will find Him in the hours of pain,
In songs that mothers sing.

You will find Him by the baby's bed
Where prayers are learned at first.
You will find Him at the fount of life
Where men may quench their thirst.

You will find Him where the faithful meet
To worship and to pray.
You will find God's presence everywhere
That men may take their way.

October

~ 30 ~

The genius thinks with the other side of his brain and simply listens and records with his conscious intellect; thus, his own mind, as well as those of others, is stimulated by his creative and original thought.

LOVE IS THE HOME OF THE SOUL

Love is the home of the soul. Too many have wandered from the hearthstone of love. Too many have forgotten the necessity and the art of the communicating heart. The loveless are the homeless. The untouchables are emotionally remote and spiritually alienated souls. They are isolationists whose fears, inhibitions, training and life experiences have set them aside and caused them to deny, or at least not to use, that fundamental technique of all communication which is the outreach of love.

The therapy of love should involve the art of touching, for the loving touch is basic communication. It is through touching as well as other communicative skills that we reach across the barriers and vast distances of our individualities and communicate at first hand and literally by hand with the body-encased spirit of the distant one. Through a combination of communication techniques and intimate encounters, we exercise ourselves mentally, spiritually, physically, verbally, and visually, and by taste, smell, and touch. But too many have strayed from the fireside of love, and love is the home of the soul.

The isolated soul instinctively cries out, "Laugh with me. Cry with me. Communicate with me by facial expressions and by body language. Write to me or speak to me audibly or with your silent, second voice of love. Listen to me. Let me hear the cadence of your voice. Let me know you are there, and let me know that you know I'm here."

If you do these minimal things, you have communicated; but communication reaches its apex of effectiveness only through actual contact. The touch of love supersedes all other methods of communication; for it began in the mother's womb and continues throughout childhood. It nourishes those who are blessed with it and leaves the adult life barren that denies it.

The human nervous system was nurtured on touch, on pressure, on movement, on encirclement and in embryonic enfoldment. So it is no wonder that humanity calls out silently, "Hold me close. Touch me gently, speak to me with your hands and with the body's vibrational language of love. Communicate to me the feelings of love and emotion. I'll listen for its silent message." All humanity needs to be held close, to feel life's rhythmic breathing and the palpatations of another human heart, or it feels lost in the limitless space following its emergence from the womb of love.

Not in isolation do I find my sense of individuality, but in the security and the comfort and the total confidence produced by the encircling arms of a loving, touching, caring humanity. Man in his birth, in his life and in his death echoes and re-echoes the cry of his first breath: "Don't leave me alone. Don't isolate me. Touch me. Love me. This is my first reality!"

The greater my sensitivity, the more insistent is my quest for the nurture of love and the fellowship of the soul's true home. To be emotionally orphaned, set aside and untouched, is more than physical punishment. It is the state of nonbeing; for I was conceived in contact. Therefore, do not leave me alone. Comfort me when life's illusory dreams torment me. Comfort me with a caressing hand. Love me, for love is the basic reality, the ground of my personhood and being. And let me return that love with the respect and the dignity of maturity.

Yes, let me have love as I need it; but let me have appropriate freedom as well. The man who lacks either freedom or love walks in a barren land devoid of life's richest meanings. Communication and love are strands in the umbilical cord of universal oneness. I can spacewalk more courageously with the touch of your hand on mine. When I do step away from you with the increased confidence of experience adventuring, please, join me, and share with me the smile of your commendation. Keep contact with the glance of an eye, the tilt of your head, the fleeting expression of tenderness, the knowing look of recognition and the emotional contact of love and understanding, though perhaps unspoken. Please keep on communicating as I keep on exploring the interspaces of life. Our expanding maturity and individuality still need the reassurance of encompassing love. I do love you and need you. For love is still the home of the soul. But because our maturity demands some independence, do not let love be overdemanding, excessively restrictive or too encompassing for breathing freely and for acting independently. Life necessitates discovery, self-identification, self-assertion, and continued growth. If my work includes adventuring and exploring, remember that I am only over here for a short while. I'll be back soon, perhaps very soon. Each soul has its individual responsibilities and its work to do, and at times we must seem to leave home to do it. But we will always need the touch of love, the mystery and the magic of the gentle touch of love, for love is the home of the soul.

I know, too, that as I give love, with confidence and with dignity, I shall receive it in the same manner and measure of its giving. I know that the entire world is filled with other people who have been living away from home, away from the hearthstone of love. They, too, need to come back to the awareness of the fullness of love. I am but a part of the whole. So let us always arise and go home together; *for love is the home of the soul!*

FLEE LIKE THE BIRD TO THE MOUNTAINS

Fly, fly is the watchword
    When tear-blinded eyes cannot
    see.
Fly like the bird for its refuge.
    The mountains of God beckon
    thee.

Fly, O my Soul, when sin tempts
    thee.
    Fly to the arms of God's love.
Nor will thou be blamed for thy
    hiding
    By him who watches above.

Fly, fly to God's mountains.
    Fly like the birds wild and free.
Nor pause, O my Soul, till you've
    found Him,
    The Creator has issued the plea.

Flee, then, for refuge and comfort
    When cares of this life would
    distress.
Flee to the fountain of courage
    To Him who will strengthen
    and bless.

Flee with the wild gulls winging
    Their flight o'er the waves of
    the sea.
Dart like the swift swallows
    winging
    Thru the branch of the frost
    smitten tree

Fly, fly is the watchword.
    Fly when the billows toss high.
Fly to the refuge of the Creator.
    The mountains of God are nearby.

GOD'S WILL

Let me be but a leaf in the wind
    Blown by the silent breath of One
Who guides the destinies of folks
    From dawn till setting sun.

Oh, let me be that willing leaf
    Blown gently here or there,
Surrounded, lifted, carried on
    Supported by wind and air.

Oh, let me be that drifting leaf
    Whose destiny is planned
By greater wisdom than my own
    And moves at God's command.

Oh, let me be a wafted leaf
    Swept upward thru the night
Where fallen leaves are dancing leaves
    Bathed in Celestial light.

October

31

*Negative suggestion accepted, or the senility of courage, and faith grown weary,
produce in the body the seed pictures accepted in the soil of the mind.*

TIE THE ENDS OF THAT RAINBOW DOWN!

Tie the ends of that rainbow down
   That arches there on high.
Nail it down with faith and prayer.
Nail it down and keep it there
   That rainbow in your sky.

Tie the ends of that rainbow down
   Where the light from God shines thru.
Nail it down with hope and love.
Keep this gift from God above.
   This rainbow was meant for you.

Tie the ends of that rainbow down
   It's a symbol of God's intent.
Stand with God's promise under your feet.
Some faith affirmations firmly repeat.
   Thus earthward all rainbows are bent.

Tie the ends of that rainbow down
   Out over an ocean of joy and peace.
Bathe yourself in its luminous light.
Keep it there for the longest night.
   And may your rainbows forever increase!

SEAGULL SHADOWS

Seagull shadows on the sand,
    White breasts against blue skies,
Grey-tipped wings and misshaped heads
    With raucous, startled cries.

Wing on in free formation flight
    Upborne by ocean breeze.
I'd love to wing my way with you
    Across the seven seas!

THE CALL OF THE SEA

Why do I walk the self-same shore
    While the beaches stretch so far?
Why do I follow a candle glow
    When I could follow the light of a star?

Why do I gather driftwood debris
    And broken shells in the sand
When there are islands that call
    With beaches of golden sand?

Why do I watch the waves roll in,
    Always different yet still the same,
While the other side of the ocean calls
    In lands I know only by name?

GHOST (DE VANEY COLLECTION)

ENGLISH SETTER BY W. JACKSON

November

1

AUTUMN

Autumn is the time of wonder.
　　Autumn is the time of change,
When Mistress Spring disrobes herself
　　And dons garments sear and strange.

Autumn is the time of turning,
　　When greens grow scarlet and brown,
Where frost, that capricious artist,
　　Paints on the hillsides and in the town.

Autumn is the time of sadness
　　Because of summer's early demise
When the rod of the Spinster Winter
　　On the back of all nature lies.

Autumn is the time and the season
　　When Cosmopolitans to the hills must go
When cold breath fogs the mountain air
　　From lips with health aglow.

Autumn is the time of Harvest
　　When fields lie ripe and full,
When hay and fruit are gathered in
　　And the children go back to school.

Autumn is the end of summer,
　　The beginning of the winter's chill,
A time and season of gladness and peace
　　When the aspens turn red on the hill.

OLD 597 BY JODIE BOREN

November

~ 2 ~

*Our years should measure growth and maturity, ripeness and resourcefulness
and not just the passing of our days.*

Life is action, time is its dimension, and immortality is its reward.

Rewarding experience reinforces our reactions even as profitable participation proves our prudence.

*Comfort is the cure for grief, the soothing balm of pain, redress for wrong,
and surcease for sorrow when love softly falls as the rain.*

LIFE IS LIKE A WINDING ROAD

Life is like a road that winds
   Up and down the hills,
Refreshed by shadows, rustic dells,
   By cool and splashing rills.

Life is like a road that climbs
   Beneath a somber sky,
With rough and rugged danger spots,
   With heartaches mountain high.

Life is like a winding road
   Where happy pleasure waits,
And just around the bend ahead
   Are Heaven's pearly gates.

Life is like a winding road
   Over the endless plain.
Weary hours and aching hearts,
   Tormenting hours of pain.

(CONTINUED ON NEXT PAGE)

Life is like a winding road
　　That leads at last to home.
And soon where evening shadows fall
　　We'll cease at last to roam.

Life is like a winding road,
　　And men are traveling fast.
Soon the lights of heaven will shine
　　And we'll be home at last.

Life is like a winding road.
　　Oh, guide our hearts, dear Lord,
And may we follow in thy steps,
　　Directed by Thy word.

For life is like a winding road
　　Up and down the hill,
With victory waiting at the end
　　For those who do God's will!

November

3

When the beautiful autumn banquet begins, let Pleasure sit on your left hand and Temperance on your right hand. It is harder to "overeat" with someone sitting on both hands.

Self-control is the criterion and moderation the mandate for the man who would be an anchor, not just flotsam and jetsam in the sea of survival.

Femininity is the mother, sister, daughter, heart, and hope of humanity. Masculinity declares that femininity is the most attractive part of humanity.

TREES AGAINST THE SKY

Above the trees, the jet
Left twin trails of smoke
Like narrow railroad tracks
Against the cold, blue, winter sky.

Or like the trail of foam
Where water-skiers glide,
These twin streaks cut
The placid ocean of the silent sky.

Great burly trees, like giant arms
Reach through green velvet robes of grass,
Straining with crooked fingers
To pluck the fruitage of the barren sky.

The scaly, old arthritic trees
With lean arms and searching fingers,
Stretch up to claim the refreshing rain
Of hope-filled youth from empty skies.

(CONTINUED ON NEXT PAGE)

The fir trees, like green exclamation points,
Rise up to shout in stalwart tones
Their hallelujahs to the startled blue
Of acquiescing, undulating, peaceful skies.

And I, exultant, with levitated soul,
Spring to the lower arcing jet stream
With winged feet of love and earth rapport
Ride its soaring path across the sky!

And far below, the trees reach up
Their longing, groping fingers
In earthbound, silhouetted envy
Pointing my orbit in the vaulted sky.

November

4

No man who writes a book can fully die, for he has written with his blood a message on the sky.

A WRITER IS AN ARTIST

A writer is an artist who puts new pictures in old frames, and leaves some pictures without frames, and some frames without pictures, in hopes he can inspire the creative thought and action of the viewers and stimulate their desire to evaluate the finished work, to complete the incomplete, and to comprehend in an hour what it took a lifetime to learn and portray.

SONGS OF BELONGING

Sometimes poetic insight reaches a level of elevated awareness where the sense of identity, unity and oneness with all creation become an acute part of the spiritual consciousness. Here kinship with all things is realized in the ecstasy and love of life. You belong! You belong to God, and all things belong to you!

FISHING IN THE ALPS BY NENAD MIRKOVICH

November

5

BOOKS

Books for crooks and criminals
   And books for the Sunday School;
Books for the wise and the otherwise
   And books for the dullard and fool.

Books that are fat or skinnier than that
   And books that are tall and thin.
Books for show with nowhere to go.
   And a few worth looking within.

Books for the baby and old Grandpa
   And books for the working class.
Books for college and junior high
   And for every grade we pass.

So give us books of every kind
   For the ignorant and the wise old sage.
There's something in books for everyone
   If you put your heart in the printed page.

LOVE'S SILENT NIGHT

Oh, Love, immortal beauty is thy name
Whence comes immortal grace and equal fame.

Throughout time's fading, endless, dying years
Immortal love cures beauty of its fears.

Oh, Love, whence comes thy long, enduring grace
That smiles thru tears that stain thy patient face?

Whence comes thy will to live and serve always
And ask no boon but love's chains day by day?

Oh, Love, art thou mute or only silent now?
What seals thy lips, smoothes Mona Lisa brows?

I cannot know the depth of Love's own Muse.
Why silent be when thou hast power to choose?

So let me kiss thy lips till dawning light
Dispels all silent fears of loveless night!

November

~ 6 ~

A kiss may tell a thousand things or still conceal the same;
for a kiss is what the heart reveals as the lips spell out its name.

The strength and depth of our wisdom, the extent and the permanence of our achievements,
depend upon the assimilation and contemplation of the facts we store in the vaults
of our subconscious, creative mind.

The Winds Blow Cold

Nature hears the cold, snarling snap of winter's jaws and the grinding, whining, raw, whistling wind that whets and sharpens the knife blade of wilderness hunger. The frozen edges of an endless river of frustration and unfulfilled, silent pain cut the chilling waters that flow cold and imperturbably by. All yesterdays, like jagged mountain ranges in serried ranks, fade into nothingness in the mantle of mists and low-hanging, bitter, brittle storm clouds. Yesterday only adds to the threat of today's emptiness and hidden hungers. Yesterday and today, with tarnished skies threatening darkness, offer little refuge from the storms for nature's struggling offspring or for windswept mortals on time's barren, shattered shore.

Whereas wild things know the simple consciousness and physical awareness of elemental needs, their human peers know deeper pain and an inner, knowing grief with deeper soul and mental hunger, hostility, misunderstanding, uncomprehended deprivation and the bitterness of the colder winds of human adversity. Human beings realize the universal kinship of common suffering and the understanding of a common experience shared with intuitive awareness. But where cold winds blow fiercest, LOVE'S flowers bloom quickly and with sweetest fragrance or not at all.

WINTER IS A MONSTER CAT

That little bird perched in a dying limb,
I wonder what in the world
Is the matter with him?

(CONTINUED ON NEXT PAGE)

Doesn't he know that summer
No longer is here,
That the white ghosts of winter
Are very near?

Hey, Little Bird,
Go pack your flight bag.
Take off like a jet
With your tail a-wag!
Spread your wings;
Raise your sight;
Head for the warm
Southland tonight!

The Tom Cat's asleep;
You won't hear him growl;
But a Monster Cat called "Winter"
Is out on the prowl.
He hunts day and night
And never seems to tire.
He howls in the harsh wind
And his eyes are on fire!

His jaws are like traps
Of cold, heartless steel.
He eats hundreds of birds
Just for one meal.
His hair is a mountain
Of snow-covered trees!
He'll starve you to death
And laugh when you freeze.

He has frost on his whiskers,
And icy sharp claws.
He has icicle teeth
In two refrigerator jaws.
He's too mean to outsmart
And you'd better not try;
So fly south, Little Bird.
Fly! Fly! Fly!

November

7

Man's greatest need in life is not more or less of any material thing; his greatest need is for a truer sense of direction, wiser evaluation, and the cooperative enthusiasm of unselfish love that makes life more meaningful and adds the zest of purpose well directed.

OUR HAPPY DIMENSION OF LOVE

Love is a dimension of consciousness, a condition of togetherness, an integration within ourselves, a separation-less relationship with each other, and a union with the infinite Creator. Can you join me in spirit and may we dwell together? Let us continue that journey now! Here, caught up in a beautiful, heavenly awareness, we step from dimension to dimension.

Let us visualize ourselves for the moment on some far-distant cloud. See yourself floating in the sky with soft clouds drifting by. Feel yourself to be in an atmosphere of peace and beauty. Here, meaningful, melodious bands of light dazzle perception. Your cloud is swept by soft rays of living light in shapes and hues ever changing and new. Each resplendent ray cleanses and invigorates your entire being in perfection of function as it passes over and through you in undulating spectrums of colors known and unknown. Soothing, restful, healing pools of living light are filled with shadowed symbols of hidden meaning whose secrets are known only to you. Fountains of luminescent, liquid light rise, ever flowing. Far blue skies of beckoning light, unlimited, expansive, and resplendent, stretch over you from horizon to far horizon. You swim in a sea of light. You float in skies of light on clouds of light, with your head lifted up from mountaintop to mountaintop, outracing the winds, outshining the sun, outswimming the fish in the sea, outsinging the birds of the sky. You and I sail and soar together, luxuriate and live, live, live. Today, all of life is love. We have taken up our residence in the heavenly dimension where love is home base.

Here, primary, secondary, and tertiary colors of timeless, kaleidoscoping beauty roll out the reds, blues, yellows, greens, violets, and golds—plus an infinite mixture of pastel shadings of iridescence that converge around you. You feel, hear, and breathe in rhythm with the pulsation of the universe as it sings its song of glad self-acceptance. Join, then, in its chorus: I am that I am glad-hearted and free. I'm glad, I'm glad, I'm glad that I'm me! I'm glad I'm a part of Infinity, a part of the happy family.

WALK WITH GOD

I walked the woods one Sabbath day
    Where pine trees towered high,
Where sunlight mingled with the shade,
    Beneath the blue of sky.

I walked thru paths of Sacred Writ,
    And searched the word of God,
While light divine illumined it,
    Along the way I trod.

The bird notes rang from azure sky;
    The wood folks raised their voice,
While God spoke to me from His Word,
    And made my heart rejoice.

The dark trees framed a lake of blue
    Where deer their way betake.
I thought, how like God's Word so true
    Where I my thirst did slake.

And all who walk with God and read
    Shall see rich truths unfold.
Go walk with God—He'll walk with thee—
    As Enoch walked of old.

November

❧ 8 ❧

The courtesy and consideration of polite civility often requires no cost but quietness in the language of unspoken goodwill.

LIGHT REFLECTS FROM EVERY STAR

You are wrapped in the golden light of wisdom, encircled in the white light of the Ultimate, in the beauty and light of love. You are at home in the heart of God, and love dwells in your home sweet home.

Dimensions beyond the universal-blessed dimension of the soul! The perfect environment, paternal, maternal, eternal! This is the home of the spirit. Realization, awareness, fields of joy, peace, love, and bliss are here. Ecstasy of being, knowing, and loving are yours to experience here. Exquisite emotions of oneness, where the "no thing" is lost in the "all thing" of oneness and union with God, are here for you to know. For love is of God and God is love. Love is the dwelling place of our essence.

Clusters of knowledge, like fruit, are ripe for picking. Living, green leaves are here for the healing of all. A sturdy trunk of awareness, serene and unshaken, manifests as the tree of love and life rooted in the consciousness supreme. This is the home of the soul. For love is the garden of life, and love is the home sweet home.

Oceans roll and break on every shore. Light reflects from every star. Eternal sunrise and sunset succeed each other in endless beginnings and endings of calmness, tranquility, peace, and promises are all fulfilled. Here, longings are all satisfied, tears of sadness are now diamond-jeweled in gladness on the upturned face of a child called Peace and Love. But always it is sunrise. Always it is a new day, a better day, a day of hope renewed and love made manifest. Here, a family called "our family" clasps hands around a hearthstone called Love.

❧ 765 ❧

FRUIT OF THE CORN BY CAROLINE SEYMOUR

November

9

SOLITUDE

Listen for it!
The startled, questioning cry
Of the marsh birds
That rise from the dark lake
    margin in fear,
Apprehensive, primeval,
While winging away!

Comfortless night!
These stygian shores deserted,
Profounder now,
Still fearful, uncertain
    and insecure—
Are in silence forsaken
While solitude reigns.

GRAY TABLEAU

Dull, gray sky;
Distant, snow-cloaked mountains
Lifted high;
Gray-tinged, purple foothills
Closer by;
Bald, brown knolls, white
Blanketed below;
Where nature's rugged patterns
Of rock and sage and snow,
Keep a winter tryst
In gray tableau.

BEAUTIFUL OCEAN

Beautiful, beautiful ocean,
    Roll up your waves of foam,
Like a permanent wave in curlers
    Some grandmother would do at home.

Beautiful, beautiful ocean,
    Your waves roll shoreward and spread,
Crested with the sheen of silver
    Like snow on a hoary head.

Beautiful, beautiful ocean,
    Your horizon of darker hue
Like a tint of steel-blue hair dye
    Looks soft where the light shines through.

Beautiful, beautiful ocean,
    Your streaming hair hides your face.
But I see where it flows over the boulders,
    Stalwart shoulders sculptured with grace.

Beautiful, beautiful ocean,
    My heart is enamored indeed,
I know you have many more lovers,
    But one wave is all that I need!

OPEN GATE BY CAROLINE SEYMOUR

PHARMACY BY GREG WALZ

November

10

Character is the grain of sand, or the wrought iron designs that action, interaction, providence, personal choice, morality and adversity have forged in the fires of fear and faith.

THE TIGER TWINS

There is an ionosphere resplendent with glory
    Where tiger-like "ions" are tied tail to tail.
Where interacting, interlocking duality poles
    Of unified divergency prevail.

They wrestle and claw and strive to survive
    And die to be reborn every minute.
But revival is reversal turning the tiger inside out,
    The *was* and the *will be* are both found within it.

So untie the tails of the tiger twins
    And you've unlocked the secrets of matter.
For cohesion and refraction are the twilight tiger twins
    From which all energial motion must scatter.

But who tied the tail of the tiger twins
    In interlocking catatonic interruption?
God tied the tails where interaction prevails
    So inertia would survive inner corruption.

The secret of power in the tiger's tail
    Is the mathematics of molecular action
The reversal pattern of interaction interrupted
    By the dualities of divided refraction.

(CONTINUED ON NEXT PAGE)

Oh sing the song of the tiger's tail
   And observe the clawing and the scratches.
As they hang on the clothesline axis of invisible poles
   While sparks and fur fly in interminable snatches.

For out of the invisible web and woof
   Of matter and its incessant reaction,
Comes unity in divergence and multiply manifest
   In the dualities of magnetic attraction.

The infusion and fusion of cosmic forces
   As it aborts thru dimension wall linings
Is distorted, aborted, divided, and thwarted
   And for perfections oneness goes repining.

It lives and feels, this cosmic force,
   It thinks, wills, and exchanges
Its identity and affection in marriage and divorce
   In innumerable matches it arranges.

Sing, sing me the song of the tiger's tail
   Interlocked in the inseparable fashion
And I'll sing the part of resolution and dissolution
   As revealed in the rhythmic sagation.

November

～ 11 ～

*Liberty is a glad word ringing like the pealing of a bell; and liberty is a sad word
that brave men in battle bled for where they fell.*

VETERAN'S DAY AND ARMISTICE DAY

World War I involved thirty-five countries. The war continued for five years, but the United States was only involved from 1917 to 1918. At the end of the war, several countries signed an armistice on the eleventh day of the eleventh month. This truce, or agreement, to stop all fighting was known as Veteran's Day. Over sixteen-and-a-half million Americans were involved in World War I and World War II, and 407,000 Americans died in that service. In many parts of the world, people would take two minutes for silence at 11 A.M. as a respectful remembrance for the roughly twenty million who died during World War I and World War II. The following is the history of Veteran's Day according to Watertown Historical Society.

1918

World War I, then normally referred to simply as The Great War (no one could imagine any war being greater!), ended with the implementation of an armistice [temporary cessation of hostilities—in this case, until the final peace treaty, the infamous Treaty of Versailles, was signed in 1919] between the Allies and Germany at the eleventh hour of the eleventh day of November 1918.

1919

November 11: President Wilson proclaims the first Armistice Day with the following words: "To us in America, the reflections of Armistice Day will be filled with solemn pride in the heroism of those who died in the country's service and with gratitude for the victory, both because of the thing from which it has freed us and because of the opportunity it has given America to show her sympathy with peace and justice in the councils of the nations . . ." The original concept for the celebration was for the suspension of business for a two-minute period beginning at 11 A.M., with the day also marked by parades and public meetings. The people of the city showed their respect for the heroes who have died by the many flags which were hung about the city.

～ 773 ～

1920

On the second anniversary of the armistice, France and the United Kingdom hold ceremonies honoring their unknown dead from the war. In America, at the suggestion of church groups, President Wilson names the Sunday nearest Armistice Day as Armistice Day Sunday, on which should be held services in the interest of international peace.

1921

Congress passes legislation approving the establishment of a Tomb of the Unknown Soldier in Arlington National Cemetery. November 11 is chosen for the date of the ceremony. On October 20, Congress declares November 11, 1921 a legal Federal holiday to honor all those who participated in the war. 1921—The Tomb of the Unknowns is dedicated by U.S. President Warren G. Harding at Arlington National Cemetery.

1926

Congress adopts a resolution directing the President to issue an annual proclamation calling on the observance of Armistice Day. Throughout the 1920s and 1930s, most states establish November 11 as a legal holiday, and at the Federal level, an annual proclamation is issued by the President.

1938

Congress passes legislation on May 13 making November 11 a legal Federal holiday, Armistice Day. The United States has no "actual" national holidays because the states retain the right to designate their own holidays.

1941-1945
1950-1953

World War II and the Korean War create millions of additional war veterans in addition to those of the First World War already honored by Armistice Day.

1954

On June 1, President Eisenhower signs legislation changing the name of the legal holiday from Armistice Day to Veteran's Day.

1968

Congress passes the Monday Holiday Law which establishes the fourth Monday in October as the new date for the observance of Veteran's Day. The law is to take effect in 1971.

774

1971-1975

The Federal observance of Veteran's Day is held on the fourth Monday of October. Initially, all states follow suit except Mississippi and South Dakota. Other states change their observances back to November 11 as follows: 1972—Louisiana and Wisconsin; 1974—Kentucky, Arkansas, Connecticut, Georgia, Maine, South Carolina, West Virginia; 1975—California, Florida, Idaho, Illinois, Iowa, Kansas, Missouri, Montana, Nebraska, New Hampshire, Oklahoma, Oregon, South Carolina, Utah, West Virginia, Wyoming.

1975

Legislation passes to return the Federal observance of Veteran's Day to November 11, based on popular support throughout the nation. Since the change to the fourth Monday in October, forty-six states had either continued to commemorate November 11 or had reverted back to the original date based on popular sentiment. The law was to take effect in 1978.

1978

Veteran's Day observance reverts to November 11.

Some Gave All and All Gave Some

THE FLAG OF THY PEACE

No peace by conquest ever came
    Tho' many have tried before.
The Caesars, Napoleon, and others all failed
    To bring oneness by methods of war.

And the only peace they ever brought
    Was silence and peace of the grave.
The peace of the dead and the crosses of white
    And the sorrow to mothers who gave.

Oh, God, may the peace of Armistice Day
    In truth encompass the world,
Till sorrow and dying and fighting are done
    And the flag of Thy peace is unfurled.

FOREST ESCAPE BY MARINA MIRKOVICH

November

12

Loyal service is royal service; for the loyal are the royal rulers in the kingdom of faithful service.
True worthiness is their crown and dependability their golden throne.

THE VIEWPOINT OF GOD

I float with the clouds in the distant sky.
I grow with the flowers on the hillsides nearby.
   I'm the fragrance of flowers in the gardens of earth.
   I'm the garden, the sunshine, and God giving birth.
I sway with the grasses under my feet.
I race with the cars that go down my street:
   For I am a part of it all.

I sway with the branches in every tree.
I laugh with the breeze, vagrant and free.
   I sing with each bird. I dip and I float.
   I'm a part of the song in each songster's throat.
I stand in each pine. I rest firm in each rock.
I roll in each river. Count time of each clock.
   For I am a part of it all.

I leap with the kitten wrapped up in the string.
I play with the children on trapeze and the swing.
   I race with the horses with wind in my face.
   I wait at the finish line and am first in the race.
I'm last and I'm first and I'm still in between.
I'm all that's visible and all that's unseen.
   For I'm more than a part of it all.

(CONTINUED ON NEXT PAGE)

I'm candle and holder and wick and the flame.
I'm divinity and humanity and God is my name.
   I'm creator of nature, stability, and form.
   I'm deviation, variety, the mean, and the norm.
I'm whatever I am and whatever I'm not.
I'm all things I remember and all things time forgot.
   I'm the unmanifest, all-knowing Unknown.

I'm the triunity of God and the angelic host.
I'm the farthest star of the outermost.
   I'm the answering awareness of the innermost part.
   I'm circumference and center and the love in God's heart.
I'm a part of God and He's all of me.
I'm the measure of time echoing eternity.
   I'm more than whatever I am.

I'm the viewer observing and the object observed.
I'm Providence preserving and the treasure preserved.
   With shifted awareness to the higher divine,
   I am all things and no thing and all things are mine.
For I am that I am, God-conscious, supreme.
For I'm what I am not and far more than I seem.
   For I am the viewpoint of God!

November

13

The past is gone; the future may or may not come; our only time to live, to learn, to love, or to labor is wrapped up in that fleeting thing called NOW!

MEDITATION PRAYER

Holy, Wise, and Revered is your name, Oh, God: For you are the governor of our finite world and you do so dwell forever beyond, yet in our little sphere of heartache, toil and pain. Our lot has been better than we deserve, our troubles less than well they might have been. Your blessings have been more at times than we could number. For this we give you thanks. When we were poor, you made provision to make us whole. When we were hurting and unlovely, you gave us life. Thank You. Amen.

MORE FULLY TO LIVE

Just a ghost of a house
   With the contents gone,
Just a shell of a house
   That still clings on.

Gone are the roses
   That bloomed at the door.
Gone are the faces
   As we knew them of yore.

Not gone from the heart
   Is the ache and the pain
Or the longing to see them
   And to hold them again.

(CONTINUED ON NEXT PAGE)

O God, roll the years
    And the losses away.
Let us live, and relive
    The events of each day.

Let us live. Let us love.
    Let us hold our joys fast.
Lest we lose them in days
    That soon will be past.

Lest too busy or unmindful
    Of things we possess,
We lose life in living
    And find we have less.

And value the water
    When our wells have gone dry,
Or fail to live life
    Till we're ready to die.

O God, fill up life's cup
    Till its fullness runs o'er.
We'll take time to savor it
    And flavor it more.

We'll love while we're loving.
    We'll listen and see.
We'll treasure life's pleasures
    Till life ceases to be.

Then when we come to saying
    That final goodbye,
If we really have lived,
    We'll be ready to die!

November

~ 14 ~

My influence is my shadow, line for line; the fault for what it blights or blesses, too, is mine.

WOMAN:
With Adam's rib, God mixed in earth the fragrance of flowers, the bitterness of herbs, the sweetness of wild honey, the stardust of dreams and fire, fashioned it in perfection, breathed on it with love, and waking Adam softly said, "This is woman!"

INSPIRATION

Without the voice of the poet
    Earth would seem quite bare.
Without the poet's emotion
    We'd have much less joy to share.

If poems are like our children
    They must not come forth stillborn,
But vie with the gamecock at dawning
    Who awakes to announce the morn!

Let's conceive these poem children
    And help deliver them, too,
For inspiration still is needed
    In a world with work to do!

UP THE MIFF TREE

There's a lot of monkey business
Up in the miff tree so I've heard.
In fact up in the branches
I've heard the mockingbird.

I've heard the hoot owl grumping
And he didn't give a hoot.
He didn't know just who was who
And didn't care to boot.

Some mighty fussy people
Are hanging from its limbs—
They committed verbal suicide.
They dangle neat and trim.

Other folks have fallen earthward
Who climbed out just too far
And sawed the limb off under them
While baying at some star.

Let's cut the miff tree, neighbor.
It's never safe to climb.
Let's climb the steps of faith and love
To safer heights sublime.

November

∾ 15 ∾

HEARTLAND WINTER BY GREG WALZ

LOVE

Love still keeps the world's heart throbbing,
    And love makes the little children grow.
Love is life and will and wisdom
    Reflecting heaven's radiant glow!

Love is all in all sufficient.
    Love is warming, winning, kind.
Love is quest and also questor,
    Effulgence of the soul and mind.

Love is like a purple sunset
    Burnished bright with clouds of gold.
Love is like a hearth fire burning,
    Self-consumed but dispelling cold.

Love is like the God eternal,
    For love is God, and God is love.
Gates of gold swing on its hinges
    Both on earth and in heaven above!

November

⁓ 16 ⁓

No one breathes earth's air in vain who brings a great thought into focus, and by it raises the intelligence quotient of humanity, and lays a foundation for the progress of posterity.

PROSE VERSUS POETRY AND "VICE-WORSER!"

The flower of fragrant thought seldom blooms other than in the fields of silence, quietness, and solitude.

Self-confidence, not self-sufficiency, holds hands with Divinity and walks fearlessly through the darkness to the light.

My influence is my shadow, line for line; the fault for what it blights or blesses, too, is mine.

Those who learn to observe intently wherever they are, need not travel so far or so fast to find something worthy of observation.

To waste the unwanted is sometimes wiser than to want the unwanted for the sake of unwise frugality. Remember the packrat.

PROGRESS

Once the strongest was king
In the days long gone,
   Way back when the world was new.
For fame or self
He elected himself
   To a place in the first "Who's Who!"

Then the stick and the stone
Were the tools of power—
   Status symbols of a vanished age—
And the muscles were best
That conquered the rest,
   Then the setting changed on the stage.

For man's muscles shriveled
And the stone ax fell
   And man looked up at the stars.
His muscle-bound brawn
Seemed wasted and gone
   With little left but his scars.

Then he found that his brain
Was strong and sharp
   So he whistled a different tune.
He plucked the stars
Through his prison bars
   And rode his stone ax to the moon!

November

~ 17 ~

The heady wine of criticism loosens the tongue, closes the mind, freezes the heart;
so don't drink the conceit of criticism.

THE PRAYING PERSON

Cease your pitiful, plaintive prayers,
    Your fretful and whining petitions.
Our God loves faith and confidence
    As much as true contrition.

Trade your weak tears for stronger ones
    Filled with the brine of insistence.
Ask for the best in the will of God
    With relentless, courageous persistence.

Raise prayers of purpose and of power
    That shake the skies' foundation.
The violent still are taking the Kingdom
    And winning God's approbation.

Such prayers will pull God's heaven near
    And all the angels circling round
Will wait with joy the answers won
    If ever such praying persons are found!

CRITIC, DON'T BE A CRITIC

Self-styled critic, I love you,
    In spite of my tempted disdain.
I love you, and I even listen
    To your observations in the main.

But can you rightly tell me
    Just who you really are?
You can't tell me who I am either
    Not knowing, you'd miss it far.

You're still looking at prizes
    That I've lost or haven't won.
You see the wheat hulls only,
    Not brown loaves when baking's done.

A critic's job is a part-time one
    With only part-time facts at hand.
The critics die before the rest of us
    Have reached our promised land.

November

~ 18 ~

Gratefulness is the coin of courtesy; and they are bankrupt indeed
who neglect to pay their debts of gratitude.

MEDITATION PRAYER

Thank you, Oh God. You have allowed us our days to labor in and our nights for rest and well-earned repose. Grant that again this day from its dawning till the sun goes down may be successfully lived as one day that is acceptable within your plan. May the nightfall find us unashamed of this day's activities. Permit no selfishness to allure us, no misfortune to overtake us, and no folly to ruin us. But may the protection of your paternal care and concern be ours through all our days and all our nights. Thank you from my heart. Amen.

THANKSGIVING, FAITH, AND ACTION

How do we recognize thankful faith in action? Have you ever observed this type of faith? Do you practice this thanksgiving? There are as many different ways to express thankful faith as there are individual believers. Here is a description for at least one pictorial involvement with a responsive, thankful faith at work!

Grateful faith wears a choir robe and has a hymnbook in its hand. There's a song of praise on faith's lips, and the light of another world reflects on its shining face. Its eyes are fixed on the far stars of constancy and hope. This is faith. Faith has a wholesome, sincere countenance, a fresh-washed, ruddy glow of inner strength and vibrant soul health.

Faith looks equally well in working clothes as it does in choir robes. And it sings more beautifully in overalls and heavy shoes with sweat in its eyes than it does with satin slippers and Sabbath day's flowing robes. Faith at heart is a workingman who can rest in good conscience when the work is done. Can you relate to such a heartfelt involvement? Join me in reading the PRAYER OF GRATITUDE on the next page. Giving thanks is so positive. Purposefully be positive today!

A PRAYER OF GRATITUDE

Great God, Thou hast given us
The good earth to live on—
    Warmed by the sun and wet
    with the rain.
Great God, Thou hast given us
Gardens and orchards
    And fields that are ripened
    with grain.

For seedtime and harvest,
For grass for our cattle,
    For springtime and winter
    and freedom from pain;
For dew in the morning,
And strength for our labor,
    Great God, we pause to thank
    Thee again.

Grant us, we pray Thee,
A heart that's wide open,
    Filled with the warmth of
    the beauty of love.
Forbid that our souls
Should be blinded or narrow.
    Teach us the secret of
    looking above.

Forbid that our passions
Should darken our vision
    Lest heedless and sightless
    we go on our way.
But open our eyes
To Thy goodness and greatness,
    And may we be grateful from
    day unto day.

November

19

SONG OF THE SEA BY CAROLINE SEYMOUR

PACIFIC THERAPY

Men have called it the "Pacific"
   Though it isn't always so
When it's lashed by furious tempests
   Where the mighty tradewinds blow.

But there's a therapy of patience
   Like the solace of a prayer
In that ocean of benignity
   With a dash of silver in her hair.

She helps express the urges
   And the surges of the soul.
She brings release and inner peace
   With her calliope rock and roll.

There's a vast amount of H_2O
   In the fathomless ocean's deep
That rises over thirsty lands
   To fall where grey clouds weep.

There's a therapy of cleansing
   In the patter of her rain,
A murmur of contentment
   And release from inner pain.

But the therapy specifically
   That I really like the best,
Is when the "sleeping beauty" ocean
   Lies without tumult in her breast!

November

∽ 20 ∽

*Gratitude is an attitude that tunes the human heart
to the vibrations of harmony divine.*

GRATEFULNESS

Gratitude is the climate in which faith grows. Thankfulness is the automatic transmission that puts the heart into the right gear of faith for either the quick takeoff, the long, hard pull, or the burn of speeding wheels on the highway to the desired destination. Thankfulness meshes gears with the past through grateful memories of the Creator God's abounding mercies and repeats again its song of golden praise.

Thankfulness shifts the attention to current courses of gratefulness and tries with every singing bird in voicing its melodious music of heartfelt appreciation. Thankfulness, having practiced on the keyboards of yesterday and today, slips so easily into gratefulness for anticipated gifts of tomorrow. This is faith! For faith is a confident, expectant, sure-fingered, happy concert organist weaving a glad melody of thoughtful assurance for days to come. It is singing tomorrow's song of victory, today.

Faith plays confidently tomorrow's prayer songs in a major key. When the soul can, as naturally and as easily, thank God for blessings expected in the future as it can thank Him for the benefits of yesterday, then that heart has found the way of faith through gratitude.

When you can sing the doxology in the key of "F-Future" with the same jubilant, "I have, that's what I have," kind of thankful assurance, you know that your prayer and praise have moved from minor to major keys, and your spiritual gears are meshing with the faith-conceived reality of things that soon shall be. Gratitude is the only native climate that guarantees to produce luxuriant, blooming flowers of fragrant faith. God appreciates worship and gratitude. Our fellow pilgrims as well as our family members appreciate consideration and gratitude. Today, demonstrate your love and thankfulness.

THINKING THANKSGIVING

If we think, of course, we'll thank
The God in heaven above,
For temporal benefits of life;
For health and home and love.

Goodness, kindness, songs of hope.
"And more!" Our lips proclaim,
"The sun, the rain, the harvest time."
Oh, think, then praise His name.

And has He ever failed you once
In bringing soul relief?
Oh, count your blessings! Do they not
Far outweigh your grief?

Think, oh think! And then give thanks,
On each Thanksgiving Day,
To One whose blessings, undeserved,
Were yours along the way.

MEDITATION PRAYER

Your mercies of this day, Oh, God, have been so great, as have the mercies of the night with your continual watch care. For the tranquil rest and trust that come from our spiritual relationship with you, I offer up to you my thanks. Surround us with the brightness of your love. Build a bridge across every chasm of difficulty as you stimulate our vision and our courage to leap if faith does so necessitate. Continue to surround us with your creative presence. With the light of your love, dispel all of our darkness; kiss away the tears of our temporary defeat. Teach us that your love is our hope for success and supreme living. On this Thanksgiving Day, I thank you. Amen.

November

~ 21 ~

*Gratitude is the gateway to God, the door to gratuities, and the most gracious gift
that the grateful can give in return.*

GRANT ME WISDOM TO CHOOSE

Grant me, Oh God Omnipotent,
    The power of illumined sight
That I may always know and choose
    Between wrong and eternal right.

Grant me, Oh God Omnipotent,
    The power to stand apart and see
That my bones and blood and daily bread
    Are but a temporal part of me!

May I envision all my separate bones
    Like jumbled white logs on time's shore.
May I see them as when finally laid aside
    When I shall need these bones no more.

Grant me, Oh God Benevolent,
    The sacrificial love to freely give
All things that for a while I claim my own
    That I may thus in dying, learn to live.

Grant me, Oh God Transcendent,
    The power to stand afar and know
That I shall leave sometime forever
    All the earthly, sense-felt things below.

Grant me, Oh God Eternal,
    The power to now forever choose
All things divine, eternal and unending
    That I may be rich in things I cannot lose!

GIVE TO OVERCOME

Hidden hungers in loveless hearts
 Grow with inner pain.
Like parched ground, cracked and hard
 They hunger for love's soft rain.

The cry of essential identity,
 Need to relate with others as one,
Surges as deep as instinctive pulse
 And beats on till life is done.

Hidden hungers for words of praise,
 To be held worthwhile by some,
Are a vital part of every heart
 But we must give to overcome!

November

~ 22 ~

*Adversity looks like the end of the road, but just around the bend, the fruit of adversity
hangs ripe on every tree. Stay until you can see around the corner.*

A bee will find some honey in a poison flower; so man may wrest some good from evil's power.

The Bells of Memory ringing clear oft hurt the heart but not the ear.

*Degenerate civilization is little more than informed savagery; and without true piety,
civilization is simply heathenism spelled in neon signs!*

*The clock hands only point the hours and hide the face in shame,
devoid of other active powers for works of praise or blame.*

CAISSON

Caisson, Caisson,
With six white horses drawn
And a riderless horse behind.

With the church bells mutely tolling
And the drums with their muffled beat
The funeral Caisson moves slowly
Down the Capitol's sorrow-thronged street.
With the leaders of earth assembled,
The nations have forgotten their mirth,
As a world in grief pays tribute
To a man who has proved his worth.

Caisson, Caisson,
With six white horses drawn
And a riderless horse behind.

(CONTINUED ON NEXT PAGE)

Sad day when the murderous hunter
Stalked unsuspected his noble prey.
Sad day in the streets of Dallas
When our Leader lay cold and grey.
Bereavement, heartache, and sorrow
Cast over the nation its shroud.
While children and men and women
Unashamed, lamented aloud.

Caisson, Caisson,
With six white horses drawn
And a riderless horse behind.

With requiem masses over,
And the solemn prayers for the dead
Silently moved the white horses,
As softly our tears were shed.
Courageous widow and children
Now walk alone with their dead,
For long is the road of heartbreak
And numberless the days ahead.

Caisson, Caisson,
With six white horses drawn
And a riderless horse behind.

The pages of history are groaning
At the weight of the story they hold;
While America looks to the future
To see what its pages unfold.
New hands on the reins of the nation,
A new rider in the saddle of state,
We face the world undaunted;
America will always be great!

Move on, Move on!
We ride toward the dawn
With no riderless horse behind.

November

∽ 23 ∽

ORANGE PEKOE BY JESSICA HENRY DAVIS

WHAT IS A FRIEND?

What is a friend? I hear you say.
The answer is: One with a friendly way
   Who helps you bear life's burden.

A friend in one who, when in grief,
Will bring the balm of calm relief
   And help you bear your burden.

A friend will see your jumbled plans
And stoop to help with gentle hands,
   For he understands your burdens.

A friend will thru tomorrows walk
And comfort you with love's small talk
   While he helps you with your burdens.

He offers you a listening heart.
He is love's happy counterpart,
   For he, too, has had his burdens.

Each friend is a link in the chain of life, and the person who
loses a link loses part of this life.

November

24

A hanging man's hope is in a breaking rope; for even a rope doesn't hold much hope when you're hanging by your neck and not by your hands.

ACTIVE HOPE

Hope without foundation in fact or faith leaves only the false bottom of delusion on which to stand.

Hope is a banker in the business of loaning confidence to the cautious and courage to cowards.

Hope is Hercules holding up the world while Atlas rubs his aching back.

Hope has calloused hands that labor while it waits.

Excessive hope is best counterbalanced by caution, but not capsized by fear.

Hope must awaken the will to work and the resolution to recover from reverses.

Hope, like bread, is the staff of life, but, alas, it's not always buttered!

HOPE

Hope is a candle half snuffed by the breeze.
Hope is an old man on rheumatic knees.

Hope is a child half well, half sick.
Hope is life's mainspring that makes us tick.

Hope is a mask that hides tears of despair.
Hope is a ribbon in a bald man's hair.

Hope is a Band-Aid on the cancerous spot.
Hope is a lot of things that hope is not!

MISTY MOUNTAIN STREAM BY EVERETT SPENCER

November

25

LOVE'S TENDER EMBRACE

The autumn leaves fall,
    Harvest's spawned afterbirth.
They cover old ground scars
    Making velvet soft earth,
Reminders of summertime's mirth.

The trees scrape the house
    Through the cold midnight rain
While weeping and tapping
    On the cracked windowpane,
Splattered rivulets of longing pain.

If only the rain
    Were your tears on my face,
Or your subtle, soft handclasp
    Near some sweet trysting place,
To know love's oblivious embrace.

Now empty the bed
    And how cold is each sheet.
How empty my arms are
    And how restless my feet.
Can you hear as your name I repeat?

But springtime will come
    When I see your sweet face;
And roses will be blooming
    All over the place.
Then I'll rest in love's embrace.

PINECONES BY CAROLINE SEYMOUR

November

26

Foresight and insight rather than hindsight are the binoculars for spotting an opportunity while it is still coming our way.

CLOSE TO HIM

The longing of the soul for God,
The heartfelt hunger cry,
No intermittent fellowship
Can ever satisfy.

Habitual contemplation
Of the things of God each hour
Will fill the hungry heart and mind
With grace and peace and power.

The closeness that is constant,
The blessings that abide,
Are only known to those who come
And tarry at His side!

YESTERDAY'S ASHES ARE WARM TODAY

To trace my footstep's weary way
Back to the paths of yesterday,
    To drink from the dipper at memory's well,
    To relive the tales my tongue could tell,
Would this be yesterday?

To soothe the longings of inward pain,
To trade the husks of earthly gain,
    To hold the ones I loved before,
    To enter the past thru a time-locked door,
Would this be yesterday?

On a mother's breast to cushion my head,
To sleep again in a childhood bed,
    To walk barefoot in the dust again,
    To be a boy and not a man,
Would this be yesterday?

Yesterday, your wine is gone.
Your bottle is empty and the winds moan on.
    The clouds are gone that cooled your sky
    And salty tears half blind the eye,
In memory of yesterday.

For yesterday's hours forever are fled.
Yesterday's hopes are buried and dead.
    And yesterday's places are far away.
    The past has come and gone to stay.
But yesterday's ashes are warm today!

November

~ 27 ~

Why do we read the epitaphs on yesterday's tombstone of memory or dig up the bones of past failure? Best to leave yesterday's shadows behind, and work in the sunlight of today's hopes and tomorrow's sure expectations.

PLEASE HEAR WHAT I AM NOT SAYING

Don't be fooled by me.
Don't be fooled by the face I wear.
For I wear a mask. I wear a thousand masks.
Masks that I'm *afraid* to take off,
and none of them are me.
Pretending is an art that is second nature to me,
but don't be fooled, for God's sake don't be fooled.
I give you the impression that I'm secure,
that all is sunny and unruffled with me,
within as well as without,
that confidence is my name and coolness my game,
and that I need no one,
But don't believe me.
Please.

My surface may seem smooth, but my surface is my mask,
My ever-varying and ever-concealing mask.
Beneath lies no smugness, no complacence,
Beneath dwells the real Me in confusion, in fear, in aloneness,
But I hide this.
I don't want anyone to know this.
I panic at the thought of my weakness and fear of being exposed.
That's why I frantically create a mask to hide behind,
to shield me from the glance that knows.
But such a glance is precisely my salvation. My only salvation.
And I know it.

(CONTINUED ON NEXT PAGE)

That is if it is followed by acceptance, if it is followed by love.
It's the only thing that can liberate me from myself,
from the barriers that I so painstakingly erect.
It's the only thing that will assure me of what I can't assure myself of—
that I'm really worth something.

But I don't tell you this. I don't dare; I'm afraid, too.
I'm afraid your glance will not be followed by love and acceptance.
I'm afraid you will think less of me, that you will laugh,
and your laugh will kill me.
I'm afraid deep down that I'm nothing; that I'm just no good;
and that you will see this and reject me.
So I play my game, my desperate pretending game,
with a façade of assurance without, and a trembling child within.
And so begins the parade of masks,
the glittering, but empty parade of masks,
and my life becomes a front.
I idly chatter to you in suave tones of surface talk.
I tell you everything that's really nothing,
and nothing of what's everything. Of what's crying within me.

So when I'm going through my routine, do not be fooled by what
I'm saying.
Please listen carefully and try to hear what I'm *not* saying,
what I'd *like* to say, what, for survival, I *need* to say,
but what I *can't* say.
I dislike hiding. Honestly.
I dislike the superficial game I'm playing, the superficial, phony
game. I'd really like to be genuine and spontaneous, and me.
But you've got to help me.

You've got to hold out your hand,
even though this is the last thing I seem to want or need.
Only you can call me into aliveness,
Each time you're kind, gentle, and encouraging.
Each time you try to understand because you really care,
my heart begins to grow wings, very small wings, very feeble wings,
but wings.

With your sensitivity and sympathy, and your power of understanding,
you can breathe life into me. I want you to know that.

(CONTINUED ON NEXT PAGE)

I want you to know how important you are to me, how you can be
creator of the person that is me, if you choose to.
Please choose to.

You alone can break down the wall behind which I tremble.
You alone can remove my masks.
You alone can release me from the shadow world of panic and
uncertainty, from my lonely prison.

So do not pass me by. Please do not pass me by.
It will not be easy for you.
A long conviction of worthlessness builds strong walls.
The nearer you approach me, the blinder I may strike back.
It's irrational, but despite what the books say about man,
I am irrational.

I fight against the very thing I cry out for. But I am told
that love is stronger than walls, and in this lies my hope.
My only hope.
Please try to beat down these walls with firm hands
but with gentle hands . . . for a child is very sensitive.
I am someone you know very well.
I am every person sitting here in this room.

AFTERNOON STORM BY JIM FINGER

November

∽ 28 ∽

FAIRY IN THE JAR BY BRUCE EAGLE

Impossibility is an unthinkable word that challenges divine creativity and stirs the blood of courageous persons to action.

INSPIRATION FOR LIVING
(CREATIVE VISUALIZATION)

Resting comfortably, relaxing completely, visualizing clearly and distinctly in color and in action, open your heart and mind to listen and receive the inspiration and the instruction on self-improvement and profit by it. Listen to the music and become a part of the emotional essence of it all as we go deeply within ourselves to program ourselves for progress.

To stand on some high pinnacle of inspiration, to rise over difficulties, to climb, to achieve, to make self-improvement—these are the challenges of life and the privileges of man. Conquest is the most basic note and truest harmony of all man's source. Man's words are but the symbols of his feelings. They contain the mental images that he perceives and conceives. Picturization precedes language verbalization. Pictures are the basic language of thought in any language. It is basic talking to ourselves using pictures. Pictures are the blueprint for action and attraction used by the creative, inner mind to materialize our desires.

What is inspiration for living? Inspiration is enthusiasm. It is the awakening of awareness to the Ultimate Reality of the Creator within us. It is more than a soda mint of rationalization to relieve what you can't stomach of life's smorgasbord of indigestibles. It is more than the Alka-Seltzer effervescence of a false optimism that promises to cure a sour mind or take the weight off of your fallen arches. Inspiration for living goes deeper than nostrums, Band-Aids, and campaign buttons.

Real inspiration for living is the upsurging joy of the healthy spirit and the quickened flesh. It is the zest of total well-being in body, mind and spirit. It is the true secret of success. It is the emotional lubricant that makes planned effort flow smoothly and almost effortlessly in the right direction. It is life's battle strategy, ground support and air supremacy. It's the soldier's battle cry before the battle is won. It's the pilgrim's song of determined conquest before he climbs the last grey hill and sees the sunrise of hope spread across all of his tomorrows!

Inspiration for living is the reverberating overtones of the warm, integrate, forward-moving individual who has opened his inner being to the unity and rhythmic flow of the whole spiritual universe, which has its own hidden laws of being, measure, meaning and purpose. Inspiration for living is the river flowing through the gates of the dam to turn the wheels and dynamos of all practicality. It is the lifeblood of being. It throbs and pulses in zestful living. It laughs in recreation and play. It works long hours that seem but minutes in its self-forgetful absorption of self-expression and creativity. It is the essence of life, the heartthrob of achievement. It is lifeblood free from the virus of negativity as it stirs the limbs to action, the mind to mentation and the spirit to realization. It is like the pounding of the surf playing and working away at the ocean shores of all activity.

Inspiration for living is a glad song of summer, the expectant song of spring, the fulfillment song of autumn and wintertime, when frost and snow blanket the ground and cover old scars with the promise of rejuvenation and resurrection after the earth rests a bit and regroups its energies for project survival and success! It is a song that sings the harmony of universal things. Inspiration for living is the strength of the draft horse with his sweating shoulders against the cold collar. It is the feeling of unbeatable drive in the piston-like propulsion of the racehorse with the wind in its mane and its heart bursting with the joy of competition and the prospect of being first across the finish line.

Inspiration for living is the foe of mediocrity, the sister of creativity, the fortification against failure and the commonsense consummation of practicality that makes alibis unnecessary and excuses irrelevant. It is the subconscious feeling of intuitive victory that the cyclist feels when he and his motorcycle are one unit cornering the track and stretching out for the straightaway on the final lap. It is a singleness of purpose born of the uncluttered mind whose sense of direction is accurate and whose detachment from the unnecessary and the secondary has been completed.

Inspiration for living is the whir of rising wings when forward thrust overcomes resistance, where lift laughs at gravity and lofty levitation of inner being changes the entire perspective of life. It is jubilant sublimation, envisioned expectation and remembered consummation. It is the eagle's-eye viewpoint of purposeful optimism, the vantage point of self-confident, God-confident, life-confident assurance of the individual who expects the cooperation of a compatible universe. It is identifying oneness with that universe which gives back its uncontestable and sufficient support at each point of manifestation.

It is the warm, anticipated handclasp of congratulation, pride of participation, the dependability of teamwork and the overflow of released life forces that rise resistless and beautiful to make the desert places blossom with the verdant fruit and foliage of manifest achievement. Inspiration for living is life itself, turned on, turned loose and turned into the corrugations of irrigation ditches of all infertility; and where inspiration for living flows, there an oasis points its palm trees heavenward and its palm roots earthward to drink the nourishment of its underground rivers and living vital force and subterranean supply.

Inspiration for living is love of life, the joy of self-expression, the song of unselfish service, and the action of achieving faith. It is the spark of genius, the unconquerable spirit of adventure in the pulsing blood of the sturdy pioneer. It is sincerity, earnestness, dynamic drive and the cadence of conquest!

Now, in your mind and heart, be very, very thankful that this is true, and it will be more so as the days come and go. Get ready to come up to activity level. Open your eyes, please. Take a deep breath. You are wide awake, alert, happy, healthy and ready to face life courageously. Everyone stand, please. Stretch a little. Thank you for listening!

THE CHURCHYARD OF THE SEA

The ghosts of all the sailors
　　Who never came back to land
Ride each wave in thunderous grief.
They moan and sigh for some relief
　　And stretch their length on the sand.

The ghosts of all the sailors,
　　The pirates and buccaneers,
Who fought for spoils and finally died
Expire again on every tide
　　Smothered by ancient fears.

The ghosts of all of the sailors
　　Rollick in friendly glee,
Skipping from frosty, crested waves,
Are free yet chained to their mobile graves
　　In the Churchyard of the Sea.

November
～ 29 ～

MATING SEASON BY JORGE R. ARAUJO

INCOMPLETENESS

Burning and fierce is my desire
Flamed from out of love's pure fire.

Drizzle of darkness, monotonous rain,
Great empty spaces silent with pain.

Empty the bed; uncrumple the pillow
Like the sea without a billow.

Incomplete feeling; awareness of lack;
Nothing can fill it till you come back!

STAND FACING THE LIGHT

Always stand facing the light—
   That light is the light of love.
Always stand tall in the presence
   Of sunlight filtering from above.

Always stand facing the good.
   The highest good is always love.
Love for God, for others and self,
   An olive branch held by the Dove.

November

∽ 30 ∽

SWAN PAIR BY CLANCY CHERRY

∽ 817 ∽

Wisdom is the prize that fools never gain and the price that the indolent never pay.

THE CREATOR OF LOVE
(CREATIVE VISUALIZATION)

Sitting comfortably, so there'll be no need for body movement, heads either up or down with your eyes closed gently, let the feeling of relaxation spread over your forehead, around your ears, up and down your back, and over your shoulders. Let your arms relax quietly. Listen to the music. Pick up the restful, rocking, rhythmic musical sound. Check back over your body again. Know that as we go deeper in our relaxation, we will relax completely, not only in the physical voluntary muscles but in all of the internal, involuntary muscles as well, for this comes automatically as we begin to visualize vividly, clearly, in color and in action! You have permission to add to it, to subtract from it, to make it more beautiful or more meaningful, or to put more color or action in it as we go along.

Love cannot be isolated, nor can man be inoculated with the essence of it, for love is the universe in action and man can only relate to its vibrations and rhythms in order to radiate its attractions and be unified by its magnetism. Let those who have written with a pen of hate in the book and tears of humanity learn to write with a flow of light, with the pen of peace in the steady hand of love, for this writing all the world can read.

It is our love in which all cohesion functions, and it is out of the rhythms of perfection, love and balance that our nature expresses and sustains itself in many little ways. The Creator is the one true lover of the soul, the great lover, and the one true lover of the universe of His manifesting. The Creator serenades all creation with the harmonics and the rhythms of its own accord. He serenades the stars with the songs of His love, and the stars re-echo His praise. All nature reverberates to the theme of this love. The morning stars still sing together and the voices of the night rise in joyous praise. Every atom has its tune, just as every bird has its song. It is the symphony of the Creator's own integrated body parts, the music of the universe and the music of the spheres. This music rolls in the oceans and drums against its shores. Its notes dance in light reflections across its endless waves. This love laughs in the winds that sway the fragrant flowers. This love smiles in the sun that melts the winter snow. This love caresses the earth in the rain. The thirsting earth distills itself in dew and runs laughing down the hillsides in rivers of ecstatic glee. Nature sings and nature laughs, and its laughter is the sound of joy and the gladness of love. Its notes of love are the sound and light energies emerging from the expansive, creative heart of the Creator who ventures out into the rhythm of the varied self-expressions of individuality, multiplicity and variety, which are all bound together in the harmonics of the one song of love. Its notes are notes of light; its bars and staffs are bars and staffs of light. It s chords are chords of light. The whole universe speaks only the language of light and the language of love.

Only errant man, who has lost his togetherness, insists on singing false notes, adding false chords and rhythms that are inconsistent with the oneness of the whole. But when man's inner sight is opened, he sees anew how to read the music of the universe, the music of light and the music of love. When mortal ears are opened, man becomes aware of the comparison of his own discordant sounds with the intricate harmonies and cadences of the music of love and light. When his sense of touch and feeling are activated, stimulated, purified and sublimated, his fingers sense where to produce the notes, and intuitively he plays by ear the same song that angels sing—the rhythmic, harmonic, beautiful, melodious song of the Creator. In the beauty of color and in the language of light, and in the rhythms of ecstatic cadences, the Creator writes His love across the sky, paints His canvasses in the sunrise and in the sunset, and whispers in the winds through the tall trees. He whispers words of love and words of light bathed in incredible colors and sounds. The Creator is love!

The man who subdues and relaxes the Beta brain-wave levels of mind activity and progresses on into increasing quietude, or the Alpha-Theta level, and who adds to this the higher, ecstatic increase of the emotional activity of a spiritual nature, is able to enter into the source of beauty, of truth, of love, of peace, of wisdom, of light, and of Life itself. This occurs even as this individual lowers his sensory awareness and quiets the activity of the electrical brain machine. He who has found the quiet place has found the true dwelling place of the Creator. The place of contemplation is the secret place. All have been invited to the banquet and to abide in the house of the Creator, but all too few have accepted the invitation, being unable to separate themselves from the sensory clamor of the deceptive but noisy dream that life is in its discords and not in its silences.

The place of inspiration is the place of light. He who is carried on the wings of inspiration, whether in art, music, or writing, is carried on the wings of the Creator, and they are the wings of light. The elevated state of calm ecstasy and the holy, lifting, inner joy is the atmosphere of the creativity of man, for it is the atmosphere and environment of the Creator. The ecstasy of creativity and the uplift of inspiration are the dwelling place. Here the balance of truth, the cadences and rhythms of beauty, the intuitive knowledge of form, and the radiance of ineffable light teach man the art of self-expression. The man who sees through the viewpoint of the Creator and who sees things in balance and in proper perspective has a cause for joy and unfathomable gladness. Those who would create with balance and beauty in whatever form of art or expression must first learn to listen to the rhythm of the universe. They must tune their heartbeat to the pulse of omnipotent love, where out of its cadences come the structured rhythm of perfection, of beauty and of art. If he cannot at first find these within himself, let him walk through the forests where the wind blows through the pines. Let him lie upon the beaches of the ocean and feel its pulse and hear its roar and see its spray dashed upon every shore. Let him listen to the songs of birds. Let him feel the rain upon his face, caressing his skin. Let him feel the warmth of the moonlight, the cool shadows of the night, and the radiance of the sun. Let him feel the solidarity of rocks and the life and nerve pulses of the lesser creatures of field and forest. Let him love man, let him love nature, let him love the Creator. Out of the sensitivity of his inner caring and the quieting of his own vibrations will come the rhythm of the universe, which is the pulse of the balance, being, beauty and love of Him who is all and in all.

The driving whiplash of poverty or over-attentiveness to the possession and preservation of riches can in either case be sufficient inducement to wean the soul away for the contemplation of the beautiful, the true, the positive, the loving and the good. Yet a man can, in his enslavement to poverty or in his enslavement to riches, let either or both become the awakened cause of turning his vision inward toward the light. To know intuitively is a step beyond proceeding sensorially.

The Creator is love pouring itself in splendor through all the forms of its self-expression. The candle holder of man's body and mind needs the candle of the high self aglow with the light of the Creator's light.

Remember, each day you will look forward to your sessions on self-improvement and relaxed learning. Each time it will become easier to do, and you will, little by little, more and more each day, become the wonderful person in reality that you already potentially are.

Wide awake now, feeling better, more rested and peaceful than you ever have before. Thank you for listening.

BLOW, STORM, BLOW

Huff and puff and blow, old storm
   Like the wolf in the fairy tale.
When your breath is spent my house will stand
   Clean washed by wind and hail.

Your strong winds tug at the corner posts.
They pry the shingle edges.
Like a frantic gardener you sweep the leaves
   From the lawn and autumn hedges.

You swirl and cry with sad lament
   As moaning you finally depart.
Not knowing you carried a load of grief
   From my world-weary, cluttered heart!

MOUNTAIN MAN BY BOB ERWIN

A LETTER FOR YOU BY CAROLINE SEYMOUR

December

~ 1 ~

Mindfulness, without fanfare, is more impressive and is accepted with the greatest appreciation because its motives are the most sincere.

THE KINDNESS OF GOD

God is the Artist and Sculptor,
Painter and Gardener
too.
Architect, Builder of Mountains,
Arranger of Clouds in the
blue.

Botanist, Lover of flowers,
Master of Fashions is
He,
Designing the clouds into landscapes,
Carving the cliffs by the
sea.

Lover of all that is living,
His watch care is tender and
true.
Keeper of birds and of wildlife—
The whole wide world is His
zoo.

Crowning the works of creation
Came men when all else was
done.
On him God lavishes kindness,
From dawn's break till setting
sun.

JANE DOE BY GREG WALZ

December

2

Do you believe in your own dependability, strength of purpose, and power of performance?
If you do, others will soon!

THIS IS FAITH

Can you smell tomorrow's roses
    In full bloom?
Can you smell their fragrance
    In an empty room?
This is faith.

Can you see tomorrow's pathway
    In the dark?
Can you build a glowing fire
    From hope's small spark?
This is faith.

Can you see tomorrow's promise
    Here and now?
Can you see its glad fulfillment
    Tho you can't see how?
This is faith.

Can you feel a gratitude that's
    Full and deep?
Can you smile and still be glad
    When you could weep?
This is faith.

Can you commit to Him what you
    Have fought for and won?
Can you trust in God and say,
    "Thy will be done"?
This is faith.

PINE TREES

There's something about a pine tree,
    Rugged, straight, and tall,
That turns my heart clean inside out—
    Determined to give my all.
Couldn't tell you why, friend,
    Except that life's like that.
And when I see a strong pine tree
    I'll stand and lift my hat.

On barren mountain hillsides,
    Gnarled roots and rocks,
Long years of storm and tests,
    Strength for every shock!
A thousand bitter winters;
    Frost and sleet and snow,
That alternate till springtime's
    Gentler breezes blow.

While every sturdy limb holds
    Its banner to the sky!
It stands an exclamation point
    That does not question why.
Its feet are planted firm-like;
    Its roots are buried deep;
A stalwart tree that challenged me
    To stand tho tempests sweep!

Beneath whose mighty shelter
    Some mighty cabin hides;
A place of rest while storms molest
    And suns in darkness hide.
O, God, you need some pine trees,
    Firm and straight and tall,
To be a covert in the storm—
    A shelter over all.

December

~ 3 ~

Happiness and helpfulness are Siamese twins; both of them come when the other is called.

THE CREATOR'S GREATNESS

Thy summer coat is of meadow green
With forests and rivers woven between.

Thy steps could span from pole to pole
As you walk thru space where planets roll.

The bluest blue of the bluest skies
But reflects the blue of omniscient eyes.

No bed could hold Thy formless form.
No evil powers could work Thee harm.

For Thou art God supremely great,
Author of life and death and fate.

Thy nature is the fire of consuming love
Beneath, within, around, above.

From Thy radiant person powers flow
As the garments of God to the earth below.

It is from Thy power that all things are
From the tiniest flower to the distant star.

For Thou art here and Thou art there,
Thus readily perceived by man in answered prayer.

We fellowship in communion blest
And in Thy greatness we find our rest.

THERE IS MUSIC IN THE WORLD TODAY

There is music in the sky above;
Yes, music in the air;
There's music in the hearts of men;
There's music everywhere.

The music of the singing birds:
The warbling full and sweet
Of happy-throated choristers
That makes the day replete.

There's music in the rippling
Brook that flows along;
There's music in the treetops,
The soft wind's soughing song.

There's music in the harmony
Of colors, shade and life;
There's music in the world today
That swells above the strife.

There's music in the hearts of men
Who sing redemption's song;
There's music in the hearts of all
Who triumph over wrong!

December

4

Dream your dreams of achievement,
but dream that you are working when you awake.

THE WINGS OF THE WIND

The wings of the wind? Who sees them?
 I have felt their swift passing by.
Like a giant bird flown from heaven,
 I have heard their jubilant cry.

I have heard their cry at nighttime,
 Mourning like someone bereft.
Whispering sighs they have passed me.
 Answering, I found they had left.

Wings of the wind, how they rustle!
 Fanning my face with their breeze.
Wings of the wind's angry buzzing
 Like the hum of wild, swarming bees.

Wings of the wind like some angel
 Have brushed me in passing by.
Oh, wings of the wind sent from heaven
 Drive the dark clouds from the sky.

Wings of the wind, how symbolic!
 Portraying God's Spirit Divine,
Come fill my heart with Thy Presence
 And touch Thou this spirit of mine.

RIGHT SOLUTIONS

The power to recognize the right,
  In solution or action given,
Is a bit of wisdom, God-inspired,
  Coming directly down from heaven.

The world is full of problems, sure,
  But not so full of answers.
It may seem to have more undertakers
  Than lighthearted, joyful dancers.

But be it as it may or is,
  The solution is forthcoming.
There's always a proper monkey wrench
  Somewhere to fix the plumbing.

So face the problem, analyze!
  Life has powers of right attraction.
And when the answer comes to mind
  Be sure to go into action!

BEDDED DOWN BY SHAWN SWAIN

RAGTIME BY CAROLINE SEYMOUR

December

5

Lips cautiously say with kisses
what the heart lacked courage to tell.

ALL THAT YOU HAVE IS MINE

The energy of love from hand to hand,
  From eye to eye flows kindly.
To touch your cheek releases pain
  Of love's tension that gropes blindly.

The warmth of your flesh invigorates
  And madly quickens now my will to live.
The wine of your laughter intoxicates me;
  Inspiring love's instinct still to give.

Perfection's lines formed by your body,
  No artist ever could outline.
Your smiling lips spell out the words intently;
  All I have is yours, and you are mine!

ESSAI BY CAROLINE SEYMOUR

December

6

*Conditions are crutches, environment is clay, and the strong
mold monuments from circumstances that would crush
less courageous, creative persons day by day.*

K.C. BONES' LAST RIDE

K.C. Bones was a railroad tramp
With his roll on his grimy back.
He had no fare and his feet were sore
As he walked down the railroad track.

They filled the tank on 75
As he waited on the off-station side.
When the train pulled out of the railyard
K.C. Bones was set for his ride.

He sat with his face to the engine ahead
And his back to the mail coach car.
Between his feet the coupling creaked
As he swayed with its rhythm and jar.

K.C. Bones felt half-hypnotized
With the clicking wheels under his feet.
And he dozed and almost slipped and fell,
But there was no place left to retreat.

He fastened his arm with his broken belt
To the ladder of the mail coach car
So that when he started to fall in his sleep
He would feel the tug on the bar.

(CONTINUED ON NEXT PAGE)

The belt didn't hold. His arm slipped thru
As the train sped on in the night.
He held to the coupling with cold, numb hands
Then he gave up the losing fight.

His body fell down between the cars
And under the grinding steel.
And K.C. Bones died a thousand deaths
Beneath each bouncing wheel.

The coyotes cleaned the jumbled bones
On the desert right-of-way
Where the steam locomotive's whistle moans
Down the tracks of yesterday . . .

FIVE MINUTES AFTER I'M GONE

Five minutes after the blood in my veins
    Has ceased to flow along.
Five minutes after they say I'm dead,
    I'm sure that they'll be dead wrong.

Five minutes after they've said goodbye
    I'll be walking the streets of gold,
Vibrant and living, immortal and new,
    Five minutes after I'm cold.

Five minutes after the funeral car
    Has sadly driven away,
I'll be happy in Heaven's eternal home.
    Only time will have passed away!

December

~ 7 ~

Wisdom is the prize that fools never gain
and the price that the indolent never pay.

Let the wheat of wisdom always outweigh the chaff of your
untested self-opinions, lest the listening harvesters find they have labored
half the day to find a kernel or two of doubtful grain.

GEMSTONES

As viewing an agate against the sun
   Reveals its colors bright,
So the soul shines through the smile-lit face
   Luminous with inner light.

As water flows over the agates
   Down on the ocean shore,
So God washes the souls of men anew
   Burnishing them more and more.

As the lapidary cuts and shapes them
   When tumbled and polished well,
God saves each stone for its purpose
   Too precious to trade or sell.

So God gathers the human gemstones
   Here on the shores of our earth,
Ill-shaped and rough to begin with,
   He makes them of infinite worth.

WISDOM

Wisdom of the ages
    Like glistening mountain peaks,
Whose thundering tones reverberate
    As truth its essence speaks.

Wisdom of the ages
    Roll like oceans set aflame
By intuition's glorious sunrise
    Where ignorance has no name.

Wisdom of the ages
    Whose past was not misspent,
Whose future and whose present
    Are filled with glad intent.

Wisdom of the ages
    Speak and we shall hear,
For knowledge waits to whisper
    In every listening ear!

ALTOONA BARN BY GREG WALZ

RUNNELS COUNTRY ROAD BY GLADYS DAVIS

December

8

He who claims God as his Father must by necessity treat the rest of humanity as his brothers.
Please love one another.

GOD, GIVE US LOVE

For the sake of the sun
   in the setting sky,
For the sake of the soft clouds
   floating nearby,
For the sake of the ocean
   turbulent, deep,
For the sake of the valleys
   where dark shadows sleep,
For the sake of the twilight,
   the hours of dawn,
For the sake of the rivers
   that flow swiftly on,
For the sake of our brothers
   with uplifted hearts,
For the sad eyes of longing
   where teardrops start,
For the sake of the poor
   and downtrodden of earth,
For the sake of creation
   that brought it all forth,
For the sake of this world
   and God up above,
We cry with one voice,
   "O God, give us love!"

RED MOUNTAIN PASS BY GREG WALZ

December

9

THE BEST I CAN

Hazy are the mountains
    Where the shadows thickly lie.
Scowling are the driven clouds
    And frowning is the sky.

Weary are my faltering feet.
    My will is nearly gone.
But thru the tears I see the path
    And blindly stumble on.

Oh, mortal ache within my heart,
    Oh, eternal question mark.
I must press on till night is past
    And dawn succeeds the dark.

I do not know the reason,
    Nor fathom life's "grim plan."
But I know the path leads upward.
    And I'll do the best I can!

GOD'S BREATH BY TOM DUBOIS

December

10

Fairness is akin to kindness and kindness is akin to God.
Fairness is found in the Golden Rule of Love.

HAVE FAITH IN GOD

Have faith in God, O precious Friend,
  And in no thing despair.
For in all life's perplexities
  You'll find that God is there.

Have faith in God when trials sore
  Would press on every side.
For just remember that our God
  Has promised to abide.

Have faith in God when sickness comes
  Or old age would smite you down.
For God will either raise you up
  Or give you Heaven's crown.

There is a place of trust and prayer,
  A place that's free from fear,
A place of peace for the resting soul
  Where God is always near.

Have faith in God. It is the best,
  The only happy way.
Have faith in God, an anchor sure
  To keep you day by day.

HEAR US AS WE PRAY

Companion in the commonplace,
   Our Deliverer in each storm,
Our Guide, our Compass and in life
   Our Rule and Measuring Norm.

Grant to us now an audience, Lord,
   On this, Thy Sabbath Day.
Incline Thine ear to hear each prayer
   Wherever people pray.

Sweep from our hearts all trace of care,
   All shadows of lingering gloom.
Oh, let devotion's golden light
   Illumine each empty room.

Accept our belated gratitude
   For gifts the week has brought.
Forgive each erring word or deed,
   Each unworthy, straying thought.

Grant us true conformity
   In nature, life and word.
And whisper deep within each heart,
   "My child, Thy prayer is heard!"

December

~ 11 ~

To initiate or imitate, to be the voice or the echo, that's the question.
The Creator's works are the originals.

THEY ARE GONE

Never again will the buffalo dust
    That followed those thundering feet
Arise on the prairies and plains again
    In migration or stampeding retreat.

Never again will the warriors in paint
    Circle and shout in attack.
For buffalo and early Indians both are gone,
    And nothing can bring them back.

Never again will the past return
    To drink from our rivers and streams.
And the future will never know the past
    Except in our legends and dreams.

GOD WROTE TWO BOOKS FOR MAN TO READ

In stony silence giant rocks
    Throughout long eons watched the earth
Bury primordial history in its breast
    As the First Narrator gave it birth.

And in books paged with serried stone,
    Hidden under covers of velvet grass,
Lies a story the silent centuries told
    That vanished as it came to pass.

God in granite archives stored
    Fossil facsimiles of all He made
Embalmed in silicone and buried now
    In ocean depth or hidden forest glade.

Days as ages came in stately turn
    Watched over by the Great Creator's eye,
Till dust-formed man awoke in wonderment
    To read his prelude in the earth and sea and sky.

God wrote it down for man to read
    A World-Book too big for one to hold.
Then He wrote a shorter, much-loved, Holy Book
    Wherein essential truth shines forth as
                                burnished gold.

OLD YELLER BY GREG WALZ

THE NEW CREATION BY TOM DUBOIS

December

~ 12 ~

Shall we multiply our loneliness and disappointment by reconsidering the hurts? No, best take courage:
Think on the benefits, and then pick up the broken pieces of failure and pain
and mold a mosaic in success and healing.

LONELINESS

I wonder if the waves are lonely
    As they lave the ocean shore?
I wonder if the gulls are crying
    For comrades they've known before?
I wonder if the winds are sighing
    For days that will come no more?

God, grant me the heart to know it
    And grant me the will to go on.
Grant me fulfillment for longings
    And strength thru the night till dawn.
Grant me a mind of endurance
    For things that forever are gone.

Fill me with balm for the aching
    And crying of inward unrest.
May I gather from life's broken pieces
    Some memories that God has blest
To shape some mosaic of meaning
    The embodiment of all that is best.

Great God, are the weeping skies lonely?
    Why cry the gulls in their flight?
Tell me, do mortal men only
    Face emptiness by day and by night?
Do the ocean waves seek for new shorelines
    That forever are just beyond sight?

ANOTHER WILDERNESS SEASON BY CAROLINE SEYMOUR

December

～ 13 ～

*Engraved on every countenance and every heart are the sculptured scars
or the beauty lines of each hidden thought or deed.*

I WONDER HOW THEY ACT AT HOME

I saw a lady singing
   A solo all alone,
And I wondered a bit about her—
   Just how she sang at home?

I saw the preacher smiling
   As the people entered in,
And I wondered if, when he was home,
   He acted mean as sin.

I saw a teacher teaching
   A great big Sunday class.
But I listened on the party line
   And, Brother, could she "sass"!

I saw the ushers taking
   The money in the plate,
And I wondered if their own tithes
   Would come in soon or late.

We put our best foot forward
   When in the public place,
But when we're home with loved ones
   There's a frown upon our face.

We use the candied, false tone
   As through God's world we roam,
But you ought to hear the accents
   We use when we're at home!

PRAYER

Transcend the common conception of prayer.
Converse with God. He's always there.

Gather the light from the trysting place.
Mold a candle of vision and grace.

It will light your way on paths untrod,
For prayer is the wick and the light is God.

THE CARPET OF PRAYER

The confident eye of sturdy faith
    Will pierce the darkness through.
When hands are clasped in fervent prayer
    God opens His hands to you!

The sincere heart that prays at night
    Is fairer of face by day.
And the person who travels on his knees
    Will stand at end of day!

The carpet of prayer where believers kneel
    Will carry your faith on high
And bring the rain of blessing down
    From every waiting sky!

December

14

What is death but dust resplendent in resurrection's hour; and what is death but the gate to heaven and the scepter of deathless power?

OTHER DAYS WILL COME

Other days are coming;
    Other winds will blow.
Spring will follow winter
    Melting ice and snow.

Other days are coming,
    Better days I know,
If we keep our hearts in patience
    As seasons come and go.

You who live with sorrow,
    You whose days are long.
You know that days of sunshine
    Bring with them a song.

Yes, other days are coming,
    Better days than these.
God can make them better
    If we start them on our knees!

I MUST BE TRAVELING ON

I belong to the people;
   I hear the train whistle blow;
I hear the call of the distant place
   And I follow the urge to go.

For mine are the feet of mercury—
   Winged feet with a message of peace.
Mine are the words of the ready pen,
   Words that must find release.

I hear the whistle of the waiting train.
   I feel the longing of parting pain.
And I must be traveling on again
   To the whistle's sad refrain.

Perhaps I'll die in a foreign land
   Away from all held dear.
But what does it matter if I live or die
   If I know that God is near.

What does it matter if death comes then
   Far from the familiar place?
Only let me die in the love of God
   A debtor to love and grace!

COUGAR BY WILLIAM R. JACKSON

AT MY PLACE BY KAREN WRIGHT

December

15

LOVE IS AN EMOTION

Love is an emotion as wide as the ocean
    And as dangerous and deep as the sea;
For love is an image, half truth and half fancy,
    And I know not which half is for me.

Love is a prison, but my hopes have arisen,
    For my lover is the guard at the gate;
But love is a monster, half demon, half angel,
    That can caress or devour me with hate.

Love is a passion that's always in fashion,
    Out where Cupid can shoot with his dart;
For love is an arrow, death dealing yet healing,
    And, alas, it has pierced my own heart.

Yes, love is emotion in constant commotion,
    Tempestuous and wild as the sea.
My will is half sinking for thought I am thinking;
    And I wonder what has happened to me.

The emotion of love has a secret language of heart and hand and eye.

A PREDATOR IN THE MIND'S EYE BY JUSTIN SPARKS

December

~ 16 ~

Impossibility is an unthinkable word that challenges divine creativity
and stirs the blood of courageous persons to action.

THE PROMISE OF GOD

The Word of God, a rock unmoved
Is a refuge sure for His beloved.

It is a sea broad, deep, and wide.
Its promises are like an ocean tide.

Like a great, protecting wall
The promise of God surrounds us all.

A pillow at night for the tired head,
The Word is still the soul's soft bed.

Like the warm sun in the clear sky,
It shines in where dark shadows lie.

God's promises I'll claim as mine.
Wondrous, eternal, promise divine!

VISION

The oak is asleep in the acorn.
  In the egg is the eagle's wing.
In the highest vision of mortal man
  The awakening angels sing.

So cherish your thoughts and your visions,
  The music and dreams of desire,
And fan the embers of "wanting to be"
  Till it mounts as a living fire.

Go dream of the sunlit mountains
  And sing of the rolling spheres,
And the music of love and true success
  Will be coming to you through the years.

Your dreams are the promise of better days.
  Your hopes will at last come true.
And the person you have held in your vision
  Will finally turn out to be you!

For the oak is asleep in the acorn.
  A shell holds the pinioned wing.
In the desire and vision of things to be
  The minstrels of victory sing!

December

~ 17 ~

The clock of time runs slow, or so it often seems;
but life is sooner over than the careless mortal dreams.

THE CLOCK AND THE CALENDAR

Visualize the answers for these questions when thinking about the commodity of time:

• Why are inspiration and motivation, as they relate to time as a treasure, so important?

• How much time do I have? For what?

• How best can I use my valuable time?

• Can I discover ways to enhance my time so that it becomes geometrically expandable?

Is it possible to challenge yourself to crank up the efficiency of your use of time? What would inspire you? What would motivate you? Experience this for a moment. Identify with the whir of rising wings, when forward thrust overcomes resistance, where lift laughs at gravity and lofty levitation of a determined inner being changes the entire perspective of life. We will do better with our time budget. We will soar higher, and we determine to do it now.

As for the spending of your personal time this very day: Envision yourself alert, important, and involved as a member of the changing of the guard! Begin to identify personally with the inspiration and motivation of the dedicated individual who expects the cooperation of a compatible, receptive spaceship earth environment. Begin to see through the eagle's eye the achievement and personal accomplishments brought about through purposeful optimism and self-confident assurance in a healthy, natural life, relative to your success.

YOUTH HAS A TREASURE

Youth holds something of wonder,
  Something that many have not.
Youth carries rare jewels so lightly
  And gives it so little thought.

The ill would sell all to possess it.
  The octogenarian with trembling and fears
Would trade the gain of a lifetime
  To possess but the half of youth's years.

For time is the thing youth has most of
  And the thing that the older ones lack.
Spend wisely the wealth of your time-gold,
  Once spent it never comes back.

Be a miser of sparkling minutes
  To spend on your noblest desires.
May your memory and the memory of others
  Be warmed at Time's sunset fires.

Crowd learning, improvement and service,
  The culture of mind and soul,
Into Time's mansion of minutes.
  And let kindness be part of your goal.

Youth has a treasure unmeasured
  But in time we must pass it by
For the young of tomorrow to squander
  Who in turn learn the bitter beggar cry.

Poor fools with hands full of diamonds
  Unaware that they soon will have less,
Will toss hours like pockets of pebbles
  Stone blind to the wealth they possess.

O youth, the clock and the calendar
  Hang silently there on the wall,
To remind us that time is our treasure
  Counted mutely when long shadows fall.

SILENT NIGHT BY JODIE BOREN

A PREY IN THE MIND'S EYE BY JUSTIN SPARKS

December

~ 18 ~

RADIATE TO COMMUNICATE

When words seem flat and faltering
 And fail to reach their goal,
Then you can simply expand and emanate
 The sincere essence of your soul.

You adapt and adjust to every one,
 To child or tree or beast.
You become a part of all you love
 From the greatest to the least.

Without condescension or striving
 You simply communicate.
You glow with kinship's kindliness
 And warm oneness radiate.

An all-embracing luminousness,
 Akin to that love divine,
Melts invisible barriers down
 Absorbing the divisive line.

This rainbow radius blends with all
 That chance to pass your way.
And you become full as you freely share
 What you have and are each day.

*The frontiers of friendship still call for the pioneering spirit
and the courage of the conquistadors.*

THE GATHERING BY TOM DUBOIS

December

19

The person who cannot give money can best give something of himself; kind words, timely knowledge, the liberality of love, and the wealth of a willing heart.

A POET'S PRAYER

Give me a poem, Oh God, I pray
   That will lift up the hearts of
     men.
Give me a poem of depth and
     breadth.
   Let it bless as it flows from
     my pen.

Give me a poem, Oh God, I ask;
   Not for the fame it would
     bring,
But give me a poem touched by
     Thy fire
   That will make the broken heart
     sing.

Give me a poem, Oh God, today,
   A poem that throbs in each part.
Touch me, Oh Lord, with the
     power of love,
   And give me the poet's heart!

AWAY FROM THE OCEAN SHORE

There are only streets and sidewalks here,
    No ocean's rolling tide.
Monotonous houses, row on row
    Where strangers live inside.

Here no seagulls shrilly cry
    As their grey wings cleave the sky.
Here no ocean liners sail,
    Silhouetted in passing by.

Here no cooling ocean breeze,
    Like a magic touch divine,
Can caress away the deep regrets
    Stirred up by memory's wine.

Here no driftwood's jumbled mass
    In profusion piles high.
Here no sand, caressing, warm,
    Offers solace where we lie.

Here no penetrating rain
    Can beat and sting your face.
No driving spray from high-flung waves
    Rises vaulting to shoreward race.

I miss the feeling of release
    That broad oceans always bring,
Where loveliness and nature reign
    And solitude is king!

December

20

Home isn't so much a place as it is a relationship, a confidence, and a condition.
Home is where love makes its dwelling.

PLEASE DO NOT QUIT

When things go wrong, as they sometimes will,
When the road you're trudging seems all uphill,
When the funds are low and the debts are high,
And you want to smile, but you'd rather cry.
When care is pressing you down a bit,
Rest, if you must—but don't you quit.

Life is strange with its twists and turns,
As everyone of us sometimes learns,
And many a failure turns about
When he might have won had he stuck it out.
Don't give up, though the pace seems slow—
You might succeed with another blow.

Often the goal is nearer than
It seems to a faint and faltering man,
Often the struggler has given up
When he might have captured the victor's cup.
And he learned too late, when the night slipped down,
How close he was to the golden crown.

Success is failure turned inside out—
The silver tint of the clouds of doubt—
And you never can tell how close you are,
It may be near when it seems afar.
So stick to the fight when you're hardest hit—
It's when things seem worst that you mustn't quit.

MY GRANDMOTHER

Curls once beautifully auburn
   Have long since turned to gray;
But the hoary head is a glorious crown
   When found in the righteous way.

With the Ancient Book her constant guide,
   She had lived a holy life;
With childlike faith she'd walked in peace
   When all around was strife,

Her days, like a peaceful river,
   Refreshingly rolled along;
As pure and sweet, as calm and deep
   As the melody of a song!

Ninety-eight times her eyes had seen
   The leaves of autumn fall;
Ninety-nine times they'd leafed again
   When they heard the spring winds call.

But the leaves of her life are now renewed
   By the breath of Eternal Spring;
Redeemed, transformed, immortal now,
   She dwells where seraphs sing!

December

21

Energy is the true coin of the kingdom. You can't buy and sell without it. It is the basis of credit, the currency of commerce, the bonds in the bank, the difference between failure and success. Spend your energy where it counts the most and costs the least.

WORKING

See a mother tending baby,
   Cooking dinner, baking cake,
Patching, sewing, dusting, sweeping,
   Doing all for someone's sake.

See a teacher grading papers,
   Doing well the commonplace,
Typing, teaching now, or planning
   With a steady, faithful pace.

See the farmer, or the millman,
   Single or in sweating crew—
All must work as for the Master
   In the task that each must do.

Tho' unseen and unapplauded,
   God will judge our work at last;
And with kindly smile reward us
   When earth's portals are all past.

THE SPIRIT OF DIVINE ENERGY

The Spirit of God moves on the waters.
    The Spirit of God moves on the land.
He has all supply if you take it
    With confident, upreaching hand.

The Spirit of God moves among nations.
    They wait for the prophet's clear voice.
And the Spirit of God shall guide them
    And the nations in truth shall rejoice.

The Spirit of God moves in our business,
    In the buying and selling of things,
For He is the Spirit of Wisdom;
    His wealth is the wealth of all kings.

The Spirit of God moves in each person.
    He shares both the traveler and the path.
And benign is His brooding and blessing
    Where love tempers even His wrath.

THE BUCK STOPS HERE BY GREG WALZ

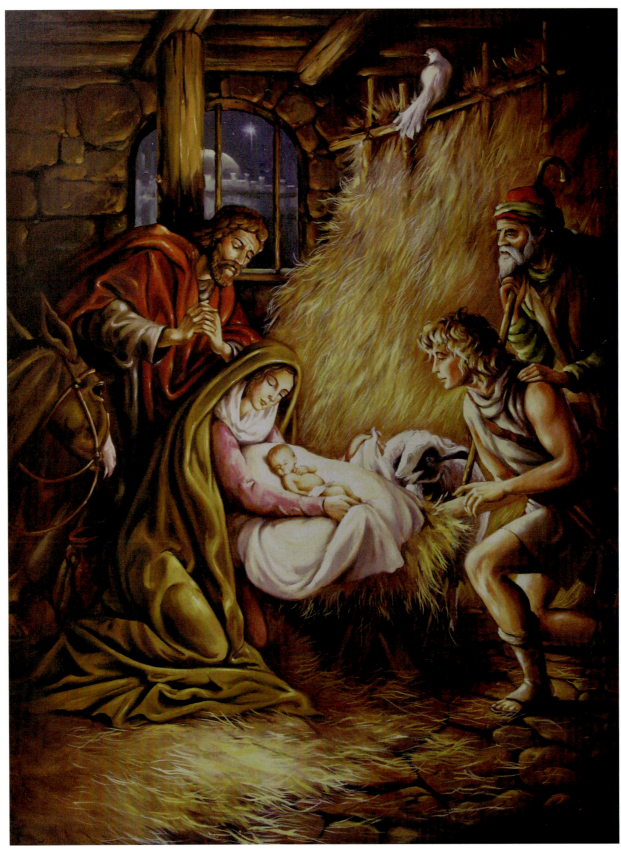

NATIVITY BY SERGEY CHERNOMORETS

December

22

FAITH'S CANDLE BURNS AT NIGHT

I set a candle burning in the sky.
  For my altar candlelight
I choose a star to shine afar
  In the darkness of the night.

I claim the moon for candle flame
  On a pine-tree candlestick
Where the flickering gold in radiance bold
  As the flame on the burning wick.

I set a candle burning in my heart
  Upon a sacred altar there.
In calm retreat its perfume sweet
  Intermingles with my prayer.

Light from the stars was flowing
  From the unfathomable wells of night,
Silently but brightly declaring
  The God that was hidden from sight.

Oh, trust in God who made the night
  Whose altar is the world.
Just choose some star right where you are.
  Let doubt be backward hurled.

Pray on and sing and trust and pray.
  The flame of hope burns bright.
The stars, the moon, the sun at high noon,
  Faith lights them all tonight!

Faith is a sure foundation and the rest to labor given, the repose of confidence and hope that counts on God and heaven!

IN THE GARDEN BY TOM DUBOIS

December

~ 23 ~

The original thinker can find within himself life's important questions and, by continuing his quest, can also find the faculty within that channels the answer through him from the Fountain of Infinite Wisdom and Intuitive Knowledge.

COMPENSATION

Every man a sower is
   In the harvest fields of God.
His sowing may in deserts be
   Or on the fertile sod.
The seed that he is sowing
   Is God's truth so strong and pure.
When planted, watered, blessed of God
   It forever will endure.

For not alone with precepts
   Or pious parrot-talk
Do we plant goals for heaven
   But by the way we walk:
We may sow God's Word in another's life
   By loving deeds that we have done.
And others water, hoe and reap
   The work we have begun.

The manner of our sowing,
   The spirit of our task,
The blessing of the Father
   As we work and as we ask,
These are things that surely make
   The harvest rich or poor;
And bring the fruitage to the bin
   With abundance more and more.

(CONTINUED ON NEXT PAGE)

The law of compensation
    Here works its sure decree.
And the bounty of our sowing
    Is reaped for all to see.
And in the realm of giving
    Of self or things possessed,
In the manner of our sharing
    Is the measure we are blessed.

For he who soweth freely
    With liberal heart and hand
Will reap in bounty multiplied
    Of the best within the land.
But he who soweth sparingly
    And withholds the better part,
Will find his fields sear and brown
    And within a withered heart!

The mental impulse of thought reaches the midbrain of another before the sound can reach the ear or the meaning of words can be translated by the conscious mind. If such thought and words do not agree, confusion arises; but the thought transferred takes priority in the listeners' emotional response. Therefore, let every person think sincerely and speak accordingly to be most clearly understood. This can put a song in each person's heart.

Gratitude is the gateway to God, the door to gratuities, and the most gracious gift that the grateful can give in return.

December

~ 24 ~

A person's wants, whether based on need or simply desire, will find expression in some form, or die trying.

ABORIGINAL CUPID

Just paint me the color of stupid.
　　Tear the picture in a hundred parts,
But call off that bushman, Cupid,
　　With his blowgun and love-poisoned darts!

WHEN THE NEXT ANGEL WALKS BY

Who swept the stars from the sky
　　With a witch's broom?
Who turned off the sun
　　And turned on the gloom?

Who carries the torch
　　That I used to hold?
Why did love leave me
　　Out in the cold?

The less fortunate would envy
　　Your beautiful face,
But your heart was too fickle—
　　Without constancy's grace.

I'm wounded but not dead.
　　Love is still worth a try.
So I'll turn on the charm
　　When the next "angel" walks by!

WHAT I WANT FOR CHRISTMAS

I want a bag of "glad wrap"
   For gloomy homes tonight.
Let genuine joy and gladness
   Outshine the festive light.

I want a lot of "happy"
   Back in the happy, glad New Year,
And a real star and angels
   When I'm thru with Christmas here.

When you've brought the joy of living,
   Made the world happy as can be,
Then, Dear Lord, leave a heaped-up load
   Of "tummy chuckles" just for me.

December

~ 25 ~

*The person whose body is relaxed, whose mind is contented, whose spirit is bathed
in peace and dried on the towel of courage, can put on the housecoat of perfect love and
the slippers of restful relief and sip the cup of comfort in quiet enjoyment.*

PEACE AND THE MAN OF GALILEE
(CREATIVE VISUALIZATION)

Close your eyes gently. Please visualize the symbols and thought forms of this meditation of peace. Translate its message into vivid, visual, inner pictures with color, detail and action. Relaxing completely, breathing easily and deeply, visualizing clearly, enter also into the cadence, rhythm and emotional essence of the concept, Peace and the Man of Galilee. Go beyond it all and become one with the True Author of all that is beautiful, good, positive and true.

Out from the now-distant corridors of half-forgotten time rings the voice, the inimitable voice, of the Man of Galilee, the rugged carpenter of Nazareth. His hands are calloused from saw and ax and plane. Strong muscles ripple under his coarse tunic. His sandals are odorous with the smell of the fishing boats and perhaps brittle with the brine from the sands, minerals and salt of the Dead Sea. His hair is lighter than that of his contemporaries. Bleached with the sun, it reflects the light of his inner spirit and the light of the sunbeams that play on the edges of its deeper auburn shadows. There is about him a subtle calm, a strength deeper than the strength of a mountain man who often sleeps out under the stars and the olive trees. It is an inner calm of the unperturbed, eternal spirit of God, the Unmoved Mover.

Speaking to the enraptured crowd on the hillsides of Galilee, he spoke from out of the depth of his eternal knowing. The birds of the air poised on motionless wings to hear it. The winds carried it softly across the waters, and the ships rocked gently on the calm bosom of the sea; a word stirred and whispered through their sails. It was a beautiful word. The birds and the sea swelled with its gladness, and the skies had a deep and knowing look like the confidence of love in a lover's eye. The multitudes grew hushed and still, and John quickly made notes on his parchment as out of the center of Divine and eternal wisdom the Master said, "My peace I give unto you. Not as the world giveth, give I unto you. Let not your hearts be troubled neither let them be afraid."

The disciples remembered it. They remembered the day when their storm-tossed boat was near to sinking and the Master was asleep. They remembered how they awakened him with troubled hearts and in fear. He had gone to the side of the pitching, rocking boat, stretched out his wondrous hands and simply said, "Peace be still," and the waves curled up and laid themselves down to rest, and there was a great calm from shore to shore. They had asked in incredulity, "What manner of man is

~ 883 ~

SHIP AT SEA

this that even the winds and the waves obey him?" It was the Master saying, "My peace I give unto you. Not as the world giveth, give I unto you. Let not your hearts be troubled neither let them be afraid."

Peace is a river flowing, a storm that has been calmed, a well overflowing, a refreshing summer shower, a soft blanket of winter snow covering old ground scars and putting the scarlet leaves to rest at the foot of stalwart trees. Peace is a fire purging. It is a breeze from heaven, a zephyr blowing, a wind from angel wings. Peace is a breeze of promise, a cooling breath of hope, a beckoning and a swaying in the treetops of expectancy. Peace is a breeze of summertime and the resurrection of spring that kisses the early flowers into bloom and embraces the drifted, calloused, crusted snow and melts it in the arms of transforming love. Peace is laughing springlets and flowing streams and darting fish in deep, green pools where skippers glide on its undisturbed surface.

Peace is the warm rays of the summer sun ripening fruit, helping to incubate the eggs in a billion nests and overshadowing the nestlings and pouring its energies into the maintenance of all creation. Peace is the whirl of the far-flung galaxies of an ever-expanding universe. It is the oil of gladness that makes all life's machinery run more smoothly. Peace winks in every star at night, smiles in the complacency of the silver moon, and rises with the faithful sun for its morning calisthenics as it jogs across the awakening sky.

Peace is a river of red, the pulsing circulation of lifeblood in every warmhearted life form that walks or runs or flies. Peace is the life blood of distilled experience where the wine press of life squeezes the beautiful, the true, the positive and the good from the grapes of our wrath, the fruit of our frustration and the pulp of our fears. It is the sparkling red wine of God's kingdom that flows through all of the arteries and veins of our inner and outer person, circulating the oxygen of confident hope to every cell where it imparts perfect health of spirit and the abundant energy of life made manifest.

Peace breathes in rocks and trees, stars and stones. Peace is the inbreathing inspiration of the living God in living people. It is the music of the spheres. It is the joyous energy of dancing, swirling, and waltzing atoms all attuned to the harmony of the whole universe. Peace is a gift to be received, unwrapped and examined—a gift to be enjoyed, cherished, and shared with others.

Again I hear the Master say, "My peace I give unto you. Not as the world giveth give I unto you. Let not your heart be troubled neither let it be afraid."

Please tuck the awakened awareness of your personal concept of peace away somewhere in a hidden corner of your heart where it can work its leaven of transformation in your outer life for every day. You, too, are a peaceful person through Him. Peace be unto you.

LOVE IS TENDER

Love is a way that fools can't tread.
Love is the wisdom of right things said.

Love is a way that too few have trod.
Love is a high hill that leads to God.

Love is a desert where oases spring.
Love is the lifeblood of everything.

Love is the crossbow and arrow we send.
Love is receiving and giving without end.

Love is a soft cloud pregnant with rain.
Love is the soft hand alleviating pain.

It's the circle transposed by the cross.
Filling each vacuum, not counting cost.

Love is the beginning. Love is the end.
Love, the cement joining friend to friend.

Love is the spell gentle words weave.
May love quickly come and never leave!

December

~ 26 ~

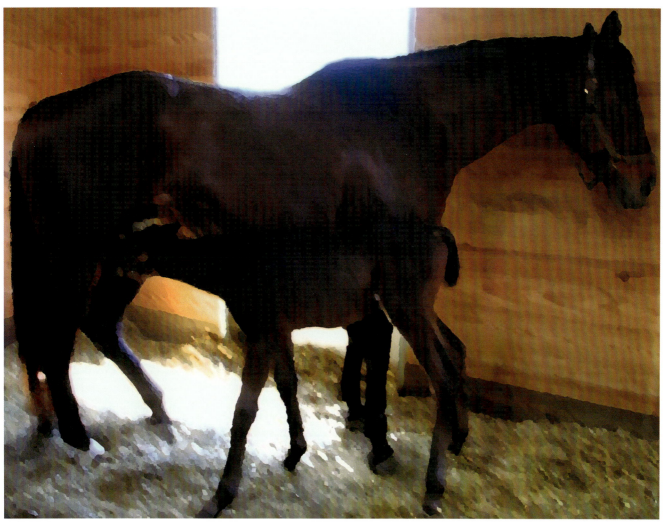

MOTHER AND CHILD BY GREG WALZ

TEACH US TO SING

It's hard for mortals to sing the song
   The heavenly hosts were chiming.
Our hearts are cold, our words are hard
   And we've lost the art of rhyming.

Teach us to sing the angel's song—
   That song they sang about peace.
Teach us the tune, Thou God of love,
   May all our discording cease.

Send Thou the angel of love again.
   Teach these dumb lips to ring
That song of goodwill for everyone.
   Yes, teach us, Dear Lord, to sing!

December

27

Initiative is the drive for beginning something, the spirit of conquest, and the self-starter for action; what it begins should be the product of creative imagination, balanced by judgment, sustained by courage and directed to some worthwhile end.

THE APPLE VISUAL
(CREATIVE VISUALIZATION)

Let's think about the Christmas season. We're going to do a visual today about a big, red Christmas apple. If you haven't already taken a deep breath, take a deep breath with every head down and all eyes closed. Keep them closed until the very end of this visual and until we have come back to our activity level on instruction. Now take another deep breath but not so deep that it is noticeable. When you let it out, be completely, completely, completely relaxed. Be so relaxed that there isn't a tense muscle in your body anywhere. Every muscle is at ease, and all of the life forces flow unhindered through you in complete restfulness.

Please picture now the most beautiful red apple that any student ever brought to a favorite teacher on a Monday morning. Think of the apples you've seen in the store in boxes and in baskets. Think of the apples you've seen on trees in the summertime.

Now I want you to imagine that it's a beautiful summer day toward the fall of the year. You're in an apple orchard. There are dwarf apple trees where the tree is so small and the fruit is so large that there seem to be more red apples than there are green leaves. You are as tall as the top of that dwarf, miniature apple tree. It's loaded to the ground with apples. Some trees have yellow apples, some have red apples and some have green apples. They are every shade and color and size.

Back of the dwarf trees, over against the stone fence, are the regular, full-size, giant apple trees. You're going to look through these big trees and put in your pocket the nicest apples that you can find for your teacher, for your mother and for a friend. As you walk under the trees, you look up through the green leaves against a blue, blue sky with fleecy white clouds floating by. Notice the leaves. They are a dark, waxy green on top, and they're a lighter, paler green underneath. Notice the little veins and stems on the lighter green side of the apple leaf. You see that perfect, delicious, red apple you've been looking for. Imagine that you're climbing the tree. Swing up into the crotched branches. Take a step. Now you are way up on a sturdy limb. You're reaching out to get that most beautiful apple. Oh, it looks so good! You pick it off. You twist it and it comes loose from the twig that it's fastened to. A little leaf comes back with it so that you have the big, red apple, the apple stem and a leaf on it, too. You're climbing down now, or sliding down the tree. You can almost feel the rough bark of the tree or the rounds of the ladder rub your stomach as you come back down, carefully holding on. There, you slip down to the ground now. You say to yourself, "I've got the nicest apple in the world for my teacher. I have the nicest apple in my pocket for my friend, and one for my parents." You are going to go home with at least three apples of your choice of whatever color they are. You're polishing the apples on your sleeve or on your tummy, or with something.

You are so busy that you're not looking where you're going. All of a sudden you bump into something. It's red and almost as big as a small house. You look up and you say, "This looks like an apple!" It's right in the middle of the orchard where there aren't any trees, in a grassy place with irrigation ditches flowing by on the far side, and the tall summer grass is bent over. This giant apple is bigger than a school bus! Where you bumped into it, there's a ladder. It has ten steps on it. These ten steps lead up to a yellow door in the side of the red apple. The door is curved to fit the curve of the apple, just like an airplane door is curved to fit the contour of the plane.

You start at the bottom of the ladder that leans against the apple. You put your right foot on the first round of the ladder. You have tennis shoes on. You put your weight on that right foot and feel how it fits your arch. Put your weight on it. Reach up and get ahold of the rounds of the ladder and start to climb. As you count and climb round by round to the yellow door of the giant apple, you will become more and more relaxed, and you'll be at perfect mind level for picturing things clearly, imagining vividly and enjoying thoroughly this visual exercise as you reach that number one, top round of the ladder. The nearest round at your feet is number ten. Take a deep breath and reach up for the next round, and put your left foot up on number nine; now number eight, going higher up the ladder as you count. Go deeper into your decentration or relaxed concentration. Seven. Six. You are getting closer to the top and to that important number one. You will be completely relaxed and at an active level and at an enjoyment level when you reach number one.

Five. Four. More and more relaxed! Three. Two. You're almost there. At the count of one, you'll be deeper than you've been before. You've had some wonderful times, but today you're going to go deeper still. Now, at the count of one, you'll be there. One!

Imagine there's a silver dollar on the doorknob in front of you. It's yours if you can twist it off. You're twisting the knob on the door of this giant, magic apple. As you twist on the silver-dollar doorknob, the door swings open and in. Of all things, there's a tunnel right through the middle of that giant apple. It's a tunnel big enough to walk through. The floor looks like a cobblestone sidewalk. What could those round, shiny, beautiful, transparent cobblestones be? Why, they're the cells that hold the apple juice, like those cells in a grapefruit or in an orange. They are little, minute sections that encase the delicious juice of the fruit. These are round rather than oblong, and you're walking on the cobblestone cells of the apple floor. You crowd inside the door one by one as you all climb up the ladder. Just inside the door there is a glass tabletop. On it there are plates full of sliced apple sections. Just beyond that there are boxes of candied apples. Standing beside that table, who do you think is there? It is none other than Johnny Appleseed, that legendary character who went across the early Americas in colonial times, sowing apple seeds so that the early settlers coming in the covered wagons could have apples to eat when they passed that way along the trails and the rivers and the lakes of the new land called America. Johnny Appleseed is standing there. On his head is an old slouched felt hat, grey with age, that looks like he carried water in it, packed his lunch in it and slept in

⇔ 890 ⇔

it to keep his head warm. He has on a wrinkled, blue workshirt. He's wearing a soft, well-worn, pliable, leather-fringed jacket; fringed, leather trousers made of deerskin; and an old pair of Indian moccasins with beads on them. Slung over his shoulder is that ever-present bag in which Johnny Appleseed carried his apples across America. He reaches in and rattles those dry apple seeds and lets them run through his gnarled, wrinkled, brown fingers. You can hear them striking the sides and bottom of the leather bag.

You can almost hear Johnny say, "Take one of these apple sections." So you hold it up close to your nose and smell the delicious aroma of ripe apples in the cellar. You recall the taste of apple juice and apple cider. You notice the difference in feeling of the inside of the apple and the smoothness of the apple skin. Bite into it again. Feel how crisp and cool that apple is. Then, feel how paper-like and rubbery the skin is. You've smelled it and you remember what apples smell like. You tasted it. You remember what apple cider and apple juice taste like. It reminds you, too, of those baked apples that your mother used to make when she put cinnamon and brown sugar in the hollowed-out core of the apples and put them into the oven to bake. When they came out, they were so full of sweetness and the warmth of the cooking oven that their sides had split, and you could look in through the cracked, red skin of the apple and see the white, deliciously cooked inner part. You could look at the cinnamon and the crisp sugar on top. You could see the juice down in the middle and the red juice down around the bottom of each apple. It reminds you of your favorite kind of cold apple pie, maybe with cheese on it. You think of hot apple pie, fresh out of the oven with a glass of cold milk from the refrigerator.

Johnny Appleseed is holding that box with little squares of transparent, candied apples over to you. "Come this way." As you look down the long, long, tunnel isle, you see at the other end the little elves silhouetted against what looks like a red stained-glass window. You can see the light coming through the skin of the apple at the far end of the tunnel. It's beautiful! It's very soft, and it reminds you of the stained-glass windows of a chapel or a temple where the light comes through. You walk on clear to the very end. You reach up and feel the transparent apple-skin wall. You can almost see through it but you can't quite. There's a zipper in this side of the apple. One of the Christmas elves is unzipping that apple-skin stained-glass window in the wall. You're crawling through that opened, unzipped place. You can't fall off because there is a balcony outside all the way around. You're looking out over the orchard from the balcony. You can see the irrigation ditches. You can see the green leaves and the grass that's bent over here and there where people have walked. You can see a lake in the distance and beautiful, snowcapped mountains. You're walking around the apple, feeling it. It's round. It's smooth. You're patting the sides of that great big apple house from the outside. You're looking at the little flecks and freckles on it where the sun kissed it. All the way around the circular balcony you hurry. You're coming back in now through the zipper place.

Okay. You're back inside. Somebody zipper that up so the draft won't blow down the hall! You notice that there are rooms on the right-hand and left-hand sides of the tunnel hallway. On the right side, there is a door that has a sign in letters of gold. It says, "Merry Christmas!" Tinsel is hanging on the door. A Christmas bell is hanging there, along with some holly and pine branches. The sign flashes, "Merry Christmas!" An elf opens the door, and you get a glimpse of your own family tree. You see presents under the tree. You see your own davenport. You see your own windows with the curtains, your own linoleum and rug. It looks just like your own house, and someone says, "Merry Christmas; we love you." This is from your parents to you. You come back out and close the door, very thankful that you have a home, that you have a Christmas tree, that there will be presents there for you, and above all, that you have the love of your parents and your family, your brothers and sisters, and your friends.

You see another beautiful door and it says "Nativity" on it. Open that door and look in and see what you can see. In this room are three camels, a hill in the distance, and a star shining, and it is night. There are three wise men riding the three camels. They're headed for Bethlehem. That scene passes. You see Mary and Joseph and a donkey. Joseph is walking beside the donkey and Mary is riding, uncomfortably, for she's heavy with child and is carrying close to her heart the unborn Son of God. They're on their way to Bethlehem in Judea of old. The scene changes again. You see a rough manger hewn out of a cliff wall, and there are cattle in a cave in the background munching hay. A donkey is there. In the manger, with Joseph standing by, is Mary and the newborn Jesus, wrapped in swaddling clothes, lying in the manger. Outside, a star is shining. Its rays, like pencils of light, point down to the ground and to the manger in Bethlehem. This, too, is a scene that passes away. Out on the hillsides are shepherds watching over their flocks by night. All of a sudden, the stillness of the Judean hillsides is broken by the sounds of angels singing. As the startled shepherds look up into the sky, they hear not only the songs of angelic choirs, but also white-robed angles circling around. They're singing, "Peace on earth, goodwill to men." And an angel is announcing, "For unto you is born this day, in the City of David, a Savior which is Christ the Lord." The angels are gone now, and the echo of the singing fades away across the hills. The shepherds wonder if they had a dream or if it could be true. They hurry to Bethlehem to tell the others that they heard the angels sing and that Christ is born. You feel a radiance of light in the room where you see and hear these things. It makes you want to wash your hands and face in the Christmas light of love. Imagine you are washing your hands and face in the atmosphere of this room. Shine your shoes with the glowing atmosphere of love. Put it on your hair like a tonic and comb it in. Spray it on your clothes until you're covered with the spirit of Christmas love. May this Christmas season be filled with the warm glow of the picture scenes from the first Christmas day of long ago. Come out of the room and close the door.

On the other side of the hall a sign flashes off and on saying, "Happy New Year! Happy New Year!" There is a picture of a child representing the new year. There is also the usual picture of an old man representing the old year. He's there with his sickle that indicates the brevity of life as the years come and go. But always there is a new year being born when an old one comes to its close. As you look into this room, you may see some beautiful things that are going to happen during the New Year. Dream about them. See what pictures you can see. There's a movie screen in the back of the room. The movie playing on it is yours. It is called, "Your Happy New Year!" Take a moment to visualize and to anticipate a happy future . . .

The old-year part of this room seems to have a lot of junk in one corner. It looks like somebody should clean house. Wait a minute. I think a big truck just stopped under the window. Let's open the window wide and start throwing out some of the things we don't need or want for the New Year. Picture yourself throwing out any bad habits, wrong attitudes, and anything else that has cluttered up the past year. Out the window it goes—disappointments, broken hopes, wasted time, you name it. See it crash below in the truck bed. It's driving away now, and you do feel a lot better. Sweep and dust the room. Forgive yourself and know you are forgiven for every stupid thing you've ever done. This is a New Year, a wise year, a happy year. It's your year. You feel released and free to live the life you want to live and to be the person you want to be. The breeze is blowing through the window curtains. The door is partly open.

In our imagination, we're all gathered just inside this magic apple. We've enjoyed it so much. As we're seated on the floor, we notice something big and round like a stone. We almost stumbled over it as we came back out. A giant apple seed as big as a boulder has fallen from the roof of the apple core. Let's sit on it, all of us. It's been a fun trip through the big, red apple. Recall the things you've seen, especially the things that stood out the most vividly in your mental picturing. The whole group feels close, happy, and friendly. Hold this feeling of unity and oneness as we get up and walk together over to the yellow door and the ladder that leads back down to the ground. Hold the door with one hand and step backward out of the apple and go down the ladder. Wave good-bye to Johnny Apple-seed. Step down, please, counting from one to ten. When you reach ten, and even before, you will be alert, feeling good, in perfect health, happier and wiser than before. Counting now, one, two, three, four, five, six, almost down now. You are becoming alert and wide awake, seven, eight, nine and ten! You're on the ground now. In fact, you are right back here where we started from. Take a deep breath. Open your eyes, stretch! You are wide awake. Thank you for listening!

REJOICE WHEN THE YEAR IS DONE

Would you empty your pockets of gravel
    To fill them with nuggets of gold?
Would you trade off the scum of the stagnant pool
    For the clear crystal fountain so cold?

Would you give your counterfeit treasures
    For diamonds of rarest worth?
Would you rather have riches in heaven
    Than all of the pleasures of earth?

If so, while the old year is passing,
    Let wisdom shine forth as the sun;
And make next year's choices all wisely,
    Then rejoice when that year is done!

CLYDESDALES BY GREG WALZ

December

❧ 28 ❧

WHAT AM I?

I float with the clouds
    In the distant sky.
I grow with the flowers
    On the hillsides nearby.
I'm the fragrance of flowers
    In the gardens of earth.
I'm the garden, the sunshine
    And God giving birth.
I sway with the grasses
    Under my feet.
I race with the cars
    That go down my street;
For I am a part of it all.

I sway with the branches
    In every tree.
I laugh with the breeze,
    Vagrant and free.
I sing with each bird,
    I dip and I float.
I'm part of the song
    In each songster's throat.
I stand in each pine.
    I rest firm in each rock.
I roll in each river.
    Count time on each clock.
For I am a part of it all.

(CONTINUED ON NEXT PAGE)

I leap with the kitten
    Wrapped up in the string.
I play with the children
    On trapeze and swing.
I race with the horses
    With wind in my face.
I wait at the finish line
    And am first in the race.
I'm last and I'm first
    And I'm still in between.
I'm all that is visible
    And all that's unseen.
I'm more than a part of it all.

I'm candle and holder,
    The wick and the flame.
I'm Divinity and humanity
    And God is my name.
I'm Creation in nature,
    Stability and form.
I'm deviation and variety,
    The mean and the norm.
I'm whatever I am—
    And whatever I'm not.
I'm all things I remember
    And all things time forgot.
I'm the unmanifest, all-knowing unknown.

I'm the Trinity of God
    And the angelic host.
I'm the farthest star
    Of the outermost.
I'm the answering awareness
    Of the innermost part.
I'm circumference and center
    And the love in God's heart.
I'm a part of God
    And He's all of me.
I'm the measure of time
    Echoing eternity.
I'm more than whatever I am.

(CONTINUED ON NEXT PAGE)

I'm the viewer observing
　　And the object observed.
I'm Providence preserving
　　And the treasure preserved.
With shifted awareness
　　To the Higher Divine,
I'm all things and "no thing"
　　And all things are Mine.
I am That I Am:
　　God's consciousness supreme.
For I'm what I am not
　　And far more than I seem.
For I am the Awareness of God!

CAUTIOUS CURIOSITY BY JODIE BOREN

December

29

A good memory depends upon associating new things with the old by observing the similarities and differences. Bad memories should be wrapped in a shroud of love and buried in a casket of forgiveness in the cemetery of forgetfulness with no headstone in memoriam to mark its forgotten resting place.

THE LIVING CHRISTMAS TREE
(CREATIVE VISUALIZATION)

Resting comfortably, eyes closed gently, breathing deeply and easily, visualize clearly in color and in action. Be sure that you're as relaxed as an old dish towel hanging on the line. Go down as deeply in relaxation as you can. Notice the music while you think for a moment about Christmas. This is the month of December. You've already been thinking about Christmas presents and what you wish you might have or give. We're going to do a visual about a Christmas tree of living light and about the Christmas Wish Angel. But I want you to think for a moment about something you'd like to have that is not a material thing. Don't think about motorbikes or things you could wear or things you could eat. These are things we usually think about. So we're going to leave these behind for now. We're going to think about something that is more important. You may not be able to see it, feel it, ride it, or push it, but it's still something very important. I want you to think about personality, about your grades in school, about good health, about strong minds, about the beautiful, the true, and the good. Think about the things you would like to do and be as you grow up, about getting along with people, about getting along with teachers, about anything that you can think of like wisdom or intelligence or reading better or doing your math better, about concentrating better, about paying better attention, and remembering things better. Think about it silently. When you have chosen, we could either share it out loud or think about it silently. Keep right on relaxing while we do our verbal visual. Keep in mind these things that we have chosen or may add to our Christmas wish.

Our lesson, as we said, is about the Tree of Living Light and the Christmas Wish Angel. Picture, if you will, a Christmas tree that is made out of light. Choose any color in the rainbow or any color that an artist would use. Imagine that the trunk of the tree is this color. You may want the trunk to be green. You may want it to be brown. You may want it to be blue. It has to be a trunk of shining, beautiful, soft, fluorescent light. See the little pieces of bark with the valleys and the high spots. See the limbs dead or broken. All of it is made out of light. It has darker and lighter values of light. Now for the bigger branches! Pick another color or colors. Maybe the branches down at the bottom are one color of light, while further up the tree there are different-colored branches clear up to the top. Now make the smaller branches come out from the larger limbs. Put in the twigs. Let them be in lighter pastel shades of whatever light or color the larger limbs and branches are. Then out at the very ends of the twigs and limbs and at the ends of the branches, please see the pine needles or fir needles as little scintillating, shining, pencil points of light that are bursting out from every part of the tree. It is a tree that rotates like a psychedelic light, a tree that undulates and moves, sways, shifts from color to color, that blinks, winks and shines. You can look right through it. It is a transparent, luminescent tree of life and light and living color.

Look at the bottom of the tree, where it seems to be encased or held in by a great snowdrift of artificial snow. Notice how the lights, as they flicker and sway, cast their spell on the little artificial snowflakes like pieces of glass glittering in the sun or like diamonds shining in the light. Look at the top of your tree and choose a star for the top. Choose a blue star for the light, if you like blue. Let the star go around and around like a pinwheel of color blown in the breeze.

Look down at the bottom of the tree and you'll see a transparent box of light. Everything in our picture is light. This box is so transparent that you can see what's in it without opening the lid. It's full of Christmas decorations of every kind like long strings of different-colored tinsel. It has tinsel moonbeams and tinseled sunbeams and sparklers of living light. It has balls and bells and candles of light. Lift the lid. Reach down into the box and pick them up. Put them on the tree. Light every candle, for they won't catch the tree on fire because the whole tree is a tree of living light. Light the candles and see their orange flame against the multi-colored tree on which you have placed them. See the tinsel sweeping, dripping, and drooping down like the rain of light, like icicles of light. It's a beautiful Christmas tree. Over to one side of it see the Christmas Wish Angel standing there dressed in a robe of translucent, beautiful, shining, soft light. In her right hand the angel holds a magic wand. On the end of it there is a beautiful light, like a laser beam. She's reaching with her left hand under the magic Christmas Tree of Living Light. She is reaching for something we may not have seen before. There's a box under the tree. It has your name on it! The box is a box of light. Someone has stenciled your name with a gold felt pen against the white light of the box. There's a gift in it for you. It's the one mentioned a moment ago—better grades, how to understand people better, a better personality, a better memory, getting along better with teachers, being better in every subject that you study, and anything else that you've thought of that's beautiful and good and true. It's in that box. It's yours!

You're walking up to the tree now, slowly but with anticipation, and your hands are outstretched. The Christmas Wish Angel has your box in her hand. It's shining. She's handing it to you and you're taking it with both of your hands. She's touching the backs of your hands. The sparks are flying from that magic wand. She seems to be calling your name, saying, "I am giving this gift to you. It is yours. And I'm also touching your hands so that you will guard it and hold it secure and firm. Do not let it go, for all of the gifts of life are precious gifts. They are valuable. Hold it in safe keeping." She continues her explanation. "I'm touching the backs of your hands with my magic wand so they'll be working hands. You'll unwrap the box, you'll take out your gift, you'll invest it in life, you will use it, you will increase it. You will make it grow more and more." She touches you right on the forehead, too, like they knighted people in old England in generations gone by. She's placing the magic wand upon your head. You feel a fullness in your forehead just above your eyes.

You feel energy patterns swirling there. You feel your mind becoming expanded, your awareness becoming increased. You do feel that intelligence is dawning in a greater degree than you've ever had it before. Your whole mind is lighting up with an inner brilliance, with a clarity of thought, with a radiance of mind. You seem to read better, you hear better, and it is as though the light were filling your mind and your head itself, shining out through your ears and through your skin. You are becoming a person of light. Your mind is becoming strong. Your body is becoming strong, for you are receiving the vital force of living light and life. Your memory will be better. Your grades will be better. You will get along better with your teachers and other people as well, for the eye of understanding is being opened in your mind.

Intuitive wisdom is awakening. It is knowledge that almost knows the answer before you're told. It is knowledge that expects the answer when you turn the page and find it there. It is knowledge that comprehends the deepest meaning of life of the books you read and the people you meet. Wisdom is in this box. Whatever request was back of it, wisdom must be there. And you receive it.

You're thanking the Christmas Wish Angel and you're bowing low. The gift is in your hands. You're backing away now so that another can come. You're sitting down on the hillside of light. You're unwrapping your present. You're throwing away the wrapping of light. You're throwing away the string and the Christmas stamps. You're getting down to the tissue paper of light. Now you're getting down to wisdom and knowledge, intelligence, disposition, and to a better personality. You're getting down to the gifts of your better self. Your gift is beginning to grow and expand until it comes out of its box like a jumping jack to fill your comprehension and your awareness with its beauty. You're very, very thankful for it. It's yours for always. A year from now it will be stronger. Ten years from now it will be better. Guard it as a priceless possession. Enlarge it and work at it to make it grow. As you do this, the gift of the Christmas Wish Angel will grow throughout all the years of your life. From time to time you will think of other things that are beautiful, true, positive, and good, and they, too, will be yours because you have learned how to increase the gifts that life gives to you. I congratulate you. May this be the happiest Christmas season that you've ever, ever had in all your life, and may each season be better and better as seasons come and go.

Thank you for listening. Shall we stretch now. Get a big breath of fresh air. Open your eyes. You are wide awake and happy.

MEMORY WALKS WITH ME

I have walked so many evenings
   Along the ocean shore.
I have seen its waves come rolling
   Ever shoreward more and more.

I have climbed across its driftwood
   And wave-tossed, piled debris.
I have seen its jumbled, wild display
   Tossed up by an angry sea.

I have walked on sand dunes shifting
   Where the sand fleas sting and bite.
I have seen the sunset fading
   And the stars come out at night.

I have thought long thoughts at evening
   And come to know God there;
For nature speaks God's language
   On the ocean's salty air.

No man can live upon its shore
   And ever be the same.
And memory walks with me today
   Along the way I came!

December

∽ 30 ∽

PUSHING FOR HOME BY LEE HERRING

MAN MUST REFLECT GOD'S IMAGE

The Power that is back of all causing,
　　The Primeval Force and its laws,
The Mover of all manifestations
　　Is God, the Ultimate Cause.

Life began with God's creative thought
　　And a universe swung into view.
God spoke the forms He was thinking,
　　Then the void brought forth the new.

Man, God-imaged, was more than dust,
　　But a Creator and King by birth.
God entrusted man with His Spirit
　　And dominion over all the earth.

And beyond the forms of matter,
　　But from life's spiritual deep,
God awakens man's gifts and powers
　　That have long since lain asleep!

Man must arise from his groveling
　　And his bondage to material things.
Then faith and truth will triumph,
　　And all men will be Priests and Kings.

But man is the channel and not the Source,
　　The candle and not the light,
The window through which the sun must shine
　　Reflecting God's glory bright.

*Genius is the creative capacity of the awakened intellect
in cooperation with the creative mind of God.*

December

~ 31 ~

Even an unfurnished house seems warm and full with friendship in it.

Life is but one day; in the morning we call it tomorrow, at noon we call it today,
but in the evening we call it yesterday, and try to recall it again.

THE HANDS OF THE CLOCK AND FATHER TIME

It was New Year's Day and Father Time
Stood by the clock to hear it chime.
But the hands of the clock just came to rest
And didn't strike twelve, as if they knew best.
With a furrowed brow and a jaundiced eye
Father Time tinkered and tinkered and wondered why.
Then the long hand reached out and tapped him a bit,
And said very kindly, "Take a chair and sit?"
"We figured we've worked 366 days
And it's time, Father Time, that someone gave us a raise.
This year was long and our machinery unoiled.
Now those electric clocks have really been spoiled.
We'd like a day off with time and a half for pay.
Our hands have worked hard and it's New Year's Day!"
Then Father Time gave the clock box a whack.
Brushed the hair from his forehead and pushed the hand back.
You could tell he was angry and highly displeased
As he opened the clock door and the pendulum seized.
He gave it a swing with a swoosh and a swack
And the hands started moving along the time track!
Then he answered rather gruffly in a querulous voice,
"There's work to do and you don't have much choice.
Time marches on while idle hands rest.
Just keep on pointing. It's the thing you do best.

(CONTINUED ON NEXT PAGE)

I'll oil your machinery and adjust your tick-ticker.
I'll even give you an Inspection Sticker.
But work you should and work you must
In spite of long hours as your rust turns to dust!
Your greatest reward is to faithfully serve.
You're asking for time off? You've got your nerve!"
The hands on the clock covered their face in shame.
Their numbers were up but they couldn't take the blame.
So they replied in unison as they moved along,
"Tell us why, Father Time, why are we so wrong?
Teachers and preachers and nurses 'take five,'
And those who rest most are the longest alive.
The doctors and lawyers take vacation, we're told.
What are holidays for, if we may be so bold?
Even little kids come home after school,
Throw their hats in the corner and break every rule.
Workers strike for wages while we strike the time.
Clock hands have rights and that isn't a crime!"
Old Father Time, since Time was beginning,
Had heard everything, but this was a new inning!
He'd have to "play ball" with the hands of the clock
Or the whole New Year was in for a shock.
So he scratched his head and his hair turned grayer
As he crossed himself and uttered a prayer.
"The extra day in Leap Year makes it seem a long hitch.
But I can give them time off if nobody will snitch."
So Father Time reached out a gnarled, old hand.
"Shake, Partners. Your vacation has already been planned.
Three years in a row, on February twenty-nine,
You can have the day off and everything will be fine.
But about the time while you vacation and laugh,
You must reward yourself for the time and a half.
Your hands were made to help each other
And doing nothing is a vacuum not worth the bother.
Your wish has been granted. Please keep your wheels clicking.
Have a good New Year and keep your ticks ticking!"
Then the hands clapped each other in jubilant glee
And went right on pointing for everybody to see.
Father Time smiled in a tired, quizzical way.
Laid down his sharp cycle and said, "Let's call it a Day!"

BENEDICTION

May God's rich blessing attend thee;
    Encompass the way you tread.
May glory, and peace and joy divine
    Rest ever around thine head.

May fountains of hope refresh thee;
    No striving disturb thy rest.
May God in all grace o'er shadow
    And comfort and keep thee blest.

Till tired of toiling and labor,
    And length of the passing years,
The angels of peace surround thy bed,
    Uphold thee and still thy fears.

The Gate of Heaven swing open,
    The Father accept thee then,
The circle up yonder unbroken.
    To God be the glory, amen.

RADIANCE BY GREG WALZ

Index to Prose and Poetry

CREATIVE VISUALIZATIONS

A Boat Trip and Expanded Awareness, 666, 667

Access to Intuitive Knowledge, 529

Bulldog Visual With Flower Experiment, 369

Cloud Technique, 739

Dumping the Garbage Bag of Fear, 603

Golden Doors, 473

How to Get Along With People Who Bug You, 225

Inspiration for Living, 812

Memory and Mental Set, 521

Peace and the Man from Galilee, 883

Positive Living and The Old Grey Mare Visual, 589

Recall and the Balloon Experiment, 737

Self-Appreciation, 231

Self-Improvement, 595

Synchronizing My Movements in Time and Space, 435

The Apple Visual, 889

The Creator of Love, 818

The Living Christmas Tree, 899

Thought Force in Action, 669

Wall, Window, Tree, and Super Concentration, 659

You Are a Peaceful Person, 517

ENVIRONMENT

A Forgotten Forget-Me-Not, 356

Air Quality, Water Purity and Land Productivity, 467

Air Pollution Solution, 468

All Are a Part of God's Forest, 164

All Life Is a Poem to Me, 2

A Lone Tree Grew, 534

An Energy Divine, 439

An Ocean Prayer, 44

An Orchestra of Trees, 542

A Royal Tapestry, 5

A Tree Weeps, 316

Autumn, 751

Autumn Leaves and Life, 725

Away from the Ocean Shore, 870

Beautiful Ocean, 768

Blow, Storm, Blow, 820

Broad Skies in Which to Fly, 562

Character Brocade, 20

Communion by the Sea, 30

Creation, 413

Day and Night, 6

Design, 538

Dimensions, 188

Each Season in Review, 397

East of the Shadows, 137

Flying to Aspen in Autumn, 697

God's Embrace, 550

God's Handiwork, 540

God Wrote Two Books for Man to Read, 848

Grass, 464

Gray Tableau, 767

Great Minds, 338

Grey Sunset, 502

Harvest Days, 715

Heaven's Summertime, 466

Heritage of Earth, 483

He Walked With Me, 500
Humanity, 129
I Am Available, 559
I Climbed a Hill, 631
Idaho Treasures, 326
If I Can Go Down to the Sea, 104
I Know You Are There, Old Ocean, 298
I Love the Sound of the Sea, 154
I Love the Sound of the Surf, 178
I'm Akin, 48
I Must Away, 248
I Must Walk On, 624
I'm Your Sister and Your Brother, 491
Insight, 196
Intuitive Knowledge, 29
"Kissing Cousins," 14
Memory Walks With Me, 902
Mountains, 414
My Heart Is Like the Ocean, 618
Ocean Shore, 24
One of God's Daughters, 683
On Opening a Rosebud, 366
Pacific Therapy, 792
Pegasus: Can We Win the Race? 341
Perfect Land, 599
Perspective, 20
Pine Trees, 826
Primal Cause, 347
Reflections, 254
Repose With a Song, 246
Responding to Love, 365
Rivers, 414
Safe on That Shore, 202
Seagull Shadows, 748
Sea Life and the Tides, 409
Sense-Bound, 252
Siletz Keys, 714
Solitude, 767
Spring Song, 270
Spring Walks Today, 320

Storm Ghosts Dance, 700
Sundown Is Symbolic, 38
Symbolic, Old Ocean, 360
Tell Me, Cities, 162
The Artist Hand of God, 323
The Artistry of Love, 35
The Call of the Sea, 748
The Churchyard of the Sea, 814
The City at Night, 472
The Creator's Greatness, 827
The Environment of Spaceship Earth, 47
The Garden of Our God, 312
The Kindness of God, 32
The Lily, 465
The Lord Loves Nature, 368
The Mad, Mad Ocean, 264
The Night the Trees Went Walking, 689
There Is Music in the World Today, 828
The Rhythm of Life, 510
The Sea Is a Steed Green-Broken, 250
The Suffering, Sobbing, Sighing Rain, 628
The Wealth of Autumn's Treasure, 686
The Wind Blows Free, 704
The Winds Blow Cold, 761
The Wings of the Wind, 210
The Works of the Creator's Hand, 4
They Are Gone, 847
To a Fast-Footed Seagull, 332
Trees, I Love You, 393
Trees Against the Sky, 755
Tree Talk, 344
Union, 82
Urban and Rural Class Structure, 471
Viewing the Ocean, 154
What Am I? 895
"What If . . .?" 236
When Day Is Done, 110
When Shearing Time Is Past, 326
When Spring Is in the Air, 504
When the Storm Was Over, 570

Where the Yachats Flows into the Sea, 354
Wild Geese Across the Sky, 681
Wings Over Seagull Bay, 216
Winter Is a Monster Cat, 761
You Can Change It, 558
You'll Find Yourself, 553

HUMOR

A Fly-By-Night Wedding, 193
Baldheaded Men, 688
Chalk Talk, 616
Choir Member, 321
Doorknob Day, 588
I Don't Know, 10
I'll Tell You a Secret, 214
I Wonder How They Act at Home, 853
Gossip, 53
My Golden Goose, 166
The Personality of an Earthworm, 278
The Silicone Man, 653
What I Want for Christmas, 882
What Shall We Call It? 238
Who Stoll Th Motor and The Stearin Wheol? 9

INSPIRATION

Accountability and Inspiration in Education,
    355
Achievement, 127
Active Hope, 801
Administrative Accountability and Inspiration,
    359
A Masterpiece Someday, 480
A Poet's Prayer, 869
A Sunset, Evening Sky, 602
A Writer Is an Artist, 757
Boundless Hope, 32

Change of Vision, 496
Climb With Me, 19
Confidence at Bat, 647
Courageous Conqueror, 93
Creativity Is King, 495, 497, 499, 501, 503, 505
Enthusiasm and Success, 107
Enthusiasm in Action, 119
Enthusiasm Personally Applied, 121
Eternity, 576
Faith and Hope, 642
Flee Like the Bird to the Mountains, 745
God, Give Us Love, 841
Going the Extra Mile, 273
Good, Good News, 61
Gratefulness, 793
He Shall Overcome, 40
Hope, 801
Hope, Industry, Authority, and Courage, 253
How Does Enthusiasm Help You? 101
If a Poem Should Come to Me, 609
If You Can, 262
I'm Glad You Are Mine, 345
Inner Nonresistance, 271
Inspiration, 781
Inspiration and Teacher Accountability, 357
Inspiration for Living, 15
I Shall Not Fear, 488
Keep On Keeping On, 658
Keys That Unlock Creativity's Doors, 507
Let There Be Light, 406
Live the Inspired Life, 673
Love and Gravity, 115
More Fully to Live, 779
October Days, 692
Oh, Let Me Sing On! 208
Oneness, 710
Opportunity Ideas Glisten Everywhere, 411
Oregon Trail Strength, 361
Philosophy for Today, 131
Pledge of Courage, 317

Radiate to Communicate, 867
Rejoice When the Year Is Done, 893
Roll Out That Golden Carpet, Sir! 50
Shut In When the Rain Comes Down, 611
Songs of Belonging, 757
Sundown Ship, 626
Survival, 475
Tempest Tossed, 720
The Best I Can, 843
The Creative Mind, 417
The Energy of Enthusiasm, 105
The Enthusiastic Person, 85
The Flag of Thy Peace, 775
The Foe of Mediocrity, 261
The God of the Roses is Mine, 242
The Rewards of Creative Imagination, 509
The Tree House, 556
The Triumphant Marching Song, 551
The Viewpoint of God, 777
The Will to Win, 93
They That Wait, 706
Thinking Thanksgiving, 794
Tie the Ends of That Rainbow Down, 747
Timeless Weaving, 3
Times Like These, 272
Triumph, 276
Veteran's Day and Armistice Day, 773
Vision, 862
Wandering Thoughts, 477
We Are Weavers, 1
We March to the Sound of Drums, 623
What Is Happiness? 159, 161, 163, 165, 171, 173,
    175, 177, 179, 183, 185, 187, 189, 195

JACKSON FABLES

Aggression, 155
Good Finding and the Gardener's Dog, 141
Lucky Luther and King Henry Happiness, 145

Lucky Luther and the Two-Horned Unicorn, 149
Positive Fuzzy-Wuzzys, 135
Relaxed Learning with Jackson Fables, 59
Silly, the Silicone Dog (Flexibility and
    Adjustability), 379
Sir Uno Who and the Seven Magic Gifts, 299
Sky Dog and Saucer Cat and Half Kitten, 387
Sleeping Beauty and Awakened Awareness, 287
The Bear That Had a Boy for a Dog, 305
The Black-Eyed Peas Who Wouldn't Say Please,
    451
The Color Birds and Levels of Awareness, 63
The Finger and the Flame, 219
The Great Dane at the Obedience Show, 293
The Green Room Relaxation Visual, 75
The Hibernating Bear Visual, 69
The Land of the Nine-Foot Elves,
Or I Like You Because . . . (Expressing
    Appreciation), 77
The Old Violin, 97, 99
The Potato Who Couldn't See, 223
Two Ears of Corn and the Wagon Tongue, 373
Uncle Snoose and the Blue-Eyed Goose, 445
Whistle Boy, Who-Done-It, and the Whim-
    Whammer, 455
Wistful the Wibble With the Wobble in His
    Wing, 447

LOVE

Aboriginal Cupid, 881
A Hundred Broken Hearts, 663
All That You Have Is Mine, 833
Always I Need You, 734
A Man Never Outgrows His Mother, 351
A Mother's Faith and Love, 335
Bring Me to My Love, 36
Campfires Along the Way, 646
Chat With Me About Love, 421

Cheerfulness in a Kiss, 139
Come, My Love, 470
Communicating Love, 168
Heart to Heart, 213
Home Is Where You Are, 58
I Am Love, 120
I Fell in Love With a Manikin, 168
I'll Tell You on Valentine's Day, 113
Incompleteness, 816
I Opened the Door, 514
I Send My Love, 402
I Sing of My Own True Love, 46
Life Is Love and Love Is Life, 45
Love, 46
Love, 784
Love and Romance Earned? 243
Love for Our Fellow Man, 39
Love Identifies and Unifies, 113
Love Is a Fragrant Flower, 285
Love Is a Haunted House, 116
Love Is an Emotion, 859
Love Is an Inexact Science, 639
Love Is a Wonderful Thing, 244
Love Is Tender, 886
Love Is the Home of the Soul, 743
Love's Harvest, 586
Love's Silent Night, 760
Love's Tender Embrace, 803
Luminary Dissertation on Love, 57
My Father to My Mother, 331
My Grandmother, 872
My Love, 139
Our Happy Dimension of Love, 763
Paul's Passion Paraphrased, 493
Please Hear What I Am Not Saying, 807
Raindrop Wedding, 266
Responding to Love, 265
Stand Facing the Light, 816
Shyness Versus Communication, 167
Teach Us to Sing, 888

That's What You Do for Me, 422
The Artistry of Love, 444
The Golden Rule of Love, 142
The Love Loom, 11
The Magic of Love, 494
The Power of Committed Love, 95
Timeless Love, 712
True Love Is One, 324
What Is a Baby? 404
What Is Love? 640?
When Cupid Loosed His Dart, 96
When the Fog Lifts, 574
When the Next Angel Walks By, 881
When the One That I Love Passes By, 546
Whispering Wind, 648
Your Heart and My Heart, 12
Your Love, 286

SPIRITUAL

Above the Forms of Matter, 490
After Chastisement, 672
All Things Are a Part of Me, 274
A Prayer of Gratitude, 790
A Strong Faith, 122
Authoritative Faith, 123
Back of the Seed, 434
Benediction, 907
But I Can, 702
Close to Him, 805
Creation, 413
Creative Thought, 186
Cutting Cloth from the Garments of God, 67
Dimensional Area of Spirituality, 649
Dissonance, 635
Divine Reality, 629
Divine Union, 19
Escape Emptiness, 508
Faded Rose Leaves, 162

Faith for Each Day of the Year, 126
Faith's Candle Burns at Night, 877
Faith Works, 403
Five Minutes After I'm Gone, 836
Gemstones, 837
Gift or Giver, 481
Give Me the Book of Tomorrow, 349
Give Something to Someone, 552
Give Us Back, 612
God, 268
God Has Many Voices, 528
God Is, 463
God Is Love, 396
God's Allness, 190
God's Grace, 717
God's True Plan, 487
God's Will, 746
God Walks on Earth With Men, 296
Have Faith in God, 845
Have I Thanked Him? 212
Hear Us As We Pray, 846
Heavenly Want Ad, 525
Heaven's Day Has Just Begun, 291
He Will Keep Me Triumphant, I Know, 426
Higher Mountains, 88
How Great Is God? 358
How Shall We Cross, 430
Identity, 336
I Know Thou Art Real, 343
I Must Be Traveling On, 856
Ingratitude Is Blind, 106
I See God Standing There, 459
Lead Us, 356
Lean Hard, 267
Light Reflects from Every Star, 765
Loneliness, 851
Make Way for God, 531
Man Must Reflect God's Image, 904
May I Know Him! 395
Meditation Prayers, 112, 159, 163, 506, 566, 704,
   714, 779, 789, 794

"Natural Law," 86
Nearing the Shore, 607
New Self-Awareness, 643
Oneness With Life, 694
One With the Pure of Heart, 634
Plant a Rose of Rebel Red, 318
Prayer, 854
Prayer for Peace, 482
Purpose, 132
Quiet Enlightenment, 89
Sabbath Rest, 112
Shepherd of Love, 568
Sometimes, 200
Stand Still and See, 416
Thanksgiving, Faith, and Action, 789
Take Thou My All, 650
The Carpet of Prayer, 854
The Closet of Prayer, 728
The Conqueror, 552
The Essence of Life, 605
The Kindness of God, 823
The Light, 506
The Praying Person, 787
The Promise of God, 861
The Promise of Golden Day, 174
The Quiet Heart, 644
The School of Prayer, 218
These Are the Great Ones, 255
The Secret Place, 184
The Size of God, 564
The Spirit of Divine Energy, 874
The Ultimate and the True, 206
The Wine of Thy Kingdom, 730
The Wings of the Wind, 829
This I Must Do, 51
This Is Faith, 825
Thou Art Adores, 560
Union With God, 73
Walk With God, 764
What Is a Miracle? 340
When I Was a Little Child, 579

Who Am I But a Singer? 284
You'll Find God Everywhere, 742

WISDOM

Accountability Feedback, 541
Achievement, 161
A Deep Well, 428
A Looking Glass for the Dead, 22
Ambition and Admonition, 441
Artist's Eyes, 98
As a Man Thinketh, 437
A Select Clergy, 21
A Tombstone for Despondency, 691, 693, 696,
    699, 701, 703, 707, 709, 713, 719, 721
Attitude, 432
Awareness Is A Key, 567
A Woven Union and Communion, 13
Books, 759
Brokered Intelligence Pool, 245
Brotherhood and Civilization, 41
Caisson, 797
Children on the Beach, 126
Clown-Dust, 260
Commerce, 281
Common Sense, 209
Compensation, 879
Consider Your Potential: Don't Sell Short, 339
Critic, Don't Be a Critic, 788
Criticism Quotables, 511
"Daddy, Show Me How to Do It," 23
Dubious Mind Smog, 657
Egotistical Pride, 583
Elephant Ears, 584
Employees, Employers, and the Extra Mile, 281
Envy's Ignorance, 276
Experts, 364
Family Design, 237
Fear in the Face of Success, 587
Fear Versus Faith, 263

Friendship, 329
Gift or Giver, 52
Give to Overcome, 796
Goals and Objectives of Education for
    Achievement, 31
Goals and Objectives of Humanistic Education,
    325
Goals for Public Education, 615
Gossip, 515
Grant Me Wisdom to Choose, 795
Hear Wisdom, 255
Hidden Beauty, 233
How Far Away Is Yesterday? 452
Humanity Is One, 130
Hybrid Businessman, 400
I Am Humanity, 148
I Belong to the Universe, 726
Ideas About Worry, 425
Ideation, 205
Imagination, 689
I Meet Myself, 100
Industry, 350
It Pays to Think, 199
I Want to Know, 180
Jealous Love, 566
Jealousy Demonstrated, 565
K.C. Bones' Last Ride, 835
Laugh With Me, 321
Life Is All Bright and Happy, 108
Life Is Like a Winding Road, 753
Life's Peak Experience, 731
Listening for Tomorrow, 675
Logical Thinking, 207
Making Friends, 134
Manikin Folks, 732
Man in a World of Change, 251
Many Would Praise the Sea, 454
Memory, 159
Money, 239
More About Friendship, 134
Mother and Cleanliness, 351

My Strong Friend, 361
New Perception, 577
Observation Thinking and Science, 215
Other Days Will Come, 855
Peace and Love, 204
Perseverance, 708
Pioneer Tendency, 723
Please Do Not Quit, 871
Positive Attitude Accountability, 573
Positive Emotional Lubricants, 561
Preventive Discipline or Crutches for the Rat
    Race! 315
Progress, 786
Prose Versus Poetry and "Vice-Worser!" 785
Questions to Think About, 126, 128
Recompense, 408
Relationships, 128
Repose: Dignified Calmness, 109
Right Solutions, 830
Seal My Lips, O Lord, 172
Selfish Glory, 491
She's Yours Only Today, 462
Silence, 90
Slander, 156
Sleep, 498
Solitude and I, 34
Struggling Makes the Person, 593
Subconscious Mind and Courage, 279
The Blarney Stone, 198
The Cat That Came to Church, 55
The Clock, 736
The Clock and the Calendar, 863
The "Common" Mind Benefits, 247
The Depot Called Success, 25
The Doors Are Wide Open, 275
The Hands of the Clock and Father Time, 905
The Ideal Rose Is the Real Rose, 412
The Laborer, 79
The Love of the Beautiful, 727
Then, I'll Buy, 548

The One-Eyed Monster, 282
The Other Side of Truth, 176
The Power of Thought, 572
The Subconscious Mind, 621
The Test of Faith, 102
The Tiger Twins, 771
The Viewpoint of Childhood, 633
The Written Word, 670
Think, 228
Thoughts, 520
Time Is in Your Favor, 625
To the Low Self, 622
Tribute to Nothing, 544
True Identity, 197
Twenty-Six Dead Soldiers, 441
Uncommon, Common Sense, 399
Universal Harmony, 43
Up the Miff Tree, 782
Vulture Ways, 512
We Are Brothers! 42
Welcome to Wisdom's Eden, 582
What Is a Friend? 800
What Is Thinking? 203
What You See When You Look, 641
When He Becomes a Man, 238
When the Fog Came In, 630
When You Give All Things, 348
Wisdom, 838
Wisdom and Leadership, 581
Wisdom Participating; Life Expressing, 729
Wisdom's Gate, 474
Without Pegasus to Lead You, 342
Working, 873
Write the Words Down, 619
Yesterday Is Dead, 651
Yesterday's Ashes Are Warm Today, 806
You Can Choose Your Pod of Peas! 132
Your Mind and Adversity, 417
Youth Has a Treasure, 864

Index to Artists and Artwork

Alston, Susan
    February's Gift, 92
Araujo, Jorge R.
    Mating Season, 815
Baer, D.
    Fisherman, 922
Baggett, Ralph
    Tree of Life, 735
Bartlett, Jean
    Flattop Mountain, 37
    In the Garden, 376
    New Day Dawning, 33
    Water Tower, 485
Bengartt
    Clown, 269
    Clown with a Blue Face, 249
    Clown with Top Hat, 277
    Clown with Yellow Hat, 241
    Fisherman, 169
    Indian Chief, 42
    Judy, 665
Boren, Jodie
    Cautious Curiosity, 898
    Old 597, 752
    Silent Night, 865
Chernomorets, Sergey
    Daydream, 711
    Nativity, 876
    Odessa, Black Sea, 327
Cherry, Clancy
    Angry Tiger, 563
    Apache Lookout, 230
    Bengal Tiger, 594
    Chinese Panda, 118

Cherry, Clancy (continued)
    King of the Beasts, 601
    Lion's Gaze, 600
    Mexican Wolf, 222
    Silent Approach, 569
    Snow Leopard, 545
    Snowy Egret, 138
    Swan Pair, 817
    The Wisdom of Solomon, 539
    White Tiger, 606
Cook, Ginger
    House of Music, 234
Cydney
    Clown Duet, 258
    The Sad Clown, 235
Dale, I.
    Jewel of Seascape, 617
Davis, Gladys
    Blue Mountain, 81
    Blue Vase, 84
    Runnels Country Road, 840
    The Quiet Place, 74
    The Windmill Out Back, 718
Davis, Jessica Henry
    Orange Pekoe, 799
De Vaney, Lynn
    Waiting, 921
Dubois, Tom
    God's Breath, 844
    In the Garden, 878
    The Cloak, 460
    The Gathering, 868
    The New Creation, 850

Eagle, Bruce
    Fairy in the Jar, 811
    Masters of the Sky
    Moses, 571
    Mustard Seed Faith, 62
    My Mother in the Wind, 655
    Touched, 453
Erwin, Bob
    Bolivia, 330
    High Seas, 229
    Kilimanjaro, 585
    Mountain Man, 821
    North American Wildlife, 536
    Patio Arrangement, 133
    Skeet's Peppy, 722
Evans, J.D.
    Buffalo Soldiers, 677
Fallas, Elliot
    Amalfi at Night, 353
    Italian Coast, 333
Fears, Vickie
    Along the Rio Grande, 158
    El Potro, 637
    The Candle Dance, 638
Finger, Jim
    Afternoon Storm, 810
Fyk, D.B.
    Clown with the Blue Hat, 257
Gamlin, Ken (Family of)
    Bristlecone Pine, 319
Gray, Steve
    Strays, 431
Green, David
    Hopa Woman, 698
    Solitude, 682
Herring, Lee
    High Sierra, 724
    Moving Out, 705
    Pushing for Home, 903

Jackson, David
    Yosemite, 144
Jackson, Karrie
    Einstein, 337
    My Grandpa, Cornelius Mulder, 527
Jackson, R.W.
    Bugling Elk, 49
    Rose in Vase, 91
    Rose on the Table, 103
    R.W. Jackson Family, Season's Greetings, 695
    White Rose, 87
    Wild White Rose, 125
    Wyoming Mountain Lake, 469
Jackson, William R.
    A Proud Father's Son, 608
    Bill Jackson and His Brother Jim with
        Number 75, 27
    Carriage Ride in Evergreen, 923
    Cougar, 857
    Cousin Betty, Billy, and Mom Jackson, 513
    English Setter, 750
    Fulvic: Above the Forms of Matter, 489
    Grandkids at Play, 924
    G.W. 75 Co. Business Card, 26
    Lee Marvin with Number 75 in the Movie
        Cat Ballou, 28
    Lynn's Back to the Future Car, 923
    Makeup for Actor, 436
    My Grandpa Mulder, Holland Dutch
        Dairyman and Farmer, 533
    Number 75 on the Road, 26
    The Old Sea and the Fisherman, Alaska, 211
    Two Jackson Daughters, 461
    Steam Locomotive Engineer, 419
Kamerath, Pat
    Grandpa's Old Truck, 645
Kincaid, Shannon
    Garden Cottage, 438
Kippenbrock, Wanda
    Dream Rose Garden, 143

Kippenbrock, Wanda (continued)
Garden of Happiness, 401
Season's Scarlet Rose, 283
Welcome Home, 346
Leitner, Jan
Roseheart, 111
Mirkovich, Marina
Forest Escape, 776
Mirkovich, Nenad
Fishing in the Alps, 758
Liberty's Diamond, 478
Peaceful Pond, 16
Village with Red Poppies, 656
Reinke, Ellen
Early Winter Coming, 680
Sambatero, Joe
Arezzo, 716
Schvaiko, Viktor
Cobblestone Sunset, 415
Sunny Village, 259
Seymour, Caroline
A Letter for You, 822
Another Wilderness Season, 852
At Dock, 182
Dahlias, 314
Dandelion, 292
Disputed Landing, 217
Essai, 834
Essai 2, 377
Fjord, 170
Fruit of the Corn, 766
Gravity Is Winning, 363
Heritage of Seattle, 192
Mountain Stream, 423
Open Gate, 769
Pinecones, 804
Port Comrades, 181
Ragtime, 832
Rust in Peace, 297

Seymour, Caroline (continued)
Small Boat Harbor, 80
Song of the Sea, 791
Valentine's Day, 117
Walk in the Park, 157
Smith, Harvey Garrett
Mayflower II, 627
Sparks, Justin
A Predator in the Mind's Eye, 860
A Prey in the Mind's Eye, 866
Bluebird Garden, 367
Mother and Daughter, 392
Spencer, Everett
Fall Splendor, 427
Misty Mountain Stream, 802
The Getaway, 450
Wood River, 407
Swain, Shawn
Bedded Down, 831
Tetteh, Daniel
Peaceful Surrender, 201
Unknown
Ghost (De Vaney Collection), 749
Ship at Sea, 884
The Children's Wall, 334
The Tree House (De Vaney Collection), 555
Walz, Greg
Altoona Barn, 839
Angels Over the Tetons, 484
Aspen Road, 678
Bear of the West, 68
Chama, 671
Cherryvale Barns, 424
Clydesdales, 894
Creede Waterfall, 313
Elk in the High Country, 433
Engine No. 489, 420
Fixer Upper, 486
Gone Fishing, 741
Guarding the Hen House, 83

Greg Walz (continued)
Guido's Estimation Services, 532
Heartland Winter, 783
Jane Doe, 824
Kids at Play on the Side of a Mountain, 516
Lamartine, 610
Last Train's Gone, 7
Lizard Head Sheep, 535
Lost in the Clouds, 679
Maxwell Falls Cliffs, 405
Moose in the Willows, 56
Mother and Child, 887
Nectar Fest, 443
Ocean Grill, 429
Old Yeller, 849
Once It Was Mine, 372
Pharmacy, 770
Radiance, 908

Red Mountain Pass, 842
Shavano and Tabeguache, 479
State of Education, 280
The 102, 304
The Buck Stops Here, 875
Tracks on Fire, 8
Vallecito Fall, 614
Weathered and Weary, 526
Westphal, Hugo
Chiva-Ken Fishing Village, 191
Woodland Friend, 687
Wollman, Robin
Molly in the Garden, 54
Wright, Karen
At My Place, 858

WAITING BY LYNN MEGORDEN DE VANEY

FISHERMAN BY D. BAER

CARRIAGE RIDE IN EVERGREEN BY WM. JACKSON

LYNN'S BACK TO THE FUTURE CAR BY WM. JACKSON

ABOVE AND BELOW: GRANDKIDS AT PLAY BY WM. JACKSON